A POLICEMAN'S LOT

A POLICEMAN'S LOT

Antony Beaden

AFM
Books

A POLICEMAN'S LOT

First published in Great Britain in 2009 by
Arguments and Facts Media (AFM)
PO Box 35
Hastings
East Sussex
TN34 1ZS

ISBN 978-1-873976-38-8

1-873976-38-0

British Library Cataloguing in Publication Data:

1. Police — Hastings 2. Africa – History 3. Police — Uganda
4. Autobiography – History 5. History I. Title

Distributed in the UK by:

AFM
PO Box 35
Hastings
East Sussex
TN34 1ZS

Email: christie@btclick.com

For my long-suffering wife
Margaret

CONTENTS

CHAPTER 1

'I remember, I remember, the house where I was born.' Thus wrote the poet Thomas Hood, who died in 1845. Well, so do I, and a great deal more besides. As the years roll by, ever more rapidly, the power of recall seems to improve. Maybe it is just the high points that stand out. I shall try to commit some of them to paper. Just for my own amusement.

The reason for my arrival was explained to me many years later by my mother — somewhat tongue in cheek I suspect. She had suffered a bout of ptomaine poisoning due to eating a tin of contaminated sardines. As a result she came out in a lot of nasty itchy lumps which failed to respond to a variety of ointments and lotions. During one of her visits to Doctor Carey, the family physician, he advised her that, should she become pregnant again, she might get rid of the itch. Foolishly, she took his advice and I weighed in eventually at eight-and-a-half pounds. I can't vouch for the truth of this but she did mention that she still had the itch even after my arrival — but I took her mind off it. There's nothing so satisfying as being wanted, is there?

The house where I was born was 46, Dacre Park, Lee, London, S.E,13. Some years later the street was re-numbered and it became number 77. I was born in the front ground floor room, though I must admit that I don't recall the actual incident, in fact my earliest recollections are at the age of two or three when my sister Kathleen, ten years my senior, force-fed me with a spoon, with various items of food which I loathed, cabbage, onions, brussel sprouts, fat meat and so on. It was at least two days before I forgave her for this.

The house was one of a rather pretentious terrace row, the front of each peaking in a gable. The front door was approached over a concrete path about 7-feet wide and 14-feet in length, then up five broad tiled steps to a porch flanked on each side by a tapering gothic column.

On the left-hand side of the porch was a circular hole sealed with a cast iron cover. This led to the coal cellar situated in the semi-basement. A half-glazed door with a brass knocker led to the hall.

On the right-hand side of the door was a brass bell-push, belonging to a bell which to my knowledge never worked. My

1

mother, however, kept it highly polished, which I suppose, compensated to some degree for its other defects. In the hall, which was about seven feet wide, were two doors on the right and a staircase on the left which led to the first floor. There was another staircase immediately below this which led to the semi-basement. The first of the two doors on the right in the hall, led to the front room — where I was born — which was normally used as a drawing room — though it was where my sister force-fed me. This was a good-sized room, probably 12-feet by 14 feet. A rather grand marble mantelpiece supporting a large black marble clock was emplaced in the wall opposite the door and a large window, complete with internal wooden shutters which, owing to the numerous coats of paint applied over a great many years, were quite incapable of being opened, looked out onto the front garden. Against the wall on the same side as the door was an upright piano. The fourth wall opposite the window was occupied by a large oak sideboard with a pannelled mirror-back. Behind the sideboard was a four-sectioned folding panel door which could be opened like a concertina to make a much larger room, should we have a party at any time.

The second room on this floor which, of course, formed the larger room on opening the folding panels, was about the same size as the drawing room and was of course used as a dining room. It also had a marble fireplace opposite the door and a large window, with similarly inoperable wooden shutters — this one looking out on to the back garden which was about twenty or so feet wide and about 60-yards long. Very big for a garden in this part of London. A back door led from the end of the hall down some rather dilapidated steps to the garden, though if one turned left before reaching the back door one would go downstairs to the semi-basement. Immediately in front at the bottom of the stairs was the aforementioned coal cellar and to the left of this was a room mostly used for billiards. A six-foot by three-foot slate bed billiard table stood in the middle of the room, mounted on a home made heavy timber support. A large black iron, coal burning stove was fitted in the chimneypiece, indicating that at one time this had been a kitchen. Indeed, from time to time it reverted to this use. A half-window gave a small amount of light to this room but it only looked out onto a small semi circular concrete area, over which one could just see the top of the front garden wall.

A passageway led from the billiard room to the scullery, from which a back door and steps led up to the back garden. A pine dresser, also weighed down with innumerable layers of paint, stood along one wall alongside a gas cooker, while opposite was a scrubbed pine table. In one corner was a big earthenware sink, below which was a bit of gingham material, hiding various basins, buckets and a scrubbing board. There was no hot water tap. Hot water for laundry purposes was provided by a circular, free-standing, galvanised boiler with a gas ring beneath it connected by a rubber tube to a gas tap on the wall. This had to be filled from the sink with a bucket, and the hot water emptied from the boiler into the sink by the same method.

If the weather was inclement my mother would hang the washing up in the scullery on a clothes line which ran the length of the room. My father, being an electrician and knowing all about these things, had draped a piece of flex across the ceiling in the same direction as the line used for the wet laundry, to an electric pendant fitted to the ceiling in the center of the room. Unfortunately, over a period of many years, the flex had become somewhat frayed. My mother sometimes used it as a second clothes line — with shocking results. To the best of my recollection my father never replaced this flex and as I got older and taller my head occasionally touched the wet washing as I passed underneath. I became somewhat wary after being thrown across the scullery several times but I never tired of inviting my friends home to introduce them to the pleasures of electrocution.

Two doors led from the scullery passage — one of these was to the larder in which, unusually for a small boy, I wasn't very interested. The other was to the wine cellar where my mother stored her home-made wine. This was a damp uninviting room, half of it being under the stairs. It boasted a tiny window and was lit by a bare bulb on another piece of flex — also installed by my father. However as I was not tall enough to reach the flex I didn't meet with any accidental electrocution. As I grew older I fitted out this room as a sort of laboratory, in which I made various deadly concoctions and bombs. More of this anon.

Returning to the hall, if one mounted the staircase it led to the first floor on which was a bathroom and a separate toilet, a linen cupboard and two rooms the same size as those below. The front room was my parents bedroom while that at the back was let out to various lodgers to supplement the family income. Upstairs led to two attic bedrooms, the back one being occupied by my sister Kathleen, while I shared the front one with my brother Ralph who was eight years my senior. I was never very close to my siblings. I suppose the age difference made this inevitable. At the back of my bedroom was a door which led to an Aladdin's Cave known as the 'long attic cupboard'. It was in fact part of my sister's bedroom which had been partitioned off with hardboard and pieces of 2' x 2' timber. All the junk was kept in this room. As a child I would sit in there in the light of a dim bulb mounted on the wall and let my imagination run riot. I was the Captain of a submarine, the Master of a ship and a white hunter. I don't remember ever inviting any of my friends up there. I was quite happy there on my own. In that way no one could spoil it for me. What I didn't know about the 'long attic cupboard' was its origin. I didn't find out till many years later that a previous lodger, a Mr Marchant, before I had been born, had committed suicide while occupying what was later my sister's room. An ex-soldier, he had been severely shell-shocked during the 1914-18 war. The unfortunate chap had never recovered from his experiences and gassed himself, his body having been found lying in that part of the room which had been partitioned off. Well I never knew at the time and there was certainly no atmosphere there to indicate that there had been a tragedy of this sort.

Just by the door of the 'long-attic cupboard' was a window which opened out onto the roof. - This was of slate construction and I remember that my father was always having trouble with the 'valley' — where the roof of our next-door neighbour met ours. It was always letting in the rain and causing damp patches on the stair well below.

The back garden was divided from our neighbours by a wooden fence on each side. My mother was a keen gardener so half of the garden nearest the house was laid out to a rockery, a lawn and flower beds. An acacia tree grew on the right-hand side and a little further on was a marginally productive pear tree followed by a cherry tree. On the left-hand side were a couple of apple trees, and an ornamental pond. At the far end of the garden was a chicken run. Overhanging the chicken run and a footpath outside the back gate, was the major feature of this garden, a vast mulberry tree, some 300-years old it was reckoned. Also, in the same area near the mulberry tree, was a shed used for rabbits which occasionally supplemented the family diet. The earliest pet I ever had was a grey rabbit which I called Edmund. It was so named from a character in a weekly comic which my mother used to buy for me. This particular tale was about King Alfred who, it appeared, had a son called Edmund. I was very fond of this rabbit, who did not live in the rabbit shed with the others, except when he was taken along to be introduced to one of the dogs. Edmund lived in the house with the dog and cat and was quite sure he was one of the same species. He lived to a great age and I remember vividly one occasion when someone came to the front door to inform my parents that my uncle Reg had died unexpectedly. My mother, busy having hysterics, called out to my father, 'Reg is dead'. Hearing this from my cave in the 'long-attic cupboard', I misheard her and thought that she had said, 'Edmund's dead'. I was terribly upset by this tragic news until I found that it was only my uncle who had expired.

I was a sickly child and rapidly succumbed to any infection which happened to be going around. When I was ill I would be moved into my parents bedroom and I well remember one hot summers day, lying in bed with the curtains closed and the window open, hearing my mother shooing away the children noisily playing in the road outside, because I as about to cash in my chips. During long periods confined to bed, I became an avid reader and picked up an unequalled fund of knowledge — unequalled, that is, by the other children of my age, who nicknamed me 'The Professor'. My weekly comics had a sort of 'General Knowledge' section in them and it surprises me to this day to find that I am still able to dredge up some gem of totally useless information from the depths of my mind, tucked away so many years ago.

I was a great fan of *The Hotspur*, *The Adventure* and *The Wizard*. I could not wait to read the next installment of 'Strang the Terrible' who fought with dinosaurs, or 'Soapy Sam' who was a popular schoolmaster. Then there was another yarn about an Afghan tribesman who used a cricket bat named 'Clicky Bar' as his weapon, striking terror into the other tribesmen as he fought with them in aid of the British soldiers in the Khyber Pass. I never discovered why he was such a traitor to his own countrymen. Another story gave an account of a cruel headmaster of a famous public school who led a sort of Jekyll and Hyde existence, stripping off to a loin cloth and terrorising the countryside, killing and eating cows raw! Yet another story gave accounts of a gallant English pilot who managed to camouflage his plane so well that it was invisible and he had a great time shooting down the evil Boche. All went well until an untimely shower of rain washed the paint off.

My parents had a large collection of fairly dilapidated books and these, in addition to my weekly comics formed the basis of my literary education. I read most of the works of Dickens, but apart from these several other titles spring to mind as examples of the Victorian authors to whose works I had access. *Christie's Old Organ, Froggies Little Brother* and *Old St Pauls* were fairly morbid examples, while light relief was provided by J.M. Ballantyne's *Coral Island*, and the *Gorilla Hunters*. Jerome K. Jerome's, *Three Men in a Boat*, and *Three Men on the Brummel*, appealed to my sense of humour.

I only remember a few of the pictures which hung in my parents home. Two of these were oil paintings, very badly executed. One of these was meant to be my maternal grandfather at the age of about 30. A ferocious chap he looked, though I gathered from my mother that he was anything but. The other was intended to be my mother at the age of two or three. Very unflattering I thought. Apparently the artist, if such he could be called, owed my grandfather some money and had offered the portraits as a way of repaying it. Clearly my grandfather, although he ran a pub, was too kind-hearted in some respects. The other pictures were a sepia print of Dante and Beatrice, (whoever they were), in Venice, which hung in the hall, and two dreadful colour prints which were in my parents bedroom. One of these was entiled 'My Hero' and featured an unfortunate soldier being packed off to war by his loving wife. The other, whose title I forget, portrayed a nauseating infant biting into an enormous red apple. Another quite good religious painting portrayed a woman looking skywards. This, I was informed, was Mary Magdelen. All the pictures were stolen when the house was vacated on being bombed during the war in 1940. By a strange coincidence, my sister recognized the painting of Mary Magdalen in a magazine in 1996. This featured the house of Maggie Philbin the T.V. personality. There, on the wall, was Mary Magdalen still looking skywards. Absolutely no mistaking it. I wrote to Ms Philbin to enquire how she came by it but, naturally, my letter was ignored!

The school which I attended was Northbrook School near Lee Green. To reach it I had to walk about a mile. There was another school much nearer in Dacre Street but my mother had fallen out with the teachers some time earlier when my brother and sister attended there. It was a mean, dirty little Church School, totally lacking in facilities, overcrowded classrooms and toilets which were indescribably filthy. My mother happened to go into one of the toilets when she was collecting my brother. She was so appalled that she went straight away to complain to the headmistress — who told her in no uncertain terms to go away and mind her own business. An unwise move on the part of the headmistress. This was just the sort of challenge my mother loved. She wrote to the School Governors, the Health Inspector, the School Inspector, the local newspaper, Old Uncle Tom Cobley and all. To such good effect that the school was closed for a month for complete refurbishment and the headmistress was sacked. My brother then went to Northbrook School, while my sister went to a private school called Lewisham College where she learned to be a lady.

By the time I went to Northbrook School, Ralph was in his final year so I didn't reap any benefit from his presence. Occasionally he would take me to school or bring me home. Usually I was out of school before him and would have to sit in the park and wait for him. Sometimes he forgot me and went off with his friends to play football or enjoy himself in some other way, while I sat for hours till my mother turned up, frantic with worry at my non-arrival home. This was not too bad during the summer but when the snow was on the ground it was no joke sitting on a park bench by the side of a frozen lake bawling because I couldn't feel my fingers. Eventually I could make my own way too and from school. This meant crossing a busy main road but usually there was a policeman on duty there. One cheery fat policeman I liked particularly was P.C. Armstrong whose hand I would grasp firmly as he took me across. He always had a kind word and knew most of the children by their names. This sort of behaviour would be unheard of in today's police force where one rarely sees a policeman on the street and certainly never on a school crossing. I must say, however, that during the years I subsequently spent as a bobby, I never felt it beneath my dignity to help youngsters across the road. Building up a rapport with them has never been a cause for regret.

When I first went to Northbrook School I was in the infants class. I was four years old when I started. My teacher was Miss Brookes whom I loved dearly. She was a kindly soul of about 50, I suppose. More like a loving aunt than a teacher. She taught me to draw and stick bits of paper together and simple writing and arithmetic. She would read stories to us and warm our milk on the radiators in the cold weather. She never minded doing up difficult trouser buttons when necessary and would tuck us down for our half-hour snooze in the afternoon. I made a severe tactical error while in Miss Brookes' class. She was called away for half-an-hour leaving us alone. Before going she gave out our little blackboards and chalk and told us to do some drawing to fill in the time. Instead of drawing I filled up my blackboard with multiplication, addition a subtraction sums. On her return Miss Brookes inspected the children's efforts. When she looked at my blackboard she took it away and showed it to Mr Fluke, the Headmaster. It was decided that I was some sort of genius and I was instantly promoted to the next class up, that of Miss Bates whom I heartily disliked. It seemed that my infancy had come to an abrupt end. It also meant that I was in a class where all of the children were older and bigger than myself so I got well and truly bullied by one and all.

Opposite our house were 'The Buildings'. This was the name by which they were popularly known. Their real name was 'Dacre Houses'. They consisted of two dreadfully ugly grey blocks of flats where a large number of the 'lower order' were housed. I suppose that most of them were decent hard-working people but I also know that there were also a number of very rough characters among them. A lot of drunkenness and wife-beating took place and most of the tenements were smelly and in a squalid condition. The boys from 'The Buildings' were considered much too rough for me to play with.

My great friend was Joan Trevas who lived in Eaton Grove, a cul-de-sac 100 yards or so further up the road. She was a couple of months older than me and our mothers had originally met when pushing our respective prams. Mrs Trevas was a poor rabbit of a woman whose face appeared to have been badly scalded at some time. She had five children of whom Joan was the youngest. Her husband was, I believe, slightly mentally subnormal, as was her eldest son. I don't believe Mr Trevas did any work. He was probably incapable of holding down a job. He had a beard and used to walk round talking to himself. He terrorised his wife who used to come running to my mother when he beat her up. He in turn was terrified of my mother who would go round and give him a good thumping. He called her 'The Hedgehog' for some reason. Joan could always be relied on to join whole-heartedly in any games I thought up. I once made an aeroplane about six feet long out of planks of wood nailed together. When I considered it finished we both sat on it and were most disappointed that it did not immediately become airborne. Many of our games centered round the African jungles. This was probably because my comics featured tales set in this area.

Much of our time was spent in hunting wild animals and shooting cannibals. We also used to go off on long walks together across Blackheath and down through Greenwich Park to the Thames. We usually rounded off the day with half-an-hour on the boating pool on Blackheath where a paddle boat or a rowing boat could be hired for three pence. Joan was a rather undernourished child. I don't think her mother got much money to spend on food. She came round to us every day and my mother would feed her up as much as possible. Strangely, when I met her many years later, she had blossomed into a very beautiful woman.

People in distress in the locality would always go to my mother for advice and assistance. Whether their sons had been taken away by the police or their children were ill, my mother was always the first to be informed. I well remember Mrs French who lived up the road, rushing down to my mother one evening because her son, John, who was about eighteen-years-old was locked in the bathroom and wouldn't answer when called. mother went back with Mrs French and broke the door open. Poor John was inside, quite dead having been overcome by fumes from a defective gas water heater. My mother administered artificial respiration, in which she had had no training whatever. I guess that whatever small chance of survival John had stood was extinguished at that point. Still, she meant well.

The road outside our house was occasionally used as an

arena for female argument. Several times I witnessed exciting slanging matches between two matrons from 'The Buildings' These would sometimes be finally settled by fisticuffs. When these events took place a crowd of onlookers would form a circle round the antagonists, offering advice and cheering them on in the event of violence. I only remember my mother taking part in this sport on one occasion when she fell out with Mrs Bumstead from 'The Buildings'. I've no idea what the argument was about, but it didn't reach a violent conclusion. My mother emerged victorious in the battle of words and a browbeaten Mrs Bumstead retreated back to her squalid flat. I know that she came over in tears later and apologized to my mother — probably because she knew that mother wouldn't let her borrow a cup of sugar again unless she did.

Sunday was an exciting day. Not because of the Sunday School which I loathed but was forced to attend, but because the winkle man came round with his barrow in the afternoon and would park outside 'The Building's. I would be sent over for a couple of pints of winkles or possibly some shrimps and we would all sit around, armed with pins, and eat them with our afternoon tea. Occasionally I would be taken to church. The nearest church was St Margaret's in Belmont Hill about a quarter of a mile away. The Rector was the Rev. Gillingham, who, in his youth had been a famous cricketer. He was a large, bald-headed man with an ugly monkey-like face, but he was very good-hearted. I believe he baptised me, but I don't remember the incident. I do remember though, after one of his Services to which I had been taken, being asked, 'What part did you enjoy most?' 'I liked the hymn about the Teddy Bear' I replied. Everyone was puzzled about this until it was recalled that we had sung a hymn entitled 'Gladly the Cross I'd Bear. In the winter the Winkle man would be replaced by the Crumpet Man and we would enjoy toasted crumpets round the fire. I remember that at the age of about three I tripped and fell backwards on to the fire, sitting full on it like a chair. Fortunately the fire had just been made up and the coals were still black instead of red hot. I was dragged off by my father and suffered no more than minor burns to the top of my legs where they had caught the fire basket. At about the same age my father bought me a little tricycle. The pedals were mounted on each side of the front wheel. I was delighted with it and lost no time in taking it out on to the pavement in front of the house. I didn't notice that the left pedal was held in place by a nail which stuck out at right angles. So intent was I in showing off my new transport that I didn't feel the first scratch as the nail caught my leg. Whether this severed a nerve or not I don't know, but I certainly felt no pain and continued to pedal up and down. Every turn of the wheel drew the nail across my leg twice, once up and once down. After a few minutes a passer-by noticed that I was in trouble —bleeding like a stuck pig, and took me home. I lost a lot of blood and to this day have two large scars on the inside of my left calf. My father was held entirely to blame by my mother and was treated by her accordingly.

A particular friend of mine was Frankie Crowhurst who lived further up Dacre Park, towards Eaton Grove. Frankie was about the same age as myself and started in the infants class at Northbrook School at the same time as I did. His father was a jobbing gardener, a very hard-working, pleasant man. He was also a Communist. The family was very poor but scrupulously clean. Frankie had two older sisters and one younger one. When I was about five I was invited to Frankie's birthday party. I took along a small toy of some sort as a birthday present. I remember we had some games and eventually sat down to tea. I had a look round the table at what was on offer and announced 'We've got better than this at home'. I then left the table and returned home. What a horrid child I must have been. Mrs Crowhurst related to my mother what had happened and of course my mother was very embarrassed. They both had a good laugh about it though. I don't remember being invited to Frankie's subsequent birthday parties.

A regular summer visitor was the Walls Ice Cream man. I preferred Walls Ice Cream to his competitor, Eldorado, and found that the ice cream supplied by the Italian Okey Pokey man was foul. The Walls Ice Cream man travelled on a tricycle built round a refrigerated box, painted in white and dark blue squares. He was a very small man with a peaked cap and bicycle clips. The ice cream was kept cold by blocks of solid CO_2. Sometimes, for a treat he would take out a piece of CO_2 and hold it against the bell on his bicycle which would then give out a strong ringing tone. I found this slightly baffling at the time, come to that I still do, but I suppose there was some scientific explanation for it.

The Walls Ice Cream man would toil up the hill and park outside 'The Buildings' where he would ring his bell furiously to attract attention. He also distributed large square cards displaying the letter 'W' which, if placed in the window, would ensure a personal call from him. I became somewhat unpopular with my father for putting these cards in the window. The Walls Ice Cream man would call, and my father, to avoid having to deny placing the card in the window would have to buy a Family Brick which, because we had no refrigerator, would have to be eaten straight away.

Another regular passer-by was the lamplighter. He would arrive on his bicycle every evening armed with a long pole which he would reach up to the lamp and pull on a ring, causing the gas to light with a satisfying plop. He would be back again the following morning to extinguish the lamp by the same means. Early every morning a man, I suppose was a knocker-up, would pass by. I never saw him but he would stand outside and shout, 'How about it?' A few seconds later and further up the road he would give a whistle, Ooo ii oo. I never heard him after I was about seven so I suppose he must have died. Living in 'The Buildings' was an old man called Fred. He was a countryman really, but then there were still a lot of fields around in South East London. In the autumn he would turn up on the doorstep with a cloth filled with horse mushrooms or chestnuts or sometimes a bunch of wild flowers for my mother. He always wore corduroy trousers with string tied round the knees, and large boots. Sometimes he would be hired to do a bit of digging in the garden.

At the top of Dacre Park was Victoria Mews, at end of which was a Carters Yard. It was owned by a man named Manchester. He had a string of magnificent Shire Horses which pulled heavy carts with the owners name emblazoned on the side. People used him for removals or carrying building materials and so on. His horses were very popular with the local small boys who would follow along behind with buckets and shovels collecting horse manure. My mother bought great quantities of this at a penny a bucket. Our garden was very productive as a result. I thought I would try this lucrative task out one day and duly went out armed with two buckets and a coal shovel. After touring the roads for several hours I managed to fill them. On the way home

I passed the home of a great friend of my mother, Mrs Helen Severez. She seemed somewhat puzzled when I offered her one of the buckets but eventually took it but didn't give me a penny. Come to think of it she didn't even return the empty bucket. I returned home somewhat disconsolately with the second bucket and offered it to my mother. She was very upset to find that her son had lowered himself to collecting horse manure and didn't give me a penny either. When I told her that Mrs Severez had been presented with a bucket she nearly had a fit. I never heard the last of that episode and didn't bother collecting horse manure again. From this I learned to be sure of one's market before going into business.

Down the hill about 70-yards was 'Jennings', the little grocers' shop. Mr Jennings was about 60 and his wife about the same. They had a daughter who was about 35 and unmarried. She was occasionally wooed by a rather unsavoury person, but I don't think they ever got married. My mother had a weekly account at Mr Jennings shop and I often went on errands for groceries. 'A quarter of ham cut thin to make it look a lot' was a favourite order. I would occasionally purchase a hap'orth of sweets. I used to like the assorted sweets, usually the remains of almost empty jars which would be lumped together and sold at a penny for a quarter of a pound. This was, I reckoned, the best bargain. I remember, one day we had a chimney fire in the drawing room. Salt was my mothers remedy for chimney fires and actually it worked quite well. No salt in the larder. 'Quick run down to Jennings and get some', said my mother. I ran down the road. Jennings shop was crowded. Forcing my way to the front I gasped, 'Quick, give us a packet of salt, my chimneys on fire'. Thus I coined a phrase I have heard repeated with variations many times since.

Further down the road from Jennings was the Post Office and Stationer. It was run by Mr Bratt. Mr Bratt was a very little man standing no more that four feet six inches. He had a little weather-beaten face and a large moustache. He was usually dressed in a grey overall. The shop had an L-shaped counter. One side of the counter held piles of newspapers and magazines and stacks of packet sweets, glue, ink and writing-paper, the other side was the Post Office behind a grill. I used to collect my comics from Mr Bratt twice a week. One day I was waiting to collect *The Hotspur*, when someone pulled out a newspaper from a pile and dislodged a stack of chewing gum which showered on me. I helped pick them up and returned them to Mr Bratt. I collected my comic and returned home. I had been home for about ten minutes when on reaching into my jacket pocket found several packets of chewing gum. I was horrified. Having been brought up to be totally honest I went straight back to Mr Bratt and said, 'Mr Bratt, these chewing gums fell into my pocket'. I handed them back and he looked at me in a suspicious way. I don't think he ever believed that it was accidental, and I'm sure he never trusted me afterwards. I learned from this that 'Honesty is not necessarily the best policy'. Another thing that Mr Bratt used to sell were sheets of heavy card with models printed on them. By cutting out the patterns in accordance with the instructions and then bending and gluing them together one could make anything from a cottage to a battleship. These were known as 'Penny plain and Tuppence coloured', and afforded hours of enjoyment.

Opposite the Post Office was a bakery run by Mr Ross. This was mainly noteworthy for the quality of its excellent doughnuts. My mother sometimes sent me down for a loaf of bread. I would loiter back home inhaling the fragrance of the hot bread and if I was lucky enough to have got one which had been baked in close contact with its neighbour, thereby leaving a soft area in its side, it was my great joy to pinch off lumps of the fragrant bread and eat it on my slow return up the hill. Often the inside of the loaf would be half hollowed out by the time I got home. Another thing I could not resist was evaporated milk. I remember, at the age of about four, taking a full tin out of the cupboard. It had been punctured on each side at the top for easy pouring and I took it under the table where, protected by the long tablecloth, I tucked into it. Having drunk my fill I was not quite sure how much remained, so I had to keep taking another swig to make sure that there was still some there. Eventually there wasn't. I got into trouble over that.

When I was old enough I joined the Cubs. A lady called Akela whose real name was Ethel Jones used to teach us to tie knots and play ball games and so on in the Church Hall at Christ Church in Lee Park. Christ Church was about half a mile from home if one went round the proper way. During the summer, however, I would take a short cut through a nursery which I reached by going up the road where Ross's Bakery was. This way was less than half the distance. It was a private path through there but no one seemed to mind. The only problem was that the gates were closed by the time Cubs was finished. I did try climbing over the gate on one occasion but got caught on some spikes at the top and tore my trousers rather badly. This made me somewhat unpopular with my mother so I didn't try it again. When the nights started to draw in, the gates of the nursery were closed early so it meant going the long way round. Lee Park was very badly lit, although it was one of the better class roads in Lee. On the way up the road, the other cubs and I used to make a loud yodelling noise at intervals to give us courage and to identify one another. Many an old lady walking up the road has been frightened, almost to death, by a cub creeping up behind her and yodelling loudly from a range of eighteen inches. This evil behaviour had to be balanced by doing a good turn every day. This varied from knocking over a box of apples outside a greengrocers shop and the picking up most of them, to the old chestnut of dragging a protesting old lady across heavy traffic to the side of the road she didn't want to be. I found one excellent good deed was to grab a passing dog, going about its lawful business, and after reading the address on the collar, dragging it off home and banging loudly on the front door till the owner arrived. Returning the allegedly 'lost' dog not only counted as a good deed but also occasionally reaped a reward of a penny.

When I got a bit older I transferred to the Scouts. My mother couldn't afford a new uniform but managed to get some second-hand stuff. I remember the hat was about five sizes too large. It had to undergo some major surgery before I could use it. It was split down the back and across the brim. A large Vee-shaped piece was taken out and then it was stitched back together again. The end result was somewhat comical since the crown, having been reduced in size, remained tall while the brim, being for a much larger head, could have been used as an umbrella.

The Scoutmaster was Mr Aspinal who, coincidentally, worked in the same office as my father's sister — auntie May — at County Hall. I had to keep my nose pretty clean there as he passed on news of my progress — or lack of it — to auntie May from which it rapidly reached my father's ears.

The Scout troop also used the Church Hall at Christ Church for their meetings. One evening the vicar of Christ Church visited our meeting. After a chat he inquired who regularly attended Church. I saw no reason to add lying to my day's evil deeds so I told him that I did not. Henceforth I was banned from the Scouts. My career with them had lasted all of six months. Just as well in the circumstances that not much money had been expended on my uniform. However, I did have the distinction during that time of being one of the Scouts who lined the route of the procession at the Silver Jubilee of King George V. Several people behind me complained bitterly because they could see nothing of the procession, their view being totally blocked by my hat.

CHAPTER 2

'Man', my father proclaimed one day, 'is the only animal to stand upright. The more upright he stands the more of a man he is.' I think, reflecting on this over a period of a great many years, that it was probably something which his father had told him, and for all I know, a wisdom which had been passed down from time immemorial. I don't want to reflect on the truth of this remark since, in my lifetime, I have known many men who stood totally upright but who could not, by the greatest stretch of imagination, be described as manly. At the time, however, I could only accept this gem as a truism. From that day on I did a very good imitation of a Pouter Pigeon. Every time I caught myself relaxing I would throw my shoulders back take a mighty breath and glance furtively round to make sure that no one had noticed the slumping Beaden. I suppose that this exercise did me no harm, since today I have a 50-inch chest.

My sister and brother had both had piano lessons. Lucy Kettle who lived across the road gave these at sixpence an hour. She was an old lady whose face somewhat resembled that of a toad. Regardless of her looks, however, she was a sweet old thing. Each of them had two, one-hour-sessions each week. We were regaled with 'The Bluebells of Scotland' and 'Stephanie Gavotte' by Kathleen and Ralph on the piano in the drawing room. Kathleen was quite tone deaf and had no interest in the piano. Ralph, however, was quite talented and could eventually play quite well. In due course, at the age of about nine, my turn came for piano lessons. I was hopeless. Worse than Kathleen if that were possible. My mother persevered for about six months, after which Miss Kettle told her that she was wasting her money. The next step was the violin. An elderly, rather dilapidated instrument was procured and a course of lessons arranged. These were at school during the lunch period. On the first occasion I turned up, the class of about twenty pupils commenced. All of them had been taking lessons for over a year. No instructions were given to me. I didn't even know how to hold the thing. However, presuming that the other pupils had it about right, I tucked the instrument under my chin and followed their example by sawing away with them. The dreadful noises I was making were drowned by the efforts of the experts. 'Well done', said the teacher at the end of the session, collecting my six pence. Subsequent lessons followed the same pattern. My mother persevered with the lessons, but after six months it was clear that Paganini need never worry about me as a rival. After that it was arranged for a friend of Ralph's —Jack Collins, who lived in 'The Buildings', to give me lessons. After a few weeks I found that I could give a fair imitation of an air raid siren. The lessons were discontinued.

My father got paid each Friday afternoon and, on his return home at tea time, came the ritual handing over of the house keeping money. In addition to this he used to give my mother a half-pound slab of Cadbury's Whole Nut Chocolate, which she referred to as her 'wages'. I don't know how much the weekly house-keeping money amounted to but it was rarely enough. Usually by Thursday morning she was skint. This would cause problems, in particular as far as the gas and electricity were concerned, since both were on 'one-shilling' meters. My mother was highly delighted when, one day, she found that a token given away by the Co-op fitted both meters perfectly. Obviously there was no intent to defraud here, since the meter was emptied each quarter by the collector, and at this stage she had to cough up the correct amount. Looking back on it though, I am astounded that nothing was ever said about this practice. The gas man or the electricity man would sit down and drink his cup of tea, empty out the coin box and laboriously count the spoil. 'You owe 18-shillings, Mrs Beaden', he would announce. Usually she would have the money saved up by the time of his arrival and she would hand this over and the tokens would be returned for later use. I suppose most of the housewives in the street were equally hard-up and probably all of them engaged in the same practice.

My cousin, Arnold Wheaton came to visit us. He was an officer in the Merchant Navy and hailed from Brixham in Devon. He was in London attending a course which, if successful, would give him his Masters Ticket. He was a little man with a beaky nose. His mother, Rose, was my father's half-sister. After six months he visited us again. 'This,' he announced, 'is to introduce Captain Wheaton.' We all congratulated him and he promised to take my mother on a world cruise when he became Captain of a cruise liner. Unfortunately he never reached that pinnacle. He did however become a First Officer and had his ship sunk under him several times during the war.

My father was a keen player of Bridge and Chess. For years an old bachelor friend of his, Bill Axham, would come every Wednesday evening and the two of them would settle down to play Chess. Bill Axham had a deep, croaking voice like an untuneful frog. He was a very poor Chess player and never won. At the end of each evening he would hold a post mortem on what he should have done to beat my father. One evening in a fit of uncharacteristic kindness and no doubt encouraged by my mother, he allowed Bill to win a game. Poor old Bill was like a dog with two tails, crowing over his victory. My father, however, soured the occasion by telling Bill that he had let him win. It was a long time before he visited us again.

Three times a week my father went to his Bridge Club. He was, without doubt, the most brilliant Bridge player ever. His memory was phenomenal. He could remember every card played and the order in which the bidding was made, not just for the previous evening but for years back. He was for ever bringing home prizes from Bridge Tournaments. When it came to Bridge he was also the most boring person I have ever known. From the age of six he explained to me the bids and play in the previous evenings games. His partners usually let him down in some way thereby cheating him out of the top prize. I made a mental note never to play Bridge and I never have.

My father was forever building wireless sets. Being an electrical genius he knew about these things. He usually started off with a piece of plywood onto which he would mount various valves and other components, connected together with bits of wire. A loudspeaker and various tuning devices were liberally scattered across the surface. Bits of flex connected other loudspeakers hanging on the walls and aerial wires were draped across the ceiling. Eventually audible music or conversation erupted from the loudspeakers and my father would step back looking pleased with himself. 'That will do temporarily,' he would announce, and so it would be left for the next twelve months, when the spirit would move him to build another set on the same lines. Woe betide my mother if she dared to dust or clean anywhere near the wireless. 'Who the hell has been mucking about over here?,' he would demand when he noticed that the set had ceased to function and that half an inch of dust was missing from the valves.

Every summer the mulberry season arrived. The old tree

would produce its annual harvest of luscious fruit and for weeks I would give a fair imitation of a monkey up in the branches. It was an easy tree to climb and it never let me down. Not so Ralph, however, when he got a bit big for climbing. He was stretched out flat along one of the branches when it suddenly parted company from the main trunk, depositing him flat on his face on the ground below. A drop of about twelve feet, as I recollect it, Ralph didn't climb the tree much after that. My mother and I had a working arrangement about the harvest. I did the picking and she did the selling. We split the proceeds. I used to climb the tree with a two-pound glass jam-jar tied round my waist. This would hold about a pound of fruit. There was an art in picking the ripe fruit without squashing it. The neighbours would pay a penny a jar full. Sometimes my mother would use the fruit to make jam or wine in which case I got nothing for picking it, but in a good summer we would each make about sixpence a day during the fruiting season. Quite a useful sum for a hard-up housewife. Even more so for a hard-up schoolboy. I remember one day an itinerant greengrocer came to the door wanting to buy some of the fruit. Unfortunately, my mother did not explain to him that it was sold by the jam-jar full, not by the pound, as we didn't possess any scales. My mother asked me to pick what I could and in a short time I had produced twelve jars full. My mother received a shilling for this and a few minutes later the man returned complaining that he had only got ten pounds. I was a bit put out by this and collected all the windfalls I could find, including those with bird-dropping on them to make up the other two pounds. I also communicated to the man that I could do without his custom in future.

The local children would come up the footpath which ran along the bottom of the garden and collect any fruit which had dropped. I had a wonderful time up the tree, where the branches spread over the path. Stretched out on a branch I was totally concealed from those below by the thick blanket of leaves. As my victims bent to pick up the fruit I could drop a large over-ripe berry on to their clean white shirts. Mulberry leaves an indelible stain on clothing and my conscience pricks me when I think of the innumerable wallopings I must have been responsible for. But not much!

During my childhood my mother encouraged me to have

many pets. Mice and white rats, green Jersey lizards, slow worms, grass snakes, gold fish, guinea pigs, rabbits, cats and dogs and even baby crocodiles. I remember once we went on holiday to Dymchurch in Kent. We stayed in a converted wooden army hut which had been erected near one of the Martello Towers. We went to a local Fair where one of the events was bowling for a pig. The idea was to bowl three balls into a number of hoops each marked with a different score. The prize was a pig or a pound. At the end of the day my father shared the top score with another man. I had badly wanted that baby pig but my father settled for ten-shillings as his share. Just across the road from where we were staying was a dog breeder and for ten-shillings my father bought a beautiful Spaniel puppy. We took it home with us the next day. It was a delightful creature but it died from distemper within a week despite expensive veterinary treatment. I was very upset by this and shortly afterwards a little white mongrel bitch arrived which I named Pat. She was a great companion and very clever. She could walk on her hind legs all round the room and do all sorts of other tricks. We also had a tabby cat which arrived as a stray. When he came he was very humble but later when he got his feet under the table he ruled the household. We called him Uriah Hepe.

I don't know why my mother bought the baby crocodile, I don't remember ever asking for one. It came from a shop at Lee Green. It only lived for three days. My mother returned the corpse and was given another one. This one refused to eat and she had to force feed it, sticking lumps of meat down its throat with her fingers. It survived for about three months. The tortoises usually did well during the summer, when they had the run of the garden, but rarely survived the winter — a smelly corpse being tipped from the box at the end of the hibernation. The slowworms were more successful. I would frequently take then to school with me. They were very tame and would curl round my wrist like a bracelet, remaining quite still except for the occasional flash of the tongue out and in. I occasionally gave lectures on my pets thereby enhancing my reputation as 'The Professor'. The slowworms normally lived in a big galvanised bath just outside the back door. This proved a good environment for them and they had a dish of water, a pile of grass-cutting and a quantity of horse manure which would attract the flies which they would eat. They were also very fond of meal worms and small red bandling worms. During the heat of the summer baby slowworms usually appeared and disappeared. Maybe the adults ate them. I never found out.

I was a child of infinite patience. One day, on going to the rabbit shed, I saw a shadowy movement in an unoccupied cage. After staying quite motionless for over an hour I saw a small brown mouse slip across the floor of the cage to a bit of discarded food. I noticed that as it fed its tail slipped down a gap in the flooring of the cage. Later the same day I sat under the cage and after a couple of hours was rewarded by the sight of the tail slipping down through the floor again. I cautiously stretched out my hand and grabbed the tail. I bet that was the most surprised mouse around at the time. I pulled it gently down through the gap and was rewarded with a vicious bite on my finger. I kept hold however and popped the mouse into a jam-jar. I took it to show my mother, after which I let it go again

My mother bought me the Green Jersey Lizards. Again, I don't know why. I can't say I really wanted them since they had a tendency to bite the hand that fed them. However, they arrived and were kept in a box with a piece of glass let into the front. They were not overly thrilled at their situation and were quite unhandleable. One day one of them jumped out of the box while my mother was showing it to a neighbour. Off down the garden it went at great speed with my mother in hot pursuit. It was lost among the flower beds in a very short time. An immediate search proved unsuccessful but a few days later mother lifted a stone on the rockery and found the recalcitrant lizard underneath. She grabbed it, only to find that the tail came off in her hand while the rest of the lizard made good its escape. Mother had hysterics and we never saw the half lizard again. The tail however, jumped about for hours, much to the amusement of Uriah Hepe.

The family summer holidays were almost always spent in Devon. My father had an old 'Matchless' motor bike and sidecar. Kathleen never accompanied us on these holidays so the motor bike was just big enough for us. It was the bright yellow sidecar from which the vehicle derived its name — 'The Flying Banana'. Dad would drive, wearing a leather motor-cycling helmet, with Ralph on the pillion. My mother sat in the sidecar with me on her lap. Various bits of luggage were tied on with string. To the best of my recollection we only crashed once, when my father took a sharp corner too fast. Ralph flew over a hedge into a field and suffered concussion. father broke his leg, the sidecar finished up upside down in a ditch but mother and I escaped with minor scratches. Poor mother took all the skin off her nose and looked a mess. I was about four at the time. I know we decided to abandon the holiday and went home — my father driving 200 miles with his leg broken in two places.

On subsequent, more successful holidays we used to stay at a village called Dolton in North Devon. A lovely unspoiled spot. My father had spent many of his boyhood holidays there. We always stayed at the local Pub — the 'Royal Oak', which was owned by Mr and Mrs Gill. They had two sons, Vic who was about Ralph's age and Ron who was a little older than me. Mr Gill, in addition to owning the pub, had a small farm. At the back of the pub was a farmyard with chickens, geese and ducks. There was also a cowshed where half a dozen cows went twice a day for milking. If it happened to rain my favourite place was the barn which was half full of hay. I would clamber up to the top of the hay and inhale the glorious country smells from the farmyard below.

I was always given my pocket-money at the beginning of the holiday and I developed a taste for rough cider which cost two pence for half-a-pint at the bar. I was about six years old at this particular time and I would sit at the bar with my half-pint jug in my hand, chatting to the locals. Eventually Mr Gill enquired of my father if this was in order. I don't think my parents were particularly bothered either way as neither of them were 'teatotal'. However, for the sake of appearances, I suppose, my activities were curtailed.

My father introduced me to the gentle art of night-lining for trout and eels which abounded in the little streams which ran through the nearby woods. To do this we would arm ourselves with three-tined pickle forks. Wading into the water we would gently pick up a stone and wait for the disturbed water to clear. With any luck we would find a Loach or a Bullhead, or Millers Thumb as it was called locally. A quick stab with the pickle fork and a wriggling fish would be lifted out. Having collected a dozen or so of these for bait, the next task was to cut an appropriate number of hazel sticks from the nearby bushes. To the end of each of these would be tied a piece of stout fishing line and a hook. With the bait attached to the hook, the stick was wedged under a stone in one of the deeper pools. On returning the following day, about half of the lines produced as good rainbow trout or an eel. This, of course, was poaching, but the fish always tasted so much better than anything that could be bought.

My parents had some other friends in Dolton —local farmers named Folland who lived in a very old farmhouse called Woolridge. This was a delightful old house and it and all the barns and outbuildings were beautifully thatched. I was allowed to help in milking the cows. Mrs Folland had a large kitchen with an enormous black iron, wood-burning stove. Each day she emptied about five gallons of fresh milk into a vast cauldron on top of this stove and after a couple of hours of gentle heat the beautiful thick clotted cream would rise to the surface. Some of this was set aside to eat with the home-baked bread and strawberry jam. The remainder would be placed in a large earthenware crock and allowed to cool. Mrs Folland would then set about this with her hand in a brisk churning motion and lo! after about a quarter of an hour, out would come some lovely creamy butter. This really was the Food of the Gods. Usually our holiday coincided with the harvest. The big field on the other side of the road was always cut first. Mr Folland or one of his sons would take two great Shire Horses up to the field and hitch them to the reaper. Then round and round the field they went, every few yards a sheaf of corn was thrown out to be collected by the army of helpers assembled for the purpose. A quick twist with a handful of corn stalks and the sheaf was tied up and then stacked together with half-a-dozen others to form a stook. Round and round went the reaper and smaller and smaller grew the square of corn in the middle of the field. The helpers grasped their shotguns firmly. Those who didn't possess shotguns stood ready with their sticks. Suddenly a rabbit or two would break out of the corn. They never got far. The stooks confused them and they couldn't run in a straight line. A blast of shot or a runner with a stick would account for all of them. As many as 50 rabbits would be caught in a single field by these methods, not to mention the occasional pheasant or fox. At the conclusion of the harvest everyone sat down on the grass. Mrs Folland and her daughters produced the harvest tea. Home-made bread, saffron buns, scones thick with home made butter, and strawberry jam and cream in great mounds. Great jugs of home-made cider. All this, followed by a share out of the rabbits. This went on day after day as the various farms gathered in their harvest. What wonderful times.

The Follands had a very attractive daughter named Margaret. She and Ralph became quite fond of one another during our yearly holidays. I think that both Mrs Folland and her daughter hoped that matters would progress, eventually, to his 'popping the question'. According to Ralph it eventually did — when she was about seventeen and he 'had his evil way' with her!

The River Torridge ran about a mile from the village and this was a great favourite of mine. Much of the river was quite deep and Ralph and I would dive and swim to our hearts content. When we sat on the banks great salmon would make their exuberant leaps after the flies and nymphs which abounded. Further up, the river shallowed and widened and we would throw flat stones and make them skip on the surface. We often picnicked on the banks and Ralph and I would explore the woods in which were scattered the remains of a few derelict abandoned cottages. Also, in the woods near the river was a water mill where lived the Misses Budd who had known my father since he was a boy. They were well into their seventies at the time and looked like two cheerful pink witches. I don't know how they survived. They didn't work and they didn't grow anything. They had a few ducks and hens and guinea fowl scratching about. Maybe they had money stashed away. We also visited Frank Johns and his wife who lived in the village. They were old friends of my father's youth. Frank was the local gamekeeper so we had to be very secretive about our poaching. I'm sure we were not he only ones engaged in this dastardly activity. At the pub we often had a meal of fresh salmon. When my father wanted to buy some to take home, Mr Gill became very reticent about his source of supply.

For some reason my mother tried to convey the impression at the pub that she was a journalist, or at least connected with the world of journalism. This was probably because of her friendship with Mrs Severez, of horse manure fame. She used to write down odd notes during conversations. I believe she used to pass these to Mrs Severez who would write poetry about them. I'm sure the country yokels were impressed! Mrs Severez lived about 100-yards away on the other side of the road. A tallish woman with a very bad acned complexion. She had supposedly been married to a Frenchman, Mr Sevrez, presumably during the war. In any case she had a daughter Betty, about the same age as Kathleen. She also had a man friend, Mr Varwell, known as Chang who stayed with her occasionally. Betty spent a lot of time with her grandmother in France. Chang was, I believe, the sub-editor of one of the provincial newspapers. Mrs Severez considered herself to be in a class well above the other residents of Dacre Park. She wrote a bit of poetry each day for the *Daily Sketch* under the pen-name Gloria Storm. My mother sometimes had a very close relationship with her. At other times they quarrelled and couldn't stand the sight of one another. One way and another she was a weird sort of character. I remember one occasion when we had been out in the Flying Banana for the day down into Kent and we came back with a mass of bluebells. My mother insisted that I take a bunch over for Mrs Severez who was blowing warm at the time. I was greeted enthusiastically as though I had presented her with a bouquet of orchids. To my horror a poem about me appeared in the *Daily Sketch* a few days later.

JUBILEE BOUQUET

A knock at the door and a ring at the bell
the sound of footsteps I know so well;
and the clear little voice of Antony John
(with his red white and blue rosette pinned on)
Antony John from over the way
(who thought of your rhymester on Jubilee Day).
Flushed and smiling there he stood
with country flowers from a Kentish wood.
English blossoms blue as the sea
that bounds the isle where hearts go free.
A bunch of bluebells ringing their chime;
Antony John's little Jubilee rhyme.
He watched me with his grave young eyes,
while I arranged them countrywise
in a gold brown crock from a southern shire
(where they'd be lighting their beacon fire).
Mixed with twigs of hazel green
a bonnier posy I've never seen:
or a lovelier smile for a Jubilee Day,
than Antony John's from across the way.
                    Gloria Storm.
                    Friday. May 10 1935

Hardly the appropriate description of a little monster who yodeled at old ladies in a dark street from a range of eighteen inches!

My mother also featured in Mrs Severez's literary outpourings from time to time when they were feeling benevolent towards one another. At other times she was a right cow. I well remember one hot summer day when I was playing with half a dozen kids in the road outside her house. I think she and my mother had recently fallen out. It so happened that the Walls Ice Cream man cycled along just at that time. It was a Saturday and I had just received my pocket-money, but before I could make a purchase the door flew open and Mrs Severez rushed out into the road — straight to the Ice Cream man. She bought all of the children a large ice cream wafer — except me. When the Ice Cream man asked if I was to be included she said, 'No not that one'. When everyone was served I went to the Ice Cream man and spent my entire weeks pocket-money on a Family Brick which I took home and ate. I was as sick as a dog. However I related the incident to my mother and to my surprise she gave me another weeks pocket-money. Poor Mrs Severez. I suppose she was a bit mental.

When I was seven- or eight-years-old my brother Ralph started to dig a trench. It was at the bottom of the garden near the mulberry tree. I was allowed to assist in the excavation. Initially it was a hole in the ground about six-feet by three-feet and about three-feet deep. Various games could be played in this and I invited my friends round to join in. We all had wooden guns and swords and hours of pleasure were had by all. The trench started to grow. Then a roof was put on it. It was deepened so that we could all stand up under the roof. The surplus earth was piled on top. Duck boards were placed in the bottom and furniture moved in. A kitchen extension was dug and an old stove installed. Two new rooms were added and furnished. Old carpets were laid on the duck boards and an electric cable brought light to our surroundings. Eventually after a couple of years one of the neighbours blew the gaff and the rating officer arrived. The trench was filled in. I still have happy memories of it though as, I am sure, have all the kids who joined in the fun of cooking underground and playing doctors and nurses!

From time to time my parents would have musical evenings. My two aunts and various friends would arrive and we would all sit round in the dining room and the drawing room, with the partition opened. Plates of sandwiches would appear and mother would take her place at the piano. My father had a good baritone voice and would sing, 'Trumpeter, What are you Sounding Now' or 'The Cobbler's Song', from ' Chu-Chin-Chow' or 'I Did But See

Her Passing By'. My mother would sing 'Londonderry Air'. Then they would both sing 'Pale Hands I Love'. When I was very young I was made to sing 'Christopher Robin is Saying His Prayers'. I loathed this and refused to participate at a very early age.

When Kathleen left Lewisham College after becoming a lady she was apprenticed to a hairdressing establishment which went under the name of Maison Maurice. I believe that this place had a good reputation and she got on quite well. In order to afford her plenty of practice various neighbours were invited over and for a very small sum had their hair cut or styled or permed. I remember one day when Mrs Smallpiece arrived to have her hair done. She was a rather small shrill woman, whose daughter, Edna, was a great lump of a thing about my age. I think she must have dozed off during the cutting process. Anyway, there was a sudden almighty shriek when Kathleen cut a lump of her ear off. I don't think it was a very big lump and some effort was made to stick it back in position by 'Nurse Beaden'. To no avail I fear. I don't think Kathleen made a charge for that.

A year or two later Kathleen joined a local Operatic Society called 'The Utopians'. To the best of my knowledge they never performed anything but Gilbert and Sullivan operas. I don't think I do Kathleen an injustice when I say that she was no Maria Callas. In fact she was invariably in the back row of the chorus. Other members of 'The Utopians' visited our house and my mother had to play the piano while the house rang to the strains of 'Two Little Maids from School', 'The Flowers that Bloom in the Spring', and many other detestable tunes. I pride myself on being a lover of good music, but as a result of being dragged screaming twice a year to sit through mediocre performances of 'The Pirates of Penzance', 'Trial by Jury', 'Iolanthie' and 'The Mikado', I loathe Gilbert and Sullivan with a deadly loathing. However, Kathleen found a husband at 'The Utopians' and they lived happily ever after, so I suppose some good came out of it.

One of Kathleen's friends was Barbara Tutt, who, I believe, she first met at Lewisham College. Her parents had a wet fish shop in Pound Place, Eltham. (What an appropriate address). Barbara was, I recollect, a petite brunette, quite pretty but fragile looking. She spent a lot of time at our house. Her brother Gene was a professional ballet dancer. A pleasant chap who had the misfortune to suffer with a terrible complexion. I never saw him dance, as ballet was not a strong favourite with me. I believe that a promising career was forecast for him but unfortunately, at an early age he died of tuberculosis.

My mother had a 'fancy man' at one time. At least that was how she referred to him. His name was Mr Gill but she always called him 'Gillie'. He was a very small man. Not at all my mother's type. I believe that at one time he was a lodger, but I'm not sure about this. He was an insurance agent and used to call in about once a month. He loved my mother's 'sad' cake and she would make it especially for him. She would make a fruitcake mixture and put it in the oven. Halfway through the cooking she had to open the oven door and slam it shut. This had the effect of making the cake go flat and gooey in the middle, which is what he liked. I don't think there was anything serious between them and eventually he stopped calling.

My father was also an admirer of the opposite sex. On one of his, not infrequent, hospital incarcerations when suffering from a duodenal ulcer, he was nursed by a 'Nurse Nicholson'. He referred to her as 'Nicky'. She was an attractive woman of about 35 with very dark short hair and a good figure. She came from the Channel Islands and my father was smitten. When he came out of hospital Nicky was a frequent visitor at home. My mother loathed her but did her best to be polite. She once varnished the lavatory seat and told everyone how Nicky had yelped when she stood up, and how a close examination afterwards had revealed a large number of whiskers from Nicky's bottom stuck to the seat.

My father had bought our house around 1913. I believe it had cost £250. Originally my father's parents and his two sisters had lived there also. My mother didn't get on with them, particularly my two aunts who, unlike my mother, were very religious. After Kathleen and Ralph were born, however, they couldn't take the continual bawling and moved out. My paternal grandmother died before I was born and my maternal grandfather a couple of years after my birth. When I first knew my two aunts they lived about half-a-mile away in Glenton Road. My mother had twelve soldiers billeted on her during the first World War. God knows where she put them or how she managed with two babies to look after as well.

One day when I was about eight years old a 'For Sale' board went up outside the house. This was totally unexpected and I thought my mother would go mad she was in such a temper. It turned out that the house was leasehold and it was the lease, which only had a few years to run, which was for sale by auction. My parents certainly didn't have the sort of money which would be needed to buy the lease so a council-of-war was held. Eventually, my maternal grandmother was prevailed upon to sell some of her 'War Loan' stock and lend my parents the money. For some weeks prior to the auction people would arrive to view the house. They had a very hostile reception from my mother. On the due date, off went my parents to the auction. My mother related the events afterwards. The bidding opened at £50 and went up in bids of ten pounds. The only opposition was from a large fat Jew sitting behind them. Up went the bidding to £200. My mother in some panic started having a row with the Jew and distracted his attention sufficiently for my father to be able to purchase the lease for £250 which was their outside limit.

A couple of our summer holidays were spent at Hastings instead of Devon. This was probably when the heat was on, after Ralph rodgered Margaret Folland. We stayed with some people named Vine. Frank Vine lived in Lewisham and worked with my father at Elliott Brothers the Electrical Instrument makers. After the week on his own in Lewisham, Frank would go off home at the weekends and make up for lost time. Resultantly his wife produced a new infant each year. They didn't have a very large house and I don't remember how they managed to pack us in during our holidays. We preferred that part of the beach near the Fish Market where the boats were drawn up and never tired of watching the fishing boats coming in with their catch. As they neared the shore a large quantity of undersized fish would be thrown overboard. I used to wade in with my little shrimping net and often retrieved a couple of dozen small plaice or dabs which we would take back to our lodgings with us for supper.

One day when so engaged there were two older boys playing and swimming nearby. One of them said to the other, 'Look out, there's a turd'. This was a term with which I was not familiar. I went across with my shrimp-net thinking that it was some kind of fish. Shortly afterwards I found out what a turd was. It was at about this time that Ralph decided that I should learn to box. He had a couple of pairs of boxing gloves and we used to spend about half-an-hour each day sparring. Needless to say, I got well and truly thumped. Ralph being eight-years-older than me had a great deal of height, weight and reach advantage —and used it. I don't think I ever landed a blow on him —except once. 'Come on,' he said, 'I'm not going to hit you'. I waded in at this invitation and caught him a fourpenny-one on the nose. 'Right,' he said, wiping the tears from his eyes, 'now I am going to hit you'. And he did. I became a great defensive boxer. When I took up boxing at school I didn't get hit very much, the trouble was that I had no idea how to thump my opponents. Any contest I took part in was usually given the slow handclap. I learned eventually though, to very good effect.

From an early age I took a great interest in science and chemistry. Neither of my parents discouraged this and the wine cellar became my domain. I rigged up Bunsen burners and bought test tubes and chemicals and various retorts. The smells which occasionally emanated from the depths of the house left much to be desired. One of my first experiments entailed the construction of an illicit still. With the aid of this I managed to turn a large proportion of my mother's home-made wine into pure spirit. I also manufactured gunpowder and made fireworks. One very effective explosive I made I fortunately decided to test at a safe distance from the house. In order to do this I drilled a hole in one of the walls of the Trench and packed the substance into it. In order to detonate it I laid an electric cable the length of the garden. I then waited my opportunity and when my mother went out shopping and I was the only one in, I connected up the cable and switched on. The Trench developed yet another room and the Church Hall about 50 yards away sustained broken windows. No one ever traced this to me and I lay very low for some months afterwards. A lot of comment was made locally about vandals.

I learned how to make hydrogen and oxygen by passing and electric current through water. Fortunately I didn't cause an explosion on this occasion as the experiment took place in the wine cellar. I also made a very effective insecticide on one occasion by using a distillation of the leaves and flowers of various plants. This was long before pyrethrum had been discovered. Previous experiments on this line had failed when the resultant mixture had proved so ineffective that the only way I could kill the insects was to drown them in it. Speaking of drowning insects, I also discovered how to bring a fly back to life. If a fly is drowned for up to 48-hours and is quite dead on being removed from the liquid, it can be brought back to life by covering it with cigarette ash. Experiments of this sort made me feel somewhat superhuman so it was poetic justice, I suppose, when I invented an electric rat killer consisting of a brushed out piece of flex connected to the mains supply and placed over, but not quite touching a rat hole near the chicken shed. It duly killed a rat but I forgot to switch it off before removing the corpse. I was thrown across the garden for my carelessness.

One of my favourite weekly comics *The Adventure*, as a regular feature, invited its readers to submit any jokes they might have thought of, offering a variety of prizes for any which were considered good enough to publish. One day I thought of a jolly good joke. I sat down and drew a picture of two elephants, their trunks entwined in a knot. The caption was 'Now I'll show you how to tie a reef knot', I must have had a very retarded sense of humour because I thought this just about the funniest thing I had ever seen. I duly sent off my drawing and, to my astonishment, it was published. My prize duly arrived in the form of a cap pistol which worked on the principle of compressed air and a roll of paper. When the trigger was pulled it compressed the air in a chamber which was eventually discharged through the paper roll with a very satisfying bang. Actually it wasn't a bad toy at all. My name and address was, of course, published below the drawing. A few months passed and I received a letter bearing a Gold Coast stamp. It was from a small black boy named Kwasi Anani Atta who had seen the comic and was writing, wanting to be my pen friend. Of course I thought this a great idea and duly wrote off to him. In double-quick time I had a reply. A package containing two monkey skins and a request that I send him a football. He had to be joking. I didn't even have a football of my own. However the correspondence continued for a considerable time. His sister joined in and started a correspondence with my mother. Over the course of the next year I received letters from no less than twelve little black boys. Most of them sent monkey skins and they all wanted footballs. Eventually I received no more letters. The last one was from a little lad who said he had found the comic in a latrine. Presumably it had finished up by being used to wipe someone's bottom. I gathered from this experience that a child's life on the Gold Coast, consisted mainly of writing scrounging letters in the hope of obtaining a vast stock of footballs. Undoubtedly however, it had to be preferable to that of the local monkey who was clearly in great demand.

When I was about twelve-years-of-age, I discovered that I had a remarkable talent. I could waggle my ears! Not a lot, to be true. Quite noticeable though. I rather wish, all these years later, that I had concentrated on this party piece. I might, with constant practice and by attaching extensions to my appendages, have become the first person to achieve flight without mechanical power! I have yet to meet anyone else who can claim to waggle their ears.

I had a nickname when I was at school. 'Donkey Beaden.' This, however, had nothing to do with my prowess at ear waggling!

CHAPTER 3

When I was eleven years old I sat for several scholarships. One was for entry to a Grammar School, another was for Technical College. I can't remember what the third one was. I managed to pass all three though and decided that my natural bent was for a Technical Education. I was then admitted to the South East London Technical College at New Cross. This was a fine modern building with well equipped classrooms, laboratories, engineering workshops and gymnasium. The College was open to both sexes though we were strictly segregated. I felt somewhat out of my depth on starting here though. From being head boy at Northbrook School, I became the lowliest pupil at the Technical College. Considerable emphasis was placed on the learning of geometry and trigonometry, neither of which subjects had been touched upon at Northbrook. Most of the other pupils appeared to have had some grounding in these subjects at their previous schools so I was out on a limb. In view of my lack of knowledge and resultant disadvantage in these subjects I decided that I loathed them both. I also developed a strong dislike of the two masters who taught them. It was a very considerable time before I caught up. The practical subjects, however, I excelled in.

Among the female students I noticed one day a most attractive dark-haired girl of about my age. She was gorgeous, and I fell in love at first sight. Making contact proved difficult but eventually I lay in wait and found her waiting for a bus after school. Unfortunately she was heading in the opposite direction to me but, to hell with it, I got on the bus anyway. I did this for several days before I managed to pluck up the courage to speak to her. Eventually I struck up a halting conversation. I don't think she had even noticed me before, but I persevered. I found out that her name was Flossie Boggis. What a terrible name, but what a wonderful creature. First Love. Every meeting resulted in what was for me a new and painful medical condition. Orchitis amorosa acuta, or lovers balls. One day Flossie didn't turn up for school. A few days later I learned that she was very ill. She had contracted infantile paralysis, poliomyelitis as it is known today. She died the following day. So ended my first 'crush'.

I rather wanted to learn French but it was advised that German would be a better language to learn if one was embarking on a career in Engineering. There were no facilities at school for learning a second language so it was decided that I should have private tuition. A most extraordinary choice was made in the selection of a tutor. A little old man named Mr Bernard. One of my aunts had found him ostensibly selling boxes of matches in the gutter at Lewisham. In fact he was begging. He was an alcoholic, very smelly and dirty. My aunt wanted to 'Give him a chance', so he was engaged to teach me for one two hour session each week. He asked me to call him Professor Bernard but I'm afraid I gagged at the idea. Mr Bernard was, I believe, quite an intelligent man, or at least he probably had been. Strong drink had undoubtedly rotted whatever intelligence he may have once had. My grandmother was living with us at this time and the smelly Bernard decided that he would try to hang his hat up there. He was about her age. He spent much time trying to pump me about her, to find out how much money she had and so on. My progress in learning German was nil and eventually I got so fed up with his attitude that I had a word with my father about him. There was a stormy interview in which my father told Professor Bernard that he had better go back to selling matches in the gutter. Professor Bernard responded by telling my father that I was no good as a student as I was intellectually bankrupt. My father then threw him down the front steps. I gave up German after this.

One year an educational visit to Belgium was arranged by my school. My parents decided that I should take advantage of this and saved up for me to go. We were to stay at the Hotel Du Soleil, Rue de Pechur, Blankenburg. The trip which was to extend for a week took in a tour of the battlefields of the First World War. The arrangement was for us to pick up a coach opposite the school at nine o'clock on the morning of our departure. My mother insisted on accompanying me to near the departure point to make sure that I got safely aboard. She didn't come with me right to the coach for fear of embarrassing me in front of the other students. One of them, when I got aboard the coach, wanted to know who it was I had come with me. 'Oh,' said I, 'that's my mother'. 'Bloody liar,' he said, 'it's your sister.' I didn't discuss the matter any further but on my return from the trip I happened to mention it to my mother. I've never seen her so pleased. Talk about vanity. She preened herself and repeated the incident to anyone who would listen. What small snippets of praise it takes to bring a little happiness into peoples lives. One of our Saturday trips on the 'Flying Banana' took us down into Kent. I don't know if my father planned it, but we finished up in a lane at a place called Culverstone, between Meopham and Wrotham. We pulled into a clearing at the side of the road and went into the woodland. Mostly silver birch and chestnut. We all got out and went into the wood for a picnic. It was a delightful spot. Rabbits and squirrels abounded, masses of birds in the trees. When we had finished our picnic and had a good wander round, we piled into the 'Flying Banana' and headed for home. At the top of Wrotham Hill my father pulled into a lay-by where, it transpired, was a site-office. Half an hour went by when he emerged and announced, 'I've bought that woodland'. It turned out that he had bought two plots amounting to about half-an-acre. I believe it cost £50 and was paid for by installments over several years. From then on our weekend habits were transformed. A bit of the woodland was cleared, and four silver birch in a convenient oblong were topped. Demolition timber was purchased, and in a few weekends a very reasonable weekend residence was constructed. No planning permission was ever sought or obtained. A couple of ancient cars were towed in and, with their seats turned down made very adequate double beds for the numerous friends who would spend their weekends with us. Later a more ambitious hut was built with a verandah and kitchen and a pleasant sitting-room. My father installed one of his temporary wireless sets and we spent all our weekends and holidays there. I obtained an air rifle and Ralph got a .22 rifle which I don't think was ever licensed. I became very expert at stalking and shooting rabbits and pigeons. With my air rifle I had to get within about twenty yards of my quarry to be effective. With practice I found that I could do this easily, even though it might take me up to an hour to get that close without startling the prey. I developed a very considerable knowledge of woodcraft and of the habits of the wild animals and birds which I am proud to say stood me in good stead later.

An adjoining piece of woodland belonged to Lady Bolster. There were always more rabbits and pigeons in her woods so inevitably we trespassed and poached. One day Ralph was caught by a gamekeeper and his gun was confiscated. My mother went to see Lady Bolster who was threatening prosecution. They became close friends and the gun was returned. We continued to poach but were more careful.

With the outbreak of war in 1939, the staff and pupils of the Technical College were evacuated to a place of safety. I was fifteen at the time. There was no way that I was going to be evacuated so I left school before taking my final examinations and went to work at Elliott Brothers, the Electrical Instrument makers where my father was employed. This was interesting work and I got into the department where instruments were returned for repairs. One of the first I had to work on was a CO^2 indicator from the submarine *Thetis* which had tragically sunk with the loss of all her crew several years earlier. While I was working at Elliotts I met a lad of around my own age, Bernard Woodman. We got on very well together and became firm friends. He frequently visited me at home and I just as frequently went over to his house. He had three sisters and I became very fond of the youngest who was about a year my junior. Now I can't even remember her name. I must have been impressed! Bernard's father was a member of the Yeomen of the Guard. As such he had to undertake all sorts of ceremonial duties. Bernard and I used to cycle down to Culverstone most weekends. A little later, however, with the fall of France and the evacuation of the British Forces at Dunkirk, the Battle of Britain started and the dogfights between the British and German aircraft took place overhead. The whole of the south of England became a restricted area and we were not allowed to go to Culverstone any more. These were desperate times and I decided that my war effort lay in joining the R.A.F. My attempt to join up there and then met with no success whatever. I was politely informed that they weren't recruiting sixteen year old pilots. I was told to try again in a couple of years! The Local Defence Volunteers were being formed at this time and I was among the first to volunteer for this Force. There were no uniforms however and our drills were practiced using broomsticks instead of rifles. I'm sure though, that in the event of an invasion, we should have sold our lives dearly. To this end, I made a spear from a pole with a large carving knife tied to the end of it. Now the blitz started. A dozen times a day the air raid siren would sound and we would all troop off to shelter. If I was at work, I would go off with the others to the substantial shelters that Elliotts had constructed. If we were at home we had to go to our next door neighbours house. For some reason they had received an Anderson Shelter while ours had not arrived. This didn't go down too well with my father. We should probably have been allocated our own shelter in due course but after the first few days and, particularly, nights of being cramped up with people with whom he didn't get on too well, we moved back into our own house and spent a considerable amount of time and effort constructing a shelter of sorts in the cellar under the stairs. I fear that, had we received a direct hit from a bomb at this time, we should have undoubtedly perished. Several times during this period, our house was struck by incendiary bombs but these, fortunately, didn't penetrate the roof, the burned out casings being found on the following mornings. I well remember standing in the back garden night after night, looking north towards the Thames. The sky was brightly lit and the whole of the rea of Dockland was in flames.

Each evening I would report to the shed near St Margaret's Church where, with the other Local Defence Volunteers, I would practice my broomstick drill. Our house had a number of near misses from bombs at this time and quite a number of our neighbours were bombed out. Our turn came about three or four weeks into the Blitz. Not a direct hit fortunately, or we should all have been killed, but close enough to blow out most of our windows and remove part of the roof. We had no alternative but to get out. There was no other accommodation to be had so our options were limited. My father's duodenal ulcers had, by this time caused him to become an invalid, and unable to work. He had been forced to take early retirement so, grabbing a few belongings, we headed for Oxford where Kathleen and George, her husband, were living. My mother had collected up a couple of neighbours who had also been bombed out. Mr Mote was a blind man of about eighty and Ethel Nugent who was his housekeeper of about 50. Somehow we all got down to Oxford and poor Kathleen managed to pack us in to her tiny house. Shortly afterwards we were lucky enough to rent a house at the village of Stanton St John about three miles away. I went back up to London and collected some more bits and pieces during further air raids, and brought them back on the coach. On a subsequent trip Ralph, who was married by this time, met me with his little car. He packed my grandmother into the passenger seat and loaded more belongings round her and we set off back to Oxford, with me following close behind on my bike. The next day I went in to Cowley and applied for a job at Morris Motors. I was taken on as a fitter in the Civilian Repair Unit. I had a most interesting job working on Spitfires which had been shot up during dogfights or had crash landed. The Battle of Britain was in full swing and I worked long hours to get the planes back into the air. A little later I contacted Bernard to let him know that I was still alive, and invited him down to join us. He arrived several days later and was likewise taken on at Morris Motors in the same Civilian Repair Unit. Our house had, by this time, received further extensive damage as a result of a land-mine which had fallen at the end of the garden, severing a large limb of the mulberry tree in the process. We now abandoned all thought of a return to London. Some while later we all moved to another house right out in the country near the village of Woodperry. This was very basic but quite delightful. Water, we got from a nearby spring and sewage was of the bucket system, the contents of which would be dug into the vegetable patch. Cooking was with logs and lighting by oil lamp.

Bernard and I both decided that the time had come to join the R.A.F. so we both volunteered for Air Crew duties. We both became members of the R.A.F.V.R. and had to attend lectures and parades with the Air Force Cadets. Bernard was called up first as he was a few months older than me. He commenced his training and was selected to become a Observer. By this time I had also commenced my aircrew training, being posted initially to Aberystwyth. Shortly after completing his training Bernard was posted to a Mosquito Squadron. He was shot down and killed over Holland on 22nd July 1944. It was his third operation. The local villagers collected his body and buried it secretly. He still lies there in Plot 1E, Row B, Grave 4 at Woobrugge General Cemetery. This is about 21 miles north east of The Hague.

On the completion of my Initial Training course I was posted to South Cerney in Gloucestershire where I learned to fly on Tiger Moths. I succeeded in making several solo flights and was hopeful of being chosen to continue my training to become a pilot. No such luck however. I suppose that my technical education together with my work as an instrument-maker and aircraft engineer made the choice inevitable. I commenced a course at the end of which I would be qualified as a Flight Engineer. The training seemed to go on for ever. The urgency for aircrew had apparently diminished as the outcome of the conflict became less in doubt. Eventually I qualified as Flight Engineer was promoted to Sergeant and looked forward to being posted to a Squadron. My final training had been on Sunderland Flying Boats and I anticipated a Squadron in Coastal Command. Instead I was sent on leave and, on my return, set out on yet another course, this time it was Air Gunnery. The venue was Bishops Court, County Down in Northern Ireland. Accommodation was in Nissan Huts which, all things considered, were quite comfortable. The next bed to mine was occupied by a young lad named Richard Attenborough. I became very friendly with him and flew many training flights in his company during the course. It turned out that he was a budding actor and on his joining the R.A.F. had been drafted to take part in a recently-completed film called *In Which we Serve*. This starred Noel Coward and was about the war at sea. Dickie was still an A.C.2 and apparently had been sent on the Air Gunners course as being the quickest way of promoting him to sergeant as a reward for taking part in the film.

Dickie was a martyr to air sickness, as was I to a lesser extent. I used to share with him various pills and potions, guaranteed to cure this horrible complaint. None of them worked but after about eight or ten flights we both got used to the motion of the plane and were, to some extent, cured. Most of the training flights were on Halifaxes and Lancasters and I can't say that they were particularly enjoyable. The rear gun-turret was the position to be occupied. This entailed getting down a very narrow corridor to the turret. There was no room for the parachute which had been issued so it had to be parked outside. Then one wriggled through a tiny sliding door into the turret itself and tried to remember to close it after one was inside. If this was omitted it was rather disconcerting as the turret was swung round to find oneself totally exposed to the elements. If the plane happened to be hit and it became necessary to bale out it was expected that the rear gunner would centralise the turret, reach out and collect the parachute from where it had been stowed, clip it on, rotate the turret as far as possible and fall out backwards. Of course, should the engines happen to have failed prior to this procedure, all of the centralising and rotating had to be done by hand with a little wheel. I believe that the survival rate of rear gunners was somewhat limited, but I guess it gave them a strong incentive not to miss any attacking fighters.

At the conclusion of the Air Gunnery Course I thought that at last I should be able to see a bit of action. Not so. I was now posted to Sywell near Northampton where I spent an enjoyable three months flying in Wellington bombers and practising air navigation, of which I had only slight knowledge, and flight engineering of which I had none on the particular aircraft. Sywell was a repair unit for Wellingtons and the perimeter of the airfield was lined with these aircraft awaiting collection after repair. One afternoon I was out on the playing field with other trainees, having a game of football. The roar of engines alerted us to another Wellington taking off. This, it transpired, had been fitted with extra fuel tanks to increase its range. It also dramatically increased its weight. The Canadian pilot had not allowed for this and his take off was not long enough. He was clearly using, as a marker, a white Wellington of Coastal Command which was parked on the perimeter. Unable to gain sufficient height, the aircraft's undercarriage clipped the cabin area of the parked plane and it somersaulted into the ground on the playing field about twenty yards away from me. I do not recollect moving, but the next thing I knew I was in amongst the debris searching for survivors. Shortly afterwards I was joined by the others. The stench of high octane fuel pouring on to the hot engines is something that still haunts me. Somehow the fuel failed to ignite. I found one of the crew members who was still just alive. He was lying face down, his head half buried in the soft ground. Lying across his back was one of the aircraft's three bladed propellers and a part of one of the engines. The combined weight of this must have been in the region of three or four hundredweight. Looking back I still find it extraordinary that I somehow found the strength to lift this weight bodily from him. The adrenaline must have been flowing in vast quantities. The task was made worse by the fact that over the top of us was a ruptured petrol tank from which high octane fuel was gushing. To pull him free I had to crawl under this cascade. I was instantly soaked with the fuel. One spark and I should have been incinerated together with the other searchers. The petrol got into my eyes and mouth, blinding me and making me gag. Somehow I pulled the injured man out of the debris and away to a safe distance. Leaving him with others who were trying to assist I went back and eventually found another two members of the crew who I similarly removed. Regrettably however, none of them survived. A couple of hours later it was found that an engineer had been working in the cabin of the parked Wellington. He had been severely injured and bled to death while the others were being attended to. Such are the fortunes of war.

Now I was finally sent to a Squadron. But the war in Europe was over. After two or three flights which I suspect were more in the nature of a consolation prize than anything else, orders arrived. I was sent to a place called Heaton Park, near Manchester to await an overseas posting. 'At last,' I thought, 'I shall soon be off to the Far East. I might see a bit of action yet'. Heaton Park was quite a pleasant place. I imagine it must have been a well-maintained public park before the War, but the R.A.F. had taken it over quite early and used it as a holding centre for overseas postings. A great many temporary buildings had been erected and, apart from attending the occasional lecture, there was little to do. A lot of spare time was available. I spent much of it in Manchester and discovered Belle Vue. This was a large amusement area, part of which was a Zoo. There was also a large arena. On Saturday afternoons wrestling would take place here, while on Sundays John Barbarolli conducted symphony concerts. I was very fond of classical music and attended these as often as possible.

After two months at Heaton Park awaiting a posting the bad news arrived. I was off aircrew and was to be regraded ground crew, and was posted to Farnborough to work on experimental aircraft. I was bitterly disappointed but had to make the best of it. Actually I found the work extremely interesting. A number of German Experimental Aircraft had been seized and shipped to Farnborough together with their German ground crews. A right surly lot they were too. One plane I recollect vividly was a fighter which had an engine mounted at the back as well as the front. The Station Commander, a Group Captain, was most keen to fly this unusual plane and spent a lot of time in the cockpit, learning the controls One day as I watched, he took off in it and, after roaring across the Station a couple of times, took it into a steep climb. Something then went badly wrong and the plane headed for the ground out of control. Had he tried to bale out he would have had no chance as he would have been chopped up by the rear propeller. He stayed with it and crashed into a school. Thus ended a distinguished career.

Even though I was off aircrew I still managed to fly fairly regularly. I worked on the maintenance and repair of various aircraft both experimental and service. I think the occasional flight in these was intended to keep one on one's toes and ensure that the work was up to standard.

Most weekends I was able to go home though this entailed a quite long train journey. I would catch the train from Ash Green Station and change at one of the London Stations for Oxford. I can't remember now which one it was but it's not important. There was a little grocers' shop near the Station at Ash Green and I entered into an arrangement with the proprietor to park my trusty cycle at the rear of his premises. On one occasion in mid-winter, I was late for the train. The rear of the grocers was pitch black. I only had a couple of minutes to spare to get my ticket and get on the train. Padlocking my bike to a railing I shouldered my pack and ran —straight into the canal. Somewhat fortunately, it had only about twelve-inches of water in it at the time and I landed flat on my back in the mud and boulders. I clambered out, soaking-wet, unhurt except for my pride and gathered my senses together. My pack was full of water and a large glass jar of peaches in syrup, which I had saved from various meals in the Church Army Canteen, and was taking home to my parents, was smashed. The sticky syrup was running all over my wet uniform and I looked and felt a mess. Worse still, I had missed the train and had another two hours to wait. I could hardly sit in the waiting room in my condition so I sat on a seat on the open platform, and froze. That was as close to becoming a casualty as I had come during the entire war! I fear I was still extremely dishevelled when the train arrived and the seats must have been a bit of a mess at the end of each stage of the journey.

After six months or so at Farnborough I was posted to another Experimental Station, this time at Beaulieu in Hampshire. This was in part of the New Forest and was most enjoyable. While I was here the atom bombs were dropped on Japan, bringing the war to an end. A few months later I had another move. This time it was to R.A.F. Locking near Weston Super Mare. For some extraordinary reason I was to undergo a Senior N.C.O's Discipline Course. This entailed a lot of 'square bashing' and arms-drill as well as extremely strenuous assault courses, lectures and various exercises. Rifle and small-arms practice was well-covered as were armed ceremonial parades. To my surprise I found that I did remarkably well at this lot. Parade work, which I loathed and, in the past had avoided like the plague, I found I had a natural bent for. I didn't like it any better mind you, it's just that I had developed a vast pair of lungs and a parade-ground voice to go with it. I found that I could literally knock a man over with it at three paces. This was not only a surprise to me, it was the cause of total amazement to the officers and Senior N.C.O's running the course. When I came out top of the course I was interviewed and offered an immediate commission in the R.A.F. Regiment if I would sign on for the peacetime R.A.F. I refused out of hand. I have often wondered since, what course my career thereafter might have taken had I accepted. I suppose it's possible that with a commission in the peacetime R.A.F. I might have got back onto flying eventually. It opens up an enormous variety of possibilities. However, I made a decision then and I guess I've no regrets about it now. I suppose my decision then was based on the frustration of still waiting for my demob now that the war was over and with no possible chance of active service.

While stationed at Locking I was able to start on a totally new hobby. Speleology or cave-exploring as it is commonly termed. The Mendip Hills were only a few miles from Locking. This beautiful limestone area was thick with natural caves formed over millions of years as water courses wore away the rock. Many of these are of course very well-known, the caves at Cheddar and Wooky Hole, near Wells in particular. There are also many others, less well-known in the surrounding hills. These became my hunting ground. My friend Eddie Bates, and I would go out most evenings and weekends clad in boilersuits and large tough boots and armed with torches and ropes. We visited and explored such places as the caves at Banwell, where vast amounts of fossilized bones of animals such as Woolly Rhinoceros, Bison, Cave Lion, Hippopotamus, Mammoth, Cave Bear, Grizzly Bear, Hyena and Wolf had been found. Swildon's Hole, Lamb Lair and Goatchurch became our happy-hunting-grounds. The latter, at Burrington Combe, was our favourite haunt and I succeeded in reaching its most remote point which entailed wriggling through a narrow 'pipe', so narrow in fact that my arms had to be extended forward, there being no room for them down my sides. Progress was by wriggling toes and fingertips. My blood runs cold to think of it now. Totally foolhardy. The 'pipe' was 40-feet long into the final chamber. No room to turn round. Retreat was impossible once the wriggle had commenced. A sudden storm and the lower reaches of the cave would have filled with water. We were nearly 200-feet vertically underground and we had not even told anyone where we were going. Such is the foolishness of headstrong youth. However, we had a good time and, luckily, survived. Having explored most of the known caves to which we could obtain access we decided to see if we could find a new one. We had noticed a pronounced depression in the ground on the top of one of the hills near Burrington Combe, so we went out equipped with a spade, pickaxe and ropes. Digging in the lowest point of the depression was hard-going. Rocks had to be dragged out with the ropes and these, we found from painful experience, were encrusted in fossilized shells, dating back to the time when this whole area had been under the sea. Eventually, after several days of effort we broke into a first chamber, full of loose rock which all had to be shifted out before we could make any further progress. Before we could get much further on this, however, my demob came through. I wonder if anyone else has continued our exploration! I must go back one day and see if I can find it.

The great day dawned. It's surprising how much gear one accumulates over a period. I dumped as much as I could but the remainder was still of considerable bulk and weight. Lytham St Anne's, just north of Blackpool was the place chosen to cast me adrift, and this is where I dragged my considerable belongings. After an overnight stay I entered the sausage factory. I had heard it was like a conveyor belt and this was no exaggeration. Some of my R.A.F. clothing like my sheepskin flying jacket, I was permitted to keep, the rest was handed in. First I was measured, then into an area where suits were hanging on racks. Not a lot of choice in my size. However, I eventually chose a brown herringbone pattern. Next, I passed to a long series of counters. Here were issued a shirt and tie, a pair of shoes and socks, a raincoat and a hat. I never wore a hat of any sort in civilian life but I took it since it was on offer and gave it away to the first needy looking individual I could find. My father chuntered about this later when I told him and said he could have done with that!

My final pay, to cover the leave I was due and I was on my way. I had decided that I would spend my first night of freedom with my sister Kathleen and her husband George who had a house in Leeds, so I made my way there. Their's was a big old Victorian house of, I think, four storeys. I was directed to my bedroom at the top of the house. This room was approached by a flight of stairs ending in a well with a final riser on each side, one of which entered my bedroom and the other leading to the bathroom and toilet. After a pleasant evening I went to my room. After undressing I went across to the bathroom. Unfortunately I forgot the step down and up the other side. My right foot stepped out. Finding nothing, it accelerated to 40-miles an hour and struck the riser on the other side. Having come through the war without a scratch I had now sustained a painful injury on my first day in civilian life. My sister learned a complete new vocabulary of curses as I hopped about nursing my toes. I suppose I should have gone straight to hospital. Instead I went to bed and didn't get a lot of sleep. The following morning my big toe resembled a large aubergine. However, I had to get to London whence my parents had removed, their house having been repaired after its extensive bomb damage. Sorrowfully, I cut the toecap out of my new shoe, this being the only way it would accommodate my foot.

My journey to London, dragging about two hundredweight of luggage with me does not bear thinking about. My toe was in agony and it complained bitterly every time I stepped on it. The train was crowded so I had to stand all the way. The worst part was changing stations. Eventually I reached Lewisham and got a bus to the stop nearest home. Never had the road seemed so long. The old saying, 'The longest mile is the last mile home', was never more true. I clambered the front steps and beat on the familiar knocker. My first words to my mother were to ask for a large whisky, which was not forthcoming because they didn't have any. I think my parent must have thought that their prodigal son had turned into an alcoholic. On the following morning I staggered off to Lewisham Hospital where my foot was X-rayed and my big toe found to be fractured in two places. Of course they could do nothing about it except put it in a collodion splint, which made it even more bulky and painful when I forced it into my shoe.

Morris Motors, where I had been employed prior to joining the Air Force were legally bound to offer me employment on my discharge. After a few days to allow my swollen toe to subside, I made my way to Cowley to see what was on offer. I had foolishly hoped that I might get a job on the development side, on new models. Some hopes! This of course was reserved for employees with years of experience.

Instead I was offered a job on the assembly line, working on Morris Eight saloons. Having nothing else in view I decided to try it. First I had to find lodgings. In this I was reasonably fortunate, being taken in by a woman of about 30 with a young child. She was a divorcee and eked out a living with boarders. There were two others beside myself. All of us worked at Morris Motors and one of the others shared her bed. As far as I was concerned he was welcome. She wasn't my type at all, though she was quite pleasant and certainly the accommodation was clean and the food good.

Work on the assembly-line did not suit me at all. The first job I tried was attaching the fabric roof-linings to wooden formers, which someone else then attached to the inside of each car body as it went past. There was quite an art to this, which entailed taking a handful of tin tacks into my mouth and then spitting them out one at a time, right way round, onto a magnetic hammer. I became quite expert at this after a day or two. I had some difficulty in equating this to job satisfaction however. I found also that I was not just doing it for eight hours a day on the assembly line, I was doing it for eight hours at night as well while I slept. My next job was adjusting the locking nuts on the accelerator and brake pedals. This proved just about as boring as spitting tacks. Added to this, the entire assembly line closed down for a while and then started up on a three-day-week. I was never sure of the reason for this, I can only put it down to union activity. I had refused to join the union and was, as a result, somewhat unpopular with the shop stewards. After a few weeks of this I decided that I'd had enough. I took a few days off and went home. I went to Woolwich to Siemen Brothers, the Electrical Contractors. Here, I was offered a job at a considerably enhanced salary installing the new automatic equipment into Telephone Exchanges. This entailed travelling all over the country, spending anything up to a year in one place and either installing the equipment in brand new exchanges or stripping out the old equipment and replacing it with new ones. This sounded to be an interesting job and I decided to give it a go. I therefore returned to Oxford and handed in my notice to Morris Motors, then, after collecting my belongings and ration book and bidding a fond farewell to my landlady I made my way home.

My parents were no longer living in our house at Dacre Park. After it had been repaired they had moved back from Oxfordshire but rapidly decided that life in the capital was no longer for them. Mr Thomas, who lived just up the road and was a Bridge-playing friend of my father, owned a large block of flats at St Leonards and offered him a job collecting rents and arranging any repairs which had to be carried out. It was, therefore, to the old house at Lee that I made my way. Most of the house had been let by my parents prior to their departure, but I had access to what had been the billiard room in the basement and my old bedroom in the attic. Living conditions could only be described as Spartan. A table and chair downstairs and a bed in the attic. However, it was a base at any time that I happened to be working in London. At other times I would be in digs anyway. The new tenants, I fear, regarded me as very much the interloper. My first assignment was at Sydenham, about five miles away from home and an easy trip on my bicycle. The Exchange had been in use for, I suppose, about twenty-years and was a spacious pleasant building. It was still a manual exchange but we didn't see a lot of the staff. During the six months it took to convert it to automatic equipment I learned a great deal, particularly the un-wisdom of putting ones' side-cutters or other metal tools down on the buss-bars which ran along the top of the racks where all the cables were supported. These carried a very high voltage and were not protected in any way. Anything metallic placed upon them would produce a great fireworks display and reduce the tool to several ugly looking bits. After my initiation, involving a few such episodes, I was taught to be cautious.

Completion of the work at Sydenham involved a change of scenery, so it was to Scotland that I made my way. My first impressions of Aberdeen were not inspiring. The granite city it was called and, indeed, so I found it. Bon Accord Street was where I found my lodgings. The Company had arranged this, though what I had done to be so afflicted I really don't know. At first sight it didn't seem too bad. The house was, I believe, number eight-hundred-and-something. The road seemed endless. Mostly of very similar detached or semi-detached houses built of granite blocks. I was allocated an attic bedroom the ceiling of which sloped from about seven-feet down to about four-feet. Consequently, I was only able to stand upright for about one third of the floor area, most of this being occupied by my bed. 'Not to worry,' I thought, 'I shan't be spending too much time up here. My landlady Mrs McGregor, was a thick-set woman with a broad Scots accent. I never saw her smile and she was built like a middleweight wrestler. Her husband was a poor thing, thin to the point of being skeletal, he was completely cowed by his wife and said hardly a word. Their one offspring was a youth of about fourteen, doted on by his mother and universally disliked by all of the boarders. My fellow residents were two lads of about my own age who were students at Aberdeen University, Angus was taking a degree in forestry, while John was taking one in medicine. George was a middle-aged commercial traveller. Margaret, aged about twenty-three, who was quite attractive and worked as a telephone operator at the exchange where I would be changing the equipment. Another resident was Rose, an old lady who had spent many years in New Zealand but had decided to come back to Scotland to die. (God knows why. Personally I couldn't see any redeeming features in the place.) Lastly there were Albert and Jean, a young couple who were expecting their first infant. Albert was a scientist employed at the Ministry of Food and Fisheries near the docks in Aberdeen. His life was spent examining fish for any diseases they might have. Jean was about six-months pregnant when I arrived on the scene. They were a very pleasant couple who, like the rest of us, were plagued by Joseph the son of the house. It was, I think, about December when I got to Aberdeen. It was snowing hard. My bedroom, immediately under the roof was like a refrigerator. There was no heating. My two blankets were totally inadequate. I did manage to get a third by complaining bitterly to the wrestler, but that was it. To get any comfort at all at night I had to pile all my clothing on top of me. I took to sleeping in my flying jacket for warmth and bitterly regretted handing in the sheepskin lined trousers that went with them.

Rose had with her a vast collection of photographs of New Zealand and these were trotted out several times a week for the benefit of anyone who had not previously seen them. Being a bit forgetful Rose never knew who had seen them and who had not. I had the pleasure of having them thrust under my nose four times during my sojourn. Eventually, on seeing the albums being brought out, I learned to make my excuses and go to the cinema or the local hostelry. I never enjoyed the latter in Scotland. The Scots, it seemed, were a dour race and would sit unsmiling all evening intent on their drink and little else. I did find one recreation which I really enjoyed. The theatre. At the time Donald Wolfitt, the great Shakespearean actor, was performing the bard's plays. His role as King Lear was unforgettable. I can't claim to be a great fan of Shakespeare but those performances were really something.

I had been under Mrs McGregor's roof for about four months when things came to a head. I had survived the bitterest weather conditions I have ever experienced, the food was just about edible, but Joseph, the son of the house, was becoming unbearable. Added to this, Mrs M had got the idea that John and Margaret were having a affair. I don't know how she arrived at this conclusion. I never saw any evidence of it myself but at breakfast one morning she came in brandishing a lace handkerchief which she claimed to have just found in John's bed. John said, 'Yes it was his, and what the hell had it to do with her anyway?' 'It belongs to that Glasgow tink', roared Mrs McGregor pointing the finger at Margaret, 'She's been sharing your bed under my roof!' A great row then erupted and crockery flew. The outcome was that John and Margaret then packed their belongings and departed. The same evening the loathsome Joseph started commenting about the morals of the two absentees. This was something I was not prepared to take from the little turd so I gave him the back of my hand and split his lip. After the ensuing uproar I packed my belongings and also departed. As I left Mr McGregor shook me warmly by the hand. 'Sorry you're going,' he said, 'I've been wanting to do that for months.'

Out of the frying pan and into the fire. My next digs were half-a-mile further up Bon Accord Street. Initially, they seemed to be an improvement. Conditions however rapidly deteriorated. My new landlady, Mrs Wilson was shorter and fatter than Mrs McGregor. My bedroom was a marginal improvement too, since it was not directly under the roof. There were only three boarders here and we got on well enough. The food, however, became more and more sparse. I was in a continual state of near starvation. I spent more and more money at cafes trying to ward off the pangs of hunger. However, winter was over, the weather was improving all the time and the job was nearly finished. Eventually I was able to pack up my belongings and thankfully vacate the granite city.

Chapter 4

The next stop was Colwyn Bay, Wales. Once again lodgings had been arranged by the Company. This time however I couldn't . fault them. I was the only boarder in a modern bungalow. My room was clean, well-furnished and comfortable. My landlady, Mrs Williams, was a friendly, middle-aged, motherly woman. Best of all the food was plentiful and well prepared. The local Exchange was a newly constructed building, quite small, in line with the requirements of the little town. Only two of us were employed in installing the new equipment, so I found myself working with Sam, a friendly little man who had been employed by Siemens for many years. At night we would put the key under a stone outside the door and whoever arrived first in the morning got the kettle on for a cup of tea. The work was scheduled to take eight or nine months.

Colwyn Bay was, I discovered, a pleasant, quiet little seaside town. The people were friendly and the beer was good. There wasn't an awful lot to do there though and the evenings and weekends tended to drag a bit. It was about this time that I started to take stock of my situation. Was I really cut out to spend my entire life leading a nomadic existence, travelling all over the country, living in lodgings of varying degrees of discomfort. Supposing I decided to get married. How would my wife feel about my being absent from home for months on end. Some of my fellow employees at Aberdeen were married. They had never said much about their married lives though. I know that at least three of them were divorcees. I decided that, while the present was O.K. the future looked bleak indeed. Siemens would no doubt be able to transfer me to another department where travelling and living away did not form part of the contract. The pay would then be considerably reduced. The solution, I finally decided, was to take a Course in Electrical Engineering and obtain a Degree. Armed with this qualification I should, no doubt, be able to land a good job with a substantial salary. Special arrangements were available for ex-service men to take university courses so I wrote off to the appropriate authority. I was shortly afterwards invited to attend an office in Newcastle for an interview. On the suggested date I arrived and was shown into a waiting room where several other applicants were already awaiting their interviews. Eventually I was called into the interview room. The only person there was a middle-aged woman who looked me up and down and told me to sit. The interview did not take long. Ten minutes to be precise. 'What,' I was asked, 'were my present qualifications.' I had to confess that they were nil. 'Did you not go to school?,' my interrogator demanded. I explained that I had indeed gone to a technical college. 'What qualification did you get in your final examinations?,' she enquired. Well, actually, I never took them', I explained. The war started so I left to go into a factory'. I received a withering glance. 'Well, you're wasting my time as well as your own,' she growled. 'Had you taken your final examinations we could have got you straight into University. In the circumstances, there's no chance at all.'

Dejectedly, I left the office. Clearly my good intentions in leaving school to help my Country had dropped me in it. The outlook now looked bleak indeed. On the way back to Colwyn Bay I had time to re-assess the situation. I had a flash of inspiration. A correspondence course. That was the answer. At the end of a couple of years of hard evening studying in my digs I should be able to finish up with the required degree and an assured future. The papers were full of adverts for suitable courses so I wrote off for one of them and, after reading the glowing prospectus, sent off the appropriate sum and duly received my first lessons. Talk about 'back to basics'. This really did start from the beginning. A ten-year-old could have done it with his eyes closed. I raced through the exercises and sent them back to my tutor. The second lot of lessons were marginally harder, but gave me no problems. So it went on for a dozen or so lessons. My evenings and weekends were fairly fully-occupied with my quest for knowledge. I decided that I was doing so well that I would have an evening off and go to a Saturday night dance at a nearby Hall. Dancing has never been my forte, but it was no doubt as good a way as any for meeting up with members of the opposite sex. The dance was moderately well attended but the female talent was pretty limited. Two girls sitting together on the other side of the hall were about the only ones in whom I could feel any interest whatever. A quick assessment and I decided that of the two the brunette was the better value of the two. Both of them were, I thought, a year or two older than me, but the brunette was definitely the more attractive. Plucking up my courage I sauntered across and asked her for a dance. She seemed more than willing and at the end of it invited me back to sit with her and her sister. She told me her name was Anne and her sister was Jenny. Anne had a pleasant, soft, Welsh accent, which I found captivating. She told me that I was the only distinguished-looking man there. Now here was a girl who was not only perspicacious and discerning but had impeccable taste.

This encounter proved to be a turning point. I fear that my correspondence course began to take second place. I still waded through the lessons and exercises but they took me longer and I found it difficult to lavish the same degree of concentration on them. I found that most of my evenings were spent with Anne, my weekends also. I felt that I was getting out of my depth. I liked Anne very much but she was clearly getting much too keen. Next thing I knew I was invited home to meet her parents. I must say I was made very welcome. A very nice spread of food was produced. I was clearly being sized up as a prospective son-in-law. Two or three home visits later and I was taken aside by Anne's father and asked what my intentions were towards his daughter. I couldn't really tell him that my only interest was in her body, or he might have been a bit upset. I therefore gave him a bit of a *spiel* about wanting to get my degree before I settled down. This seemed to satisfy him and I breathed a sigh of relief. I began to feel trapped however. Also, I was now making very slow progress with my course. Once again I decided to take stock of my situation. What I needed, I felt, was a job in which I could live at home, where I had plenty of spare time for my studies and where I was not going to be pressurised by a prospective father-in-law. After giving this very considerable thought I could only think of one job which would suit. I decided to join the Hastings Police.

Having decided on my course of action, I set the wheels in motion. I did not tell Anne of my intentions as I thought it unnecessary to raise the inevitable objections till things were much further advanced. I felt a bit sneaky about this, but I'm sure it was the sensible thing to do. I wrote a letter of application to the Chief Constable at Hastings and in due course received a formal application form which I completed and returned. My landlady started looking at me a bit oddly as letters marked 'Hastings Borough Police' began to arrive. Eventually I received a letter asking me to attend on a certain date to sit the entrance examination.

I was due a few days holiday so I made my excuses to Anne that it was time I went home to see my parents. She was a bit upset about this and implied that it might have been an opportunity for me to have taken her to Hastings to meet them. With a bit of effort I managed to dissuade her from this idea. I made my way to Hastings. I felt really sorry about leaving her behind but decided that sorting out my future was a bit more important than non-stop nooky. After a relaxing weekend at my parent's new flat, I made my way to Hastings Police Station on the Monday morning. I expected to find a number of other applicants waiting there. In the event I was the only one. I was greeted by the Administration Sergeant, Frank Dunster, who was friendly in a formal sort of way. I was then handed mathematics paper. 'Here you are young 'un, you've got an hour to finish this so you'd better get your skates on'. I glanced at the paper. It was ludicrously simple. I would have had little difficulty even had I not been doing my correspondence course. As it was! 'Do you want me to show the working or can I just write down the answers?' I enquired. 'Please yourself, young'un,' said Frank. Five minutes later I handed in the completed paper. Frank looked a bit startled about this. 'You sure you've checked all this,' he said. A paper on 'General Knowledge' followed, which I completed with similar ease. This was topped off with a final paper which was a predictable essay on 'Why I want to join the Hastings Borough Police'. I felt that the time had come to tell a few convincing lies. It would not be politic, I felt, to say that I wanted to join the Police in order to have enough spare time to study for a Degree in order to get a different job.

My lies were clearly sufficiently impressive to convince the Chief Constable of my sincerity. After waiting about an hour while my papers were assessed, I was asked to return at ten o'clock the following morning for an interview. It looked as though my cunning plan was going to succeed. Angus Cargil, the Chief Constable of Hastings Borough Police, was a canny Scot and nobody's fool. He was about 45-years-of-age and during the war had risen rapidly to the rank of Lieutenant Colonel. He questioned me closely about my reasons for wanting to join the Force but was eventually satisfied by my untruths. He then asked me what jobs I had been doing since leaving the R.A.F. When I mentioned my sojourn in Aberdeen I was closely interrogated about what I thought of the Scots. Naturally I lied through my teeth. I did tell him the truth about my admiration for the acting abilities of Donald Wolfitt, which seemed to impress him no end. I did not, however, mention my feelings for Scottish landladies. The interview came to an end and I left the Police Station feeling reasonably confident.

My return to Colwyn Bay was greeted warmly by Mrs Williams and even more warmly by Anne. I felt a proper heel. For a couple of weeks I slipped back into the old routine. Then one morning arrived an official looking letter with the familiar marking, 'Hastings Borough Police'. Mrs Williams handed me the letter while I was having my breakfast. She flitted around the room hoping that I would open it and was most disappointed when I tucked it in my pocket and left for work. Once out of sight of the house I tore the letter open and scanned the contents. I was offered an appointment as Police Constable at a starting salary of £240 a year, to include two increments for War Service. This was a bit less than I was currently getting, but since it wouldn't cost much to live at home it didn't sound too bad. My joining date was eight weeks hence. That evening I wrote to the Chief Constable accepting the appointment. I also wrote to Sieimen Brothers submitting my resignation. I then went to meet Anne. Tears flooded forth when I told her the news. Then she cheered up. 'I could come to Hastings and get a job,' she suggested. 'I don't think that would be a very good idea,' said I. 'I shall be going away for three months to the Police Training School at Sandgate,' I said. 'I don't even get away at weekends,' I lied. She was quiet for a while after this. 'You won't get yourself another girl will you,' she asked. 'Of course not,' said I, crossing my fingers. The next three weeks passed quickly. Anne was, if anything, more passionate than ever. I thought her father eyed me a bit dubiously. He didn't ask me what my intentions were though! Mrs Williams was, I think, genuinely sorry to see me go. Anne accompanied me to the train. Tearfully she said her farewells. 'I'll come to Hastings as soon as you finish at the Police School,' she promised. 'Of course', I lied.

I arrived in Hastings in February 1948. My first day at Hastings Police Station was spent filling in forms and being issued with my uniform and equipment. Bob Tester was the

Stores Sergeant and he spent a lot of time ensuring that I looked my best. Of course I wasn't allowed to wear my new finery around the police station until I had completed my three months training at Sandgate, near Folkestone, Kent. However, I attempted to make myself useful around the Station, collecting prisoners' meals and so on. After a few days of kicking my heels, the great day arrived and I left on the bus for Sandgate.

It was about 3 o'clock on Sunday afternoon when I arrived. I was shown to a large dormitory which I was to share with about 20 other recruits sent from a variety of Forces throughout the South East. I found that there were two classes of recruits in my intake, totalling around 40-odd in all. Three intakes of recruits of a similar size were under training at any time.

Having grabbed myself a bed in one of the better positions in the dormitory, I set out to have a look round the School. The main building was set in a raised position and approached by a long winding drive from the main road. It had been built in the 1920s and had originally been used as a Star and Garter Home, catering for disabled ex-servicemen. The entrance foyer was manned each evening and at weekends by several of the students on duty, checking the other students in and out. The dining room which was large enough to seat well over 150 pupils and staff had a stage at one end, behind a curtain and was sometimes used as a theatre or lecture room or for the very occasional social function during the course. The two upper storeys of the building were used as dormitory accommodation while the ground floor was designated as classrooms and offices. There were also a number of temporary buildings scattered around the grounds which were likewise used as classrooms. In the basement was the gymnasium. The grounds of the school were quite extensive, amounting to around eight acres, maybe more. Part of this was left as woodland. About an acre immediately in front of the main building had been constructed as a parade ground. The remainder was flower beds and shrubbery's with paths winding through them. Altogether it was a very pleasant layout. At the eastern end of the grounds were the houses occupied by the Commandant and his Deputy, together with their wives and families. Here a second road exited onto the main Folkestone road. We were warned at an early stage that this entire area was out of bounds on pain of severe punishment.

By four o'clock all of the new intake of recruits had arrived and tea was served in the dining room. We were them welcomed by one of the officers and told that, once we were settled in and had sorted out places in the dormitories we were free to go out and look around the town. In the foyer I had noticed a list of names of all the new recruits. Scanning through them I noticed one Peter Godber from Hastings Borough. I lost no time in seeking him out to compare notes. Peter was in the second class of the intake and predictably in another dormitory. At an early stage in our acquaintanceship we formed a close friendship. He was a couple of years older than me and had served in the Navy during the War. He was married to a Scots girl, Jean and they had a young son.

The next three months sped by. I am not going to claim that I enjoyed it. Most weekends I got home if I was not required for the inevitable security patrols or foyer duties. Most days I received affectionate letters from Anne and I began to fear that she really would emigrate to Hastings when my course was at an end. I wrote irregularly, making the excuse that the course was so intensive that I had very little time to spare. In this I was telling no more than the truth. The course certainly was intensive. My correspondence course went totally by the board. I continually promised myself that on my return to Hastings I would make a big effort and catch up. Each morning I was up with the lark and in company with virtually every other student perambulated around the paths and roads muttering definitions under my breath until I knew every one of the 100-odd by heart. These, it appeared, formed a major part of the curriculum. In many ways I suppose that they were quite important, in as much as they covered every facet of an offence and formed a guide when deciding what charge was appropriate. Nearing the end of the course I received a letter from Anne. She was sorry to tell me that she was going out with someone else and did not intend coming to Hastings after all. I breathed a sigh of relief. Much as I liked her, she had proved much too keen on getting married and I had no intention of tying myself down for several years yet. At the end of the course a final examination was held. In this I came third. I was a bit put out about this having become used in the past to occupying first place in any examination I took. Still the opposition was quite fierce so I suppose it wasn't too bad. I decided to do better next time, when the refresher courses were held after one and two years respectively.

On our return to Hastings, Peter and I were paraded before Angus Cargil and given a bollocking for not coming first. Peter had only managed sixth place so he got a rougher ride than me. We both had to promise to try harder next time. Was it my imagination or did I see a slight flicker of a wink from the Chief Constable as we were marched out.

Peter and I were both posted to the same shift. The shift system being worked involved seven days on duty followed by one day off. This meant having one weekend (Saturday and Sunday) off in eight weeks. Not the most convivial working arrangement. In addition we were entitled to two weeks off each year but this was allocated, not chosen. The hours of duty on each of the shifts was from 6 a.m. to 2 p.m. then from 2 p.m. to 10 p.m. and finally from 10 p.m. to 6 a.m. At the end of each period of seven days and one day off the shift was changed, working backwards so that one would finish at say 2 p.m. and start at 10 p.m. on the following day. Needless to say this constant changing of the sleeping and feeding habits was found to play havoc with the digestive system and the majority of policemen got stomach ulcers or something worse as the years went by. The system was complicated by being occasionally put backwards or forwards by four hours for administrative reasons like additional cover for special occasions or to cover for sickness in the ranks. The shift times then ran from 2 a.m. to 10 a.m. and so on.

Our shift Sergeant was Les Finch with whom I got on very well. Our Inspector, on the other hand was Mr Pilbeam, a pig in police clothing if ever I came across one. He was not the least bit interested in catching the local criminal fraternity. His efforts were directed entirely at detecting minor infringements of the rules by the uniformed constables. At night he was in his element and it required a great deal of ingenuity to keep one jump ahead of him. One of our most important jobs on night duty was to physically check the security of each of the shop and commercial premises on our beat. Every door-knob had to be twisted and if there was any access to the rear of the premises this had to be checked as well. Pilbeam's favourite ploy was to tie a bit of cotton round the door knob and check several times during the night to see if it had been disturbed. He was universally disliked by everyone he came into contact with. He was also one of the most ignorant and ill-mannered policemen I have ever come across.

He delighted in using long words which he invariably mis-pronounced 'Of course,' he proclaimed, 'I edjamicated myself.' 'Profilic' was another oft-used word. He delighted in explaining that this meant, 'There's a lot of 'em'. When reporting anyone for an offence we had been taught that copious notes had to be made in our pocket book of any conversation entered into. I well-remember one occasion when a list had been placed on the notice-board, inviting anyone to apply for overtime duty in connection with a fair which was to take place. I put my name on the list hoping to get a few extra shillings. However, I heard nothing further about it so assumed that I was not one of the fortunate few. I came on duty at 10 p.m. the day the fair had been held. On this occasion I had been instructed to report on duty at a police box in Magdalen Road. At 9.45 p.m. I telephoned in. John Cox who was a most unpleasant sergeant on duty in the office, took my call. 'Oh', he sneered, 'you've finally turned up.' I enquired what he meant. 'You were supposed to be on duty this afternoon at the Fair', he said. 'You're to stay there until Mr Pilbeam arrives'. Forewarned is forearmed. I made sure my pocket-book was up to date. Pilbeam arrived. 'I'll have a look at your pocket book', said he. I handed it to him and he perused it closely. 'You weren't on duty this afternoon', he demanded. 'That's true', said I. 'So you admit it', he said. 'Yes', I said, 'I can't deny it.' He handed my pocket book back and I immediately wrote in it the conversation we had had. 'Why are you writing that?', he demanded. 'Why?', said I, 'Have you any objection.' 'Right', he bellowed. 'P.C. Beaden, you are charged that you failed to report for duty at 4 p.m. today. I caution you that you are not obliged to say anything, but whatever you say will be given in evidence'. I don't know if he thought I was going to give the time honoured chestnut 'Its a fair cop'. but if he did he was disappointed. I said nothing, but wrote in my pocket book what he had said. He waited till I had finished writing. Pencil poised over his pocket book. A minute passed. Then another. Eventually he could contain himself no longer. 'Aren't you going to say something?', he begged. I shook my head. He stamped out of the police box.

The following evening I came on duty at 10 p.m. This time I was on duty at the Central Police station. My beat kept me in the town centre. After about half-an-hour a well-known car drew up alongside me. 'Hop in', said Angus. 'We'll have a drive round.' There was no doubt in my mind that he had been fully informed of my alleged misconduct. 'Well', he said, 'how are you getting along?' 'Oh, all right I think', I said non-committally. 'I believe I shall be coming up to see you in the near-future though.' 'Oh', said Angus, 'can I have a look at your pocket book?' I handed it to him and he perused it closely. 'Were you told that you were to be on duty at the Fair?' 'No, of course not', said I, 'I put my name down for it, hoping to get a bit of paid overtime out of it but I was never told that I had been chosen for duty so I assumed that I was not required.' 'Right', said Angus, 'out you get then'. I was never called to appear before him on the charge and Les Finch told me that it had been dropped. He also told me that Pilbeam had had to go in front of the Chief Constable and had received a hell of a bollocking. However making an Inspector eat humble pie doesn't go unpunished and for a long time things were made as awkward as possible for me.

My parents flat was at St Leonards, to the west of Hastings. Week after week I found myself working the beat at Ore Village to the east of the town, which entailed a cycle ride of over four miles. This was not too bad when the weather was good but when it was pouring with rain and a strong easterly wind was blowing it was purgatory, particularly since the last mile was up a steep hill. However there was nothing I could do about it. Clearly it would be useless complaining that I was made to travel too far to work. 'All part of the job', I would be told.

First appearances in Court are a testing time for any young constable. Indeed I don't think I really enjoyed Court appearances during my entire career. Generally speaking the Bench of Magistrates are sympathetic in such circumstances. It can still be a trying experience even though it had been practised a multitude of times at the Training School. My first Court case came about as the result of a traffic accident. One of the drivers involved was clearly in the wrong and I duly reported him for driving without due care and attention. When the case was called I made my way to the witness box and took the oath in the approved manner. Halfway through giving my evidence I happened to catch the eye of the Chairman. He was surreptitiously picking his nose. Instantly my mind went a complete blank. Panic. What came next? The Chairman continued his surreptitious picking. After a pause of what seemed a lifetime but was in fact about half a minute he got the bogey he was after and glanced up at me. 'You may continue constable', he remarked. 'May I refer to my pocket-book?', I gasped. 'Were the notes made at the time?', he demanded. I affirmed that they were and took my pocket-book out. However, before I had time to open it the remainder of my evidence sprang to mind. I rattled it off before I had time to forget it again. Cross-examination proved no problem as I had suddenly overcome my feeling of inferiority. Why indeed should I have any qualms about speaking up in front of people who picked their nose in public. After all the Chairman was only the manager of a Building Society. My offender was duly found guilty and fined. A major hurdle had been cleared. A few weeks later I happened to be in Court when another young probationary constable was making his first appearance. He had just started giving his evidence when he suddenly disappeared from sight. The ordeal had been too much and he fainted. The case had to be abandoned.

In some mysterious way a year had passed since my joining the police. Where had it gone. I had been enjoying myself so much that I had hardly noticed it passing. Glancing through Daily Orders I found that I was to attend a refresher course. This was a two week course and was to be held at Brighton. Three of us were detailed for it, Peter Godber and myself plus Peter Austin who had been on the intake after ours at Sandgate. There was nothing particularly memorable about this course except that this time I managed to resume my usual place at the top when the results were announced. Peter Godber came third and Peter Austin fifth. Not a bad result I thought. We returned to Hastings and as usual were marched before Angus. The two Peters both got a bollocking for not trying harder. I was congratulated and out we marched.

Back to the same old grind. Les Finch was still the Section Sergeant and Pilbeam was still the Inspector. I don't know if there had been some divine intervention during my temporary absence, but my trips up to Ore Village were now an event of some rarity. I wasn't sorry about this, not least in view of the fact that finding something to do during the eight-hours stint was becoming more and more difficult. This was without doubt the most law-abiding area of Hastings. Since our progress was invariably judged by the number of offences we detected, it was not a very popular beat with young constables. There was of course St Helen's Hospital with its copious supply of desirable young nurses, but at the time I didn't seem to be having a lot of luck in that direction.

From time to time I thought about my correspondence course and my ambition to get a degree in electrical engineering. In fact there were times when I actually put pen to paper and did a few lessons. To my everlasting shame however, there came a time when I began to wonder if it was all worth while. I quite enjoyed being a policeman. I had no intention of remaining a constable to the end of my days. If I could get up to say, Inspector, life would be a lot easier and the salary would be quite satisfactory. Plus, there was a pension waiting at the end of 25 or 30 years. After mulling this over for some months I decided to cease work on the correspondence course and I became yet another statistic among the drop-outs.

Since becoming a policeman my life had been practically one of enforced celibacy. I determined to do something about this. I took to going to dances on Hastings Pier. As I have remarked before, dancing is not my forte. Neither is chatting up the girls. However, 'needs must when the devil drives'. I met Eve. Quite an attractive girl but with rather thin legs. 'Still', thought I, 'you don't have to look at the fireplace when you're stoking the fire'. Eve didn't live in Hastings. She was from the southern outskirts of London where she lived with her mother. When I met her she was visiting her sister and brother-in-law who had a little shop in Plynlimmon Road. I had never met a nymphomaniac before. It was quite a revelation. Each weekend she would come down to Hastings and I would meet her at every opportunity. Poking around while on night duty I had come across some excellent places where we could go, and be guaranteed no disturbance.

With an eye to the future I decided that I ought to start thinking about promotion prospects. One essential to this ambition was to pass the promotion examination. There were in fact two examinations to be passed. The first would qualify me for promotion to the rank of Sergeant, the second to Inspector. Each examination was in two subjects: education and law. I commenced attending classes in the education subjects. These were conducted at one of the local schools, the instructors being drawn from the teaching staff at the particular school.

Naturally one of the subjects was mathematics. I became a bit unpopular with the instructor when I challenged his method and result in a particular problem. I immediately regretted doing this as it could have badly undermined his position to be proved wrong. I therefore withdrew my remarks and agreed that he was undoubtedly right. At the conclusion of the class, however, I took him to one side and pointed out the error of his ways. I don't think the poor chap ever really forgave me. People don't like having a 'big head' in their class who could 'show them up' at any time.

The other subjects being studied included English and Current Affairs. Fortunately, I had no problems with any of these subjects and in due course sat and passed this part of the Sergeants Examination. For some extraordinary reason the regulations precluded me from taking the law examination until I had completed my probationary period at the end of two years. I suppose there was some slight logic in this when one considers that, at the end of the initial three months course at Sandgate, the majority of recruits could have immediately passed their Sergeants examination had they been permitted to sit it. This would have led to a ludicrous situation where newly-joined probationary constables could have passed their promotion examinations while being shown the ropes by senior constables who had not. The next indication that progress was being made was being taught to drive. Angus had decided that better cooperation with the motoring public might be achieved if more policemen knew how to drive. I have no doubt that he was right in this. After all, a constable with a knowledge of driving would be far more likely to understand the problems faced by the motorist. I was among the first to attend these classes. This did not amount to a formal driving course, but an elderly Wolsely saloon was set aside and one of the traffic sergeants was detailed to spend his time instructing the ignorant. I was given two one-hour sessions each week for six weeks. At the end of this I was judged ready to take my driving test. My examiner was Inspector Rodgers. All went well until I was driving along Bexhill Road. I was faced with a slow-moving lorry. The road ahead was clear so I signalled to pull out, accelerated and overtook. Unfortunately during this manoeuvre my speed momentarily touched 33-miles an hour. I was failed. My punishment was to wait for a further six weeks before taking another test. This time I was a little more cautious and passed. That, however, was the end of the matter. I only ever drove one other police vehicle during my service in the Hastings Police.

My relationship with Eve was reasonably static. She came to visit her sister most weekends and we went out together if my duties permitted. I was not keen for anything to progress beyond this stage. I found that she worked as an assistant in a dental surgery. She was surprisingly open about her relationship with her employer. He was a married man but had been bedding her on a regular basis over a period of a couple of years. When she eventually found herself pregnant he paid for her to have an abortion. She assured me that should she find herself pregnant again she was quite prepared to have a further abortion. Somehow I could not foresee a permanent relationship coming about here, but I considered her O.K. for practise purposes.

Once again it was high summer. Hastings was crowded with visitors. It was time for the annual Hastings Carnival. Personally, I have little time for festivities of this sort. Invariably parts of the crowd lining the route become over boisterous. Water and other things are sprayed at the nearest policeman and fights break out among drunks. Maybe the children and summer visitors get some pleasure out of it but I never have. This time I was on duty at the Memorial. For a change everyone in the crowd appeared to be behaving themselves. The procession started to pass by, each group with its band. All very colourful. Eventually the float containing the Hastings Carnival Queen and her two attendants passed by. The Queen this year was a local girl, Jean Horsfall whom I had met several times. She was very attractive but not quite my type. My attention was drawn to the gorgeous creature sitting just in front of her. Now here was beauty I could really admire. 'Why', I wondered, 'had she not been chosen as Carnival Queen?' She was ten-times better than Jean. Then she was out of sight. How was it that I had never noticed her before! I must be less observant than I had thought. Two weeks went past before I caught sight of her again. Again she was near the Memorial but this time on foot. At a safe distance I followed her. In doing so I had to leave my beat. I hoped I wouldn't meet Inspector Pilbeam or I would be having a lot of explaining to do. Her route took her round the back of Hastings Railway Station into Braybrook Road. I kept at a safe distance not wanting to alarm her.

Eventually she went up some steps and into a house. I sauntered along in the rear and made a quick note of the house number. Then I returned to my beat by the quickest route. On getting back to the Station I got out the voters list from the front office and quickly turned to the address I wanted. To my considerable consternation I found that it was the house where Sergeant Ben Hunt lived. 'My God', I thought, 'Surely she's not his wife!' Ben Hunt was one of the traffic sergeants, and one of the ugliest men I have ever met. I'd never had a lot to do with him but had always got on reasonably well when we had any dealings. The last thing I wanted to do was to enquire of him who it was I had seen entering his house. It looked as though I was going to have to bide my time again. 'I wonder if she goes to dances on the pier'. I thought.

The following Saturday I fortunately finished duty at 2 p.m. That evening, keeping my fingers crossed, I made my way to the pier. The dancing had been in progress for about an hour when I arrived. I hoped that I wouldn't bump into Eve who, I had told I would be on duty. My luck was in. Eve wasn't there, but the object of my admiration was. She was sitting on the far side of the dance hall chatting to another girl. I took a deep breath. This was it. I made my way over and was greeted with a smile. At my invitation she got up and we danced. I'm no great shakes as a dancer but suddenly I was transformed. I couldn't put a foot wrong. I was the best dancer on the floor. The music came to an end and we sat down. Her name, she told me, was Joan. I told her who I was. 'Yes, I know', she said, 'you're the policeman who followed me!' Had I been so transparent, I wondered. I was pleased to find that Joan was not Ben Hunt's wife but his sister-in-law.

My life now took a rather different course. One of my less pleasant tasks was to break the news to Eve that all was over between us. She took the news philosophically I thought. I'm pretty sure that over the months that we had been going out together she had been continuing her relationship with her dentist employer so I guess the news was not a total disaster. I wonder how things finally turned out for her. I never saw her again. Joan had a flat in Magdalen Road, a couple of hundred yards from the police box. She worked at an electronics firm in West Hill Road at St Leonards. I was able to see her at some time practically every day, either on or off duty. Had I been able, at this time, I should undoubtedly have married her almost immediately. This, however, proved impossible. Why? Well there was the small matter of her husband to consider. Joan had got married during the War. Her husband was in the R.A.F. like myself. It was one of those many wartime marriages which had just not worked out. She was now separated from him. There were no valid grounds for divorce and the only way appeared to be to wait the appropriate number of years and then apply on grounds of desertion. It seemed to be an awful waste of time. 'Maybe', I thought, 'her husband would sue for divorce if we gave him grounds to do so'. I discussed this with Joan but she didn't seem too keen on the idea. She had been separated for nearly four years so only had to wait a further three years before commencing divorce proceedings.

Another year was rushing past. Daily Orders informed me that the time was nigh to commence the second-year's refresher course. The two Peters and I were to undergo this four-weeks course at Maidstone. We would be able to return home every weekend if we were not required for duty. On the due date, off we went. Again there was nothing very memorable about the course that springs to mind, except the celebration dance at the end of the fourth week. I invited Joan to attend. Fortunately, she had some relatives who lived in Maidstone and she arranged to stay with them overnight. When I escorted her into the hall where the dance was being held there were bulging eyeballs all round. She really looked lovely and I was the object of considerable envy. At the beginning of each dance there was a mad rush to try to get her away from my grasp. No one succeeded however. After the dance I heard a lot of comment about how greedy I was. I escorted Joan to her relatives' house and arranged to meet her the following afternoon when we should travel back to Hastings together.

The following Monday I was back on duty. Up to see Angus again. This time he was happy with the results. I had come first, Peter Godber was second and Peter Austin third. Angus was like a dog with two tails. That day there was a special announcement of the result in Daily Orders. 'This is the first time members of this Force or, as far as is known, of any Force, to have occupied the first three places.' The future looked quite rosy.

Chapter 5

My probationary period was now at an end. For some time I had been thinking of joining one of the local Masonic Lodges. I had been initiated into Freemasonry while I was in the R.A.F., when I was twenty-one. My brother Ralph, having been a Mason for some years, was able to propose me into his Lodge which was in London. During the past couple of years I had attended a few meetings, but, since they were held on a Saturday afternoon and I was on duty seven Saturdays out of eight, it had not been easy. I had determined to make no move in this direction until I had completed my probationary period.

From certain remarks which I had overheard in the canteen and such places, I gathered that the Admin Inspector, Richard Dann, was the Secretary of the Lodge of St George, which held its meetings at the Masonic Temple in St Leonards. I decided that in this instance a direct approach was preferable. To this end I made my way to his office one morning when I judged he might not be too busy. 'Could I have a word with you Sir?', I enquired. I had always got on well with Mr Dann and, beaming at me, he told me to take a seat. 'What can I do for you P.C. Beaden?', he asked. 'I understand, Sir, that you are the Secretary of the Lodge of St George. I am thinking of joining a Lodge and I was wondering if you would be so kind as to propose me'. If I had hit him in the face I don't think he could have appeared more shocked. His face, from its smiling pink became bright red and angry. 'How dare you approach me on this matter', he bellowed. 'I'll have you know that no policeman under the rank of sergeant is permitted to be initiated into Freemasonry. Don't you ever approach me on this subject again or I'll make sure that your career in the Police Force is rapidly terminated'. He continued to rant on in this vein for several minutes, becoming more and more angry. Eventually he bellowed, 'Now leave my office'. I rose to leave. As I reached the door I turned and said, 'I'm sorry that you have taken this attitude Brother Dann. It's not one I am accustomed to from a Brother Mason. I must tell you that I have been a Mason for some years and that I belong to the Lee Kent Lodge. I was not asking you to propose me as an initiate but as a joining member'. With this I left the office. I had gone about three paces down the corridor when he ran after me. 'I'm sorry about that', he said. 'I never realised that you were a Mason. Please come back to my office'. I returned with him. I felt really sorry for him. It must have been a terrible shock to find this out after his display of ill-temper. He questioned me about my Masonic career to date and then told me that the Provincial Grand Master for Sussex had issued an edict that no policeman under the rank of sergeant could be made a Mason. 'How can this possibly be?', I enquired. 'This is totally against the precepts of Freemasonry. He'll either have to rescind this rule or I shall take the matter up with Grand Lodge through my Mother Lodge.' 'You put me in a very difficult position', he said. 'I shall have to take advice about this. Please don't do anything until I've had a chance to sort it out'. I agreed to this and left the office. It was many months before I heard anything further, but more of that anon.

Dealing with sudden death was a not infrequent part of my duties in Hastings. At that time there was no designated Coroners Officer and any officer dealing with a sudden death of any sort was expected to see the job through to its final conclusion. The mortuary was at the end of Rock-a-Nore in Hastings Old Town. At night the constable on duty was expected to check the mortuary for security. I feel it was fairly unlikely that anyone would voluntarily wish to break into the place and even more unlikely that anyone, once having been placed on the slab would have the inclination or ability to break out. Most of the customers we had in the mortuary were sad cases. I remember being called one day to attend to a body which had been found on the beach. When I arrived I found the remains of an aircrew member, killed during the War. From the condition of the body the Police Surgeon, Dr. Nesbit Wood deduced that the body had been trapped in the cockpit or fuselage of an aircraft when it went into the sea. From being immersed so long in salt water and with practically no contact with fish or other foragers the body had turned to a waxy substance called adipocere. An identity disk was still attached to the body indicating that this was an American airman. It was assumed that he came from a Flying Fortress known to have crashed into the sea a few miles out. It was probable that the trawl from one of the local fishing boats had torn away part of the fuselage thus releasing him from his watery tomb.

One day I was called to the top of the cliffs at Fairlight,

where an old jacket was lying on the grass. There was nothing to indicate the identity of the owner. I crawled face down to the cliff edge. Lying on the rock 300-feet below was a body. I sent one of the bystanders for further police assistance and made my way along the cliffs until I could get down to the beach. Fortunately the tide was out and I was able to walk along to where the body was lying. It was an old man of around eighty years. He had recently lost his wife and, I suppose, in a fit of depression had chosen this as his way out. A boat arrived while I was at the scene and the body loaded into it and taken along to the mortuary. When I undressed the body ready for the post-mortem I found that both ankles were broken and both femurs had been driven up into the abdomen. The old boy had simply jumped feet first and held his upright position all the way down. The Coroner returned a verdict of accidental death though I had no doubt that this was a clear case of suicide. The Coroner often took this course of action where no note was left by the deceased, I suppose this made the relatives feel better about it. Also it made it easier where an insurance claim was later made.

Dickie Stevens was a naughty boy. He lived with his mother in Frederick Road. Several times I had to tell him off in the presence of his mother. I believe his father had gone off with another woman and as a result young Dickie was getting out of control. 'Couldn't you give him a good hiding Sir?', his mother begged. 'He's too big for me to do it'. I had to explain to her that this was not part of my duty, though I sympathised with her. One afternoon I had a call to attend at the cliff bottom just east of Rock-a-Nore. Dickie and a couple of his friends had been climbing the cliffs collecting gulls' eggs. He had, unfortunately, lost his footing and plunged 200-feet onto the rocks. Later that day I had the unpleasant duty of breaking the news to his mother. She answered the door to me. 'What's he been up to this time?', she said. 'I'll kill the little bugger'. Imparting such tragic tidings to relatives is just about the worst part of police duty.

The mortuary attendant at Rock-a-Nore was named George. He was, I think, a bit mentally unbalanced. I suppose he had to be to do his particular job. There were not enough sudden deaths requiring post-mortems to keep him occupied so his main job was attending to the sewage pumps which were also in Rock-a -Nore. He was a natural for both of these jobs since he had no sense of smell and some of the bodies brought in, which had been lying around for a month or two during the summer, were a bit ripe.

Dr. Nesbit Wood, the Police Surgeon who performed most of the post-mortem examinations was always delighted if one of the constables was sufficiently interested to attend one of his autopsies. Most of the policemen would dodge this experience if they could. However, I always found it intensely interesting, and attended whenever I could. The body was always prepared by George who would make the major incision from throat to pelvis. He would then cut the skin at the back of the head and pull the scalp forward over the face. Next the top of the skull was removed with an electric saw and the brain removed. I must say that for someone totally unqualified George certainly knew his way round a corpse. At this stage Nesbit Wood took over, slicing through the brain with a carving knife, looking for any disease or injury. The heart, liver, kidneys and lungs were similarly dealt with. 'Ah!', Nesbit would exclaim, 'look at this!' A cancerous tumour or a ruptured aorta would be pointed out. Not a job for the squeamish. At the end of the post-mortem George packed the brain cavity with newspaper and sewed the skin back in position. The brain, together with the other various organs were poked back into the abdominal cavity and the main incision roughly cobbled together. I never saw Fred wear gloves either during post mortems or while engaged on his sewage job. He always ate his sandwiches in the mortuary and even offered them around. For some reason no one ever accepted them. If only people realised the manner in which their body or that of their dear ones was treated after accident or sudden death, there would probably be far less opposition to the removal of organs for transplants today.

About this time an old lady who lived in one of the ground floor flats in Winchester House died. She left one or two nice bits of furniture to my mother who had been looking after her for some time. When the flat was cleared my parents decided that they would like to move into it, so arranged with the owner to do just that. They still continued to collect the rents from the other tenants and arrange repairs as necessary. This left vacant the small flat which they had been occupying. I took this as a heaven-sent opportunity. I rented the flat from them and Joan moved in. For the sake of appearances I continued to occupy a room in my parents' flat but I purchased adequate furniture at the auction sales and made the flat very comfortable.

C.I.D. in Hastings was very much a closed shop. Detective Chief Inspector Longhurst was in charge while under him was Detective Inspector Copper. There were a couple of Detective Sergeants and half-a-dozen Detective Constables. Most of them had been on C.I.D, for many years and had found a cushy little number. Since the C.I.D. establishment was fixed there was practically no possibility of joining the club. However, it had been arranged that each constable, on completing his probation would be attached to C.I.D. for a period of two weeks, to see how the other half lived. Eventually my turn arrived. I reported for duty in plain clothes at the C.I.D. office one Monday morning and was studiously ignored by everyone. Eventually Norman Church, one of the D.C.s took pity on me. 'Come on young 'un', he aid, 'We've got an enquiry to do'. The C.I.D. had been allocated one small Ford 8 saloon for their use, and this we took. We made our way to Silchester Road at St Leonards. 'Right', said Norman, 'we had a break-in last week at a shop in Queen's Road. We pulled in a suspect, Gordon Catt who gave this as his address. We had to let him go, but I want you to make some enquiries and see if anyone here knows him'. He pointed out the house where Catt claimed to live. 'What am I supposed to ask him if he's in?', I enquired. 'Oh, you'll think of something. We're pretty sure he doesn't live here anyway. Don't let anyone know that you're a policeman though', he said. I got out and went to the door. A woman answered it. I recognised her immediately. 'Good morning', I said. 'Does Gordon Catt live here?' 'Yes, he does but he's not in. He's at work. What do you want him for', she said. I desperately tried to think of something convincing that would not betray my identity in case she had not recognised me. 'Oh', I said, 'I met him the other evening and I just thought I'd call round for a chat'. 'I know you', she said. 'You're a policeman. What are you up to?' I retreated down the steps. 'I'll call back another time', I called out as I fled. Norman glanced at me as I got back in the car. 'Well?', he demanded. 'He lives there, but he's not in. He's at work.' 'Did you find out where he works?' said Norman. I had to admit that I had not. 'I hope you didn't let her know that you're a policeman', he said. 'She already knew me', I confessed. Norman was a bit annoyed that I had blown my first assignment but I wondered if he could have done much better in the circumstances. We returned to the C.I.D. office.

The next day, on my arrival, I found that I had been allocated a desk. The 'In' tray was full of old files. Each one had been chewed over by its original investigator and finally put aside in the 'Don't know what to do next' collection. 'Have a look through this lot', said one of the sergeants. 'You should be able to solve one or two of them.' 'Thanks a lot', said I, commencing my mammoth task. The vast majority of the files had clearly come to the end of the road. Why they hadn't just been filed as 'undetected' I don't know. However, one of them I found of interest. This was a recent case of 'obtaining goods by false pretences'. The miscreant, a woman giving the name of Richards, had gone to half-a-dozen shops one Saturday afternoon and had selected clothing and other goods, paying each time by cheque. On the cheques being presented the following Monday they had all been returned, the cheque book having, in the meantime, been reported lost. Statements had been obtained from each of the shop assistants and one of them claimed that the woman had been in her shop several times previously. There the investigation had ended. The woman's description had been circulated, but without success. I pondered this over. If 'Mrs Richards' had been in the shop several times before, I felt it likely that she lived in the town. Would she chance being recognised by any of the shop girls who had been her victims? I thought it unlikely. If I was right it appeared probable that she had committed these offences just before moving out of town. I got the Directory out and looked up the local removal firms. I made a list of these and left to make my enquiries. The first one I went to was Pickfords who had an office in Cambridge Road. It was my lucky day. I explained to the manager what I was looking for. 'Yes', he said, 'I think I know the woman you are after. Unfortunately, I can't give you any information as all of our clients moves are confidential.' He produced a large ledger from a drawer and opened it. 'I'm just going out to get a cup of tea, I expect you'd like one. Of course I must ask you not to look at this ledger while I'm out. I shall be about ten minutes I expect'. Off he went and I grabbed the ledger. There it was. Mrs Emily Farmer had been moved out of her flat at Kenilworth Road, St Leonards on the day the offences took place. Her furniture had been placed in store and she had gone to join her husband who was an officer in the occupying forces in Germany. My next move was to visit the vacated flat in Kenilworth Road. The owner of the house opened the door to me. I explained my mission without specifying the reason. 'Yes, Mrs Farmer had moved out leaving the flat in total chaos'. The landlord was furious about this and showed me up to it. Debris lay everywhere. I spent half- an-hour sorting through the rubbish. At the end of it I had found two documents containing specimens of her handwriting. These I checked against the signatures on the cheques and even my inexpert eye could tell that the writing was the same. There was also an application form for a passport. This had been spoiled and discarded. I reasoned that if she had recently applied for a passport she would probably have needed a photograph to be taken. My next place of call was the Sunlounge Photographers, on the sea-front. Here again my luck held. The photographer remembered Mrs Farmer and was able to produce a copy of her photograph. I returned to the C.I.D. office in triumph. Before I could make my report I was sent for by the Detective Inspector and given a bollocking for taking the C.I.D. car and keeping it all morning. However I was partially forgiven when I explained my first success. The other files were taken away from me in case I should solve any more. No one was prepared to risk his job by letting a constable on attachment have successes. However, the photograph of Mrs Farmer was identified in due course. I hoped to be sent to Germany to arrest and escort her back, but no such luck. The case was not considered that serious. I did get a commendation for clearing it up though. The rest of my attachment to C.I.D. was uneventful. The others made sure of that. That then was the sum total of my attachment to Hastings C.I.D. 'T'was but a poor thing but t'was mine own!

I was doing a stint on the Clive Vale beat. This was a quiet residential area adjoining the Ore beat. Clive Vale was, by and large, a quiet and law-abiding area which is another way of saying that it was downright boring. Les Finch, my beat sergeant, met me when I was making a point at one of the telephone boxes used for that purpose. 'I've got a little job for you P.C. Beaden', he said. 'Get a statement from a young lady at 41, Barley Lane, about a traffic accident involving her brother. Should be just up your street, you being a single man and all that'. This sounded fine to me so I made my way to the address given. The door was answered by a delightful young creature of about eighteen. She introduced herself as Margaret Sutton. She was a student nurse in her second year of training. She really was a breath of fresh air. Pity she was so much younger than me! Otherwise, if I wasn't already courting pretty heavily! I dismissed the thought. I was already promised to Joan! I obtained her statement, taking as long over it as I could. She had been out for a walk with her young brother David, when he had suddenly run into the road in front of a taxi and been knocked down. No serious injuries fortunately, and no offence by the taxi driver that I could see. With a feeling of regret I returned to my beat. I had never noticed Margaret around the town previously. After this she seemed to pop up all over the place. Maybe I was just getting more observant.

Hastings was in the throes of a crime wave. Clearly we had at least one experienced professional criminal living on us. Around the town and in adjoining St Leonards were some very good class houses. One after another they were being burgled, ransacked from top to bottom. Only comparatively small valuable articles and cash or jewellery were being stolen. The dreadful thing was that practically every house so attacked belonged to someone who had gone on holiday, leaving their premises under police supervision. Unlike the present day slapdash attitude of the police, very strict rules were enforced about the security of property in those days. These insisted that every house placed under police supervision had to be visited at least twice during each eight-hour shift, as were all shop or other commercial premises on each beat. This meant that every unoccupied house was visited six times each day, yet no break-in had been found in progress during any police visit. How were the criminals getting away with it. It was clear from the extent of activity which had taken place at some of the burglaries that a considerable amount of time had been taken up in perpetrating the offence. I was as puzzled about the whole business as everyone else.

One night I was on duty at St Leonards. This was a beat I had not worked for a considerable time, mainly because it was almost the nearest one to where I lived and I had to be in very good favour with whoever allocated the duties to deserve this. This was the most vulnerable area of the whole town, since it contained the highest proportion of good-class detached residential property. At 9.45 p.m. I booked on duty at the police box at the bottom of Filsham Road. On the shelf was the book in which were listed all of the houses under police supervision. There were about a dozen of them. I was going to have my work cut out to cover this lot twice in the night in addition to two visits to each lock-up shop on the beat. I decided that I had better get cracking and start by visiting the houses. The first one I visited was at the top end of Filsham road, about half-a-mile from the Police Box. The owners were taking a holiday in the Mediterranean and had been away for several days. I admired the house. It was set in its own grounds of about half an acre. Beautifully landscaped garden complete with large fish pond and fountain. 'Lucky buggers', I thought. All was secure, and mounting my trusty police bicycle I went on my way. I visited all of the other houses and shop premises before I went back to the box for my sandwiches. I fully intended repeating the whole process during the second half of my duty, however, before I had taken more that a couple of mouthfuls of sandwich the telephone rang. 'Get along to Bulverhythe Road', I was instructed, 'R.T.A. ambulance on its way'. I dropped everything and dashed along to Bulverhythe about half a mile away. The ambulance passed me on the way. On my arrival I found a car crashed into the front of a house. The driver must have either been drunk or gone to sleep. He and his two passengers were not badly injured but were nevertheless taken along to the hospital to be checked over. I followed along behind and spent the next two hours taking statements and filling in forms. Eventually I got back to the Police Box. It was nearly five o'clock. Something had to go by the board. By 6 a.m. I was back at the Police Box to go off duty. 'I've not managed two visits to them all', I told my relief, 'but I've done as many as I could'. I booked off duty and went home to bed. At about 9 a.m. I was awakened by my mother. 'There's a policeman wants to see you'. she said. I struggled wearily out of bed. One of the traffic constables stood in the lounge. 'Sorry to get you out', he said, 'you're wanted down at the nick. There was a break-in on your beat last night. What was the last time you visited 28 Filsham Road?' I shook my head trying to get my thoughts into some sort of order. 'Well I only managed one visit. That would be about 10.30 p.m,' I said. 'I've got a note of it in my pocket-book'. 'Well I hope you've got a good excuse for not making the second visit', he said. I made my way to the police station. My greeting was frosty. The Detective Chief Inspector was there. He held out his hand for my pocket-book. 'Only one visit I see', he said. I pointed out that I had been tied up with the traffic accident for most of the rest of the night. He didn't look convinced. After about an hour I was permitted to return home, but I didn't get much more sleep. On my return to duty that evening I found that I had been shifted back up to Ore Village. Clearly I was not to be entrusted with anything as important as St Leonards.

Over the next couple of months the spate of burglaries continued. They were the major subject of conversation among all of the police. One day I was eating my sandwiches at the old police station at Bohemia. I was talking to Jim Brinkhurst, one of the old-time coppers. He had lived for years in a flat over the police station and was coming up for his well-earned retirement after nearly 30 years of service. We were discussing the spate of burglaries and he commiserated with me about the Filsham Road job. Jim was a dour old character but was well-liked among his colleagues. He was faced with the prospect of having to find alternative accommodation on his retirement. 'I don't know what I'm going to do young 'un', he said, 'I suppose I might stand a chance of a council house. I've not managed to save anything'. Jim's son was also in the police. He was a sergeant in the West Sussex Force.

My next spell of night duty was spent on the Town Centre. I noticed that there seemed to be a lot of C.I.D, activity for some reason. At 1.30 a.m. I went in for my refreshments. The Police Station seemed to be alive with activity. Seated in the Interview Room was Jim Brinkhurst. His face was ashen. I have seen a few people in a state of shock but never any to compare with the condition of Jim. 'What on earth is going on?', I asked Les Finch. 'C.I.D. set a trap and watched him go into a tobacconist in London Road. They arrested him when he came out with cigarettes and marked money'. Shortly afterwards Jim left with the C.I.D, officers to search his flat over Bohemia Police station. There they found the entire proceeds of all of the burglaries which had taken place over the previous months. Jim had certainly made up his mind that when he retired he was going to have a nice little nest egg to fall back on. Looking back with hindsight, it now seems obvious that the culprit had to be a policeman. All the inside knowledge that was needed was there.

It transpired that Jim had been working with one Reg Westover, a retired C.I.D. officer who was engaged on private detective work. The perfect cover. Jim and Reg would watch when the beat constable started his rounds, following at a discrete distance on Reg's motor bike and sidecar. As soon as the chosen premises were checked, in they would go in the full knowledge that they would be undisturbed for at least a couple of hours. Instead of an honourable retirement, Jim went to prison for five years, accompanied by Reg. Both forfeited their pensions. They had never managed to dispose of any of the loot.

Around September 1950 Inspector Dann called me to his office. 'Sorry this has taken so long', he said, 'I've had a hell of a fight over this but in the circumstances the Provincial Grand Master has had no alternative but to rescind the rule about no police constables being Masons.' 'Quite right too', I said, 'it was a disgraceful rule anyway'.

'You realise that it will open the door for lots of other policemen to join a Lodge', he said. 'Well I can't see anything wrong with that', said I, 'they'll raise the tone no end!' He handed me an application form to fill in. A couple of months later I was admitted to the Lodge of St George as a joining member. As I stood up to answer the speech of welcome which had been extended to me I saw the glances of apprehension on the faces of some of the members of Provincial Grand Lodge who were present. I made no mention of the difficulties which had been placed in my way and the atmosphere noticeably relaxed. My attendances at the Lodge were, however, few. Those who arranged my duties saw to that.

I was on duty on the Town Centre beat. At the bottom of Cambridge Road was the Orion Cinema. It was showing a film called *Brighton Rock*. A familiar face looked out at me from one of the photographs. Dickie Attenborough! I stopped and examined the posters. He was playing the lead role. Old Dickie, my mate from R.A.F. days —a film star! Not only that, he was due to make a personal appearance on the following day. The following morning I was again on the same beat. I wandered into the foyer of the cinema. There sat Dickie signing autographs, surrounded by reporters and photographers from the local newspapers. I produced my pocket book and sidled up to him. He did not look up from his task. I thrust my pocket book under his nose. 'Who would you like me to sign it for?', he enquired. 'Why me of course', I said. He glanced up. 'Good God', he gasped and jumping to his feet he shook my hand and embraced me. Being in uniform I was a bit embarrassed by this show of affection. The photographer had a field day. Dickie abandoned his task of signing autographs and we spent the next ten minutes talking over old times. He told me that he was about to commence acting in Agatha Christie's play, 'The Mousetrap' at a London theatre. He later sent me complimentary tickets and Joan and I went to an evening performance and met him afterwards in his dressing room, where we helped him finish of the best part of a bottle of whisky.

The winter of 1950 seemed particularly bitter. I was never over-fond of night duty, but pounding around in sub-zero temperatures for eight hours when everyone else was tucked up having nookey seemed an exceptionally hard way of earning a crust. My friend Peter Godber was having a particularly hard time of it. Just before Christmas he had developed a dreadful chest infection. Coughing and sneezing all over the place. As usual there were the cynics with their snide comments. 'Going sick just in time for Christmas I suppose', I heard one of the sergeants remark. In the event he managed to complete his Christmas duties, but shortly afterwards collapsed with pneumonia. He was off-duty for several weeks and eventually returned looking like death. He had evidently been doing some serious thinking during the time he was laid up. 'I hope', he said, 'that you are going to enjoy your 160,000 mile walk'. 'I', he added, 'am not'. Seeing my puzzled look he elucidated. 'If we walk the beat at the regulation three miles an hour for say seven hours a day for 30 years it comes to 240,000 miles. Take off rest days and leave, plus time spent in writing reports, etc, and I reckon that 160,000 miles is about right. I had to agree with his logic. It sounded an awful lot of miles.

I had also been doing a bit of thinking recently. I was out of favour again and banished to the beat at Ore Village. Battling through the snowdrifts to the back of beyond. Pushing my bike most of the way because the roads were too icy in most places to ride it. I had to allow almost an extra hour to get there and the same when I came off duty the following morning. 'I'm feeling a bit fed up', I announced to Peter. 'The thought of another three months up at Ore is enough to try the patience of a saint. Some bugger has got it in for me all right. I've a good mind to apply for this'. This last remark was made somewhat jokingly since, at the time, I was glancing at a copy of *The Police Review* lying open on the table in front of me. 'The Crown Agents', I read, 'invite applications from serving police officers for appointment as Assistant Superintendent of Police in Malaya!' The salary offered, while not princely, was well over twice what I was currently receiving. The thought of Peter or myself as Assistant Superintendents or even applying for such posts seemed, however, beyond the realms of possibility, so discussion of the matter was rapidly exhausted and the subject closed. However, the seed was sown. My knowledge of Malaya was negligible. It had been overrun by the Japs during the war and, from what I read, there were the murmurings of communism to be heard. Still, from what I gathered, it was nice and warm and would make a pleasant change from the arctic conditions we were currently experiencing.

After a couple of days I decided to broach the subject again with Peter. 'Look here', I said, 'I've been thinking about that Malaya lark and I really think I might apply for it. After all, the advert simply asks for serving police officers. It doesn't say you've got to be a Sergeant or Inspector. We're no longer probationers so we should be eligible'. Somewhat to my surprise Peter was quite enthusiastic. 'Why not?', he said, 'they can only turn us down and it might be interesting to see what sort of reaction we get'. 'Right', I said, 'I shall write off today.' 'Do you think we ought to tell Angus we're applying?' said Peter. 'Not bloody likely', I replied, well able to anticipate the likely comments of our Chief Constable. Our letters to the Crown Agents were followed by two weeks of tense anticipation. The letters of refusal which followed were something of an anticlimax. The contents were abrupt and to the point. 'The posts of Assistant Superintendent of Police in Malaya have now been filled', we were informed. No reason was given as to why we had not been chosen to fill them. Our disappointment was bitter indeed.

Some weeks went past and another advertisement appeared in *The Police Review*. 'The Crown Agents invite applications from serving police officers for appointment as Inspectors of Police in Uganda Protectorate', I read. The salary was £480 per year. Not a lot, but almost twice what I was getting as a police constable at the time. The rank of Inspector wasn't as grand as that of Assistant Superintendent, but either were preferable to that of constable. I wasted no time in conferring with Peter. He needed little persuasion from me. The weather was still foul and Peter was still recovering from the pneumonia which had laid him low. The thought of another twenty-seven years endlessly rattling door handles was appalling. Hot tropical sun was just what was needed to cure the winter blues. We wrote out our applications the same evening.

A week went past. Suddenly on the doormat lay the letter. A bulky brown envelope marked C.A. on the flap. Trying to contain my excitement, I tore it open. Together with the application form it contained a most interesting publication issued by the Uganda Tourist Board. What a tropical paradise Uganda seemed to be, with an altitude mostly over 4000 feet. Never too hot or too cold. Snow-covered mountains to the west, luxuriant rain forests, sterile deserts, vast waterfalls and immense sluggish lakes. Truly a land of contrasts. For a keen angler like myself there were Nile Perch to be caught, up to 250 pounds in weight, while game and birds abounded everywhere. I could hardly wait to get there. First however there was the small matter of the application form to be completed. I filled it in without hesitation. Looking back at me from my completed application my qualifications seemed meager to say the least. Technical College till the age of 15¾ when, at the outbreak of war, I had left prematurely. An instrument-maker for a year until our house was made untenable by a land mine, necessitating our move to Oxfordshire. Aircraft Mechanic repairing Spitfires for a couple of years and then, into the R.A.F. where, as a Flight Engineer, I had reached the exalted rank of Flight Sergeant. No degrees, no languages, just three years as a humble copper, shaking hands with door knobs. My confidence waned a little. None the less, I lost no time in posting the application. Later the same day, I found that Peter had also received his application form and had completed and posted it. He, it appeared, was as delighted with the prospect as I was. We spent a considerable amount of time during the next couple of weeks optimistically discussing our forthcoming careers, with myself at least, mentally crossing my fingers over my lack of qualifications and hoping they would not affect my chances too greatly. Meantime we decided to say nothing to our colleagues since, without exception, they were notorious chatterboxes, and anything mentioned to one of them would ensure a total circulation of the Police Station personnel within 24 hours. After two weeks of nail-biting tension I was greeted one day by an exultant Peter. 'I've got an interview', he said. 'Have you got yours?' 'No', I replied sourly, 'not a word'. Peter, it seemed had been selected for an interview at the Crown Agents' offices at Millbank in London, a couple of weeks hence. A week passed while I watched every mail and then one morning it arrived. A thin envelope marked C.A. Crossing my fingers I tore it open. Incredible. I also had been selected for an interview. Mine was to take place three days after Peter's. 'Not bad', I thought, 'I'll be able to get advanced information about it'.

Now the cat was out of the bag. Peter had no trouble about attending his interview. The day coincided with his weekly rest day. Mine, however, would require a change of duty in order to attend. To change duties would require a report and reasons would have to be given. Everyone would know of my intentions. What then if I didn't get to Uganda after all. There would be knowing grins and snide remarks if I wasn't mistaken. I submitted my report, carefully avoiding the true reason for my request.

The following day I reported for duty at 1.45 p.m. 'Ah! P.C. Beaden', the Section Sergeant said during the briefing. 'Now you're for it. The Chief wants to see you at 3 p.m. What have you been up to my lad?' At 3 p.m. after a final polish of the toe caps of my boots on the back of my trouser legs, I was marched into Angus's office. 'Ah!, P.C. Beaden'. he said as I stood to attention in front of his desk. 'Relax man. Take a seat.' 'Alright Sergeant', he went on, 'you can go now'. The Sergeant, clearly aggravated at not being able to listen to the interview, saluted and went out. 'I wondered when you would let me in on it', said Angus. 'On what Sir?', said I. 'Oh, come off it', he said. 'You don't think the Crown Agents would invite you to attend for an interview without asking for my opinion of you first.' So, he had known about it all along. I wondered if the Crown Agents had written to him about my Malayan application as well. 'Didn't cross my mind really', I said, deciding to put a bold face on it. 'There didn't seem to be much point in spreading it around before at least the first hurdle was cleared.' 'That's alright', he replied, 'I just wanted to let you know that your change of duty is approved and to wish you the best of luck with your interview. If I was a bit younger I would be doing exactly the same'. Breathing a sigh of relief, I returned to my beat followed by the curious eyes of my Section Sergeant who was obviously itching to know what it was all about. I didn't enlighten him.

Peter went to the Crown Agents on the Monday. The following day I received a full account from him. The interview, he told me, had been tough, but afterwards he had been sent to Harley Street for Medical Examination and X-ray. 'The porter at the Crown Agents told me that you only go for the medical if you have passed the interview satisfactorily, so it looks as though I got through that anyway', he said.

Thursday arrived and I set off for London. On my arrival at the Crown Agents' impressive premises at Millbank, I was ushered into a waiting room where four other applicants were already waiting. To my eyes they looked an impressive bunch. I tried not to feel too inferior. No conversation took place during our wait. One after another the applicants entered the interview room. One after another they came out. Some of the interviews were lengthy, others painfully short. One unfortunate emerged after about ten minutes, red in the face with anger and shouting over his shoulder to the panel of interviewers, precisely what they could do with their appointments. My name was called and, somewhat nervously I entered the interview room where four impressive looking individuals were seated. I was motioned to a seat on the opposite side of the table from where they were sitting and the grilling commenced. 'What made you choose to apply to go to Uganda?', I was asked. 'The hope of improving my police career', I replied.

'Why Uganda?'

'I've always had an urge to go to Africa. I like the idea of a hot climate'.

'Why didn't you apply three years ago when you joined the Hastings Police?'

'Well, I don't think I would have stood much chance then. After all the advertisement does call for serving police officers'.

'Do you think you could cope with living in a tent on safari. Not much comfort you know?'

'The prospect sounds most exciting and I shall look forward to it'.

'Have you given any thought to your employers. Three years has been spent in training you, and as soon as you become a useful policeman you want to go somewhere else. How do you think Mr. Cargill is going to like that?'

'I've already discussed the matter with him. He has no objection to me trying to improve my prospects'.

'Hoping to get rid of you maybe?'

'I doubt it', I replied, feeling the hairs beginning to bristle on the back of my neck. 'I've earned my pay while I've been in Hastings. Now I want something to improve my prospects and broaden my outlook.'

'What gives you the idea that you would be any good in Uganda?', remarked my chief inquisitor, the Chairman of the Board, Sir George Abyss. 'After all you're just a semi-literate cockney.'

That did it. 'Now look here my friend', I replied, 'In the first place, although I was born in London I'm not a cockney. Secondly, I'm a good copper even though I don't have any university degrees, and thirdly, what's the matter with cockneys anyway. I consider them to be equal, if not better than —'

'Yes Mr. Beaden', my tormentor interrupted. 'Thank you for sparing us your time. Just wait outside will you?'

I left cursing myself under my breath. 'I've blown it', I thought. 'All that build-up and then I have to lose my temper at the crucial time'. I sat down and waited. Twenty-minutes went by and a porter appeared. He handed me an envelope. 'Take this to 32 Harley Street', he said. 'You've got to have a medical and an X-ray.' My jaw fell open. 'What does that mean', I asked, stupidly. 'Have I passed the interview?' 'Well I don't know about that', he replied, 'but I don't suppose they'd spend out twenty five guineas on a medical if you hadn't'.

The medical examination proved no problem and I returned to Hastings in a most optimistic frame of mind. Two weeks went by. Each time I saw Peter we had long conversations about our forthcoming life in Africa. Peter, being a married man was making plans to dispose of his household effects. I had no such problems. Finally the long-awaited letter which would decide my future arrived. I tore it open.

'The Government of Uganda is prepared to offer you an appointment as Inspector of Police in Uganda', I read. 'Your salary will be £480 per annum plus two increments of £20 in respect of your War Service. The appointment will be on contract for a tour of 30- to 36-months with the opportunity of joining the permanent and pensionable establishment after a probationary period of two years, subject to your passing the Government examinations in Law and Kiswahili. You will be required to travel by air from London to Entebbe on 1st May 1951. If you wish to accept this appointment you should complete the attached Form of Acceptance and return it to this office within the next seven days'.

Enclosed with this letter were a number of pamphlets about baggage allowances, kit allowances and suggested equipment to take to Uganda on first appointment. I decided to peruse these later at my leisure. Meantime I went to see Peter to give him the good news and to see if he had also heard from the Crown Agents. Indeed he had and was in a dreadful state of shock and depression. His letter, instead of offering him an appointment read, 'It is regretted that we are unable to offer you an appointment in Uganda. We strongly advise you to consult your local tuberculosis specialist without delay'.

Peter was shattered. What could I say. All his plans of a career in Uganda were in ruins. This was clearly the parting of the ways. Peter went to hospital where he was X-rayed and shortly afterwards was told by the specialist that he was suffering from milliary tuberculosis in both lungs. His prognosis was nil. A maximum of six months to live. He was immediately confined to bed and a week later was transferred to a sanatorium at Darwell Hall near Robertsbridge.

Meanwhile, I accepted the appointment offered and in due course received my air ticket and a kit allowance of 50 pounds. On examining the suggested list of equipment to take with me to Uganda I discovered an astonishing miscellany of items considered as necessary. The list was headed by a galvanised tin bath. A pith helmet and spine protector were most desirable as were khaki shorts and mosquito boots. A water filter and mosquito net were high on the list of priorities, together with camp stools, folding table and cooking utensils. About the only thing not mentioned were beads for trading with the natives. A strange omission in the circumstances. Uganda was undoubtedly a most primitive part of the world. Since my baggage allowance was limited to 40 kilos I decided to limit myself to khaki shorts and shirts. Off I went to Millets where I bought three pairs of army-surplus khaki shirts and the same number of shorts. I regretted this later when I tried them on. They were cut very long and narrow, and looked rather is if they had started life as long trousers and had had part of the legs cut off at knee level.

In due course I went to the Hospital for Tropical Diseases where I duly had my jabs to prevent cholera, smallpox, yellow fever and other unpleasant diseases. My resignation was now submitted and I faced a barrage of questions from my colleagues, some envious, some wanting advice on how to apply for a similar post, but mostly incredulous and scoffing. 'You'll be back in a couple of years', said my arch enemy Inspector Pilbeam. 'You'll come crawling round trying to get your job back. Fancy chucking up a good job with security like this to go to wogga-wogga land'. I stifled an inclination to tell him to get stuffed, since I still had a month to run before my resignation became final. He could still make things awkward for me if he was so inclined. I gritted my teeth and continued my exercise of door-knob rattling. 'Well', I thought, 'I shan't ever have to do this again!'

In a surprisingly benevolent move, the Crown agents wrote to me to impart the information that a police officer from Uganda was at present in London on leave. I was invited to contact him. Thus I first met Brian Peskett. Brian turned out to be a heavily-built chap a couple of years younger than myself. He seemed a quiet, unassuming individual. I found that he had been born in Kenya where his father was a serving Police Superintendent. He was forthcoming with his information and over lunch answered a lot of the questions which had been plaguing me. Our meeting had considerable benefit for me and I must acknowledge a debt of gratitude to Brian for giving up his time and advice.

The past few months had, to say the least, been somewhat traumatic. I had, of course kept both my parents and Joan fully informed of my intentions and the occasional progress in the direction of a total break with my present mode of life. My father and mother had, I think, mixed feelings on the subject. On the one hand, I was a handy sort of bloke to have around the place, strong as an ox, very useful when it came to decorating or carrying out repairs around the place and, not least, a useful source of income from the money I paid my mother for my board and lodgings, plus the rent I paid for the flat in which I had installed Joan. On the other hand there would be a considerable degree of reflected glory if they were able to tell their cronies that I had been promoted to the rank of Inspector of Police. I don't, however, think that they really believed, until the appointment actually came through, that I might in fact achieve my stated intention. Joan, on the other hand was devastated at the thought of my intended departure. She would have been more than satisfied for me to have remained in Hastings, ploughing along as a police constable, with the hope, in the distant future of becoming a sergeant or inspector. She had just less than two years to go before she would be able to obtain her divorce. I pointed out that she would have the use of a comfortable flat, rent-free, and that my parents, who were very fond of her, were nearby to offer any assistance which might at any time become necessary. The two years would undoubtedly fly by and, as soon as she was free of her husband, she could fly out to Uganda and we would be able to get married out there. I bought her an engagement ring and, suitably mollified, she agreed to the idea.

I visited Peter a number of times during my remaining few weeks. He looked fit and relaxed as he sat in the spring sunshine at Darwell Hall. Not at all the dying man I had expected. Skin tests were being carried out every few days but so far no reaction had occurred to indicate that he had tuberculosis. Just before I was due to leave England I visited him for the last time. He had just received the result of his last X-ray. It was completely clear. He had never had the disease. The marking on his lungs, diagnosed as milliary tuberculosis had in fact been caused by the pneumonia he had suffered earlier in the year. He was over the moon at the thought that his number was not up after all, but distressed at the thought of having, as a result of a faulty diagnosis, missed the opportunity of an overseas career. 'What do you think I should do?', he enquired. 'Keep applying', I advised. 'After all, had it not been for the mistake of their specialist you would be on your way to Uganda by now. It's my opinion that they owe you a job overseas for the worry they've put you through.' He followed my advice and I was glad to hear from him some months later that he had been offered and accepted an appointment as Sub-Inspector in the Hong Kong Police. Many years later, when he had reached the rank of Superintendent, Peter, in common with the majority of Hong Kong police succumbed to the temptation of bribery by the Tongs who ruled the criminal element there. He netted half-a-million-pounds before he was caught and an example was made of him as a warning to the others. He spent a year in a Hong Kong prison. On his release he returned to England and, learning that the Hong Kong Government was intending to pursue him to recover the half-million, fled to Spain. I have not heard from him since. On such minor variations in fortune do our entire lives hinge.

CHAPTER 6

The early departure of my flight on 1st May necessitated an overnight stay at a cheap hotel in London. Now that the moment of departure had arrived, I boarded the train at St Leonards station with very mixed feelings. My parents were upset and I persuaded them not to come to see me off. Joan, however, insisted on accompanying me to the station where we said our last fond farewells. The imminent change in my lifestyle caused me to have some last minute doubts as to the wisdom of my action. However, the die was cast so, for good or bad, I boarded the train with confidence and two heavy suitcases containing what was, for all practical purposes, my entire worldly possessions, most of which I was to find totally useless in my new environment.

Early the following morning I passed through the Customs and Immigration formalities at Heathrow and boarded the plane which was to carry me to my destination. This was an Argonaut. A four-engined, propeller-driven job. A bit crowded and a bit noisy, but a great improvement on anything I had flown during my career in the R.A.F. There were, I suppose, about 100 passengers on board. The plane taxied to the end of the runway and the pilot went through the final engine check. Eventually it lurched forward, rapidly gathering speed. I muttered the small prayer I had been accustomed to murmuring under my breath during the innumerable similar take-offs in more dangerous times. Suddenly we were airborne, looking down on the airport buildings and Staines Reservoir, rapidly diminishing in size. Then, banking to port we were away and heading for the coast. Our route lay across France for our first landing at Rome. Unfortunately low cloud obscured the view most of the way and eventually I dozed. An announcement woke me and, glancing through the window, I saw Mont Blanc passing below slightly to our right. An extraordinary and beautiful sight. The sea of cumulus cloud billowing far below while the mountain, with its folds, peaks and valleys, glaciers and crevasses rose like a mighty island. All around, near and far, other peaks broke through the clouds like the hands of drowning men. How small and insignificant it felt, perched far above them, like a fly, our progress seemingly so slow as to be negligible.

Once clear of the Alps the clouds below us vanished. Italy was bathed in bright sunshine. After a perfect landing at Rome Airport we trooped across to the passenger lounge where we had a splendid lunch while the plane was being refuelled. Back to the plane we went and, after the usual preliminaries, we were off again and, in a short time, were heading out over the Mediterranean for Cairo. I had never realised that the 'Med' was so large. Hour after hour we droned across a vast waste of sea, the occasional ship showing up against the blue grey water, more as a result of its wake that its bulk, and looking for all the world like a water beetle on a pond. The monotony was broken by the frequent free drinks and refreshments of various kinds. From time to time I surveyed the other passengers as far as I was able. 'Were there', I wondered, 'any other new appointees to the Uganda Police on board?' I suspected that there probably were, but there was no way of telling. I engaged the passenger sitting next to me in conversation. He was going to Uganda. This was his third tour. He loved the place. He was not in the police but one of the other government departments. He didn't enlighten me as to which one. His name, he confided, was Pottie. Funny sort of name, I thought. I wondered if he worked in the loony bin. I did hear years later that he had changed his name by deed poll — to Chambers.

By the time we reached Cairo Airport it was dark. Peering through the window of the plane as it circled over the city preparing to land, I could see the myriad of lights below. 'Just like fairyland', I thought. How I wished we could stay here for a while, just long enough, maybe, to visit the Sphinx and the Pyramids. No chance though. We were scheduled to stop here just long enough for refuelling before continuing our journey. Once again we disembarked and trooped across the tarmac to the airport lounge, where we had our evening meal and examined the many souvenirs offered for sale. Then, after an hour, back to the plane where several of the unwary found that their cameras and binoculars had been stolen. Eventually we were away again, lumbering off the end of the runway and up into the darkness. Turning south we sped out over the desert. I glued my face to the window wondering if I should see any lights indicating a village or other human habitation below. None whatever. What I did see about ten minutes later however, was a sudden streak of flame coming from the starboard inner engine, As I watched, it rapidly grew in intensity. It didn't take a lot of my flight engineer's experience to realise that we had a bit of trouble. I got up from my seat and went to the nearest stewardess. I anticipated that the engineer or the pilot was already aware that he had a problem. The stewardess certainly didn't know and shot into the flight deck when I pointed it out to her. She emerged a few minutes later, thanked me and asked me to return to my seat. By this time several of the other passengers had noticed the fire and were looking a bit apprehensive. 'It's all O.K', I announced, resuming my seat. Shortly afterwards the propeller was feathered and the fire was extinguished. We banked slowly to the right and an unpleasant stench of high-octane fuel filled the cabin. 'No smoking', read one warning notice. 'Fasten your seat belt', read another. The lights of Cairo reappeared and we circled the city for half-an-hour while the heavy load of petrol was jettisoned. The stewardesses buzzed around like bees, reassuring the nervous passengers and handing out yet more free drinks. Eventually we made a totally uneventful landing and taxied to a parking area. Again we trooped back to the passenger lounge. More food and refreshments were produced and we all settled back to see what the outcome of our mishap was going to be. An hour passed. Then an announcement was made. A new engine would have to be flown out from London. Meanwhile, we would be taken to the Heliopolis Palace Hotel where overnight accommodation had been arranged for us at the expense of B.O.A.C. First we had to go through the Customs and Immigration formalities. Coaches had been arranged and away we went to the hotel. What a delightful place. It was my first taste of a top class foreign hotel. I was impressed. It was palatial. The drive up to the entrance was through an avenue of hibiscus and bougainvillea in full bloom. Flame trees and other beautiful flowering vegetation, all illuminated by concealed lighting. The impressive entrance flanked by palm trees. A vast marble entrance hall flanked by a double marble staircase rising to the first floor. Large numbers of menials in their *tarbooshes* and *khanzus* flitted about on naked feet. I was shown to my room. What magnificence. Not the sort of thing a hard-up copper was used to. The marble floor strewn with Persian rugs. Marble bathroom. Superb. I was bloody glad not to be paying for this lot! 'Would I care to attend a nearby open-air cinema at the expense of the Airline?' I was asked. I declined. A glance out of the bedroom window showed me the cinema screen about 100-yards away. The film was already in progress. I had seen it! By eleven o'clock after quite an eventful day I was under my mosquito net and asleep for my first night in Africa

During a pre-breakfast stroll through the suburbs of Cairo the following morning I found that the streets had lost a little of their eastern promise when viewed by the warm light of day. To be true, they held that touch of the mystic east which one might expect, but in addition, the seamier side was also apparent. Here opulence and squalor rubbed shoulders. Smart modern shops filled with exquisite jewellery and native craftsmanship lined the streets while outside small boys vied with one another to offer their very clean sisters for jig-a-jig. Scruffy-looking Arabs whispered their offers of filthy postcards. The streets were strewn with dust and rubbish. Half-built, and apparently abandoned, blocks of flats and houses rose among the squalor. I ceased to reflect on the social situation and instead thought of my good fortune in having the opportunity to experience all this.

Back at the hotel I tasted Paw-paw, Guava and Mango for the first time during the course of a delightful breakfast. Afterwards, all the passengers were asked to assemble in the lounge. Transport was to be laid on to take all those passengers who wished to go to the Sphinx and the Pyramids. I don't think anyone declined this invitation, especially since the airline was footing the bill. One or two of us clambered to the top of the Great Pyramid. I found it hot going but eventually reached the top. The coaches below looked like toys while the passengers were the size of ants. Afterwards I went into the pyramid and clambered up into the burial chamber. I found it a bit disappointing once there. Still at least I could say that I'd been. The stench of camels carried in on the clothing of the various guides was very strong. We returned to the hotel for lunch.

After an afternoon spent wandering the streets of Cairo and repelling the natives who were insistent on selling me genuine artifacts, straight from the tomb of Tutankhamun we were whisked back to the airport by about 9 o'clock. Once again we took off and headed out over the desert. No blazing engine this time, just the velvety blackness of the desert by night, relieved only by the occasional spark of light from the cooking fire of some Arab family far below. Some hours later my sleep was interrupted by the landing preparations which heralded our landing at Khartoum. Once again we wandered like zombies across the tarmac to the airport lounge. Khartoum airport was, I found, basic in the extreme and the whole area smelled like an open sewer. Coffee in the lounge was served by the most villainous-looking group of ruffians I had yet encountered. A large assortment of tourist souvenirs were on sale: poufs made of genuine camel skin, handbags made from baby crocodiles, snakeskin wallets and handbags, all at what appeared to be ridiculously low prices. However, I managed to resist the temptation.

Eventually we were off on the last stage of our journey. I slept fitfully and woke as breakfast was being served. Far below the landscape appeared to be an endless uninteresting desert of grey sand with darker patches of scrub and thorn bush. As far as the horizon in every direction no roads or signs of human habitation could be seen. By mid-morning a popping in my ears warned me that we were losing altitude. Glancing through the window I could see a brilliant green landscape passing below me, criss-crossed by a multitude of red roads and paths. Thatched huts were scattered everywhere. Ant-like figures could be seen walking and riding bicycles. Ahead I could see the shimmering inland sea of Lake Victoria. I tried, unsuccessfully to spot a crocodile. After a wide sweep over the lake we came in for a perfect landing at Entebbe Airport. The luggage was finally sorted out and we went through the formalities of Customs and Immigration. Waiting for me outside was a friendly individual dressed in the uniform of the Colonial Police. 'I'm Paddy Erskin', he said, shaking me by the hand. There should be a couple of other new arrivals around here somewhere. Seen anything of them?' I had to confess that, if I had, I should not have known them. Eventually however they were traced and introduced themselves as Johnny Walker and Jim MacGillivray. Somehow the four of us, plus a vast amount of luggage piled into Paddy Erskin's car and we set off on the 20 miles or so of murram road to Kampala. Entebbe, I discovered, was the centre of Government for Uganda. Kampala was the capital city but Government House, the official residence of His Excellency, together with The Secretariat and the Headquarters of several of the more

important Government Departments were all at Entebbe. As we
drove through the town on our way from the Airport, I noticed
that it was a most attractive place. The surrounding countryside
sloped down towards the vast expanse of Lake Victoria. Dozens
of beautiful colonial style residences were scattered along our
route, each standing in its own grounds and each with its
beautifully landscaped gardens. On the well manicured grass
leading down to the lake couples strolled with their families and
ayahs congregated with their prams and infant charges. The
temperature, which I had thought might be oppressive was in
fact that of a pleasant English summer day. A light breeze drifted
in from the great expanse of water. It was altogether an idyllic
scene. The roads in Entebbe Township were of tarmac
construction and well maintained. Once out of the town
however, the scene changed. Here the road, while quite wide,
was constructed from the local soil. This was of a startling red
colour which contrasted vividly with the brilliant green of the
foliage on each side. On each side of the road were groups of
mud huts, some of circular construction but mostly built in the
rectangular European style. Most had roofs which had been
thatched with grass or reeds. Here and there however, were the
houses of the better off, roofed with corrugated iron. I could not
but help wondering which would be the cooler and the more
comfortable in this climate. Outside the huts were groups of
women in their brightly-coloured dresses, some sitting around
talking, some pounding grain in their wooden pestles while yet
others cultivated the bright soil with their *jembies*, a sort of
mattock. All appeared good-humoured, greeting us with a smile
or a wave as we passed. On the road were numerous bicycles,
the riders mostly toiling under vast loads of produce or other
goods. Women in their bright dresses walked along the road
verges, many carrying great bunches of green bananas, *matoke*,
on their heads. In the trees and bushes on each side of the road
were a multitude of brightly coloured birds. Apart from a few
native dogs, I saw no animals, however I did see a thin brown
snake about five-feet in length, slither rapidly across in front of
us out of the path of the car wheels. Paddy Erskin treated us to
a running commentary on our way. Uganda, he told us, was
divided into a number of Provinces, roughly adhering to the old
tribal boundaries. We were at present in Buganda, which

encompassed a large part of the countryside to the north of Lake Victoria. The Kabaka or hereditary king of Buganda was Sir Frederick Mutesa, known as King Freddie, who lived in a palace at Mengo just outside Kampala. On the outskirts of Kampala we passed through the Village of Katwe. This was an untidy-looking dump which looked as it would be much improved by being burned down. Here, I was informed, flourished a large criminal community. A modern tarmacadam by-pass was in the course of construction, which, when completed, would avoid the necessity of driving through the village. A police station had been built during the past few years on the outskirts of the village. It was manned by a European officer but was so awful that no one lasted more than six months. I kept my fingers crossed and hoped I would never be sent there.

We passed through a modern shopping area, of which virtually every shop was run by an Asian, we reached the European Quarter. Finally we drew up outside the Speke Hotel where accommodation had been arranged for us. The Speke was one of two European hotels in Kampala. The other one was The Imperial, which was the more modern of the two. The Speke was a real old Colonial-style building, single-storey with a broad verandah running round the front and one side. It was run by a middle-aged couple who had lived in Uganda for many years. What a pleasant place it was. The cool, shady lounge with its slow-moving electric fans suspended from the ceiling. Outside, the brilliant sunshine, while in the cool of the hotel bare-footed African waiters moved noiselessly around in their spotless white *khanzus*, red cummerbunds and *tarbooshes*. Opposite the hotel was King George the Fifth Park, where there was a bandstand at which the Police Band played every Sunday morning.

Paddy introduced us to the proprietor of the hotel, and in answer to the snap of his fingers and a murmured order, three of the waiters picked up our belongings and bustled off to the rooms which we had been allocated. 'I'm sure you chaps could do with a beer', said Paddy, 'I know I could'. We sank into the deep comfortable armchairs in the lounge and sampled our first taste of the local brew. A delightful lager-type beer brewed at nearby Port Bell on Lake Victoria, from which it got its name. It slipped down the gullet like nectar. 'Boy', called Paddy and a silently-moving African appeared as if by magic, '*Lete beer ngini*'. Flashing his teeth in a brilliant smile the waiter produced a further four bottles of 'Bell', the icy contents producing a film of dew on the outsides. What a useful phrase, I thought, tucking it away into my memory bank. How right I was. Over the years which were to follow I can't think of a more useful phrase than *'Lete beer ngini'*. During the short session which followed each of us tried out the phrase and became proficient in its use. Later we made our way somewhat unsteadily to our rooms to recover. 'I'll pick you up at 9.a.m. tomorrow', said Paddy, 'you're to see the Commissioner first thing'.

The room which I had been allocated was at the far end of a newly-built annex. It was a large room with a private verandah and faced out on to the park opposite. I was sharing this with Johnny Walker. I hoped he didn't snore. I lay on my bed and snoozed the afternoon away. By four o'clock I was refreshed and into the lounge for afternoon tea. Afterwards I donned my long shorts and went out for a stroll. I must admit that I felt somewhat conspicuous. No one else had shorts like mine. I saw a number of European police officers and, in common with Paddy Erskin, their shorts were cut well above the knee and the legs were wide, not skin tight as mine were. I decided that I wouldn't wear these on my visit to Police Headquarters on the morrow. A wise decision.

The rapidity of the change from daylight to dark took me somewhat by surprise, and found me a couple of miles from the hotel. In no time, friendly nubile young African ladies were approaching me, presumably offering to show me the way. However, being somewhat naive and not being able to understand a word they were saying I could only smile and walk on. My sense of direction didn't let me down however, and half-an-hour later I found myself back at the park and so to the hotel. As I made my way along the corridor leading to my room, I became conscious of the teeming insect life around me. The trilling of the cicadas was deafening and infinite in its variety. Praying mantises lay in wait for the unwary moths, beetles and mosquitoes, turning their heads and watching me in an almost human manner. I found their behaviour fascinating and stood watching them for a while. As their prey moved near them they would turn their eyes to gauge the distance. Once within range their fate was sealed as a lightning pounce would be followed by swift dismemberment and munching of the powerful jaws. In their turn the mantises would, from time to time, fall prey to the pale, fat tailed geckos who ran up the walls and across the ceiling defying gravity in their search for food. Occasionally a gecko would pick an adversary as large or larger than himself, then a battle royal would take place, the outcome seemingly in doubt as the contestants fell to the floor with a plop. 'I shall never be able to sleep with this racket going on', I commented to Johnny Walker.

Dinner at the hotel was a fairly informal affair with the choice of a roast or a spread of cold meats to which one was expected to help oneself. I chose the latter. After years of frugal living, I found myself looking at an apparently limitless supply of magnificent joints. No rationing here. 'Take as much as you like', said the hotel manager. He was evidently used to the reaction of the new arrivals from the austere U.K. I took him at his word and piled my plate from this unaccustomed cornucopia. Returning to my table I asked one of the waiters to bring me a beer. The manager accompanied him on his return with the foaming nectar. He suggested that it might be more convenient to open a monthly account for drinks, rather than bothering with the payment each time. I thought this was a wonderful idea, especially since my finances were very strictly limited. After dinner Johnny and I sat and chatted for a while before returning to our room. Tucked in under my mosquito net I wondered if I would ever get used to the trilling of the insects. Fortunately soon after midnight the hotel lights were dimmed and the racket became more subdued.

The following morning started pleasantly cool. '*Chai Bwana*', said the room-boy as he poured out a cup of tea for me. 'My God', I thought, 'tea in bed no less. I could get to like this given time'. I arose and donned my totally unsuitable garb, slacks, shirt, tie and jacket, and went along to the dining room for breakfast. What a spread. Delicious local coffee, paw-paw, grapefruit, oranges, bananas, bacon, eggs, ham, kippers and a host of other delights were available. I fear I made a bit of a pig of myself. At 9 o'clock sharp, Paddy arrived and took us to Police Headquarters, a low, rambling single-storey building with a red tiled roof. Inside was a little on the warm side, but electric fans kept a current of air circulating. Paddy took us into an office and introduced us to the occupant. 'I'm Stan Fortt, the Staff Officer',he said. 'Settled into your hotel O.K.? You'll be there for a week or two I expect, till we decide what to do with you.'

A little later we were ushered into the Commissioner's office. Joseph Deegan turned out to be a rather short, squarely-built man who looked more like a farmer than a Commissioner of Police. His attitude struck me as being pleasant, if somewhat vague. You'll spend the next few weeks at the Police Training School at Kibuli'. he said, 'Teach you a bit of drill, Swahili and Law and then we'll decide where to send you. Any of you got any previous Police experience?' he demanded. We all had. 'Oh well, that might be an advantage', he allowed. 'Any questions?' A myriad of questions flooded the mind, but no one voiced them. How could one, at this stage, ask what the job consisted of? Whatever it was, it was now too late to have second thoughts. Better not make an ass of oneself by asking the Commissioner a host of petty details. All would, no doubt, be explained in the fullness of time. We were dismissed from 'the presence' and piled into Paddy's car. Next stop, Police Training School. Here we were shown into the office of the O.C. John Thomson who held the rank of Senior Assistant Superintendent of Police. He was a lean man of military bearing and kindly disposition. After the introductions he got straight down to business. 'Right', he said, 'we'd better get you fitted up with uniform to start. You look bloody uncomfortable in that lot'. The day was becoming distinctly warm and my shirt and jacket were beginning to stick to me. The other two appeared to be suffering from the same trouble. 'I'll get someone to take you along to see the Quartermaster and then the tailor. Sorry we've no transport to spare, but it's not all that far'. We left his office and went outside to await our escort. On the parade ground squads of Africans were being marched round in double-quick-time, with or without rifles. About 200-yards away from us was an open-sided drill shed measuring about 80-yards by 30. Here the police band was having a practice session. The rhythmic beat of their instruments creating havoc with the marching of the squads outside. John Thomson, it turned out, was a great man for drill and liked nothing better than putting a squad through its paces.

Bill Bruce arrived. A slightly built, cheerful individual, he had been in Uganda only a couple of weeks longer than ourselves. He looked smart and cool in his new Inspector's uniform. We introduced ourselves and, after a short chat, set off to meet the Quartermaster. The stores was situated about a couple of miles distant on the top of Nakasero Hill. It was, in fact, within the walls of a Fort, one of the original strongpoints built by Lord Lugard, when Uganda was being brought under the protection of the British Crown in the days of Queen Victoria. Its enormously thick brown stone walls and the great reinforced timber doors provided excellent security for the very considerable armoury of weapons and ammunition stored there. The approach road to the top of the hill wound like the coils of a snake but, by climbing the steep footpath worn between each road level, we were able to cut a very considerable distance from our journey.

George Blyth, the Quartermaster was an ex-military man, of lean and dour appearance. He sported the badges of rank of an Assistant Superintendent. For some reason, which I never discovered, when he was appointed as Quartermaster he reverted to his Army rank of Captain. In all the years I knew him his title never varied, though he finished up with Superintendents' Crowns on his shoulders. Like all quartermasters, George greeted new arrivals to his domain with dubious enthusiasm. His dour exterior betrayed no welcoming smile. In this, however, he belied his true nature. He could not have been more helpful and in the many years acquaintanceship which followed I had good reason to bless him on many occasions. During the hour which followed he issued us with a vast amount of equipment and uniform, and topped it off with 30-yards of khaki drill from which our uniforms were to be made. Quite a lot of the equipment was issued on loan on the understanding that it would have to be paid for in due course, if and when we passed our probationary period and were admitted to the permanent staff. The rest of it, including our cap, boots, shoes, stockings and the khaki drill had to be paid for. 'It's O.K', said George, 'you'll get the bill in due course, but there's no great hurry'. What an understanding chap. He rounded off his kindness by giving us a lift back to the Speke Hotel where we dumped everything except the khaki drill and made our way to the tailor's shop which was only half-a-mile distant.

The tailor was Mr Mehta, an Indian, whose grandfather had come out from Calcutta as a labourer when the Kenya-Uganda railway was being built. He greeted us obsequiously on the verandah of his workshop. Two Africans working at ancient treadle sewing machines, sat on the verandah. One was making trousers, the other, brassieres of various dimensions, mostly very large, from brightly-coloured materials. Breast holders, I found they were called. I wondered who did the measuring. Our measurements were now being taken and we were promised two bush jackets and four pairs of shorts within three days. A ceremonial uniform consisting of a long sleeved jacket and trousers was to follow later. I wondered what would happen about payment. I had £50 to my name. I was living in a hotel at £20 per week and I had just run up a tailors' bill of a further £25. This was my first day in the country and the shadow of imminent bankruptcy was already looming before me. I couldn't expect any salary to be paid for at least a month. Turning to Bill Bruce I enquired if there happened to be a Bank anywhere near. 'Not far', I was told. 'I dare say you want to change some Travellers Cheques! Which one do you fancy'. Not having had a Bank Account before I decided on Barclays and was duly escorted there. 'I'd like to open an Account', I said to the manager, into whose presence I had been ushered. 'Splendid', he replied. 'How much do you want to deposit?' 'I had thought about 40 pounds'. I replied. His face dropped a bit. 'Which department are you in?', he enquired'. 'Police', I replied. His face dropped further. 'That won't go far out here', he said. 'I was wondering about an overdraft', I said hesitantly. I thought for a moment that the manager was going to have a fit. With a great effort he recovered himself. 'You've made my day', he said. 'I've never had an account opened with an overdraft before.' However, he was either very kind or very foolish because, after ten minutes of lecturing me on the perils of unwise expenditure and bouncing cheques, he agreed that I could overdraw up to £50. I breathed a sigh of relief and left.

By now it was too late for us to return to the Police Training School before lunch. The four of us went back to the Speke and sampled the delights of the products of the second brewery, that at the township of Jinja, about 50 miles to the east of Kampala and also on Lake Victoria. This one was aptly named the Nile Brewery since Jinja was of course the site of the Rippon Falls, the source of that ancient waterway. The major product of the Nile Brewery was Tusker Beer. This proved to be a similar lager-like beer to that which we had already sampled and, after the exertions of the morning, tasted equally good. Following an extremely good lunch we made our way somewhat unsteadily back to the Police Training School, where we spent the rest of the afternoon watching the recruits at their drill and other activities under the watchful eyes of their instructors.

Back at the hotel I eased myself out of my jacket and slacks and donned, once again, my long shorts. After tea I set out for a further tour of exploration. The well-stocked Asian-owned shops along the main roads, with their broad covered arcades over the pavements were well worth lingering over, but the clutter of beggars squatting or lying on the pavements outside added a somewhat jarring tone. Some of these unfortunate creatures were suffering from the most appalling deformities and, in many cases, were totally unable to move. Their relatives, I learned, were in the habit of dumping them there early in the morning and collecting them in the evening together with any *baksheesh* they might have accumulated during the day.

As dusk began its rapid onset, I noticed the African night-watchmen taking up their positions in the door of each shop. Most of these were ex-*askaris* who had served in the Kings African Rifles during the war. Their night-watchman's uniform if such it could be called, invariably consisted of the ancient, smelly, army greatcoat which they had been permitted to retain on discharge, a shapeless black felt hat and a stick. The only additional item they carried was the cheap blanket in which they wrapped themselves, as they lay in the doorway of their employers shop, where they would hopefully lapse into uninterrupted sleep for the next twelve hours.

'How would you fancy coming for a swim in the Kabaka's Lake this afternoon?' said Tony Frisby. It was Saturday and I had met Tony and his attractive wife Pat in the lounge of the Speke. Tony was something of an old hand in the Colonial Police, having served for a short time in Singapore before transferring to Uganda in 1950. He had married a nurse and they had a baby son a couple of months old. They didn't live in Kampala but at Bombo, about twenty miles outside, where the Police Service Unit was located. This, I found, was an armoured unit kept in readiness to go anywhere, anytime, if trouble flared up. I must say that I had taken an instant liking to these two youngsters, though, clad in my long shorts, my face and knees still pale after the English winter, I felt somewhat overshadowed. Tony was a burly, good-looking lad in his early twenties, and a very good rugby player, where he could use his weight to advantage. He was a little shorter than me but considerably heavier. His wife, Pat, was a stunningly pretty, dark-haired girl. They were clearly very much in love. Johnny Walker, Jock MacGillivray and I decided that there were few things that we would prefer to a swimming party in company with Pat. Clearly, the alacrity with which we accepted the invitation, combined with our admiring glances, caused Tony to have momentary second thoughts about his invitation. However, we all piled into his car and set off for the lake which was about two miles distant. The Kabaka's Lake covered an area of about 30 acres. It had been constructed many years earlier when a wall had been built across a shallow valley by the then Kabaka's subjects. It was fed by water from a nearby swamp. It was said that human sacrifices had been made to crocodiles living in the lake at that time, but these had all been killed off years ago. It was now a popular resort for Europeans and Africans alike. 'Let's have a run round the lake', said Jock. So quickly slipping into our bathing trunks we set off, leaving Pat and Tony to get changed. All went well until we reached the top end of the lake where the outflow from the swamp commenced. Here a mass of floating vegetation formed a crust over the water. A few tentative steps on this proved that it would bear our weight, one at a time, providing we kept moving all the time. Any hesitation would result in our sinking through the crust and into the unknown depths below. I set off, the others following at intervals of a few yards. A hundred yards out from the bank and my gaze was riveted on a fast-moving shape a few yards ahead. What I had at first thought to be a log turned itself suddenly into a crocodile. Not a big one to be sure. Maybe six- or seven-feet in length, but big enough to do considerable damage, given the opportunity. However, it clearly didn't relish our company any more than we did its'. It slid off into the water and vanished, to appear a few seconds later about twenty yards away, where it regarded us malevolently. Meanwhile, our enforced stop had had a disastrous effect. We were up to our armpits, the crust having refused to support our weight any longer. There was no way we could climb back out again as each effort at extrication resulted in further areas of the crust giving way and sinking under us. After a minute or two we took to the water and set off in the direction the croc had taken, reassuring ourselves that it was less likely to take a crafty bite if it thought we were pursuing it. It rapidly vanished from sight and we swam the intervening stretch of water to where Tony and Pat awaited us. Our account of the crocodile was greeted with some scepticism since it was well-known that none had been seen in the lake within living memory. We were, however, vindicated a few weeks later when, as a result of our encounter the croc was sought out and shot. Meanwhile, as we lay sunning ourselves on the banks of the lake, Pat and Tony frolicked in the water. Our afternoon was made even more delightful when Pat emerged from the water. Her white silk costume, so attractive when she went into the water, had become completely transparent. Yes, Tony was certainly a lucky chap!

Monday found John and myself again walking to the Police Training School. At this time of day the two-mile walk was very pleasant. A scattering of cotton wool clouds drifted across the brilliant blue sky. The Baganda women on their way to the market passed us like oversized butterflies, clad in their highly coloured *basutis*, voluminous ankle-length national dress, gathered in a series of folds, giving the appearance of enormous thighs and backsides, which were apparently sought-after features. On their heads they carried great bunches of *matoke* or baskets containing groundnuts, pineapples, mangos, avocado pears or oranges. Their friendly, beaming smiles as they passed, and the low pitched voices wishing us 'good morning' or *jambo bwana* or *bulungi sibu* made me feel most strongly that this was the country where I would love to spend many years.

This was to be our big day. Our uniforms should be ready for collection from Mr Mehta. After making our initial appearances therefore, we set off back to Kampala. Mr Metha greeted us, flashing his mouth full of gold fillings, and ushered us into the back of his shop. What a fine job he had done for us. The Khaki Drill which we had supplied had been laundered to pre-shrink it and the garments he had made were well-fitting and extremely comfortable. Even more satisfactory was the fact that he didn't insist on immediate payment. 'I will send you a bill in due course', he promised. 'Splendid', I thought, 'if I can go on living on credit like this all might yet not be lost'. Back at the Speke I enquired of the manager, where I could get my uniforms laundered and starched. 'Oh', he said, 'leave it with me. I'll get it done in time for tomorrow. He was as good as his word. On going along to my room an hour later I saw my uniform, together with those of John and Jock, lying out on the grass between our corridor and the staff quarters, having already been laundered.

Back at the Police Training School we spent a couple of hours of the afternoon with Mr. Abubaka, who tried to teach us the rudiments of Kiswahili. Mr. Abubaka was a small thin-faced individual, an Arab from the coastal region of Kenya. It might have been more helpful had he spoken better English. As it was, I could barely understand whether he was talking in English or Kiswahili. I picked up a few phrases from him but it was soon clear to everyone that I was no linguist and never would be. The following day, in addition to morning tea, our uniforms were produced. The boy responsible for their condition had excelled himself. Starched and polished, the creases razor sharp, the chrome buttons and badges of rank sparkling in the morning sunlight. Somewhat self-consciously we strode along to the dining room for our morning repast. Not a soul took the slightest notice. Oh well. At least we looked like policemen, and after the discomfort of the past few days of slacks, ties and jackets we felt on top of the world.

On our arrival at the P.T.S. we presented ourselves to John Thomson to show off our new finery. 'That's more like it', he said. 'Now you look more like policemen. We'll see what your drill's like later this morning'.

Now we were able to join the other newcomers in the various activities at the P.T.S. In all there were seven Inspectors newly arrived, plus a large Asian, Sub Inspector, Ram Gopal. A locally recruited officer he was the son of a Kampala doctor and appeared to have a distinct advantage in that he spoke fluent Swahili. Those of us with previous police experience had the edge on him however, when it came to the law subjects. Much of the law taught was very similar to what we already knew. The Uganda Penal Code, Criminal Procedure Code and Evidence Ordinance were virtually identical to those used in India, which in turn, had been drafted on the lines of British Law. The local laws however, covered a multitude of subjects of which there were no British equivalents. Their unfamiliarity undoubtedly added interest. After all, who could be bored when learning the intricacies of such subjects as the Witchcraft Ordinance, The Waragi Ordinance or The Game Ordinance. One of our instructors at the P.T.S. was John Docherty. He was a very pleasant ex-Army officer who had, after the war joined the Palestine Police and later still transferred to Uganda. He now held the rank of Assistant Superintendent. In addition to being an efficient police officer, John had the distinction of being a natural linguist. Having passed, in double-quick-time, his examination in the Government Lower Standard Swahili which was the obligatory examination, he immediately went on to pass the intermediate and higher examinations in the same subject, and was now a member of the Examining Board in this subject. I fear that poor Sub Inspector Gopal had a very hard time with him. Not only did he get a regular bollocking for his inability to comprehend the Law subjects, his fluent Swahili was found to be of the 'Kitchen' type used by shopkeepers and housewives. Understandable, but totally lacking in the essential grammar so necessary when it came to the passing of examinations. My sympathy went out to Gopal, since he was clearly going to have a harder time forgetting the habits of a lifetime than we were going to have starting from scratch.

Kampala was reputedly free of malaria so none of us bothered with taking prophylactics during our first week or so. Bill Bruce who had been in the country a couple of weeks longer than we, went down with a very unpleasant attack of it. Thereafter we all took our daily dose of mepacrin which, in the course of time, imparted a yellowish tinge to our complexions. Fortunately by the time this happened we had acquired a healthy tan which helped to disguise it.

During our first few weeks at the Police Training School a great deal of parade ground activity was going on. The Kings' Day Parade was being rehearsed. This was an annual event, always attended by His Excellency The Governor, who took this opportunity to present medals and awards to police officers. The police band played an important part in this. The bandmaster was Teddy Bear, a jovial, red-faced individual who ranked as an Assistant Superintendent. In common with all bandmasters he had trained at Neller Hall and had succeeded in producing, from the rawest material, not only an extremely good military band but also a tolerable dance band whose services were in frequent demand. We new arrivals were, fortunately, not expected to take part in the parade. This afforded me considerable relief. Although I had developed a vast parade-ground voice during my service in the R.A.F, drill was a subject which I found difficulty in enthusing over as, from my earliest experience in it, I had found difficulty in differentiating between my left and right feet. Worse still, when faced with a squad of men, I had equal difficulty in identifying theirs. Thus, when attempting clever things like making people go the other way the law of averages ensured that I gave the command on the wrong foot at least 50-per-cent of the time. This would cause most of them to fall over or bump the chap in front, whereupon I would have to shout loudly calling them idiots and other unfriendly terms, knowing all the time that the balls-up was entirely my fault.

The main parade consisted of four Companies, drawn from police recruits under training, plus a number from the nearby police barracks at Nsambya. The parade was, of course, commanded by John Thomson, who loved doing it. Each of the Companies had an European officer in charge, drawn from the Police Training School staff. I must say that the standard achieved was very high indeed, but I hoped that I would never have to take part in any of the subsequent performances.

Among the officers on the staff at the Police Training School was an Inspector, Alan Hussell. A pleasant chap of about the same age as myself, I got to know and like him well during my stay at the P.T.S. Some months later he was appointed A.D.C. to H.E. The Governor, Sir Andrew Cohen. The Cohens had only recently come to Uganda and, having young twin daughters plus two small boys, had brought with them a nanny, Miss Williment. Alan and the nanny were living in close proximity at Government House and the inevitable happened. They decided to get married. The ceremony took place at Entebbe and the Cohens insisted that they spend their honeymoon at the Governors' Lodge at Makindye Hill, near Kampala, with its magnificent views over Lake Victoria. At the end of the honeymoon they returned to Government House to find that Mrs Hussell had been sacked from her position for breaking her contract while Alan was removed from his appointment and, at the end of his tour, his contract with the Colonial Office was terminated. All this however was in the future. When I heard of it though I fervently hoped that I should never receive a similar appointment.

Life at the Police Training School had become a fairly easy routine. We even found ways of avoiding the long walk to and from the hotel by timing our departures to coincide with that of our more senior colleagues who had transport of their own. 'Can any of you chaps drive?' asked John Thomson a couple of weeks after our arrival. I was the only one to respond. My sparse series of lessons in Hastings and my passing of the test on my second attempt were the sum total of my experience. I didn't go into details on this though but simply produced my U.K. Driving Licence. 'Right', said the O.C., 'I've managed to scrounge an elderly patrol car. You can't take it on the road of course, but you can spend a few hours a day teaching the others to drive on the parade ground. Stay round the edge though. I don't want any ruts where the parade is being held'. For the next few weeks Johnny Walker, Jock MacGillivray and the others enjoyed the dubious benefit of my tuition. Oddly enough no one was killed or maimed, and although the car received a few more dents to its battered body and squads of recruits had to run for their lives on more than one occasion, one person at least benefitted. That was me. I was taken for a driving test by the Inspector of Vehicles, Fris Crossen, and astoundingly, passed!

After lunch one Saturday we adjourned as usual to the lounge bar of the Speke for coffee and a beer. A few minutes after our arrival we were approached by a very ancient, portly old chap clad in khaki shirt and shorts, who enquired if he might join us. 'Just arrived?', he asked, and introduced himself. 'Came out here in 1919', he informed us. 'Living out at Masindi now I've retired.' For the next hour or so we were treated to a potted history of his life in Uganda. Elephant and rhino-hunting, croc shooting, lions, snakes and malaria. Very exciting it seemed and we sat enthralled, for all the world like an updated tableau of Milaise's 'Boyhood of Raleigh'. Well worth the few pints of Tusker we bought him.

Inevitably the subject of language arose. I had by this time confirmed that I had absolutely no talent for learning foreign languages. I did not view the prospect of taking the written and oral examinations in Kiswahili with any great enthusiasm. I consoled myself with the thought that it would be nearly two years before it became essential for me to pass these examinations. Meantime I felt I could cope with just about making myself understood.' 'Heard of this chap the other day', said our new-found friend, 'took his oral exam in this very room. Examiner said, 'Tell that waiter to come over here', Fella said *Kuja hapa*. Over came the waiter. 'Good', said the examiner. 'Now make him go over there.' Fella thought for a moment, got up and went to the other side of the room. *'Kuja hapa'*, he said, and over went the waiter. 'The rest of the party rolled about with mirth at this yarn. Not so myself. I was busy tucking away this snippet of information into the recesses of my mind. After all it could come in very useful on the dreaded day if I was faced with the same examiner.

At about this time I was offered alternative accommodation which I thankfully accepted. Not that I hadn't enjoyed living at the Speke. Truth was that I simply couldn't afford it. I was living way above my means and I couldn't see even the most imbecilic Bank Manager extending my overdraft any further. Johnny Walker was also moving out. He had been allocated a flat, by the simple expedient of saying that his wife was pregnant and medical advice was that she should join him. This subterfuge worked well enough, though the expected addition never arrived. I packed my few belongings and moved to 10 Ternan Avenue. This turned out to be a delightful old bungalow in the European quarter of Kampala. its main claim to fame was the enormous jacaranda tree in the garden. It was said to be the largest in Uganda and I could well believe it. Unfortunately, it wasn't in bloom while I was there and it was several years before I got my first viewing of this most beautiful of all tropical trees in its full glory.

I was to share this domain with three other European officers who were already in residence. These were Roy Mackinson who was, from his appearance, totally unsuited to being a policeman. No apparent harm in him though, but I formed the impression that he was unlikely to make the grade. In this at least I was proved correct. The other two were Ron Mead and Derek Barnes. These proved friendly and, having been in Kampala for about a year, were able to give me a lot of useful advice. In common with all junior officers in Kampala they were very hard-up. Derek had been appointed accountant and purchaser of food supplies. Meals were frugal in the extreme and the fare was very different from that to which I had become accustomed at the Speke. Derek bought meat from the Police Training School where it was part of the recruits' diet. P.T.S., in turn, had bought it from the cheapest source available, a Somali butcher who had his business under a tree near the market. It was invariably beef which had died of old age or disease. Under normal circumstances it would have been totally inedible, but when one is hungry and broke it's surprising how strong the teeth and jaw muscles become.

The bungalow had four large bedrooms and a thoughtful Government had provided basic furnishings. Each of us had a solid-looking mvule wood bed and an even more solid mattress and two pillows, a vast wardrobe and matching dressing table and chest of drawers. An easy chair and bedside cupboard completed the furnishings. I certainly couldn't afford curtains but my depleted Bank Account had to be stretched to allow the purchase of a cheap blanket and a pair of sheets. Fortunately the weather was warm enough for these basics to be adequate. The next problem which arose was regarding the cooking, cleaning, washing and ironing. Each of the other three had a houseboy who looked after their employers needs and shared a communal roster for cleaning and tidying the house, preparing the meals, shopping and so on. No one was keen on my paying a part-share for these services so, somewhat unwillingly, I became an employer. I was now introduced to Kesi Rusoke who was to be my guide and mentor for the next three years. He also stole my food, paraffin and whatever else he thought he could get away with over the same period. Never, though, in quantities which would become unacceptable. All this, however, was in the future. Kesi was the brother of Mackinson's houseboy and he turned up on the day following my arrival at No 10. Afterwards I wondered at the alleged relationship, since the two were from different tribes. The African philosophy appeared to be 'All men are brothers'. Who was I to gainsay this?

Kesi was a Mutoro from the Western Province —around Fort Portal. He was about 18-years-old and had a cheery face and ready wit. His knowledge of English was as limited as was mine of Kiswahili. He produced several references from previous European employers, all of whom commented on his honesty, cleanliness and drunkenness. I agreed to employ him at the princely wage of 50-shillings a month for a trial period of two months, to rise then to 60-shillings should he prove satisfactory. Later the same day he came to see me and Ron Mead obligingly translated. 'He wants some soap and starch and matches and charcoal and a charcoal iron. Also some boot polish and an advance of ten-shillings to buy some matoke for himself.' 'Christ',

I said, 'what's all that going to cost?' 'Give him a couple of quid', Ron advised, 'he'll get it a lot cheaper than you will'. I grudgingly parted with two twenty-shilling notes. With luck I would be paid within the next week. I might just last out without exceeding my overdraft.

The next morning I was roused from my slumbers by Kesi with early morning tea. *'Chai bwana'*, he said, *'Ni me lete uniform' yako*. I sat up. My uniform shorts lay on the chair. The jacket hung over the back. It was immaculate. So much starch had been applied that the garments could literally have stood up unaided. Moreover he had somehow managed to impart a mirror finish to them. My shoes sparkled in the morning sunlight streaming through the window. I wondered idly how much of the night Kesi had spent achieving this result. I complimented him on his efforts and wondered how long the standard might be maintained.

The next couple of weeks passed uneventfully. Kesi performed adequately. Complaints were sometimes heard from the others when he turned his hand to cooking but this didn't happen very frequently so the situation was reasonably satisfactory. Bearing in mind the poor ingredients he had to use I suppose he did very well really. He managed to teach me a few useful phrases in Swahili, imparting the most dreadful grammar in the process.

I began to chafe a little at our inactivity at the Police Training School. We were left very largely to our own devices apart from an hour each day, devoted to learning the intricacies of Kiswahili. A break in this routine occurred when we were taken on the rifle range for a day. Firearms were something at which I had excelled during my service with the R.A.F. My eyes had lost none of their sharpness in this respect and I was graded as marksman immediately. Then came the revolver shooting. I had had several sessions on this while on the Air Gunnery Course during the War. The weapon used was the .38 revolver and I achieved all bulls and inners. This aroused considerable comment from John Thomson. Apparently the Uganda Police entered each year for the East and West African Cup, which was an inter-Force revolver competition. Uganda were the current holders of the Cup but new talent was constantly being sought.

The time was now approaching when we should be getting

our postings. Rumour was rife regarding our probable destinations. Some of the earlier arrivals had already departed. Off went Bill Bruce to the Police Service Unit at Bombo. Others went to Mubende, Mbale, Entebbe, Kampala and Jinja. Their place was taken by new arrivals from the U.K. We began regarding ourselves as old hands able to impart our superior knowledge to the new boys. Finally John, Jock and myself were called to the O.C's office. 'Right!' said John Thomson. 'Here's what you've been waiting for. MacGillivray, you're posted to Bombo. Walker, you're off to Headquarters, Traffic. Beaden, you're going to Karamoja, and the best of luck!' The news took me a few seconds to absorb. I just couldn't believe my good fortune. Karamoja! I knew little about the place, but the very sound of its name was like a roll of drums. All I knew was that it was the largest and the most primitive part of Uganda. Adventure! The very stuff that figured so large in all of the boys adventure books I had ever read. My thoughts were interrupted by Teddy Bear. 'Karamoja', he said, 'I wouldn't like that. Noel Caunce is O.C. up there. He was an instructor here before he went on leave. Been up there a couple of months now. Loves everyone, providing their name is Caunce!' I ignored him, determined that no one should spoil my dreams of darkest Africa. What had I done to deserve such a wonderful posting? I found out later that it was due to my having a driving licence.

CHAPTER 7

Over the next few days I found out as much as I could about the District in which I was to serve. Uganda, for administrative purposes was divided into several different Provinces. Karamoja was one of a number of Districts which came under the control of the Provincial Commissioner of the Northern Province, based in Gulu, Acholi District. Currently this was Rennie Beare, whom I had yet to meet. Each District was administered by a District Commissioner who usually had one or more Assistant District Commissioners under him. I already knew that Karamoja was the largest District in Uganda, covering an area of around 12,000 square miles. It also had the sparsest population and was the most primitive. It was classified as a Closed District, which meant that no one could enter it without being in possession of a pass issued by the District Commissioner. This was apparently to protect the unsophisticated tribesmen from the crafty Asian traders. Looking back I feel that this probably didn't work very well, since there were already a considerable number of Asian and Somali traders within the District who were able to take advantage of the tribesmen's ignorance of the outside world without let or hindrance. Its two main tribes were the Karamajong and the Suk. Both were semi-nomadic pastoralists. The former had come south from the Sudan many years earlier, accompanied by their flocks of cattle, sheep, donkeys and goats. At the end of many years travelling they had come upon this delightful area of permanent water, long grass and almost inexhaustible supplies of game animals. On reaching the place the elders had announced *KARAMOJA* which meant, 'The old people can go no further', Thus Karamoja got its name. The members of the two tribes wore little or no clothing and were engaged in an almost continuous state of warfare against one another, and against the more civilised tribes living along their borders. Being such a large District it had many such borders. To the north was the Sudan and to the east, Kenya. Its internal borders were with Acholi, Lango, Teso and Bukedi Districts. Frequent minor incursions across these borders by raiding parties, made the Karamajong and Suk the least popular tribes in Uganda and the resultant thefts of cattle and occasional spear bloodings kept the Police busy. Fortunately these problems rarely resulted in any major conflagration.

Karamoja was also the driest area in Uganda, though, in common with the rest of the country it had the long and short rainy seasons. If one should fail however, conditions of drought and famine could easily result. However, a benevolent government was always at hand in the background to assist. As a result of its isolation the Karamajong were still a backward, though totally unspoiled, tribe having few desires beyond that of being left to get on with the important sport of raiding their neighbours, blooding their spears when the opportunity presented itself, this being the way of proving manhood, and building up a sufficiently large herd of cattle to buy a wife or two. This latter custom was the cause of much of Karamoja's trouble. The bride price was high. Possibly 80- or 100-head of cattle had to be paid by the suitor to the bride's father, and the only way to get these was to raid a neighbouring tribe and steal them. Cattle were wealth and not to be lightly disposed of. Resultantly the grazing areas were grossly overstocked and overgrazed. With the loss of the grass the heavy seasonal rains swept away the topsoil, creating large areas of erosion. In the early part of the 20th century Karamoja was a Garden of Eden. Long grass and permanent rivers with vast herds of elephant and other big game roaming from end to end. Now, every rainy season washed away more of the fertile soil. The rain, instead of penetrating and acting as a reserve, ran off in raging torrents and was gone. The provision by the government of a series of dams to create permanent water, if anything aggravated the situation, since the vast herds which congregated cleared every blade of greenstuff within twenty miles. The benefit of each rainy season lessened as each year went by, but the efforts of the government to persuade the tribesmen to dispose of more than a small fraction of their stock, met with little success. Twenty years earlier, the problem of overstocking would almost certainly have been solved by Nature herself. At that time rinderpest, the cattle plague, struck about once every decade, This would almost certainly reduce the cattle population by at least 75 per cent, reducing them to a point at which the countryside might have had a chance to recover. Now, however, inocculation schemes had been introduced and rinderpest was virtually a thing of the past. Although it may sound a cruel thing to say, Nature usually knows best in these things. The benevolent government had much to answer for.

Kesi received the news of our imminent departure from

Kampala with equanimity. I had fully expected him to resign, rather than go to such a fearsome place, where *matoke* was unobtainable. Instead, he accepted my offer of an extra ten-shillings a month and asked for a further advance to purchase those items which might be in short supply when he got there. The night before our departure he went on a bender of mammoth proportions. One of the other houseboys brought my tea the following morning. *Kesi iko wapi?* ('Where is Kesi?') I enquired, *Huyu mgonjwa sana.* ('He is very ill'.) was the reply. I cursed, thinking that he was down with malaria or something. I dressed and went to his quarters. Kesi sat on his straw mattress holding his head and looking very sorry for himself. His normally chocolate brown complexion had a grey green tinge to it. A girl of about fifteen, stark-naked, sat on the mattress beside him, beaming at me. *Shauri gani?* ('What's the trouble?') said I. *Huyu mlevi sana.* ('He was very drunk') she replied. Kesi groaned and I handed him two Aspirin tablets. 'You can't take her with you'.I said. *Ndio bwana.* ('It is so Sir.') he replied. 'It is only my sister, come to visit me.' I looked at the comely lass and wondered if Kesi knew that incest was against the law. Then I remembered that since all men are brothers, it follows that the female of the species must therefore be their sisters.

A little later a staff car arrived and my few belongings and those of Kesi were bundled in. Kesi appeared to be making a gradual recovery though he was still green around the gills. A few minutes later, all farewells having been said, we were away to our new life. Our route took us first to the township of Jinja, situated on the north east side of Lake Victoria. The road was of the usual murram soil construction, deeply corrugated at intervals of about two feet. I had found that this peculiarity was due to the circular motion of the air caused by the passing of high speed vehicles. Progress over such roads was very uncomfortable at low speeds, when one's teeth were shaken loose by the bumps. However, if a speed of about 50-miles-an-hour was maintained, the car leapt from crest to crest of the corrugations and a comparatively smooth ride resulted. For this reason, all motorists and lorry drivers drove like bats out of hell, leaving a red cloud of dust a quarter of a mile long in their wake. Overtaking other vehicles in these conditions was, to say the least, hazardous, and resulted in a high rate of fatal accidents.

The road to Jinja took us through the Mabira Forest, a remnant of the vast rain forests which used to cover a large part of Africa. The depredation of these forests over the years had brought about a complete climatic change. When the forest covered thousands of square miles of the continent, the condensation of moisture from the foliage brought about conditions so humid that rain fell almost continuously. The gradual advance of the desert is the direct result of de-aforestation. At one stage our road followed the line of a deep gully cut through the red soil of the forest floor. I was startled to see a family of vervet monkeys suddenly race down the slope into our path. They were too close for any evasive action by our driver and one unfortunate individual, being chased by the others, was struck by the front of the car and was thrown under the wheels. We stopped and I got out and returned to the small body lying in the road. It was quite dead so all I could do was to lift it to the edge. Of its companions, I saw nothing.

We reached the road and rail bridge which crossed the Nile, and stopped. A short distance up-stream were the Rippon Falls, discovered by John Hanning Speke in July 1862, the source of the Nile which had been sought for well over two thousand years. Speke had named the falls after Lord Rippon who was President of the Royal Geographical Society when his expedition had been formed. I gazed in awe at the rushing torrent and wondered how long it would take for the water I was looking at to make its 4,000-mile journey north to the Mediterranean. A dozen or so natives with crude fishing rods stood on the rocks and islets which formed the falls, casting into the turbulence and, surprisingly frequently, pulling out a silvery fish. I walked down the track to the waters edge to get a closer look. The fish being caught were all of the barble family and weighed anything up to five pounds. The hooks were baited with bits of water weed or, in some cases, lumps of posho-maize meal cooked into a thick breadlike porridge. On another occasion I bought one of these fish and, on tasting it, found that it resembled cotton-wool stuffed with darning needles. On this, my first sight of their activity, I envied the fishermen the success they were getting with their primitive gear. We continued our car journey, and by lunch-time had arrived at Tororo, not far from the border with Kenya. The town was dominated by a large volcanic outcrop, springing up from what was otherwise a fairly uninteresting landscape.

Industry was beginning to cast its shadow over the landscape and a large cement works was already under construction, its chimney at odds with the surrounding countryside. Our driver pulled up outside the Tororo Hotel where I partook of a frugal lunch.

North from Tororo could be seen the vast bulk of Mount Elgon, rising out of the plains. This was a large, extinct volcano over 14,000 feet in height. Mbale, the next town on our route, lay on its western flank. Not a lot seemed to go on in Mbale but it was, nevertheless, the provincial centre of the Eastern Province. We drove through the township without stopping and pressed on towards Soroti, 80 miles to the north. An hour later we arrived at the Awoja Ferry. This crossed a narrow arm of Lake Salisbury, about 300-yards wide. Blue lotus blossoms grew in profusion from the water. Dragonflies and brightly coloured birds were everywhere. One irridescent jewel which I found to be the malachite kingfisher enthralled me with his darting flight, hovering and suddenly diving into the water, almost invariably to emerge with a tiny fish in his beak. The water was crystal clear and shoals of tilapia could be seen cruising in the shallows while mudfish scavenged on the bottom. The local children stood on the banks trying their luck with crude rods and lines but seemed to be less successful than the kingfisher.

The ferry, when it arrived from the opposite bank, proved to be constructed from oil drums and planks. There was just room on board for two cars or one lorry. A couple of lusty natives poled us across to the far bank and we were away again towards Soroti, where we were to spend the night. Half-an-hour later we drew up outside the police station, a sprawling, low, brick building with a red-tiled roof. It was of simple construction where offices, cells, stores and a garage surrounded a central courtyard. I made my way in to meet Dick Hook, the O.C. Police of Teso District. He was a thickset dark-haired individual who I judged to be in his late thirties. Like many others in the police, he had served in Palestine before transferring to Uganda. He had a bluff, friendly manner and shook me warmly by the hand. 'There's no room at the Rest House', he said, 'so I've arranged for you to spend the night at my house. Give me a few minutes to clear up and we'll push off.'

Dick's house proved to be a modern and extremely

comfortable bungalow with a semi-circular patio in front, on which were set tables and easy chairs. He introduced me to his wife, Katie, a homely, friendly woman who had been a nurse prior to getting married. Twin baby girls completed the family. As we enjoyed tea and cakes on the patio, Dick looked the picture of domestic bliss. A splendid meal and several bottles of beer rounded off the day. 'See you at the border conference next month', were Dick's parting words as I left the following morning.

The final leg of the journey was well under way when I first caught sight of Napak Mountain. An extinct volcano, it had been riven in two by some past cataclysm. It formed the boundary between Karamoja and Teso Districts. Our road ran though the cleft a few miles wide between the two halves of the mountain range. As we passed the border an enormous volcanic plug, looking as old as time itself, appeared from the plain on our left. Akisim Rock rose like a champagne cork, 1,200-feet of sheer unclimbable rock. We had now arrived at the police post, sited to prevent unwanted visitors from entering Karamoja. The post comprised three or four mud huts set in a clean swept earth compound. A few chickens scratched around the huts and a hen with a family of chicks shepherded them to cover as a hawk flew overhead.

The staff car pulled off the road beside the police post. I got out to stretch my legs, followed by Kesi and the driver. A sleepy face appeared at the door of one of the huts and immediately disappeared. Ten seconds later the same face appeared, this time crowned by a police fez, and a body struggling to get into a jacket bearing corporal's tapes on the sleeve. 'Out, out. Fall in *pesi pesi*', roared the corporal and strode over to me, halting with such force that his feet must have smarted within the unlaced boots that he wore. '*Jambo effendi*', said he, beaming so broadly that the top of his head nearly fell off. '*Jambo* corporal', I replied and decided on the spur of the moment that, since he clearly intended turning out his staff, I had better do him the courtesy of having a look at them. 'Fall in your men. I'll have a look at them in five minutes.' '*Ndio effendi*', he roared, saluting with the precision of a guardsman, and sped away to the huts, where he chivvied the others with such good effect that three minutes later they had fallen in, all three of them, rigidly at attention. 'Parade *tayari effendi*', he roared at me, giving the butt salute on the .303

rifle he carried. I accompanied him to the three constables. No one could have said they were immaculate, but I wondered how many men in a British Army camp could have done better at three minutes notice. I inspected them and then, to my astonishment, the corporal gave the order, 'For inspection, port arms'. The rifle bolts were drawn back and forth thrice with precision, one pace forward and a shiny thumb nail inserted into the breech. I peered down each rifle barrel and found them spotless. A display of rifle drill and marching followed which, I am sure, would have continued for half-an-hour, had I not insisted that I had seen enough. To say that I was impressed would have been an understatement. Corporal Okeng certainly had his unit under control. I made a mental note to recommend him for a promotion course at some convenient time and expressed my satisfaction with his performance in the station diary which he produced for my inspection. The only problem with this book was that it was all written in Swahili and in appalling writing. I didn't understand a word of it. One of the constables spoke reasonable English and through him I discovered that the other three constables stationed there were out on patrol to the quarantine a mile or so away, where cattle were kept to fatten them up and to ensure that they were not carrying disease, before walking them down to the railhead at Soroti, en route to the markets at Kampala and Jinja. No other problems were reported except that a leopard had taken a dog belonging to Corporal Okeng the previous evening. 'It does not matter Sir, it was an old dog', said the constable. I wondered how the corporal viewed the matter. I also decided that I would keep my tent flap securely closed should I have the occasion to spend a night there. We returned to the car. Corporal Okeng insisted that his men fall in again and, as I was driven away he was roaring, 'General salute, present arms'. I waved through the open window and knew exactly how the King must feel.

Fifty miles away across the plain, through the heat haze, I could dimly see the outline of a great mountain. I knew that this had to be Mount Moroto. A similar distance to my right was another mountain of equal proportions. My map told me that this was Kadam or Debassian Mountain. I believe the two alternative names were those given by the Suk and the Karamajong tribes. It was always referred to as Kadam by Government officers. Both names sounded equally impressive and certainly this range deserved a name in keeping with its grandeur.

The road we now travelled was in a much poorer state than that on the Teso side of the border. we bounced from pothole to pothole. the road ran through scrub and thorn bush. It was dry and arid, and little grass remained. Large areas were completely devoid of vegetation, but across these bare patches, flocks of guinea fowl and partridge scampered and small groups of Grants Gazelle were occasionally seen. A couple of miles on we came to a small group of huts about 50-yards from the road. I told the driver to stop, and got out of the car. A palisade of thorn branches about six-feet in height surrounded the huts. These were about eight in number and very small. Constructed of mud and sticks with crude thatched roofs they were clearly intended to be of only a temporary nature. Away through the thorn scrub, which made up most of the surrounding vegetation, the clunking of bells told of the presence of a herd of cattle, but they were too far off to be seen. An elderly African sat on a tiny wooden stool outside the entrance to the thorn boma. He was naked except for a dirty black cloth slung over one shoulder. His ten-inch penis dragged limply in the dust as he sat. He stood up as I approached and I saw that his left eye was opaque. He peered at me through the other one. Flies crawled over his face but he made no attempt to brush them off. His skinny, wrinkled belly was encrusted with dust, while his matted hair fell almost to his shoulders. In contrast to this pathetic figure another individual now emerged from within the compound. He was a real dandy. In his early twenties he stood only an inch or two below my own six-foot-two-inches. His well-muscled body shone with health. He was as naked as his companion and as well hung. His lower lip was pierced and a plug of polished metal was inserted in the hole. His outstanding feature was however, his headdress. This appeared to be a cap made of his own hair, dressed with various coloured clays and adorned with ostrich and other feathers. He was followed by two young women of about 20-years-of-age. One was heavily pregnant, the other clasping a child to her breast. Both wore knee-length leather skirts, split to the waist and decorated with beads and cowry shells. Around their necks were large numbers of iron and brass rings. Their wrists were similarly adorned. Their lower lips had similarly been pierced and their broad grins showed that their front teeth had been removed. One thing I noted they all had in common, none of them attempted to brush away the flies that crawled all over their faces. All of them appeared well disposed towards me and the younger man greeted me in Swahili. This appeared to be as far as our conversation was going to go however. The old man held out an upturned palm to me and pointed to his mouth with his other hand. I had no food with me however so I returned to the car. 'Bwana', said the driver, 'these people are *shenzi*. (uncivilised) You should not go to them. ' 'I'm sure I shall learn to love them', I replied. Some miles further on the car arrived at a major river. This was the Mani-mani. It was completely dry, and the bed, strewn with boulders and tree trunks bore witness to the power of the torrent during the rains. A concrete ramp about ten feet wide carried traffic across this obstacle. I estimated from marks on the banks that, at times, the river must run up to ten feet deep and 30-yards wide. We drove down the sloping bank. I saw that the downstream side of the concrete had been undercut by the flood water to a depth of about three or four feet. Negotiating this track with any depth of water flowing across it would be a bit fraught I decided. A few hundred yards from the river was the village of Kangole, a small settlement which, I found, had grown up round the county headquarters of Bokora County, through which we were passing. This consisted of a scatter of semi-permanent mud huts with rusty, corrugated iron roofs, and including a shabby shop run by a Somali, who sold beads, maize meal, cheap plastic trinkets and jaggery, an unrefined sugar formed into lumps each weighing about three pounds. Centrally situated within the village was a large imposing compound enclosing a series of large round mud huts where the County Chief, Yakobo Lowok, resided. He was away I found, so I didn't make his acquaintance on this occasion. I didn't find the settlement very attractive however so we pressed on towards Moroto, a further twenty miles distant. The mountain was now taking up a large segment of the horizon and, as we got nearer, I could see that there were a number of different peaks, each with its folds of ridges and valleys, reaching out like so many fingers onto the flat plain. The lower slopes were covered with scrub and trees. Although at this distance I could not make out any individual buildings, the occasional glint of the sun reflected on windows showed that I was again approaching civilisation. A quarter-of-an-hour later and a few mud huts with corrugated iron roofs indicated that we had reached the outskirts of my new home-town. On our left we came to a garage, with the legend Pandit Puran Chand emblazoned outside. Adjoining it were half a dozen Asian *dukas* (shops) set in a crescent. The road bypassed these and continued on with an open area of grassland scattered with acacia trees on the left. We passed a post office, also on our left. Immediately opposite were the police lines with their straight rows of grass thatched mud huts. Next came the parade ground and finally the car turned to its right and pulled up outside the police station. This had been designed by someone who had mastered only the basic elements of architecture. It consisted of a long single-storey block with a verandah about eight feet wide running along the entire frontage. The first room was the office of the O.C. Police, shared by the Second in Command, the post I had come to fill. Next in line was the clerks office housing two clerks, Mr Otwao and Mr Sentamu. Then came the charge-office followed by three cells. The armoury came next and finally the store in which exhibits, found property, records, paraffin and camping equipment were housed.

Lying on the verandah outside the O.C's office was the biggest bull terrier I have ever seen. His shiny jet-black coat covered layers of rippling muscle and his good-tempered piggy face was laced with dozens of white scars. He rose to his feet and advanced to the edge of the verandah wagging his tail and grinning a friendly welcome. I wondered who owned this monster. As I got out of the staff car a khaki clad figure appeared at the door of the office. 'Greetings', said a precise, friendly voice. 'Inspector Beaden, I presume. I'm Noel Caunce.' 'Morning, Sir', I replied, saluting. I mounted the steps to the verandah. Noel shook me warmly by the hand. I ran my eye over him. He was probably about five years older than me and was of medium height with a plumpish face and an air of efficiency about him. I thought he looked a bit bookish to be in charge of a wild District like Karamoja. 'Had a good trip?', he enquired. We chatted for a while and were interrupted by the arrival of a second khaki-clad figure who emerged from the office. Noel introduced him. Ian Fergusson was a dapper young man of about 23-years-of-age and standing about five-feet-eight-inches. 'My dear chap', he said shaking me warmly by the hand, 'I'm delighted to meet you. Now

I can start my packing'. Noel glanced at his watch. 'Time for lunch', he said. 'By the way, I've not booked you into the Rest House. I thought you'd be more comfortable at my place for a few days. Just till we sort out some housing for you. I'll give you a lift. The Staff Car can follow on'. We left the office and headed off towards the mountain. The European houses were set out delightfully on each side of the earth track. Bungalows, some new, some very mature were set out in plots, each of about half-an-acre and about 100-yards apart. The whole area was scattered with mature trees, acacia thorns with flat tops like umbrellas and euphorbia candelabra looking like green, spiky multiple candle sticks. At the top end of the European quarter where the mountain reached out its fingerlike ridges, a flat space had been cleared of the scrub and thorn bush. Here a bungalow had been built within a few yards of the excavated bank where the bush commenced.

It was of an attractive appearance with white plastered walls and a red-tiled roof. At one end was a concrete drum about eight-feet tall and of similar diameter. The roof guttering led into the top of this so storing water during the rains. A small central patio with a glazed door led to a cool lounge with a red polished concrete floor.

Kesi and the driver now alighted from the staff car which had followed us. My two suitcases and one cardboard box were unpacked and taken into the house. 'My boys will sort out a place for him to sleep', said Noel. 'I expect the driver will want to get away as soon as possible'. He was right in this assumption. The driver, a Muganda, implied that there was nothing he would like less than having to spend a night in this land of naked people and wild animals. He didn't even bother to stay for a meal. I was taken to the spare bedroom at the east end of the bungalow. One window looked out onto the rock wall of the mountain, the other across the valley to another mountain spur pointing out onto the plain. A couple of vultures circled lazily above the valley and the sun beat down onto the sea of acacia thorn. 'Care for a beer before lunch?', called Noel. I joined him in the lounge. The beer was cool and refreshing. Through the lounge window we looked out over most of the European quarter. 'That first bungalow is Tom Hinett's', said Noel. 'He's Public Works Department. His wife Vi is the only white woman in Karamoja apart from Doris Clarke the wife of Bob Clarke the C.M.S. Missionary out at Lotome. They've got four children, but the three girls are away at school in Kenya. Next bungalow down is unoccupied. That's where you will probably be housed. It's a condemned Asian cottage but the P.W.D. are working on it to make it habitable. the next one down belongs to Dick Baker, the A.D.C. Ian Fergusson shares with him at present but he's decided he doesn't want to share any longer — hence the housing problem. On the other side of the road lives Arthur Brown the Agricultural Officer. Next to him is Sandy Taylor, the Vet, and the bungalow you can just see through the trees is occupied by Sandy Field the D.C. Dick Heron lives a bit further on, but you can't see his house. He's the boreholes officer. There's a building programme going on and the doctor's house is nearly finished. We have a African doctor at present but he lives down near the hospital.'

Lunch arrived, interrupting this potted geography of the European quarter. It consisted of a roast bird about the size of a chicken, roast potatoes, fresh peas and cauliflower. 'I see that you've got a supply of fresh veg then', I said. 'Not here', said Noel, 'We get a twice-weekly bus up from Soroti. It brings the mail and we all get our veg, bread, butter, bacon and so on from De Souza's store down there. You've got to decide well in advance what you're getting short of so that you can send a list with the bus driver. You'll get used to it.' I could foresee some difficulties already. With no fridge the supplies of fresh food wouldn't last very long. 'What's the bird?', I enquired. 'Oh that's guinea fowl', replied Noel. 'Place is thick with them. Take a .22 rifle out of the armoury any time you want. Just wander up the mountain and help yourself.'

The meal ended and we had another beer in the lounge 'Well', said Noel, 'I'm going to push off back to the office. I'll leave you to unpack and I'll see you in a couple of hours. By the way, the D.C. is having a sundowner this evening, so you're invited along to meet everyone'. I watched as he left. He had a large maroon-coloured Chevrolet estate car which rode effortlessly over the rough roads. I unpacked my meagre belongings and settled to my daily task of writing letters to Joan, weekly to my parents. I already had plenty to tell them of my new life. At about 4.p.m. Noel returned. 'Let's have a quick cup of tea', he said, 'then we can go for a swim'. We got into his car and set off along a track leading further up the mountain. After about half-a-mile we stopped in a grassy clearing under the acacias. We walked for a couple of hundred yards along the bank of a small stream. A concrete wall had been built across the gully and a pool, some 30-feet long and 15-feet wide was formed behind it. The water was discoloured but not stagnant. Two great mahogany trees and a fig tree overhung the pool and the water looked cool and inviting. 'No need for costumes here', said Noel, and stripping off we dived in. The water was about eight-feet deep and delightfully refreshing. 'The locals aren't allowed to water their cattle above this point so it's reasonably clean. Mind you, they try it on occasionally and then we have to deal with them.' He didn't specify the punishment meted out. We lay on the grass at the side of the pool and the warm sun rapidly dried us out. As I lay there I caught a glimpse of movement in the undergrowth. I raised my head and saw, about three feet of the tail-end of a large brown snake sliding away into the scrub. 'Christ!', I said, 'there's a bloody great snake over there.' 'Probably a puff adder', replied New Yellie. 'There's a lot of them about. Saw one at the front of my house yesterday.' I found later that Noel's knowledge of snake identification was nil. According to him, all snakes were puff adders. I got dressed and decided that at an early opportunity I would cut a stout stick and carry it with me at all times.

The sun was sinking rapidly and darkness approached as we arrived back at the house. Twilight didn't exist here. At 5.55 p.m. it was daylight. At 6.05 p.m. it was dark. The mountain hanging over us accelerated the process of nightfall. '*Bafu tayari bwana*', said Kesi. 'Don't be too long', said Noel, 'we've got to be at Sandy Field's in 20-minutes'. I bathed and donned a shirt and slacks.

Sandy Field, the District Commissioner, lived in an old, typically Colonial style bungalow. It was enclosed by a verandah some 12-feet wide on each side. It was raised about six feet off the surrounding ground on a concrete base. Its corrugated iron roof was painted green and its cool interior was lit by half-a-dozen paraffin pressure lamps. Mosquito gauze was fixed over the diamond-shaped expanding metal panels at the sides of the verandah, and the usual geckos ran up and down the walls capturing any stray insects which managed to find their way in, attracted by the lamplight. Outside in the garden, with its

124

frangipani and bougainvillea the cicadas fiddled away merrily. Sandy Field looked for all the world like a gnome. In his early thirties and about five-feet-three-inches tall he was as thin as a lath. His thin, cheerful face sported a large pointed nose and an equally large pair of ears were attached at ridiculous angles on each side of his head. 'H-H-H-Hallo', he stammered in an Oxford accent, 'I'm S-Sandy Field. S-so pleased to meet you. Come in and have a b-beer'. I accepted gratefully. 'Let me introduce you to D-Dick Baker. He's my A.D.C.' Dick Baker was a large, dark-haired, fleshy young man with a ready grin. Until a few months earlier, I discovered, he had been A.D.C. to the previous Governor of Uganda, Sir Hathorn Hall, at Entebbe. That was until he crashed the Governor's car. Then he left Entebbe at a great rate of knots and was posted to Karamoja as a punishment. He didn't seem perturbed about it though, and seemed to have accepted the fact that his career in the Colonial Service was unlikely to be long or distinguished. Certainly, when I saw him driving his Citroen sports car around the township, I gathered that the lesson which he should have learned from his earlier crash had not been fully absorbed.

Ian Fergusson arrived, accompanied by Barney, the bull terrier, whom I had met earlier at the police station. Ian greeted me and helped himself to a beer. Barney lay beside him on the carpet and slept, with one eye open. Ferguson had been in Karamoja for about 15 months and his one regret seemed to be that he had had three wet seasons and only two dry ones. 'Still', he said, 'I'll be able to dine out on my experiences for many years to come'. I could quite believe him. 'When are you leaving Uganda?', I enquired, knowing that this was to be his first and last tour in the Country as his services were being dispensed with. 'In about three weeks time', he replied. 'I've got a bit of a problem', he confided. 'I can't take Barney with me. I suppose you wouldn't like to take him over would you? He's a good chap —look after you and all that.' I didn't need to be asked twice. 'Of course I'll take him', I said, 'I was just going to ask where you got him so that I could try to get one like him!' 'Well, he's all yours then', said Ian. 'Not yet though, I'll hang on to him till I'm ready to leave'. Thus I came to be owned by a four-legged friend who would play a major part in my life for the next few years.

The next arrival was Sandy Taylor. He was not much bigger in build than Sandy Field and was about 35-years-of-age. He had a broad Scots accent and was very full of himself. He spoke authoritatively about rinderpest and anthrax and of the problems of getting the Suk and Karamajong to have their cattle inoculated and of grazing and water and worm infestations. Most of all he spoke of Sandy Taylor, and what a brilliantly good chap he was. I felt however that he would be good company if kept in check.

Dick Heron was on safari and Tom and Vi Hinett had gone to Kitale to collect their daughters from school for the holidays, so the final arrival was Arthur Brown the Agricultural Officer. He turned out to be a likeable, thickset lad of about 24. Not long out of university and obviously knowledgeable in his field. His main problem was to persuade the local tribesmen to settle down, be less nomadic and farm the land. He spent his time demonstrating ploughing with teams of oxen and trying to work out irrigation schemes. He had quite a large staff of African assistants scattered throughout the District, helping with these laudable schemes. His success was, I gathered, somewhat limited.

The evening progressed and the effect of the beer began to manifest itself. Voices became slurred and conversations incomprehensible. Every so often one or two of the party would make their way on to the front lawn, 'To see Africa', as they would genteelly remark before relieving their bladders. No one went to the toilet as this only consisted of a bucket, which would quickly have overflowed. Toasties of various sorts were produced in profusion by Stephen, Sandy's cook, and the party eventually broke up at about midnight. Noel drove home, somewhat erratically, to be greeted, somewhat glumly I thought, by Noel's cook and Kesi who were awaiting our arrival with a large meal. '*Sitaki chakula*', '(I don't want any food') said Noel. 'I don't suppose you're hungry either are you?', he enquired as an afterthought. 'No thanks. Couldn't manage another thing', I murmured. I said goodnight and tumbled into bed. I slept immediately. After what seemed like five minutes but was probably a couple of hours I was suddenly awakened by the most diabolical noise I had ever heard. 'Oooo ip, Oooo ip', came roaring through the open window within about two feet of my ear. I leaped out of bed and peered through the mosquito gauze. The full moon overhead made the outside almost as bright as day. Two large shapes, hump shouldered and sloping backed, with vast pot bellies looked up at me. Mouths opened in hideous grins and rounded ears cocked in my direction. 'Oooo ip, Oooo ip', said one of them in a loud voice. 'Piss off', I shouted and the two hyenas loped off up the slope, gurgling and chuckling as they went. Noel, as far as I could make out, hadn't stirred. I heard his snores continue uninterrupted from the next room. I climbed back into bed and after about an hour dropped off again.

'Did you hear those bloody hyenas', I enquired at breakfast the following morning. 'No, I can't say I did', said Noel. 'I know they come round here most nights but I guess I'm probably used to them by now. There's a price on them if ever you shoot any, Five-shillings for each tail. Nasty blighters. Liable to eat you if you sleep outside'. I decided that I would earn myself a lot of money and do everyone a favour by reducing the hyena population when I got settled.

I accompanied Noel to the office. 'Fergusson is off on pay safari tomorrow, so you can go with him. Help you get an idea of the District. Anyway, this morning we've got a pay parade here so you'll be able to give a hand.' Ian Fergusson arrived, quite chirpy considering the amount of beer he had consumed the previous evening. He was, of course, accompanied by Barney. Since he was to be my new owner I took more interest in him than I had the previous day. After greeting Noel and myself he took up his usual position on the verandah where he could watch out for any trouble that might arise. One of the local shenzi dogs came into view. He had evidently already made Barney's acquaintance since he walked with a pronounced limp. A deep rumbling growl from Barney was sufficient. The interloper fled. Barney relaxed.

A constable arrived with the Station Diary which Noel scanned to satisfy himself that nothing required urgent attention. A second constable brought a sheaf of radio messages. Again, nothing serious. I found that at the back of the police station was a radio office which was manned for 12-hours each day. Messages were sent in Morse Code and a network of transmitters and receivers linked Moroto with the more distant police outposts as well as with other units. I made my way to the radio office. The radio constable was receiving a message. I glanced over his shoulder as he decoded it. Nothing earth shattering. 'P.C. Obonya requests that an extra Shs 5/- be paid to his wife Teresa on pay parade.' I glanced through the file of message copies. there was certainly going to be enough to keep me interested.

Over the past couple of months there were messages about cattle raids, murders, woundings, cattle trespass in closed areas, marauding wild animals, poaching and a mass of domestic matters. I didn't see anything about thefts or burglaries however.

On my return to the office I found that a group of women and children had started to collect and were squatting on the grass at the edge of the parade ground. 'Who are all these?', I enquired. 'Oh they're wives of the chaps on outpost duty', Noel informed me. 'Their husbands do six months at a time out there. Most of the outposts are unsuitable for wives and kids to accompany them so they either send them home to their parents or keep them here. They have to allocate a certain amount of their monthly salary and we take them the rest when we go out on pay safari.'

The pay parade started. It was rather more complicated than I had expected. First the police personnel formed up outside. Head Constable Musoke reported. 'Pay parade *tayari* Sir', said he, saluting smartly. 'Two-hundred-and-eighty-two-shillings- and 24-cents', said Mr Sentamu, the African clerk. Noel counted out the cash from piles of notes and coins in front of him. The Head Constable collected his money, stepped back and saluted and then went over to the camp table which had been placed in one corner. Here sat Ishverbhai Patel the proprietor of one of the local *dukas*. He was the approved supplier of what might be termed canteen supplies. For a small percentage of his income he was permitted to extend monthly credit to the police personnel, up to about half of their monthly salary. The paying officer in turn had to make sure that the debts were fully cleared each pay day. The only exception to this was for the purchase of bicycles, where the debt could be spread over a period of six months. At the door of the office stood a corporal, whose task it was to sell copies of the police magazine, *Habari*. This was a monthly publication produced by the O.C. of the Police Training School in Kampala. It was printed half in English and half in Swahili, and contained articles, stories, news of Courts in various parts of the country and District Notes. It was heavily subsidised but not terribly popular amongst the junior ranks.

About 40 constables and N.C.Os paraded for their pay. The Head Constable marched each one in and then supervised the payments to Mr Patel. There were few arguments. One or two wanted to carry over part of their debt till the next month. Noel was quite adamant about this. 'Pay up', he said. Now came the turn of the wives. All were dressed in their Sunday best. A few wore the voluminous *basuti* favoured by the Baganda, but most wore simple cotton dresses. Most of them had several small children with them and, as they squatted on the edge of the verandah awaiting their turn, some breast-fed their infants to keep them quiet. A separate pay sheet had been prepared for the wives. A few could sign their names but most of them dabbed their right thumb onto an ink pad and pressed it on to the pay sheet where Head Constable indicated. As each approached the O.Cs' desk she would sink to her knees, murmuring unintelligible greetings. Some had applied cheap scent for the occasion but most relied on their natural B.O.

Finally, it was the turn of the porters. These were a fairly transient lot. Very few Karamajong took employment for any longer than it took to earn the cash to pay their Poll Tax of 30-shillings. Almost invariably once this sum had been accumulated they would return to their nomadic existence. About 15 were employed by the police in Moroto. Their work included cutting the grass on the parade ground and in the police lines, building, repairing and thatching of huts and any odd jobs that the officers or N.C.Os could think up for them to do. Each received about 35-shillings a month which was slightly more than the one-shilling a day paid by the D.C. to the Township porters for grass cutting and road repairing.

Throughout the entire proceedings Barney had maintained an aloof disinterest. He had seen it all before, many times. One or two adventurous toddlers escaped the watchful eyes of their mothers and stroked his sleek coat. He smiled and wagged his tail tolerantly but otherwise took no notice. Screams of alarm from the mothers usually terminated each sortie.

For the hour which followed the pay parade Noel and Ian were hard at work, counting the cash which remained and calculating the amount which still had to be paid out. 'Damn it', said Noel, 'we're 16-cents up'. Another 20-minutes went by. 'Found ten of it', he said, 'Can't put my finger on the other six cents though. 'Oh well', he finally announced, 'it will probably sort itself out at the end of the pay safari. If it doesn't it will just have to go into the goat bag'. I was somewhat mystified at the panic over 16 cents. It was, after all, only about twopence. Also,

what was this goat bag which had been mentioned? Noel
explained. 'It's only six cents now, but it's just the sort of thing
the auditor would pick on. You never know when the bugger's
going to arrive and once they find a small discrepancy they start
turning the place upside down. Then you start getting 'Please
explain' letters for months afterwards. As for the 'goat bag', that's
totally unofficial. Everyone has one but it's never admitted to.
We've got about 53-shillings in ours. It's mostly from paraffin
debis', I still looked mystified so he explained further. 'We indent
on Headquarters Stores for paraffin for the oil lamps in the
charge office and at the outposts and safari and so on. It arrives
in five-gallon tins called *debis*. When they are empty they are in
great demand among the locals for carrying water, brewing
waragi and repairing holes in roofs — so we sell them to the
duka for two-shillings each and that goes into the goat bag.
Sometimes we might be ten or 20-shillings light on a pay safari
if a couple of notes get stuck together. Then the goat bag makes
good. Some bloody fool once included it as an item in the
handing over certificate when he was posted to another Station.
'In the goat bag, 23-shillings-and-73-cents.' There was absolute
hell to pay over it. Questioned all the previous O.Cs for years
earlier to find out where it had come from. The auditors had a
field day. 'Speaking of auditors', he went on, 'There was an old
D.C. up here years ago. Hated auditors and they reciprocated. He
was a law unto himself. One time they found he was 60-cents
short on the petty cash. They wrote lots of nasty letters which, of
course, he ignored. Finally they wrote and complained to the
Provincial Commissioner who wrote to him, 'WHAT HAPPENED
TO THIS MONEY?' He wrote underneath it, 'I STOLE IT'. That
was the end of the correspondence. They had it in for him
though. Another time he went on foot safari. He hired 40 porters
to carry his gear. The auditor sent him a letter enquiring why it
had been necessary to hire this number. He ignored this for a
while but after three or four reminders he wrote back, 'BECAUSE
39 WERE NOT ENOUGH.' On yet another occasion he had to hire
three canoes to cross a lake in the south. When the auditors
wrote to enquire why it had been necessary to hire three canoes
he was ready for them. 'BECAUSE I AM NOT JESUS CHRIST.'
Never got any further than D.C., of course, but what a character.
I wondered if I would ever have enough courage to deal with the

bureaucrats in such a cavalier manner and thought, probably not. Tempting though.

'We've got lines inspection this afternoon', Noel announced after lunch. 'You can come round with me to see how it's done.' At about 2.30 p.m. the Head Constable arrived to report. 'Lines ready for inspection, Sir'. he announced. We accompanied him the 200-yards or so across the parade ground. Many of the huts were unoccupied or were occupied only by the wives and children of the outpost men. We did not include these in our tour. The 40-or-so men who had been on the pay parade were however, stationed at the doors of their huts, smartly dressed and awaiting our arrival. The earth roads between the huts were swept and immaculate. I could find nothing to complain about with the cleanliness of the inside of the huts.

Clearly a lot of effort had gone into the preparation for the inspection and I felt the Head Constable was to be congratulated. While the inspection took place the wives sat outside their huts still dressed in their Sunday best and giggling to one another. I wondered what comments were being made about the new arrival.

At the top end of the lines the porters were rebuilding one of the huts. The old hut had been dismantled and the grass thatching and what remained of the poles lay to one side. I noticed that the poles were partly eaten through, apparently by some insect. Progress on the new hut was rapid and at the end of the inspection I decided to stay on for a while and watch the work. A number of wooden poles had been set into the ground about a foot apart and in a circular shape. Pliable sticks were woven in and out of these and a doorway about two-feet wide was left at one point. Another structure of poles built into a conical shape lay nearby. All the poles had been bound together with strips of bark torn from the poles themselves. As I watched, the porters collected round the conical structure and lifted it bodily. Then, with it held above their heads, they walked across to the wall of poles set in the grass and placed the one upon the other. It fitted like a glove. A little more work with the bark strips and the two structures were bound firmly together. Two of the porters then climbed onto the roof and the thatching commenced. This was not the neatest piece of thatching I had ever seen and did not compare with the job which might have been done by an English thatcher. Still, it was effective in keeping out the rain and since the hut was only intended to last a couple of years before being destroyed by the insects there was not a lot of point in creating anything with a more artistic finish. When I next visited the lines about a week later the walls had been completed by filling them in with mud, a door had been fitted and a smooth layer of cow dung had been plastered over the inner and outer surfaces and the floor. It made a cosy, if somewhat smelly residence and was already occupied by a police constable and his family who appeared more than satisfied.

The pay safari scheduled to start the following day was to be of four-days duration. I thought I had better have a chat with Fergusson to find out what was involved.'Well', he said, 'we hire an open lorry from Puran Chand. He supplies a driver and a turn boy, plus all the petrol we may need. The camping gear is loaded by the store man, who's done it so often that he rarely forgets anything important.

You've no need to take any food this time. I know you're not organised yet so I'll see to all that. You'll need a couple of blankets if you've got them, and make sure you take slacks and a long-sleeved sweater. It can get quite cold in the evenings at times and there are lots of mosquitoes about. I don't suppose you've got any mosquito boots have you?' I confirmed that I had not.'If you get to Kitale or Soroti any time you'll do well to get yourself a pair made. They're only about 60-bob. They'll stop the mosquitoes making a meal of your ankles and they're a bit of protection against snake bite as well'. I decided that I couldn't do better than accept this advice. After tea I called Kesi and told him that he would be accompanying me. He accepted the news philosophically and went off to see Fergusson's boy to find out what he would need.

'I'd better take you to meet some of the *duka* owners', said Noel. You'll have to open a monthly account with one of them anyway. I suggest you go to Ishverbhai Patel. He runs the canteen account for the police staff. Most of us deal with him and he won't rook you too much.'We drove down to the bazaar area. Our first stop was at the garage. A dapper little Asian with a balding head and a beaming smile which displayed half-a-dozen gold teeth, bounded out to meet us. He greeted Noel in good English. Noel introduced me.'This is Madan Tandon', he said.'He runs Pandit Puran Chand's. Supplies all our transport requirements, repairs our cars, runs the bus and robs us at the end of each month.' 'Oh no Sir', said Madan. 'I would not rob you. You are my good friends. Come inside for a beer Sir, or whisky if you prefer it. 'We went into the living quarters at the side of the garage. It was clean, not very tidy but full of the nick-nacks so beloved by the Asians. Madan called out in Hindi and a couple of other Asians came in from the garage area. He introduced me to Mr Tandon senior, Madon's uncle, and Mr Sharma, and they beamingly shook me by the hand murmuring their welcomes. 'Will you have beer or whisky Sir?', enquired Madan. I accepted a bottle of beer straight from the fridge. Cigarettes were produced, which I declined. Within a few minutes a variety of Indian delicacies were produced. Samoosas, roasted groundnuts, pakhoras, and dishes containing a mixture resembling spaghetti, peas and chillies. Who produced these delightful bits and pieces at such short notice I never discovered. I did find out later however, that the Asian community have a habit of keeping their hard-working wives very much in the background and giving little credit for what they do. Before I had finished my beer another bottle was open and standing on the table beside me. Noel had gone on to whisky which was being dispensed by the tumblerful. We eventually escaped at about ten o'clock very much the worse for wear. The drive home was, if anything, more erratic that it had been the previous night. Noel's cook and Kesi were awaiting our return, dinner having been kept warm for several hours. '*Sitaki chakula*', announced Noel again, turning to me for confirmation. 'We'll just have another beer before turning in', he said. A couple of hours later we eventually rolled into bed. I don't know if the hyena visited again that night. I certainly didn't hear it.

Chapter 8

'Do visits to the *dukas* always finish up as drunken orgies?', I enquired of Noel the following morning, nursing my head. 'Well no', he replied. 'I suppose they just thought they were making you welcome so it's entirely your fault. Anyway, it's a pity we didn't get round to meeting Ishverbhai and the others. We'll have to do that when you get back from safari. I'll let them know we'll be along, so that they can get plenty of sustenance ready.'

On our arrival at the police station we found that a lorry had already arrived and was being loaded. Its battered exterior failed to arouse much confidence in its ability to complete its journey, but Fergusson, who arrived a few minutes later, didn't seem worried. 'Hear that you had a heavy session last night', he commented, looking at my bloodshot eyes. 'I've only packed a couple of crates, so we'll have to ration ourselves this trip.' He went to the store and emerged a couple of minutes later with two canvas bags called chaguls. These had narrow necks like a bottle but had been split just below the neck. These he proceeded to fill with water. They were then hung on the side of the lorry and a bottle of beer placed in each. 'The surface evaporation causes a considerable drop in temperature', he explained, 'By lunch time you'll think they've just come out of the fridge.'

On the open back of the lorry just behind the cab, two wooden armchairs had been placed. Ample kapok-filled cushions ensured a comfortable ride. Two 44-gallon steel petrol drums were loaded onto the back of the lorry and the safari gear was stored in other parts. Four policemen with their belongings clambered aboard, and Barney leapt nimbly over the tailboard. The load was completed by Kesi and Fergusson's boy. Saying 'cheerio' to Noel we clambered aboard and settled into our armchairs. The driver climbed into the cab and the turnboy cranked the handle until the engine burst into life.

It was nine o'clock in the morning and I was off on my first African safari. This was the life. Not exactly as I had imagined it but near enough. No porters with head-loads, chanting as they marched across the bush and mountains. Maybe, one day, even that might happen.

Our route took us east along the road which skirted Moroto Mountain. This was little more than a rough track, from which

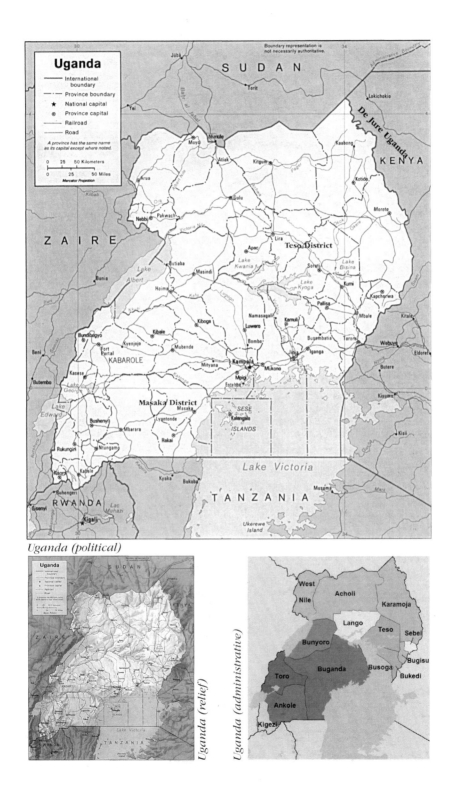

Uganda (political)

Uganda (relief)

Uganda (administrative)

Tony Beaden, Hastings, 1965

Margaret Beaden, Ward Sister, 1951

'Barney' — The Bull-terrier Tony Beaden 'inherited' from Ferguson

The author's police house in Moroto

The author with his first car

July 1951: transferred to Moroto

Camel Patrol

Land Rover Patrol

Murdoch MacKenzie, O.C. Kenya Police at Lokitaung   *Leslie Whitehouse, D.C. Turkana (nobody's friend)*   *Arthur Kessel, my house-mate for 3 months*

First safari in Karamoja District   *On the peak overlooking Moroto*

Thomas Hinett with a baby Dik-dik

Curious Karamajong tribesman   *Tappo. Chief of the Merrile tribesmen*

Kenya Police Askaris at Lokitaung

Uganda Police detachment during Suk/Karamajong tribal war

Parade of Kenya Police at Lokitaung

Uganda Police detachment at Lodwar

Moroto Police Station

District Commissioner's Office, Moroto

Government House, Entebbe

Field shelter used by tribesmen   *Karamajong Witch Doctor*

Top: Karamajong women. Right: Nanyero, county chief of the Pian, killed by Suk raiders in May 1953

Top: Karamajong tribesman. Below: Suk tribesmen

the boulders had been cleared. The frequent water courses which carried flood water from the mountain during the rains had been filled over with the red murrum soil which covered the entire area. No bulldozers or other mechanical devices were used in the road maintenance here, but gangs of naked Karamajong were occasionally encountered filling in pot holes or carrying on their heads iron bowls called *karais* filled with murrum. Their pay for this labour was only one-shilling a day, so they only worked when they were being watched. Karamoja roads thereby lived up to their reputation of being the worst in the country. Seated on the back of the lorry, the rush of air past our faces made the travelling conditions reasonably pleasant. The bumping and lurching over the potholes and stream beds caused some discomfort, but the ample cushions on the armchairs absorbed most of it. The policemen and our boys were not quite so fortunate since they had to sit on the rather hard safari boxes or on the rolled-up tents. Barney was quite clearly used to this mode of transport since he lay fast asleep on a cushion at his master's feet.

A gang of baboons scampered across the track ahead of us, pausing to peer curiously at us as we lurched past. The big males bared their fangs and barked defiance at us 'Nasty brutes' said Ian, 'I've seen them tear a dog to pieces. They don't just bite, they bite with their teeth and push with their hands, tearing out lumps of flesh. Try not to let Barney tangle with them.'

Flocks of red-legged francolin, a partridge-like bird, ran in front of us and stood in small groups on the verge. 'Damned good eating', said Ian. 'We'll shoot a few later on for tomorrow's breakfast.' A little further on a couple of minute buck about the size of hares, stood watching our progress. 'Dik-dik', I was informed. 'Meat has a rather strong flavour since they rarely drink. Always in pairs, or a pair and a youngster. They mate for life. This is ideal territory for them, though you'll find thousands of them throughout Karamoja.' Sure enough, I spotted pairs of Dik-dik every few minutes as we drove along the track. Our first call was at Katikekale Police Post, about 20 miles from Moroto, and still at the base of the mountain. This was manned by four constables and a corporal. All were present and fell in smartly as we drew to a halt in front of the group of mud huts. The post itself had little to commend it. It didn't even boast a fence round it, and water was drawn from a pump nearby, which was set atop a borehole. Twin spurs of the mountain, heavily clad in scrub, groped their way down towards the plain, cradling the group of huts between them. Above us Soglimuk, one of Moroto Mountain's three peaks, peeped from the fluffy clouds which lay near the summit. To the south-east lay the plain, with its lines of acacia thorn and the occasional wild fig marking dry watercourses. Through the trees the clunking of cow bells betrayed the whereabouts of a nearby herd, and a few hundred yards distant two or three crude grass shelters a thorn boma showed where the herdsmen spent their nights. The police post was sited in a sparsely-occupied area between the Karamajong and Suk tribes and was intended to reduce the risk of cattle raids between the two tribes. From here on no Karamajong would be found unless it were a scouting party or a band set on a raid.

On Ian's instructions a folding camp table and two folding camp chairs were set up beneath a nearby fig tree. The metal cashbox was retrieved from beneath one of the armchairs and the pay parade commenced. Barney woke up and leaped from the lorry and, after peeing against the corporal's front door, lay down at his master's side. The pay-out followed the same pattern as that at Moroto the previous day, save that no wives and children presented themselves. It took but a few minutes to deal with the policemen and their two porters. The task of the latter was to was to keep the compound swept and tidy and to collect firewood from the nearby mountain. They would also go out on patrol with one or other of the policemen should an interpreter be needed for recording statements and so on.

Leaving Ian to the mundane tasks I wandered over to a rocky outcrop, and was rewarded by the sight of a pair of brilliant blue agama lizards sunning themselves on the rocky surface. They regarded me with interest, raising their heads and watching every movement then, when I was about 20 feet away, they departed at lightning speed to their shelter under a nearby boulder. In their hurry they disturbed a small group of brown and blue butterflies which had been poised on the top of a pile of white hyena droppings. They flew around for a few moments before returning to their previous positions, where they commenced probing with their long proboscis. 'No accounting for taste', I thought and returned to the pay table.

'Any *shauris*?' Fergusson enquired of the corporal.'Only one,

Sir.' he replied in Swahili.'Three Karamajong were seen by a herdboy at Cholol Hill about two miles from here yesterday.' 'What have you done about it?' he was asked. 'Sir, I went with P.C. Oyot to the spot together with a tracker. We found the tracks of three men but they headed towards Okodat.' 'Right', said Ian. 'Send out patrols daily with the tracker for the next week, and report any sightings to Moroto.' He turned to me. 'Probably nothing in it, but these people are forbidden to carry more than one spear, and shields have been banned for ages now, except for very small ones used in dances. They've all got war shields hidden away of course but the only time they are ever carried is when they are on a raid or a scouting party prior to a raid.' 'What do you do if you catch anyone carrying them?' I enquired. 'Well, if it's just a second spear we simply confiscate it. A good spear costs them a cow so its loss is a punishment in itself. If it's a shield though, that means trouble so the carrier is arrested and taken to Moroto where the shield is confiscated and he is fined or imprisoned.'

The table and chairs and cash box having been safely placed aboard the lorry, Ian and I clambered aboard. Barney leaped over the tailboard and settled onto his cushion, and we started off again. Our track took us further from the mountain now, and the dry watercourses were deeper but less frequent. A few miles further on we came to a T-junction. This was where we met the main road from Kitale to Lodwar in the Turkana District of Kenya. 'This is now, in fact, part of Kenya', said Ian, 'but for convenience it is administered by us'. He pointed to a jumble of peaks away to the east. 'Those are the Karasuk Hills. They stretch as far as the escarpment below Kapenguria and Kitale. Miles and miles of sod all. There are no roads or tracks there. Most of the inhabitants have never seen an European and very few Europeans have ever been there. I've never heard of one anyway. We never seem to get any news of happenings there. I suppose things must go on from time to time but nothing is reported by the chiefs.' Our lorry now turned to the south-east, away from Moroto Mountain. The road we were now on was marginally better than the one we had just left. For the most part it was flat as it headed over the plain. Stream beds became less frequent but the few we encountered were considerably wider than those we had left behind. The murrum surface was heavily corrugated by the passing traffic. The lorry accelerated to some 30-miles-an-hour over the featureless landscape. Featureless that is to say, apart from the occasional rocky outcrop and the increasing number of red termite mounds. At the roadside, pairs of Dik-dik stood, watching this thundering giant with wide-eyed amazement and scampering off into the bush as we passed. A wart hog, its tail stiffly erect like a pennant, ran across the road ahead of us trailing its five ugly piglets, exact replicas of itself. Behind us the vortex stirred the dust which rose in a dense red cloud, trailing for half a mile to indicate our progress. Half-an-hour later we drew up outside the next police post, Kanyengereng. A name to play with. To roll around the tongue, each syllable to be savoured to the full. Its appearance, unfortunately, was, if anything, even less inspiring than Katikekele. Here, however, a small community had grown up alongside. Presumably the police presence had created a degree of confidence in not being raided by the Karamajong. Half-a- dozen roughly-thatched huts lined the road, each with its quota of naked children and semi-naked women. The Suk women were, I decided, not as handsome as the Karamajong. The married ones wore a leather apron or short skirt, decorated with cowry shells and suspended by a belt at the waist. Around their necks and shoulders were several dozen iron-wire hoops. Their hair was dressed liberally with sheep fat and plaited into small ringlets. In common with Karamajong women their lower lip was pierced and the front teeth of the lower jaw were removed. On enquiry I found that this custom was universally practiced by the Karamajong, the Suk, the Turkana and the Tepeth. The object being to give them an opportunity of survival should they contract tetanus. In this disease, commonly known as lockjaw, the muscles become rigid, making it impossible to open the mouth. By removing the front teeth and piercing the lower lip it was possible to feed the patient with milk and blood, the staple diet of these tribes. Usually a plug of ivory or metal was inserted into the pierced lip, causing a grotesque deformity. Those who failed to wear a plug dribbled liberally through the hole. The smell of the rancid fat, even in the open air was somewhat unpleasant. The Suk men were, generally speaking, shorter in stature than the Karamajong, though their headdresses, different in pattern, were just as intricate. As with the Karamajong the men went completely naked except for, in some cases, a black cotton cloth (*shuka*) around their shoulders.

The object of the cloth was made clear to me a little later when the rains started. They covered the head to protect the intricate hairdo's which might otherwise have melted away. I had an impression of shiftiness among them — a first impression I never had reason to alter.

Ian explained that the Kanyengereng salient was an area of bush about ten miles square which had been closed off to allow the grass an opportunity to recover. It was largely experimental and the District Council, under the direction of the D.C. and the Agricultural Officer, permitted entry by the Suk tribesmen, only towards the end of the dry season, when all other grazing was exhausted. Frequent police patrols were made in the area to ensure that no grazing took place at other times. Needless to say, the temptation of all that lovely grass was far too much for the tribesmen who would drive their cattle in, often at night, in the hope that the patrols would not catch them. Very often they got away with it but just occasionally they would be caught, their cattle seized and they would lose about ten per cent of the herd as a fine. When the salient was officially opened for grazing, vast herds of cattle and goats would move in from the Karasuk Hills and then the Karamajong would have a series of field days, often making off with herds of several hundred cattle at a time. A raiding party amounted to anything up to a 100 warriors. Once the cattle were secured they would be run for anything up to 50 miles non-stop, spears pricking the flanks of any who showed signs of flagging. About half the party would remain as a rear guard to deal with the infuriated band of owners who followed up within a very short time. The actual theft often resulted in the death of one or two children herding the cattle. These would be surrounded or chased, and speared by as many of the raiding party as could get to them. Such spear bloodings were much admired. No man could be a fully-accepted warrior until he had blooded his spear. The subsequent chase by the cattle owners would often result in a pitched battle in which many casualties would occur on both sides. Usually the raiders would win, they being composed of selected warriors, while the offended owners were invariably a scratch lot. Counter raids would then be mounted by the Suk on the Karamajong, following the same ground rules, and a raiding season without at least a 100 deaths was rare indeed. This had been going on for as long as anyone could remember and was regarded as the equivalent of the British football season. From time to time some of the raiders would be arrested, tried and sentenced to be hung. The deterrent effect was however negligible. Executions were carried out in Kampala and relatives or fellow tribesmen of the condemned men never bothered to find out their fate. The culture of the tribesmen and the conditions under which they lived made life very cheap indeed.

The pay parade at Kanyengereng followed very closely the pattern of that at Katikekele. I left Ian seated under the solitary acacia tree and wandered over towards the thatched huts that made up the small community. A Somali trader had one of the huts. He greeted me at the door. He spoke rapidly in some totally unknown language. I replied, greeting him in my halting Swahili. The conversation faltered. I glanced inside his store. A meager stock of beads and cowry shells, iron-wire and Pepsi-cola appeared to be his sole wares. A small pile of goat skins at one side indicated that he bought as well as sold. How, I wondered, could he possibly make a living out of this in such an area. 'Kwa heri', said I, and left. As I came out into the bright sunlight half-a-dozen naked toddlers who had been playing in the dust scampered back to their mothers. The smell of cow dung was even stronger than that of the rancid sheep fat. One of the toddlers, about two years of age grabbed its mothers pendulous breast and started to feed. She made no attempt to restrain it. I was told later that children were encouraged to breast feed as long as possible as it was believed that this reduced the chance of another early pregnancy. As far as I could make out, this was the only form of contraception that was practised among the Suk or the Karamajong.

Several shenzi dogs lay scratching in the dust. These unfortunate creatures had a pretty hard life of it one way and another. They survived on any scraps which might be thrown their way plus any odd rodent or lizard they might catch. I suppose their function was to set off an alarm should a raiding party arrive during the night. I shortly noticed another function they performed. One of the infants of about 18 months excreted in the dust. The nearest shenzi dog immediately got up and devoured the mess. It then went to the child and licked the remnants from its backside with every indication of enjoyment. Cheaper than toilet paper, I thought, and probably more effective.

I returned to Ian, who was just finishing the pay parade and was receiving the corporals report. 'Any *shauris?*' he enquired. 'Sir, I have charged P.C. Longok with losing five rounds of .303 ammunition while on patrol.' 'Right', said Ian, 'bring him in.' P.C. Longok, it transpired, was a locally-enlisted police constable, who had two years service. These locally-enlisted men did not undergo the usual police training in Kampala but went through a very basic form of training at Moroto before joining one of the outposts, where their local knowledge was often invaluable. The corporal marched him to the table where Fergusson sat. An unprepossessing specimen I thought. His left eye had a pronounced squint and a scar alongside it indicated that this was due to an old injury. He wore no lip-plug so a line of dribble ran down his chin, where several flies partook of a light refreshment. He did not even seem to notice them. The charge was read over to him. 'Sir', he said in Swahili, 'I had ten rounds when I went on patrol. When I returned I had only five. They must have fallen from my ammunition pouch.' 'Where's the pouch?' demanded Ian. P.C. Longok produced it and Ian examined it. 'I don't see anything wrong with the catch', he said. P.C. Longok said nothing. 'Bloody carelessness', said Ian, 'You'll be fined five-shillings.'

'Yes, Sir', said Longok. As he turned to march away I noticed a smirk on his lips. 'Got off pretty lightly didn't he?', I enquired. 'Well, I suppose he could have lost them accidentally', said Ian. 'In any case, he only gets about 50-shillings a month and since this is my last pay safari I'll give him the benefit of the doubt.'

While the parade had been taking place, Kesi and George, Fergusson's boy had been preparing lunch. They now brought this to our table. My hangover had been gone for several hours and the fresh air had produced a healthy appetite. Cold roast guinea fowl, cold boiled potatoes, a can of baked beans, all washed down with ice cold beer. A feast fit for a king. Ian was dead right. Those *chaguls* certainly did their job well. I noticed that two more bottles had replaced those which we had been drinking and would no doubt go down equally well later in the day. The meal completed, we climbed back onto the lorry and settled in our armchairs for the final part of the day's safari. The landscape continued in its familiar pattern of rocky outcrops and dry stream beds. Ahead of us a small herd of Grants Gazelle rushed startled across the road, their hooves raising small dust clouds. As we passed through the point where they had crossed a larger herd could be seen walking away through the trees. Herds of cattle, bells clunking around the necks of the herd bulls, were frequently encountered as they sought out the sparse dry grass which sustained them. Birds were everywhere, from the Bateleur eagle soaring high above, conspicuous by its apparent total lack of a tail, to the weird looking crowned hornbill wandering about among the termite mounds in its search for food and looking like an artists caricature. A flock of guinea fowl meandered across the road ahead of us and Ian banged the top of the cab. The lorry slowed and stopped about 30 yards away from them. Some of the flock made off into the bush while others stood around in a muddled sort of way. Ian reached for a .22 rifle and dropped two of the birds where they stood. He glanced at me. 'Not terribly sporting, I suppose, but we've got to get something for tomorrow's lunch and this is the quickest way of getting it.' A little further on a dozen or so red-legged francolin stood around a large termite mound. 'Have a go if you like', said Ian, handing me the rifle. I didn't get much of a thrill out of dropping two of the birds. It was too much like target practice at a fair. I dropped the first bird who was standing on top of the termite mound. He rolled forward with a brief flutter. Within seconds a second bird took his place and received a similar fate. 'Fine', said Ian, 'that's tomorrow's breakfast taken care of.' A few miles further on the road was cut by the bed of a large river. One or two pools of standing water indicated that the threatened rains had already started in this area. The rocky bed lay about 12 feet below the level of the road, which had been graded on each side to allow vehicles to pass. In an attempt to prevent the continued erosion, the bed of the river where the road passed had been concreted over and, although the concrete had broken away in places, it would clearly have been passable for a lorry when two or three feet of water was flowing. A herd of cattle, sheep and goats together with several donkeys were drinking from the pools of water while three small boys sat nearby. Our lorry lurched its way down the bank and across to the other side of the river. We were on the outskirts of a small village. This was Amudat where we were to spend the night.

Amudat proved to be a settlement of several hundred people. Indeed it was the headquarters of Upe County and the seat of the *Ekapalon* or County Chief, Amiri. Groups of Suk women and children sat in front of their mud huts which lined the roads. As we got further into the village we came to a series of shops, built of mud and wattle but with roofs made of corrugated iron or flattened paraffin debis. Most of the shops were run by Asians or Somalis and a later examination showed that they held a comprehensive stock of everyday goods from corrugated iron, nails, and iron-wire to ornaments, ostrich feathers, cloth, sandals and foodstuffs. A couple of hundred yards past the *dukas* and we drew up at the police post. This stood in its own compound and was somewhat different to the other two we had visited. Most of the buildings were rondavels made from prefabricated aluminium sections, bolted together. The aluminium roof was thatched over in an attempt to keep the interior cool. These huts had the advantage of being proof against the ravages of the termites and being easily transported. Their main disadvantage, however, was that during the day the temperature inside could rise to well over 100-degrees. For this reason they were not very popular with the policemen living in them. As our lorry stopped, a police sergeant appeared and, marching smartly up to the side of the lorry, saluted Fergusson with military precision. '*Jambo* sergeant', said Ian, returning the salute from his armchair, 'pay parade in ten minutes.' '*Ndio effendi*' said the sergeant and, saluting again ,he marched off to the huts where he could be heard roaring to his corporal and ·constables to get on parade. The pay parade followed the now familiar pattern. A sergeant, two corporals and eight constables formed the establishment here, though one of the corporals and two constables were away on patrol. A quick inspection of the huts showed them to be spick and span. One of the rondavels housed the radio equipment, a Morse receiver and transmitter, together with the operator. Contact was made every two hours during the day with the police station at Moroto. No messages awaited us however, so at the conclusion of the parade and inspection we handed the cash box over to the sergeant who locked it away in the armoury box for safe keeping overnight. Then climbing back aboard the lorry we made our way to the rest camp which had been built about half-a-mile away on the river bank. This was available to all government officers on safari but on our arrival we found that there were no other occupants. It consisted of half-a-dozen tent-shaped thatched shelters, each measuring about 16-feet by twelve at the base, open at each end, plus a number of mud huts. A cooking area was set at one side and, on the outskirts, near the river, was a pit latrine surrounded by a thatched wall. Our two safari tents were unloaded and were swiftly erected under two of the thatched shelters. The thatched roof plus the large trees along the river bank provided a welcome relief from the heat of the sun. The camp chairs and table were set up outside and camp beds, complete with mosquito nets were placed in each tent. The whole operation was completed by practised hands in about 15 minutes, by which time Kesi had produced tea and biscuits. Ian and I sat down and relaxed. Meanwhile, the lorry, with its driver and turnboy drove off towards the police post where they would spend the night.

'There are quite a few snakes and scorpions around here', said Ian, 'so don't forget to knock out your shoes and clothing in the morning before you get dressed.' I thanked him for the information. 'Have you been bitten or stung since you've been out here?', I enquired. 'No, but I've found scorpions in my shoes a couple of times', he replied. 'The big black scorpions are not too bad I understand, but the little yellow ones are deadly.' I made a mental note to be extra careful when dressing from now on. I decided to attend to the calls of nature and walked over to the pit latrine. This consisted of a hole dug in the ground, about twelve feet deep and four feet across. Branches were laid over the top in a criss cross pattern and mud applied over these to form a floor. A hole, about one-foot square was left and sometimes a cover was provided. In this case it was missing. A mouse scuttled into the thatched wall as I entered and I could hear it rustling as it made its way round the thatching. I stamped heavily on the floor of the latrine to make sure that it was sound. I didn't fancy it giving way while I was crouched over the hole. A rattling sound came from the pit as the termites, busily eating their way through the timber construction showed their annoyance at being disturbed by gnashing their mandibles. I wondered just how much of the support they had consumed, and how long it would be before some unsuspecting individual fell through. However, I had more pressing matters to attend to. Crouching over the hole with my shorts around my ankles I spent a fairy uncomfortable five minutes. Nothing untoward occurred but I thought I heard some odd noises emanating from the depths. I returned to my tent and collected a torch. Retracing my steps to the latrine I shone a beam of light down the pit. Coiled at the bottom was a large cobra. Several smaller snakes lay nearby. I consoled myself with the thought that, even had the cobra been able to stand on the tip of its tail, it would still lack about five-foot in length between it and my backside. 'Not a terribly pleasant existence', I thought, 'being shit on from a great height every so often, but I suppose that food was no problem with rodents, insects and other snakes dropping in from time to time.

I decided that while there was still a couple of hours of daylight I would take a walk along the river bed. A recent storm up on Kadam Mountain had brought the first flood-water of the season down the previous day so although the river bed was mainly dry there were plenty of pools of standing water. The bank was a sheer twelve-foot drop by the camp but, by walking a couple of hundred yards along I found a suitable place to clamber down. The rocky bed was strewn with trees and branches, washed down by the spate during the last rainy season. It soon became clear that some of the pools had survived right through the dry weather, since the surface of the water was rippled by the activities of a myriad of tiny fish. The occasional swirl on the surface of the water, indicated that bigger fish also existed in the pools. Much of the water was murky from the cattle which had been drinking there. From the overhanging trees malachite kingfishers like crested jewels darted into the water and came out with their small captures. I sat on a nearby rock to enjoy the scene and was rewarded a few minutes later by the sight of a magnificent chestnut-and-white fish eagle swooping over one of the pools, its talons outstretched. It hit the water with a mighty splash and almost immediately took off again grasping a struggling mud fish. Landing in a nearby tree it threw back its head and uttered a laughing scream before settling to tear and eat its prey. I sat, unmoving, to see what else would appear. I didn't have long to wait. A flock of guinea fowl fluttered down from the bank nearby and hurried across to the pool. While they were drinking their fill a mud turtle crawled from the water and lay on the edge sunning itself. Brilliant butterflies fluttered around, settling every so often to drink from the damp surface. I felt most privileged to be able to enjoy the scene. I was going to enjoy my time in Karamoja. Eventually, tearing myself away from the spot, I made my way back to the camp. The sun was sinking low behind the trees and Kesi had lit a campfire near the tents. Two bottles of beer, fresh and cold from the *chaguls* stood on the table awaiting my arrival and a dish of freshly-roasted groundnuts accompanied them. 'I think a cold beer, followed by a hot bath, followed by dinner will be the order of the day', said Ian. 'I hope you don't mind roast *kanga* (guinea fowl) again', he said, 'It gets a bit monotonous I know, but we'll have lamb tomorrow evening for a change.' We sat down at the table. The beer tasted splendid. 'I've only one regret', said Ian, 'I've only had two dry seasons here. Safari isn't quite so much fun during the rains. It can get a bit tedious pushing lorries out of the mud or getting marooned on the wrong side of the river. Best to bring a good book with you and then sit it out.'

The brief African twilight was now over and I could hear the ping of the mosquitoes. Kesi appeared with a couple of paraffin pressure lamps, which gave out a brilliant light and a terrible roaring noise at close quarters. He placed these on the table and immediately began the bombard of flies, mosquitoes, beetles and moths. Ian yelled and his boy shifted the lamps and hung them on nearby branches. We started to extract the struggling insects from our beer but decided that there were too many. Sadly we threw away the contents of our glasses. The warm beer from the crate didn't taste as good, but would have to do. We killed a bottle each. '*Lete bafu*', yelled Ian. His boy hurried over with a paraffin *debi* filled with boiling water. He tipped it into a canvas folding bath which had been set up nearby, and brought another *debi* of cold water to add to it. Ian went for his bath. He reappeared a quarter of an hour later clad in slacks, sweater and mosquito boots. 'They've just refilled the bath for you', he said. 'Soon as you're ready, we'll have dinner.' I bathed. The canvas bath was about three-feet square, held up at the sides and corners by a folding wooden frame. Clearly, when it had been designed, comfort had not been foremost in the mind of the inventor. Sitting down, one's feet had to be on the soil outside, which by this time was mud. Also, sharp objects on the ground underneath precluded any thought of a lengthy soak. Nevertheless, at the end of it I felt refreshed and ready for dinner. The evening was turning chilly so I followed Ian's example and donned slacks and a sweater. On my return I found that a dining net had been erected under one of the shelters. This was a mosquito net about ten-feet square and seven-feet in height. The table and chairs were placed inside it together with the pressure lamp and the remains of the crate of beer. Ian and Barney were already within and I joined them gratefully. Inside, the effect was very cosy. The roar of the single pressure lamp was tolerable, the mosquitoes pinged outside the net and beetles banged around in their efforts to reach the lamp. A few geckos appeared outside and started to feast on the moths as they dropped to the ground. A couple of beers later and Kesi appeared outside the net with dinner, consisting of roast guinea fowl, roast potatoes and tinned peas, followed by tinned peaches and cream. He shoved these under the net. A few insects got in at the same time by a quick squirt with a Flit spray soon dealt with these.

By 9.30 the beer and food had produced a soporific effect. Bidding goodnight to Ian I made my way to my tent. I was asleep almost as soon as my head touched the pillow. Some hours later my slumbers were shattered by some idiot sawing wood nearby. I cursed whoever it was and tried to get back to sleep. The sawing continued for about half-an-hour and I was just about to get up and sort the culprit out when it ceased. I dozed off and a little later was aroused again, this time by a gang of hyenas laughing their heads off nearby. Eventually they made off and I was permitted to sleep again. No time at all seemed to pass before Kesi arrived with my morning tea. I stumbled, bleary eyed from the tent.

The morning was clear and fresh. A light dew covered the grass and leaves and the bird calls were deafening. A canvas washbasin was set up on the same frame that had held the bath the previous evening. Hot water steamed in it. As I washed Ian and Barney emerged from the other tent. 'Who was that bloody idiot who was sawing wood during the night?', I enquired. He looked puzzled and then his brow cleared. 'Oh', he said, 'that was a leopard on a kill on the other side of the river. Yes, they do sound like sawing wood come to think of it. The hyenas cleared up the remains after him so there won't be much left now.' While we had our breakfast of cold roast francolin with baked beans, toast and Kenya coffee, I noticed a small group of Suk tribesmen approaching from the direction of the police post. 'Here comes tonight's dinner', said Ian. I made no comment as I didn't know what he was talking about. As the party drew closer I saw that one of them was leading a sheep. One of the group approached and I noticed that he was about 40-years-old, well-built and clad in shorts, an army jacket and a pair of sandals made out of sections of a car tyre. His lip was pierced in the traditional manner and a small ivory plug was inserted. His head was close-cropped instead of the usual Suk hair style. *'Jambo bwana'*, he said, *'Jambo Amiri'*, replied Ian and introduced me. Another chair was produced and the Ekapalon joined us for a cup of coffee. The next half-hour was spent discussing the grazing, cattle raids, poll tax collection, supplies of meat to the local police posts, marauding lions and hyenas and a multitude of minor problems. I had the impression that Amiri was a good-humoured, intelligent individual who liked nothing better than a good gossip. 'You owe him five-shillings', said Ian, as the conversation drew to a close. 'What's that for?,' I enquired. 'Well, the sheep is four-shillings and 100 eggs are another shilling', he replied. 'It's customary to supply a sheep to government officers on safari. Four shillings is the going-rate. You can sell the skin to one of the traders in Moroto for a shilling when you get back, so you won't be much out of pocket.' I handed over a five-shilling note to Amiri and thought of my parents in England where meat was still rationed to a few ounces a week and very expensive to boot. By the time Amiri left, the sheep had been slaughtered, gutted, skinned, and jointed. 'We may as well have lamb chops for lunch instead of roast kanga', said Ian, and gave the necessary instructions.

The lorry arrived with the sergeant bearing the cash box. The chairs and table were loaded aboard. 'Right,' said Ian, 'we've a long way to go and I want to be back in time for lunch'. It was 9 o'clock and the heat was just beginning to build up again on the next stage of our journey. Katabok was the police post we headed for, 20 miles distant and nestling at the base of Kadam Mountain. This was another post whose function was to discourage raiders. The area in which it was set was sparsely inhabited and lay in a sort of no mans land between the two tribes. It was thick with game and birds. The soil here was totally different from the red murrum I was used to. The track led across a broad plain composed of black cotton soil. This was a sort of alluvial deposit, black as soot and many feet thick. It contained no stones or pebbles and, although there were termite mounds they also had the same dark colour. When it became wet during the rains, lorries could not pass because they sank in up to their axles. Deep ruts along the track showed where the unwary or unlucky had been caught in the past. 'It dries out very quickly', said Ian. 'You can get bogged down in the morning after a storm and within two hours its dried out and is passable again. It's just as bad after a shower. Then the soil collects on the tyres like a snowball and the wheels get bigger and bigger until the mudguards stop them from going round.' I glanced at the sky. A few clouds were gathering over the mountain but it didn't look as though we were in for any appreciable rain in the near future. I couldn't shake off the feeling that the time was likely to come in the not distant future when I should be making this journey on foot. Meantime, I relaxed in my armchair as the lorry lumbered forward. Herds of Grants gazelle, kongoni and topi were everywhere. The occasional solitary eland watched us before charging off into the bush. A herd of zebra galloped away, barking like dogs, while a large male ostrich, resplendent in his black plumage and white tail feathers, shepherded his flock of drab females away from the noisy vehicle, his legs and neck glowing pink with his excitement. The lorry stopped and the driver pointed. Fifty yards away a pair of cheetah rose from the termite mound where they had been lying and walked unhurriedly away twitching their tails. Birds were everywhere. Gorgeously-coloured, raucous-voiced turacos sat in the wild fig trees, plucking the fruit, while brilliant bee eaters darted about catching their prey before settling in thorn bushes to eat them. Flocks of guinea fowl were everywhere. High in the air tiny specks wheeled in the rising air currents — vultures, patiently waiting for some small tragedy on the ground far below to provide them with their meal. I felt at peace with the world. What a privileged person I was to be sure. This was somewhat better than rattling door handles of shops on a dark wet night.

The journey to Katabok took just over an hour. We drew up at the police post consisting of four thatched mud huts at the foot of one of the spurs of the mountain. The scenery was magnificent. Above us the mountain dominated. The police post was in a slightly elevated position and commanded a view over the surrounding plain. A rough thorn hedge surrounded the post and nearby a borehole and pump supplied water. I noticed that one of the constables even had a garden growing in which I could see tomatoes, chillies, several varieties of grain and groundnuts. Very enterprising I thought.

The camp table and the chairs were unloaded from the lorry and set up under one of several thorn trees growing within the *boma*, and Ian set to with the pay parade. Meanwhile, the clouds I had noticed earlier, forming over the mountain were growing in size and beginning to look a bit threatening. After having a look round the huts, which I found as immaculate as ever, I decided to take a stroll a little further up the spur coming from the mountain above. 'Don't be too long', called Ian. 'We need to move fairly soon if we are to be back at Amudat in time for lunch.' I did not need to go far to reach higher ground. Within a couple of hundred yards I had gained 100-feet of height. I was rewarded with an unbroken view for many miles over the plain below. Everywhere I looked I could see herds of game. Apart from the Grants gazelle, topi, kongoni and eland which I had already noticed, there were roan antelope and waterbuck. After absorbing this scene for about ten minutes I could see Ian getting the table and chairs back onto the lorry. Regretfully I made my way back. I related what I had seen as we set off in the lorry. 'Do you know', he said, 'I've never climbed up there during the 18 months I've been in Karamoja. I don't suppose I shall ever do it now.'

As we left the police post the first spots of rain started. Glancing back I saw that over the mountain a great storm cloud had formed. 'We'll be lucky to get back to Amudat in time for lunch now', said Ian. The journey now turned into a race between the lorry and the advancing rain. All the time we could keep just ahead of the rain we were alright. Gradually, however, we were being overtaken. After ten miles the black cotton soil over which we were traveling was wet. Our progress slowed. Glancing over the side of the lorry I saw that the front and rear tyres were now encased in about four inches of soil. Somehow the driver kept us going. From time to time great lumps of black sticky mud dropped from the wheels and we surged forward at a greater speed until the build-up again slowed us to a walking pace. As suddenly as it had started, the rain stopped. The lorry crawled forward for a few more miles until we reached ground where there had been no rain. 'Looks like we are in luck', said Ian. 'These short, sharp showers often happen at the start of the rains. We shall probably have rain every day from now on. Anyway that's the dicey one out of the way. The other police posts are more or less easily reached providing the river crossings are not too deep.' By mid-day we had reached Amudat and drove up to our camp. 'I think we'll take the afternoon off', said Ian. 'We could press on and do Kacheliba, Karita and Loporokocho but it would make a bloody long day of it so we'll do that tomorrow.' Relaxing in my armchair with a cold beer at my elbow I thought back over the morning. 'How much would it cost for a tourist to do what I had just done?', I thought. 'What further incredible sights and adventures lay ahead.' Lunch arrived. Half-a-dozen delicious lamb chops each, with mashed potatoes, carrots and tinned peas. Having demolished this we retired to our tents and enjoyed an hours siesta. Later, I repeated my walk down the river bed. This time I found that the morning rain on the mountain had created a small flow of water. Several pied crows were busy clearing up the oddments left from the leopard kill of the previous night. A flock of Burchell's Starlings chattered in the overhanging thorn trees and several of them flew down to bathe in the pools of water. The malachite kingfisher and his mate were still busy diving for the small fry but this time I saw no sign of the fish eagle. I turned and walked back in the direction of the camp. Instead of climbing the bank again I continued downstream, past other pools of water. A rustling in the undergrowth at the side of the river drew my attention. I froze and, as I watched, saw a great lizard slide down the bank and make its way unhurriedly across to one of the pools where it drank its fill. This was my first sighting of the monitor lizard. I estimated it to be about four-feet in length and quite heavily-built. It looked capable of giving a nasty bite, given the opportunity. After a few minutes it noticed me and made its way back up the bank and was lost to view. Clouds of butterflies, which were sucking up the moisture from the damp sand, flew into the air as I disturbed them in passing.

Arriving back at the camp I found Ian settling down to the first beer of the evening. Shortly after I had joined him we were aroused by the arrival of a truck. The driver, an European climbed stiffly down from the cab, and came across to where we sat. Ian introduced him as Dick Heron, the local officer of the Geological Department. He was one of the officers from Moroto who I had not yet met. Dick was of stocky build, about five-feet ten-inches and a very pleasant character. He was a bit reserved to start off with but soon thawed and told me about his job. He was in charge of the programme of drilling boreholes and building dams throughout Karamoja. Consequently, he spent most of his time on safari. His wife was living in Kampala but he told me that he hoped that she would soon be joining him in Moroto. The rest of the evening was spent yarning round the camp fire. After a bath and a dinner of roast leg of lamb we turned in for the night. In view of the close proximity of the leopard the previous night I slept with my revolver under my pillow.

CHAPTER 9

The following morning we were up at daybreak. Our lorry arrived shortly afterwards and after a light breakfast of toast bacon and eggs our safari gear was packed aboard and we were away. Our route took us along the main road towards Kitale in Kenya. The landscape consisted of the usual thorn scrub, wild figs and *sansivaria*. This was a type of wild sisal. The stems were about an inch in diameter at the base tapering to a needle sharp point at the tip. The stems were about two- or three-feet long and very tough. Each plant had 20 or 30 stems set like fans, and where they grew thickly were almost impenetrable. Plenty of game was to be seen. Dik-dik were passed every few hundred yards. Several groups of warthogs crossed the road in front of us and a herd of zebra standing at the side of the road suddenly decided that it wanted to get to the other side before we reached them. Our driver had to brake sharply to avoid ploughing into them and the lorry swerved wildly on the loose dust lying on the road surface. Four giraffe viewed us unconcernedly from the roadside where they were browsing from the tops of the acacia thorn. The road surface was in reasonable condition and we were able to make good progress. A little over two hours after leaving Amudat we were entering another quite large settlement. This was Kacheliba, the border settlement between Uganda and Kenya. The demarcation of the border was the Suam River. This, like the river at Amudat, had a certain amount of water in it most of the year. The Suam drew its water supply from Mount Elgon some 30 or 40 miles to the south-west. The police post was several hundred yards from the river. Like the one at Amudat it consisted of four or five straw thatched aluminium rondavels, plus several mud huts. The sergeant in charge, warned of our visit by a message from Amudat, already had his men drawn up on parade. While the table and chairs were being unloaded I wandered down to the river. Being a fairly important settlement and a border between the two countries a substantial bridge about 40-yards long had been built across the river. A few pools of water with a thin trickle between them indicated that as yet little rain had fallen on Elgon. Clouds gathering in the distance threatened that this situation was likely to be changed in the not too distant future. Most of the settlement had been built on the

Kenya side of the border. I crossed the bridge, as much as anything to be able to say that I had been in Kenya, though I anticipated that it would not be long before I would be making regular trips across. The Asian *dukas* were duplicates of those at Amudat. The same commodities were on sale. I purchased a crate of beer and the shopkeeper dispatched a nearby African to carry it back to the lorry. By the time I returned to the police post Ian was in the process of packing the table and chairs back on board. Very soon we set off to our next destination.

Karita lay about 20 miles from Kacheliba and to reach it we had to retrace our tracks for about five miles before turning east. Once on the new track the difference in the surface soon became apparent. This was really rough. Our lorry lurched from pot-hole to pot-hole, Kesi and George hanging on for dear life. Game was, if anything, even more prolific that it had been previously. Flocks of guinea fowl wandered all over the road, scuttling out of our way at the last minute. About an hour later we drew into the police post at Karita. The corporal in charge reported to Ian.'We are going straight on to Loporokocho. Hopefully we shall be back by about four o'clock so have your men ready for pay parade then.' Without any further delay we were off again. Immediately after leaving the police post we were crossing a dry river bed. This was the Keriki River which also drew its water from Mount Elgon. This appeared to be quite a major river, about 30-yards wide and eight or nine-feet deep. Boulders and rocks had been placed on the bed of the river and boughs of trees placed over the top to smooth out the crossing.'I hope it doesn't rain before we get back', said Ian, 'this one can be a bastard when the rains start. The bed is mostly sand and when it gets wet you can sink in up to the axles. You can be marooned on the other side for days when you get heavy rain.' We lurched across the river. The main track continued towards the west but we turned almost immediately to our right. For a couple of hundred yards the track was clearly marked then it petered out. Now we were literally driving through the bush.'Loporokocho is a dry season post only', said Ian, 'We shall be closing it down any time now.' Our route was marked only by the slight indentations left by the few previous vehicles. In fact the surface we were driving over was reasonable smooth. From time to time we crossed over dry stream beds. The distance between Karita and Loporokocho was only about ten miles but it was a wonderful journey. I had thought I had seen a lot of game on the previous journeys. Now that we were completely out in the bush the numbers and variety of animals and birds increased dramatically. Several small groups of Lesser Kudu were encountered. Bush buck were frequently seen as were oribi. From time to time large slow-moving tortoises were passed on the side of the track. Greater and lesser bustard were occasionally seen but these tended to be solitary birds. Occasionally the thorn bush gave way to large areas of grassland. Here the bigger herds of animals congregated. A herd of around 100 buffalo grazing 50-or-so yards from us looked up as we passed but otherwise showed complete disinterest. What struck me most was that the animals and birds appeared to be totally unafraid. Clearly they had never been hunted or disturbed. The police post, when we eventually reached it, consisted of three aluminium rondavels. It was manned by a corporal and four constables whose job it was to continuously patrol the area seeking signs of raiding parties, either Suk or Karamajong. Two of the constables were on patrol when we arrived. The corporal reported to Ian and he and remaining two constables paraded and received their pay. 'Any *shauris*?', enquired Ian. 'Sir, we are having lion around the huts every night', said the corporal. 'May we have permission to shoot some of them. We fear that they will get into the huts and eat us!' 'Certainly not', said Ian. 'You will only be here for a few more days, then the post will be closed until the rains stop. The last thing we want are wounded lions roaming about.' If we have problems when we re-open the post, Mr Beaden can come out and shoot them.' 'Thanks a bunch', I thought. Loporokocho did not have the refinement of a radio. It appeared that if any messages were to be passed it entailed one of the constables cycling into Karita and sending the message from there. Oddly, none of them seemed in the least worried about cycling ten miles through the bush, apparently infested with lions and buffalo. Rain clouds were again threatening as we set off back to Karita but this time we were fortunate and crossed back over the Kerike before any problems were presented. It had turned three o'clock by the time we arrived back at Karita. 'Time for lunch I guess', said Ian. The lorry was unloaded and while Ian got on with the pay parade Kesi and George started to prepare our meal. Meanwhile, I had a look round the police post. This was roughly half mud huts and half rondavels. About four of each. The establishment here was a sergeant, a corporal and six constables. No fence surrounded this post. An area had been cleared from the thorn scrub, leaving half-a-dozen large trees for shade. Hens with their chicks scratched around the huts and I was surprised to see about a dozen guinea fowl walking round with them. On enquiry I was told that these were from eggs found in the bush, which had been hatched out under a hen. They were completely domesticated and were kept for their meat. A small settlement was nearby with the usual tin-roofed *duka* owned by a Somali and a dozen or so huts comprising the local inhabitants occupation. An area of the post had been set aside for the tents of officers on safari. The sergeant supervised as the constables erected our tents. A nearby mud hut was for the use of our boys. Our table and chairs had been set up under one of the trees and a couple of bottles of beer were opened. Ian and I sat and relaxed. Shortly afterwards Kesi arrived with our lunch. He set a vast saucepan on a framework of branches which had been erected nearby, to act as a table. The smells coming from the saucepan were delicious. I had noticed this utensil at our previous camps, boiling away each evening and had thought that it was food for Kesi and George. Now, however, all was revealed. Stew. Anything left over from our previous meals was cut up and popped in the pot. Water was occasionally added plus a few carrots, onions and potatoes. Here then was a mixture of *kanga* (guinea fowl), *francolin* and lamb. 'This gets better as you go on', said Ian. 'You've got to make sure it's boiled up every time you make camp, otherwise it goes off, but provided you can keep it sterile, by the end of a week it's quite incredible.' I could quite believe him. On the other hand I could quite believe that if it wasn't closely supervised it could result in a nasty dose of food poisoning. However I was quite peckish by this time so got stuck in. It tasted as good as it smelled. I managed three helpings.

Later, Ian and I accompanied by Barney, crossed back over the river. Ian took a .22 rifle with him. 'We'll see if we can pick up a buck for dinner tonight', said Ian. We had walked about half a mile. A movement in the bushes about 30 yards away attracted my attention. A brown form could be seen moving behind the branches. Ian slowly raised the rifle to his shoulder. A shot rang out and the buck collapsed. Barney was like an arrow released from a bow. Within a few seconds he had the buck by the throat.

His activities were not needed, however. The animal was quite dead. 'Oribi', said Ian. 'Very good eating, and not too heavy to carry.' The animal was about the size of a small dog and weighed about 25 pounds. On its head were a pair of small, straight horns about five inches long. I picked it up and we retraced our steps to the camp. Here we handed our victim over to one of the camp porters who rapidly skinned and butchered it. 'We'll have one of the legs roasted tonight', said Ian. 'The boys and the *askaris* can have the rest.' Tea and biscuits arrived. 'Are you interested in shooting?', enquired Ian. I explained that my early youth had been largely spent poaching in the Kentish woods. 'It will pay you then to get a game licence before you come out on your own', he said, 'It only costs 100-shillings and you can shoot unlimited birds and practically unlimited buck. If you want to shoot elephant and rhino you have to get additional licences. The first elephant costs £10, the second £15 and the third £20. A rhino licence will cost another ten. I don't bother with them myself, but if you're interested, it's a quick way of making money. There are plenty of big tuskers up in the Kidepo Valley in the north. The ivory fetches two pounds a pound and a good tusker can carry a hundredweight of it. A rhino horn can weigh 20 pounds and will fetch several hundred quid.' In my present impecunious state I was almost tempted. I thought of a big bull elephant with tusks of 80 or 90 pounds each. Then I thought of the years he had taken to grow them to this size. Why should I, purely for greed, snuff him out in a split second, leaving his carcass to rot or be eaten by hyenas and vultures. The same argument applied to the rhino. The mere thought revolted me. In the case of buck and gazelle no such qualms moved me. There were millions of these. They bred every year and matured in two. I was able to look on them as a pleasant feature of the landscape and a convenient meat supply and not much more. I decided to get a game licence on my return to Moroto.

The following morning after a breakfast of oribi liver and kidneys and eggs we set off on the next stage of our journey. Returning to the main road we headed back towards Amudat arriving there at about eleven o'clock. After a quick visit to the police post, to make sure that nothing untoward needed our attention, we continued on towards our next destination. Namalu. Instead of taking the road towards Moroto we now headed west and after about 15 miles struck off south-west again down a rough track. Namalu, our next port of call, was, like Katabok, situated in no-man's land. In fact it was only about 15 miles from Katabok over a couple of the spurs of Kadam Mountain. The ground in between was, however, far too rough for motor vehicles. The track to Namalu was far more open than the one to Katabok. A number of volcanic outcrops were scattered across the landscape. Game was still reasonably plentiful, but nowhere near as much as that around Loporokocho. Namalu, when we arrived, was found to consist of the usual mixture of mud huts and aluminium rondavels. After lunch and pay parade, Ian dealt with one of the constables who was charged with damaging his equipment. It appeared that he had left one of his pairs of boots under his bed for three days without checking them. When he did get round to doing this he found that the only parts left were the rubber soles. The rest had been eaten by the termites. 'When were these issued?' demanded Ian. 'Sir, they were not my best boots', said the constable. 'I have had them for two years.' 'Fined five-shillings,' said Ian. 'No excuse for leaving them like that to get eaten. You should know better.' Shortly afterwards we were off to our next port of call, Nabilatuk. This was back in Karamajong territory, and was the headquarters of Upe County. The police post was another large one consisting of a sergeant, two corporals and eight constables. Most of the buildings were aluminium rondavels. After the pay parade, while we were drinking our afternoon tea, a figure arrived at the post. *'Jambo Nanyiro,'* said Ian. I was introduced to the County Chief. He was an impressive figure, about 50 years of age and dressed in shorts, shirt, tyre-sandals and khaki puttees. On his head was a khaki bush hat which had seen better days. His bearing was military and I gathered that he had seen army service in the middle east during the war. While we were chatting, a second figure approached. This was Lorika, the Government Agent. I was never quite sure who was the more senior figure of these two. He was of a similar age and build to Nanyiro but was an Acholi by tribe. I gathered that he was a sort of A.D.C. who lived permanently at Nabilatuk and reported back directly to the District Commissioner. Both of these old boys were likeable characters with a lively sense of humour. They joined us for tea, which they sucked noisily from their saucers. We discussed with them the usual problems of raiding, rain, grass, cattle and taxes.

A little later Ian handed them a cigarette each. These they lit and then did something I had never previously seen. They put the lighted end in their mouths. How they didn't burn their tongues I've no idea, but they appeared to enjoy smoking this way. I later found that it was a fairly common practice among the Northern Tribes. At the conclusion of our discussions we settled down for a relaxing evening and the remains of the roast oribi.

The following morning we set off at around nine o'clock for a fairly leisurely trip to Iriri, the post I had visited on my way in. Our route took us back in the direction of Moroto Mountain and we had to pass the Christian Missionary Society mission at Lotome. This was run by Bob and Doris Clarke. Bob was an ex-blacksmith, a very practical man for a missionary. Unlike some of the missionaries they made no attempt to ram religion down ones' neck. Their five children were all away at school in Kenya. The mission school taught largely practical subjects but the children were taught English and simple maths as well. Doris taught the girls to sew and knit and cultivate the ground. Bob taught the boys carpentry, animal husbandry, building, ploughing and so on. Bob and Doris seemed pleased to see us and we had morning tea with them. Then we were off once again to Iriri. The river Mani mani at Kangole had a fair amount of water flowing over its ramp from a recent storm on Napak, but not enough to make crossing dangerous. On arriving at Iriri I was greeted like a lifelong friend by Corporal Okeng. After the pay parade we had a beer and a few more helping of the excellent stew, then it was all aboard and off to Moroto. During our safari we had dropped off the four constables at various places on route but had picked up another four who had served their six months out in the bush and were now due for a spell at Moroto. As we entered the town and passed the police lines the wives and families of the four rushed out, ululating in their pleasure and excitement at the return of the wanderers. Noel met us at the door of his office. 'Had a good safari?', he enquired. 'I'm just knocking off. Time for a drop of refreshment I think.' Pausing just long enough to put the remains of the cash into the safe, we made our way up to Noel's house, where I related the details of the trip. Noel seemed pleased at the way I was settling in. 'You'll be away again tomorrow morning', he said. 'There's a couple more police post up in the north at Kotido and Kaabong. You'll probably make it in a day though, weather permitting.'

The safari to the Northern Police Posts proved fairly uneventful. Our lorry had been checked-over and refuelled overnight and was awaiting us when we arrived at the police station at about 7 o'clock the following morning. The full quota of safari kit was packed as, although it was anticipated that we should be returning by the same evening, there was no guaranteeing the weather at this time of year. 'See if you can bring back a sheep for me', said Noel as we departed. 'Some eggs too if you can.' Neither Ian nor I had had time for breakfast. 'We'll have brunch when we get to Kotido', said Ian. We headed out towards Iriri, but just before reaching Kangole we took a right-hand fork and headed north-west. We were now gradually climbing to a higher altitude. Already the surrounding countryside was looking greener, though some of this might have been due to recent showers of rain. There was less thorn bush here. About mid-morning we pulled in under the shade of a sausage tree, where we had a bottle of beer. I later found that this was the 'kigalia'. It was quite remarkable. I had noticed similar trees previously as we were driving along, but this was the first opportunity I had had of examining one closely. It was about 30-feet tall, the leaves broad and about three inches long. From the branches hung numerous sausage shaped fruit. These were generally around 18-inches long and hard-skinned. I should think each one must have weighed ten or twelve pounds. I was a bit dubious about sitting under this tree. Had one of the fruits dropped off, it could have brained anyone it hit. I asked Ian if the fruit was edible and was told that the only use that he knew it was put to was in making beer, when it was added for its bitter flavour. By mid-day we had arrived at Kotido which was the County Headquarters of Jie County. The police post here was similar to that at Nabilatuk and about the same size. The sergeant in charge paraded his men and Ian got on with the pay parade. I could see nothing out of the ordinary in the settlement nearby. There were about seven or eight *dukas* of which two were run by Asians, the remainder being Somalis. I was surprised however when a Chevrolet truck drew up outside one of the *dukas* and an European got out. This proved to be Father Farina, who was in charge at the local Catholic Mission. He was an Italian but spoke good English. Clearly he was quite keen to have a chat with someone new and invited Ian and myself along to the

Mission for lunch. We gratefully accepted the invitation and, as soon as the pay parade was ended, followed his truck up to the Mission which was half-a-mile or so from the police post. The Mission, when we reached it, was quite spectacular. The Church was large and brick-built, surrounded by modern brick-built bungalows occupied by the various brethren. On enquiring I was informed that all of the bricks were manufactured locally by Father Farina and his flock, as were most of the other building materials. After an excellent lunch, accompanied by a considerable variety of alcoholic beverages, Father Farina would, I am sure, have been happy to spend the rest of the day showing us over the Mission but we made our excuses and returned to the police post. Ian gave the necessary instruction to the sergeant regarding the sheep and eggs and we started off again for Kaabong, the last of the police posts to be dealt with. This was a further 50 miles distant and only about 40 miles from the Sudan border. Our road was cut through an area of volcanic hills and outcrops. These were the Labwor Hills. One vast rock rose practically sheer for 1,500 feet from the surrounding plain. This, I was informed, was known as Rwot. It had never been climbed. On our way to Kaabong we took the opportunity of collecting half-a-dozen kanga to take back to Moroto. The Labwor Hills were traditionally the area where the blacksmiths lived. Large deposits of iron ore and other minerals were found here, which the blacksmiths used to mine and smelt. From this were made spears, knives and a variety of other weapons. Of recent years, however, the traditional smelting of the ore had gone. In its place old lorry springs were now used for the purpose. The Karamajong spear was quite an interesting weapon. It was made in three parts: a razor-sharp, leaf-shaped blade with a thin round shaft about three feet long connected to a central wooden shaft of about the same length. An iron tailpiece of similar length completed the weapon. This could be thrown with unerring accuracy for up to about 30 yards. It was quite a heavy weapon and would easily penetrate a man's chest and emerge the other side with little effort. Traditionally, the blacksmiths were also wizards and very respected members of society. An ox was the usual payment for a spear. Blacksmiths also became very rich!

Kaabong police post was another of those which had been established to prevent raiding. This time it was raids made by the Turkana from Northern Kenya on the Karamajong of Dodoth, and vice versa. Within a few miles of Kaabong was the escarpment, dropping down nearly 3,000 feet into the Great Rift Valley where Turkana began. For the most part this drop was almost sheer. In places. however, tracks existed, sufficient for raiding parties and cattle to be driven up or down as the case might be. For some time, however, peace had reigned in the area, but patrols were continually made to ensure that raiding didn't start up again. A corporal and four constables were considered sufficient for the needs of the area, so the pay parade didn't take very long. I promised myself that my next visit would be of longer duration as the whole area looked fascinating and I couldn't wait to see what the view was like from the top of the escarpment.

Our trip back to Kotido was quite rapid and, stopping only to collect the sheep and eggs, and pay the agreed five-shillings, we pressed on towards Moroto. It was just beginning to get dark by the time we reached the police station. Noel had left his office some time earlier so, leaving Ian to lock away the cash box and firearms, I walked up to Noel's bungalow. 'Glad you're back', said Noel. 'The *duka* owners have fixed a going-away party for Ian. It's also a welcome party for you.' I gave a mental groan. Having already experienced the hospitality of the *duka* owners, I could see that we were in for yet another boozy evening. I quickly bathed and changed and was ready to be off as soon as Noel. By half-past-seven we were down at the bazaar and being greeted by the various Asian and Somali shopkeepers. Ishverbhai Patel I had already met, also Madan Tandon and messers Tandon senior and Sharma. I was introduced to Ambalal Patel, Manibhai Patel and Tarin Shah. Of their wives and families there was no sign. The party was being held at the rear of Ishverbhai's shop. His small living room had been cleared of everything except chairs and tables and we were invited to sit down. A very considerable assortment of alcoholic beverages had been assembled. I stuck to beer. Shortly afterwards the other European officers, including Ian, started to arrive. Ishverbhai's small room rapidly filled and then overflowed outside where a number of pressure lamps had been hung up. A vast assortment of samoosas, pakhoras, and bhargies were produced together with roast groundnuts and curly toasties made from gram flour. It was fatal to put one's glass down as it was instantly filled again. Little speeches were made emphasising what a good and helpful chap Ian was and how badly he was going to be missed, and what a good chap I appeared to be and how helpful it was hoped I would be. Everyone got more than slightly pissed and at about 11 o'clock we all drove somewhat unsteadily home. '*Sitaki chakula*', said Noel as we entered. The boys cleared away the roast lamb and vegetables they had prepared for us. We sat down and, over a beer, discussed the safari, the party and the other officers.

The following morning I helped Ian do the final accounting on the pay safari. At the end of the day we were still six cents up so this found its way into the goat bag. 'I hardly like to mention this', said Ian, 'but do you by any chance want to buy any of my household gear? If I don't get rid of it here I shall have to dispose of it next week in Kampala before I push off, so if there's anything you want, I shall be only too pleased to flog it to you. I shan't be wanting much for it since you're taking Barney.' I had been wondering how I was going to be able to take over my own cottage with practically no household effects. This seemed a golden opportunity. Ian and I left the police station and made our way in his car to the house he was sharing with Dick Baker. In the course of the next hour I bought cushions, curtains, cutlery, crockery, pots and pans, four assorted oil lamps, a portable gramophone and a number of glasses. A refrigerator which ran on paraffin which I could have done with had already been purchased by Dick Baker, as had a radio. Still, by and large, I had not done too badly I felt. I gave Ian a cheque for ten pounds for the lot and hoped that my friendly Bank Manager would remain friendly.

After making these purchases I decided that it was time for me to inspect the cottage which I had been allocated. It was about 100-yards from Ian's house so we walked over. The work appeared to have been finished. The doors were locked, but on looking through the windows the rooms appeared to be in quite good order and everywhere inside had been freshly painted. A new mud hut had been erected in one corner of the garden which would be occupied by Kesi. While we were looking around a small bald man appeared from the bungalow next door. He introduced himself as Tom Hinett, in charge of the Public Works Department. I took an immediate liking to him. 'I'll get the keys so that you can have a good look at the place', he said in a pronounced Northern accent. He returned a few minutes later and we went into my new domain. It was certainly fairly basic but it was clean, and I felt I could make a remarkably comfortable home here. There were two main rooms, the bedroom and the sitting room. A door connected the two. Directly off the bedroom was the bathroom. The bath and wash basin were made of concrete. Quite cleverly done I thought. Bath water discharged directly outside on the ground where at some time a previous occupant had tried to grow a few vegetables. There were no taps. Water had to be brought in buckets from an outside wood-fuelled boiler, which was a 40 gallon tank mounted on a brick base. Next to the bathroom was a toilet, for which the Swahili term is *choo*, also made of concrete, with a wooden lid. Under the lid was placed a large bucket which had to be emptied via a flap at the rear, by a member of the township labour known as the abominable *choo* man. I soon discovered that one had to time one's visits to the *choo* rather carefully, to avoid being found there during the *choo* man's visits. If one was unlucky enough to be caught with trousers down the results could be quite painful. The *choo* man seemed quite used to this and would call out '*Jambo bwana*' or '*Jambo memsahib*', as the case might be. He was never known to be wrong! At the front of the bungalow was a wide verandah which ran the length of the two rooms. This was covered with mesh to prevent mosquitoes getting in. About ten yards from the rear of the building was the kitchen, brick-built and raised on a concrete base about 18 inches off the ground. This was equipped with a wood-burning stove. A large pile of *kuni* (firewood) stood in one corner. The bungalow was equipped with basic furniture, table, chairs, sideboard, wardrobe, bed with a rather hard mattress, also, four easy chairs were placed on the verandah.

'Come and have a drink and meet the family', said Tom. I accompanied him round to the next building. His bungalow was of a similar style to that of Noel's. A homely woman of about 35 greeted me. Tom introduced his wife Vi. Next came the children, three attractive girls, young Vi, Yvonne and Joyce and a small boy, Thomas. A tray of tea and biscuits and home-made cakes was produced. I breathed a sigh of relief. At least there was one person on the Station who did not automatically assume that beer was the only drink. 'You can move into your cottage any time you feel like it', said Tom. 'Hopefully you won't have to be there too long anyway. There's a building program on for several new houses, so it shouldn't be too long before you get something better.' I assured him that I thought the renovated cottage was just fine for my present needs and that I was looking forward to living next door to him and his family. I was not, of course, in a position to move into the cottage until Ian departed and I came into possession of the various bits and pieces I had bought from him.

The next couple of days flashed past. Saturday came and Ian departed. Barney was totally miserable at being left behind, but I made a fuss of him he cheered up a bit. I was duly installed into the cottage. My purchases were taken into use and Kesi moved into his thatched hut. I had expected him to protest at this but he appeared resigned to the idea. I suppose, having lived most of his life in a similar building it came as no great change to move back into one. I assured him that it would be only a temporary measure and he was quite happy at once more having a place of his own. Rain had started to be a regular feature each day. Nothing very heavy or prolonged as yet, and it was fairly predictable. Each day at about 3 o'clock, heavy clouds would come overhead, followed by a short, sharp shower, usually lasting for about half-an-hour, then the sun would appear once more and the rest of the day would be sunny. This was apparently the pattern the rainy season took in this part of the world. As the season progressed the rains would get earlier and more prolonged, but even in the wettest part of the season, most of the day was fine. This seemed to me to be an ideal weather situation. One could at least plan ahead which is more than can be said for English weather. During the rains the cattle-raiding season was at a low point, so little was reported apart from a couple of very minor incidents which were dealt with by the staff at Amudat. My time in these few early days was spent in going through various files which Ian had left for me to deal with. These mainly related to old cattle raids involving spear-blooding which had been investigated as far as possible but without any conclusive result. I found that quite a high percentage of these files ended up as 'undetected' due, in the main, to the lack of experienced investigation staff and the lack of reliable information which could be obtained.

One of my daily duties as 2 i/c Police was to visit the prison, which was situated a few hundred yards from the police station. The O.C. Police was also O.C. Prison here, a situation which existed in many of the outlying Districts of Uganda. There was a lot of extra responsibility attached to this post but no extra money was forthcoming. The prison was a depressing building entered by a large, reinforced timber gate which opened onto central courtyard. Blocks of cells were built around the outer wall. These were, for the most part, small and overcrowded. One section was for remand prisoners, mostly those arrested for cattle raids involving murder. These would be held, sometimes for months, waiting first for a preliminary enquiry which was carried out by Tony Hatch-Barnwell, who came up from Soroti for two or three days each month, and secondly for the High Court which came round on circuit for about a week once every three months. The remainder of the prisoners were short-term convicts who had, for the most part, been arrested and convicted locally for offences involving cattle theft, Game Ordinance or *Waragi* Ordinance. *Waragi* was a locally brewed spirit, the brewing, sale or possession of which was an offence. Occasionally a cattle raid offender would receive a comparatively light sentence if his part in the raid did not involve blooding his spear. In such cases he might receive only two or three years which might be served in Moroto Prison. Longer-term prisoners served their sentences in Luzira Prison at Port Bell on the outskirts of Kampala. My daily visits would involve a physical inspection of the prisoners, dealing with their complaints, holding enquiries into alleged misconduct with the resultant loss of remission, examining the prisoners' food, checking their rations to ensure that the staff wasn't nicking any of them and supervising corporal punishment when it was meted out. All of the prisoners had their exercise each day under the watchful eye of the warders, and those who were considered unlikely to try to escape would be taken out on working parties, cutting firewood, cultivating the fields in which green vegetables were grown and, if considered particularly trustworthy, working in the gardens of the O.C. Police and his 2i/c. One lunchtime shortly after I took over from Fergusson, I arrived home to find Kesi, beaming widely as he ordered a Karamajong prisoner to do the washing. From then on my tame Karamajong, who was serving two years for killing his wife during a drunken fight, was a regular feature of the Beaden menage. Never employ a thief, was the maxim followed in such cases. A murderer is O.K. as it's unlikely that he will repeat the offence. A thief will always be a thief.

Barney had accepted me as his new master and, of course, followed wherever I went. He also tolerated Kesi who fed him. Having thoroughly examined his new domain he settled down quite well and made sure that no unwelcome dogs were allowed anywhere near the premises. One lunchtime, shortly after moving into the cottage I was aroused by a great deal of angry shouting going on nearby. Going outside I saw Tom Hinett on the other side of the hedge. Barney had obviously been over there and was on his way back, smiling broadly. I walked over to see what the fuss was about. To my horror I found that Barney had torn open the mesh on top of Young Thomas's guinea pig run and had killed the guinea pig. Thomas was in tears and the whole family were clearly taking a dim view of the event. This was something that I was not going to put up with. There was absolutely no excuse for it. I apologised to Tom and Vi and promised to pay for a new guinea pig as soon as one could be obtained. With a sinking heart I took a length of rope and tied Barney to a tree next to the run. This was going to be a case of kill or cure. I cut a stick from the hedge and beat Barney till my arm ached. It seemed that he was never going to give in, he was such a strong dog. Eventually he yelled and I stopped. A very sore Barney limped back home. I followed and found him sitting dejectedly in a corner. I ignored him and eventually after thinking things over for about half-an-hour he came up to me and put his head in my lap. I felt a right bastard, but what else could I have done. He had to be taught that he simply couldn't go round killing anything that took his fancy. Anyway, the medicine worked. Barney, afterwards, never touched another animal unless he was either attacked or I told him to.

Each afternoon after finishing at the office I made my way up to the swimming pool. Barney always accompanied me on these trips. Usually Tom and Vi and their family found their way up there as well. Tom had an Austin van, from which he had cut the side-panels and inserted windows. Seats had also been installed for the children. The van looked somewhat old and battered but I found that in fact he had only had it for about a year. The damage was merely the result of Tom's frequent accidents. He was, it transpired, the world's worst driver. Although I got to know him very well, and we became the best of friends, his driving never improved.

The pool was without doubt, the most popular place in Moroto at that time. Sometimes over a dozen of its residents would gather there in the late afternoons and at weekends numbers would swell even further as lunches were taken there. At times numerous vervet monkeys would gather in the trees near the pool and some of them became sufficiently adventurous to climb down to collect morsels of food thrown to them. Barney didn't even turn a hair in response to these visitors. Clearly he had now learned his lesson. On my way up to the pool I invariably wore plimsolls and made my way quietly. This way I saw far more game than most of the others who usually announced their approach with maximum disturbance. On entering the clearing around the pool I often saw snakes making off into the bushes. These were usually cobras but there were a variety of others I could not at the time identify. Anyway, they seemed to follow the behavioural pattern of snakes in England and, if given the opportunity, would get out of the way as fast as possible. Nevertheless, I felt that it would be wise to carry a firearm of some sort with me in case I found something that would not give way so easily.

I had by now obtained my game licence, but the .22 rifle from the police armoury was much too heavy to be comfortably carted around. It was in fact a standard military .303 rifle which had been converted to .22 caliber by having a Parker Hale tube inserted in the barrel. Each evening great flocks of guinea fowl moved through the undergrowth at the foot of the mountain, on their way to their roosting sites. During a chat with Dick Baker he told me that he had a spare .22 rifle which he wanted to dispose of. After examining and testing it I decided that this was just the weapon I needed. It had a magazine which held ten shots, open sights and was deadly accurate at up to 100 yards. I went to the D.C's office where Dick himself issued me with a gun licence at a cost of five-shillings and I gave him a post-dated cheque for the gun for the agreed price of five pounds.

About a week after I moved into my cottage I became aware of the major disadvantages of having no fridge. I was plagued with tiny sugar ants which swarmed all over the place whenever food was available. These were a real pain in the arse. Putting the food away in the sideboard was no deterrent. The little buggers climbed up the wooden legs, under the doors and covered everything. I found a partial cure to this by standing the legs in tins of paraffin, but a few particularly crafty ones climbed to the ceiling and then dropped to the top of the sideboard. It was necessary to be very vigilant and have the faithful Flit spray handy at all times. Furthermore, any perishable food rapidly perished. Worst of all, I had no cold beer, so no one would visit me. I assumed that I would be able to do nothing about this until I was able to get to Kampala or one of the larger towns. This could be months away. One day while making my meager purchases from Ishverbhai Patel I happened to mention my problem. 'Sir, let me get you a fridge from my brother in Mbale. What size would you like?', said Ishverbhai. I explained that I shouldn't be able to pay him for a couple of months but he was quite happy about this and, lo and behold, two days later there arrived a brand new fridge, together with a four gallon *debi* of paraffin to run it. I invited Noel round for a couple of beers to celebrate the evening after my new acquisition arrived. Unfortunately, on opening the first bottle I discovered that I had misjudged the size of the flame required for working the fridge satisfactorily. The beer was frozen solid. However, fortunately some of the other bottles stored in a different area were still drinkable so these, together with freshly-roasted groundnuts, prepared by Kesi, meant that my first effort at entertaining a guest was not a complete failure.

Karamoja was now experiencing some very prolonged thunder storms. Heavy rain was now falling in various areas. These made safaris somewhat hazardous. Not having had any experience of the power of the many river crossing in spate I was, therefore, somewhat perturbed on going in to the office one morning to find a message from Kacheliba reporting a suspected murder. 'Here you are', said Noel, 'In at the deep end.' And in at the deep end I was. First, down to see Madan Tandon about transport, then home to inform Kesi and instruct him in collecting up food, bedding and so on. Meanwhile, Noel had been busy, and on my return to the office I found the storeman already loading the lorry. In view of my inability to understand either Karamajong or Suk or Kiswahili I was allocated a young constable who could at least translate for me from Kiswahili to English. We had to hope that we would be able to find some local who could translate for us from Suk to Kiswahili, when the investigation commenced. I had serious misgivings about this. Single translation in the hands, or rather the mouth of someone undoubtedly inexpert in the process, could lead to mistakes. Doubling the translations could, I felt, probably treble the chances of errors arising in the process.

However, it appeared that this was considered normal procedure in such cases so I could only hope for the best. Doctor Musoke the local G.P. had been alerted and on his arrival I was introduced to him. He had with him not only his medical equipment, for use should we come across someone needing his expertise during our safari, but also his autopsy equipment for carrying out the necessary post mortem on the victim, if there were any remains left to examine. It seemed unlikely that the long journey and the investigation would be completed in one day so the full safari kit had to be packed on board. Dr Musoke and I climbed aboard and settled into the armchairs. Barney took up his usual position, but this time by my feet. Kesi and two additional constables completed our party. Within an hour of arrival at the office I found myself on my way to investigate a suspected murder. My previous most serious investigation had been the false pretences job by Mrs Farmer.

Fortunately the weather was fine when we set out and we made good progress. Most of the rivers we came to had plenty of water flowing in them, but none had enough to impede our progress. Several times it was considered necessary to fit a rubber pipe over the end of the exhaust so that, should we get stuck in the middle of the river, and the engine cut out at least the water wouldn't flow back and flood it. We decided not to stop on route for sustenance but to press on to Kacheliba, time being of the essence. We reached our destination at about mid-day. Here the river was in full spate and almost up to the level of the bridge crossing it. Obviously there had been some very heavy rain on Mount Elgon. I was informed that it had been flowing like this for the past week. The sergeant at the police post reported to us. The suspect, one Korit, had been arrested and was being kept handcuffed in one of the rondavels. The body of the deceased was lying about a mile away down stream where it had been taken from the river. The local chief was in attendance at the police post. I decided that my first step would be to interview him with the object of getting some idea of what had happened. Here I was fortunate inasmuch as he could speak Swahili so the translation was made a bit easier than anticipated. The deceased was one Alobut who was the brother-in-law of the accused Korit. There was a history of animosity between the two, arising from an argument about the bride-price of Alubot's wife. Two days earlier they had gone out together on a hunting expedition. Korit had returned carrying Alubot's weapons and saying that Alubot had fallen into the river and had not been seen again. His body had been recovered the following day a mile downstream from Kacheliba, being about eight miles from where he was reported to have fallen in. The accused, Korit had, I found, been badly beaten-up by the relatives of the deceased. I interrogated him. Here problems arose. Cautioning him, 'that he need not say anything unless he wished to do so but that anything he did say would be taken down in writing and might be used in evidence', proved cumbersome to say the least, even translated once. Translating it twice from English into poor Swahili and finally from poor Swahili into the primitive Suk dialect was asking altogether too much. All the unfortunate accused understood, eventually, was that under no circumstances was he to say a word or he would undoubtedly be hung. Needless to say he shut up like a clam. I decided to start again abandoning any thought of cautions, but just trying to get him to tell me his side of the story. With considerable effort I persuaded him and wrote down what I gathered had happened. 'Alubot and I decided that we would go out together and try to kill some *nyama* (animal, bird). This was in the morning, two days ago. We each took our spear and a bow and arrows. At about 9 o'clock in the morning we were in the bush about eight miles from here, not far from the river. We did see some animals and tried to get near enough to kill them but they saw us and ran away. Alubot then saw a honey guide (a bird about the size of a thrush). We decided that we would see if we could get some honey instead. We followed the honey guide for a mile, till we came to the bank of the river, which was flowing very fast. Here we saw the bees nest in a dead tree leaning out over the water. Alubot made a fire with some sticks and then took some lighted grass up the tree to the nest. He then blew the smoke from the grass into the bees nest and after a few minutes broke away the dead wood and started to get out the honey. He threw several pieces of honey down to me. Then the bees attacked him and as he tried to get out of their way he fell off into the water.'

'He shouted several times and waved his arms. I know he could swim a bit and thought that he would get out of the water further downstream. I ran down the river bank following him. Then he went under and I lost sight of him. I never saw him again till his body was found the following day. I went back to my *manyatta* and reported the matter to the *mukungu* chief. Alubot's brothers came along and beat me because they thought I had killed him. I know I had not been on good terms with Alubot but I did not kill him. In fact we had become quite friendly recently and were planning to kill an ox to celebrate our new understanding.'

On the face of it the story seemed quite plausible, but first it was necessary to examine the body. Accompanied by Doctor Musoke, various policemen, the *makungu* chief and about 50 hangers on we made our way downstream to the point where the body had been found. A pile of brushwood had been placed on top of the corpse to protect it from the attentions of the vultures and hyenas. Nevertheless the trees all round were thick with the various carrion-eaters. Marabou storks, with their pendulous crops hanging from their necks, Egyptian vultures, Griffon vultures and several others I was unable to identify sat around. Guests awaiting the funeral feast. Nearby I saw several silver-backed jackals lurking in the undergrowth, hoping to take their share.

The branches were cleared away and I saw a naked bloated body lying on its back on the ground. The corpse had blown up like a Michelin Man. The *makungu* chief assured me that this was Alubot. I first took a number of photographs from various angles and distances. Numerous marks about the size of peas were still visible on the face and abdomen of the corpse, particularly around the eyes. Many of the marks still contained the stings of the bees which had stung him, and which had detached from the insects after the damage was done. There was no doubt at all that Alubot had been badly stung prior to his death. Doctor Musoke then examined the body and agreed that these marks were bee stings. 'Do you want me to carry out a post mortem?' He asked me. I most certainly did! I felt a bit sorry for Musoke. His was a lousy job at the best of times. Cutting up a body in this condition was not going to be all fun. I stood away at a safe distance as he made the first incision. The policemen and hangers on crowded round for a better view. The scalpel penetrated the bloated abdomen. The body literally burst like a balloon, showering stinking guts, blood and mucous in all directions. The audience fled. The stench was appalling. Poor Musoke, crouched over the body, had copped the lot. I must give him his due. He had a very strong stomach. Smiling somewhat desperately he invited me over to view the rest of the proceedings. In the circumstances I felt that I could hardly do otherwise. The stench was still ghastly but the worst was over. I stood by the side of the corpse as the trachea and lungs were removed. Musoke pointed out the various bits of river debris still embedded in these organs. There was no doubt that Alubot had died of drowning. Almost certainly his death had been accidental. Only one thing remained. I wanted to have a look at the bees nest. We returned to the police post, leaving the corpse to be disposed of by the local sanitary squad in the traditional manner of the Suk. Within an hour nothing would be left, and a lot of heavily-laden marabou storks and vultures would be flapping their way home. Leaving Musoke to clean himself up, I boarded the lorry together with the prisoner, the *makungu* chief and three policemen. Fortunately we were able to drive to within a couple of miles of the scene of the tragedy. Korit then guided us the rest of the way. The scene was just as he had described it. Bees in their hundreds still flew in and out of the hole in the tree trunk about 20 feet above the water. I could clearly see where the dead wood had been broken away to enlarge the hole. There was no honey to be seen but this was no doubt due to the honey guide and the local ant population clearing it up. The remains of the fire which had been built were clearly visible. The final verification of Korit's story came when the honey guide appeared on a nearby branch and for several minutes flew up to the bees nest and back to his perch in the hope of getting someone else to obtain some honey for him.

I returned to the lorry and back to Kacheliba. The time was now 4 o'clock. The radio at the police post was out of order. Had I overlooked anything? This was my first major investigation. I could find no evidence of a crime having been committed. Was I safe in letting the accused go free? I wished I could have a chat with Noel to get his opinion. I made my decision. If we left immediately we could get to Amudat before the radio closed down. I could send my report and see what advice was forthcoming. Everything was packed back on the lorry and we were away. To be on the safe side I took along the *makungu* chief and Korit. As we set off the rain started to sheet down. It turned out that there was a well-tried procedure for this. Our armchairs were turned to face backwards. A heavy tarpaulin was rigged over the back of the lorry as far as it would reach and some degree of protection was obtained. Sitting in these confines I rapidly became conscious of the fact that Doctor Musoke had not made a very thorough job of cleaning away the remains of the burst corpse. I had to make the best of this though. I guess it was worse for him than it was for me. Fortunately we were able to negotiate the various river crossings on the way and at half- past-five drew into the police post at Amudat. By this time I had composed a message covering the outcome of the investigation and requesting further instructions. Handing this to the radio operator I sat down in the rondavel being used as an office and gratefully accepted a cup of tea which Kesi brought me. An hour passed. On my instructions the radio operator stayed on the air. Eventually the reply came. 'Well done. Come home', it read. I breathed a sigh of relief. Just one small snag. What about the *makungu* chief and Korit? I certainly wasn't going all the way back to Kacheliba with them. I gave my instructions to the sergeant. 'You'll have to find accommodation for them overnight. In the morning tell them to start walking!' If there was any remaining animosity between then they had 60 miles to sort it out! This final detail being settled we all boarded the lorry and set off. With luck I should be able to spend tonight in my comfortable bed after all. Alas, it was not to be. Twenty miles out of Amudat we came to a river. Crossing it was clearly out of the question. Another lorry, belonging to one of the traders from Moroto was already in trouble, stuck in the middle and in danger of being washed away. Ropes were rapidly produced and the turnboy from the other lorry threw the end across the flood. Somehow or other the ends of the rope were attached between the two vehicles and our lorry backed off taking up the slack. Everyone, including myself got out and pushed and shoved and gradually the other lorry was drawn back out of the river. Eventually it was back on the bank, high and comparatively dry. Now we all settled down to wait. Four hours went by. Musoke and I consumed a couple of bottles of beer each and I tried to disregard his dreadful stench. Now the water level was noticeably dropping. Within a further half-hour it was considered safe to make the attempt. First the other lorry went. It had to because there was no way we could get past it. Lurching and revving, it eventually managed to get to the other side where it pulled in and waited in case we needed assistance. Our turn came. The rubber pipe over our exhaust belched smoke and fumes into the air. We bounced about on the dislodged boulders on the river bottom and were eventually across. With much shouting and sounding of hooters the two lorries started off again towards Moroto. The rest of the journey was comparatively without incident and at 4 o'clock in the morning we pulled in to the police station at Moroto. First I called into the station office and dispatched a constable to rouse the storeman. While he was arriving the lorry made its way to my bungalow where Kesi and one of the constables unloaded my gear. By five o'clock I was in bed, but unable to get to sleep. I lay awake turning over the events of the past twenty-four hours. As soon as it was light I got up and roused Kesi. Half-an-hour later I was wallowing in a hot bath and with a cup of tea by my side. By 8 o'clock I was down at the police station. Shortly afterwards Noel arrived, looking somewhat surprised at seeing me. 'You didn't waste any time did you', he commented. I thought you'd be away at least three days.' I gave him an account of the events. 'Well', he said, 'very well done. I certainly couldn't have done better. Now, I think you ought to pop off home and get a bit of shut eye. I'll see you this afternoon if you feel up to it.' Thus ended my first bit of police work in Uganda.

CHAPTER 10

After a refreshing sleep and a hearty lunch I made my way down to the police station. Noel arrived shortly afterwards. I noticed that he was in a particularly good mood. At first I flattered myself that this must be due to the successful outcome of my investigation. I was wrong. He was obviously bursting to tell me some news. Eventually I asked him what it was. 'Our troubles are over!' he said. 'We shan't need to hire lorries from now on. Headquarters have decided to give us a Land Rover and trailer, together with a driver, so we shall now be able to go out whenever we need without the trouble of hiring transport.' He produced, for my inspection, the signal from Kampala imparting the good news. From this I gathered that our new vehicle was due to arrive four days hence. All seemed joy and contentment. I then started to have a few thoughts on the subject. The Land Rover was undoubtedly a wonderful vehicle for rough terrain. But how would it stand up to crossing flooded rivers. It wouldn't have sufficient weight to hold on the bottom in deep water. Moreover, would this affect my own position? I had been hopeful of eventually getting a car of my own. There was a special scheme whereby officers could obtain a government loan at a very low rate of interest, for the purchase of a motor vehicle, after they had been in the country for six months. A monthly vehicle allowance and mileage allowance covered the cost of repayment of the loan. If a Land Rover was provided it might be considered unnecessary for me to have a car of my own. I voiced my feelings to Noel. On the first point he had no doubt that the Land Rover would cope very well with the river crossings. 'If the water's too deep we'll just have to wait a bit longer for it to go down.' He was quite sure that the acquisition of the Land Rover wouldn't affect my entitlement to a car loan. I was sufficiently reassured to join in a celebration drink that lunchtime, which meant that not very much work was done during the afternoon.

'What about a garage for the Land Rover and trailer?' I said to Noel, shortly after the news of its arrival had sunk in. 'No chance', he replied. 'I'll put it in the estimates at the end of the financial year. If it's approved we might get it built in a couple of years' time. Headquarters don't like spending money unless they really have to and they are bound to take the view that there are far more important things to spend money on.' I made no reply to this but determined to have a word with my friend Tom Hinett to see if he could think of a way round the problem.

The following evening I made my way over to Tom's bungalow. He and his family greeted me warmly. They even allowed Barney in. 'You'll stay for supper.' said Vi. and without waiting for my agreement laid another place at the table. After a couple of bottles of beer and an excellent meal, I was inveigled into playing canasta with them. Not my favourite sort of pastime and I got thoroughly beaten. I suspected that there was some degree of teamwork being used to my detriment, but made no comment. Eventually I broached the subject of a garage. Tom was immediately enthusiastic. 'Can you supply any prison labour for digging out?' he enquired. 'No problem', I told him. 'Right', he said, 'what I propose is something like this.' He drew out an enormous building, and included a large inspection pit. 'Hang on a minute Tom', said I, 'I haven't got any money for this you know.' 'Not to worry', said Tom, 'I've got a bit left over from one or two of my votes. We'll see what we can do.'

The following morning I was at the office early. I had a quick look round at the proposed site for the garage before Noel arrived. Some time later when we had settled into the office routine, I again broached the subject. 'Now it's no good going on about it', said Noel. 'I've told you I'll put it in the estimates and see what happens.' 'What happens if we just build it without reference to Headquarters?', I enquired. 'Now be sensible', said Noel. 'In the first place we've got no money. I'm sure that Headquarters would be delighted if a garage just appeared by magic, but such things don't happen. In any case you can't go around building things without telling the D.C. He has to approve any plans before anything can be done.' 'I can get a garage built for nothing', I said. 'Moreover it will be large enough to use for vehicle examinations when the Inspector of Vehicles comes up for his annual inspection and licensing of all the lorries. And it will have an inspection pit.' 'I don't believe what I'm hearing', said Noel. 'What the hell have you been up to.' I told him of my conversation with Tom. 'Well, I don't know what sort of pull you've been exerting', he said, 'but it sounds bloody marvellous. Do you think you can get some rough plans drawn up?' If you can I'll take them over to show Sandy Field. I'm sure he won't raise any objections.'

At lunchtime I again went to see Tom and as a result he

arrived at the office at about 3 o'clock. Together with Noel we had a look at the proposed site. 'We shall have to put in another couple of tracks', said Tom. 'One to drive in and the other straight out at the other end after the inspection.' By the following morning Tom had prepared the plans and Noel took them over to Sandy Field who was as enthusiastic as the rest of us. The only people who were not informed were those at Police Headquarters. 'We'll keep it as a surprise for the next visit by the Commissioner', said Noel. I wondered what sort of reaction we should get to this bit of unauthorised initiative. I hoped that Tom would make a good job of it. If not I could see that my job was going to be on the line! Progress was rapid on the new project. Tom marked out the lines for the footings and I organised labour parties from the prison to do the digging. Meanwhile Tom was up at the brickfield organising the making and burning of thousands of additional bricks. I decided that I could leave the whole project in his capable hands. While these preliminaries were going on a signal arrived from Headquarters. 'Land Rover and trailer leaving Kampala 06.00 hours 12-8-51. Also consignment of 30 new .303rifles and ammunition. Driver Kintu. E.T.A. 12.00 hours 13-8-51.' So, at last our new vehicle was on its way.

During the night I was awakened by torrential rain. This was about as heavy a downpour as I had ever experienced. In my sleepy state I wondered what this would do to the Mani-mani River. It crossed my mind that, if this weather hit Napak Mountain the river crossing at Kangole was going to have a fair amount of water in it by morning. Still these storms were generally pretty localised. Napak was 50 miles away and probably wasn't affected. I went back to sleep. The morning dawned, bright and sunny as usual. The stream bed on the opposite side of the road from my cottage, usually dry as a bone was a raging torrent, but apart from this everything was completely normal. I started to walk down to the office. Noel caught me up on the way and gave me a lift. We went to look at our new garage site. The trenches dug for the footings were practically full of water. The gang of prisoners was already hard at work, bailing out. Back in the office we settled into the daily routine. Mid-day came and we began watching the road for the arrival of our Land Rover. At half-past-twelve we gave it up and went home for lunch. Two o'clock and we were back in the office. At half past two a naked Karamajong arrived with a note tucked into a cleft stick. Our Land Rover was in the Mani-mani. Washed half-a-mile down stream. The driver and two constables with him had managed to swim ashore! Send help!

Poor Noel. I thought he would never come down off the ceiling. The names he called Driver Kintu don't bear repeating. Down we went to Pandit Puran Chand and hired a lorry, together with some heavy tow ropes. 'I'm not worried about the Land Rover', said Noel, 'but if any of those rifles and ammo have gone missing there will be hell to pay!'

Noel and I went out to the Mani-mani in his car, the lorry following behind. The road was sticky with mud but passable. The Mani-mani when we reached it was in flood. A solid five-feet of water was rushing over the concrete ramp. Of our Land Rover there was no sign. A couple of lorries were parked on each side of the river, waiting for the water level to drop before attempting the crossing. A very bedraggled-looking constable met us as we got out of the car. His hat was missing but he saluted us just the same. 'What the hell happened?', said Noel. 'Sir, when we reached the river the lorries were waiting. The drivers told Kintu that we could not get across till the water dropped. Kintu said, 'I've got a special gear for crossing rivers.' He drove into the water and next thing we were upside down and our Land Rover was being rolled over and over downstream.' 'How did you manage to get out?', was Noel's next question. Apparently one of the doors flew open as the vehicle was progressing downstream and the three occupants managed to scramble out. 'Pity that bloody Kintu wasn't drowned', said Noel. 'I'll make the bugger wish he had been by the time I've finished with him.' We made our way down river and after about half-a-mile came upon the Land Rover, caught up behind a fallen tree. It looked very sad. Even sadder looked Driver Kintu who sat on the bank crying his eyes out. The second constable stood beside him. I spent the next ten minutes taking photographs of our drowned vehicle. The river at this point was a bit shallower, about three feet of water. Fortunately, the vehicle had finished its watery progress right way up and on our side of the river. Furthermore, there was a rough track along the river bank along which the lorry was now making its way. 'I don't see why we should get wet', said Noel. 'That bloody driver can go in and hitch up the ropes.' Driver Kintu was only too keen to try to make amends and waded in to the front of the vehicle. I noticed then that a trailer was bobbing about in the water behind the Land Rover. I hoped that the rifles had not been in that or they would be miles downstream by now. The rope now safely hitched onto the front of the vehicle, the other end was attached to the front of the lorry. With much revving and complaining from the lorry, the Land Rover was gradually drawn out of its watery grave. Noel and I immediately looked inside and were relieved to find that the boxes containing the rifles and ammunition were all present and correct. Apart from the mud and debris festooned all over the vehicle, it didn't look too much the worse for wear. The rifles and ammunition were transferred to Noel's car and Driver Kintu resumed his seat in the Land Rover while it was being towed to Moroto police station.

Our first job, of course, on reaching the office, was to compose a suitable message to be transmitted to police headquarters. Next, a fatigue party was summoned to unpack and clean the rifles. Fortunately, the metal containers full of ammunition were watertight so no harm could have come to them. The rifles, however, had to be dealt with fast. All of them were well covered with grease and by the time the fatigue party had finished six hours later we were able to report that the arms were all present and correct. Meantime, Noel and I had been hard at work filling in the accident report and recording statements from every one who could conceivably have had any information to impart. All of the witnesses to the incident were agreed that Driver Kintu had been repeatedly warned not to try to cross the river. All of them also agreed that he had insisted that 'he had a special gear to enable him to do so'. The evidence was incontrovertible and when it came to Driver Kintu's turn he also admitted that it was the case. Noel immediately suspended him from duty to await the next visit of the District Magistrate when he would appear on a charge of dangerous driving.

The following day Madan Tandon sent one of his mechanics to the police station and the Land Rover engine was drained of oil and river water and filled with clean oil to avoid as far as possible, further corrosion damage. Meantime, a message arrived from police headquarters informing us that a breakdown vehicle would be dispatched immediately to collect our Land Rover for repair in Kampala. A new vehicle and driver was being sent on the same transport. Two days later our replacement vehicle arrived without incident, together with Driver Odongo, a cheerful little man who spoke no English and, being a Moslem, called all officers *effendi*!

Our new garage was progressing apace. The foundations were in and the inspection pit had been dug and lined with brick. The oversite concrete was down and bricklaying had commenced on the walls, the ends of the building were being left open for vehicles to drive in and out. Once Tom had made up his mind to do a job he certainly got stuck in. I was happy to leave it all to him after this.

Noel decided that it was time that he had a look round the outposts to christen our new vehicle. The policy was for both the O.C. Police and his 2 i/c to each spend a minimum of ten days each month on safari. This ensured that the outposts were adequately supervised and that the officers collected their night allowances, which amounted to 12-shillings per night. I liked the idea of this since it cost practically nothing in food while on safari and it would also assist in a most practical fashion to eliminate my overdraft. He was sufficiently confident in my ability by this time to let me take charge. 'After all', he said, 'if you have any problems you're not sure about you can soon get in touch. You've got a note of my itinerary.' And so, loading up the safari gear into the trailer and accompanied by his houseboy and one constable, he was off on his travels.

On the day following Noel's departure I was busily going through the various files and books in my office when the prisons' sergeant reported to me. He was as tall as myself, an Acholi by tribe, an ex-army N.C.O. strict disciplinarian and as tough as old boots. Unfortunately he spoke no English and my Swahili was not yet sufficient to understand precisely what he was talking about. I could get the word '*Nyoka*' repeated frequently, and I knew this to mean snake. I called Mr Sentamu, the clerk, who translated. 'Sir, one of the prisoners had been bitten by a snake', he said. 'The snake is dead.' It crossed my mind that this should be the other way round. 'What about the prisoner? ' I said. 'He is outside.' I was told. I went out. On the verandah was a rough stretcher made from a few branches lashed together. On it lay a prisoner, already unconscious and looking as though he could only last a few minutes longer. Also, lying alongside, was an enormous puff adder which had had its head crushed. The puff adder, I knew was one of the most deadly snakes in Africa. This one was well over five feet in length. Probably a record size for the species. It was as thick as a man's leg and probably weighed about 20 pounds. The prisoner had been bitten on the left ankle. 'When did this happen?', I said. 'About half-an-hour ago.' I was told. 'He was working in the prison *shamba* and trod on it.' I felt sure that medical aid would at this stage be too late, but nevertheless I grabbed a piece of rope from the Charge Office and bound it tightly above the wounds. Then together with the party carrying the stretcher we set off at a run for the hospital, about half-a-mile away. I took the precaution of sending one of the constables on ahead on his bicycle and by the time we arrived Doctor Musoke was waiting for us with a syringe of anti–venine at the ready. After administering the dose and examining the victim, Musoke said, 'I don't give much for his chances. The venom of the puff adder is a blood coagulant. If he lasts the next 24 hours he might make it but I can't see it happening.' I returned to my office. The Prison sergeant accompanied me. 'Why did you not get him straight down to the hospital?', I enquired. 'Sir, I could not take him to hospital with informing you. The doctor would have sent us away again.' I spent the next few minutes telling the. sergeant what he would do in similar circumstances in the future, and wondered what the Coroner would make of it if the prisoner died! Meanwhile, I examined the great snake. I had been interested in these reptiles ever since I kept slow-worms and grass snakes as a youngster. What a beautifully marked skin it had. I decided that I would remove the skin and stretch and dry it. 'Are there many of these around? ' I enquired. 'Oh, yes Sir, very many', I was told. 'Right, if you kill any more, send them round to my house. Meantime, you can get this one up there. Tell my houseboy to take care of it and I will attend to it when I get home.' Thus, to the horror of Kesi, a succession of snakes of various sorts began to be brought to my bungalow, and I started gaining a reputation as a herpetologist. On my return home from the office that afternoon I set about skinning the snake. I commenced by making a cut from the underside of the lower jaw, down to the tip of the tail. Then I carefully peeled the skin from the body at about mid-line. Tom Hinett and his family arrived about this time to view the proceedings. Once I was able to get my hand round the back of the serpent, under its skin the process became quite simple. The entire skin from mid-line to the tail peeled away easily. 'Ooh, how can you do that? ' said Vi. I couldn't touch the beastly thing.' I explained that I had a fair amount of experience in skinning rabbits and this was not that different. I then recommenced the skinning process, this time from the mid-line up to the head. Skinning the head was not so easy, but with a bit of cutting I eventually succeeded. Having got so far I decided to examine in some detail the fangs on this monster. I found them to be two-and-a-half inches in length. This was something of an eye-opener for me. I never dreamed that any snake could have a killing apparatus anything like this size. The fangs were hollow down their entire length, just like hypodermic syringes. Anyone bitten by this creature would get the entire contents of the poison ducts injected at least two inches deep into the flesh. How on earth could the prisoner hope to survive? As I was examining the fangs, quantities of yellow venom were oozing from the tips. I was careful not to get any of this onto my hands as I didn't know if it could have any effect if it came into contact with the skin. Probing a bit deeper I found no fewer that two additional sets of fangs waiting to grow out should the first set be damaged in any way. Seeing what I had in mind, Tom produced a wide wooden board and some small nails. I stretched the skin and tacked it into position. Finally I rubbed quantities of salt into the damp surface to preserve it. Having got thus far with my examination I decided that it might be interesting to examine the stomach contents to see what the snake had been feeding on. I split the tissue over the stomach area and tipped the contents out. These consisted of a ground squirrel and two rats, plus a quantity of other debris which was too decomposed to identify. The stench was appalling. Almost as bad as the decomposing corpse I had dealt with a few days earlier. Tom and his family beat a hasty retreat!

On the following morning, after dealing with the office routine, I made my way to the hospital. Doctor Musoke greeted me. 'How's the prisoner?', I enquired. 'Still alive, and he's regained consciousness', I was told. I went into the ward where there were about 20 patients. My prisoner sat up in bed looking sorry for himself. Of the prison warders there was no sign. 'Where's his escort?', I enquired. 'Oh, there isn't one', I was informed. 'I guess they thought it unlikely that he would run away.' I wrote a quick note to the prison sergeant and sent it off with a runner. The next half-hour I spent at the hospital. I certainly didn't intend allowing a prisoner to escape and with the progress he appeared to be making he could have been up and away in double-quick-time unless a guard ensured his continued presence.

For the past few days I had been too busy to visit the swimming pool. The weather had, anyway, been a bit dull and overcast, but today was fine and I fancied a nice cooling swim. Taking my rifle and accompanied by Barney I made my way up the mountain track. On reaching the pool I was appalled by the sight. The torrential storm of a few nights earlier had brought down great quantities of mud from the stream bed higher up the mountain. The pool was totally filled with it. What a mess. On my way back I met Tom and his family. I told them what had happened. The kids were, of course, most disappointed. Faced with the remainder of their school holidays and no pool to swim in. Clearly something had to be done. I sent a message to the prison sergeant and within half-an-hour he was waiting outside my house. I went with him up to the pool. Yes, he could supply a gang of prison trusties on the following day, but no warder was available. I sent a message to the Head Constable and in due course he arrived. I gave him the necessary instruction and, on the following morning, as I walked down to the office, I was passed by a gang of ten prisoners and a constable on their way to the pool. At lunch time I went to see what progress had been made. The clearing job was nearly finished. The constable stood knee deep in the mud and gave me a butt salute with the rifle he carried. I left rapidly before he got out. I had no wish to see the state of his boots which were undoubtedly ruined! Sufficient unto the day! The job was finished by mid-afternoon and by the following evening, much to the delight of everyone on the station, the pool was once more back in use.

I had taken to playing my gramophone most evenings. I must now confess to being strongly moved by some music. A particular passage will have tears starting from my eyes and I find great difficulty in hiding my emotions. Having brought with me from England my favourite records I had fallen into the habit of playing one or two each evening. I have always been very fond of classical music and I suppose that my selection from the many records I had was an early form of 'Desert Island Discs'. Debussy, Dvorak, Tchaicovsky, Brahms, Greig, Elgar, Sibelius, I sat back and enjoyed the lot. Happening to glance up at my gramophone during a particularly moving passage of Bruch's Violin Concerto, I was startled to see what appeared to be a tiny fat squirrel sitting on the edge of the gramophone case, apparently closely studying the revolving turntable. I didn't move for fear of disturbing the little creature. Its colour was grey, its size, that of a large mouse and a great fluffy tail stuck out at the back at just the angle that a squirrel would carry its tail. When I made a move at the end of the record, it vanished. I rubbed my eyes and wondered if I had been hallucinating. I went over to the machine. There was no sign whatever, but I was quite sure that, had it run away, I would have seen the movement. I wound up the gramophone and changed the record. I sat back and watched. After a few minutes the little animal appeared again — out of the sound box. Evidently Chopin was not to its liking because after a minute or two it clambered down the table leg and out under the door. This, then, was my first encounter with the Grey African Dormouse. A charming little creature. How it has never become a popular pet animal I shall never understand. Much later I kept one as a pet and found it ideal in every way.

Each Tuesday and Saturday a bus run by Madan Tandon of Pandit Puran Chand's garage arrived at the end of its run from Soroti to Moroto. In addition to the mail which it carried this also brought the twice-weekly supplies of perishable foods from De Souza's, a Goan-run grocers in Soroti. The European officers would send their orders down by the bus on Mondays and Thursdays and the goodies would arrive on the bus in cardboard boxes at the garage from where they would be collected by the claimants. This had to be done as soon as possible after the bus arrived as fresh butter, fish, meat and vegetables soon spoiled in the heat. I had taken to getting a small order each week, now that I had my fridge. Saturday arrived and Noel was still swanning around on his safari. Knowing that I was without transport Tom called round and offered me a lift to the garage to pick up the supplies. I accepted gratefully. On our arrival I found that a box was also awaiting Noel. I collected this as well as my own, and Tom drove me home. Having disposed of my goodies I took the other box round to Noel's house. Of his boys there was no sign. I went to the kitchen door intending to deposit the perishables in the fridge. Somewhat to my surprise I found an attractive Muganda girl of about 25 years sitting in the lounge. I think she was as startled as I was. She was well-dressed and clearly way above the standard of woman one would have expected to find living with the servants. 'Hello', I said, 'who are you? ' She informed me that her name was Sophia and she was the bwana's *bibi*. I must admit that I was a bit shaken by this information. I had no inkling that Noel had taken an African mistress. Still it was none of my business so I disposed of the groceries and returned home.

Noel returned later the same day. The following morning he called round at my house for a beer and to tell me about his safari. I didn't raise the subject of my earlier discovery but he obviously knew that I had been round to his house and knew all about the situation. Eventually he spoke about it himself and was quite open about it. 'She's been with me for the past three years', he said. 'You know what they say about learning a language. Get a good dictionary, take it to bed and open it at the same page each night! 'Sophia could speak practically no English but Noel, over the past three years had learned good Swahili and more than a smattering of Luganda. 'Fortunately she can't have children, which is an advantage for me, but she's no good on the marriage market. I paid her father some money and I've also paid for her to have a house built, where she lives when she goes to see her family or if I'm away on leave. It's a good system. You should try it!' I tried not to look too disapproving, but said that I thought, probably not, as I was already engaged to be married. On subsequent visits to Noel's house, Sophia made no effort to hide away, but always greeted me with a welcoming smile and word. Maybe she thought that she could encourage me to take on one of her sisters!

The border conference which Dick Hook had mentioned to me was scheduled to take place the following week. 'I don't think we should both attend, ' said Noel. 'One of us had better hang on here in case anything blows up. I'll attend the conference and you can do the pay parade the week after. I'll leave the Land Rover here for your use. I'll take my car and that will give me a bit of extra mileage.' This suited me fine. I couldn't help feeling though, that the timing of the conference left something to be desired. The rains were lessening but there were still the odd storms around, and rivers had a habit of rising dramatically within a few minutes. However, I had no doubt that Noel knew what he was doing. He wouldn't be on his own anyway. Sandy Field, Arthur Brown, Sandy Taylor and Dick Heron were also attending the conference, as were their opposite numbers from Teso District, and all were taking their own transport. Apparently the object of the exercise was to iron out any problems about border raids and other incursions, grazing, forestry, boreholes and so on. It was also a good get-together which took place annually and enabled officers to renew old acquaintanceships and drink a few beers.

I was surprised to see Dick Baker in my office the following morning. He didn't seem to be in a particularly good mood. 'I don't know what things are coming to', he said. 'I've been in Moroto now for over a year and never had a thing stolen in all that time. I never lock up my house. As far as I was aware the locals are totally honest. Now some bastard has pinched a couple of cushions off my verandah. It's got to be one of the houseboys. There's no way that a cushion would be any good to a Karamajong.' I enquired if anything else was missing. 'Well I've not checked completely, ' said Dick, 'I left in a hurry to report the matter to you. I'll slip back home in a few minutes and make a more thorough check.' I promised that I would be up at his house in about half-an-hour and settled down to finish off the oddments I was working on, then I made my way up to Dick's house. After examining the scene of the crime we settled down for a couple of beers. 'Nothing else has gone', he told me. 'They were here when I turned in about 10 o'clock last night.' 'Did you hear anything during the night?' I enquired. 'Not a thing', he told me. 'Funny old business', I thought. 'I can't see much chance of getting a result here. Karamoja's a big place and two cushions could soon be disposed of.' Looking over the edge of the verandah I noticed a couple of hyena droppings. I had a sudden thought. 'I'll just have a bit of a wander round', I said. 'See if I can spot any tracks.' 'What do you think you are', said Dick, 'A Red Indian?' Leaving him on the verandah I made off down a well- marked animal track. Hyena footprints showed up occasionally in the damp soil. Suddenly, after about 200 yards I came to a gully. There were the cushions. Ripped open. Feathers in all directions. Dick hadn't told me that the cushions were not the usual kapok or I might have tumbled to the truth a bit earlier. I'll bet that the hyenas were a bit fed up when they found that there were no chickens inside after all. I picked up the tattered remains and made my way back to Dick's house. 'Property recovered', I reported, 'but no arrest!' To celebrate the successful conclusion to my investigation we each had another beer.

During the afternoon I made my way to the hospital to learn

how the unfortunate prisoner was progressing. 'Ah!', said Dr Musoke. 'I'm glad to see you. I was just about to write you a note. I'm not too happy about his condition.' I accompanied the doctor to the bed where the victim lay. The warder on duty saluted smartly and stood aside. There certainly didn't seem a lot of chance of an escape here. He was conscious but that was about all one could say. He was a nasty grey colour and moaning loudly. The doctor pulled back the sheet which was covering him. The left leg was swollen up like a long balloon. 'There's no circulation you see', said Musoke. I'm afraid he's going to die. The only possible thing which might save him is to amputate the leg.' It didn't take a medical expert to see that this was true. Without amputation within a very short time, gangrene would set in and death would be a certainty. 'Has anyone told him yet?', I enquired. 'No, I wanted to consult you first', replied the doctor. 'Well lets get an interpreter and break the news to him', I said. A Karamajong-speaking orderly was called and the bad news was imparted to the prisoner. Oddly enough he seemed quite unperturbed by the news, and signified that he wanted the leg off. 'What are the chances of a successful outcome if you amputate?', I enquired. 'About 50-50', was the reply. 'Let me have this in writing straight away, and then get on with the operation', I said. Half an hour later I had the written report in my hand and the amputation was under way. The following morning I again made my way to the hospital. 'The operation was successful', said Dr Musoke, 'but I'm afraid the patient died half-an-hour ago.' I cursed under my breath. This meant an inquest. Any prisoner dying in custody, regardless of the reason why, necessitated a full enquiry. 'I'll send along a Post-Mortem Request form straight away', I said. 'You won't want to hang about with the autopsy!' I departed thinking to myself that at least I'd got the doctor's report in writing before the amputation. The post-mortem would be interesting though. I'd never seen one resulting from a snake bite! I returned to the police station and made the necessary entry in the occurrence book and the sudden death register. Later I returned to the hospital mortuary where Musoke was about to perform the P.M.

On viewing the liver and other organs I was surprised that the unfortunate man had lasted as long as he had. Apart from the massive blood clots being present, the organs had begun to break down. 'That's one of the effects of snake bite', said Musoke. 'The tissues are pre-digested. There is no way that he could have survived, given the condition of the body.' I made my way back to the office.

Around lunchtime a few days later a large American car swept past the police station on its way up to the Rest House. I was in time to see a thin-faced bespectacled individual in the driving seat. 'Who's that?', I enquired. 'Oh, that's Tony Hatch-Barnwell', replied Noel. 'He's the Resident Magistrate from Soroti. Miserable bastard! I forgot to tell you. He's up here for a couple of days to hear three preliminary enquiries and whatever else you've got ready for him. He'll be sitting tomorrow so you had better have a sort through the cases to see what there is and make sure it's all ready. You'll have to prosecute. I shall be too busy.' This I must admit rather took the wind out of my sails. I was totally unprepared. I had never prosecuted any cases in my life, let alone conduct a preliminary enquiry into murder cases. Why the hell hadn't Noel remembered to give me a few days notice to familiarise myself with the evidence. I expressed my feelings on the subject. 'Oh, don't give it a thought', said Noel. 'You won't be expected to say much. Hatch-Barnwell likes to do it all himself. Just make sure the interpreters are there at the beginning of the day, and leave the rest to him.' I called for the files on the various cases due to be heard. Fortunately the sergeant in charge of the prosecutions had been a bit more efficient than Noel and had sent out the summonses for the various witnesses. Apart from the three preliminary enquiries there were two cases under the Waragi Ordinance, one for growing *bhangi* or Indian Hemp (cannabis), one under the Game Ordinance and our Driver Kintu for dangerous driving. As an afterthought, I added in the inquest on the dead prisoner and sent a note down to Dr Musoke to warn him that he would be required to give evidence.

The same evening I received a note from Noel. 'Come over and have a drink. Hatch-Barnwell is coming so you'll be able to meet him.' I made my way across to Noel's house. Shortly after my arrival the large American car pulled up outside and Noel greeted the R.M. and escorted him inside. I was introduced. Tony Hatch-Barnwell was always known as Hatch, never as Tony. We sized one another up. Hatch was about 40 years of age and about five-feet-ten-inches tall. He was about the thinnest man I had ever met. A pair of spectacles sat on the end of a large beaky nose and I was strongly reminded of a vulture, sizing up a meal. He had a most precise manner of speech and an air of superiority. There was something about him that I couldn't put my finger on. I felt that I could probably tolerate him, but never become on friendly terms. Over a few beers I found that he had been in the Indian civil service and on his premature retirement on that Country's independence had made his own way to Uganda and been locally employed as a Magistrate. He was now endeavouring to have his terms of employment varied to enable him to be classed as a Crown Agents' employee so that he would become entitled to a pension.

Court was due to commence the following morning at 9 o'clock. On his arrival at the office Noel warned me to leave Barney behind in the office. Hatch had brought with him his own dog a mean-looking cross-bred type which also had a bit of Bull Terrier in it. This always sat under the table where he worked. Barney and he did not get on at all well. I then found that Hatch had devised a most extraordinary method of working. He was provided with a complete set of all statements which the police had recorded. As each witness was called he would scan the statement, lead the witness through the evidence, and then type out his own version of the statement. The typing was necessary since his handwriting was so appalling that no one, not even himself, could read it. I felt a bit dubious about the legality of this system but no one else had ever questioned it so who was I to rock the boat. In the event it appeared that a certain amount of time was saved, so what the hell. The accused were never legally represented at this stage so were not in a position to object. Invariably Hatch enquired of them whether they wished to give evidence on their own behalf or call any witnesses but it was practically unheard of for any of them to bother with these niceties. Conviction rates for minor crimes were high indeed. One hundred per cent to be exact. My role as police prosecutor proved to be confined to ensuring that the witnesses were called in the correct order and to cross-examine witnesses or accused should their evidence vary in any way from that which had already been recorded. At the end of the scheduled cases the eight accused in the three murder cases on which the preliminary enquiries were being held, were further remanded for the next High Court Circuit, the *waragi* offenders received three months imprisonment with hard labour each, the cannabis grower got two months, the

Game Ordinance offender who had killed a rhino with the aid of a wheel trap got 12 months and Driver Kintu got one month which was to be served in Luzira Prison in Kampala. I must say that I felt a bit sorry for Kintu. True he was a bloody idiot, but I could well imagine the Inspector of Vehicles in Kampala, enthusing to him about the Land Rover. 'This vehicle is guaranteed to go anywhere', he would have been told. Probably if Kintu had come to a cliff after this promise, he would have driven over the edge in his blind faith.

At the end of these proceedings I slipped in the inquest on the dead prisoner. This took Hatch somewhat by surprise and he enquired of me if it could not be postponed until his next visit. I felt justified in insisting on it being heard straight away, however, as a full report on the death had to be sent as early as possible to the Commissioner of Prisons in Kampala. After a short argument I got my way. I then had the opportunity of dealing with the witnesses myself and gave my own evidence. At the conclusion a finding of 'Death by Misadventure' was recorded. No comment was made about the undue delay in getting the unfortunate victim to hospital. In fact I don't think this aspect was ever mentioned. Life, it appeared, was very cheap in Africa. However, I felt that, by and large, justice had been done.

On his return from the border conference, Noel had given me a full account of his activities. Fairly uneventful apparently, apart from getting stuck on river crossings on two occasions, but with the help of his houseboy and constable plus a few of the local Suk who had been pressed into service, he had got out on each occasion without undue effort. As predicted. the meeting had been a fairly boozy affair and had lasted two days. I was not sure from his account whether any worthwhile conclusions had been drawn from the exercise. Probably not! What was really needed to control the raiding between the Karamajong and the Itesot was a substantial all-weather road running to the south of Kadam Mountain. The likelihood of getting this was remote indeed.

Pay parade was once again due. The pay sheets were produced by Mr Sentamu and handed over for me to check. These were of course complicated by the supplementary sheets required for the various amounts to be paid to the wives, plus the further sheets for the porters and so on. How much simpler this would all have been today with pocket calculators to help. However, the totals tallied and the next thing to be worked out was the breakdown of the denominations of notes and coins so that the pay out could be conducted with the minimum of trouble. I managed this without too much of a problem and the list together with the imprest for the money was sent over to the cash office at the Boma, as the D.C's office was known. On the following morning Noel and I, together with Mr Sentamu and a couple of constables, collected the cash and the pay parade commenced. It followed the same pattern as the previous month with Ishverbhai Patel collecting the debts due to him. At the conclusion Noel and I set to, checking what cash was left and calculating how much was needed to complete the pay out at the outposts. Hurrah. This time it was correct to the last cent.

Bright and early on the following morning I made my way to the police station, accompanied by Kesi and Barney and a variety of foodstuffs and utensils. The Land Rover was already being loaded as I arrived, the bulk of the equipment fitting quite snugly into the trailer. I drew my revolver and a .303 rifle from the armoury, collected the cash box from the safe and by half-past-eight we were away with Odongo driving, myself in the front passenger seat and Kesi, Barney and a constable in the back. The route we followed was the same as that taken the previous month. I noticed that there were a number of bird species around which I had not noticed on the previous trip. A number of pools of standing water were passed from time to time and a number of hammercop storks could be seen, presumably looking for small frogs and tadpoles. These had a peculiar shuffling gait when in the water which I believe they use to disturb their food.

The first day of the safari passed uneventfully. We passed a good number of herds of various buck and zebra and large flocks of guinea fowl. I took the opportunity to shoot a couple of these. Early on, I shot a Grants Gazelle and left quantities of the meat at the police posts we visited. The local Mkungu chiefs were supposed to supply meat to the posts but invariably there were problems in this respect. The odd goat would occasionally be produced but these were often on their last legs either through age or disease. The N.C.O's and constables seemed glad to get a bit extra anyway, though some of them were Moslems and said they couldn't eat any meat unless it had been properly slaughtered. 'Shauri yako', I said. 'That's up to you.' I've no doubt they had their share as soon as I had gone. Naturally I retained some of the meat for Kesi and Barney.

On the second day we made camp at Kacheliba. I finished the pay parade at about three o'clock and made my way to the rest camp where my tent had been erected. I was busy deciding whether to slake my thirst with a cup of tea or a beer when an ancient lorry drew up. An elderly European got out of the drivers seat and made his way over to me. This could only be Wreford-Smith, the Government cattle buyer. He was about 70 years old, six feet tall and heavily built. A bush jacket and baggy trousers topped off by a broad brimmed bush hat. A lined, weather beaten, craggy face with a great beak of a nose. His entire appearance shaped by years of experience in the African bush. He greeted me warmly. 'I heard we'd got a new policeman', he boomed, enveloping my, by no means small hand, in his vast paw. I introduced myself and he wandered over to inspect the Land Rover. 'Handy toy', he bellowed. 'Too small for me though.' We chatted for a while and he joined me for a cup of tea. 'I'll be off then', he said. 'Come and have a bite at about seven.' I had no idea where he was off to. 'About half a mile up the road', he said. 'Right-hand side. You can't miss it.' At the appointed time I drove the Land Rover to Wreford's camp. 'Can't miss it', he had said. I missed it three times, driving backwards and forwards, searching. Eventually an African came out of a gap in the bush and waved at me. I drove into the bush 100-yards or so and eventually came to a clearing where Wreford had set up his camp on a semi-permanent basis. He certainly liked his comfort. I expect at his age he felt entitled to have things about right. A large open-fronted thatched hut the size of a small house. Inside, a number of pressure lamps. Wreford was having a bath. I sat outside awaiting his appearance. Eventually he arrived. '*Lete* beer', he bellowed. A houseboy arrived with bottles of ice cold beer, straight from the fridge. Dishes of roasted groundnuts. A lump of what I thought was wood was laid on the table together with a .fearsome looking knife. Wreford picked up the knife and started to cut slivers off the wood. 'Help yourself.', he said, filling his mouth. 'What is it? ' I enquired. 'Well *biltong* of course', he roared. I took the knife and cut off a tiny slice. I popped it in my mouth and chewed. It practically melted. Firm, but not rock hard, salty, dark red, almost black but absolutely delicious. What a thirst it created too. The first two pints hardly touched the sides as they went down. 'What meat is it?', I enquired, stuffing my mouth. 'Eland, ' he replied, 'That makes the best *biltong*, though you can use practically any meat, except possibly waterbuck and zebra.' During the evening he instructed me in the art of making *biltong* and I resolved to make my own supply as soon as possible. The evening was spent chatting with Wreford about a variety of subjects. He dominated most of the conversation while I sat back and listened to his words of wisdom.

Wreford had arrived in Kenya in 1919 as one of the ex-servicemen sponsored by a grateful government after the first World War. He had been able to raise a loan to enable him to purchase, over a period of 20-or-so years, a large tract of land about 15 miles out of Kitale. He had named his farm Kipkulkul. He employed a number of Africans to help run the place, each of whom had brought their families with them. Each family was allocated several acres of land on which to grow their own crops and to build a small house to live in. As the children grew up they were largely absorbed into the labour force and, over the years, Wreford had become a sort of patriarchal figure. His wife, Dos, an ex-nurse, cared for her large and growing family of Africans, running a small school for them and looking after them, should they fall ill. On his farm, Wreford ran herds of dairy and beef cattle and grew crops of coffee as well as maize and other cereals. The day-to-day running of the farm was left largely to Dos, as Wreford was on safari for at least half of each month, traveling all over Karamoja buying cattle from the unwilling Karamajong and Suk tribesmen, on behalf of the Uganda Government. Resultantly, he also employed many of the tribesmen as porters and cattle drovers, shifting the herds from where they had been purchased to the quarantine station at Iriri. As though this didn't keep him sufficiently occupied, Wreford had taken out prospecting rights in a number of areas throughout Karamoja where he mined mica and certain other minerals. These mines he left in the hands of a number of capable employees who, in addition to scouting around to find new areas to exploit, would dig out the blocks of mica and stack it ready for his monthly visits. On finding suitable sites Wreford would drill and dynamite the deposits and leave the extraction to his miners. He never trusted them to do their own blasting and I can't say I blame him either. I shall never know where he got so much energy at his age. Even as we sat relaxing and drinking beer he was busy with the current batch of mica from the local mine. Each lump of mica had to be trimmed and split with a sharp knife and then graded by size and quality. One of his favourite miners, whose virtues he was constantly extolling, was named 'Shitott'. Wreford had christened him so. This one apparently had a nose for mica and was able to unerringly pinpoint large deposits of the mineral.

Our meal was finally served. The first course appeared to be a sort of porridge. Wreford helped himself to a large plateful. 'Dig in', he commanded. I didn't like to appear rude by enquiring what it was so I helped myself to a small portion. Meanwhile, Wreford had reached for a large earthenware jar and was extracting quantities of what appeared to be butter from the depths. This he placed on top of the porridge and topped it off with rock salt out of a grinder. I followed suit and took my first mouthful. Ambrosia! Undoubtedly the food of the Gods. I helped myself to a further plateful. This was my first introduction to *posho*, maize meal, grown and ground on Wreford's own farm. The butter was made by Dos with cream from their own cattle. This was unlike any butter I have ever tasted, before or since. Kenya was known as the producer of the finest butter in the world, having for years won the gold medals at every international exhibition. Dos, in her turn, won all the local competitions with her butter. Undoubtedly I was partaking of the best butter in the world, and acknowledged as such. I could happily have made a complete meal of this, but as soon as I had finished, a large plate of roast beef was thrust in front of me. The Yorkshire pudding and vegetables would have done justice to a top class London hotel. Apple pie and cream completed the meal. 'By God, Wreford, you live well', I commented. 'Well, it's O.K. for the first couple of days', he replied. 'After that I have to shoot whatever meat I need, same as you!'

CHAPTER 11

On the following morning we packed our belongings into the Land Rover and trailer and set off for Katabok. My intention was to complete the pay parade and any *shauris* here before going on to Amudat where I was going to spend the night. About a mile from the police post I saw a large flock of guinea fowl off to the right. Instructing Kesi to keep Barney in the vehicle, I set off in pursuit. after a careful stalk of about100-yards I got within range and fired. One guinea fowl dropped. A second which had been standing behind ran off trailing a wing. The rest flew off.

The great snake lay basking in the sunlight. She had recently caught and eaten a small rat which had been unwary enough to have strayed into her path. She had recently shed her skin and had mated a couple of weeks earlier. She was carrying 12 eggs which she would soon be ready to lay in the nest which she had already chosen. Now she dozed in the pleasant warmth, her eyes open as she, like all snakes, had no eyelids. Neither had she ears, otherwise she might have heard the noise of the shot about 50 yards distant as the group of guinea fowl came under fire. She was however very sensitive to vibrations and within a few seconds became aware of approaching feet. Too late she made some movement to trace the source of her disturbance. She raised her head a few inches above the ground but before she could make any decision on whether to retreat or attack, a human shoe trod heavily on her coils.

Unaware of the danger that lay in my path, I ran after the wounded bird rapidly gaining ground. Suddenly I was aware of a sinuous dark brown body under my feet. In my haste I had not noticed the enormous snake coiled up in front of me. I then performed a series of agile contortions the like of which have never since been repeated. Leaping about five feet vertically and waving my legs vigorously I finally landed a few feet away from the reptile which was obviously as startled as myself. I had an impression of the snake striking at me somewhere about waist height but everything happened so fast that the sequence of events was blurred. Where the fangs struck I didn't know, probably around the belt of my bush jacket. Suffice it to say that the several layers of stout khaki drill or maybe the belt itself, absorbed the blow and I finished up untouched by the fangs. I was unaware of this at the time, however. Never having been bitten by a snake I was unsure what to expect. I assumed that it would be a bit like being stung by a wasp, possibly worse. However I got no such feeling so I assumed that I was O.K. By the time I had recovered my balance the snake was away at great speed. As I watched, it seemed to flow over the top of low shrubs and thorn bush, rather that going round them. I was fascinated to know what sort of snake it was that I had encountered. I ran after it! Fools rush in! I suppose that it was travelling at about ten or 12 miles an hour so I had no difficulty in keeping up with it. I think it must have been puzzled by my behaviour. After all, who in their right mind, having just had a brush with death, would set off in pursuit of the source of that brush. After a chase of about a couple of hundred yards the snake came to a dry stream bed, about four or five yards across. I was a few yards behind it, awaiting an opportunity to get a clear shot when it slowed down. At this stage my quarry obviously decided that enough was enough. It stopped in its tracks and turned, raising its body up about four feet off the ground to get a good look at me. Then without hesitation it launched itself in my direction. This all happened too fast for me to be alarmed by the change of events. Here was the hunter suddenly become the hunted. I had no time to take aim but fired from the hip, hoping that the noise of the shot might divert the snake from its course. In my hurry I had, of course, forgotten that snakes cannot hear anything. The next second the reptile was keeling over backwards. My shot had taken it in the neck, a couple of inches below the head. I think that I can claim that this was the luckiest shot I have ever made. In fact I probably used up a major supply of my available luck on this occasion. Maybe, like a cat, I have nine lives. Certainly I must have lost one of them on this occasion. I made my way to where the serpent lay writhing on the ground and crushed its head with the butt of my rifle. To my regret I had now lost sight of the wounded guinea fowl so, picking up the snake, I made my way back to the Land Rover. Driver Odongo had meantime collected the first bird. I was faced with mutiny when I wanted to put the snake into the Land Rover down by Kesi's feet. However I found a suitable home for it in the well of the spare wheel mounted on the bonnet. On reaching the police post I was greeted by oohs! and aahs! when the constables viewed the corpse. I had no idea what the snake might be but was informed that it was terribly venomous. 'Were their many snakes like this around?' I enquired. 'Oh yes, very many indeed', I was informed.

At the conclusion of the pay parade we made our way back to Amudat where I paid out the staff and porters. Word of the encounter with the snake rapidly spread and a crowd of onlookers formed to view the corpse. Well, there might be a lot of similar snakes around but the event certainly raised a bit of local interest, with the women ululating and the men shouting and chattering. I took the opportunity, while they were all feeling so brave, of taking a photograph. I induced Driver Odongo to stand on the bonnet of the Land Rover, holding the snake by the tail. With his arm as high as possible its head just touched the ground. On measuring it I found the length to be a little under ten feet. Next I settled down to the task of skinning the body and examining the stomach contents. I found a newly devoured rat and, interestingly, a number of soft eggs in the body. I noted that the fangs were completely different to those of the puff adder, being grooved down their length instead of hollow like a hypodermic. Copious amounts of venom were ejected as I examined and skinned the head. On completion of this operation I covered the skin with salt and pegged it out in the sun to dry off for a couple of hours.

The remainder of the pay safari was a bit of an anti-climax. Eventually two days later I reached Moroto where I related my narrow escape to Noel. 'Why not go over to the D.C's office and have a look at the snake book? You might be able to identify it', he said. I made my way over to Sandy Field. I produced the skin which I had rolled up and placed in a cardboard box. 'Goo-good heavens', he exclaimed, 'what a m- monster'. So saying he produced a tome entitled *Snakes of East Africa* by Captain Pitman, who had been Chief Game Warden in Uganda until his retirement a few years earlier. This proved to be a beautifully illustrated volume in full colour. The top and underside scale markings of each specie was accurately represented, as were the head, front and side view. From this I was able to identify the snake beyond any doubt. It was a black mamba. I was interested to learn that it had never previously been recorded in Uganda and never previously at heights above 3,000 feet. Katabok, where the incident had occurred, was well over 4,000 feet above sea level. Later, I sent the skin to the Coryndon Museum in Nairobi, where the curator was able to confirm my identification and note the newly discovered area of occupation.

A rather amusing sequel to this occurred a month or two later when I sent a copy of the photograph of the snake, being held by driver Odongo, to my mother. 'This is a black mamba my son shot', she proudly proclaimed to Mrs Bourne, who lived over the road. Mrs Bourne was not only a bit short sighted, she was also a bit deaf and possibly a bit racist in outlook. She thought that my mother had said 'black man'. After examining the photograph closely for a while she said, 'Well I can't say I blame him. It must have been terribly annoying to have him jumping on the bonnet of the car like that with his great boots'.

My brush with death during the mamba incident set me wondering what would occur should one actually get bitten. Survival after a mamba bite was considered practically impossible even should it occur right outside the hospital with medical aid instantly available. There were however many other types of snakes around of less venomous varieties where treatment within a short time might ensure at least a chance of survival. After discussing the problem with Noel I addressed a report of the Commissioner of Police, describing the incident which had occurred, and requesting that a full anti-venine kit be issued for use by officers on safari. Noel endorsed this suggestion and the report was sent. Some weeks later came a reply. Three anti-venine kits were being issued — to Moroto Hospital, where the phials of anti-venine could be kept in refrigerated conditions, where they could be issued as required to officers of all departments, and from whence the phials could be exchanged for fresh ones as they became time-expired, the refrigeration life being only about nine months. This scheme seemed admirably sensible to me and the matter was circulated to all departments. Thereafter, I never went off on safari without first collecting one of the kits. To the best of my knowledge I was the only government officer to take advantage of their availability.

Noel came back from a meeting of the District Team a few days later. 'Do you know anything about athletics?' he demanded. I confessed that I knew quite a lot having been involved in competing in various events at the White City and at Oxford for many years. 'Splendid', he said. 'We want to hold a District Sports Meeting, open to all the Counties in Karamoja, plus all the government departments. Maybe it will take their minds off cattle raiding. You can be in charge.' When I had recovered from the shock of this news I began to consider the organisation which would be required. First I would have to work out a programme of events. There should be no difficulty in obtaining the services of the various government officers to fill the posts of starters, timekeepers, referees and so on. Then there was the problem of a suitable venue. Prizes would have to be decided on and funds to purchase them. I could foresee that the majority of the competitors in the government team would have to come from the police and prison staff. Somehow I would have to get hold of a heavy rope suitable for the tug-of-war, also Tom Hinett would have to be spoken to nicely with a view to getting hurdles made and stands for the high jump. Pole vault would be out. I could think of nothing that would be suitable for the poles.

Anyway, landing from about 16 feet onto sun-baked earth, hard as rock, would only generate ill-feeling when the onlookers roared with laughter as the casualties occurred. I decided that I had better form a committee. This way I could at least farm out some of the responsibility. Noel clearly didn't want to be involved. If I fixed him up with a job he didn't fancy he would be off on safari so fast that his feet wouldn't touch the ground, which would leave me to do the job myself! With this in mind I drafted a letter to a number of government officers. Tom Hinett was an obvious first choice as were Arthur Brown, Dick Baker, Doctor Musoke, Sandy Taylor. I decided to include Madan Tandon and Ishverbhai Patel. Maybe they could be prevailed upon to fork out for some of the prizes. I asked each of the officers I circulated, to nominate whatever of their African staff they considered sufficiently reliable to carry out the various jobs which would invariably need doing once the details were sorted out.

The committee met a couple of days later. The open-sided Court was decided on as the venue for the meeting as there was plenty of room to place the table and chairs required. It was also central for the convenience of all involved. Since I appeared to be the only one with a clue as to the requirements of an athletics meeting, I was elected Chairman. I suggested Dick Baker as secretary and this was duly agreed. I had come armed with paper and pencil so I passed these over to him and the meeting got under way. I commenced by outlining the thoughts I had had on the subject and continued by enquiring if anyone had any ideas on a possible venue. In the absence of any flat open areas in the whole of Karamoja it was suggested that the area between the D.C's Boma, the Post Office and the Bazaar might be appropriate if a quarter-mile circuit could be drawn out among the numerous acacia thorns that littered the area. This was, at least, kept in good order by the Station porters who were continually wielding metal slashers and pushing lawn mowers over it. Since the available space measured some 800 yards by 300 I thought that a suitable spot might be found to mark out the circuit. This job was duly left to me with Tom Hinett to assist since he could provide the whitewash. Between us we decided of the events to be competed. Suitable prizes were considered and it was decided that rather that allocate a particular prize to the winner of a particular event it would be best to have a selection of prizes to include iron- and brass-wire, beads or cowry shells and black americani cloth from which the *shukas* were made, should any of the local tribesmen win the events. These could be obtained on a sale-or-return basis from Madan and Ishverbhai. Small cash prizes could be allocated for events won by members of the various government departments. I managed to extract a promise from Dick Baker on behalf of the D.C. for the allocation of Shs 1000/- for prizes and on my prompting, Madan Tandon and Ishverbhai Patel each promised Shs 100/-. I felt that with this I could do the competitors proud, since the going rate for the locals was Sh 1/- per day while the government employees averaged about Sh 3/- per day.

Having sorted out the mass of foreseeable details the meeting was closed. The following morning, armed with a large bundle of sharpened pegs and a hammer, Tom and I made our way to the area decided upon. This was not going to be easy. There were far more trees there than I had thought. Several attempts were made to pick a spot where we could get an uninterrupted circuit of 440 yards. Hopeless. Eventually we compromised. After all, who was going to know anyway. There was only one person with any expertise in the matter, that was me. So whatever I decided upon was going to be O.K. We commenced our pegging-out and eventually had a rough oval shape. True, there were a couple of dog legs in it, where we had to avoid the odd tree which, no matter what we did, insisted in popping up in the middle of the track. Tom and I then paced out the oval we had marked. Me with my long legs and he with his short ones. I made it 342 yards. Tom made it 391. We split the difference and decided that the circuit was 367 yards. Our quarter-mile would have to be a lap and a bit. The longer races would vary accordingly. A bit complicated, undoubtedly. Still, who would know! I did manage to get an uninterrupted space for the 100 yards event and I was pleased about this since I had every intention of competing in this myself. It was decided to hold the athletics meeting in about four weeks time since it would take this long to circulate the County Chiefs and get the various teams in to Moroto.

Life for me at Moroto had settled down into a fairly regular routine by now. My cash-flow worries were at an end. There was very little outlay on food, since I was self-sufficient for meat, and eggs were so cheap that my conscience almost pricked me every time I purchased 100 or so. True, I had to buy sugar, flour, vegetables, kerosene and so on, but this didn't really amount to much. On the credit side I was spending about ten nights each month on safari and was able to claim 12-shillings a night for this. This was a most useful supplement and practically paid my grocery bill. One thing I really missed was a nice freshly-baked loaf of bread. Vi Hinett gave me the occasional loaf if she happened to be doing some cooking, but Kesi didn't have a clue on the bread-baking art. Enquiring round I found that every other officer of the Station was self-sufficient on this front. Their cooks were all expert bakers. I was left with the twice-weekly loaf which arrived on the bus from Soroti, and which was stale even before it arrived. The time came when I decided that this situation must be rectified. 'Kesi', I said, 'It's high time you learned to make bread. All the other boys on the Station can do it so you'd better find someone who can teach you. I shall pay you Shs 10/- when you produce a loaf of quality which you have made yourself.' '*Ndio bwana*', said Kesi, beaming. On my return home from the office the following afternoon a splendid aroma was issuing from the kitchen. Shortly afterwards Kesi brought me my tea on a tray. Accompanying it was a superb loaf of bread, still hot from the oven. A dish of butter and a pot of jam stood alongside. '*Mkati bwana*', he said, holding out his hand for the ten-shillings. 'I'll try it out first', I said and proceeded to cut a thick crusty slice. It was superb. A bit on the hot side, but as to quality I had no complaints. I cheerfully passed over the cash to him. In return he passed me a list. On it was written in appalling English, Stanley for teaching 2/-. Underneath was a short list of requirements, baking tin, yeast, flour, all obtainable from Ishverbhai. This was accompanied by a request for five-shillings a month increase in salary. I passed over the two-shillings which had to be paid to Stanley, the D.C's cook, and indicated that I would consider the rise if subsequent loaves turned out as successfully. Kesi went off with my note to Ishverbhai while I made my way to the pool. On my return at dusk I found no sign of Kesi. I poured my usual beer and one for Noel who had accompanied me back from our swim. I was intending to suggest that he stay for a bite of food but time went by and still Kesi did not arrive. Noel examined the loaf of bread and after trying a slice gave it his approval. 'I gave him ten bob when he produced it', I explained. Noel looked knowingly at me. 'I doubt you'll see him again this evening', he said. 'He's a Mutoro. The worst drunks in the country. He'll be off celebrating.' Another hour passed and still no sign of Kesi. Eventually Noel suggested that we adjourn to his house for a meal and I gratefully accompanied him. I returned home about ten o'clock. Kesi had arrived, very drunk and looking very sorry for himself. I cursed him roundly but he was obviously in no condition to appreciate the bollocking he deserved. I decided to deal with him in the morning and made my way to bed. My morning tea arrived as usual and I later administered the desired bollocking plus a fine of five-shillings for his misbehavior. 'It was all Stanley's fault', I was informed. On receipt of his two-shillings he had suggested going for a glass at the local beer house. The glass had been the first of many and the two had eventually staggered home rather later than anticipated. I could well imagine Sandy Field's wrath when Stephen failed to appear. He wasn't as tolerant as me!

The next few weeks passed rapidly, my time being well filled with the odd safari to investigate a cattle raid or murder, or both. In this the Land Rover was proving its worth. I had got into the habit of doing most of the driving myself, leaving the routine maintenance and cleaning to Driver Odongo. Sometimes I didn't even bother to take him along with me. The vehicle wasn't all that big, even with the trailer for the camping gear. I usually took Kesi and Barney along but occasionally I left Kesi behind and travelled light, taking only a couple of police *askaris* to assist in the translating and recording the statements. Barney however, always accompanied me.

The details of the forthcoming athletics meeting had by now been sorted out. I received offers of help from far more volunteers than I had dared hope for. Everyone seemed very keen on the idea and were determined to make it a success. Each of the County Chiefs had decided to enter a team of competitors, with the exception of the Suk who, it appeared, were less than enthusiastic, partly because they feared that any team they entered might get severely trounced by the opposition and partly because they weren't too keen to get them all annihilated by the various Karamajong tribes with whom they were still very much at odds. The team entered by the government departments were, as I had predicted, mostly drawn from the police and prisons. I was informed that there had been many volunteers, keen to compete from among the prison inmates, including many Suk tribesmen. Mostly they wanted to take part in the long-distance running events. I regretfully had to discourage them from taking part. In any case, being handcuffed to a warder would be a terrible handicap when trying to outdistance the field. There were, however, a few exceptions including a very promising hurdler from the Veterinary Department. This one had received a secondary education at Buddu College near Kampala, where athletics had been much encouraged. In the police team I had discovered P.C. Ogwang, also secondary educated who could not only speak and write remarkably good English but was also first class when it came to putting the shot, throwing the javelin and high jump.

The great day dawned. Warm and dry as usual. My team of helpers gathered and received their instruction and we got under way. All went well until the Javelin event started. The Karamajong spear, made in three parts, was intended for short distances only At twenty yards it was a fearsome weapon indeed. The tribesmen insisted in using their own spears and were not interested in trying out the javelins which I had borrowed from the police stores in Kampala. P.C. Ogwang opened the event with a throw of about 70 yards. All the bystanders, including the entire population of the nearby police barracks, were suitably impressed and greeted this first throw with a chorus of oohs and aahs! He was followed by couple of other contestants entered by the other government departments. Neither of these came near to the distance set by Ogwang. Next a Karamajong tribesman swaggered to the throwing mark. He was completely naked except for the black cloth *shuka* worn round his shoulders. I noticed the police wives eyeing his magnificent physique with some anticipation. However, they were well used to the local tribesmen displaying their nakedness. The warrior grasped his spear firmly and tried not to look too conceited. He hefted it a couple of times to make sure he had it properly balanced and then took a mighty run to the throwing mark. The spear left his hand like a lightning bolt, flew into the air and disintegrated into its three component parts, landing about 30 yards away. Somewhat self-consciously our hero collected the damaged remains. The soft iron blade and the tailpiece had distorted so much that they resembled a couple of giant hairpins. A great cheer went up from the onlookers, and a second tribesman stepped up and gave an identical performance. This was a tricky situation. Clearly the Karamajong spear was not intended for treatment of this sort. Our warriors were bound to lose face since their spears were their proudest possessions. Not that they had as strong feelings about these sort of things as some nationalities. I had a quick conference with the assembled County Chiefs, pointing out the shortcomings of the spear in this sort of contest. Then taking one of the borrowed javelins I went to the tribesman who had first thrown and taking him by the hand led him back to the throwing mark. I pressed the javelin into his hand and he examined it scornfully. I indicated that he should try out a throw with it and after some hesitation which was resolved when his Chief gave the O.K. He ran up to the mark and the javelin hurtled into the air and landed not far short of a group of spectators who were standing almost 100-yards distant. He beamed his thanks to me and the next tribesman stepped up and gave a similar performance. P.C. Ogwang was not quite so pleased at the outcome. 'My God', said Sandy Field, 'I hope they don't think about redesigning their spears now, or we'll have a blood bath on our hands.'

The events now went forward without incident until the high jump. P.C. Ogwang gave an immaculate and scientific performance of this event followed by several other competitors from the various departments. Having seen how it was done, one of the naked warriors tried his hand at it, with disastrous results.

His wedding tackle caught on the cross bar and he staggered away grasping his balls. Several others then tried their hand but the sight of so much bum and bollocks flying around was too much for the police wives, several of whom collapsed with mirth and had to be escorted away. This time I couldn't think of a way of intervening since I could hardly issue each tribesman with a pair of police shorts. The hurdles events which followed were even more hilarious and the sight of a dozen sets of wedding tackle at a time, flying in all directions moved everyone to tears. Eventually the time came for the 100-yards sprint. I took my place at the start line with about ten other competitors. I had no running spikes with me and in any case they would have given me an unfair advantage. I took off my shoes and hoped for the best. My start was appalling. My bare feet slipped on the dry grass and I was ten yards behind the field. However, thankfully, I soon caught up and eventually finished a yard or two in front. At the end of the day Sandy Field presented the prizes. I declined my few shillings and it went to P.C. Ogwang, which helped to make up for him not winning the Javelin event. Everyone involved decided that the day had been a great success and we adjourned to Sandy Field's house for liberal liquid refreshment.

On my arrival at the office one morning Noel handed me a signal which he had just finished reading. 'Compolice arrives yours for inspection Tuesday next, by air e.t.a. 10.00 hrs. Arrange overnight accommodation. Parade required a.m. Wednesday.' 'Bugger', said Noel, 'I wanted to go on safari for a few days on Wednesday.' 'Maybe you could take him with you', I suggested. 'Well, we'll see what he wants to do when he arrives', said Noel. 'Anyway, he wants a parade. You'll have to be on it. How's your drill?' 'Awful', said I, 'I hate it!' 'Well we'll get a squad out this afternoon and you can have a practice.' I wondered if I could go sick without it looking too obvious.

During the afternoon a squad of about a couple of dozen police constables and N.C.O's formed up outside the office and I drilled them under Noel's supervision for nearly two hours. At the end of this time we were all hot and sweaty, but at least I had managed to perfect a series of commands which would keep the Commissioner amused for ten minutes or so. 'You've got a good drill voice', said Noel. 'I can't think what you were worried about.' 'Christ. I'm not worried about it. It's just that I loathe it.

It's such a bloody waste of time and effort. Also I've got two left feet!' 'Never mind', said Noel, 'The Commissioner will never notice.'

The next few days were given over to checking files and exhibits, armoury and stores, giving the outside of the police station a fresh coat of whitewash, painting the stones lining the path between the police station and the police lines and ensuring that the police barracks were in pristine condition. At the end of all this activity Noel pronounced himself satisfied and we sagged into a state of relaxed preparedness.

Tuesday arrived and I was up with the lark. Noel took the Land Rover out to the airstrip, five miles out on the road to Iriri, together with a couple of constables to drive off any cattle, sheep or goats which might have encroached onto the runway. I remained at the police station attending to the last-minute details, and hoping against hope that a murder or a serious raid might be reported, giving me an excuse to absent myself for a few days.

Just before 10 a.m. a light aircraft flew overhead. The Commissioner was having a look at us from the air before heading back to the airfield. I kept my head down and stayed in the office. Half an hour later the Land Rover drew up outside the police station. I made my way outside and threw up a smart salute as Joe Deegan got out of the passenger seat. 'Ah. Inspector Beaden', he said, shaking my hand. 'How are you settling in. I've been hearing great things about you from Mr Caunce.' 'Thank you Sir', said I. 'I'm finding my way about. I've got a good instructor.' I thought I had better say kind things about Noel since he had clearly done the same for me. 'We're going up to my place for a coffee in ten minutes or so', said Noel. 'Join us. We'll start off this afternoon with the parade instead of tomorrow morning. Then we'll follow that with lines' inspection. That'll give us some extra time tomorrow. You had better tell the Head Constable.' The Head Constable, I knew, was lurking in the Charge Office. I gave him the necessary instruction. Meanwhile, Noel had disappeared round the end of the police station accompanied by the Commissioner. They reappeared a few minutes later, Joe Degan was grinning broadly but didn't say a word. We all got into Noel's car and set off for his house. On the way past my cottage Noel pointed it out. 'That's not much of a place', said the Commissioner. 'I hope it's only going to be temporary.' 'I'm quite happy with it', I said, 'It's a bit on the small side, but I'm quite comfortable.' 'I don't see why my officers should be expected to have second-best', was the reply.

Over coffee the Commissioner questioned me about the unauthorised construction of the garage at the police station. I thought for a minute that I was in trouble. Then he beamed at me. 'That's exactly what I like to see. Initiative. You've saved us quite a bit of money there, not to mention getting the Land Rover under cover. I'd better not mention it to the Provincial Engineer though or your friend Hinett's feet wouldn't touch the ground.' Noel winked at me broadly. The inspection had got off to a good start.

After lunch the inspection started with the parade. I performed my ten minutes of drill without making too much of a hash of it. The rest of the afternoon was taken up with the barracks and police station inspections. At the end of the day it was decided that the Commissioner would go off with Noel in the Land Rover on the following morning to visit a few of the outposts before returning to Moroto for the night and flying back to Kampala on the following day. The Commissioner was staying overnight with Noel, so Sandy Field, Dick Baker and I were invited round for drinks and a bite to eat that evening. This function went off without incident. Sandy Field enthused to Joe Degan about the athletics meeting and I could see my stock rising by leaps and bounds. However, pride goeth before the fall.

On the Saturday following the Commissioner's visit, I made my way in the Land Rover down to the bazaar area where the bus had just arrived with the groceries from Soroti. After packing away those of Noel together with my own in the back of the vehicle, I made my way to the post office where the mail was being sorted. I collected the bundle addressed to the police station and started off towards Noel's house. Barney was seated beside me. Passing the *boma* we started to drive past the Agricultural Officer's office I noticed a slight movement over by the office. A large rat was scuttling around outside. Barney also saw this at the same moment and without the slightest warning leapt across on top of me and out through the open window. Fortunately, having just come round a right-angled bend in the road I was only travelling at about 15 miles an hour. Nevertheless, the sudden impact of an 80 pound dog ripped my hands from the steering wheel and the Land Rover swerved violently to the left straight into a two-foot deep ditch at the roadside. There was one hell of a thump. My ribs struck the steering wheel a violent blow and my head caught somewhere in the same area cutting my mouth. The engine stalled and the vehicle tipped over at a precarious angle. Fortunately it couldn't tip right over as the ditch wasn't wide enough. Cursing and trying to get my breath, I put the vehicle into low ratio, low gear and with a horrible grinding noise, reversed out. Barney meanwhile was trying to catch the rat. I bellowed my threats at him. If I could have got hold of him I truly think I should have killed him. Clearly he took me seriously for, without much hesitation, he headed for home like the proverbial long dog. I got out and glanced around. No one about. No witnesses to make snide remarks later. I opened the bonnet. The radiator appeared to have been pushed back a couple of inches on the nearside. Also the dumb iron on the chassis was buckled. The steering was probably out of true. The steering wheel, having taken the full impact of my chest and face, was looking decidedly the worse for wear. I was having a bit of difficulty in getting my breath. I found later that I had broken a couple of ribs. There was no way that I could get out of this one. I made my way to Noel's house and explained to him what had happened. To my surprise he was quite calm about it. No hysterics, no cursing. 'Good job it didn't happen before the Commissioners visit', was all he said.

On the following day I made the acquaintance of Doug Essex. Noel drove his car, I drove the Land Rover. Doug was a few years older than me, a bachelor and, one of those rare breed who can live in the bush on his own, perfectly happy with his own company but grateful enough should anyone take the trouble to visit him. He was shortish, fair-haired and barrel chested. Tanned a chestnut brown and clad in begrimed shorts and sandals. Doug worked in the same department as Dick Heron but lived in a mobile caravan in the bush where he had a selection of heavy road construction machinery. Currently he was living about 20 miles out of Moroto, where he was grading out a track so that a drilling machine could be got in to sink boreholes for a water supply for the local tribesmen and their cattle. Part of Doug's equipment was a mobile workshop where he carried out the repairs and maintenance to the heavy machinery. After the introduction, Noel related the sorry story. Without a word Doug lifted the bonnet of the Land Rover and peered inside. 'Come back on Tuesday. I'll have it ready for you', he said. After a couple of beers Noel and I returned to Moroto. No mention was made of the mishap to anyone. After work the following Tuesday, off we went again to Doug Essex's camp. There stood the Land Rover in pristine condition. Even the nearside wing which had been buckled, had been straightened out and repainted in an identical colour. I made a mental note to drop in a couple of bottles of whisky next time I was out in this direction. 'Oh, think nothing of it', said Doug as I tried to thank him. 'Any friend of Noel's is a friend of mine. Glad to have been of help.'

The following week Noel announced that he was going to Kampala for a few days. He duly departed in his car, leaving me in charge. The following day the Head Constable made his morning report. 'Driver Odongo is very ill', he reported. 'What's he ill with?' I enquired. '*Sijui!*' (I don't know) replied the Head Constable. He then informed me that Odongo had been taken to hospital on a stretcher the previous night and had been kept in. I had become quite fond of Odongo since his arrival in Moroto and decided to go down to the hospital to have a chat with Doctor Musoke to find out what the trouble was. 'He's got a severe attack of amoebic dysentery', Doctor Musoke informed me. He'll be in about a week but I don't think he's going to be back on duty for a couple of weeks after I release him. I made my way into the ward where Odongo lay looking sorry for himself. 'Cheer up', I said. 'I'll save the cleaning of the Land Rover so that it's ready when you come out'. Odongo didn't even look mildly amused. 'These people haven't got much of a sense of humour', I thought.

As I was leaving the hospital I heard a commotion going on nearby. A tribesman and his wife had arrived with a young child. I wandered over to see what was going on. The little crowd which had gathered drew back as I approached. On the ground, whimpering, lay a young girl of about five years. A dirty bit of cloth covered her head. Her mother drew back the cloth. The sight which met my eyes caused a sharp intake of breath. The child's face had been mutilated beyond recognition. Her nose was completely missing as was one eye and the left cheek. Her facial bones and jaw were laid open and flies buzzed around feasting on the raw flesh. 'What did this?' I demanded. '*Fisi*.' (Hyena) I was told. It appeared that during the previous night the hyena had managed to get through the thorn *boma* surrounding the *manyatta* where these people were sleeping. The slumbering child had been an easy target and, with one snap, most of its face was removed. The animal had been speared while trying to find its way out through the thorn fence. Its tail had been brought in as proof so that Shs 5/- could be claimed from the D.C. I didn't fancy the job now facing Doctor Musoke. There would be little he could to for the child. There wasn't even enough flesh left to sew up the wounds. In any case, if it should survive, what would its future be. I was relieved to hear on the following day that the child had died, no doubt helped by the doctor. I found that this sort of incident was by no means rare. It probably came about mainly as a result of the tribal custom of putting out corpses to be disposed of by the vultures and hyenas. These animals became so used to feeding on human flesh that they could see little difference between a sleeping child and a dead one. I was later to see some horrific injuries caused in an identical manner in which the unfortunate victim had survived. But for what a future?

Noel returned from his Kampala trip a couple of days later. When he came into the office I got a distinct impression that he was trying to convey something to me. He was walking in a most peculiar manner, sort of lopsided. I tried to ignore this odd behaviour and eventually he gave up and sat down. It wasn't until about ten minutes later when I had practically finished giving him a run down on the current state of the station, that I suddenly saw what all the stooping and funny walking was about. An extra pip sat on his shoulder. Where there had been two, now there were three. Noel was now a Senior Assistant Superintendent of Police. I got to my feet and shook him warmly by the hand, profuse in my congratulations, and apologising for not having noticed earlier. In return he invited me to come round that evening for a celebratory drink, or two.

A week or two later I decided that it was time for me to be a bit adventurous and climb the mountain at the back of Moroto Township. I suggested to Noel that he might care to accompany me, but he was less than enthusiastic. 'I'd better stay around just in case anything serious happens', he said. I mentioned the idea around the other officers, but none of them seemed the least bit keen. 'Lazy buggers', I thought. Sandy Field was at least helpful, even if he didn't fancy the climb. 'I'll lay on a guide for you', he said. 'It will have to be one of the Tepeth tribesmen,' he added. 'They don't like carrying much though, but at least they know the best route.' The Tepeth were a Sub Tribe of the Karamajong who had confined themselves to living in the mountains hundreds of years before. They found this existence preferable since they didn't get raided as much as the others. The nearest Tepeth village was several miles away, perched on one of the spurs of the mountain well above the altitude of Moroto. I decided to make the climb on the following Sunday. In view of the fact that my guide would be traveling light I decided that I had better follow his example. I confined myself to a packet of sandwiches a couple of bottles of beer and a flask of water. To be on the safe side I took my .22 rifle and hunting knife.

Kesi brought my morning tea bright and early on the Sunday morning. Barney was keen to accompany me on this expedition but I decided that it would be best to leave him behind on this occasion. I told Kesi to keep him locked in for the next hour or so. My guide was already waiting at the back door and by 7.a.m. we were on our way. At this time of day the weather was pleasantly cool. For the first hour our progress was good. The route we followed was past the swimming pool and more or less in line with the bed of the stream though several hundred yards from it. We were very soon into an area which was totally new to me. From time to time, through gaps in the trees, I could catch glimpses of the officers' houses, the police lines and the township *dukas*. The climb was not hard in these early stages, more like a prolonged uphill walk. There was at this time no rock climbing, not even rough scrambling over the strewn boulders. Gradually the tree line grew more sparse and the going got steeper. The day grew hot and I started to sweat. I began to feel the pangs of thirst. So did my guide apparently. He made a detour over to the left for about half a mile, followed by a sweating Beaden. He didn't bother to let me know the reason for this, indeed he didn't appear to be able to speak or understand Kiswahili, so if he had informed me I shouldn't have had a clue as to what he was talking about. Eventually we reached a rocky outcrop and my guide buried his head under this. When he got up I found that he had been drinking at a tiny pool of dew. He had finished the lot. Not that I would have partaken in any event. I didn't think I was sufficiently thirsty to chance the possible bugs which might have been lurking. Still, he at least was refreshed and on we went. I decided not to start on my water or beer supply as I would probably need it more urgently later. I learned something from this experience though and on subsequent walking safaris I invariably took a small phial of permanganate of potash crystals with me, to sterilise any unexpected water supply that might show up.

So far we had not come across any sign of life with the exception of a troop of baboon and a few francolin and guinea fowl. Without warning however a large black cat, the size of Barney rose from a nearby rock where it had been lying and loped off across the grass. The Black Caracal had been described to me before but had never seen one. It was apparently exclusive to Moroto Mountain. The Caracal is a small lynx with tufted ears. Normally they are a sandy-brown colour, but the Moroto variety was pure black and very handsome. It is not large enough to be a threat to humans but could no doubt be a dangerous adversary if cornered. Also in the vicinity was plenty of evidence in the form of white droppings, of the presence of hyenas.

Our route now skirted close to a belt of scrub trees which followed the line of a dry stream bed. A disturbance in the undergrowth caused me to look round in time to see a magnificent Greater Kudu buck bounding away through the shrubs. This great antelope had a pair of beautiful spiral horns nearly five feet in length. This was the first time I had seen one up close, though the Lesser Kudu was comparatively common.

By this time the climb had developed into a hard rocky scramble. I decided that the time had come to take a drink of water. I was ready for it. In the sun it had warmed up to above blood heat. Never had a drink tasted so good though. I got through about half-a-pint before I decided to ease off. After all I had a long way to go yet. My pack of sandwiches and beer began to feel very heavy indeed. I cursed myself for bothering with the rifle. After all we had seen nothing which could be construed to be a threat. A little later however, a leopard with three cubs loped off from behind a boulder. Maybe I had been wise after all to come prepared.

Shortly before mid-day we came to the final sharp climb to the peak. Breath was coming in gasps. I began to wonder if I should make it to the top. My guide wasn't even out of breath. I determined to make it there or die in the attempt. Fifteen minutes later I was there. The peak ended in a little flat patch of grass about 20 feet square. In the middle of this was a pile of stones about three feet tall. The trig point, placed there long ago by the early surveyors.

I gazed around me. Far below was Moroto Township. I could make out the tiny houses, the *boma*, the police lines and the shopping area. Turning round I gazed in wonder at the other peaks and valleys of Moroto Mountain in each direction, stretching away as far as I could see. In the distance, 50 miles away across the plain I could make out Napak and Kadam Mountains just visible through the shimmering heat haze. We had only walked about eight miles from Moroto but had climbed from an altitude of around 4,000 feet to around 10,500. I felt buggered! Time for lunch. First though I pulled out a little hand mirror which I had carried in my pocket. I spent a few minutes flashing the mirror in the general direction of the Township. Shortly afterwards I was rewarded by an answering series of flashes from Sandy Fields house which I could just make out through the trees. At least someone knew that I had made a successful climb! I sat down and opened my pack. Taking out one of the bottles of beer I took a deep swig, followed by a couple of the sandwiches. The beer was hot and quite awful, but even so it tasted like nectar. A yard or two away sat my guide. He was begrudging me every mouthful. I suppose I owed him something for bringing me this far. I couldn't forget however, the detour for him to get a drink though, while I got nothing. My conscience pricked me and I handed him a sandwich and my second bottle of beer. A little voice inside said, 'What a mug you are Beaden. You've carried it all this way because that lazy sod wouldn't carry anything. Now you've given it away. Talk about the white man's burden!' I can't even claim to have experienced that warm feeling which one is supposed to get from doing a good turn.

The return trip down the mountain was a doddle. One of the empty bottles I left behind under the trig point, with my name and the date on a scrap of paper inside. My guide was more than happy to carry his empty bottle back to get the 20 cent deposit back from the *duka*. That left me to carry the rifle and a half-empty water flask. I didn't stint myself with liquid on the way down. After all anything I drank lightened the load. About a mile before reaching the swimming pool I was greeted by delighted barking and Barney bounded up to me. 'Bloody old fool', I said. 'You might have been taken by a leopard, coming up here on your own'. Barney beamed at me. Clearly he didn't mind being scolded now that I had returned. By 3 o'clock in the afternoon I strolled in a leisurely fashion up to my house. Kesi was there to greet me, the kettle boiling in readiness and a welcome cup of tea was soon on the table. Barney, he told me, had taken off for the mountain as soon as he was let out, so had clearly spent five or six hours looking for me.

Chapter 12

A day or two later Sandy Field sent a message across to the police station. With considerable difficulty we deciphered his dreadful handwriting. 'Would we both come over for a conference?' 'Get the coffee ready. We'll be over in ten minutes', we replied. We made our leisurely way across to the *boma*. Sandy Field and Dick Baker were awaiting our arrival together with several other officers. Cups of coffee awaited us. 'We-we've got a small pro-problem', stammered Sandy. This slight impediment always surfaced when he became agitated. 'It's about the appointment of the new County Chief of Jie. The tribal elders don't like the choice I've made and they're coming in for a *baraza*.' I fear that this was all over my head. Most of the others seemed to know what he was talking about and I was loath to show my ignorance. For once, however, I felt that I'd got to know what was going on. If there was going to be trouble I should undoubtedly be involved and I wanted to know what was entailed. In answer to my questions Sandy enlarged on the subject. The post of County Chief or *Ekapalon* as it was known, was not an hereditary rank. If one of them died or retired, nominations were made by the *Ejakaits* or Secondary Chiefs for the new appointment to be made from one of their number. Almost invariably each Ejakait nominated himself and it was then left to the D.C. to make the final choice of who would be promoted to the vacant position. On this occasion, however, the final choice had not met with the approval of the local tribesmen. In fact, it appeared that they wouldn't have the chosen individual at any price. Poor old Sandy was in a cleft stick. If he insisted on sticking to his guns we might find ourselves with a full-scale uprising on our hands with possibly considerable violence against the new County Chief and ourselves to boot. On the other hand, if he conceded that he had made a wrong choice and rescinded the appointment he would lose face and the tribesmen might be encouraged to stir up trouble about any other Government decisions which they might not approve of.

'How many tribesmen do you think might be attending the *baraza*?', I enquired. 'No idea', replied Sandy. 'Might be a couple of hundred, could be a thousand!' 'Mind if I make a suggestion', I enquired. 'Send out to the Ejakaits telling them that anyone carrying a spear will be arrested as soon as he enters the township!' This notion was rapidly agreed to. Noel and I then decided that we would have to denude the outposts for a couple of days to ensure that we had sufficient strength in Moroto to contain any violence which might take place.

The *baraza* was due to take place on the following Saturday so the next few hours were spent sending off signals to the various outposts instructing all but a skeleton staff to make their was to Moroto. By Friday evening the police lines were bursting at the seams. Many police wives were to be heard celebrating the unexpected return of their husbands from the bush! Early on Saturday morning Noel and I made our way to the parade ground where all available staff were drawn up. The position was explained to them, though I suspect they already knew why they were there. Rifles and ammunition were issued to half of them, the remainder were issued with riot shields and batons. I hoped that all this would prove unnecessary but it was as well to be on the safe side.

By 9 o'clock the first groups of tribesmen started to arrive in the township and make their way towards the *boma*. I was relieved to notice that none of them carried spears, though virtually all of them carried stout sticks. I wondered if we should have banned sticks as well. Too late now!

Among the first arrivals was the newly-appointed County Chief. He had a retinue of about 30 or 40 followers but appeared uneasy. He and two or three others went in to see Sandy Field. By 10 a.m the area between the *boma* and the *dukas* was crowded with a milling throng all decked out in their ceremonial garb. This made a wonderful spectacle. Hundreds of them wore leopard skin cloaks with head-dresses of black and white ostrich feathers. One or two wore conventional European style clothes but these were in a minority of half a dozen. A conservative estimate of the number was three to three and a half thousand. About half of these were women. These were clad in their tribal attire, bare-breasted with leather aprons, their necks and arms adorned with an enormous weight in copper bangles and their hair liberally dressed with sheep fat. By and large they seemed to be in a good mood. Just as well. If they turned nasty our 130 police wouldn't stand a chance.

Noel sent off a situation report to Kampala. This was a real classic. He finished it with the comment. 'Am sending in a plainclothes constable to report on the general feeling. Further message to follow.' In this he was a good as his word. We only had one constable of the Karamajong tribe. P.C. Engatun, (Karamajong for Lion) was sent for. He was divested of his trousers and sent to mingle with the crowd. This was the first and only time I ever saw a Karamajong appear embarrassed. I don't know why. From what I saw he hadn't anything to be ashamed of. Half-an-hour or so later P.C. Engatun returned to report that violence was not anticipated, not in the immediate future anyway. Noel duly passed the good news to Kampala. Among the crowds were a number of individuals even more sumptuously dressed that the others. These I discovered were the witch doctors. The crowd divided into groups and squatted under the thorn trees, from where I could hear the chiefs and witch doctors haranguing them. From time to time bands of women broke away from the groups and ran around jumping high in the air, swinging their leather skirts and ululating and chanting. This, I found, was an attempt to urge the men on to more drastic action than was being taken.

Eventually Sandy Field emerged from the *boma* and the vast crowd gathered around. Sandy could speak Kiswahili and was fluent in the Acholi dialect but was lost with Karamajong. The *baraza* was therefore somewhat protracted with multiple translations going on. From time to time one of the witch doctors or an Ejakait would leap to his feet and wave arms and fists in the direction of the new *Ekapalon* who, for his own safety was seated near to the D.C. Continual ululation's by groups of women tended to disrupt the proceedings. Sandy Field was quite adamant that his choice of *Ekapalon* was final. The tribesmen were quite adamant that they would not accept this choice. Their objections seemed to be based on two factors. First the *Ekapalon*, when an *Ejakait*, used to take the best girls without payment. Second, that he was known to confiscate cattle from the tribesmen for imagined offences. Eventually an old man got to his feet. He was not dressed in any finery. He was not a witch doctor or a chief. He was just the oldest person present. He looked to be well over 100 years old, but it was difficult to be certain on this. He didn't have a lot to say either. What he did say was to the point. He spoke directly to the *Ekapalon*. 'You are not fitted to be a chief. You have two choices. You can resign or you can be killed. I shall not kill you but you will not last a month.' He sat down. The crowd was silent. I wondered if I should arrest the old man for incitement to violence, but this did not appear to be incitement. It was more a statement of fact. Eventually the new *Ekapalon* rose to his feet. He looked rather grey. His statement was short and to the point. 'I resign', he said. The crowd started to clap. A deep chanting came from the throats of the assembled warriors. Rising to their feet they started their leaping dance. The women commenced their ululation. Then they joined in the dance. What could have been a very nasty situation had been averted. They had come into Moroto determined by one means or another to reject or dispose of the new *Ekapalon*. They had achieved this object. They had won. Sandy Field had, however, not lost face in the process. Gradually they started to disperse. 'Who was the old man?' I enquired. 'Oh that was the father of the *Ekapalon*', was the answer.

As the thronging tribesmen started to make their way out of the town the weekly bus arrived outside the post office with the mail. The postmaster had barricaded himself inside and refused to open the door since around 500 tribesmen had surrounded the building. I don't think they were hostile in any way, but they were interested to see the mail being unloaded. I decided to clear them off so calling Barney I left the police station and wandered as nonchalantly as I could towards the post office. A remarkable thing then happened. One look at Barney was enough. The crowd started to melt away. By the time I reached the post office they had broken into small groups and were making their way peacefully out of town.

Having got the embarrassing incident of the *Ekapalon*'s selection out of the way, Sandy Field decided to take a spot of local leave. Most government officers in need of a break made for the Kenya coast, around Mombassa or Malindi, or at least a change of scenery. The high life in Kampala or up to the Murchison Falls. Not so Sandy Field. He had one great aim in life. This was to slaughter his annual quota of three elephants and one rhino. No other European accompanied him on these expeditions. He would set off in his American Ford truck together with his cook and gun-bearer. His tracker and porters he would hire locally. Being well-known in the area he usually got the same team and he would send a message to the local *Ejakait* a few days before his arrival to ensure that all was laid on and the initial search for suitable elephants was well under way. The Kidepo Valley up on the Sudan border was his favourite venue. This was an area alive with game of all sorts. The great elephant herds which had roamed the whole of the District at the end of the 19th century when they were hunted by Karamoja Bell were, of course, a thing of the past. However, there were a number of large elephant herds in Kidepo, many of the old bulls carrying good ivory. Personally speaking I viewed with repulsion the thought of destroying in a split-second a great animal which had taken 70 years to reach maturity. However, it was perfectly legal and a lot of other people did it. Maybe Sandy Field, being of such small stature, got a thrill from dropping such a large creature. On the other hand, ivory and rhino horn fetched a high price so maybe the money was the attraction. A week later he was back, very cheerful, having taken his full quota. The six tusks in the back of his truck weighed a total of 450 pounds and would fetch a great deal of money. He was a bit disappointed with the pair of rhino horns though. 'Not up to the usual standard I'm afraid, there's a lot of poaching going on up there. The buggers are coming over from the Sudan and taking the best ones. You'll have to make a trip up there and see if you can catch them!' I wondered how one went about catching gangs of armed and desperate poachers without the benefit of an army unit and aircraft. I said I would give it a bit of thought. I accompanied him round to his house where we enjoyed a celebratory drink and I was shown the rather smelly sets of elephant and rhino feet which were in the process of being dried out before they went off to be turned into stools and door stops.

The next week an evening party was held at Pandit Puran Chand's garage. This, it turned out, was a farewell party for Dr. Musoke. I was sorry to see Musoke leave. We had got on well together on the various times he had accompanied me on murder investigations. He had never turned a hair at performing post-mortem examinations on the smelliest corpses. I hoped that his replacement would be as efficient. On enquiry I found that his replacement, Dr. Lubega had arrived that day. 'I'll come down to the hospital tomorrow and you can introduce me', I said.

The following morning I made my way to the hospital. Dr. Lubega turned out to be a plump little Muganda. Pleasant enough but a bit out of his depth I thought. Dr. Musoke introduced us and we chatted for a while. As I was about to leave there was a commotion outside in the hospital compound. A woman shouting and ululating. I made my way out to see what was going on. The two doctors accompanied me. The woman who was making all the fuss was accompanied by a man, apparently her husband. She was carrying a bundle in her arms. This turned out to be a baby of about 9 months of age. A deep gash on the child's head penetrated the bone and laid open the brain tissue. Remarkably it was still alive although the wound had started to suppurate. As soon as the cloth covering the infant's head was removed the flies started to swarm around, feasting on the living tissue and busily laying their eggs. With the aid of one of the hospital orderlies interpreting, the tale was told. Two days earlier the man had come home drunk and had started to beat up his wife. She happened to be carrying the child. He had made a wild swipe at her and naturally she dodged. Unfortunately he was wearing a wrist knife, a fearsome weapon, used during cattle raids and very useful in hand-to-hand combat. The weapon was produced by the man himself. A steel disc, cut and split to fit over the wrist. I had seen these weapons before. Normally the razor sharp blade is protected by a leather cover. This time, however, the cover had come off and the blow had caught the child on the head causing this horrific injury. Remorse showed in the man's features and anger and the lust for revenge in those of his wife. The doctors took the child and its mother into the hospital. I bundled the husband into the Land Rover and removed him to the police station. The following day the child was dead. After the due process of the law the husband was convicted of manslaughter and spent the next three years in prison.

Following his successful hunting trip, Sandy Field decided to go on leave to the U.K. Normally a tour for a government officer was two-and-a-half to three years, followed by between five- and six-months' leave. For reasons best known to himself Sandy had decided that 18 months was sufficient this time and so he was away for three months leave. In these circumstances it was not considered necessary for him to pack up all his belongings, since he would be returning to Moroto at the end of his leave. He simply turned the key in the lock of his front door, sent his cook and houseboy on leave and departed after the usual mandatory parties at the *dukas*. Dick Baker was considered too junior to hold the fort during his absence so a day or two before his departure a relief D.C. arrived. This was Peter Gibson. Peter turned out to be a bachelor, about three years older than myself. He had been in the Uganda Civil Service since around 1941. I took an immediate liking to him and rather wished that he was going to be in office here rather more permanently.

A couple of days after Sandy Field's departure, Peter made his way across to the police station. Clearly he had not been advised about Barney. He was accompanied by his dog, an enormous grey rough-haired creature of unknown origin, about the size of a large Airedale. Barney lay snoozing on the verandah in front of the police station, at peace with the world. He awoke suddenly, to find himself the victim of a totally unprovoked assault. I suppose that all dogs have evolved their favourite method of dealing with their adversaries. Peter Gibson's animal attached itself to Barney's right ear before he had even opened his eyes. Not unnaturally Barney was a bit miffed about this, since it tended to inhibit his own opening gambit which was to clamp his jaws around one front leg, and wave his adversary about like a flag, until the bone disintegrated. In the event all he could do was to slash around with his teeth hoping that he would catch a sensitive part. After a few seconds he succeeded in this and the combatants broke apart momentarily and then clashed again in a battle royal. Blood started to spurt in all directions. Peter who was carrying a heavy walking stick started to belabour Barney whenever he saw an opportunity. Not to be outdone I picked up my own stick and commenced belabouring Peter's dog. Neither of the combatants took the slightest notice. Seizing his opportunity Peter grabbed his dogs collar. Personally I would have preferred to have let the two sort the matter out for themselves. That way the pecking order would have been decided and future peace assured. However, in the circumstances I unwisely felt I had no alternative by to try to grab Barney. This I did. Which of the contestants was responsible, I don't know to this day. A searing pain in my left hand and a jet of blood sprayed up the wall. My hand was laid open from the wrist down to the tips of two of my fingers as neatly as though a razor had been used. 'Sod this', I thought and retired from the conflict, leaving Barney to sort matters out. Seeing that I had received a *coup de grâce*, Peter also thought better of it and let go of his hound. Within seconds Barney had secured his favourite hold and the aggressor was being used in the traditional flag-waving ceremony. Crunch went the front leg and the grey hound retired from the battle as fast as its three remaining legs would carry it. Noel, who had emerged from the office alerted by the rumpus outside, wrapped a towel round my hand and bundled me into his car where I bled copiously over the upholstery. At the hospital Dr. Lubega made a neat job of stitching up the wounds and I returned to the office. I never did find out the reason for Peter's visit to the police station which was the cause of all the trouble.

The following week the blow fell. A signal from Kampala. 'The following postings will take place. S.A.S.P. Caunce from Moroto to Kampala as O.C. Nsambya Barracks. A.S.P. Peskett from Kampala to Moroto.' I think that Noel was as fed up about this as I was. On the other hand I might have been mistaken. I had long had the impression that Noel was happier seated behind a desk or out on the parade ground, than roughing it in the bush. Unlike myself who couldn't get enough of the outdoor life. Still I like to think that we had each learned something from the other. I had certainly benefitted from Noel's advice and expertise in administration. He, in turn, had learned a bit about building skills and how to get people to do things to ease life's path. Possibly my small experience in investigative techniques had helped also. Noel could not even equal my limited expertise in this field since he had joined the Uganda Police direct from his Army service.

The news of Noel's imminent departure provoked the usual hectic round of farewell parties. Fortunately the posting was not to be effective for about three weeks so I had time to put into effect an important task I had in mind, prior to the arrival of a new O.C. with whom I might or might not hit it off. This was making the formal application for the purchase a car. The mandatory six months had almost elapsed since the date of my arrival and I felt myself reasonably well-off these days. I had accumulated a bit of money in the bank and had now completed the purchase of all the essential items I needed for my comfort. A car was next on the agenda. Never having owned a vehicle of any sort I was at a bit of a loss as to what sort to plump for. My choice was narrowed when a new Force Order was published, limiting cars purchased by new officers to vans and trucks. I presume that this was to stop the practice by some young officers, down in the fleshpots of civilisation, of buying expensive passion wagons to impress local nurses and typists. In my own case a panel van appeared to be an ideal mode of transport. Plenty of room for carrying my equipment should I decide to take my own transport instead of the Land Rover. If I so fancied, I could adapt the back of the vehicle to take a mattress and thus could doss down in it any time I felt so inclined. After weighing the options I decided on a Standard Vanguard van which was priced at about £500. An excellent system was in operation whereby a loan could be obtained to purchase the vehicle. Repayment of the loan was by monthly installments over a period of five years. A monthly mileage allocation was then granted for which so much was paid per mile. The first 3,500 miles was paid at the top rate, the next 5,000 at a slightly lower rate and anything over that at the lowest rate. Very few officers managed to get a mileage allocation which took them into the second band. However, Karamoja was special. Not only did the 2i/c get a very substantial mileage allocation of some 480 miles a month, but the roads in Karamoja were classed as being 'rough track' i.e. so bad that they warranted a special rate per mile. The mileage allowance was of course based on the engine capacity of the car purchased. In my case the Standard Vanguard was, I believe, classed at Grade 2, having an 1,800 cc engine. As I recollect it, the rate I would get, assuming my application was approved, was Shs 1-23 per mile for the first 3,500 miles, dropping to Shs 1-03 per mile for the next 5,000. A quick calculation informed me that 480 miles a month amounted to 5,760 miles a year. I was unlikely to get this full amount since any unused mileage at the end of each month could not be carried over to act as a bonus for the following one. On the other hand if I exceeded 480 miles in any month my claim would not be met without there being very special reasons. However, I felt that I would manage very nicely with this allocation which could be regarded as manna from heaven. Visions of untold wealth dazzled me. With a new car the running expenses would be very low, the cost of the insurance and the oil and petrol being virtually the only outgoings. With a bit of luck I might be able to pay off the loan within about 18 months, after which the cash from the mileage would become a second income, tax-free too. I duly made my application on the appropriate forms and Noel had no hesitation in making the necessary recommendation for approval.

Only a couple of small clouds loomed on the horizon. Examinations. My efforts at learning Kiswahili were making but slow progress. True, I could make myself understood. By and large I could also understand what was being said to me. That was no problem. Grammatically, however, a lot was left to be desired. There was no one in Moroto to whom I could turn in order to get any instruction on the technicalities of this language. In fact, had I been in a position to use what was known as '*safi Swahili*' that is, grammatically correct, I very much doubt if I should have been understood by anyone at all. This, however, was not an argument which would have been accepted by the powers that be. As regards written Swahili, the situation appeared to be totally beyond my control. Again there was no one to turn to. Whereas my colleagues in the big cities had the benefit of classes, which they could attend at any time they felt so inclined, no such facility was available to me. For hours I poured over my books in the evening, both at home in my cottage and at the camp fire on safari. I picked up the odd phrase here and there. In fact I was able to assist Tom Hinett who was also facing a language crisis. Tom was approaching the end of his tour of duty and had to pass the Swahili Elementary Oral examination. Poor Tom had far less of a clue on the subject than I had. His was what was disparagingly called 'Kitchen Swahili'. It contained no grammar at all and was merely a series of words strung together. I suppose it could be likened to the pidgin English spoken in such places as Borneo. I made it my business to impart to him such small knowledge as I had.

The second cloud on the horizon was the Law Examination. There were five different subjects to this. Penal Code, Criminal Procedure Code, Police Standing Orders and Procedure, Evidence Ordinance and Local and Special Laws, which covered such subjects as Game, Witchcraft, *Waragi* and many others.

The next Law examination was to be held in Mbale shortly after Noel's departure. The Swahili examination had to be taken in Kampala at the end of the year. I decided that I had better show willing and duly submitted my application to participate in both examinations. I privately decided that since the Law examination could be taken a few subjects at a time I would concentrate my efforts on the Penal Code and the Criminal Procedure Code and leave the other subjects till a later date when, maybe, I would have had more time to brush up on everything.

We had visitors in the Rest House. Half-a-dozen of them, four men and (wonder of wonders) two women. When I first saw them they were wandering past my house heading in the direction of the swimming pool An opportunity such as this was not to be missed. True, the women could not be described as being young and glamorous, but to one who, apart from Vi Hinett, had been starved of female company for months they looked like Helen of Troy. I grabbed my swimming trunks and headed for the pool. On my arrival, to my disappointment there was no sign of them. I supposed that they must have missed the way and headed up the mountain. I dumped my trunks in the changing cubicle and started after them. As usual I had brought my .22 rifle with me in case I saw any guinea fowl. I didn't really like the idea of strangers wandering around on the mountain unprotected. True, they were unlikely to come to any harm, but there were leopard around as well as cobras and puff adders. After a short while I heard voices ahead of me. Barney ran ahead and by the time I reached the new arrivals he had already made their acquaintance. Introductions were made. I decided, on closer inspection, that the two women were not worth bothering with. They were pleasant enough, but I hadn't reached a degree of desperation sufficient to warrant quite such an effort. I found that the party were in fact scientists from the World Health Organisation. They were researching Yellow Fever. 'Why come to Moroto to study Yellow Fever', I enquired. 'Moroto is known to be one of the places where the local population of vervet monkeys were carrying the disease', I was told. Well, this was news to me. I mentally counted my blessings. At least I couldn't get it. I had been inoculated against it before leaving England! Just as well, since the chances of survival by a European getting the disease were about four to one against. I returned to the pool and enjoyed a solitary dip. During the next few days our visitors were active in the area of the swimming pool. Traps were laid and a number of vervet monkeys were caught alive. A number of others were shot and various organs removed for examination.

Eventually the party departed back to Entebbe after the mandatory party, this time at the Rest House, since that was where Peter Gibson was residing.

It was lunch-time and I was just relaxing with a glass of beer on the verandah prior to returning to the office when I heard a commotion going on at the back of the house. I rapidly made my way there. Tom Hinett's houseboy was gesticulating wildly to Kesi. For a moment I thought that Barney had been at the guinea pigs again. Then I caught the words '*Bwana na kufa*', (The Bwana is dead'). Without waiting to hear more, I rushed over to Tom's house. Before I reached the door I saw Vi Hinett on the other side of the road where there was a deep gully formed over the years by flood water from the mountain rushing down during the rains. Of Tom there was no sign. I ran over to where Vi stood. The gully lay back about 15 yards from the roadway. At this point it was probably about 20 feet deep. Large tree roots extended from the red murrum soil and swinging from one of these was Tom's van. It was quite clear what had happened. Tom had put his van into reverse instead of forward gear and instead of driving forward and out of his drive, he had suddenly gone out backwards at a great rate of knots. There was nothing between him and the gully and he had gone straight over the edge backwards. Well, I did mention that he was the world's worst driver! Fortunately, and by a complete fluke, one of the roots sticking out of the bank had become entangled with the front axle of the van, suspending it in mid air. Poor old Tom as lying back in his seat with his bald head sticking out of the window shouting for help. I rapidly sized up the situation. For the moment Tom was safe. The root seemed sufficiently substantial to hold the weight of the car, for a while anyway. Getting Tom out presented a problem however. His door was about 12 feet above the bottom of the gully. If he scrambled about too much he might dislodge the van from the root. A ladder was needed. I said as much to Vi. 'There's one over at the back of our house', she said. I ran over and found a ladder about ten feet in length leaning against the back wall. 'Not really long enough, but better than nothing', I decided. I carried the ladder across the road and climbed down into the gully. Propping it as near as possible to the side of the van, I clambered up, hoping the root would continue to support the weight. Of course the ladder was too short as I had known it would be. However, I was within a few feet of the van door. Tom poked his head out as I arrived. 'Open your door and slide out', I commanded. 'I'll take your weight until you are on the ladder.' Tom did as instructed and slid out towards me. Fortunately, he being a small man, I was able to support him. The van swayed ominously. as the weight shifted and I breathed a sigh of relief when we were both on the ladder. Soon we had scrambled down and out of the gully to safety. Poor Vi was in tears of relief to have Tom safely back at her side. Later the same afternoon Madan Tandon arrived with a breakdown vehicle and Tom's van was winched out of the gully without so much as a scratch on it, apart from the many already there. A few days after this Brian Peskett arrived. We had, of course, already met in London. I wondered how he would settle down to the Karamoja life style. For the next three or four days both he and Noel were busy with the handing over. I kept a low profile. Each evening a boozy party took place at one or other of the *dukas*, each vying with the other in their efforts to say farewell to Noel and welcome to Brian. Hangovers followed each morning. Noel took Brian out for a quick tour of the outstations, but managed to get back each evening in time for the celebrations. Eventually the handing-over was completed. A large lorry arrived from Kampala and Noel's property, packed in wooden crates, was loaded aboard. Noel's cook, houseboy and Sophia climbed into the back of his car and off they went. 'Come and stay with me any time you're in Kampala', Noel called as he drove away. Approval for the purchase of my car arrived. The Uganda Company in Kampala were the agents for this make and a short correspondence followed. The model I wanted was not in stock. They could, however, obtain delivery around Christmas time. Also for a few extra pounds I could have side windows fitted into the panels but this would take an extra day or two to complete. I thought it was a good idea to incorporate this refinement and gave the necessary instructions. Arranging collection would present no problem. I was going to have to travel to Kampala to sit the Swahili examination at the end of the year anyway. I could collect my car at the same time. The Land Rover was due for a major service which had to be done in Kampala. I could combine the lot. Down to Kampala in the Land Rover with Driver Odongo, stay overnight, take the Swahili exam the following day, stay overnight. Odongo could then take the Land Rover back to

Moroto. Meanwhile, I pick up my car and also return to Moroto. Sounds good. I gave the necessary instructions to Uganda Company to have my car ready on the due date.

Brian Peskett seemed a bit out of his depth in his new environment. Feeling something of an 'old hand', I helped him settle in as far as I could. After a few days he started to relax a bit. We took the odd day trip out together and did a bit of bird shooting and viewing the scenery. The grass was now bone dry, what there was of it left. The herds of cattle had consumed most of it. Grass fires were burning in many areas. These raged out of control for days at a time. Unlike the popular conception of bush fires as seem at the cinema, these fires travelled relatively slowly. It was rare for any animals to be caught unless this was deliberately done by the tribesmen who sometimes used what was known as ring-burning to trap a few unwary buck. To do this they would wait for a day when there was little wind, and then surround a herd of buck or other animals, setting fire to the grass in a complete circle round them. The animals would then mill round in panic, the ring of fire gradually becoming smaller. Eventually, blinded by smoke and flames they would make a break for freedom to be met by the spears of the tribesmen awaiting them. The small grass fires at present burning created an interesting picture of life in the African bush. As the flames crept forward, a multitude of insects could be seen flying up ahead of the flames. Mostly these would eventually be overtaken and roasted. As soon as the ground had cooled sufficiently, hundreds of kites and buzzards would descend on the prepared meals awaiting them. In addition, gangs of mongooses would pop up out of the nearest termite hill, where they had taken shelter from the fire. In every direction they would scamper, eating as many of the roast insects as they could stuff down themselves, and always keeping a wary eye open for the birds of prey which would take them for a meal if the opportunity presented itself. Lizards also formed a substantial part of the casualties of these conflagrations, as did the occasional snake, though it seemed rare that the latter were entrapped. Mostly, I think, they took shelter underground along with the mongooses. An amusing sight I saw on a number of occasions was that of a Secretary Bird strutting around a newly-burned area, picking up the occasional lizard or snake if it was lucky. Occasionally they would be seen to stand on a still-glowing patch of grass or bush, when they would leap into the air with much wing fluttering and foot-stamping. This experience didn't. however, seem to deter them from continuing their meal.

Often at this time of year the heat of the equatorial sun concentrated on the dusty surface of the bush would create violent up-currents of air. These would start to spin, carrying the hot dust into the vortex and increasing the temperature in so doing. This dust, together with the ash and debris from the grass fires, would suddenly be whirled into the rotary movement. Tall columns would whip into the air for all the world like water spouts. These were the famous dust devils. Sometimes they would rise several hundred feet into the air before collapsing as the altitude of the column caused a decrease in temperature. At times a remarkable landscape would present itself with dozens of dust devils swirling in all directions. Another interesting phenomena which occurred at this time of year when the high winds sometimes blew through the bush were the whistling thorns. A type of thorn tree growing in vast numbers in the bush and possessing evil-looking thorns up to three inches in length would be attacked by an insect pest which bored into the wood at the base of these thorns. As a defence, the trees would produce a gall about the size of a large marble. In this cosy home the insect would reach maturity and then burrow out of the gall to commence the cycle all over again. The galls, with their attached thorns and each with several holes bored into it, would emit an eerie whistle as the wind caught them.

The desert rose was yet another feature of the dry season. These strange plants were, of course, not roses at all. In fact I have no idea to what genus they belonged, but desert rose was the name commonly used for them. They could grow to a height of about five feet, although two feet was more common. A fleshy-looking tapering trunk emerged from the soil, dividing into a number of smaller limbs. From these dark green leaves rather like those of a camellia sprouted. At the height of the dry season, gorgeous scarlet and cream blossoms would emerge, making a startling contrast to the surrounding dry vegetation. During my stay in Karamoja I dug up a number of desert roses and replanted them in Moroto at my house. They readily accepted their changed location. The extraordinary thing about these plants was the root which formed a great sphere in which liquid was stored to last through the dry season. On smaller plants this would be the size of a football, but of the really big ones, the root could be several feet across. Digging up these monsters was out of the question.

The Law Examination was now on me. Having no transport of my own, I had to take the Land Rover. This made me less than popular with Brian. However there was no alternative. 'Suppose we have a murder or a cattle raid?', he enquired. 'You'll just have to hire a lorry as we used to', I told him. 'Anyway, I'll be back tomorrow night.' With this advice I was away. Mbale was about 160 miles away, via Soroti and across the Awoja Ferry. I didn't bother with taking Driver Odongo with me for such a short trip. I just took enough with me to see me through the night and with a clean uniform for the following day. I had arranged to stay overnight in the Mbale Rest House and here I met up with a couple of other officers also there for the examination. During the evening and over a couple of beers we discussed our varied experiences over the past months. Fairly hum-drum was the impression I gained from the others. All were envious of my life in the bush. I did, however, point out that it was not all beer and skittles. A lot of hard work was involved, with very little time for studying for the various examinations. It appeared that the others were prepared to sit all five papers.

There was no way I could do this. I had done a bit of preparation for the Penal Code and the Criminal Procedure Code which, in any case, were not too different to British Law with which I was conversant. The conversation turned to the Local and Special Laws, which I had made no attempt to study. Various aspects of the Witchcraft Ordinance and *Waragi* Ordinance and others were discussed and I suddenly realised that I knew the answers to the various problems being posed. On the following day I sat this paper in addition to the ones I had already entered for. When the results were published a few weeks later, I found to my delight that I had sailed through all three subjects.

Christmas was nearly on us. I wasn't sure how much of a celebration might occur in a place as remote as Karamoja. Peter Gibson's mother had arrived at the Rest House to spend Christmas with him and invitations were sent out to those officers who would be available to join him for a party on Christmas evening. I thought it might be politic to invite Brian Peskett and Dick Baker around to have Christmas lunch with me.

They accepted my invitation and I went down to Ishverbhai and got a good stock of booze. I thought he looked at me a bit oddly, but he said nothing. Then I had an idea, a brainwave. Out at Rupa, about eight miles west around the mountain from Moroto itself, I had seen Greater Bustard on a number of occasions. If I could get one of these birds it would make a magnificent roast for Christmas lunch. On the afternoon before Christmas Eve I got into the Land Rover and headed west along the rough track to Rupa Village. The landscape varied little from that of Moroto itself, the bush cover being somewhat heavier. No Bustard were to be seen, though there were large flocks of Guinea Fowl. Rupa itself consisted of a small cluster of roughly-thatched mud huts on the slope of one of the mountain spurs. Small herds of cattle under the guard of children were scattered over the area. Most of them waved as we drove by. A few ran behind the vehicle for a short distance, then I was out of the populated area and into the bush again. Shortly afterwards I saw my first Kori Bustard. A vast bird, having a wing span of around eight feet and weighing some 30 pounds. He was some 200 yards away through the bush. I got out of the vehicle and started a stealthy approach but he had been alerted by the noise of the Land Rover engine and was away well before I could get into range. I decided to continue walking quietly through the bush and had gone nearly a mile when my attention was drawn to a movement over to my right. Here was another Kori Bustard or maybe the same one. Fifty yards away. I carefully raised my rifle and fired just as he was getting airborne. The great wings ceased to flap and he plummeted to earth. By the time I reached him, all movement had ceased. My shot had taken him in the back of the neck and he must have been dead before he reached the ground. I returned to the Land Rover carrying my prize.

On my return to Moroto I set about plucking and dressing the bird. With some satisfaction I popped the Bustard into my fridge. Fortunately I had taken the precaution of getting a large capacity one so there was still plenty of room for a good stock of beer. Of course, I had completely overlooked ordering from Soroti the sausage meat to use for the stuffing. Never mind, I felt sure that the bird would be marvellous on its own. I had remembered to order a tinned Christmas pudding so a good meal was on the cards.

The following day was Christmas Eve. I went to the office as usual, hoping that we would have a couple of days clear of murders or raids so that Christmas could be celebrated in peace. On my return home at lunchtime I was greeted by a strange gobbling noise. Barney was all for going to sort out whatever was responsible but resisted the inclination at my command. I made my way to the back of the house. A large turkey was tethered to a small shrub growing near the kitchen. Kesi came out to greet me grinning broadly. *'Jambo Bwana'*, he said. *'Mahindi a me lete kuku kubwa kwa Christmas.'* (An Indian brought this large chicken for Christmas.) I felt glad that the bird was still on the hoof. At least I could return it to its owner. There had clearly been a misunderstanding somewhere. I certainly hadn't ordered a turkey. In answer to my questions, I gathered that the Indian was none other that Ishverbhai. What on earth was the man playing at? As I stood talking to Kesi, my attention was drawn to the sound of another turkey gobbling from the direction of Tom Hinnet's house. The tethered turkey answered back and was interrupted by further gobbling noises from the directions of all the other European officers' houses. What was going on? I could only presume that everyone else had ordered a turkey for Christmas and that, in the confusion, one had mistakenly been delivered to me. I was surprised that no one had mentioned to me that they were ordering a turkey. It might have saved me the bother of shooting the Bustard! I made my way into my house. A large cardboard carton stood on the floor of the sitting room. 'What is this?', I enquired of Kesi. *'Sijui'*, he replied, *'Mahindi a me lete.'* (I don't know. The Indian brought it.) I started to empty the box. A bottle of Dimple Haig whisky, a bottle of Courvoisier brandy, two bottles of sherry, a bottle of vodka and one of gin, boxes of chocolates, a dozen bottles of beer, a tinned Christmas pudding, two bottles of liqueur and an assortment of boxes of dates, figs and so on. My eyes popped out of my head at the sight of all this. I should have to go down to Ishverbhai straight away to sort this business out. First I wandered over to Tom's house. A similar box stood on his verandah. Tom came out to greet me, beaming. 'I see your Christmas goodies arrived as well', he chortled. 'I'm doing very well this year. Do you think you could give me a hand killing the turkey later on?' In addition to the a box similar to the one at my house, there were presents for Vi and the four children. 'Tom', I said, 'would you mind telling me what is going on. I never ordered any of this stuff.' 'Do you really mean to say you don't know', he replied. 'It's Christmas. It's customary for the *duka* owners to bring round presents.' 'A present is all very well', I said, 'But surely not a bloody great boxful of booze.' 'You wait and see', said Tom, 'There's a lot more yet.' I made my way down to see Dick Baker. I found him busy unpacking his box of booze. He seemed to have even more than me, I requested an explanation from him. 'It's the custom', he said. 'The Hindi's love it. It's their way of saying thank you for your help durng the year and for keeping them and their families safe. Just accept it with dignity and stop making a fuss. All the officers on the station get it. They don't expect preferential treatment as a result.' 'Do you think I ought to write a thank-you letter', I enquired. 'Certainly not', was the reply. With this I had to be satisfied. During the afternoon, from my office, I could see heavily-laden lorries heading up to the European quarter. On my return home at tea time, I found yet another tethered turkey plus another half-dozen boxes of assorted booze. I walked over to Brian's house. He was busy unpacking his boxes. He seemed to have done just as well even though he had only just arrived in Moroto. I returned home. What on earth was I going to do with two live turkeys? My Christmas dinner was already taken care of. I certainly had no further room in the fridge. I should somehow have to keep them alive till I was ready to use them. If I kept them till I went down to Kampala, I could pass one over to Noel. I instructed Kesi to keep them in the kitchen at night and to let them out to wander round the garden during the day.

My Christmas lunch went off well. A couple of beers each to start off. Both Brian and Dick were somewhat surprised at my choice of the roast. Neither of them had tried roast Bustard before. Neither had I for that matter. However, the meat was lean and tender. The breast meat was a little on the dark side but it was moist and delicious. Kesi had made a good job of the roast potatoes and the meal was completed with tinned peas and carrots. The Christmas pudding followed, washed down with copious draughts of the wine which had been included in the Christmas boxes. After coffee and liqueurs, the three of us settled down to a semi- drunken snooze.

During the evening, I wandered down to the Rest House to

join the festivities which Peter was organising. His mother was a dear old bird, well into her 60s but very spry. She seemed to be more responsible for organising the evening than Peter in fact. She kept popping out to the kitchen to supervise the cooking. Surprise, surprise, the main dish was roast turkey! After the blow out at lunch time, I had problems doing justice to the spread which appeared. Somehow I tucked away a sufficient quantity to avoid being scolded by Mum. After the Christmas pudding, the coffee and liqueurs, I was about ready to flake out in a chair and go to sleep. Not a bit of it. We had to play party games and charades. I had done nothing like this since I was a child and felt a bit embarrassed by the whole proceedings. Eventually, we each had to act out the title of a piece of music while the others had to guess what it was! The excessive booze had loosened me up and I enacted a rather rude rendering of 'Aire on a G string.' After this the party broke up in confusion and we all went home.

CHAPTER 13

The next few days passed quickly. In no time it seemed I was off to Kampala. As far as the Land Rover was concerned it was none too soon. At high speeds it had developed a most disconcerting front wheel wobble that at times threatened to wrench the steering wheel from one's hands. I was a bit worried in case this was found to be due to the unfortunate damage it had received during the accident in which I had been involved. However, I had written to the Traffic Department in Kampala who had informed me that this defect had been found in all of this particular batch of Land Rovers. The placing of a special shim in the steering system was found to cure the problem. This was to be done as part of the major servicing which was due. In order to make the run to Kampala in one day we set off at about 5 o'clock in the morning. A most ungodly hour. As we drove out of Moroto the Bush Babies were still bounding about from tree to tree in their search for insects. Their eyes glowing like coals in the headlights. We were about 30 miles out of Moroto when it started to get light. Odongo was driving. The turkey was tethered in the back, gobbling sleepily each time we hit a bump. I had become quite attached to my two turkeys which were very tame and had started to follow me around each time I went into the garden. I felt quite relieved that I shouldn't be responsible for killing this one anyway. A great flock of guinea fowl were suddenly all over the road in front of us, wandering around still half-asleep. 'I'll take a couple down for Noel', I thought. No sooner said than done. Grabbing my .22 rifle from the back of the vehicle I got out and waited till two birds were lined up, one behind the other. A quick shot and the two dropped fluttering on the track. I went to pick up the birds as the others fled into the bush. On we went, the journey being uneventful. At Mbale we stopped for lunch at which stage I took over the driving. As the darkness was falling we entered the Mabira Forest between Jinja and Kampala. Clouds of butterflies rose from the verges as we drove along. As they struck the windscreen their bodies squashed. An attempt to clear them with the windscreen wipers was disastrous. The screen became totally obscured as though it had been sprayed with paint. I pulled up and we got out with cloths and cleared the greasy mess from the screen. I found that the only way of dealing with this problem was to drive at such a slow speed that the insects were pushed out of the way by the air flow, rather than being squashed on the glass. After about half- an-hour, however, the swarms of butterflies ceased and we made better progress.

Noel greeted me on my arrival at his house. As O.C. Nsambya Barracks he had been allocated a very fine, newly-built, three-bedroomed house at the top of the barracks complex. He showed me to one of the bedrooms while his houseboy carried in my case. He was delighted to receive the two guinea fowl and even more so when I produced the turkey from the back of the Land Rover. He made a rather snide remark about Christmas presents from the *duka* owners. I got the impression that he was a bit miffed at having missed out on his share by being transferred so soon before Christmas. I decided not to add to his chagrin by telling him of the vast quantities of booze which had recently come my way. Still I have no doubt he was pleased that I had brought the turkey along.

Early the following morning Driver Odongo reported to me and we went off with the Land Rover. Noel then drove me to the Examination Centre, where I joined a group of some 20 hopefuls for the written part of the Kiswahil examination. The papers were handed out and the exam commenced. I was horrified. On most of the questions I hadn't a clue. I made a stab at some of them but knew as I was writing that I had failed miserably. Translating from Swahili to English wasn't too bad since I was able to roughly guess the context of the set piece. From English to Swahili was a very different matter and I made a total hash of it. My grammar was, of course, a complete disaster. I left the examination room a worried man! After lunch it was back to the Examination Centre for the oral examination. I thought I hadn't done too badly on this. I more or less understood what was being said and replied to the best of my ability. Part of the examination was to carry out a conversation with one of the instructors from the Police Training School. His grammar was of course immaculate. Mine, far from it. The examiner listened intently to the conversation but made no comment at the end of it. Finally, my ordeal was over and I was permitted to leave. I was given no indication of whether I had passed or failed but I feared the worst.

It was about 3 o'clock when I got away from the examination. I went straight round to the Uganda Company. There stood my new car, sparkling in its polished blue paintwork. I could hardly believe that such a beautiful creation was actually mine to drive away. After a short test drive and the completion of the paperwork it really was mine. I drove to Nsambya Barracks. Noel had just arrived home and we mutually admired my new possession. It was too late in the day for me to commence my return to Moroto so I stayed for the second night with Noel. After dinner we made our way to the Police Club which was quite near Noel's house in the barracks complex. A few of my cronies came into the club during the evening and I was able to catch up on all the news of my friends. Without exception, I found that they were on the verge of bankruptcy. It was the done thing to join a couple of clubs and this was the major cause of their downfall. I thanked my lucky stars that I had got the Karamoja posting. At least I was reasonably sound financially. On the debit side was the difficulty in passing the mandatory exams without access to some sort of instruction. I had a couple of years to do this, but if I was unable to achieve it within this time I would be out on my ear, which had been the fate of my predecessor, Ian Ferguson. I left the club with mixed feelings.

The following morning I packed my belongings into my car and, saying cheerio to Noel, set off for police headquarters. It was customary, I had been given to understand, for officers from the outstations to report to headquarters during any visit to Kampala, in case there was anything of an urgent nature to discuss. After the Commissioner's visit I fancied that my stock at headquarters was riding reasonably high, so anticipated no problems. The visit would be a formality and I should soon be on my way back to Moroto. I passed one or two of the officers I had previously met. From most of them I received a nod of acknowledgment, but not the friendly greeting I had anticipated. Something was up! Raised voices reached me from Stan Fortt's office. I was just about to knock on his door to announce my presence in case Joe Deegan wanted to see me before my return to the sticks. Before I could do so however the door flew open and Stan Fortt bounded out. He was purple in the face with temper. His short, bull-neck bulged over the top of his jacket. He looked as though he was about to be struck down with apoplexy. His eyes bulged at the sight of me. 'I suppose you'll refuse to go as well!', he roared. I was totally astounded by this sudden attack. What the hell was he talking about? What had I done to deserve such a reception? 'Pardon me', I said, 'would you mind very much telling me what I am supposed to have done?' At this he calmed down a bit. 'Haven't you heard?', he said. 'Frisby's dead. I'm trying to get someone to go to Hoima to pack up his belongings. I've just detailed Inspector Mackinson to do it and he's refused.' I was stunned by this news. Frisby dead. He was the last person I would have thought of as succumbing to ill-health. Strong, young, active, a terror on the rugby field. What about his wife and young son. What a tragedy. 'What on earth happened?', I enquired. 'Was it a car accident?' 'No it was polio', said Stan. He then told me the full story. The rains had come early and with unusual severity around Hoima. The resulting flash floods had raised the level of the swamps over which the main Hoima-Kampala road passed, cutting Hoima Township off temporarily from outside help. At this crucial time Tony Frisby had fallen ill with a high temperature leading rapidly to paralysis. The local doctor had diagnosed poliomyelitis but was helpless to do much about it. Tony's only chance was to get to Kampala where an iron lung was available to assist him to breathe. The doctor had packed Tony, his wife and son into a car and set off for Kampala. The inevitable happened. The car stuck in the swamp and Tony died before the party could be rescued. I could well imagine the dreadful scene. Pat Frisby must have been absolutely devastated watching her husband suffocate at her side and being unable to help in any way. 'Of course I will go', I said. 'Tony Frisby and his wife were good friends of mine. Anything I can do to help, I shall only be too willing to do.' 'Right', said Fortt. 'You've got half-an-hour to get ready. A lorry will pick you up from wherever you are and take you to Hoima.' 'Two things', I said. 'First, I shall want the lorry to pick me up from Nsambya Barracks where I am staying with Mr Caunce. Second, send signal to Brian Peskett in Moroto telling him the reason for my delayed return.'

I left Headquarters and returned to Nsambya. Noel was in his office and looked a bit surprised when I walked in. 'Back already', he said. 'Haven't crashed your car I hope.' I explained the situation to him. 'Would you mind looking after my car for a couple of days?', I enquired. 'Yes of course', he agreed. Shortly afterwards the lorry arrived laden with empty wooden crates, cardboard boxes and a good supply of newspaper for packing. Tossing my case in among them I climbed into the cab with the driver. The journey to Hoima was uneventful. The floods had subsided and the road over the swamp to Hoima was wet but passable. By lunch time we had arrived in the township and, calling at the police station, picked up a constable to show us where Frisby's house was. As we approached the house the constable indicated it. Two Africans were walking away from it carrying large bundles. 'Who are those', I demanded of the constable. 'Oh they are Mr Frisby's cook and houseboy', was the reply. 'Well, just see what they are carrying', I ordered. The constable got down from the lorry and started to question the two. An argument started and I joined him. Eventually the two were persuaded to open the bundles and various items which clearly belonged to Frisby and his wife were discovered. 'Take them down to the police station and charge them', I ordered. The lorry drew up outside the door of Frisby's house. The driver and I unloaded the crates and I started the sad job of packing up my friend's belongings. The bed lay unmade, just as Frisby had left it. I decided that the bedding had better be burned as I was not too sure what degree of infection might be residual in it. I was well on with this task when the doctor and the D.C. arrived. After a short conversation and they promised to return later to give a hand with the packing. In this they were as good as their word and by nightfall the packing was well advanced. I directed that a police guard to be placed on the house and made my way to the Rest House where overnight accommodation had been arranged. While I was getting cleaned up a car drew up outside the Rest House. I heard a female voice and shortly afterwards there was a knock at the door of my room. I opened it to find a middle-aged woman. 'I'm Miss Hastings', she announced. 'Community Development Officer. We don't get many visitors here and I was wondering if you would care to join me for dinner this evening?' I didn't feel much in the mood for polite conversation but, on the spur of the moment I couldn't think of a suitable excuse. 'Fine', she said, 'I'll pick you up at about 8 o'clock!' Sharp on eight o'clock her car drew up and I was taken to her bungalow. She had clearly gone to a great deal of trouble and a very pleasant candlelight dinner followed. Later she moved over to an upright piano which stood in the corner, where she played and sang romantic songs. She finished up with a rendering of 'Foggy foggy dew.' About a weaver who takes a young maid to bed and finishes up living with his son!

The following morning I recommenced the packing and by mid-day had the last crate sealed down. By tea time I had delivered the crates to George Blyth the Q.M. for safe custody and made my way to Noel's house.

Before leaving Hoima I had been warned by the doctor that, in handling Tony Frisby's bedding and other belongings, it was more than likely that I had picked up the virus which had killed him. It was probable that I had some degree of natural immunity to the disease but, should I be carrying it I would not develop any symptoms for a couple of weeks. Meantime I could be in a condition to pass any infection on to other people, especially to children. I decided that it was only fair to avoid contact with other people, as far as I could, for the crucial period.

Accordingly, instead of spending the night at Noel's house, I phoned him to let him know the situation. Then. having been dropped off at Nsambya, I simply dumped my case in the back of my car and started off on the drive to Moroto. It was about 5 o'clock when I left Kampala with a drive of about 350 miles of rough road ahead of me. A couple of times during this drive I felt myself dropping off to sleep at the wheel and, on each occasion, drew in to a suitable spot and slept until the chill night air awakened me again. As the sun rose, I was just leaving Soroti on the last leg of the journey. By 9 o'clock I was driving into Moroto township and, as I reached the police station, Brian Peskett was arriving. 'Glad to see you back', he said. 'There's just been a big cattle raid reported. You're just in time to go off to investigate it.' 'Sorry', I said. 'I'm off for a bit of shut eye. I've not slept for two days and, having driven all night from Kampala, I'm feeling all in.' I then explained to him about being possibly contagious at which he drew back a couple of paces. He looked a bit fed up with this and said 'Well, I expect you could go out this afternoon to investigate the raid. I'll expect you down here at 2 o'clock. I'll get the safari gear packed ready for you.'

I made my way home. Kesi greeted me with a cup of tea. I felt too tired to eat so, after a hot bath, tumbled into bed and was dead to the world for the next four hours. Kesi roused me and demanded news of Kampala. How was *Bwana* Caunce? How were his cook and houseboy? How was Sophia? I told him that we were away on safari immediately. Leaving him to pack my personal safari gear and the food and kitchen equipment, I wrote a quick note to Tom Hinett to explain to him that he and his family, the children being home from school, would not be seeing much of me for a couple of weeks.

Before leaving Moroto I called on Brian and told him the score. 'I've decided, in view of the possibility of passing on infection I should undertake some self-imposed form of quarantine. I shall stay away from Moroto, as far as possible, for the next couple of weeks. You'll have to do the best you can without me for a while. I shall probably base myself at Amudat where you can contact me by radio should you wish to do so. I'll investigate this latest raid while I'm there and, if there are any other serious crimes reported you can pass them on to me and I'll deal with them as far as possible.' So saying I got into the Land Rover, taking with me Driver Odongo, Kesi and Barney.

The investigation into the raid took about five days and a great deal of walking was involved. It was necessary to follow up the tracks of the raiders and the cattle through the bush, accompanied by the cattle owners who would be needed to identify their cattle should we trace them. It seemed that about 20 Karamajong raiders had been involved and around 300 head of cattle stolen. Tracking the cattle was made difficult by the cunning of the raiders who, once they had reached friendly territory, had herds of Karamajong cattle driven over the tracks of the stolen animals to obliterate them. Eventually, however, we were successful in tracing about half of the herd and arresting four of the raiders who were still in possession of them. The remainder of the investigation would be carried out at Moroto where the captured raiders would be interrogated and would, with a bit of luck, eventually give the names of the others involved.

I was on my way to Kacheliba a day or two later. We were running short of food and I decided to shoot a couple of birds to help matters out. Odongo was driving while Kesi and Barney were in the back of the Land Rover. Off to the left I saw a large flock of guinea fowl so, alighting from the vehicle, I cautioned Kesi to hang on to Barney in case he spooked the birds before I could get a shot in. As I approached the flock they started to move off into the bush. The terrain here consisted of fairly open thorn bush with patches of thick grass about five feet tall. Suddenly the flock took fright and flew off through the bush. They were evidently uneasy and it was quite useless to follow them further. As I turned to make my way back to the Land Rover, a Grants Gazelle broke cover and made off. This would be the answer to our food problem. I took a quick shot at the buck before it reached the safety of the long grass, aiming for the neck. For once my aim was a little out and the bullet took the animal in the chest. It leapt into the air and made off into the grass cover. By now I was about half-a-mile from the Land Rover. I ran into the grass cover and, after about 100 yards found the gazelle lying dead. The animal, a female, weighed about 40 pounds. I hoisted it onto my shoulder. Suddenly I was alerted by the sight of an animal leaping into the air about 20 yards in front of me. An African Hunting Dog! As it got sight of me over the top of the long grass, it gave voice to a sharp bark. An answering bark came from behind me and another from the left. To my horror I realised that I was surrounded by a pack of Africa's most feared animals. The Hunting Dog is a merciless killer. It hunts in packs of up to 30. Once it has singled out its prey, nothing will deflect it from the final kill. The hair rose on the back of my neck and I dropped the gazelle to free my hands for the battle ahead. As I glanced round I could see the dogs in a circle around me, leaping to get a sight of their quarry. I realised that I was going to be lucky to get out of this situation with my life. To have a chance every shot would have to count. The magazine of my .22 rifle held 12 shots. One of these had gone on the gazelle. I judged that I was surrounded by some 20 dogs. As they jumped I could see that the circle was closing in. I got ready and, as the next dog leaped above the grass, I quickly fired. I heard the bullet smack home and, at the same instant, re-loaded and fired at a second beast. Another hit. The next minute was like sharp shooting at a fair ground. with the targets appearing and disappearing. Then it was over. The leaping targets ceased. I stayed ready for a further minute anticipating an overwhelming rush. It didn't come. Picking up the gazelle I made my way out of the grass. Corpses littered the bush. A couple of wounded dogs were limping away. I checked my rifle. I had one shot left. I could hear the Land Rover driving through the bush to join me. Kesi and Odongo had heard the fusillade of shots and anticipated that I might need help. Barney came rushing to me. He had leaped out of the back of the Land Rover and, probably having heard the pack of Hunting Dogs giving cry, had decided that he wasn't going to be left out of the fight. I mentally gave thanks that he hadn't arrived much earlier. He wouldn't have stood a chance against this lot.

The first rains began. A heavy storm up in the Karasuk Hills spreading out onto the parched plains and to the foothills of Mount Elgon to the south. Within a few hours water was flowing again in the previously dry bed of the Suam River at Kacheliba. Flash floods caused the dry stream beds crossing the roads to become raging torrents, totally impassable for an hour or so and then subsiding to a trickle and finally dry again. Wherever we went, clouds of multi-coloured butterflies sipping at the moist soil, flew up as the Land Rover passed. Flocks of bright green pigeons flew from tree to tree, feeding on the wild figs and other fruits. The air smelled clean for a change instead of the dusty atmosphere usually found on the murrum roads. I spent the next few days visiting the outposts, carrying out inspections and hearing disciplinary offences.

A few days before I was intending to return to Moroto, I drew up at Kanyengereng police post. The corporal in charge saluted smartly as I got out of the Land Rover and reported, 'All correct Sir.' I accompanied him into the hut he used as an office. He produced the Station Diary for my perusal. I turned back a few days. What was this? P.C. Longok reporting the loss of five rounds of .303 ammunition! I seemed to remember a similar report the first time I visited Kanyengereng in company with Ferguson. P.C. Longok seemed to be pushing his luck somewhat. I questioned the corporal closely. P.C. Longok had been patrolling the salient together with another locally-recruited constable. On his return he had reported having accidentally lost the clip of five rounds. The story had a familiar ring to it. P.C. Longok was called for. Questioned, he repeated the story. The second constable backed him up. I was not too happy about this and asked the corporal to accompany us to the hut which Longok shared with the other man. I noticed that the two glanced furtively at one another as we made our way across the hut. I commenced by searching the box in which Longok kept his belongings. Nothing! Then I searched the other constables box. Nothing! A search of the bedding and mattresses followed. Nothing!

I was about to give up the search when an inspiration struck me. Taking the hunting knife from my belt I stabbed it into the thatched roofing. Nothing! I continued to probe and suddenly my knife struck something metallic. Reaching my hand into the hollow revealed, I pulled out two clips containing ten empty .303 bullet cases. A further search produced a tin containing Shs 420/. A large sum for a constable earning around 80/- a month. What I had discovered was not only the rounds now reported, but also those from the previous occasion. Faced with this overwhelming proof the two constables made statements each blaming the other. For months they had been shooting Eland and other large buck and selling the resulting meat to the local tribesmen. I thought it unlikely that the corporal in charge had no inkling of what was going on., but neither of the two would implicate him so I was unable to take that aspect any further. My self-imposed quarantine came to a halt and, packing the miscreants into the Land Rover, I drove to Moroto where they were placed in the cells to await trial.

I had been absent from Moroto for ten days. I wondered if my exile could now be brought to a close. I said as much to Brian. 'We've got a new doctor', he informed me. 'Arrived yesterday. Name of Gareth Mitford-Barberton. Why not slip down to the hospital and have a word with him.' No sooner said than done. I made my way to the hospital and sought him out. Gareth Mitford-Barberton was a dark, slim young man of about 26 years. He was busy taking over from Dr Lubega. I wondered why Lubega's appointment as District Medical Officer had been of such short duration. It turned out that his appointment was a temporary one until Gareth's return from leave. Lubega was remaining as 2 i/c. I explained to Gareth the reason for my visit. For a moment he seemed dubious. 'Have you had any symptoms?', he enquired. 'Any aches or pains or sweating or nausea?' I replied 'No,' to all these. A short examination followed. 'Well you certainly seem fit', said Gareth. 'I should think it's O.K. to re-join the fold, but keep away from Hinett's children for a few more days.

It was pleasant to be back in my own home after what seemed an age. I returned to work in the office but sent a note round to the other officers on the Station, advising them that I shouldn't be fit for mixed company for a few more days. The only one to visit me at home was Gareth who called in to make sure that I had no symptoms yet. Somewhat to my surprise I found that Gareth's wife Pat had accompanied him on his posting to Moroto. Even more surprising was the news that she was pregnant and expecting their first child in about three months. They were now occupying one of the new, very posh bungalows which Tom Hinett had recently completed. I had viewed these dwellings. They really were excellent. For a moment I felt a pang of jealousy. It had soon passed however. The rent for my bungalow was Shs. 20/- per month. That for the new bungalows was at least ten times that figure.

One refinement was, however, missing from my cottage. I felt that I should have a garage for my new car. I didn't want the paintwork getting spoiled by being left out in the hot sun all day. Eventually I raised the subject with Tom. Regrettably there was no chance whatever of a permanent garage being erected there. 'Why not have a word with the D.C. He could get a pole and thatch shelter erected by the station labour?' What a good idea. I had no sooner mentioned it to Peter Gibson than a gang of porters appeared with poles and bundles of thatching grass on their heads. A day later I was the proud possessor of a garage.

During the temporary absence of Kesi and myself, my turkey had been looked after by Tom Hinett's houseboy. Now it was once again Kesi's responsibility to lock it in the kitchen each night. All the other turkeys on the station had, by this time gone to the great turkey farm in the sky. My turkey was so tame that I felt loath to dispatch it. After all, I didn't need it to eat. Any time I wanted a roast bird, I simply had to take my gun out on my evening walks and come back with as many as I needed. At the same time I felt that, eventually, Kesi was going to get fed up with cleaning the kitchen each morning. The problem was resolved at the end of the month when Kesi received his salary. As usual he went missing. By the time I realised that I was not going to get an evening meal it was quite dark. I wandered round the garden with a torch but could see no sign of the turkey. Eventually I gave up the search. After a scratch meal I went to bed. At about two o'clock, I was awakened by the chuckling whoop of a hyena outside my bedroom window. Barney went mad, barking and scratching at the door to get out. I kept him inside, however.

Leopards were known to prowl around the Township during the hours of darkness. After a short while the sound of the hyena faded away into the distance. Kesi awoke me with my usual cup of tea. '*Wapi kuku kubwa*', he enquired. I replied by cursing him for going missing. I then told him that I had been unable to find the turkey the previous night. I got dressed and we both searched the garden. There, under a low growing tree was a scattering of feathers. The reason for the outcry by the hyenas during the night was now clear. My turkey had been sitting on one of the low branches hidden from me while I had searched. It had proved easy meat to the hungry hyenas who had come around scavenging during the night.

Tom and Vi Hinett had a new member of staff. They had engaged an *ayah* for young Thomas. She was a Mutoro girl about 15 years old. Quite pretty. At least Kesi thought so. So, apparently, did every other houseboy and cook on the station. Admiring glances followed her everywhere she went on her daily walks with Thomas. I gathered from Kesi that she reciprocated, not only with the Africans. '*Huyu malaya*', (She is a prostitute) said Kesi. I could not but notice as she passed any European officers, the downcast eyes, the simpering smile and the invitation in the murmured '*Jambo Bwana*'. I took it upon myself to mention the subject to Tom. He bridled at the idea. 'Nonsense', he replied. 'She was strongly recommended by the White Fathers at the mission in Mbale.' I shrugged and let the matter pass. A month or two later Tom and Vi had a visitor from Kampala. I was invited round to Tom's house for dinner one evening to meet him. A pleasant, cheerful individual about the same age as Tom. Fortunately, his name now escapes me! He was the life and soul of the party. The houseboy being away on leave, the nubile *ayah* was pressed into service to bring food to the table. I could not help noticing the covert glances passing between her and the visitor. It didn't seem to register with Tom or Vi however. I honestly believe that they were two of nature's innocents. The evening was a great success and broke up at about half-past-ten. Several days later the visitor departed in the greatest of good humour. A month later he made a return trip. Seeing him driving around the town I noticed that he didn't seem quite as cheerful as he had when I had last seen him. He smiled and returned my wave but he seemed slightly distracted when I spoke to him. The reason was revealed to me a week or two later when I was attending one of the many drinks parties. Gareth Mitford-Barberton was present and had had one or two too many drinks. 'Poor old ———— . Came to see me on his last visit. He'd picked up a dose of clap from Hinett's *ayah* on his previous visit.' I think that Gareth regretted blurting this out as soon as he said it. Hippocratic oath and all that. But it was such a gem of gossip that he couldn't contain himself. I wondered if any other European officers had collected a dose from the same source. I doubted if Gareth would have known. Presumably any so affected would head to another area for treatment as had Tom Hinett's visitor. Not the sort of thing that one wants passed round one's home Station. 'Surely', I said, 'she shouldn't be working as an *ayah* if she's got clap?', I said. 'Well, I can hardly go along to Tom and tell him that she's infected his visitor', replied Gareth. The subject dropped but I felt I had a duty to warn Tom before any damage was done. The following day I went to his office. 'Tom,' I said, 'please take a friendly warning. Your *ayah* has infected half the houseboys in Moroto with the clap. I really think you should get her along to Gareth to get her treated.' Tom's ruddy complexion turned three shades paler. 'My God', he said, 'are you sure about this?' 'Absolutely certain', I replied. Shortly afterwards Tom's van sped off towards the hospital carrying Vi and Thomas and the *ayah*. Sure enough the *ayah* had gonorrhea. Fortunately young Thomas was in the clear. The *ayah* was on the next bus out of Moroto. Tom hadn't a lot of faith in the recommendations of the White Fathers after this.

I had just finished work one afternoon and was sitting at home relaxing over a cup of tea when a warder arrived accompanied by a prisoner who was carrying an enormous puff adder. I was making quite a collection of the beautiful skins of these deadly creatures. I gave the warder the usual tip of one-shilling and set to work to remove the skin from the corpse before it got too dark. I made the usual incision from throat to vent and set about carefully peeling back the skin starting at the tail end. I completed the removal as far as the neck and was just about to start on the more difficult task of skinning the head when a constable arrived with a message from Katikekele police post. A murder was reported. 'No peace for the wicked', I thought. I dumped the corpse into a bucket and, collecting the equipment I thought I might need, set off for Katikekele. With luck I should be able to complete the first stage of the investigation and be back in time for a night's sleep. The investigation could then be continued tomorrow. Katikekele was only a matter of 20 miles out of the town.

On my arrival at Katikekele, I found that the murder was fairly straightforward, apart from the fact that there was no body. A handcuffed prisoner sat outside the hut used as an office, guarded by a constable. A glance showed me that the individual was mentally defective. This was very unusual. In the vast majority of cases where a child is born with a defect of this sort death follows fairly rapidly, either as a result of the mother refusing to feed the infant or as a result of some violence bringing its existence to an early conclusion. This time, however, it had survived and had reached the age of about 18 years.

Enquiries revealed that a boy of about seven years of age had been out herding his father's cattle. He had been accompanied by the prisoner. Eventually, when neither the child nor the cattle nor the lunatic returned to the *manyatta*, a search was mounted by the boy's relatives who, understandably, feared that a raid had taken place. However, after about an hour, the cattle were found. No sign of the boy or his companion. An unsuccessful search was made, after which the cattle were driven back to the *manyatta*. Shortly afterwards the lunatic arrived. No sense could be gleaned from him regarding the boy. It was now dark. The following morning the lunatic was again interrogated. This time he admitted that he had strangled the boy and left the body lying in the bush. A search was made of the area where the body was said to have been left. Extensive bloodstains were found, but of the boy there was no sign.

Packing the prisoner into the back of the Land Rover, together with his escort, I gave instructions for the relatives and witnesses to make their way to Moroto the following day when the investigation could be wrapped up. I then drove back to the police station, arriving at about half-past-ten. After making the necessary entries in the various registers and ensuring that the prisoner was safely locked up, I made my way home and turned in for a well-earned nights sleep.

The following morning I was awakened by screams emanating from the direction of the kitchen. The kitchen door stood open. Inside, Kesi was standing on the table, shouting at the top of his voice. Slithering around on the floor was a naked puff adder, its skin following it around like a cape flying in the breeze. Clearly, having regained consciousness the puff adder felt somewhat aggrieved to discover that some rotten bugger had nicked its skin while it was out for the count. Its annoyance was probably made worse by the fact that it was being eaten alive by a swarm of ants who were having a whale of a time. Kesi, on entering the kitchen ,had become the obvious target for the serpent's ill temper and had been rather lucky to notice that he had company in the kitchen before falling victim to its fangs. Fetching a piece of wood from a nearby pile, I succeeded in finally dispatching the unfortunate snake before it could do any real damage. Kesi was looking a bit fed-up with the situation. I got the impression that he was seriously considering resignation. I was strongly reminded of the old adage, 'If you can't take a joke you shouldn't have joined!' Unfortunately, I didn't know how to put these words of wisdom into Swahili.

The day was spent on the murder investigation. The case appeared to be simplicity itself. My murder team recorded the statements from the witnesses while I personally recorded a statement under caution from the accused. I gathered that he had the intellect of a child of five or six years. There was no possibility of his being hanged for the offence which he readily admitted, giving a detailed account of how he had killed the child. The next High Court was scheduled to take place in about a month so, with luck, I could get Hatch Barnwell to hear the preliminary inquiry in time to fit this one in. I didn't much want the responsibility of the special arrangements required to house a lunatic in the prison for any longer than was necessary.

A couple of days later a runner, carrying a note in a cleft stick, arrived at the police station. This turned out to be a message from one of the *Ejakait* chiefs living near Kotido and reported the death of a woman. No details were given, just the bare facts and a request for the police to come and investigate. I could only assume that this would be a murder enquiry. This would be a splendid opportunity to see how Gareth coped with performing an autopsy on a smelly corpse. I drove down to the hospital to see him. Sure enough he was only too willing to grab the opportunity of getting away from the hospital for a day or two. Returning to the police station, I gave the necessary instructions to get the safari gear ready, after which I went home to collect Kesi and Barney and my personal food and equipment. By the time I got back to the police station Gareth was waiting for me. There certainly wasn't going to be any room for Driver Odongo this time so I sent him back to the police lines. Arriving at Kotido Rest Camp that evening we set up camp and got Kesi to start preparing the couple of guinea fowl which I had shot during our journey. The *Ejakait* arrived while Gareth and I were starting on our first beer. I invited him to join us and the tale unfolded. This wasn't going to be a murder enquiry after all. The woman had been knocked down by a man on a bicycle. She was drunk at the time and had staggered out in front of him while he had been cycling home on a pitch black night. It appeared that she had not been badly injured and had been taken to her home. However she had died two days later. The cyclist had been arrested but nobody could think what to do next. The body had started to smell. The *Ejakait* knew that such matters should be reported to the police, so had sent off a message three days previously. Eventually no one could stand the stink any longer so the body was buried. Poor Gareth was looking a bit green round the gills on hearing the news. We decided to leave the investigation till morning.

Bright and early the following day we were shown where the body had been buried. A large crowd had collected to view the proceedings. No one seemed very keen on digging it up again. I felt that, legally, I should obtain an exhumation order before going any further. On second thoughts, I decided to dispense with the niceties. I enquired who were the husband and sons of the deceased. Three naked men stepped forward. 'Right', said I, 'get digging.' Somewhat unwillingly they turned to their task. The body was about four feet down. As the hole got deeper the stench got worse. Eventually the corpse was uncovered and lifted onto the roadside. When the cloth covering it was removed I found that it had burst and was practically liquid. Lumps of putrid flesh fell away as the woman's clothing was removed. Swarms of flies appeared from nowhere and started to feast.

Puffing vigorously on his cigarette, Gareth set about the autopsy. His examination was hurried and somewhat perfunctory. 'Ruptured spleen', he announced and retreated hastily for a breath of fresh air. The corpse was shoved, or rather, poured back into the grave and rapidly covered over with soil to blanket the frightful smell. We returned to our camp to consider matters. Clearly there would have to be an inquest so I set about obtaining the necessary statements from the various witnesses. I couldn't see any charge sticking as far as the cyclist was concerned so, after recording his statement, ordered him to be released. In due course the inquest was held and a finding of 'Accidental Death' was recorded. Whether the cyclist paid the customary compensation to the family of the deceased woman, I am not sure. I suspect that native custom forced him to do so.

A week or so later I was at Amudat on the first leg of the monthly pay safari. On this occasion I was travelling in my own car, accompanied by Kesi and Barney. Dick Baker was also camping nearby and the Administration lorry was parked alongside his tent which, like mine, had been erected under one of the grass-thatched *bandas*.

Dick joined me for dinner and, afterwards, at the blazing camp fire, we sat putting the world to rights over a few beers. At about 10 o'clock I was just about to make my excuses and turn in for the night when my attention was attracted to a bit of a commotion taking place about half-a mile-distant. One of the local donkeys was braying madly. It almost sounded as though it was screaming rather than braying. A most peculiar noise, unlike anything I had heard before. This was most odd. Almost invariably the tribesmen kept their donkeys within the thorn *boma* of their *manyattas*. Even stranger, the sound was getting rapidly closer. I could now hear the thudding of the animals hooves. I rose quickly from my chair and grabbed my rifle from close by, together with the big six-cell torch which I had taken to bringing on safari with me. Shining the torch in the direction of the noise, I soon saw a donkey running towards me. Something was clearly wrong with it. Hanging from its rump was a large hyena, being dragged along by the terrified animal. Three more hyenas were loping along behind, also trying to get a hold with their jaws. The donkey was heading for the camp fire, I suppose with the hope of getting human help. As it ran into the camp area, the hyena which had a jaw hold on its rear, let go and stood waiting for its victim's next move. The other three circled the camp at a safe distance in the expectation that the donkey would make a break for freedom on the other side. Not a bit of it. The animal clearly realised that it had found sanctuary. Now I had an opportunity to deal with some of these disgusting pests.

Holding the torch under the stock of the rifle, I took aim at the first hyena. Its eyes shone like beacons and I aimed just below them. The first hyena bit the dust. 'That', I thought, 'is for my turkey!' I rapidly turned my attention on the others and succeeded in dispatching two more in quick succession. 'That's for the child who had its face bitten off.' The fourth animal turned and made off as fast as its legs would carry it. The donkey, at this stage, appeared to realise that it was safe and, turning, trotted off through the bush. As it left I could see that it had an horrific wound on its rump, Whether it eventually survived or not I never found out. I collected the tails from the three hyenas and handed them to Dick. 'I'll have my 15-bob when I next see you in Moroto', I said.

A few weeks later in Moroto I was having a bit of a problem. I was being plagued by one of the big cats which occasionally found its way off the mountain and down into the township for an easy meal. There were already reports of dogs being taken down near the *dukas*. Soon, it was feared, a child or even an adult would be taken. Now, for several nights, my bungalow had been targeted. The time was 2 a.m. when I glanced at my watch. A familiar sawing noise from under my bedroom window had roused me from a deep slumber. The leopard was early tonight and I was getting fed up with the continual disturbance. Every visit caused Barney to go mad. He could only think of getting outside to sort out the intruder. Unfortunately, I didn't think he would come off too well in such an encounter. Leopards have excellent night vision and their favourite snacks are dogs or baboons. I have no doubt that Barney would have put up a good fight, but a big leopard, and this was a big one, would have weighed at least three times as much as Barney and its armoury included sharp claws as well as teeth. These visits forced me to keep the window closed, which was a bit of a bind as the nights were quite warm. Kesi, sleeping in his mud hut near the kitchen was starting to complain. Really, I don't think I blamed him.

During the following morning, I called at the *boma* to see Peter Gibson. During the course of our conversation I mentioned to him the problem I was having. 'Why not set a trap for the bugger?', he suggested. 'Where would I get a trap big enough for such an animal?', I enquired. 'Well I saw one in the store the other ·day', he replied. We went along to the store. There, on a shelf, was the biggest and most horrible looking lion trap I have ever seen. It's overall length was about five feet and the jaws, armed with great teeth, were nearly two feet long. Anything getting its foot caught in this would suffer the most terrible injury. A great chain at each end was intended to secure the trap to a tree or some such object to ensure that the captured animal didn't escape. I must admit to being less than enthusiastic about using such a terrible method for disposing of a fine animal. However, I was faced with a stark choice. A leopard on the prowl was not a pleasant prospect so close to the house. Barney invariably wandered around the garden for a pee before turning in for the night. He could easily fall victim to the hungry predator. Kesi was also vulnerable particularly when staggering home after one of his drinking sprees. Then there was Thomas and the three young girls next door. It would be unusual for a leopard to take a human being but by no means unknown. I salved my conscience with the thought that, should the leopard get into the trap, I should be able to finish it off within a couple of minutes anyway. I thanked Peter and put the trap into the back of my car.

The next stop was Tom's office. I explained the problem to him and, during the afternoon, one of his Asian carpenters came to my house with some strips of timber and a piece of strong expanding metal. It wasn't big enough to cover the entire window, so a gap of about six inches was left at the top and the bottom. 'No leopard could get through that', I thought. After work I fixed the trap outside, just under the protected window and, just before going to bed, I levered the jaws open and the hellish contraption was set, ready for the prowler. For the first time in a week I was able to sleep with my bedroom window open. At about three a.m. I was awakened by the sound of a scrabbling noise. In the dim light of the moon I was able to see an animal squeezing through the space left at the bottom of the expanding metal and into the room. I grabbed my torch from the chair and my rifle from nearby where I had left it to be handy. The beam of the torch flashed on, and Barney smiled at me as he eased his hindquarters through the gap. How on earth had he managed to get his barrel chest through such a minute space still eludes me, but somehow he had managed it. Clearly he had jumped from the window, evading the great jaws below him and, having had a pee and a wander round, had returned by the same route, again avoiding the trap on his way. My blood ran cold at the thought of the fate he had so narrowly escaped. I closed my bedroom window to avoid any repetition of Barney's wanderings and returned to bed. Half-an-hour later I was awakened by the most appalling screeching. The leopard had arrived and was in the trap. I had no time to feel any regrets at having caught the animal in this underhand way. Barney was going berserk and I was trying to drag on a pair of trousers and shoes before rushing outside to finish the job off. Within a few seconds I was outside. My torch showed me the great male leopard caught by one of its front legs. It's fangs were bared as it tried to reach me. I wanted to take a shot from the side through the heart, but every time I moved around the animal moved with me. I wasn't going to prolong the unfortunate creature's agony any longer so I fired from the front, the bullet entering at the base of the throat. This, I knew was not a killing shot. However it had the effect of bringing the animals head down and my next shot was through the brain. Total time from putting its foot in the trap to being dead, about sixty seconds.

Kesi, awakened by the noise, now appeared from his hut. With his assistance I moved the dead leopard from the trap and into the kitchen where, the following morning, I skinned it. The news of the dead leopard spread rapidly. I had hardly finished the skinning before a couple of the local witch doctors were on my doorstep with a young heifer, wanting to make an exchange for the skinned corpse, which they would use for making medicine. Well I certainly didn't want the corpse of the leopard, neither did I want the heifer, particularly since it was forbidden to keep cattle in the township. Kesi looked pleadingly at me. I accepted the swap and, as soon as the two witch doctors were out of the way handed the animal over to him. I believe he got Shs 200/- for it, followed by the usual drunken celebration. Well, this was an episode which I wanted to put behind me. I didn't feel at all happy about the method of disposal of the leopard. Still I had got rid of a potentially very dangerous beast.

A letter arrived for me. It bore a British stamp but I didn't recognise the handwriting. To my astonishment it turned out to be from no less a personage than Charles Pitman, the retired Chief Game Warden of Uganda and author of *Snakes of East Africa*, the definitive work on the subject. Apparently he still retained his interest in herpetology and had heard of my own interest in snakes. I can only assume that he had been informed by someone at Entebbe where my request for the anti-venine would have gone. The object of the letter was to ask me if I would collect snakes for him, sex and measure them, preserve them in formalin, list the stomach contents and any parasites found on them and do some scale counting on the bodies. I must say that I was a bit chuffed at being asked to do this and readily accepted his request. I had a word with Gareth and he supplied me with a quantity of formalin and some bottles. My first capture took place within a couple of days, when I noticed a bright green boomslang, five feet in length lying along the branches of a frangipani shrub growing just outside the police station. I caught this without any trouble. In fact I was probably a bit too nonchalant about it. Once I recognised it for what it was, I simply grabbed it by the neck. It was, I knew, one of the back-fanged group, and classed as mildly venomous. It wasn't till much later that I read that a woman in Entebbe had been bitten by one and had nearly died. Thereafter, the reptile was classed as highly venomous. From then on I spent a lot of time during the evenings and weekends, armed with a forked stick and a cloth bag, catching whatever snakes I could find. I fear that most of the European population then started giving me a fairly wide berth. After sending off several packages, I eased off on this. After all I didn't want to become known as being a bit eccentric!

The High Court was due to make its periodic circuit. Judge Stewart was to preside. Known as *'Pesi'* Stewart from his habitual use of the Swahili word meaning 'hurry up'. The list of cases to be heard included about a dozen murders of which about half had occurred during cattle raids. Consequently there were some 30 accused, including one young chap who claimed to be 18 but looked more like 14 years of age. Also, there was the lunatic who had murdered the child whose body had never been found. Hatch Barnwell had heard all of the Preliminary Inquiries and I didn't anticipate any difficulties in obtaining guilty verdicts on them all.

The evening before the High Court was to commence, I was strolling up towards the swimming pool for my evening dip, when I was joined by a well-spoken Asian who introduced himself as Loyola Saldanah. He was a cheerful individual several years older than myself. I invited him to join me in my swim and was pleased when he accepted the invitation. Loyola was, I found, a barrister. Until recently he had been practising in Kampala, but he had now been appointed to the Crown Prosecution Service. He was, I found, a Goan. Born in Jinja, he had studied Law in the U.K. and had returned to Uganda when he qualified. Over the following years we became close friends.

The High Court Session commenced, as was customary, with a Guard of Honour. Clad in my best uniform, complete with Sam Browne belt and sword, highly-polished boots and puttees, I marched out from the parade to where 'Pesi' Stewart stood, halted and commenced my hastily practised 'sword salute', and exercise consisting of four distinct movements. Halfway through it 'Pesi' started forward hand outstretched, clearly expecting me to shake hands with him. This took me somewhat by surprise. As I raised the sword to the 'recover', I came perilously close to impaling him under the chin. This, in turn, took him by surprise. 'Guard of Honour ready for inspection', said I. Recovering from the shock of his close shave, 'Pesi' accompanied me round the ranks formed up for his benefit. 'Thank you', he murmured at the conclusion, as I once again narrowly avoided executing him. I quickly marched the guard off and handed them over to the Head Constable. The Judge, together with Loyola and the defence counsel then adjourned to the D.C's office for coffee, while I sped home to get into something a bit more comfortable.

On my return to the Court House, the Judge and the counsels, together with the usual interpreters, made their way from the D.C's office and the Court commenced its session. The High Court was somewhat unusual in its makeup. Instead of having a Jury, this was replaced by a number of local chiefs and tribal elders. These were known as Assessors and their function was to advise the Judge and to give their opinion as to the guilt or otherwise of the accused. The Judge was not bound by their opinions or advice, but it seemed a democratic process nevertheless.

The defence counsel was a solicitor from Soroti. P.B. Patel by name. His knowledge of the Law was abysmal. He was appointed by the Crown to defend the accused but he had never been known to get anyone off. He was, of course, given copies of the depositions which Hatch Barnwell had recorded. From time to time during the proceedings he would rise to his feet to ask some fatuous question. He would be quickly put in his place by the Judge and eventually hardly bothered to speak.

Eventually, however the lunatic was brought before the Court. This one, I had mentally marked down as routine. He had made a statement admitting his guilt. As a mental defective he would not be sentenced to death. The result was a foregone conclusion. Or was it! P.B. Patel entered a plea of 'Not Guilty' on behalf of his client. The witnesses were called and gave their evidence. I was called and produced the statement which I had recorded under caution. Eventually the accused was called. P.B. Patel stood up and stated that his client was saying nothing. Then he sat down again. The case collapsed. There was no body. The only evidence against the accused was his own statement. With a plea of 'Not Guilty' and being unable to examine the accused, we had no case. P.B. Patel preened himself. At last he had got someone off. The prisoner was thereupon released and handed over to the tribesmen. A couple of weeks later when I was on safari in the area, I called in on the local chief where the murder had occurred. I asked if I could have a word with the lunatic. He looked quite blank. 'Oh he went away shortly after the case', I was told. I didn't bother to enquire further or, I felt sure, I should be investigating another murder.

Meanwhile, back at the Court, the final case was called. This was a particularly nasty murder involving a cattle raid in which three children had been speared as they ran away. There were six accused including the lad who looked to be about 14 but insisted that he was 18. At the conclusion of the hearing all six were found guilty. '*Pesi*' Stewart then pronounced the death sentence on them all. Before they could be escorted away however, he asked that medical evidence be obtained regarding the age of the youngest accused. I popped him in my car, together with his warder escort, and we set off for the hospital. Halfway there he started squealing and struggling. It transpired that he thought he was being taken to be hanged straight away. With some difficulty we managed to get him into the hospital where Gareth examined him. After looking at his teeth and other bits, Gareth gave his opinion that the youth was about 15-years of age. Too young to be hanged. Back into the car and to Court. '*Pesi*' then sentenced him to be detained during his Majesty's pleasure. I'm sure that the accused never knew what that was all about, or what a close brush with death he had had.

CHAPTER 14

It was time for another pay safari. I decided to take the opportunity of earning myself a bit of mileage so, loading up my car with the bare necessities of kit and accompanied by Kesi and Barney, I set off on my journey. As usual I spent my first night at Amudat. This time there were no other officers staying at the Rest Camp. After my usual dinner of roast guinea fowl I sat in solitary state at the camp fire and, after a couple of bottles of beer, decided to turn in. Barney was curled up on the canvas floor by my bed. I had been asleep for, I suppose, a couple of hours when I was awakened by some heavy breathing nearby. Then a growl. Something was clawing the canvas side of the tent. What the hell could it be. I grabbed the revolver from beneath my pillow and the torch from beside my bed. Barney, for some reason, didn't seem to be too keen on seeing off the intruder. Suddenly a ear splitting roar came from the other side of the canvas. A bloody lion was trying to get in. I could see where the canvas was bulging. I was able to hear the claws tearing the outer canvas. I pointed my revolver in the general direction of the animal but, as I was about to pull the trigger, I hesitated. The last thing I wanted was a wounded lion on the loose. If I didn't kill it with my first shot, which was most unlikely with a revolver bullet, especially since I would be firing blind, I should be faced with the prospect of searching for a wounded lion in the morning, armed with nothing better than a .303 rifle. Not a very satisfactory weapon for dealing with a charging lion. I lowered my revolver and fired into the ground. Fortunately this had the desired effect. The roar finished in a sort of hiccup and the canvas of the tent swayed as the lion broke off its attack and ran away. I didn't get a lot more sleep that night. The following morning I inspected the damage. The outer canvas of the tent was ripped in a number of places. Large pug marks in the dust around the tent showed that the intruder had been an adult male lion. Interestingly enough, about a week later we had a message from Amudat to Moroto informing us that a boy herding goats a few miles away had been killed and eaten by a lion. A party of tribesmen had followed up and speared the man-eater, an old male, practically toothless. I related this incident to my parents a little later, who in turn informed my Aunts May and Mary. Some months later I received from them, a parcel containing two bibles, one in English, the other in Swahili. An accompanying message suggested I put my trust in God. To my everlasting regret I sent a curt reply saying that I preferred to trust my revolver. Poor old dears. I'm sure they meant well.

Following the incident at Amudat, I continued my pay safari in the direction of Kacheliba. About 20 miles along this route I noticed a new track had been cut off to the left in the direction of the Karasuk Hills. this was an area which I had always intended to investigate but had never got around to. I decided to take the opportunity of seeing where the track led. Clearly it had been cut into the bush by some heavy machinery. Probably Doug Essex had been here preparing a road so that a drill could be transported to bore for water. The track was in good condition, the numerous stream beds having been filled and graded to allow the heavy machines to get in. Flocks of guinea fowl and herds of antelope and zebra were in profusion. The wildlife was clearly totally unused to vehicles and practically refused to get out of the way as my vehicle approached. After travelling about eight miles we came to a group of mud huts. A crowd of surly looking Suk tribesmen came out as I stopped. Nearby was a brand new pump. Set on a new concrete base. Evidently the benevolent government had decided to spend a few hundred pounds to give these lucky people a supply of pure water. Strangely enough no one seemed to be using this asset the government had so thoughtfully provided. The concrete base was quite dry. As I watched, some women came walking through the bush with *debis* of water balanced on their heads. 'Why are they still collecting water, when there is a supply laid on?' I enquired. 'The water has an evil spirit in it', was the answer. 'What bloody nonsense', I thought. I got out the tankard I used for my beer and pumped out a glass full. Clear as crystal, slightly fizzy. I tasted it. Delicious. Evidently this was a sort of mineral water. Probably very beneficial. The tribesmen gathered round murmuring to one another as I drained the glass. 'That will prove that there's nothing wrong with it', I thought and drained a second tankard full. My enquiries revealed that the driller who had installed this supply of delicious water, had moved on about ten miles further into the bush. I decided to call on him while I was out in this direction. I had driven about three miles when I started to experience the most dreadful stomach ache. After a further mile I was convinced that I had been poisoned. A bit further on I stopped and staggered off into the bush. Hidden behind the bushes I suffered a terrible attack of diarrhea. 'Those buggers were right', I thought. There is an evil spirit in the water. Magnesium sulphate, pure Epsom Salt. On the way to see the driller I had to go off into the bush twice more before I got rid of the effects of the glass of water. No wonder the tribesmen wouldn't drink it! 'I'll stick to beer in future', I thought.

On my arrival at the drilling site I was met by a beaming young Swede. Willie Hagstrom was as tall as me and of similar build. Blonde hair and deeply sun-tanned he was clad only in shorts and canvas shoes. Nearby the diesel engine was thumping away, raising and dropping the drilling bit far underground, connected by its steel cable to the tall gantry. Willie greeted me like a long-lost brother, effusive in his welcome and speaking good English, though with a very pronounced Scandinavian accent. His living accommodation was a large caravan, parked nearby, into which I was invited. Seated outside I noticed an attractive African girl, possibly Muganda or Mutoro by tribe. Evidently this was Willie's recreational facility. I can't say I blamed him. After all there wouldn't be much else to do, living in the bush with no other Europeans for 100-miles. Over a couple of bottles of beer and a meal of roast buck and tinned vegetables, Willie and I exchanged news. I mentioned to him the borehole which I had found earlier. He roared with laughter when I told him the result of my drinking a glass of the water. 'I'm not very popular there', he said. 'They had a big feast when I fitted up the pump for the first time. It turned into a disaster when everyone got the squitters. Took them a couple of days to realise what was causing it. By that time I had moved on.'

A couple of days later I was nearing the last lap of this part of the pay safari. I was heading for Nabilatuk. About halfway between Amudat and Nabilatuk was a small dam which had been constructed a couple of years previously. It was only three or four acres in extent and lay at the base of a rocky volcanic outcrop. It occurred to me that there might be the odd duck or goose on it which would make a nice change of diet if I succeeded in potting it. I pulled the car in about a quarter of a mile distant and made my way up a dry stream bed which took the overflow from the dam in the rainy season. I cautiously popped my head over the spill way. No ducks. I stood up and started to make my way round the side of the dam. Suddenly, to my amazement a crocodile slithered into the water on the far side, about 100-yards distant. True, it was not a very big croc, possibly seven or eight feet in length, but where had it come from? The nearest permanent water was probably 50 miles distant, a tributary of the Suam River. The only explanation was that it had made its way across country during one of the rainy seasons since the dam was constructed. It must have smelled this water supply from that distance. 'How enterprising', I thought. Anyway, there was nothing I could do about it this time. The croc had vanished. I decided to have another look next time I was in this direction.

The next day I arrived back in Moroto. I drove up to the police station at about mid-day expecting to find Brian, only to discover that he had gone off in the Land Rover earlier that day in response to a report of a cattle raid and spear-blooding near Nabilatuk. I must have missed him somewhere on the road. This caused me to alter my plans. I had intended to go off the following day to finish the pay parade at Iriri and then up to Kotido. I felt that in the absence of Brian I had better remain in Moroto, barring emergencies, until his return. After a quick look through the mail I went back to my cottage for a bath and change of clothing.

Everything appeared to be in order when I opened the door of the cottage. It was only when I went to the wardrobe that I realised that something was terribly wrong. Half of my clothes lay on the floor of the wardrobe. Murrum 'pipes' ran up the timber and along the wooden poles from which the coat hangers should have been suspended. The hangers themselves had been reduced to wire hooks. I had been attacked by termites. An immediate investigation followed to ascertain the extent of the damage. Underneath the wardrobe, when it was moved, was a seething mass of termites. They had come up through the cracks in the concrete floor and had burrowed through the timber base of the wardrobe and up inside. During the six days I had been away on safari, about half of my clothing had been eaten. Most of that remaining had suffered minor damage but would at least be wearable. I was reduced to two working jackets and three pairs of shorts. My highly-polished boots had been reduced to a pair of rubber soles. There was only one answer to this emergency. Tom. I wandered over to his house. Fortunately, he had just come home for lunch and he accompanied me back to the cottage. 'Oh dear', he said. 'I'm afraid there's not a lot we can do about this. Trouble is that this cottage just isn't worth the expense of putting in a new floor. Still you can't stay here. We'd better go along to see the D.C. this afternoon to see what we can do. You'd better leave things as they are so that we can bring him along to view the damage.'

After lunch, Tom and I went along to the *boma* and then, accompanied by Peter, returned to my cottage. Peter was appalled by what he saw. The outcome was that two days later Tom and his family moved into one of the posh newly-built houses while I moved into Tom's house. This was superb luxury as far as I was concerned. Three bedrooms (as if I needed them), a vast lounge, dining room, splendid bathroom, large kitchen and proper boys' quarters (three of them). Kesi was particularly pleased at being able to move out of his mud hut and celebrated in his usual way by getting stoned out of his mind.

Meanwhile a signal to George Blyth, the Quartermaster, had ensured the prompt dispatch of a goodly supply of khaki drill, and it wasn't too long before a tailor, in the employ of Ishverbhai, had knocked up replacements for my destroyed uniforms.

On the return of Brian from his murder investigation I made an early start to complete my pay safari. First to Iriri where, as usual, I was greeted by Corporal Okeng who insisted in treating me to half-an-hour of immaculate drill. I finally managed to extricate myself from the police post and set off for Kotido. After paying out the men on the post here, I made a courtesy call on Father Farina at his Mission. The usual hospitality was extended and I was about to make my excuses and leave for Moroto when an Alsatian bitch and six beautiful pups bounded into the room. The pups were about six weeks old and one of them, a little female, made a terrible fuss of me clambering up on my lap and licking my face. 'Looks as if you've found a friend', said His Holiness. 'Would you like to take her with you or shall I send her along later.' Having a second dog was the last thing I had thought of. Still, she was very lovely, and she would be company for Barney, and I was a soft touch! Thus I acquired Randy. Bloody silly name. I told Joan about her in my next letter and this was the name she suggested. Randy was not a pure-bred Alsatian. Her father was one of the local Shenzi dogs. Still it was a good mixture. She had the strength and looks of an Alsatian and had inherited a degree of immunity to the various dog diseases from her sire. Barney was not at all impressed by the new arrival. He growled and snarled as she fussed around him, finally barking in his efforts to intimidate her. She took not the slightest notice of this unfriendly behaviour, climbing all over him and licking him every time he lay down. I think Barney had an eye to the future really and after a short time accepted the new arrival and they became firm friends. Kesi entered the lounge where I sat reading one evening. '*Bwana*', he said, 'now that we have spare boys' quarters, could we have a kitchen *toto* to help out with the work?' I had been expecting a request of this sort for some time. All of the other European officers had a cook, a houseboy, a *shamba* boy, and a kitchen *toto*, to clean the pots and pans, fetch the firewood and generally make himself useful. However, I determined not to give in too easily. 'What's wrong with the prisoner who comes up each day?', I enquired. '*Bwana*, he's being released next week', was the reply. 'Well I can get another one to replace him', I said, determined to make him work hard for any concession I might make. '*Bwana*, a kitchen *toto* could light the fire in the morning, before the prisoner arrives.' 'What's to stop you from lighting the fire as you do now?', I countered. This conversation went on for another five minutes. Eventually poor Kesi was practically in tears. What he really wanted was someone he could order about. All the other cooks and houseboys in the employ of the officers had their minions and he badly wanted one to give him status. 'O.K.', I said. 'You'd better enquire round to see if there's anyone available', '*Bwana* he is waiting outside now.' Cunning little bugger. He knew damn well that I would give in eventually! After interviewing the applicant, who turned out to be a small Karamajong who had been at Lotome Mission until his family ran out of cash for his education, I agreed to employ him for Shs 30/- per month.

Arthur Brown came into my office one morning. His usually cheerful face was solemn. 'I've been robbed', he stated. I thought he was kidding. Theft was unheard of in Karamoja. I remembered the occasion when Dick Baker had come along with a similar complaint, when the culprit had turned out to be a hyena. This time, however, it had actually happened. The Agricultural Office had been broken into during the night and a locked cupboard ransacked. A canvas bag containing about Shs 800/-, which represented the pay for a number of field workers, was missing. Who on earth could have perpetrated such a dastardly deed. The Karamajong tribesmen had little use for cash, apart from the small amounts they needed to pay their annual poll tax. The finger of suspicion had to point to one or other of the cooks or houseboys employed by the government officers. After an unprofitable visit to the scene of the crime I visited all of the officers present on the station. Without exception they vouched for the total honesty of their employees. The next group of suspects had to be the government employees. There were quite a few of these in the town. Medical orderlies at the hospital, police and prison staff, tradesmen employed by the P.W.D., and of course the agricultural staff themselves. These last would have had the knowledge of the fact that money was kept in the cupboard. They had to be the prime suspects. My enquiries however came to nought. Arthur Brown became more and more depressed at the thought of one of his staff being responsible for this crime. 'I can't think of one of them who would do such a thing', he said. 'I would stake my life on the honesty of any of them.'

Things looked up shortly after this when one of my detectives brought in Loyem, a Karamajong tribesman who had been convicted of cattle-raiding some six years earlier and had served his prison sentence at Luzira, near Kampala. This struck be as being a possibility. At Luzira there was no telling what bad habits he might have picked up. The place was full of bad characters. He had been released from prison a couple of months prior to the burglary, and had returned to his *manyatta* at Rupa, not far from Moroto. Rumour had it that he had been spending more money than was usual, down at the *dukas* in Moroto. I felt that the evidence was flimsy in the extreme. Still, this was a case of grasping at straws, so Loyem was questioned closely, but admitted nothing. He was still in the cells when Arthur paid another visit to my office. 'Any progress?', he enquired. I had to admit that there was none. 'One of my staff has suggested that we try a witch doctor who lives out on the Kangole road', he said. 'Oh, really Arthur! Be sensible', I said. 'You surely don't expect me to believe in that sort of thing?' 'Well, I hope you're not going to take offence', he said, 'but I'm prepared to try anything to clear this up.' Under protest I agreed to accompany him on his visit to the witch doctor. After all, it would be an experience if nothing else. We got into my car, taking with us P.C. Engatun to translate for us, and Mr Okello from Arthur's office who would show us where the witch doctor lived.

Leaving Moroto, we headed out on the main Iriri road. We had travelled about 12 miles when Okello directed us off to the left and into a *manyatta* where the witch doctor lived. I had been prepared to encounter one of the striking figures I had seen at the Moroto *baraza*, decked out in leopard skins ostrich feathers and other finery. Instead I was guided to a small mud hut in the centre of the compound, well away from any other buildings. Two little shrivelled old women sat outside, chewing tobacco. One of them was pointed out to me. 'This is the witch doctor', I was informed. Arthur looked as disappointed as I felt. 'Oh well,' I thought. 'Having come this far, I suppose we will have to complete the charade.' We were invited into the hut and sat on little wooden stools. P.C. Engatun told the old lady what was wanted. She sat in the middle of the floor armed with a gourd. First she tipped the contents onto the mud floor and spread them out. I could see teeth, bits of dry skin, various seeds, knucklebones, claws, and all sorts of other unidentifiable bits and pieces. Chanting in some unknown language she placed these items back into the gourd, sealed it with a cap and started shaking the whole thing vigorously. The second old woman sat near me against the wall of the hut. The noise of the chanting and, in particular, the shaking of the gourd was deafening in the confined space. I wondered what was going to happen next. I was soon to find out. I suddenly realised that instead of one voice, there were now two distinct voices coming from the old woman. The second voice was quite different from the first and it had come in so gradually that I was unable to be sure how long it had been there. Now the two voices were overlapping. There was no possibility that the witch doctor could be responsible for two distinct voices both speaking at the same time. I looked closely at the old woman sitting behind me for any sign that she was throwing her voice. Not a chance. She appeared to be asleep. If she had been responsible I would have known, since I was seated between her and the witch doctor. I got to my feet and quickly went outside. There was no one anywhere near the hut. Could there be anyone in the thatch? No.

It was much too thin. Was there someone secreted under the hut, in a hole or a tunnel. I checked this afterwards. The floor was totally solid. P.C. Engatun was looking a bit grey. 'It wants to know if we have any questions', he said. 'Ask it about the stolen money', I directed. He did so. The old woman chanting and the voice replying. 'It says we have already arrested the man responsible for the theft. We should bring him out here and it will the be able to tell us where the money has been hidden.' The session was at an end. I was puzzled but impressed. How had it been done? We returned to Moroto and collected Loyem. I feel sure that what we were doing was totally illegal and would never have stood up in Court. However, in for a penny, in for a pound. We returned to the witch doctor's hut with the prisoner. He seemed very ill at ease. This time I checked the hut and its surrounds very thoroughly before the session started. Finally I was satisfied that no deceptions could be practised on us and the same procedure followed. Again the chanting and the rattling of the gourd. This time I was listening closely for the answering voice. Gradually it started, gaining in strength as the chanting continued. There was no doubt. The voice was overlapping the chanting. P.C. Engatun, at my direction, started asking his questions. Slowly the story unfolded. Loyem had broken the window of the office, had climbed in and searched. He had broken open the cupboard and had stolen the money together with the canvas bag, leaving the same way that he had entered. Going back to Rupa where he was living, he had passed the bazaar area. He had then taken some of the money out of the canvas bag, secreting the remainder inside a culvert which was used to carry away rain water.

The session ended. Arthur handed over Shs 20/- to the witch doctor for her services and we set off for Moroto. After returning our prisoner to the cells we went to the culvert described to us. Sure enough, hidden in the culvert was a canvas bag which Arthur immediately identified as being the one in which the money had been placed. There was no money though. What was the answer to this extraordinary phenomenon. Looking back on it, I feel that it was probably an example of thought-reading. The witch doctor had read our thoughts when she said that we had arrested someone. She read the suspects thoughts when she described what had occurred. What she couldn't know, because the prisoner didn't know himself, was that someone else had found the cache of money and had removed it before we arrived. Where did the second voice come from. I haven't a clue! I had no evidence to take our prisoner before the Court and to Arthur's disgust I had to release him. The money was never recovered.

The next few months were fairly uneventful, if life in Karamoja could ever be termed such. Tom Hinett and his family were going on leave. He had now completed his first tour of three years in Uganda, and had earned quite a reputation for himself, especially as a driver! After many tries he had succeeded in passing the Swahili, Elementary Oral examination, which was the only one he had to qualify in. Lucky bugger! I felt in some part responsible for his success as, although my own command of the language was abysmal, it was better than his and I had primed him, to the best of my ability, prior to his eventual success. Although he was going to be away for a full six months he had the promise of returning to Moroto at the end of his leave, and therefore didn't have to face the prospect of packing up all his belongings. He simply had to turn his key in the lock and drive down to Jinja, where his car would be stored during his absence. The usual round of boozy parties were arranged before he left, but they were fairly low key affairs, firstly because he was coming back, and secondly he was not being replaced during the temporary absence by another European officer, as it was felt that his African 2i/c could manage on his own for this period.

I, for one, was very sorry to see the departure of the Hinett family. They were helpful, very pleasant, people. However, I knew that I had not seen the last of them. I gave them my parents address and I was pleased to hear later that they had spent a few days with them at St Leonards.

One day a signal was brought to me. This imparted the dreadful news that the Inspector of Vehicles would be unable to make his annual visit for the purpose of examining the local lorries. This was a task which had to be carried out each year prior to the lorries being licensed. Notification had already gone out from the D.C's office, where Vehicle Excise Licences were issued, to the owners of all heavy vehicles being used within the District. All of them were expected in Moroto during the forthcoming week. I showed the signal to Brian. 'Don't look at me', he said. 'I know sod all about the workings of lorries.' 'Well, that's about the extent of my knowledge too', said I. 'Sorry', he said, 'I'm off on safari tomorrow for a week. He hadn't mentioned this before and I had a strong suspicion that he had made a 'spur of the moment' decision. I made my way to the D.C's office. 'Could he notify the lorry owners of the cancellation of the inspection.' 'No he couldn't.' I was literally and metaphorically up the creek with no paddles.

The following day saw the departure of Brian with the Land Rover, followed shortly afterwards by the arrival of the first of the lorries, driven by no less a person that Father Farina from Kotido. I went outside and tried to make my apologies. 'Sorry, but the inspections are canceled', I said. 'The I.O.V. is sick and no one else is available.' 'That's perfectly alright' said His Holiness, 'my lorry is in very good order, all I need is your signature on the Form. I certainly don't want to have to make another trip all the way down here.' I felt myself weakening. 'Well, I don't know anything about lorries', said I. 'You wouldn't want me saying that I had inspected it when I hadn't?' 'Well, just have a quick look at it to salve your conscience.', he replied. I had a quick look round. Maybe just this one! 'Put it over the inspection pit quickly then.' I said. I stripped off my jacket and hopped into the pit. It all looked alright. 'Try the brakes', I said. He did so. No fluid leaks as far as I could see. 'Turn the steering.' Again he did so. Seemed pretty positive. I got out of the pit. 'Check the lights', I shouted. All appeared to be in order. 'Windscreen wipers', I suggested. O.K. Was there anything else I should look at. I couldn't think of anything. Maybe a quick run down the road and back. I got into the driving seat and off we went. Down to the *dukas* and back. What was this. Three more lorries were queueing at the pit. I was trapped. I had passed His Holiness's lorry. Now I would have to look at three more. The rest of the day was total chaos. In between inspecting the multitude of lorries which kept arriving, I tried to deal with the normal working of the police station. By the end of the afternoon I had inspected no less than 23 lorries, passed 18 of them and learned a great deal about the mechanics of vehicles. 'That's it', I thought. 'I'll make sure that I'm not available tomorrow.'

The best laid plans of mice and men, etc. On my arrival at the police station the following morning 12 lorries were already queueing, headed by Wreford Smith. I couldn't very well refuse to do his lorry so, once again, down underneath I went. Having inspected Wreford's I was again trapped and had to inspect all the others. By the end of the day I had inspected a further 20 lorries. The failure rate was up though. I had thought of more things to look at! During the next two days I completed the inspection of every lorry in Karamoja including most of the government vehicles and Bob Clarke's from Lotome Mission. They must have thought me a real soft touch. I'm sure that I didn't spot even half the glaring faults on the vehicles. Still, to my great relief, none of then crashed due to poor mechanical condition, as far as I know.

The D.C. arrived in my office one morning. He was in a rather flustered state and was carrying a note which had just arrived in the usual cleft stick. 'I think this concerns you rather than me', he said handing me the note. I read it. It was from the driver of one of the D.C's lorries which was used for picking up casual labour and transporting to wherever they were required for road repairs. It appeared that one of the men had fallen from the lorry and was dead. 'O.K.', I said, 'Leave it with me.' I sent a note down to Gareth at the hospital, asking him if he could accompany me out to the scene of the accident. This would save me the necessity of hiring a lorry to bring in the deceased for post-mortem. Shortly afterwards Gareth arrived, ready for the fray. We got into my car and headed out towards Iriri. The incident had occurred about 25 miles out of Moroto so we were there within the hour.

On our arrival we found the lorry involved parked at the side of the road, 100-yards or so from a *manyatta* where, we were informed, the deceased had resided. We examined the corpse. It had been dead about four hours and was already beginning to bloat. Gareth commenced his autopsy, while I started making enquiries among the bystanders. The deceased was a young man of about 18 years of age. He had, I gathered, never been on a vehicle of any sort in his life. Together with half- a-dozen labourers he had got onto the back of the open lorry to be taken off for his day's work. He had squatted down by the tailboard. When the lorry had started forward he had become so alarmed that, by the time it was traveling at about 30 miles an hour, he decided that it was far too dangerous to continue on in this manner. Rising to his feet he had leaped over the tailboard, instantly hitting the back of his head on the road as he turned a back somersault.

I reported my findings to Gareth who, by this time was half way through performing a full autopsy at the roadside. The friends and relatives of the deceased gathered round full of interest as the corpse was split open and its organs removed. The only sign of grief, came from the deceased's father who shed a tear or two when his son's brain was removed. Either the deceased wasn't very well liked by his family or life was regarded even more cheaply in Karamoja that in other parts of Uganda. 'Fractured base of skull', Gareth diagnosed. I recorded a couple of statements and the family carried off the corpse to be disposed of by the vultures and hyenas. Within a few hours only a handful of bone splinters would remain.

I had been spending a few days on safari, inspecting the outposts and dealing with the inevitable problems which arose. On my arrival back in Moroto I drove into the police station compound. Brian was looking a bit glum as I entered the office. He said nothing but handed me a signal which had just arrived. 'The following transfers will take place,' I read, 'A.S.P. Peskett from Moroto to Jinja. Acting S.S.P. Allen to revert to his substantive rank of Superintendent and transfer from Mbale to Moroto.' I felt that there was something ominous about the wording of the message. Moroto certainly wasn't a Superintendent posting. What had Allen been up to, to warrant being not only reduced to Superintendent but, transferred to Karamoja. It sounded like a punishment posting to me!

I was sorry in many ways to see the departure of Brian Peskett from Moroto. We had not got particularly close during his sojourn in Karamoja. He had only been in the District for four months, and I was never really sure whether he enjoyed the somewhat uncivilised way of living or not. He was probably more used to a life in the bright lights. Maybe the lack of female company didn't suit him. For that matter, there were times when I might have felt that way myself. The inevitable round of parties followed and then Superintendent Allen arrived. I had never met him previously and none of the other officers on the station knew anything about him. A large car rolled up to the police station forecourt and a cheerful looking individual got out. He was in his late 40s, of stocky build, sun-tanned, had a matt of dark, unruly hair and a broken nose. I instinctively liked him on first appearance. He wore no uniform and on entering the office boomed 'Hello there. I'm Allen. I believe you're expecting me.'

He shook Brian and me warmly by the hand and sat himself down in the spare chair. For some odd reason which was never explained to me he was invariably called Barr Allen. I could see no logical explanation for this since his initials were R.K. Maybe it was 'Bar' Allen. He could certainly put away the drink. After chatting for 20 minutes or so, he got to his feet. 'Point me in the direction of the Rest House', he said. 'I'd better unload the wife.'I looked at him in astonishment. This was the first I had heard of a wife! Moreover he had left her sitting in the car, slowly roasting, while he yarned with us in the office. 'His wife is either very long suffering or a bloody fool', I thought. In fact, I found that I was correct on both counts.

The handing-taking over process proceeded apace and in three days was completed. Barr Allen was very laid back in his approach to this. Half-way through checking inventories or records he would announce, 'That's fine. Don't want to see any more. Take your word for it.' He didn't bother to visit the outposts. 'I'll go round later on with Mr Beaden', he boomed, and roared with laughter at our surprised looks.

Over the period of our acquaintance I found that Barr had originally joined the Kenya Police in 1928, where he had served for over 20 years, apart from a few years in Somalia. He had transferred to Uganda as recently as 1950. His broken nose was explained by the fact that that from 1929 to 1939 he had been middleweight boxing champion of East Africa. During his service in Somalia he had taken into his employ a fearsome-looking tribesman who apparently performed the function of bodyguard and general factotum. During a recent home leave he had attended a Course at the Police College at Ryton-on-Dunsmoor, in Warwickshire. His search for liquid refreshment had led him to the Kenilworth Castle Hotel, where he had found the attractions of the barmaid so irresistible that he had married her. Barbara was blonde, with a trim figure and in her late 30s. Poor creature. She can't have known what hit her when she arrived in Moroto. What a change in lifestyle, from the bright lights of the Kenilworth Castle Hotel, to the oil lamps of Moroto where, until recently, European women had not been allowed! During her stay in Karamoja she never once left Moroto Township. She was totally under Barr's thumb and, should he go on safari, the Somali bodyguard was ever present to ensure that she got up to no mischief. As a result, she was hitting the bottle in a fairly determined way.

Barr was as good as his word. No sooner had Brian departed for Jinja than he and I were off on safari round the outposts. I found him very good company on our trips. His great booming laugh echoed around the camp fire in the evenings as we exchanged yarns.

Having visited all of the outposts Barr expressed very little further interest in the running of the place. He would occasionally take himself off for a few days to do a bit of shooting, leaving me to get on as well as I might. He did take over a certain amount of the prosecution work, for which I was duly thankful. Apart from this I was left very much to my own devices. He did leave one lasting mark on the station by constructing a tennis court, with the aid of prison labour. He spent days supervising this, and days following playing on it. Barr loved curries and never missed an opportunity of getting invited to one or other of the *dukas* to partake of the genuine article. He would always take Barbara to these. She was far more interested in the liquid refreshment and within a comparatively short time would collapse into a drunken stupor while Barr enlivened the proceeding with his booming laugh.

A signal arrived from Kacheliba reporting a double murder. I was at home enjoying a well-earned evening drink when it was handed to me. Too late to set off until morning. Anyway, the culprit had been arrested, so the difficult half of the job had already been done. I sent a message round to Gareth and soon had a reply from him promising to be ready to come and examine the bodies the following day. Hopefully I should be back by the following night so I decided to travel light. Gareth and I would travel in the Land Rover. I would leave Kesi and Barney behind this time and survive on a few bottles of beer and whatever I could easily take with me from the fridge.

Early the following morning we were away. I took with me a couple of constables to assist in the translation and recording statements, and to act as escorts should I decide that there was enough evidence to bring the accused in. By mid-morning we were at Kacheliba where the suspect was in custody. I then had the story from the local chief. Ongora was a Suk tribal policeman employed by the native authority. Quite a number of local tribesmen, both Suk and Karamajong are employed in this capacity and assist the local chiefs in such mundane tasks as tax collection and arresting offenders for minor infringements for which the chiefs are empowered to administer punishment. He resided at a small community between Kacheliba and Karita. His menage was unusual in as much as, in addition to his wife, his mother-in-law, a widow, lived with him. His wife, it transpired, was barren and this lack of offspring, intended to support him in his old age, was a source of constant friction between the three of them. Under normal circumstances Ongora would have had the option of returning his wife to her father and reclaiming the bride price. Unfortunately the father had been killed while participating in a cattle raid on the Karamajong and he was stuck with this somewhat unsatisfactory situation. After a few drinks, intended to deaden the frustration caused by his nagging wife and mother-in-law, a brilliant solution occurred to him. He got his *panga* (machete) and chopped open the skulls of both women. That this was a fairly drastic solution became clear to him when he sobered up and was faced with two corpses, becoming smellier by the hour. He went to the local chief to enlist his aid, and was promptly arrested.

Having taken the accused into our custody, we drove to Ongora's village. The two victims were still in the mud hut in which they had been killed. On inspecting the scene I found the wife lying on the floor and the mother-in-law half on and half off a rough mattress. The entire dwelling was heavily bloodstained, indicating that the first blows had not been fatal and that Ongora must have chased both women around the hut, slashing at them with the *panga* until they had fallen to the ground and bled to death. We had the bodies removed from the hut and Gareth performed autopsies on both of them before a large and interested audience. The cause of death was as clear to him as it was to me, but he was very thorough as the bodies were not too ripe.

Ongora readily agreed with the chief's account of events, in fact he seemed rather proud of the brilliant way he had disposed of his problem. He was quite cheerful about it and, in many ways, I found him rather more pleasant than most of the Suk I had met. After recording half-a-dozen statements from the various witnesses, we were ready to leave. The bodies of the two victims were taken off into the bush to be disposed of in the time-honoured manner while we climbed into the Land Rover and started for home, the prisoner in the back in the custody of the two constables.

We had driven about 20 miles when a large flock of guinea fowl appeared on the right hand side of the track. There was no point in returning from safari without taking a few birds with me so I grabbed my .22 rifle and slipped out of the driving seat. I dropped a bird with my first shot and hit two with my second. One of these dropped immediately, the second made off trailing a wing. I ran after it through the bush. After about 60 yards I was overtaken by one of the constables, then the second. I stopped. Who the hell was looking after the prisoner. I need not have worried. He had also joined in the chase and rapidly overtook the policemen and caught the wounded bird. Roaring with laughter the three of them made their way back to the Land Rover, the prisoner carrying the guinea fowl, the constables slapping him on the back in congratulation. Ongora was really enjoying his day out until I insisted that he be handcuffed for the rest of the journey.

In a sequel to this, Ongora duly appeared before Hatch Barnwell for the preliminary enquiry and was remanded in custody for the next High Court circuit. I think someone in the prison must have mentioned to him that he was likely to be strung up because, a few days later, when being escorted by one of the warders, he made a run for it and got clean away. The idiot headed straight back to his village, however, and was duly re-arrested by the chief. A couple of months later, before the High Court, he was found guilty of the double murder and sentenced to be hanged. I felt quite sorry later when his appeal failed and he was duly executed at Luzira Prison.

Something a bit odd was going on. My gin seemed to be going down. Not just the odd tot either. I was a bit perturbed by this. I had never found Kesi knocking off the spirits previously. Or if he had, he had topped it up with water so that I shouldn't notice. Was it the kitchen *toto*? I decided to make a secret mark on the bottle so that I could tell if anyone got at it. I examined it the following day. No change. And the next. No change. When I came in at lunch time on the following day however it had been got at. Not just a couple of tots. At least a third of a bottle was missing. Kesi would have been paralytic on this amount. But he was apparently cold sober. I called him in. 'Where is it?', I demanded, waving the bottle in a threatening manner. 'Memsahib O.C. drank it', he replied. I demanded an explanation. It appeared that Barbara was in the habit of calling in two or three times a week, sitting down in the lounge and knocking off a few gins and tonics. When she didn't call at my house she was known to visit the houses of the other bachelors where, no doubt, she raided their supplies.

I was in something of a quandary as to what action to take about this. I didn't want to fall out with Barr Allen by telling him to stop his wife nicking my booze. At the same time, I didn't see why I should have to underwrite her drunkenness. I took the unprecedented step of locking it all away in the storeroom. Poor Barbara. I found out later that Barr had locked up his own booze in an attempt to keep her sober. I believe that she continued to get access to it though even, at times, going to the local *dukas* and demanding drinks from the Asian proprietors.

We had visitors on the station. Two Europeans had booked in to the Rest House. This was sufficiently unusual to warrant comment among the officers. Enquiries at the *boma* revealed that one was from the British Museum, the other from London Zoo. On my return from work I was sitting in the front of the house drinking a cup of tea when the two strangers walked up the road. They came to where I was seated. 'Mr Beaden?', one enquired. I got to my feet. 'Yes, that's right', I replied. 'I'm Jack Lester', he said. 'I'm curator of reptiles at London Zoo. This is Arthur Loveridge. He's from the British Museum', I invited them both to take seats and called Kesi to bring some more tea. 'What can I do for you?', I enquired. 'We were told by Charles Pitman in London, that you are interested in collecting snakes. We wondered if you would give us a hand in catching some.' I was a bit taken aback by this. Probably my face showed it. 'One of the snakes you sent to Captain Pitman seems to be of a hitherto unknown species. I believe he intends calling it Psamophis Beadenii, but we would like to see if we can capture a live specimen.' I wasn't too sure if I wanted to have a snake named after me. It seemed a bit of a back-handed compliment, like a scientist having some horrible disease named after him. 'Well,' I said, 'I can point you in the right direction, and I can give you a hand collecting a few as well, but I've a job to do so my time will be limited. What I will do though, is to find one of the local tribesmen I have heard about. He has a reputation for catching and handling snakes. He will no doubt catch as many as you need.' So saying, I sent the kitchen *toto* with a message to the local chief and the following day the local snake man appeared and was more than willing to catch as many snakes as were required, at one-shilling each. I don't think they captured a specimen of Psamophis Beadenii, but they did get a large black mamba on the track leading to our swimming pool. I hadn't realised that the mamba was quite so close to home.

Jack Lester and his friend were in Moroto for about ten days and, during this time, spent a couple of evenings with me. Over drinks I related to them the episode of the witch doctor. Both of them were fascinated by the subject and begged me to take them out to see the old woman. 'I had my wristwatch stolen when we were down in Jinja', said Arthur. 'I wonder if she could throw any light on that.' I thought that this would be asking rather a lot. After all, Jinja was nearly 300 miles away. No suspect had been arrested either. I didn't suppose the old woman would even know what a wristwatch was. I said as much to my guests, but their keenness was undiminished. Eventually I agreed, and the following day we set out, accompanied by P.C. Engatun to translate for us.

The scene was unchanged. The *manyatta* surrounded by its thorn fence. The hut, set in the middle of the compound. The two old women sitting outside. They had not been informed of our intended visit so could have made no special arrangements. Through P.C. Engatun I told them the purpose of our visit. As before, we entered the thatched mud hut and seated ourselves on the little wooden stools which were provided. The gourd was produced and its contents tipped onto the floor. My visitors examined the contents with interest as they were replaced in the gourd and the cap placed in position. Then the performance commenced. The rattling gourd was deafening in the confined space. Neither Jack nor Bob were prepared for the overlapping voice when it commenced. Knowing what to expect however, I had noticed it as soon as it started. It gradually built up in strength and they suddenly recognised it for what it was. Both of them got to their feet and searched the hut, inside and out, as I had done on my first visit. The old woman was totally unperturbed by the activity. Re-taking their seats they asked me to question the old woman about the missing wristwatch. I told

P.C. Engatun, in Swahili, what was required, and he translated my questions into Karamajong. Needless to say this was a bit time-consuming, but to my astonishment the voice appeared to be answering my questions with some accuracy. The old woman knew precisely what a wristwatch was, in fact I was wearing one so there was no problem there. In answer to my questions we were informed that the watch had been left by Arthur in a large white room where he had been working. 'That's right. The laboratory', he said. It had been stolen by a large fat Muganda who had since sold it in the local market. 'I knew that bugger had it', said Arthur. 'Well, if he's sold it, there's no chance of getting it back now.'

Both of my visitors appeared most impressed by their encounter with the witch doctor. Arthur Loveridge insisted that he would write up the incident for the *National Geographic Magazine*. I don't know whether in fact he eventually did. I personally felt that my own opinion on the matter had been reinforced, and that the old woman had done a bit more mind reading, this time probing Arthur's innermost thoughts. He had already suspected the Muganda of stealing his watch, she had merely read these suspicions and confirmed them. I was still puzzled as to how the voice was produced though. Arthur and Jack asked me to contact the police at Jinja to ask them to investigate the theft further, now that this new 'evidence' had been produced. I was having none of it though. I didn't want to get the reputation of believing such twaddle. Still, there might have been something in it!

I was called out to Amudat for a disciplinary hearing. One of the constables had assaulted a corporal and had subsequently been charged. Quite a serious offence and one which might well cost the constable his job if proved. I decided to travel on my own this time. I should be back in Moroto well before sundown so there was no need to take anything apart from sufficient refreshment to last me the day. In the event, it transpired that at the time of the assault the corporal had been drunk, and the blame lay on both parties. I duly administered a reprimand to both of them and arranged to have them transferred to different stations.

On my way back to Moroto I decided to see if I could have a crack at the croc I had previously seen at the dam on the road to Nabilatuk. I stopped my car about a quarter-of-a-mile short of the dam and, as previously, made my way cautiously up the dry spillway. I carefully raised my head over the embankment. There were no ducks or geese to give the alarm. I glanced around the dam. There it was, lying about five yards from the water, about 100 yards away. Clearly I should only get one shot at this, so it had better be made to count. I decided on my favourite. The neck shot. All animals have a vast bunch of nerves running down the neck and a bullet into this mass would inevitably create instant paralysis, leaving me time to get round the dam to administer the *coup de grâce*. I took careful aim and fired. The croc twitched spasmodically and moved forward about six inches, before its legs collapsed from under it. I moved round the edge of the water till I stood over the corpse. It certainly looked quite dead. Still I had better make sure. A bullet through the brain would settle matters. Where was a crocodile's brain? I guessed the approximate position and put a bullet through it. The croc twitched. As I had thought, it was about seven or eight feet in length. I took hold of the tail and dragged the corpse back to my car. For its size it was quite heavy. Those jaws could do a lot of damage if they got a grip. I opened the tailgate and heaved the body into the back. Then I set off for Moroto. I had travelled about 40 miles when, without warning, there was a thrashing in the back of the car and the head of the croc appeared over the top of the front passenger seat. It quite clearly had only one thought in mind, that was to remove my ear and as much else as it could reach. I dodged my head to one side and skidded to a halt. I was out of the driving seat before the wheels had stopped turning, closely followed by the extremely angry crocodile. My rifle was still inside the car and the croc, instead of making off into the bush was actually chasing me. This was very much a case of the biter bit though, fortunately, not literally. I managed to dodge the slashing jaws and ran back to the car, grabbing my rifle. The croc had now given up and was making off as fast as it could go. I chased after it and after a minute or two managed to get in a couple of shots which finished the job off. This time I secured the jaws with a piece of cord before replacing the body in the vehicle, just to be on the safe side.

Barr Allen was going on one of his infrequent safaris, leaving Barbara at home as usual, under the ever-watchful eye of the Somali bodyguard. 'I'll be away three or four days I expect', he said before his departure. He didn't enlighten me as to where he was going or what the purpose of the trip was to be. He was taking his own car so I thought it likely that he was heading for Kitale, over the border into Kenya.

The evening after his departure there was a knock on the door of the verandah at the front of my house. I thought it was probably Dick Baker, popping in for an evening drink. To my considerable alarm, I found, on opening the door, none other than Barbara. She appeared to be sober for a change. 'Oh Tony', she said, 'I'm so lonely. There's no one to talk to with Barr on safari. Could I come in for a chat?' Poor thing. She was practically in tears. I could see trouble here, with a capital 'T'. However, my options were a bit limited. I could hardly tell her to bugger off. 'Of, course', I said, 'Come along in.' She didn't need a second invitation. She was inside the door and sitting on the settee before I could turn round. The hair on the back of my neck bristled. I could feel the presence nearby of the Somali bodyguard. I carefully pulled the curtains open so that anyone outside could have a clear view of what was going on. No way was I going to get the boot for rodgering the O.C's wife. 'Would you like a drink?', I said, vainly hoping that she wouldn't. 'Yes please. I could do with a large gin and tonic', she replied. As I was getting it for her Kesi poked his head knowingly round the door. '*Chakula tayari*', (Food is ready) he said. I turned to

Barbara. I was trapped. 'Would you care for some dinner?', I enquired. She accepted with alacrity. Ten minutes later we were sitting down to a roast leg of Grants Gazelle, with the usual vegetables and a glass of wine.

I was hoping that I would be able to get rid of her after dinner. Not a bit of it. Down she sat on the settee, insisting that I sat beside her. During the next couple of hours she demolished half a bottle of gin, becoming more and more drunk in the process. Meanwhile, she poured out her troubles to me. How unhappy she was with Barr. She should never have married him. She hated living in the bush. She wanted to go back to Warwickshire. Barr had locked up all the booze so that she shouldn't get it. That horrible Somali was always spying on her. And so on, and on, and on. The horrible Somali, I had a pretty good idea, was at that moment peering into my lounge, to make sure I got up to no mischief with his boss's wife. Poor Barbara kept edging closer and closer to me on the settee. The situation was getting out of hand. I got to my feet. 'Well', I said, 'I've got to be up early in the morning. I'd better run you home now.' I didn't give her a chance to object, but went to the garage and got my car out. Finally I got her home. The Somali was there waiting. It was only 100 yards from my house so he must have dashed across from my house as soon as he saw we were on the move. As I started to get out of my seat, Barbara leaned over and grabbed me, kissing me passionately on the mouth. I fully expected to get a knife in the back at this juncture but all I got from the Somali was a toothy grin. This would all be reported to Barr on his return. Sure enough, in the office a few days later Barr raised the subject with me. He was quite apologetic about Barbara's behaviour. 'I've got a few problems', he said. 'Shouldn't have got married I guess. Thanks anyway.'

The prison sergeant reported to me one morning. A prisoner had escaped. Lokwal was on remand, charged with murder, during a cattle raid. He was a Suk and came from a village some miles from Amudat. It transpired that while being taken to the D.C's office together with three other prisoners for a further remand he had somehow slipped the handcuff and was away before his escorting warders realised what had happened. I gave the necessary instructions for a search to be mounted, and for the erring warder to be placed on a charge. I didn't hold out much hope of Lokwal's capture, however. Being a Suk, every local tribesman's hand would be against him. If he was spotted he would, no doubt, be speared out of hand and nothing said. This he would be fully aware of. He would travel at night, at least until he got into Suk territory. Then he would go to ground. Probably back to his own village where he would be protected. As I had anticipated the search proved fruitless. The next step was to send a message to Amiri, the County Chief at Amudat. With a bit of luck he would be able to apprehend the escapee.

A week later a message was received from the police post at Amudat. Amiri was reporting that Lokwal had been seen near his home village, but had not been around when the Native Authority policemen went to arrest him. I suspected that there might have been some collusion here and decided to take firm action. The short rains had just started so, getting to Lokwal's village which lay midway between Amudat and Katabok, was not going to be easy, owing to the deep black cotton soil. The Land Rover was not going to be adequate for this operation so I hired a lorry from Pandit Puran Chand's garage. Then, late at night, I set off from Moroto with 20 armed constables and N.C.O's aboard. The lorry reached Amudat at around 2.a.m. and we pulled in to the police post for a couple of hours rest. At 4.a.m. we were on our way again, taking with us a couple of the constables from the police post to act as guides. Progress was agonisingly slow. The black cotton soil kept collecting round the wheels of the lorry, slowing and finally stopping it. Everyone out to clear away the great lumps of soil, then on our way again for another half mile. We were going to be too late at this rate. There was no alternative. The last three miles would have to be made on foot, at the double if possible. It was purgatory. Every step we took gathered more mud onto our feet. However, as dawn was just breaking, there was the *manyatta* in front of us. Try as we might, our stealthy approach awakened the shenzi dogs within the *manyatta* and they started to bark. By the time we had reached and surrounded the thorn fence, there was activity within. I wondered if Lokwal had been sufficiently aroused to make good his escape. The headman appeared rubbing the sleep from his eyes. Protesting, he let us into the *manyatta*. A thorough search was made but the bird had flown. Into force came 'Plan B'. In the nearby compound were the cattle. Around 100 of them I guessed. I told the headman that we were going to seize the lot.

He would get them back when Lokwal was produced. A great wailing and gnashing of teeth then arose from the women of the *manyatta*. I was adamant. Anticipating that this was the time when, if ever, trouble might explode. I instructed my party to load their rifles. This had the desired effect and all opposition evaporated. The cattle were then taken out of the compound and we started off towards Amudat, the constables driving them as fast as possible. The occupants of the *manyatta* followed close behind, occasionally attempting to head off the odd animal from the herd. On reaching the lorry where we had left it I instructed the driver to return to Amudat. By this time the soil had started to dry out a little, and with a little help, the lorry turned and started its slow return journey. Three hours later, somewhat tired and weary, we arrived at Amudat to be greeted by Amiri. There, I handed over to cattle to him for safe custody. The herd was duly counted and signed for. Amiri was more than happy. Any calves born during the period of seizure would, no doubt, become his property, as would the milk produced daily. The owners would have plenty of incentive to hand over Lokwal at the earliest opportunity. I have no doubt that my action was totally illegal but it worked. Three days later Lokwal was handed over by his relatives. In due course he appeared before the High Court, where he was tried for murder, sentenced to death and duly executed. Cattle were far more important to his kin than was the life of Lokwal.

A message arrived at the police station. The traditional cleft stick was used but this time the messenger had scrounged a lift on the lorry of one of the Asian traders from Kotido. The message, however, was not from the chief, but from Scottie. Frank Scott was the Tsetse Fly Officer from the Kidepo Valley in the north of Karamoja where the boundary with the Sudan existed. Sandy Field's happy hunting ground! I had never had the pleasure of meeting Scottie, but knew him well by reputation. I had no idea what methods were used to clear Tsetse fly, but I was aware that a scheme was in hand to eradicate them from the Kidepo and open it up for human habitation.

Scottie's message contained the news that a bunch of poachers from the Sudan had recently crossed into the Kidepo Valley and had set about ring-burning a herd of elephant. This was a very cruel method of hunting and involved a large band of poachers, maybe 30 or 40 in number armed with spears, poisoned arrows and the occasional rifle, surrounding a herd of elephant in long grass, and simultaneously firing the grass, thereby trapping the entire herd. The herd would mill round in the ever decreasing ring finally either perishing in the flames or, if they made good their escape receiving dreadful burns from which they would be crippled or so injured as to make easy prey for subsequent killing. If they bolted for safety the poachers would be waiting to kill or maim the maddened and usually blinded animals as they passed. Any that survived and escaped in an injured state would become rogues, and a constant danger to anyone unlucky enough to come across them.

The good news was that, when the fires had been lit the wind had changed, trapping six of the poachers who had fried. The herd of elephant had escaped unharmed. However, there were six cooked Sudanese, awaiting my examination and subsequent report to the Coroner.

I had not yet been to the Kidepo Valley and was looking forward to viewing it at first hand. I rapidly set the wheels in motion to get the safari under way. Within an hour everything was ready. I left Kesi and Barney behind this time as I was not keen for Barney to get bitten by the Tsetse flies. I knew they could be fatal to cattle. They could also cause sleeping sickness in humans. I was unsure what effect they could have on dogs but thought it best to be on the safe side. There was no way that I should be able to get to the Kidepo in what remained of the day. I decided to get as far as I could before nightfall. In the event we reached Kaabong, well to the north of Kotido before having to make camp. The rest camp at Kaabong was a very pleasant spot. Neat, thatched huts spaced well apart, a cooking area and a couple of porters who's job it was to keep the place tidy and collect firewood and water for anyone staying at the camp. My tent was quickly set up under one of the thatched roofs. I sent one of the porters to fetch the local *mkungu* chief. He arrived half-an-hour later, the porter dragging the usual goat. He appeared quite pleased when I declined it and I invited him to join me for a bottle of beer. After the usual exchange of small talk I got round to my purpose in having called him. 'I would like to have a look at the famous view from Kamion', I said. 'Would you provide a guide to show me the best spot to see it as the sun comes up tomorrow morning?' He certainly would. In fact the guide would be himself, even though it would mean getting up at 4 a.m.

Kamion was an uninhabited location some eight miles from Kaabong and was reputed to have the most superb view in the whole of Karamoja. I missed not having Kesi to produce my early morning cup of tea, and decided that the view had better be something out of the ordinary to make up for the loss of this spot of luxury. In the event, I managed to rouse myself at about 3.30 a.m. Bleary-eyed I got the tea for myself and awaited the arrival of the *mkungu* chief. He arrived at about 4.30 a.m. and together with a couple of constables we got into the Land Rover and set off. The track was a bit rough but we reached our destination, or as far as we could go, just as the first streaks of pale dawn were appearing. We still had about half-a-mile to walk to the best location. The morning was cool and I shivered as I walked across the heavy dew lying over the grass and scrub. A myriad spider webs festooned the surrounding bushes. During the day they would have been invisible. With the dew lying on them they were transformed into a delicate tracery.

Little could be seen as we arrived at the view point. I could see that the ground dropped sharply away in front of us but that was all. On the horizon the sky grew gradually brighter. Suddenly, the first rays of the morning sun appeared. Instantly the scene changed. We were in bright sunlight. The valley below us was still dark. As the sun leaped upwards over the hills which had hidden it, the darkness below was transformed. The vast valley we could now make out below us was Turkana. It stretched away as far as the eye could see. This, then, was the Great Rift Valley. Created countless millions of years ago when the African Continent had split lengthwise, it runs from the Red Sea, forming the great lakes in its path. The altitude where we sat was nearly 5,000 feet above sea level. The valley wall dropped away, almost sheer, down to what was virtual desert 3,000 feet below. Far away to the east was Lake Rudolf, but even from our great height we could see nothing of this. Below us were numerous ancient volcanic outcrops scattering the valley floor. As the sun's rays struck them, vast shadows were thrown out across the desert. At the speed of an express train the shadows retreated back towards their rocky origins as the sun sped into the sky. Within ten minutes the spectacle was over. Below us now, the scene was tranquil. Smoke began to rise from the scattered *manyattas* as the Turkana tribesmen commenced another day. Through my binoculars I could make out the herds of cattle milling around in their thorn *bomas*. Far away the dull clunk of the cow bells could be heard. Herds of gazelle and kudu could be made out as they browsed, oblivious and quite close to the *manyattas*. An incredible scene of pastoral serenity. This then, was the famed view which, once seen, could never be forgotten. It had been well worth the effort involved in getting to see it at daybreak.

By 8 o'clock I was back at my camp. The early morning activity had given me an appetite and I quickly knocked up a plate of fried eggs, bacon, baked beans and tinned tomatoes. Then we were on our way once more to the Kidepo Valley.

By mid-day we had reached our destination. A couple of grass thatched huts at the side of the road indicated a check-point. A couple of natives approached us carrying what appeared to be butterfly nets and Flit sprays. These were Fly Boys. There function really was to check any vehicles traveling in the other direction to prevent any Tsetse fly being transported out of the Kidepo area. I rather doubt the efficiency of this employment. They could hardly guarantee that 100 percent of the flies traveling on a vehicle would be eradicated with a butterfly net and a Flit spray. However, it bore the air of some authority! A few miles after passing this checkpoint we pulled into a permanent looking encampment at the roadside. A figure emerged from a nearby house and came forward to greet me. Scottie was about five feet three inches tall and about the same width. His beaming face was surrounded by a vast beard. He was clad in an open-necked shirt, very short shorts and sandals. He was the colour of old teak. 'Come on in', he boomed. 'I've been expecting you. Lunch is ready. Have a beer.' I introduced myself and accompanied him into his house. A concrete floor ensured that no termites could penetrate. The walls were open around the top, ensuring a free flow of air throughout. A heavily-thatched roof maintained the cool interior. The furniture was of excellent quality. No government-issue here. Much of it appeared to be antique though very solid. Several large bookcases were placed around the walls and these were filled to overflowing with splendid books, many of them dealing with natural history and scientific subjects. A large gun case filled with rifles and shotguns of various caliber's stood nearby. The floor was scattered with expensive looking rugs. Scottie reminded me strongly of an arab potentate with his life-style. Minus the harem of course.

As soon as we had entered the house a tankard of ice-cold beer was thrust into my hand and I was motioned to a large comfortable chair. For half-an-hour or so we chatted. Scottie clearly wanted to make as much as possible of this opportunity to talk. His guests were few and far between. Eventually we got round to discussing the party of poachers who were the reason for my visit. 'Don't suppose there will be much left now anyway', he said. 'I had a few tree boughs cut and put over the corpses, but I expect the hyenas will have got at them!' 'Splendid', I thought. 'If there are no corpses, I shan't have the bother of taking them back to Moroto with me.'

After a leisurely lunch of roast gazelle and tinned vegetables we climbed into the Land Rover and made our way to the scene of the incident. It was about 20 miles from Scottie's camp. On our way we passed great herds of kongoni and topi, zebra, buffalo, eland and various gazelle. As we arrived, a few vultures flew heavily away from the nearby trees. The grass fire started by the poachers had burned itself out after about a mile or so. Piles of tree boughs indicated the whereabouts of the cooked poachers. I got out of the Land Rover and made my way to them. A few crushed bits of bone were all that remained. I counted six piles of boughs each with a few fragments. 'Hardly worth bothering with', I decided.

On our way back to Scottie's camp we took a different route. A small herd of elephant meandered off out of the way of our vehicle. Every so often we passed elephant remains lying at the side of the track or off in the bush. The skulls looking like primitive armchairs. No tusks on any of these. Mostly the work of the poachers, though some might have been down to Sandy Field, or to Scottie himself.

From time to time a Tsetse fly would land on some exposed part. There was no mistaking the bite when it came. Far worse than the most vicious horse fly. Slapping the fly had no effect on it whatever. The only way to kill them appeared to be to catch hold of them and crush the body between the thumb nails.

Having completed the small amount of paperwork required by the investigation, Scottie and I relaxed on the verandah of his house with a beer. I then learned what Tsetse control was all about. The Kidepo consisted of hundreds upon hundreds of square miles of fertile land which had once been farmed and grazed by tribesmen. However, since the arrival of the Tsetse fly from the north many years earlier, it was closed to human settlement since cattle could not survive and humans developed trypanosomiasis or sleeping-sickness. The idea was to eradicate the fly and re-open the entire area to human habitation. To this end a number of options were open and were being tried. The first of these was to cut down every tree in the valley, since the Tsetse needed shade in which to breed. This had already been tried in a large pilot area, but with limited success. The next option was to eradicate every grazing animal within the area, since this would leave the Fly nothing to feed on. I think the horror I felt as these methods were explained, must have shown in my face. There were probably several million grazing animals within the Kidepo. The thought of slaughtering these vast herds on the off-chance that it might re-open the area to the dubious benefit of human habitation was appalling. The Kidepo, from the small area I had visited, appeared to be unique in its wildlife habitat. What a wonderful area it would make if, instead of the ruination imposed by over grazing, it could be opened as a National Park. In fact, this is precisely what eventually happened. Only, however, after vast herds of animals had been exterminated and great areas deforested. Today, the Tsetse fly still reigns supreme.

On my return to Moroto I found that another raid had been reported from the Amudat area. Barr Allen clearly had no intention of going out to investigate the incident and had been awaiting my return. 'I thought I'd better not go off while you were away as well. Still, now you're back you may as well deal with it.' This suited me well enough since it meant another couple of nights safari allowance, plus a few hundred more miles to be claimed. Financially, since the acquisition of my car, I was now well and truly in the black. It seemed that the days of rude letters from the bank manager were behind me — I hoped. I left instructions for the safari gear to be made ready and went home to give Kesi the good news that we were away again on the morrow. Randy was still not old enough to accompany us on safari, and had to be left behind with the kitchen *toto*.

The cattle raid turned out to be a fairly routine affair and I was able to leave the following up to the staff from Amudat Police Post. They had, in fact, left with the tracker shortly after the raid had been reported. While I was awaiting their return I busied myself with inspecting the police post and dealing with one or two disciplinary offences which had been awaiting my arrival.

During the evening as I was relaxing with a beer at the camp fire the Ekapalon, Amiri, arrived. He joined me at the fire and I gave him a beer and a lump of *biltong*. He seemed to be in the mood for conversation so I broached a subject which I had been thinking about for some time. Arrow poison. I knew that some of the casualties which had occurred during the raids which I had investigated had been caused by wounds inflicted by arrows. Invariably these had proved fatal and I was interested to know what poison was used. Amiri was only too pleased to tell me all about it. 'You look for a particular type of thorn tree', he said, 'under which no vegetation will grow. Several branches are removed and the bark stripped from them. Then the bark is pounded to a pulp and boiled. After boiling for many hours the liquid is strained off and simmered until the residue is of the consistency of tar. This is the arrow poison. To test it, the maker cuts a small vein in his arm and allows the blood to flow. An arrow, tipped with the poison, is then allowed to touch the blood. If the poison is good it will be seen flowing back up the arm through the stream of blood. If the poison reaches the wound the man will die, so he wipes the blood from his arm before this happens.' Amiri went on to tell me that before going on a raid, the warrior armed with the bow and arrows will fire an arrow into a sheep. 'The sheep will run about 100 yards before falling dead. After its death, all of the wool falls from the sheep's body.' I didn't know whether to believe all this or not. Amiri, however, had no need to lie about the subject, and he assured me that his account was totally true. Having got him started on the subject, Amiri went on to tell me of some other interesting customs. 'If a man falls out with his neighbour and decides to kill him, this can be done in a manner totally undetectable. He will kill a leopard or lion, or, if he can't do this himself he will go to the witch doctor, from whom he will obtain the long whiskers from around the lips of one of these cats. The whiskers are chopped up finely and introduced into the food of the intended victim. From then on it is just a matter of time. The chopped whiskers work their way into the lining of the stomach and cause cancerous tumours, from which the victim dies.' I had cause to think on this matter some months later when P.C. Engatun, one of our few Karamajong constables and as strong as an ox, developed cancer of the stomach and was dead in a very short time.

The investigation into the cattle raid was completed the following day. However I decided to spend a further night at Amudat and return to Moroto early the following morning. Two prisoners had been arrested for having taken part in the raid, so I sent a message to Moroto, to arrange for the Land Rover to be sent out with an escort to collect them.

At about five o'clock I decided to take Barney and go off with my .22 rifle into the bush to collect a bird or two to take back with me. Twenty minutes later I was cautiously making my way along a track in fairly heavy bush, when suddenly Barney's hackles rose, and without warning he rushed ahead of me. Ten yards from me was a thick bush and Barney disappeared round the back of this. Sounds of snarling and growling came from his direction. I ran forward. Barney had a leopard by the throat. It wasn't a very big leopard fortunately, or he would have stood no chance at all. As it was, the big cat had been taken by surprise. It had no doubt seen or smelled the dog and had decided that this was an opportunity for an easy meal. In this, it had made a big mistake. Barney had got in first and was intent on tearing out the throat of the leopard. There was little I could do to intervene. I raised my rifle in the hope of getting in a telling shot but the activity was all too rapid. A shot could just as easily have hit Barney. The leopard couldn't get its jaws into Barney but it suddenly rolled onto its back and ripped with the terrible claws on its back feet. Poor old Barney. He was split open the full length of his belly. He still wouldn't let go of the leopard's throat and I ran up and swung my rifle clouting the cat's head as hard as I could, but without noticeable effect. Finally Barney could hang on no longer. His jaws fell open and with a final snarl the leopard made good its escape. Barney lay on his side, trying to get to his feet. His guts were protruding from the ripped flesh. I suppose I should have put a bullet through his head at this stage, but I couldn't bring myself to do it. Instead I gathered him up in my arms and made my way back to the camp. Kesi came running forward as he saw me carrying the dog. 'Bring me some warm water with salt in it', I said. He ran off to carry out my instructions. I carried Barney into the tent and laid him on the ground sheet. On examination I found that the torn flesh was bleeding profusely, but I could see no actual damage to the protruding intestines. Barney lay still at my command. I bathed the injuries with the warm salted water and gently pushed the intestines back into the cavity. Then with needle and cotton I carefully stitched up the wounds. Barney made not a sound, but grinned at me and weakly wagged his tail. Finally, I wrapped a clean vest over the injury and carefully placed Barney into the back of my car. Kesi accompanied me in the back to hold Barney still, should he start moving around. We headed for Moroto, stopping at the police post on the way, where I gave instructions for my safari gear to be packed up ready for later collection. Three hours later I pulled up outside Sandy Taylor's house. Fortunately he was not away on safari. I explained what had happened and he examined Barney where he lay. 'Well, I'm not going to open him up again to see if the guts are punctured', he said. 'We'll just have to hope for the best in that direction. I'll put in a few proper stitches to reinforce those you've already put in. The claws are bound to have been full of filth though so I'll give him an injection of penicillin. If he survives the next 24 hours he may pull through. Keep your fingers crossed.' Twenty four hours later Barney was still alive though running a high temperature. More penicillin injections followed. A week later and Barney was on his feet, weak but alive. To my great relief he made a full recovery.

Since my early meeting with Wreford Smith and the account of his activities in mining the numerous mica deposits, I had been keen to try my hand at some similar activity. So far I had restricted this to a bit of gold panning in the river beds at Karita and Amudat. Neither place had produced even a smell of the precious metal. Maybe I just wasn't doing it right. Now it occurred to me that the stream bed above the swimming pool might be a useful place to investigate with a view to discovering a deposit of gem stones of one sort or another. Not that I should readily be able to recognise anything I found, but it seemed a good idea at the time.

Barney was now fully fit and ready for action after his brush with the leopard. I set out with him after Sunday lunch and soon reached the swimming pool. There was still a trickle of water feeding the pool, but a few hundred yards further up the mountain the stream bed was quite dry. With Barney in the lead I made my way up the gully. The width varied between six and ten feet, being narrower where the stream had cut the soil and rock path to a greater depth. I had my .22 rifle slung over my shoulder and carried a trowel to dig out any likely-looking rocks. After about a quarter of a mile of fairly steep scrambling, I came to a particularly narrow stretch. The bank on each side was totally sheer and around 14-feet in depth. A few tree roots stuck out from the banks at intervals but apart from these the sides were featureless. Barney had run on ahead and was out of sight round the next bend in the stream. Suddenly I heard his furious barking. It was rapidly drawing nearer. I had visions of a hyena or a bush pig charging round the corner towards me. Neither prospect appealed much. I struggled to get my rifle off my back and into a ready position. No chance! The next second Barney appeared about 20-yards away, chasing after a snake. No ordinary snake this! I instantly identified it. Only one specie had these characteristics. 14-feet if it was an inch. Slim as my wrist and moving at twelve to 15 miles an hour. This was a black mamba and considerably bigger that the one I had killed near Katabok. There was no way I could get up the side of the stream bed. Neither could the great snake. Even had I had my rifle at the ready, my chances of making another lucky shot as it came towards me were nil. My last thought was, 'That bloody dog has got me killed.' The next few seconds were a whirl of activity. Barney, barking furiously, was within an inch or two of the snakes tail. I was the same distance from its head. Then it was over. I can only imagine that the mamba, in its hurry to get out of Barney's way, failed to see me. It passed straight over my feet brushing my ankles in the process. I stood rooted to the spot. A few yards further on, the snake reared up the bank and slithered into a hole under a tree root. Within a couple of seconds it was out of sight. Barney, clearly considering that he had done a great job, leaped up towards the hole but found it just out of his reach. The mamba had disappeared by now anyway. I felt a bit shaken by this incident. I wasn't sure whether to curse Barney or praise him. I suppose he thought he was helping by giving the snake the fright of its life. In the event he'd given me an equal one.

The news of Barr Allen's transfer came as no great surprise. I think that reports of his wife's various activities had finally reached Headquarters, probably via the D.C. whose drinks had been raided on more than one occasion. Poor Barbara. I think everyone on the station felt some sympathy for her. She was totally out of her depth in Moroto. There were no kindred spirits to whom she could pour out her troubles. Her marriage to Barr was undoubtedly on the rocks and booze was her only consolation. I think that, had she been left in Moroto much longer, she would probably have hanged herself. Anyway, Barr and his wife were off to Kampala and Roy Pearman was to be the new O.C. Karamoja. I knew nothing of Pearman apart from the fact that he had been in the prosecution branch at Kampala. Not, I thought, a very good grounding for running a district like Karamoja. The usual round of parties followed. Barbara was, for once, in her element. Each night she became paralytically drunk and had to be carried to Barr's car and taken home. Eventually the Allens left for Kampala. I was relieved as far as Barbara was concerned. I felt it could only be a matter of time before some big trouble overtook her if she remained in Moroto. In a way I was sorry to see Barr depart. I was now on my fourth O.C. within a year. Was this normal, I wondered. I heard later that Barbara had departed for the U.K. within a very short time of arriving in Kampala. Barr himself retired from the police two months later and took up a bachelor existence on Lamu Island a couple of hundred miles north of Mombasa. Here he managed to get himself murdered within the year. I never found out the gory details of his demise. It would not have surprised me to find that his faithful Somali bodyguard had been responsible.

Pearman's arrival in Moroto was delayed by outstanding Court cases so I had to take over temporary command of the District. Big deal. For a few days after his departure I was O.C. Police. Any celebration which might have attached to this was, however, short-lived. I awoke one morning feeling like death. High temperature, dreadful headache, aching in every joint, vomiting. You name it, I had it. I was unable to get out of bed, let alone go to the office. I just hoped that nothing serious would blow up since the police were now under the control of a totally illiterate Head Constable.

Gareth called in to see me. 'You've got a nasty bout of malaria.' He said. 'Have you missed taking your chloroquine?' he enquired. I didn't think I had, but I suppose it was possible I had missed the odd dose during a safari. After a week of treatment I began to feel a bit better, but not much. I crawled down to the office. It was still there. I went through the books. Nothing of earth-shattering proportions had occurred. Breathing a sigh of relief I crept back home and returned to bed. Shortly afterwards a message was brought to me. Pearman was arriving the following day. I sent a message down to the Rest House to book him in for a couple of days while he was sorting out his house. The next morning I again crawled down to the office to spend half-an-hour. While I was there a car drew up outside and Roy Pearman came into the office. 'No uniform?' These were the first words he uttered. I extended my hand to him. It was ignored. 'Actually, I'm off sick at present', I said. 'I've just called in for half-an-hour to make sure that everything is O.K.' 'Well, I hope you're on duty tomorrow', he said. 'I shall want to start taking over without delay.' 'What a c**t.' This was my first reaction to Pearman. I had no reason to change this first impression. During the next few days, Pearman and his wife Illa, moved into his house and I managed to hand over command to him. I was still feeling pretty groggy after the bout of malaria, but this made no difference to Pearman. Off we went on safari each day, checking all the outposts. Eventually the handing over was completed. Meanwhile I had been given the opportunity of sizing him up. He was about the same age as myself, three or four inches shorter, round face, dark-haired and clean-shaven except for a moustache. His build was best described as fleshy. A tendency to run to fat rather easily, I guessed. His voice was what grated. A sort of high-pitched, whining, whinging sound. His wife was about the same age as himself, and Polish. At the beginning of the war a number of Polish refugees had got to Britain. For some extraordinary reason they had been shipped out to Uganda of all places, where they were housed in a camp. Most of them were eventually found work and integrated after a fashion. Mrs Pearman was one of them. I never discovered how the two had met. I wasn't sufficiently interested to enquire. Actually she was quite a pleasant sort of woman. She definitely deserved better than Pearman, but I suppose it was a case of 'Beggars can't be choosers'.

The first thing Pearman did on inspecting his house was to

demand that it be re-decorated throughout. Most of the government-issue furniture was removed into storage and his own furniture installed. He was very proud of having his own furniture and never tired of telling anyone who would listen, how much each piece had cost. I wondered whether Illa had managed to bring out some cash from Poland.

Eventually some sort of normality returned to my life. I began to wonder if a couple of weeks at Mombasa would not be a good idea. The malaria, coupled with Pearman's arrival had left me feeling somewhat below par.

I was due some local leave and broached the matter with Pearman. 'Not a chance', he said. 'You can't expect to be allowed leave so soon after my arrival. Maybe in a few months time when I have got to know the district better. After all, you must realise that leave is a privilege not a right.'

With this I had to be satisfied.

With the arrival of Pearman, some of the sparkle had gone out of life in Karamoja. No more was I able to go off on safari at the drop of a hat. Everything had to be discussed at length and reasons given for every action I took. My mileage and safari claims were closely examined and usually returned for alteration. Anything the idiot could do to be obstructive he would do. He was as unpopular with all the other officers on the station as he was with me. I wouldn't have minded so much if he had known what he was about. He was totally ignorant of running a large district and had to rely on my good offices to get him out of trouble. Eventually I felt fully recovered from my bout of malaria and most weekends would find me up on the mountain. I usually climbed alone on these trips, and eventually succeeded in scaling each of the major peaks. As a result of this exercise I reached a new peak of fitness.

A letter arrived in the mail about six weeks after Pearman's arrival. It was from Johnny Walker. 'Would it be convenient for him, and Nan his wife, to spend a week with me?' I wrote back straight away. 'I would be delighted for them to visit and spend as long as they wished.' The following day I discussed the matter with Pearman. I wanted to have a week off so that I could show my friends over the district. Grudgingly he agreed, providing I was available to deal with any serious incidents that might arise! I sent to Soroti by the next bus, ordering a good supply of extra food, including such delicacies as kippers which I hadn't had since I left England. The day that John and Nan were due to arrive I awoke feeling dreadful. Surely not another dose of malaria! I had taken my chloroquine with religious regularity since the last bout. I crawled down to the office. 'Hangover I suppose', said Pearman. 'Best thing is to work it off', and work it off I did. Or rather I tried. But at the end of the day I felt worse if anything. John's car drew up outside my house. I went outside to greet them. My legs felt like lumps of jelly. My head was splitting and I was already running a temperature. Nan took over. 'Off to bed', she commanded. I gratefully obeyed. I had little option really. I must say I felt a right miserable bugger in the circumstances. Here were my friends, who I had not seen for over a year, come to visit me, and all I could do was to retire to bed and leave them to their own devices. 'Sorry about this', I said. 'I'll probably be O.K. in the morning and we'll be able to go off on safari.' It was not to be however. In the morning I was unable to get out of bed unaided. John helped me to get to the toilet, but as soon as he let go of me I collapsed on the floor. I was bright yellow from top to toe. My urine was orange with traces of blood in it. John helped me back to bed and sent for Gareth. Unfortunately, he was away on safari so Dr Lubega eventually arrived. I was sufficiently compos mentis to notice a look of some alarm on his face as he examined me. He went off to confer with John and Nan, and on his return, gave me a large injection of something. He then took a blood sample and instructed me to remain in bed. He visited again later in the day and administered a further injection. My recollection of what happened after that was a bit hazy. I know that I became delirious for a while and that Dr Lubega made several more visits. I had various officers arrive to view me and to make clucking noises. 'Yellow fever', I heard Dr Lubega saying. 'Sod this', I thought. 'I'm too young and too lovely to die.' I later heard that Dr Lubega had decided that he was not prepared to shoulder the responsibility for my treatment and he sent out a message to Gareth to return to Moroto. Gareth duly arrived a couple of days later. More injections followed, and I gradually returned to the land of the living. A couple of days later I heard a party going on in my lounge. John and Nan appeared to be entertaining half the Station. Drinking my booze. And not even enquiring if I felt like joining in! Well I jolly well did want to join in. I hadn't had a beer for over a week. I shouted till someone heard, and eventually I was brought a beer. The party then moved into my bedroom and I decided that I wasn't going to die after all. How had I managed to get Yellow Fever. It was anyone's guess. Certainly there was enough of it about. All the monkeys in Moroto were carrying it. The mosquitoes carried it from the monkeys to humans, but I should have been immune, having been inoculated against the disease before coming to Uganda. Maybe the serum was a bad batch. I did hear later from Gareth that all those who had received the same batch had been traced and given another dose to be on the safe side. Anyway clearly the disease had been fairly mild, otherwise I shouldn't have lived to tell the tale. Possibly the inocculation I had received had helped in some way though it hadn't been totally effective in preventing it. The only one who had not seen fit to visit me was Roy Pearman. He did call in once I was up and about, to find out when I proposed to return to work!

The frustration which I had begun to experience in having to work with Pearman was relieved by the return of Tom and Vi Hinett and their family. Having made the acquaintance of Pearman I found that they heartily endorsed my opinion of him. I had returned to duty after an absence of some three weeks and much against the advice of Gareth. Relations between Pearman and myself were somewhat strained. I had the distinct impression that he was going to ask headquarters to transfer me out of Karamoja as soon as he felt capable of coping with the district on his own, or rather, with the assistance of a different officer. In the circumstances I would have welcomed a transfer to get away from the idiot. Again my request for some local leave had been refused, even though I was feeling distinctly 'under the weather'. I was quite pleased when Sandy Field, who had returned from leave, came to the office one day and enquired if Pearman, as O.C. Police, would care to accompany him on safari to liaise with the D.C. and O.C. Police from the Sudan. The conference, if such it could be called, was to take place on the northern border of the Kidepo Valley. The stated object of this exercise was to discuss the incursions by the poachers from Sudan into Uganda. Looking back on it I feel it likely that the Sudanese D.C. was interested to find out whether the last lot of poachers died as a result of the unfortunate change of wind during the ring burning or whether they had been assisted to their happy hunting grounds by more direct methods. Sandy Field was dead keen on the meeting, as it would enable him to check up on his favourite area, with the added bonus of a possible further elephant or two. Pearman accepted the invitation with alacrity and it was agreed that they would start off two days hence, accompanied by Sandy Taylor, the Veterinary Officer. The transport was to be provided by the D.C., using his truck plus one of the lorries to carry the tents and equipment. It was not, however, made clear to Pearman that the transport would only be able to take them part of the way. The final 25 miles would have to be undertaken on foot, using porters to carry the equipment. One thing I was sure of was that Pearman was not going to forget this one in a hurry.

The final stage of the foot safari was later related to me by Sandy Taylor, who had a wicked sense of humour and revelled in the discomfort of others. He had the advantage of being fit and very used to long walks, as was Sandy Field. Pearman, I was told, started bleating as soon as everyone got out of the transport and started to sort out the head-loads for the porters. 'I wasn't told that there would be any walking involved', he whined. 'If I'd known, I would have sent Beaden.' However, he had little sympathy from anyone and was given the option of walking or being left behind. Eventually he joined the party and the walk began. Of course his shoes weren't suitable for this sort of treatment and he was soon reduced to hobbling. He dropped further and further behind but no one would wait for him. Eventually the group halted for lunch. Half-an-hour later Pearman finally caught up, just as they were moving off again. By now he was in dire straits. No one took any notice, but set off again. After about half-an-hour Sandy Field set off on a diversion, climbing a steep incline for a couple of miles to a high point some 400 feet above the surrounding countryside. At the top they all sat down and waited for Pearman. Twenty minutes later he limped up to them. Sitting down he asked Sandy Field, 'Why have we come up here?' 'Oh', said Sandy, 'I just wanted you to see the view from here. Terrific isn't it. Also there's a herd of elephant a few miles over there. I might try to get one of them on the way back.' Pearman literally wept. 'Do you mean to tell me you've brought me miles out of the way to admire the bloody view?', he whined. 'Well, you could have waited for us back there', said Sandy. 'Anyway, we're just going back now', and so saying everyone got to their feet and started off again. Eventually the Sudanese camp was sighted. The tents and other safari gear was sorted out while Pearman lay on the grass taking no part in the proceedings. The following day was spent chatting, sorting out the odd problems and generally having a pleasant time. Pearman took little interest. He was, no doubt, contemplating the following day when he would have to walk back to the transport. The blisters on his feet had burst and he had difficulty getting his shoes on. However, on the morrow he had no option but to start walking. In the event, Sandy Field didn't bother about going after another elephant. Pearman would probably have expired had he been forced to chase after elephants for an extra ten miles or so. Pity really. I felt some sympathy for him when this was related to me, but not much.

Chapter 16

It was now October in 1952. Rumours of trouble in Kenya had filtered through to us for some months and the atrocities perpetrated by a band of terrorists known as the Mau-mau had been related at sundowners by those 'in the know'. Casual listeners, like myself, found the details of the atrocities, alleged to have been committed by them, beyond belief. 'Some minor incidents', I thought, 'highly embellished and exaggerated in the telling.' Surely the disgusting ritual murders, coupled with cannibalism of parts of the bodies of the victims and the taking of oaths, couldn't be happening in peaceful East Africa.

Shortly however, we doubters were proved tragically wrong. Official action and reaction to events in Kenya was being kept very secret. I had finally got Pearman to agree to my taking some local leave and was keenly anticipating a couple of weeks down at Mombasa. It came as something of a shock when the message arrived. It was in code and I had the task of de-coding it. The police code was quite interesting and ingenious and at this distance from the events I don't think I shall be doing any harm in disclosing it. Basically it consisted of a secret nine-letter word, in which none of the letters were repeated. Take for instance, PERUVIANS as being a possible codeword. To de-code a message one wrote this word down, followed by each of the remaining letters in the alphabet, on two lines one above the other. Thus-

P E R U V I A N S B C D F
G H J K L M O Q R W X Y Z

By transposing these letters the message became clear. The shock was, however, in the content. I was ordered to be ready to leave on the following morning for Turkana, the adjoining district in the Northern Province of Kenya. A detachment of police, under the command of A.S.P. Wells, had already left the Police Service Unit at Bombo, near Kampala and, after a night stop at Soroti would be arriving in Moroto by 8 a.m the following morning. By the time I had finished de-coding the message Roy Pearman had gone home for his tea. I drove to his house. This was going to be interesting. He read through the message and then gave a great guffaw of laughter. He continued to roll about with mirth for several minutes at the thought of getting rid of me. I rather spoiled the joke for him by pointing out that the message made no mention of a replacement. He was going to have to run the district on his own, do all the safari work and crime investigations plus all disciplinary investigations and the administration of the prison. Now it was my turn to laugh. He rushed down to the office to send off a signal querying this aspect of the order. I was delighted to hear later that no replacement was contemplated for the foreseeable future.

In the meantime I had a great deal to occupy me. No indication had been given in the message, of the possible duration of my secondment to Kenya, nor of the reason for moving to an out-of-the-way place like Turkana. There was certainly no Mau-mau activity in that neck of the woods. Postings to other districts within Uganda could be expected, but one to a totally different territory were, as far as I knew, unheard of. The reasons for the move were clearly so secret that they could not even be entrusted to a coded message. However, I assumed that I should be returning within a week or two otherwise, I felt, mention of a replacement for me would have been made. I was by no means disheartened by the move. My life in the primitive conditions of Karamoja had become totally fulfilling. When I was out in the bush I felt no need to seek out the company of other Europeans. I had not, however, reached the condition of some of the old-timers who, if they found another European already in occupation at one of the camps, would hastily move on a few miles to preserve their privacy. I found, on reflection, that the independence built up by a life in the bush was completely suited to my temperament. With the exception of the absence of warlike tribes and major health hazards, the early explorers must have experienced very similar conditions during their great journeys. I envied them and welcomed the opportunity to emulate them even in a minor degree. Also I should be rid of Pearman for a while.

The message had indicated that no private transport would be taken, all personnel and equipment would be carried on police lorries. My car would be safe in its garage. I went to see Tom Hinett and explained the situation to him. Of course, he would be delighted to help in any way he could. He would make sure the battery didn't go flat and that the tyres were periodically checked, should I be away for more than a week or two. He promised to check the house from time to time. Obviously I should be taking Barney with me. Randy, however, was still too young to be taken on a trip of this sort. Tom promised to take her in and look after her during my absence. A friend indeed.

I then hastily assembled my usual safari outfit, plus the small amount of tinned food and booze I had in the house. I had no idea what the supply situation might be in Turkana, but it certainly wouldn't be any better that that in Moroto and could well be a great deal worse. Obtaining further supplies from Soroti at such short notice was out of the question, so I would just have to make the best of it. As an afterthought I collected one of the snake-bite outfits from the hospital. To my certain knowledge none of the other officers had made use of any of them since they had been supplied.

Kesi received the information of our impending departure stoically. Knowing his original feelings when I was posted to the wilds of Karamoja from the fleshpots of Kampala, I had fully anticipated industrial action on his part when faced with the prospect of an indefinite stay in even wilder parts. I gave him the option of returning to Kampala and looking for another job, or of accompanying me to Turkana and receiving an extra Shs 5/- per month. 'Am I not your son?', quoth he, in true biblical manner. 'Are you not my father?', he continued. 'How could I leave you in your time of need. Also, it is very hard to find another job.' Clearly, he knew he was on to a good thing in my employ, the biggest advantage clearly being the fact that there was no memsahib to chase him around and check up on his stealing and drunkenness. However, I decided to accept his early decision to stay on as a compliment.

In the circumstances I could hardly refuse his request for an advance of salary to purchase food at the local *duka*. Having secured this he busied himself in packing his few belongings and arranging to hand over to his best friend, the prostitute from Soroti, on consideration of payment of Shs. 20/-, who had been living with him for the past couple of months. These details having been taken care of he excused himself after my evening meal and made his way to the P.W.D. lines where he proceeded to get blind drunk on illegal *waragi*. I subsequently heard him at 3 a.m. the following morning, staggering back to his quarters and singing loudly in the hope that this would scare off any hyenas or leopards which might be on the prowl at this time of night.

In the few hours remaining to me in Karamoja I made it my business to find out what I could about Turkana. A visit to Sandy Field resulted in the production of an elderly tome. From this I found out that originally Turkana District had formed part of Rudolf Province. The entire province, now known as the Northern Frontier Province, had been part of Uganda. Count Teliki having discovered a vast lake in 1887 had named it after Crown Prince Rudolf of Prussia, and the entire province had subsequently taken the same name. In 1926, however, the province had been ceded to Kenya. The total area of Turkana District amounts to 45,000 square miles and the population around 90,000. To its west is Uganda and it is bounded on the north by the Sudan and on its north-east by Ethiopia. Its eastern boundary is Lake Rudolf, stretching north to south nearly 200 miles, its breadth varying between 40 and 50 miles. The entire Northern Frontier Province forms part of the Great Rift Valley, that great scar, running north to south across the face of the African Continent. On each side of the valley is a great escarpment, rising some 3,000 feet, in places practically sheer. This vast cliff forms the natural boundary between Karamoja and Turkana, but does little to hinder the almost continuous incursions by one tribe or the other into the opposing territory in search of livestock or victims for spear-blooding.

The non-arrival of morning tea at the accustomed hour led me to realise that Kesi was sleeping off the effects of his overnight binge. After dressing I made my way to his quarters and kicked the door open. The naked prostitute beamed at me from beside the still recumbent form of my cook. He stirred when I kicked him and eventually rose somewhat groggily to his feet. He accompanied me outside where I threw a bucket of water over him. Eventually he was sufficiently recovered to set about preparing my breakfast. Leaving him to collect up his final oddments, I walked the half-mile to the police station, Barney, full of good nature and anal wind walking alongside.

A check of the Occurrence Book showed that, with the exception of a small raid involving the death of one of the raiders and the theft of ten head of cattle, the district was quiet. This incident had taken place up in Dodoth in the north, the raiders being none other than Turkana. Roy Pearman would have to go out on that one. I smiled to myself at the thought of him walking the last 15 miles, sweating and cursing on his sore feet. 'Serve him right', I thought. Shortly afterwards Roy turned up and I had the pleasure of handing over to him all the uncompleted investigation files plus the contents of the cash box and the goat bag. I was ready to go.

Shortly before 9 o'clock three large troop-carrying vehicles arrived outside the police station. These were packed solid with nearly 70 constables and N.C.O's, together with their safari equipment and personal belongings. The passenger in the front of the first lorry was Lofty Wells himself, while the other two lorries had Sub-Inspector Balinda and Head Constable Buluma, respectively in the comfortable seats. Lofty Wells hopped down from his perch and greeted me. I had expected to meet a gigantic figure of at least six-and-a-half feet. In this I was disappointed. He was at least two inches shorter than myself. He later explained that he received his nick-name during the war when serving in a platoon consisting mainly of midgets. Talking to him I got the impression that he was a really genuine character. Good will exuded from every pore and he was, for all the world, like an overgrown schoolboy or a puppy, anxious for everyone to like him.

Over a cup of coffee in the office Lofty gave me a run-down on the situation leading to our imminent departure. Jomo Kenyatta and half-a-dozen known leaders of the Mau-mau had been arrested two or three hours earlier and, even as we sat there, were appearing before a Special Court in Nairobi. They were to be detained in custody and flown to a special detention centre which was being set up in Lokitaung in the northern part of Turkana. Later they were to be tried on charges of managing an illegal society, among other things.

At the same time, most of the Kenya police stationed in Turkana were being transferred to Nairobi and other areas where Mau-mau terrorism was becoming a serious problem. The Uganda police were now to take over most of the responsibility for security on the northern border with Sudan and Ethiopia. In addition a number were to be stationed at Lodwar, the Turkana District Administration Headquarters where a prison camp was to be constructed and where, in due course, all those found guilty of being members of a proscribed society or of any terrorist activity would be detained.

All thoughts of being back in Karamoja within a few weeks

were thus dismissed. This was going to be a long safari, with the prospect of danger and discomfort around every corner. 'How splendid', I thought. But what about the installments to be paid on my car loan. With no mileage allowance coming in, it wouldn't be too long before my bank account was once again depleted. 'Sufficient unto the day', I decided. In the time-honoured phrase of Mr Micawber, 'Something might turn up'. The next major problem was to find room on the already overcrowded lorries for my safari equipment, plus my cook and of course Barney. Finding a seat for myself presented no problem. I simply took over that occupied by Head Constable Buluma in the third lorry. He, in turn, took over that of Sub-Inspector Balinda who, although he was superior in rank, was much smaller and was able to perch somewhat uncomfortably on the gearbox cover between the Head Constable and the driver. This position had the additional hazard of being continually groped by the driver in his constant search for the right gear. However, Balinda made no complaint. Kesi squeezed himself and his belongings, together with my, not inconsiderable, safari equipment, into the lorry in which I was travelling, necessitating the redistribution of several constables to the other vehicles. Finally Barney leaped over the tailboard and, miraculously, found a large unoccupied area which, until a few moments before had been held by several policemen. Into this he sank with a grateful grin. Thus we found ourselves, within a short space of time, ready for the road.

We set off in the direction of Katikekele, to the accompaniment of the blasting of horns and the ululations of admiring groups of police wives standing nearby. It rapidly became clear that travelling in close convoy was out of the question. I was travelling in the leading lorry, owing my favoured position to my reputed local knowledge — even though I had never been into Turkana. Those unfortunates travelling behind had to suffer the disadvantages of the dust storm stirred up by the leading vehicle. Consequently, a good mile had to be left between each vehicle for any degree of comfort. Even so, the open backs of the lorries caused the dust to be sucked into the back of each vehicle. On reaching the police post at Katikekele I decided to stop for a five-minute break. On going to the back of the lorry I was confronted by an extraordinary sight. The entire interior of the lorry was covered with a good quarter-of-an-inch of red dust. Each individual had tied a handkerchief of similar piece of cloth over the lower part of his face, so that they looked for all the world like a gang of Mexican bandits. Faces, hands, clothing, boots and Barney were a uniform red brown colour, with red-rimmed eyes peering out from their encrusted sockets. Oddly, no one complained. Not to me anyway. Presumably all were resigned to the discomfort which had to be endured for many hours. However, in an attempt to alleviate the discomfort in some degree, I arranged to have the canvas at the front of the truck, rolled up thus producing a strong through draught. This seemed to do the trick though conditions were still far from ideal.

A few miles further on we reached the top of the escarpment and the view over the desert far below, while hardly breathtaking, held an air of primitive grandeur. Volcanic outcrops shimmered in the heat with the occasional thorn bush being the only vegetation able to survive. The track down which we had to traverse had been built some years earlier by an Italian engineer, using local labour. Far below and stretching into the distance, the course of the Turkwell River, dry for most of the year, could be picked out by the belt of trees which lined its banks, driving their roots far down in the search for life-giving fluid. A passing glance had to suffice however, as the track, just wide enough for the lorry wheels, wound down and round in a series of hairpin bends, for mile after mile, with frequent sheer drops to one side or the other. A termite-ridden board at the top of the escarpment announced in red wording, 'Private Burial Ground Ahead For Careless Drivers.' The burned-out remains of vehicles far below, reinforced the warning. I don't think they had been careless though. Just unlucky in most cases, when a boulder had slipped from under them at a crucial moment, sending both vehicle and occupants to an untimely end. From my seat in the cab of the lorry I had a disconcerting view, every so often, of the drop, hundreds of feet, to the rocks below. Not the most enjoyable ride I have ever taken, but at least exciting enough to take one's mind off the ever-increasing heat. On reaching the bottom of the escarpment we paused for a break, while looking back, we could see the other two vehicles, threading their way down the track, the size of dinky toys, throwing out the occasional puff of dust and, from time to time, dislodging a rock which would bound away into the depths, taking with it an ever increasing quantity of pebbles and scree.

Having ensured that our entire party had successfully negotiated the escarpment, we set off again along the desert track. That maintenance on this stretch was at a minimum was amply demonstrated by the pot-holes, ruts and protruding rocks. At times the track would cross dry watercourses, the lorries bouncing from boulder to boulder, while the engines roared their disapproval at the harsh treatment being meted out. I found myself feeling relieved that I had been unable to bring my car.

We were ten miles from the foot of the escarpment before we came across any sign of human habitation. A crude shelter constructed of branches of thorn tree. Remnants of other similar branches forming a partial fence round the area, indicated that at some time in the past months, probably during the short rainy season, some nomadic herdsman had kept his goats here. These, together with donkeys and camels, were the only domestic animals able to survive the harsh conditions hereabouts. A few miles further on we saw our first camels. A group of four. Thin scrawny creatures they were too. Much smaller in stature than those to be seen in Egypt.

The policemen miserably bumping about in the back of the lorry commenced banging the side of the lorry on catching sight of these creatures. Thinking that some dire emergency had arisen, I ordered the driver to stop. Immediately a deputation leaped from the back of the lorry and requested me to shoot some *nyama* (animals) for food. None of them had ever seen a camel before. I had to explain that, although these appeared to be wandering wild, they all, in fact, had owners. Barney, however, didn't seem to understand this fine legal point. Without waiting orders, and no doubt egged on by the constables, he leaped over the tailboard and made for the startled beasts standing about 100 yards away. They were off immediately at a great rate of knots. Barney, however, having endured hours of inactivity, needed some exercise. Fortunately, the camels set off more or less in the direction we were heading so the lorry set off in pursuit. After half-a-mile in the blistering heat, Barney had had enough. The camels were out of sight so he sat down and waited for us to arrive. Panting he scrambled back over the tailboard and resumed his seat.

At about 1 p.m. we stopped for a meal. The heat by now resembled the inside of an oven, and the sparse shelter afforded by some palm trees alongside a dry watercourse brought little relief. The other two vehicles now caught up with us and everyone alighted and set about cooking. Kesi produced some excellent tinned corned beef, the jelly content of which had turned to gravy, together with a tin of cold, or rather, unheated baked beans. Lofty shared this Spartan fare with me, with every appearance of enjoying it. 'Well', I thought, 'at least he's not a finicky eater.' We topped of the meal with a bottle of beer, practically ice-cold, it having been hanging on the side of the lorry in my *chagul* all morning. Dust devils danced all around us during our short break and several swept straight through the small area in which we congregated, much to the annoyance of all. Half-an-hour later we were on our way again on the last lap to Lodwar.

Homosexuals are, generally speaking, an anathema to policemen. Although I had no idea at our first meeting, of his various deviations, the District Commissioner of Turkana proved no exception. Forming a friendly relationship with him was not helped by Barney of course. My lorry arrived at Lodwar at about 4 p.m. after a thoroughly filthy journey. Sweaty, covered with dust, as indeed were our entire party, and as dry as a nun's crutch, we drew up outside the D.C's office, a large, single-storey building with a deep verandah running the entire way round it. The corrugated iron roof had been heavily thatched with palm leaf, or *makuti* as it was locally known, in an effort to insulate the inside of the building from the oven-like exterior. Visibility on our arrival was about 25 yards, since a sandstorm was blowing. I was to find that these were a feature of the place, and a day without one was rare indeed. After my journey my temper was as gritty as the inside of my mouth. One might have thought it polite for the D.C. or at least one of his two Assistants, to have ventured from the building to greet us. After all we had turned up to support them in their hour of need. Not so. The doors and windows remained firmly shuttered. I climbed wearily from the cab, flexing my aching limbs to ease away the stiffness caused by hours of bumping and jolting. Barney leaped from the back of the lorry and lifted his leg against a border of whitewashed stones, marking a path which appeared identical to the surrounding sand. He then squatted and deposited and enormous mound of excreta which he had clearly been saving up for hours. No respecter of men was Barney, nor of footpaths which appeared to have no function other that leading from the D.C's office to the flagpole 25-yards away where the Union Jack looking somewhat the worse for wear, waged a somewhat unequal battle against the unfriendly elements.

I walked stiffly up the steps to a door marked 'District Commissioner'. Barney, his tail stiff as a ramrod, following behind. A smart rap on the door, followed by a pause. I waited and then rapped again. 'Come', commanded an indifferent voice from within. I opened the door and was immediately confronted by a snarling monster. Whitehouse, the D.C., had quite the ugliest dog I have ever seen. It appeared to be a cross between a dalmatian and a bull mastiff, with a few other breeds thrown in for good measure. Its bared fangs left me in no doubt about what might happen should I happen to venture a step inside the office. This was too much for Barney. He had no intention of letting such an obvious threat to his master go unpunished. He went through the door like a thunderbolt and in an instant had the monster by its snout. This old trick of Barney's worked as well this time as I had seen it on previous occasions. His adversary was completely helpless, and the more it struggled, the more its nose was torn. Barney having secured his grip then engaged in a rapid head-shaking exercise. Blood sprayed liberally all over the office, including the documents on Whitehouse's desk. All this before Whitehouse or I could utter a word of greeting. Having learned from bitter experience the wisdom of standing back and letting nature take its course during such dog fights I was quite happy to take as little action as possible. Not so Whitehouse. With a bellow which resembled the braying of a donkey he leaped to his feet and, grabbing a stick, began belabouring the combatants. After receiving a few blows Barney decided to let go of the monster and deal with this new adversary. Whitehouse jumped on to his desk. Barney then chased his now screaming victim out of the door and renewed the combat outside by seizing its front leg and crushing the bone. This was ever Barney's second line of attack. Very effective too. The monster fell to the ground on top of the freshly deposited excreta on the path and, in the course of the next few seconds was liberally covered in it. Seeing his now totally demoralised creature begging for mercy at the hands of the much smaller Barney, Whitehouse leaped off his desk and rushed after the combatants wielding his stick. Sensing that the battle was now well and truly won, Barney released his foe and to cheers from the assembled policemen wandered off to the flagpole to finish his pee. Incensed by this, Whitehouse ran after him wielding his cudgel. Unfortunately for him, his terrified hound, in running back to the safety of the office, tripped him up and the two of them fell onto the remains of the turd. Whitehouse got more than his fair share of this, both from the path and from his dog. Meantime Barney hopped agilely back onto the lorry and smiled his biggest smile at the approving *askaris*. '*Mbwa ngumu sana*', (the dog is very strong), they chorused. 'Good afternoon', said I, helping Whitehouse to his feet and scraping off some of the turd with a handy whitewashed stone. 'My name's Beaden. I've come to give you a hand! '

We were interrupted in what might have been an interesting conversation by the arrival of the second lorry. The one containing Lofty Wells. The condition of the occupants was, if anything, worse than our own, they having had the benefit of our man-made dust storm for many miles before running into the natural one around Lodwar. A broken leaf spring in the suspension about 20 miles back, hadn't helped in alleviating the bumps either. Lofty climbed stiffly down from the cab. The policemen now disembarked from both lorries and proceeded to relieve themselves against the walls of the verandah. This had an electrifying effect of Whitehouse, who ran among them bleating like a goat. 'Hello', said Lofty, extending the hand of friendship. 'My name's Wells, but you can call me Lofty. Dreadful weather for the time of year. You seem to have got up against something', he added, wrinkling his nose as he observed the remains of Barney's turd adhering to Whitehouse's shirt.

An hour after our arrival in Lodwar, the dust storm abated and I was able to get a clear look at the township. Apart from the *boma*, which stood on a ridge, about 100 feet above the surrounding area, there were about half-a-dozen other buildings each spaced about 200 yards from its nearest neighbour. These were the residences of Whitehouse and his two A.D.C's or District Officers as they were locally known, the Locust Control Officer and a guest house, for the use of officers on safari, an infrequent and, in Whitehouse's opinion, unwelcome intrusion on his privacy. A new house, nearing completion, stood further away from this group and was, I later found, destined to become the residence of a prison officer. Clearly the present state of emergency, with its need to accommodate a great many detainees, had been anticipated some time previously to enable the building to be so far advanced. A further building turned out on inspection to be a small swimming pool, roofed over with *makuti* to stop the water from getting too hot. Half-a-mile away stood a group of corrugated iron huts, the residences of the local tradespeople — a few very low-caste Asians and Somalis with their drab wives screeching at their semi-naked offspring like a group of excited monkeys. These poor creatures eked out a precarious existence selling sugar, *posho*, tobacco, cloth, iron wire and beads to the local tribesmen who, in their proud nakedness looked very much the superior beings.

To the west of the township 1,000 yards distant, rose several volcanic outcrops, each some 300 feet in height, their surfaces leached by the desert winds of thousands of years, exposing a rubble of broken boulders covering every inch. To the east, a belt of palm and other trees marked the dried-up course of the Turkwell River, its presence offering the only relief in an otherwise totally inhospitable landscape. This, then, was the place which had been chosen to house what eventually amounted to several thousand Mau-mau prisoners. I envied them not. Neither did I envy the contingent of 20 of my policemen who, under the command of Sub-Inspector Balinda, were to be responsible for the safe custody of the detainees.

The two district officers were George Grimmett and David Sharp. They were pleasant enough individuals, of much the same age as myself, but were completely under the thumb of the D.C. Leslie Edward Whitehouse. He was about 50 years of age, three or four inches shorter than myself, of spare build, angular features and with a shock of grey and white hair. I discovered later that he had come to Kenya in 1920 to join his elder brother who had embarked on growing flax. After a short spell in this field he had been offered the post of schoolmaster at Narok in the Maasai area of Kenya. A few years later he became headmaster and later still joined the Administration. He was, therefore, classed as having been locally recruited, which had some considerable disadvantages. He had little conversational subject matter outside his own little world. He was currently embarking on his fifth three-year tour in Turkana. Having realised that his many peculiarities prevented any possibility of further promotion, he had created for himself a little kingdom in the desert region and had no intention of being dislodged until forced to retire, for which exigency he had had a house built at Ferguson's Gulf on the south shore of Lake Rudolf where he proposed to spend the remainder of his existence.

Lofty Wells and I were accommodated for the night at the Guest House. This proved to be a pleasantly airy building with high arched doorways between the rooms, but no doors to restrict the through-draught. No beds or bedding were provided but, as we had full safari equipment with us, no difficulties were presented. A small paraffin refrigerator stood in the kitchen and into this we placed half-a-dozen bottles of beer ready for use later on. Firewood and a stove had been thoughtfully provided, as was a good supply of water, both in the drinking tank and the boiler.

Leaving Kesi to get on with organising the food, bath and bed, Lofty and I made our way across to the swimming pool, to find it already occupied by David Sharp. The formality of swimming trunks were not needed, since no white women were permitted in Turkana, and a more delightful swim I had never had. The water, while tepid, was nonetheless mightily refreshing after our day's travel. Whitehouse did not put in an appearance, either at the swimming pool, or later in the evening. Neither did his dog. I gathered from David that both were at home licking their wounds.

Lofty and I enjoyed an uninterrupted night's sleep and awoke to a welcome cup of tea the following morning. By half-past-nine we were once again on our way, minus Sub-Inspector Balinda and his contingent of 20 constables and N.C.Os. The journey to Lokitaung where we were to be based was around 80 miles, but progress was slow and it was mid-day by the time we drew up in front of the police station. We were greeted by the dapper figure of Harry Jones, the Senior Assistant Superintendent in charge of the district. After exchanging introductions he accompanied us to the building which was to house us, on and off for what would finally extend to eight months. This turned out to be a large, ugly structure built on two levels, constructed from concrete blocks, with a corrugated iron roof. The reason for its two levels became clear when one went to its far end. It was on the edge of a great gorge which dropped away in a series of dry waterfalls down to the main river bed half a mile further down-stream. The view from the back window during the rains, when the waterfalls were carrying the flood water at full spate, must have been most impressive. It transpired that this had been the Officers' Mess during the war when the Kings African Rifles had been stationed here. God knows what they found to do, but I suppose that the presence of the Italians in Ethiopia to the north may have been a contributory factor. A large wooden table occupied part of the top level and Lofty and I decided that this would be best for a dining area. The lower level approached by two steps would make an ideal sleeping area. The kitchen was a separate building at the side, which included an annex where Kesi would have to sleep. Our bedding and the rest of our safari equipment was unloaded and brought into our new quarters. We should be roughing it here but it was better than sleeping in tents.

At his invitation we accompanied Harry to his quarters for lunch. This turned out to be a pleasant modern bungalow similarly sited on the edge of the gorge, but further down-stream. About 80 yards upstream from the bungalow, at the top of one of the waterfalls, was a large pool of water, which, because it was fed by an underground stream, was permanent, and served as a swimming pool for the local children. It also acted as a breeding ground for mosquitoes which, we later found, were plentiful.

Over a cold beer and a lunch of cold meats and salad, Harry told us about the policing problems of the district. Apart from the headquarters at Lokitaung, the major part of policing consisted of manning a series of forts, scattered at intervals around the Ethiopian border and up into the Sudan, the object of these was, in similar fashion to Karamoja, to prevent cross-border raiding by the opposing tribesmen. The Sudanese forts were manned by police from Kenya as a matter of convenience since road communication to this area from Lokitaung, while primitive in the extreme, was a shade better than that from the Sudan itself, where it was non-existent. Thus, this area was considered *de-facto* Sudan but *de-jure* Kenya. The major problems of the entire border area arose during the dry season, which was most of the time, when large-scale incursions would be made by both sides into each others tribal areas for water, which was available by digging deep into the sand under the dry river beds. At such times vast flocks of goats, donkeys, camels and a few cattle, would cross the borders, together with their owners and the complete tribal unit of possibly 100 people. The existence of the groups were made doubly precarious, facing as they did, violent action from the tribesmen into whose grazing grounds they had trespassed, and punitive action from the police, who would swoop and seize the entire herds driving them off to one of the forts, where they would be held until the arrival of one of the district officers who would authorise the seizure of 20 per cent of the animals as a punishment for the trespass. Regardless of these risks the trespass had occurred for many years and, it seemed likely, would continue to do so. The work of the police therefore fell into two main areas: first to catch the trespassers and second to apprehend the tribesmen from both sides who were responsible for the killing which inevitably resulted from the armed clashes. Unlike the similar raids in Karamoja, however, where firearms were few and far between, these clashes were more bloody owing to the possession on both sides of the borders of numerous rifles which had been left behind by the Italians when they had been driven out of Ethiopia during the war. This all sounded pretty exciting stuff to me, at least it would be more so than guarding a bunch of Mau-mau detainees.

During the afternoon Lofty and I inspected the township. A certain number of the Kenya police had remained behind in Lokitaung, though the majority had been transferred down country to areas vulnerable to Mau-mau activity. The police barracks consisted of a number of permanent buildings, a few of which were unoccupied, though the wives and children of the departed constables and N.C.Os still occupied most of them. It occurred to me that the newly-arrived Uganda police would soon be consoling these grass widows. The lucky few of the new arrivals were allocated the empty permanent buildings, the remainder were busy erecting their tents. Most of these would be moving out the following day anyway to reinforce the depleted staff at the forts. An innovation at the barracks was the provision of a classroom, where the children of the police staff were educated by a corporal. He proved to be a most intelligent and well-educated individual. I wondered why he was not at least of Sub-Inspector rank. However he didn't seem to be particularly worried about this. In addition to the Kenya Police there was a large body of locally-enlisted tribal police also housed in the barracks. These were, of course, used in the stock seizures as well as in tracking, investigation and translation. They struck me as being a much smarter body of men that their equivalents in Karamoja. They all wore navy blue kilts and their hair was dressed in a particular fashion incorporating pompoms of ostrich feathers, chicken feathers and coloured clay. The rank of the N.C.Os was indicated by an arm band on the right arm. Most of them wore a lip ornament of some sort and all were physically well built.

In addition to the police station the district officer had his office nearby. This was Eric Fox to whom I was introduced later in the day. He turned out to be a pleasant, dark-haired individual about the same age as myself. Much better value than Whitehouse, I thought. He and Harry Jones were the only Europeans on the station. There was a small hospital, staffed by an Asian doctor and a number of African orderlies. The doctor's house was several hundred yards from the office complex and nearby were houses accommodating a number of Goans, the office staff from the police station and *boma*. In the same area was a small cottage occupied by one Markan Singh, a well-known communist agitator who had been rusticated to Lokitaung by the Kenya Government as a result of his political activities. He turned out to be a most unpleasant individual. Fortunately, my contact with him throughout my stay was of a limited nature and confined mainly to occasionally censoring his mail when the D.O. was not present to carry out this task.

Near the police station and *boma* a couple of aluminium rondavels had been erected. This area had been enclosed by a double fence of barbed wire. The rondavels housed Jomo Kenyatta and three of his senior henchmen who had also been charged with 'Managing an Illegal Society'. This surly gang had only arrived the previous day and were still sorting out their pecking order. They were not provided with any comforts. Food and water was given to them each day, together with firewood. The food preparation and cooking had to be decided between themselves, as was the daily emptying of the latrine buckets, the laundry and so on. The aluminium rondavels turned into mini-ovens in the heat of the day, so a quantity of *makuti* had been thoughtfully provided. The thatching was however, up to them. I was interested to notice, the following day, Jomo Kenyatta himself climbing on the roof of one of the rondavels, securing the *makuti* in place. He also had to take his turn at emptying the latrine buckets and sweeping up the compound.

Half-a-mile to the south of this government area was a small native village consisting of three or four mean little *dukas* which stocked the usual *posho*, tobacco etc., and a number of mud huts thatched with grass or *makuti*. The tribesmen, it seemed, had little use for coins or notes, preferring to trade in tobacco or cowry shells, which had to be brought up from the coast.

Lokitaung itself was a barren outpost. Very little vegetation grew on the bare rock surface. The few hardy shrubs which were able to survive these conditions were being made the target of numbers of locusts. These were not of the swarm proportions which one hears about though, I was told, these appeared from time to time. They were, more or less, permanent residents.

Returning to our quarters, Lofty and I were surprised to find a well-built Turkana tribesman hobbling about outside. He was busy sweeping up the compound outside our house. He was somewhat remarkable in that he only had one leg, the right one being amputated above the knee and replaced with a wooden stump. He was a cheerful individual and, it turned out, filled the roll of caretaker. His duties were confined to bringing firewood and sweeping and generally tidying the place up. Together with his wife and two young children, he occupied a nearby hut built of concrete blocks and corrugated iron. Kesi seemed pleased to have him to help out around the place and very rapidly found plenty of other duties for him to fulfill.

On investigating the gorge below our house I discovered a second deep rock pool quite close, and about 200 yards upstream from the one we had previously seen. This one I found was reserved for the use of the European officers. The one near Harry Jones's house being very fully used by the local children. I was rather glad about this having seen them urinating in the water as well as swimming in it.

Inevitably, Kesi raised the subject of pay. Not only was he having to work in somewhat harsh conditions, he was also having to cook and look after two individuals instead of one, Lofty having had to leave his own staff behind in Bombo to look after his wife. I felt that he had a point here and raised the matter with Lofty who was only too pleased when I suggested that he chip in an extra Shs 30/- each month. Kesi in turn was delighted with this arrangement which, to him, represented wealth beyond his wildest dreams and would enable him to get drunk at even more frequent intervals.

Lofty and I seemed to hit it off well enough, which was just as well, since we should be in fairly close contact most of the time. It would be unfortunate if we found that we disliked one another intensely after a few days. The only thing that got up my nose about him, was a tendency to burst forth into the operas of Gilbert and Sullivan. Not that he didn't have a reasonable baritone voice. In fact he had been a keen member of the Kampala Operatic Society. It was just that I couldn't stand Gilbert and Sullivan at any price. After a week or two I found that a good way to shut him up was to play my Desert Island Discs whenever I couldn't stand G and S any longer. I suppose he must have found some of my idiosyncrasies equally annoying, though he never mentioned any.

The day after our arrival our transport departed back to Kampala. Shortly afterwards a large truck belonging to the Kenya Police at Lokitaung picked up the majority of our remaining Uganda reinforcements and set off to distribute them round the border forts. There were seven of these forts at intervals around the border. Namaraputh, right on the shores of Lake Rudolf, was the nearest, being about 40 miles from Lokitaung. This was followed at intervals by Liwan, Lokomorinyang and Kokoro, all of which were within Kenya, and then Kamathier, Kibish and Mogilla which were in fact in the Sudan.

Having made myself as comfortable as possible in the house, I settled down to write my usual full account of my activities to Joan and my parents. I was becoming a bit worried lately about the letters I was receiving from Joan. When I had first come to Uganda she had written at least four times a week. Now this was reduced to once a week if I was lucky. I had mentioned this to my mother on one occasion but was informed that she was sure that Joan was just as fond of me as ever. I felt, however, that there was a subtle change in the tone of her letters. Nothing I could put my finger on. Anyway, there was little I could do about it now. In any case, it would only be a few months now before Joan's divorce proceedings would be heard, after which she would be joining me in Uganda. I wondered if Bob Clarke at Lotome Mission would marry us. I rather doubted it though. Since Joan would be a divorcee the ceremony would probably have to be a civil one rather than in church. Anyway, with the influx of white women into Karamoja, there seemed to be no reason why I should need to be transferred to another district. Possibly by the time I returned to Moroto, Pearman would have been sent elsewhere. He had certainly not endeared himself to any of the other officers on the station, a situation which would no doubt be mentioned by the D.C. to the Provincial Commissioner. Quite a store was set on the manner in which any departmental officer fitted into the hierarchy of a small unit. The end of the month arrived a few days after we had settled in to Lokitaung. Lofty had already been called out to Liwan where a minor incursion had taken place. He had returned a couple of days later, the trespassers having removed themselves from their illegal occupation of one of the water holes before he arrived. It was decided that I should have the next outing, which turned out to be the monthly pay safari. By mutual agreement we had decided that both of us would keep on the move during our sojourn in Turkana. This way we should become entitled to a night allowance for every night we were away from Uganda. The regulations only permitted night allowances for five days in one location. By moving around at least once during this period we could circumvent this ruling quite legally, thereby at least compensating to some degree for our loss of mileage allowance on safari, which Lofty as well as I, depended for payment of our car loans.

Kesi would be left behind in Lokitaung during our absences. This was only fair, since he would have to be available to ensure the comfort of whoever was not out roughing it. Barney would, of course, accompany me on all safaris.

On the morning of the pay safari one of the police lorries arrived to pick up my safari equipment, after which we went to the police station for the cash box and to pick up our firearms. I had decided to take a .303 rifle with me on this occasion since, should an incursion be reported during our safari, shooting might become necessary. There would be little point in chasing a gang of Merille raiders armed with heavy rifles, if I only had a .22 to reply.

In the event, however, the trip was without incident. The drive through the gorge must not however pass without comment. This was a dry river bed. In times of rain the torrent of water coursing down here might be 20-feet deep in places. Great boulders were tumbled in every direction. Up-rooted trees lay at the sides forming an impenetrable barrier in many places. After each rainy season gangs of labourers from Lokitaung spent weeks carrying out the essential repairs. Even so, the drive was punishing in the extreme. The lorry bouncing from rock to rock. It was an unusual trip which did not result in some damage to the wheels or suspension of the vehicle involved. Our Asian mechanic, Ajiit Singh, was kept busy the entire time trying to keep the fleet of vehicles, to some degree, roadworthy. The road through the gorge was of some 30 miles. At the end of it every limb ached from the pounding it had received. Eventually we broke out of the gorge and I could see Lake Rudolf sparkling in the sunlight about six or seven miles ahead. I had been told that the lake was gradually shrinking. Many years earlier there had been an outlet which had connected up with other lakes, eventually finding its way to the Indian Ocean. Now, however, even though there was a permanent inflow of water from the River Omo running into the north of the lake from the Ethiopian Highlands, plus the seasonal rain from the Lokitaung River and the Turkwell, all of this additional water was counterbalanced and more by the continual evaporation from the surface. Once out of the gorge the surface became quite reasonable, the hard flat surface having once been the lake bed. It was therefore not long before we came in sight of the fort at Namaraputh.

About a mile before the fort we came to a small village of grass huts sited on the lake edge. This was the encampment of Maskini fishermen. The Maskini were a sub-tribe of the Turkana, who made their living from a primitive form of fishing. They had no canoes or boats of any sort. To catch fish they relied on a type of basket, woven from reeds. These were cone-shaped, about three-feet wide and having a hole in the top. Fishing involved a party of 20 or 30 tribesmen or women wading into the water to a depth of about two feet, then forming a semi-circle and making their way back towards the shore, plunging the baskets through the water in front of them. When the basket landed over the top of a fish it would thrash around inside until an arm, thrust through the hole in the top, extracted it and threaded with a cord through its gills which was strung around the shoulders. Mostly, the fish caught by this method would be of a few ounces in weight. Occasionally, however, a real whopper of a Nile Perch would be captured. There was reputed to be more fish per square mile in the brackish waters of Lake Rudolf that anywhere else in the world, with Nile Perch going up to 600 pounds in weight. As a direct consequence there was also the greatest concentration of crocodiles. However, it seemed that they never touched the fishermen. Probably they were too full up with fish!

My arrival at the fort with the monthly pay was greeted with enthusiasm by the Kenya police who were well-used to the miserable existence they had to tolerate. The recently-arrived Uganda police were full of complaints. The conditions they were expected to live under were too dreadful for words, I was informed. Food was unobtainable, the local Maskini fishermen unfriendly and the mosquitoes 'big enough to carry off a camel' were so numerous that it was impossible to breathe without inhaling them. I could see not a single mosquito on my arrival so I rather doubted the whole story. However, I listened sympathetically to their complaints and promised to spend a few days with them later on to ascertain the truth of the matter. Meantime, I commenced a rather protracted pay parade, made even more complicated than usual by having a second set of pay sheets for the two groups of policemen. Eventually this was done and I then had to dole out the rations of *posho*, sugar, salt and tobacco. This last was apparently the most important since none of the local tribesmen would accept cash in any form, in exchange for fish or any of their meager produce. I promised that I would endeavour to shoot some meat for them, to be delivered on my return journey.

At the conclusion of the pay parade I inspected the police lines. I was pleasantly surprised at the standard I found. The accommodation was in white-painted, conventionally round huts with grass thatched roofs. Unlike the mud and wattle construction used in similar police accommodation in Uganda, however, the walls of these were constructed of rock and cement on proper concrete foundations, and with the outside plastered with cement. This had the advantage of making them more or less proof against the ravages of the termites. I was later to find a similar type of construction used on all the forts throughout the district. There were no wives or children at the fort but, by and large, the place was clean and tidy and the men well disciplined. I was shown a rather larger hut of similar construction which, I was informed, was used by officers when they stayed at the fort. The entire fort was surrounded by a double-fence of barbed wire and in one area was a further enclosed compound which, it was explained, was for holding any seized livestock, pending its transfer to Lokitaung. There was also a watch-tower, about 30-feet tall, constructed of timber and having, at the top, a box-like structure about six-feet square, with grass sides and roof. This was manned twenty-four hours a day to watch out for raiding parties of Merille tribesmen who would come across from Ethiopia. Occasionally, an alarm would be raised, shots would be exchanged, and a party of police would sally forth to do battle with the intruders. Casualties were few in these encounters, but a couple of the raiders had been shot and killed during the past month.

About 100 yards from the fort was a grass structure that turned out to be the officers' latrine. I decided to visit this before I continued with the pay safari. I wandered across carrying my roll of toilet paper. The latrine was of the conventional 'long drop' type, with a hole over which one had to crouch. A bit undignified but at least it was private. The 'long drop' was screened from view by a woven-grass wall about ten-feet square. While I was busy communing with nature I heard a rustling in the grass behind me. Glancing round I saw a lizard working its way through the grass. A sudden flash, and the lizard was firmly in the jaws of a brown and yellow snake. I recognised it as being of a deadly poisonous specie. Well there wasn't a lot I could do about it. I was far too busy. The snake was about four feet from me but was evidently far more interested in the lizard it was engaged in swallowing than in me, so I just carried on. I was in two minds after this whether to go back with a stick and dispatch the snake or whether not to bother. In the end I decided on the latter course. After all it had not attacked me. I had no means with me of preserving the corpse to send to Charles Pitman. Also, if I killed this one, I had no doubt that another would take its place. In this environment with its proximity to the lake, the place was undoubtedly alive with the creatures. One thing I was relieved about though was the fact that the latrine was un-roofed. At least I shouldn't have snakes dropping on my head.

The pay safari continued during the afternoon to the next fort at Liwan. The Uganda policemen here were not so vociferous in their complaints as those at Namaraputh had been, but again there was a plea for meat to be provided. Eventually, towards the end of the afternoon, I came within sight of Lokomorinyang Fort which was strategically-sited on the top of a hill about 300 feet above the surrounding countryside. Here I intended spending the night. The hill was one of a number in the area and about a quarter-of-a-mile from its base were a series of pools of crystal clear water which were fed from an underground source which no doubt originated from the nearby rising ground. Around this permanent water was a delightful oasis of trees and long grass. Grazing nearby were herds of topi, kongoni and gazelle. I wondered if the staff at this fort would have similar longings for meat as had been expressed elsewhere. If so the answer was right on the doorstep. Sure enough, such a request was made as soon as I arrived. It seemed that officers on safari usually turned up with some meat of one sort or another. There was general disappointment that I had not already got some with me. I promised to see what I could do at the conclusion of the pay parade. Meanwhile, there were plenty of volunteers to unload my safari gear and prepare my bed in the officers' quarters, which were similar to those at Namaraputh.

At the conclusion of the parade, I judged that there was just time to walk down to the oasis at the bottom of the hill to see what was available. I deemed it unwise to take Barney with me as he would probably spook the herds. He looked at me a bit miffed when I shut him up in my quarters. Taking the .303 rifle, which I had made my property after zeroing it on the range, I made my way carefully down the track eagerly watched by the policemen at the fort. With this audience, I had better make this a good one. When I was about 400 yards from the nearest herd of kongoni they started to become rather agitated. Some of them started to move off. It looked as though this was going to have to be a long-range shot. I didn't like the idea of this too well. In the first place there was a strong possibility that the animal would only be wounded which would entail an undignified chase of maybe a mile. With dusk coming on, I might even lose the wounded animal altogether which was against my principles. At the same time, if I returned empty-handed having not even tried a shot my reputation would suffer badly. I adjusted the sights to 400 yards, adopted the prone position and, cushioning my forearm on a rock, took careful aim. A young bull kongoni became my chosen target. Not wanting to chance a wounding shot I aimed at the neck. If I missed this comparatively small target no harm would be done. A hit of any sort however, would bring it down. After taking a deep breath I fired. The kongoni dropped as if pole-axed, A cheer went up from the fort and the truck drove out of the compound and reached the animal at the same time as myself. Sure enough the bullet had severed the spine four inches back from the head. I breathed a sigh of relief, and made my way back to the fort. By the time I reached it the butchering was well under way. There was enough meat here for each man to have several pounds. This should put a stop to the complaints here at any rate. It occurred to me then that I was going to have little alternative to supplying meat wherever I went. I didn't mind this particularly. At least there appeared to be a plentiful supply of animals to meet any requirement.

The following morning, bright and early I was on my way to the remaining forts. These were at Kokoro, Kamathier, Kibish and finally Mogilla. The last three were in the Sudan. Anticipating the requirements of the policemen at these outposts I shot three buck during the day, distributing the meat on my rounds. Some did better than others but at least everyone got some meat. The terrain over which we travelled varied between unbroken desert and lush pastureland at the lower slopes of the hills we gradually encountered. After spending the night at Mogilla we started on the return journey. On this we made good progress and I was able to drop off a carcass at each of the forts which had not been provided on the outward journey. Finally, I dropped a Thompson's Gazelle just before entering the gorge on the final phase of the journey. This was distributed around on my arrival, some going to the driver and other police staff on the lorry, the remainder being distributed to Harry Jones and Eric Fox and our own kitchen.

CHAPTER 17

During the walks I had taken in the vicinity of our house I had been struck by the number of cast snake skins that I had seen lying around. It was impossible for me to identify the type of snakes from which they came, but they seemed to be of a fair size, four- to five-feet in average. It being an area of broken rock, the snakes had plenty of hiding places to stay during the heat of the day. I wondered what they found to feed on. The second part of this problem was made clear soon afterwards. I had noticed that from time to time the locusts, which were so plentiful on the vegetation outside, occasionally made their way into our house under the bottoms of the badly-fitting doors. One evening, while sitting with Lofty, enjoying a chat and a bottle of beer, I heard a rustling, nibbling sound emanating from under the sideboard in the dining area. On going to investigate I saw a small. grey shape scamper across the floor and out under the door. It was a mouse of some sort and it had caught and had been eating one of the locusts, which was almost as big as itself. Here then was the food chain. Locust eats vegetation, mouse eats locust, snake eats mouse. I wondered what sort of mouse it was. The following day I decided to investigate further and started by lifting up a number of the large flat rocks which littered the area. I was soon successful. Under one of the rocks was a small, grey mouse looking up to see who was disturbing its slumbers. The extraordinary thing about it was that instead of having fur on its back, it had spines, like a tiny hedgehog. It soon recovered its composure and ran off to the next rock. On lifting this I found, not one mouse but a family of them. The tiny babies were active, although they had clearly only just got their eyes open. I caught the entire family without too much effort and popped them into a handy box. The spines, I found, were not hard and sharp like those of a hedgehog, but quite soft in consistency. I couldn't imagine what could be the advantage in having these instead of a fur coat. I wonder if it was something to do with their keeping cool in such arid conditions. I continued lifting the rocks around the house and soon came across the second reason for my search. A large snake, nearly six-feet in length skidded out between my legs and, finding its way blocked by the wall of the house, it reared up and opened its hood. It was a cobra. Not the ordinary cobra, however. This was of a type known as a ringhals. It had quite a small hood, and it was an extraordinary pink in colour. It spat a stream of venom in my direction, but fortunately missed my face. Before I could take any action, it had dropped back to the ground and made its way off to another pile of rocks nearby. I suppose that after an experience such as this, most people might have signed the pledge. This was what Lofty suggested when I related to him the incident of the pink snake. 'I suppose there weren't any elephants of a similar colour under the rock as well?,' he remarked, somewhat unkindly I thought. 'Maybe, one of these days, I'll find another one', said I. 'I'll try to collect it next time to prove it to you.'

Before leaving Moroto, I had made my application to sit the final two Subjects of the Law Examination, and the written part of the Kiswahili, which was due within the month. On being transferred to Lokitaung I had thought, initially, that I might still be back in Karamoja in time to sit it. When it became clear that this was not to be, I wrote to headquarters to enquire what arrangements they proposed to make to enable me to sit these exams. The result of this was that Harry Jones duly received a letter, enclosing the relevant Law Examination papers. Having found the time and opportunity to study the two outstanding subjects, I was confident of passing them with flying colours. The day of the examination dawned and I presented myself in Harry's office at the police station. 'Look', he said, 'I really haven't got time to sit around invigilating you all morning. Just go and sit in your office and get on with it. I'll have to trust you not to use your books. If I have time, I'll pop in from time to time.' 'What a pity this isn't the Swahili Exam', I thought. 'I don't need to look at my books for this. I'm sufficiently genned up to walk the exam. It would be different with the Swahili. I would cheat on that with a clear conscience, since I've been at such a disadvantage in learning it.' The exam proceeded and I finished both papers in good time. Of Harry I saw no sign. On completion of the two papers I took them to his office. He wasn't even there. I got on with my work for the rest of the day. Harry arrived late in the afternoon. He winked at me and packed the completed papers into their envelopes without comment.

Word arrived from Kokoro Fort of a serious incursion by Merille tribesmen from Ethiopia. Some 200 of them had taken over one of the waterholes and were challenging the local

Turkana to oppose them if they dared. I set out for the fort taking
with me a dozen Kenya policemen as reinforcements. We arrived
at the fort late in the afternoon. Early the following morning we
left and made our way to the waterhole which was around 15
miles distant. The final five miles of this was covered on foot. This
was the first occasion I had experienced walking on the soft dusty
sand. I found that it was not easy. My feet sank in to the ankles.
The sand filled my shoes and socks, rubbing the skin till it
became quite sore. I noticed that all the Kenya Police had been
issued with open leather sandals. They wore no socks at all. This
had a distinct advantage inasmuch as, although the feet still sank
in to the ankles, by giving a sharp kick on the ground every so
often, the sand simply fell away leaving the sandal completely
clear. I would have to arrange to get a pair of these sandals!

On our arrival near the water hole I was able to clearly hear
the clunking of the cow-bells from the stock as they were
watered. Our total strength was around 40 policemen and I split
these so that we could approach the area from both sides. My
instructions to this patrol were that no shots should be fired
unless the Merille fired first. Fortunately, our arrival came as a
complete surprise to the Merille. The sight that met my eyes as I
emerged from the scrub lining the dry river bed was akin to a
biblical scene. Several great holes had been dug into the dry
sandy bed, down to the water some 12 feet below. Containers of
all sorts were being used to raise the water to the surface.
Standing in the water were half-a-dozen naked tribesmen. Leather
bucket, paraffin *debis* and gourds were being lowered down to
them on ropes, pulled to the surface full of water and emptied
into large hide containers from which the animals were drinking.
Scattered over the river bed and the surrounding area were
around 2,000 goats, camels and donkeys. Many of the tribesmen
in the area made off into the bush as soon as they spotted the
police party. Our object, however, was not to apprehend them,
but merely to seize as large a number of the stock as possible. We
did, however, succeed in seizing two Italian rifles at the same
time, the owners having dropped them in their flight. Now we
had the problem of driving the animals back to the fort. This was
made difficult by the Merille constantly trying to head off parts of
the herd whenever they thought they had an opportunity.
Eventually we arrived back at the fort and made a count of the

number of animals we had seized. They amounted to nearly 1,500 in all, which was a pretty satisfactory result. My feet were raw and I had been glad to get aboard the lorry when we came to it. Having got the stock safely corralled I sent a radio signal to Lokitaung requesting the D.O. to attend the following day to authorise the seizure of the 300 head of stock to be taken as the fine, prior to their being driven to Lokitaung. At 3 o'clock the following morning the attack began. The Merille tribesmen, now reinforced, had decided to attempt to recover their stock. As the opening rounds were fired at the fort the bugle sounded the alarm and all personnel grabbed their rifles and headed for their prepared positions. It was impossible to see the attackers but flashes of fire from the guns betrayed their position. A few of the bullets whistled past my head but the tribesmen were firing as blind as we were. On my orders the fire was returned and the engagement lasted for about half-an-hour. At the height of the firing I ordered the machine-gunner in the watch tower to open fire. This he did, firing several long bursts in the direction of the incoming fire. This had the desired result and the Merille broke off their attack. No police casualties were suffered but several large patches of blood found at daylight indicated that the Merille had not been so fortunate. A search of the area failed to reveal any trace of bodies so I assumed that none of the Merille had been killed. The following afternoon Eric Fox arrived. A few of the stock-owners, somewhat cowed I thought, turned up for the judicial hearing and were permitted to remove that part of their herds which were not forfeit. I stayed overnight at the fort in case there was any further trouble. There was none and the following day the seized stock were driven off to Lokitaung under heavy police guard. The remainder of the herd and all the Merille trespassers, were escorted back over the border.

Harry Jones was on his way. His transfer to Isiolo was totally unexpected but, during the present State of Emergency, nothing could be taken for granted. Harry's place was taken by Murdoch Mackenzie. He proved to be no stranger to the Northern Frontier having served in Wajir as well as Moyale, from where he now arrived after a bone shaking journey of about 1,000 miles. Murdoch turned out to be a cheerful, outgoing Scotsman with a broad accent. Of medium height and sporting a vast moustache. He was also very fond of his native tipple. He brought with him a small menagerie consisting of a small shenzie bitch, a serval cat and a pygmy mongoose named Donald. The serval cat walked with a pronounced limp, it having suffered from rickets when it was a kitten. Donald led the other two a terrible life. He would hide under a chair and wait until they were fast asleep. Then he would leap out like a flash of brown lighting, nip the dog and the serval and be back under the chair before either of them saw him. The dog and the serval would then have a scrap while Donald squeaked encouragement from the safety of his hideout. Murdoch had a supply of table-tennis balls. He would give one of these to the little animal who thought it was an egg, its favourite food. Maneuvering this into position between its back legs it would suddenly flick the ball backwards against the wall. Its puzzlement when the 'egg' didn't smash was comical to behold. I was impressed by Donald's courage. He had the run of the house and surrounding area. He rapidly enlarged his domain, however, and frequently made his way down to the police station half-a-mile distant where he soon became well-known. Not content with this he would accompany Murdoch down to the *duka* from time to time. Here he found what he was seeking. Eggs. Having been given one by the *duka* owner he proceeded to demonstrate his skill in smashing it against the wall. After this there was no holding him. Unaccompanied he would make his way to the bazaar each day and, arriving unnoticed, would locate the box of eggs and break as many as possible before the *duka* owner could drive him off. Poor Murdoch! He was forever being approached by irate *duka* owners demanding payment for the broken eggs. He never quibbled over this, however, in case one of the *duka* owners disposed of Donald to stop his depredations.

One evening. shortly after Murdoch's arrival, he invited Lofty and myself up to his bungalow for a meal. At about 7 o'clock we set off along the path leading to his home. The night was quite dark, but the outline of the sandy path could be just made out. I had a torch with me but it was only necessary to flash it on from time to time. Suddenly, in front of me, I saw what appeared to be a log lying across the path. Lofty, who was just ahead of me, hadn't noticed it and was about to step on it when I grabbed him and pulled him back. He had just started to protest at my rough handling when I shone my torch. There, lying across the path, within a foot of him was an enormous puff adder. It was well over five feet in length and as thick as my thigh. It made its way unhurriedly across the open space to the vegetation on the other side. Neither of us were carrying a stick so we could only watch as the serpent made its leisurely way and was lost in the undergrowth. One more step and it would have been good-bye Lofty!

The day arrived when I was to sit the Kiswahili Exam again. My efforts in the law exam had met with success and I breathed a sigh of relief to know that that particular hurdle was passed. Now for the big one. I had made as much effort as possible in studying for this but was not very confident. What was lacking was a competent teacher. Lofty had tried his best but was no great shakes himself at the language. Murdoch was a different matter. He was a natural and had passed the Intermediate Examination. I wondered if he would be as cooperative as Harry had been and depart for the day, leaving me to invigilate myself. No such luck. The examination commenced. I looked at the paper and sighed. No hope here. I was going to fail this as I had before. The chances of passing it while living in the bush were clearly nil. However, I set pen to paper and commenced. Murdoch watched me closely. Occasionally he got to his feet and stood behind me to inspect my efforts. 'Tut tut', he said finally, 'That's not right. You'd better start again.' So saying, he handed me a fresh sheet of paper and dictated the answers to the various questions. I started to raise a half-hearted objection to this. 'Look, do you want to pass or not?', he enquired. I shut up. My major fear was that the paper would be too good. Someone would smell a rat! Murdoch however assured me that he had ensured that it would pass muster, just, and so it did. A few weeks later I received notification that I had now passed the written examination. Only the oral remained!

The monthly pay safari was again due. As luck would have it, it was my turn again to make the bone-shaking trip through the gorge. I took the opportunity of knocking down a buck to supply the fort at Namaraputh. The staff there expressed their gratitude for this, but continued to complain of the mosquitoes. I sympathised with them but there was nothing I could do about it. Anyway, I hadn't seen any mosquitoes so I thought they must be exaggerating.

The safari continued without particular incident, with my shooting an occasional animal to supply the needs of the various forts. Eventually we were on the last lap to Mogilla. The countryside here was in stark contrast to that of the desert on the Kenya side of the border. Here the rolling low hills led eventually to the western wall of the escarpment. The land had lost its parched appearance and the low thorn shrub had given way to wild figs and mopani. The lush appearance of the land had led to a corresponding increase in the number of animals roaming the area. Great herds of kongoni, topi, zebra and gazelle were to be seen in every direction. A banging on the side of the lorry alerted me. Over to the left, at a distance of around 1,000 yards stood a large antelope. I was able to identify it as an oryx beisa. Up to that time I had not seen this type of antelope. While by no means rare, they did not congregate in herds as large as those of the topi, kongoni or wildebeest. These were the animals which had given rise in ancient times to the myth of the unicorn. Their straight swordlike horns around 40 inches in length ended in needle-like tips. Standing sideways as this animal was, it was easy to see how the two horns could be mistaken for a single one. I knew that, like the eland, the flesh of the oryx was deep red like beef, as opposed to the pale flesh of most of the other buck. I decided to see if I could get this animal both as a trophy and also to satisfy the needs of the police staff at the fort. I got out of the cab of the lorry and made my way carefully towards the point at which I had seen the animal standing. Fortunately, the wind was in my favour as the oryx is notorious for being shy, and the least hint that I was approaching would stampede it well before I was within range. Crawling on hands and knees, I next saw the animal at a range of around 200 yards, well within the distance at which I knew I should be able to make a clean kill. The antelope had turned and was facing me so I was unable to make a shot at the neck. I decided to take it full in the chest, the bullet would then pass into the chest cavity, with luck, hitting the heart. It would in any case be a quick killing shot. Holding my breath I fired. The animal lurched and staggered off behind a nearby bush. I got to my feet, confident that I had made a successful kill. To my amazement, the next second it was out from the other side of the bush and running like the wind. What on earth had happened? Here was an animal which I was sure was mortally wounded, yet running as though nothing had happened. The way it was moving it looked as though I was in for a chase which might last for miles. I certainly couldn't allow it to escape in the wounded condition I knew it to be. If it escaped it would die in agony and I was not prepared to let this happen if I could prevent it. I raised my rifle and quickly fired at the rapidly diminishing target. I heard the bullet thump home and the animal lurched but continued to run. I fired again. The range was increasing and I could not be sure if the bullet hit or not. At this moment I realised that I had only two bullets left in the magazine. At extreme range I again fired and the oryx stumbled onto its knees. I made my way towards it. As I passed behind the bush where the animal had stumbled when I first shot it, I was saddened to see it lying there. The first shot had been a clean kill. My subsequent shots had been at a different animal which was now some 400 yards further away. I made my way to where it had fallen. It was clearly badly wounded and was lying in an upright position on its knees, its head down and its great pointed horns pointing forwards. At this stage, I should have finished it off with my single remaining bullet. However, I was a bit dubious about the wisdom of this. The area was alive with lions and I was at least a mile from the lorry where I had left the rest of my ammunition. I decided that I should have to finish the animal off with my hunting knife, reserving the bullet for my walk back to the lorry. It appeared to be practically dead anyway. I made my way towards the oryx. When I was about three yards from it, it suddenly came to life and hurtled forwards towards me, its horns suddenly becoming twin rapiers. It had been shamming, waiting for me to get within range. I leapt to one side the horns narrowly missing me, then the chase was on. The slashing horns were after me, and I did the first thing that came to mind. Ran, as fast as I could. The oryx was still very agile regardless of its wounds, which didn't seem to worry it a bit. About 40 yards away was a palm tree. There was no way that I could climb it, since it had no branches low enough to afford a foot hold. There was no other cover available however and I sped towards it, the twin swords of the oryx a couple of feet from my backside lending wings to my feet. I reached the tree and dodged around it. The oryx swung round after me. From a range of six inches I blasted the animal through the neck. It sagged and was dead. I also sagged, but was alive and very shaken. I made my way back to the lorry. Fortunately, any lions who might have been in the area had been disturbed by the gunfire and pushed off. I then directed the lorry back to the two animals. The vultures were already beginning to circle overhead in anticipation of a feast. I was suddenly very much aware that I might have been forming part of that feast had the Beaden luck not held. A few days later the mail arrived. A letter from Joan, and one from my father. This was unusual. He invariably left the letter writing to mother. I opened Joan's letter.

> Dear Tony,
> I am writing to tell you that I no longer love you. I am sorry about this, but there is no other way of telling you. I have met someone else and we are going to be married as soon as my divorce is through. I don't think I could have settled to life in Africa anyway.
>
> Joan.

I felt slightly stunned at this. It was not altogether unexpected. There had been something about her recent letters which had caused me to be uneasy, but my mother had continually encouraged in me the belief that all was well. Well, no use in crying over spilt milk. She was probably quite right. On reflection I couldn't see her settling to life in a remote spot like Moroto any more that poor Barbara had. She liked the comforts of civilisation too well. I was undoubtedly as much to blame for this breakup as she was. I had related to her as well as to my parents, the various adventures I had encountered, as well as the various trials and tribulations, illnesses and dangers which I had undergone. Clearly this had been a major factor in her thinking. Well, I was now unencumbered. I would have to start thinking about someone else to share my life! I opened the letter from my father. Joan had evidently informed my parents of her decision at the same time that she had written to me. The gist of his letter was that he hoped that I wouldn't be doing anything silly on receiving the news, and that he had evicted Joan from the flat in which I had installed her. In the event I had a few beers with Lofty and celebrated my narrow escape from what might have been a disastrous marriage. I heard, years later, that Joan had married a railway labourer and had produced two daughters, both of them slightly sub-normal. Later still her husband divorced her. The Beaden luck continued to hold!

A week or two later, Whitehouse visited Lokitaung. The

object of his visit was to interview Jomo Kenyatta. Why he should have been chosen to do this I am still at a loss to understand. The interview took place in an office at the police station set aside for the purpose. Jomo spoke perfect English but Whitehouse, presumably in an effort to humiliate him would only use Swahili, in which language, to give him is due, he was a master. Jomo would have none of it. Each question Whitehouse asked, he would reply to in faultless English language. Whitehouse became more and more angry as the interview progressed. Jomo remained calm and collected. Eventually the interview was terminated. There was no doubt in my mind who had won. Nor in that of Mackenzie. His only comment was, 'That man must have a death wish. It's quite on the cards that Jomo could be in charge here one of these days.' A prophetic remark as it transpired.

Christmas arrived. No Christmas presents from the *dukas* up here. They were far too poor. The goat bag was raided and Lofty and Mackenzie and I put our hands deeply into our pockets and, pooling our resources, purchased large quantities of sweets which we packaged and on Christmas day distributed to the multitude of children from the police barracks and, as far as I know, to many other local offspring as well. After this we had a shooting competition. Eric Fox captained a team composed of the tribal police. Lofty captained the police team from the P.S.U. at Bombo while I captained the Moroto police team. In the event my team won hands down with a score of 123 out of 160. Lofty's team was next with 82, while Eric's team could only achieve 33. Modesty prevents me from saying who had the highest score. Later in the morning a great celebratory dance was held in which both the police and the local tribesmen and women joined. Christmas lunch was enjoyed at Murdoch's bungalow to which Eric, Lofty and I were invited. I provided the main dish, having shot a greater bustard for that purpose the previous day. Murdoch consumed great quantities of whisky after which he staggered onto his verandah and started taking potshots with his revolver at children using the swimming pool just upstream. They appeared to think this great fun as the bullets ricocheted off of the rocks surrounding the pool. I rapidly disarmed him before any damage was done, after which he became very abusive and the party broke up in disorder. The following day he could remember nothing of the incident, or so he maintained, and was quite surprised when I returned his revolver to him.

Rations for the forts were getting very low and it was suggested that I might like to make a trip to Kitale some 280 miles distant. Naturally, I jumped at the chance and set off in one of the lorries with a couple of the Kenya police. Our Asian mechanic, Ajiit Singh, was driving. Lodwar was our first destination, where I made a quick visit to Sub-Inspector Balinda to ensure that all was well. Apart from continual interference from Whitehouse, I was assured that all was under control. I noticed that considerable progress had been made in the construction of the prison camp in which the Mau-mau detainees were housed. Then we were on our way again. The journey across the desert was a continual grinding, bumping, nightmare. The heat in the cab was around 140 degrees. Visions of glass after glass of ice cold beer flashed before me. All these would be mine when we reached Kitale. The day progressed and eventually late in the afternoon we reached the base of the escarpment and commenced the tortuous climb to the summit. As we climbed the 3,000 feet, the air became cooler. By the time we reached the top it was dark and the temperature had dropped dramatically. By half-past-seven we had reached Kacheliba and here commenced another climb a further 2,000 feet to the 'White Highlands'. Kitale was reached at about 9 o'clock by which time I was shivering with the cold. Gone were the thoughts of the glasses of ice cold beer. In their place were visions of a large glass of warming brandy. I staggered, covered in a heavy coating of dust, into the foyer of the hotel. Smartly-clad Europeans were dining in the brightly-lit dining room. I made my way to the reception to be met by a supercilious female who looked me up and down and sniffed down her nose. I signed the register and was handed a key. An African porter carried my case up to the top floor where I had been allocated a room. On looking in the mirror I could quite understand the reason for the receptionists reaction. I was filthy dirty. Under the quarter-inch of dust that covered me, I was tanned to the colour of mahogany. My eyes were red-rimmed from the dust, my uniform grubby and untidy and my hair had not been cut for nearly four months. I was still wearing the open leather sandals which I had scrounged and apart from these my legs were bare. My revolver, which I now wore habitually, hung in its holster from my belt. Hardly the image of the clean-cut police officer which I was supposed to represent, rather the picture of a half-cut vagrant. I wallowed in the hot bath, filled to overflowing, shaved and donned a clean uniform, then I made my way to the dining room to find it closed. Only to be expected I suppose, after all it was nearly 11 o'clock. I was starving! Off to the reception. The receptionist viewed me with a more kindly eye. 'Any chance of a bite to eat?', I enquired. 'Sorry', she said, 'I'm afraid the kitchen is closed.' 'Never mind', said I, 'I'll have to make do with a drink at the bar.' Shortly afterwards, however, a delicious ham sandwich arrived. The receptionist had after all taken pity on the weary traveller.

The following day after a delightful breakfast I met Ajiit Singh outside the hotel. Our first call was the police station where a large assortment of vehicle spares were awaiting collection, after which the lorry was driven round to various suppliers and vast quantities of *posho*, sugar, tobacco, palm oil, salt and *matoke* were purchased. Since there was no point in commencing our return journey until the following morning I spent some time walking round Kitale. It was reminiscent of a small town in a Western movie. I was by no means the only person carrying a revolver in a belt holster. Many of the people frequenting the local European-staffed shops were farmers from the surrounding area. All of these appeared to be prepared to withstand a full-scale war. There had been no Mau-mau activity reported in the area around Kitale, though there had been a number of terrorist attacks in the vicinity of Eldoret some 20-miles distant. There was no telling how far this canker would spread and the settler farmers were very vulnerable on their isolated farms. I began to realise how fortunate I was in the wilds of Turkana. There, at least, the tribesmen were reliable to some degree and, what Mau-mau there were were safely locked up. Wreford Smith lived about ten miles out of Kitale in the direction of Eldoret, at his farm, Kipkulkul but not having any transport I was unable to visit him, though I know I should have been given a warm welcome. As it was I returned to the hotel. Early the following morning, clad in my newly-laundered safari clothes, I joined the waiting lorry and we were away back to the wilds. My return to Lokitaung was greeted with great enthusiasm by all concerned. Especially by Barney and Kesi. I had brought the latter two great bunches of *matoke*, the cooking banana, his favourite food, which he had not been able to enjoy since leaving

Kampala. Barney was enthusiastic just because it was in his nature to be so. Lofty was enthusiastic when I told him about the terrific time I had had in Kitale, and how I had managed to bed three different women, including the hotel receptionist. He stated his intention of being the next one to make the trip down there.

My account of the fleshpots of Kitale had an unfortunate effect on Lofty. He commenced by confiding in me about his marriage. Lofty had married late in life, his wife being a little older than himself. He told me that his marriage was not a particularly happy one. This I could quite believe since, while I had found him one of the most genuine individuals it had been my good fortune to encounter, there was no doubt that he had a number of irritating little habits, not merely his tendency to burst forth into Gilbert and Sullivan operas at the drop of a hat, but also his habit of making the most dreadful puns at the slightest provocation — and repeating them as frequently as possible. Fortunately, we were in one another's close company at infrequent intervals, one or other of us being out on safari most of the time. His wife would not have had this advantage. She, he told me, had her own bank account, into which she paid the small salary she received from an office job she had in Kampala. She referred to this as her 'running away' money and threatened, at frequent intervals, to leave Lofty and return to England when he became too much for her. I would never have thought him to be a highly-sexed individual, but my account of activities in Kitale certainly put him in a new light. During one of my absences he asked Kesi to procure a woman for him. Kesi clearly thought that quantity was more important than quality and presumably he imagined that Lofty's tastes would follow a similar pattern to his own. After making some judicious enquiries he turned up with the fattest, sweatiest Turkana woman I had encountered. Unlike the other Turkana women, she wore a cheap cotton dress instead of the traditional leather skirt and uncovered breasts. She reminded me strongly of a pink-flowered bell tent. Her name was Falua and she was very popular at the police barracks. I had returned home by the time Kesi produced her and I made my excuses and departed for a long walk while Lofty dealt with her. She had gone by the time I returned. Lofty was grinning and had a sort of defensive look on his face. He obviously felt much better. 'If I were you,', I said, 'I should go and see the doctor as soon as possible. If you haven't picked up a dose there I'll eat my hat.'

Some days later we had retired to bed on our camp beds on the lower level of the house. Barney, as was his habit, was snoring gently on the concrete floor at my bedside. At around 3.a.m. I was rudely awakened. My bed was being buffeted about. My first thought was that an earthquake had struck us. First the foot of the bed rose and fell back with a crash, then the head of the bed went through a similar gyration. My mosquito net was waving about madly. 'What on earth was going on?' I reached under my pillow and grabbed the torch and my revolver. It was difficult to make anything out from inside the net so I pulled it off and shone the torch in the direction from which the activity was coming. There was Barney. And one of the pink snakes I had previously seen. It had evidently made its way under my bed, disturbing Barney in the process. Poor Barney had, not unnaturally, taken exception to this and a battle royal was in progress. In the circumstances I deemed it wise not to put my foot out of the bed until the combatants had moved off a bit. I shouted to Barney to get away but this time he took little notice. The ringhals slithered under my bed and Barney got it by the tail and shook it vigorously. The snake coiled back and darted at him with its fangs wide. Barney saw it coming a dodged away. The battle then moved away from my immediate vicinity and I took the opportunity of sliding out of bed. Bearing in mind the closeness of the fight taking place and the proximity of Lofty in the other bed, my revolver was of little use to me. A fast-moving snake in the darkness was hardly a good subject for target practice. I then remembered that Kesi had been chopping up some firewood earlier in the day and I had noticed that he had left the axe on the other level, near the door. I ran to it and picked it up. Leaving my revolver on the table I raced back to where the fight was taking placed. The snake was now under Lofty's bed with Barney still doing his best to deal with it. Lofty told me later that he had awakened in a similar manner to myself with his bed's violent movements. Looking up he had seen me advancing upon him swinging a twelve pound felling axe. Not unnaturally he thought that his renditions of Gilbert and Sullivan had finally caused me to flip. He didn't even have time to say his prayers. My first blow missed completely. I had the axe by the extreme end of the handle in case the snake managed to use it to launch an attack on me. This didn't make for much accuracy. My second blow cut one of Lofty's leather sandals neatly in half. The third try was successful. The snake was severed in two. The head and a couple of feet of the body still wriggled round, striking at anything near it. The major part of the body threshed about bleeding copiously over Lofty's clothes, which had fallen to the floor in the struggle. I then took the opportunity of crushing the head of the snake with the heel of the axe, and threw the body to one side.

After a few minutes, Lofty got shakily out of his bed. I invited him to have a look at the pink snake to ascertain whether he too was suffering from delirium tremens. While he was engaged in this I got the pressure lamps lit and set about examining Barney for damage. As far as I could see, he had been bitten on the shoulder and venom had been spat into his eyes. Poor old chap. His eyes were already swelling up and closing. I got the anti-venine kit out and injected 10 c.c. of it into and around the shoulder wound. The remaining 10 c.c. ampoule I started using as eye drops, first having washed his face and eyes with clean water to dilute the venom as much as possible. I remained awake for the rest of the night, dripping the anti-venine into his eyes at half hourly intervals. In the morning his face was puffed up like a balloon, his eyes were practically closed and he was clearly having difficulty in seeing out of them. As soon as it became light I carried him down to the doctor's house and pounded on the door to rouse him. I must give him his due. He made no complaint about his rude awakening, but examined Barney, gave him a further 10 c.c. injection of anti-venine, plus a large one of penicillin and gave me another ampoule for use as eye drops. 'Nothing more I can do.' he informed me. 'Maybe he'll live, maybe not.' I carried Barney back to the house and laid him on a blanket. He wagged his tail weakly. 'I'm afraid that's going to be the end of the old chap', I said to Lofty. Kesi, brought us our morning tea and I told him what had happened. I saw the tears welling into his eyes. He was almost as fond of Barney as I was. Lofty and I made our way to the office. At lunchtime we returned home. I fully expected Barney to have departed for the happy hunting grounds. Not a bit of it. He was on his feet, staggering a bit it's true, but his swollen head had started to subside. He gingerly made his way to me, wagging his tail in greeting. A week later and the old boy was as good as new. I thanked my luck stars that I had brought the anti-venine with me.

One of my first actions after this was to write to a chemist in Kitale, requesting them to supply me with a further anti-venine outfit. This arrived on the weekly bus in due course. Meanwhile, I had written to Gareth in Moroto, relating the incident to him, as I thought he might be interested. He in turn told various others on the station and eventually news of it got back to Pearman. A couple of weeks later I received a letter from him full of abuse. 'In the first place', he wrote, 'you had no right to take the anti-venine with you. It was issued for the use of officers on safari from Moroto, not to be taken to Kenya. In the second place, it is government property and as such you could be dealt with disciplinarily for misusing it by injecting it into your dog.' There was much more in the same vein. I'm afraid I saw red at this and, throwing caution to the winds I wrote him a real humdinger in reply. 'The anti-venine was issued to the D.M.O. as a result of a report which I submitted, and is for the use of any government officer on safari, wherever he is going. It is one of three outfits which were supplied. To my knowledge no one but myself has ever been sufficiently interested to carry them. I certainly used the anti-venine on my dog, and would do the same again in similar circumstances. The dog, in attacking the snake, may well have saved the lives of one, if not both officers stationed here. The anti-venine was, in any case, nearing the end of its useful life and I have since replaced it at my own expense. As for my facing disciplinary action as a result of my alleged misuse of government property, I can only suggest that, if you think you have cause to complain, you'd better go ahead and lodge your complaint at headquarters!' Now the gauntlet had been thrown down. I was probably most unwise in taking a belligerent attitude in the matter, but I was incensed at the disgraceful tone of Pearman's letter. I still smarted from the manner in which the idiot had treated me when I had worked with him in Moroto. Now the die was cast. I should never be able to work with him again. If he was still stationed in Moroto when I left Kenya, I should have to request an immediate transfer. I thought it unlikely that I should be returning to Moroto anyway, since I had noticed in the monthly police magazine *Habari*, that another Inspector, Les Peach, had been sent in my place after the first four weeks of my absence. He had only lasted a month though before being replaced by yet another Inspector, Peter Oades. It looked as though I was not the only one to find Pearman's attitude impossible.

The Merille tribesmen were at it again. This time they had crossed the Ethiopian border into northern Turkana, to the west of Namaraputh. A full-scale war being waged. Not only had they occupied one of the waterholes, they had also murdered an entire family of Turkana tribesmen. Grandparents, parents and children, 11 in all, by shooting them from a range of about six inches. As it happened, all but one of our lorries were undergoing major repair so, once I had been dropped at Namaraputh I should be without transport, since the single remaining lorry would have to return to Lokitaung. It was anticipated that this would only be for one day, or two at the most. Unfortunately, it was at the end of the week and our food supplies were sadly diminished. 'No problem', I thought, 'I've got a bit of tea, plenty of condensed milk, four large pineapples and I can shoot a bird or a buck on the way out. If I get desperate I can probably get some fish from the Maskini fishermen.' With this in mind I set off to investigate. For the first time ever, I didn't see a single bird or animal on our way through the gorge. If I couldn't get anything in the immediate vicinity of the fort I should have to rely on fish from the Maskini. My first report, indicating the scale of the carnage was passed by signal to Lokitaung and thence to police headquarters in Nairobi. This resulted in a directive that any Merille tribesmen found carrying firearms within Turkana were to be summarily shot.

My camping equipment was set up within the large hut used by officers. This was about 15-feet square and constructed of stones cemented together and plastered over the outside. The roof was of thatched grass which ensured that the inside was as cool as possible. My dining net, a square construction some ten feet by twelve was hung from the roof and my camp bed and table enclosed within this area. I made myself a cup of tea and, as it was beginning to get dark, lit my pressure lamps, and settled down to read. As darkness fell, the entire place became alive with the whining of mosquitoes. Barney, who had gone outside for a pee, came flying in covered in the creatures. He burst his way through the dining net, bringing hundreds of them with him.

Shaking his head in a frenzy as they bit him. I suddenly realised that the complaints had not been exaggerated after all. These were not ordinary mosquitoes. They were at least four times the size of any mosquito I had ever come across. I grabbed my Flit spray and vigorously pumped it in all directions. I managed to kill off the mosquitoes who had come into the dining net. Outside the night was hideous with the whining buzz of millions upon millions of the insects. There was no way that I could go outside to cook anything, even had I had anything to cook. Neither could I go out to have a bath. I was trapped inside the mosquito net and here I should have to stay. I hoped that there would be no night attack. I didn't mind the thought of the attacking Merille but didn't fancy exposing myself to the mosquitoes. The bright light from the pressure lamps had the effect of attracting so many of them that the entire outer wall of the dining net became a black seething mass. Inevitably some of them started finding the weak spots and breaking into the dining area. Barney started going mad again as he was bitten. There was no alternative. The mosquitoes had won. I put the lamps out and retired to bed. Eventually I dropped off to sleep. Something woke me. I looked at my watch. It was 2 a.m. I listened. Nothing. What had happened. Then I realised what it was. Not a sound. The mosquitoes had gone. Back into the vegetation round the lake. I got out of bed and walked outside. Not a single mosquito to be seen or heard. A fresh breeze blew in from the lake. All was peaceful. I dressed and decided to take a walk down to the lake shore. I collected my torch and the .22 rifle and, followed closely by Barney made my way over the 100 yards of sandy clay surface. The sentry on guard at the entrance to the fort compound looked at me oddly as I passed him but made no comment apart from saying 'Jambo Efendi' as he saluted me. On reaching the lake edge I shone my torch onto the surface of the water. An extraordinary sight met my eyes. This particular spot was cleared of reeds for a distance of 200 yards. The water was obviously shallow and a broken bank of reeds lay some 100 yards off shore. Beyond this the waters of the vast lake sparkled in the moonlight. Floating around on the surface of this enclosed bay were dozens of red lights. By studying carefully those nearest to me, I was able to make out that they were the eyes of crocodiles, their heads just above the water and the remainder of their bodies submerged. I judged, by the size of the heads, that they were not very big crocs. An average of around six or seven feet was my guess. Big enough to give a nasty bite though. My immediate reaction was that a small fortune was floating around in front of my eyes. Crocodile skins were fetching around £2 per inch-width for the belly skin. These, at about six- or seven-feet long would be worth £30 to £35 each. Definitely not to be sneezed at. The nearest croc was about ten yards out. I raised my rifle and fired smack between the eyes. The water threshed for a few seconds and became still. My torch showed nothing. If I had hit it, and I was sure that I had, it must have sunk to the bottom. The other crocs did not seem unduly disturbed by the shot, so I repeated the process. Again the water threshed, and was still. During the next few minutes I shot six of the beasts, after which the remainder got the message. The only trouble was that I could see none of my victims. I knew almost precisely where the first croc lay so I took off my sandals and waded in to see if I could find the body. No luck. What I did experience however, was something slimy rubbing against my ankles. Shining my torch into the water I was amazed to find dozens of large eels swimming round my feet, evidently attracted by the torch light. I decided that, maybe wading around in these unknown waters was not the wisest of moves so retraced my steps to the shore. How was it that there were eels in Lake Turkana? I had always understood that all eels need to go to the sea to breed. There was no way that these could have performed this miracle Turkana was hundreds of miles from the sea, surrounded by desert and with no outlet. However, I have found a report by scientists more recently confirming that I was not mistaken and that there are indeed eels in Lake Turkana and. in fact, in all the other great landlocked lakes of the Rift Valley. I can only suppose that when they became cut off from the sea millions of years ago some of them adapted to the changed circumstances and altered their breeding habits. Maybe I could claim to be the first to discover this.

I made my way, empty-handed, back to the fort. '*Bahati Mbaya*', (Bad luck) said the sentry as I passed him. I made no comment, but on getting up the following morning I went to the scene of the night's activity. There floating on the surface were six good sized crocs. The local Maskini fishermen were soon on the scene and set about removing the belly skins for me. In return they enquired if they could have the meat. I assumed they wanted it for some sort of medicine. Not a bit of it, they wanted to eat it. I suggested that they could swop it for some fish. Unfortunately, the fish had been practically non-existent of recent days, so there was none to be had. My success with the crocs would prevent them starving though! 'What about me?', I thought. I was starving as well, having nothing to eat but condensed milk and pineapple.

After pegging the croc skins out to dry, I had breakfast of the only two commodities available and set out on a foot patrol to see if we could find any of the marauding Merille tribesmen. I already knew that they had moved off from the water hole they had been occupying, so it was a matter of trying to guess their next move. Conditions were, to say the least, trying. By mid- morning the temperature in the desert stood at 140 degrees in the shade. That's a laugh, there was no shade but I stood my thermometer in the shadow of a large rock and that was the temperature recorded. At least it was a dry heat. Had it been humid it would have been unbearable. Lunch time came and I ate pineapple and condensed milk. By 3 p.m. we were back at the fort. A message awaited me. 'Regret no vehicle available to collect you. Don't anticipate a lorry being ready for at least four days!' I just had time for a light snack consisting of pineapple and condensed milk before the mosquitoes arrived. I reviewed my situation. Things were now serious. True, I still had another two pineapples and plenty of condensed milk, but I began to feel that the sight and taste of these were abhorrent. Another couple of days and I should resemble a pineapple! My supper now consisted of a bottle of beer. Even my last bit of *biltong* had disappeared weeks earlier and I had no equipment to make more. I managed to scrounge a handful of *posho* from one of the constables. This was Barney's supper. He didn't look too pleased about it!

The mosquitoes gathered in force as they had they previous night. This time I was prepared for the onslaught and was under my dining net before they arrived. Again, the pressure lamp attracted them in their hordes. I took the inevitable step and went to bed. By 3 a.m. they had again vanished. Taking my gun and torch I made my way to the lake. There seemed to be even more red eyes reflected in the torch beam than there had been the previous night. However, this time I only succeeded in potting four of them before they made off. Maybe they just put their heads under water and waited to see if I would wade in among them again. This time I decided that discretion was the better part of valour. I returned to the fort. At daybreak I was again down at the waters' edge and gathered in the night's harvest. A few more days of this and I should be a rich man! As before the Maskini fishermen collected the corpses after removing the belly skin. 'Wait a minute', I said, 'I can use some of that meat. At least it will make a meal for Barney if I cook it well.' I enquired which was the choice cut and was told that the tail was best. On my instructions the largest tail was removed and skinned for me. I took it back to the fort, together with the four belly skins. There were about 20 pounds of meat here and I should have to cook it if it was to feed Barney for the next few days. I cut off the first steak and popped it in the pot. I boiled it for 20 minutes or so and then allowed it to cool. Barney loved it. It looked like chicken. I wondered what it tasted like. In my present state of starvation I could have eaten a horse. In fact I could no doubt eat a horse without being in a state of starvation. I popped a piece of the meat in my mouth. It was delicious. I cut another steak and grilled it over the flames. Just like grilled chicken! My prayers were answered. I shouldn't starve after all!

During the day, I made a further safari in search of the Merille raiders. In order to cover a wider area, I decided that we should make this patrol on camel back. I had already tried out the camels. It was an acquired skill, I found. Clinging on tended to rub the skin from my knees. Still it was easier than walking and at least we should be able to cover more ground. Feeling rather like Beau Geste, I set off on the patrol. At about mid-day our tracker pointed out some fresh tracks in the sand, which he said were made by the recent passing of a group of Merille. Now that I was faced with the prospect of shooting down the members of an armed gang without giving them the benefit of a trial I began to be a bit dubious about the enormity of the task. If they were shooting at us I should have no hesitation in killing as many as was necessary, but to act as Judge, Jury and Executioner, merely because they were carrying firearms went against the grain. An hour later, our quarry were sighted. Eight in number, all armed and on foot. The patrol broke into a trot. I very nearly fell of my mount. We had not yet been spotted. When we were about 600 yards distant I ordered a volley to be fired into the air. If they replied to the fire I was prepared to go ahead and shoot them down. In the event, and much to my surprise, they dropped their guns and put their hands into the air. We rode up to the group and dismounted. On checking the rifles I found that only one was loaded. The group had, fortuitously, practically run out of ammunition otherwise, no doubt, blood would have been spilled. Two of the group were recognised by members of my patrol as being the sons of the Merille Chief Tappo. All of the group were now arrested and escorted back to Namaraputh.

A surprise awaited me on my return to the fort. The Maskini fishermen had called, bringing with them not the hoped for fish, but half-a-dozen eggs. These would make a welcome change of diet, so I boiled a couple for my supper. I notice that they were a bit longer in shape than most hen eggs but thought nothing of this. I opened up the top of the first one and spooned out the contents. Delicious. A most pleasant change from the pineapple and condensed milk. I opened the second egg. Curled up inside was a perfectly formed boiled crocodile. I finished my meal with pineapple and condensed milk!

The message I had sent to Lokitaung on my return from the patrol had a remarkable effect. Three hours later, a lorry arrived at the fort to collect the prisoners. Not one of the police vehicles as these were still undergoing repair, but one of the Admin lorries, supplied by courtesy of Eric Fox. I lost no time in packing my safari kit and climbing aboard. I was just in time to avoid the nightly onslaught of the mosquitoes. I was more than glad to shake the dust of Namaraputh from my feet. Even the thought of adding to my collection of croc skins didn't tempt me to prolong my stay a moment longer than necessary.

CHAPTER 18

A few weeks after the arrest of the armed band of Merille, we were delighted to be provided with a Land Rover to ease our reliance on the police lorries. This had the added advantage releasing the Asian mechanic and the lorry drivers for other duties, since Lofty and I would be responsible for driving our new vehicle ourselves. On journeys where little or no equipment or men needed to be transported the Land Rover would be adequate. On such trips we stood far less chance of being marooned out at Namaraputh or any of the other forts. Our situation was thereby greatly improved.

Shortly after this, Lofty had to go off on the monthly pay and ration safari. Because of the bulk of the provisions to be carried he had to take one of the lorries. This left me with the Land Rover. As luck would have it, shortly after Lofty's departure a signal arrived from Sub-Inspector Balinda at Lodwar. 'We are having problems with Mr Whitehouse', said the message. 'Please come to Lodwar to assist.' Without further ado I set off for Lodwar. There seemed little point in leaving Kesi behind with nothing to do, so I took him in the back of the Land Rover along with Barney and my safari kit. I anticipated that, whatever the problem was, a couple of days in Lodwar would be sufficient to sort it out.

On my arrival I was amazed to see the difference which had taken place at the Mau-mau encampment. A vast area had been fenced off, below the hill on which the *boma* stood, by the erection of a double fence constructed of posts driven into the ground at intervals of 12 to 15 feet, to which barbed wire was fixed at close intervals. The area so enclosed was divided into long sections by the provision of further double fences of similar construction. Each section was about 30-yards wide and contained numerous long huts constructed of corrugated iron. Latrine and ablution blocks stood nearby. The Mau-mau detainees clustered around the huts or sat on the ground nearby. Guards patrolled the lanes formed between each section by the double fences. On the bluff overlooking the encampment, about 30-yards from the *boma* a neat lookout point had been constructed of brick and concrete, with a *makuti* roof. In this a machine gun was mounted in prominent view of the prisoners. I drove up to the lookout point, which I saw was manned by one of the Uganda constables. As I got out of the Land Rover, Sub-Inspector Balinda appeared from nearby. He approached and saluted. 'What's the problem?' I enquired. 'It's Mr Whitehouse', he said. He's arrested two constables, who were on guard duty for not saluting him!' I could hardly believe this. 'Are you sure of the facts?', I said. 'Were there no other circumstances to cause him to take this action?' 'No sir. I have had words with him, and he told me that if I interfered or released the men, he would have me arrested as well.' Fuming I went to Whitehouse's office and threw the door open. No sign of him. David Sharp came out of his office. 'Where's Whitehouse?', I said. If you are referring to the D.C. it's Mr Whitehouse. He gone out for the day', he said. I turned to Sub-Inspector Balinda. 'I'll have a word with the two constables', I said. We went to the cell block where the two were detained. David Sharp followed along behind. The two constables stood up as I approached. 'What are you doing in there?', I said. 'The D.C. placed us under arrest for not saluting him', was the reply. 'Any reason for not saluting him?', I enquired. 'No sir. It's just that he wasn't in uniform so we didn't think it was necessary.' 'Keys', I said. Sub-Inspector Balinda fetched them. I opened the lock and beckoned the two constables out. 'You can't do this', said David Sharp. The D.C. will be furious.' 'Well he can be furious with me if he likes', I said. 'I shall be spending a few days here to sort things out with Whitehouse. Meantime I shall require somewhere to sleep. 'Well, you can't have the Rest House', said David, 'It's booked.' I turned to Sub-Inspector Balinda. 'Will you arrange to get my tent erected under the trees down by the river', I said. I then drove down to find a suitable site about half-a-mile from the *boma*. Having sorted out my tent to my satisfaction plus another small tent for Kesi, I walked up to the newly-erected house where the prison officer was now installed. He came to the door at my approach. Paddy McKinney was of medium height, and stout build. He beamed at me in greeting. 'Come along in', he said. 'Splendid to see a different face. I'm fed up with the ones I see around here.' Over a glass of ice cold beer he poured out his woes to me. Whitehouse was continually interfering in the running of the prison. 'Time someone put him in his place!', he said. I told him the reason for my visit. 'I propose sorting him out', I said. 'Well watch him. He's a nasty bastard', said Paddy.

Sub-Inspector Balinda came to my tent during the evening. Over a glass of beer he told me of the problems Whitehouse was causing. The Uganda contingent were of course living in tents in conditions of great discomfort. Keeping their uniforms and equipment clean and smart in these circumstances was most difficult. If Whitehouse saw them down at the *dukas* he made a point of criticising their appearance in front of the local tribesmen. Anything he could do to be difficult he was happy to do. The men were almost at the point of mutiny. It had become a well-known fact that Whitehouse was a practising homosexual, which in itself was a serious offence. He slept with his houseboy and insisted that he be buggered by the boy each night. Thus he had forfeited any respect which the police might have had for him. I decided that now was as good a time as any to have a chat with Whitehouse. I made my way to his house and was met by the houseboy. On my enquiring if Whitehouse was in he informed me that he had gone to his office. I made my way there and knocked at the door. 'Come', said a voice from within. I went in. Whitehouse sat at his desk. He looked up as I entered. 'Ah. Beaden', he said, 'I wanted to have a word with you. What do you mean by releasing the two prisoners?' 'It's about my two men that I have come to see you', I said, trying to contain my anger. 'Might I enquire why you arrested them?' 'Well, they didn't salute me', he replied. 'Actually, I'm not sure that you are entitled to be saluted', I said. 'Had you been in uniform you might have been, but you weren't. In any case, even had you been entitled to a salute, failure to give you one would be classed as a minor disciplinary offence, certainly not one which would empower you to arrest them.' Whitehouse glared at me, his mouth dropping open. 'Now an offence which does carry a power of arrest is that of false imprisonment, which it seems has been committed by you! How would you like it if I arrested you now and stuck you in the cell for the night? Your houseboy might enjoy a night off from what I hear too.' Whitehouse's face paled. 'You couldn't do that. I'm the D.C.', he said. 'Don't try me too far or I might', I said. 'Now I want to tell you a thing or two. These men have been sent here to assist the Kenya police during the present emergency, as have I. They are living in most trying conditions with no comforts whatever. Sub-Inspector Balinda is an efficient officer and is able to carry out his duties without your interference. I shall thank you in future to leave my men alone to get on with their job without the constant chivvying from you and your staff. I hope I make myself clear.' I turned to leave the office. 'Thank you for your open discussion', said Whitehouse, 'I'll make sure there's no further problem.'

The following morning Kesi brought my morning tea. I started to get dressed. It had by now become a habit to knock out my sandals before putting them on. Nothing had ever dropped out, however. This time was different. Out dropped a small yellow scorpion. I quickly crushed it. These little ones, I had been told, were the worst of the lot. Their sting was as deadly as the bite of some snakes. It was evident from the tracks in the sand that the tree covered area around the river was infested with the creatures.

I spent the morning in Lodwar trying to cheer up the Uganda contingent. During the afternoon I was invited by Paddy to be present at a punishment session. It was the first I had heard of these. Apparently, when the prisoners appeared before the magistrate in connection with their Mau-mau activities they were sentenced to be detained for an indefinite period. They were usually sentenced to corporal punishment as well. Anything from six to 30 strokes of a cane on the buttocks. I wondered if this would be effective as a punishment for grown men. Anyway, it was laid down in the prison regulations that an officer and the prison doctor should be present during the beating. There were six newly-arrived prisoners to be dealt with and they were brought out one at a time. The prison sergeant stood with his cane, a length of rattan about four-feet long. The prisoner had his shorts removed and was placed over a long bench. Warders held his hands and feet and a wet cloth was placed over the buttocks. The caning commenced, six from each side. A few of the prisoners were able to keep quiet but most of them were screaming at the end of the punishment. The cane was replaced several times as it split at the end. At the end of each caning the cloth over the buttocks had been split by the force of the blows, and the skin underneath was a mass of bleeding weals. At the conclusion of each man's punishment, he was examined by the Asian doctor, and taken to the nearby building being used as a temporary hospital. Not the most enjoyable experience I've ever had, but I salvaged my feelings with the knowledge of the sub-human behaviour of these people. Their diabolical cruelty in the manner in which they murdered any Europeans unfortunate enough to fall into their hands. The disemboweling of cattle and sheep on the European farms. The hanging and disembowelling of pet dogs and cats. Raiding and killing any villagers who would not take their oaths. Ripping the living foetuses from pregnant women and eating parts of them in the course of their oaths.

In the evening Paddy McKinney invited me to his house for a curry. It was superb. A multitude of side-plates contained everything I could think of, chopped pineapple, tomato, cheese, cucumber, groundnuts, even sardines. Goat meat was the only flesh available, but somehow he had managed to make it so tender that it fell apart. Very different to the usual goat flesh which I had tried in Lokitaung, which was so tough that it was practically impossible to chew. The curry was so hot that the sweat started to drip from every pore. I noticed that Paddy was prepared for this. He had donned a *kikoi*, a lightweight cloth which was wrapped around the waist. He wore nothing else but wrapped a bath towel around his neck to soak up the sweat. As the sweat poured out he replaced it with beer. 'You've got a bloody good cook', I gasped. 'No, not really', he said, 'I make the curry myself.' Paddy, it turned out, was a member of the Nairobi Curry Club, and had learned his art from experts.

At daybreak the following morning I was aroused by the sound of the 'Alarm' being blown on the bugle. 'What the hell was going on.' I leaped from my bed and dressed rapidly. Within two minutes I was in the Land Rover and heading for the *boma*. I went to the constable on duty at the machine-gun post. 'Where's the trouble', I said. 'Down at the prison', he replied. I drove down there. Sub-Inspector Balinda had just arrived and was being briefed by one of the guards. He turned to me. 'Sir, the prisoners have seized two of the constables and are beating them in the compound.' By now it was light enough to see what was going on. The trouble was fortunately confined to one section only, but I felt sure that if it was not nipped in the bud rapidly we should be faced with a massed breakout and possibly a massacre. By now the entire Uganda contingent had arrived. I was startled to see the D.C's truck, with Whitehouse at the wheel, speed past us and out on to the road leading to Lake Rudolf at Ferguson's Gulf, where his retreat had been built. Whitehouse was evidently not going to take any chances on being involved in the massacre.

The two constables who had been seized had fortunately been unarmed, so the prisoners had not managed to get hold of any rifles. The two were cowering against the barbed wire fence trying to escape the blows which were being rained upon them. Clearly the situation had to be rectified without delay. I gave the order to load the rifles. 'I am going inside', I told Balinda. 'You will remain outside with your men. If there is any attempt to seize me, you will open fire, shooting to kill. Try not to hit me', I added. So saying I took a riot baton in my right hand and my revolver in the left, and entered the compound. I rushed at the group holding the constables, flailing the riot baton as I went. I managed to break several heads of those not quick enough to get out of my way. The rest fled. Had there been any resistance, I was quite prepared to shoot them down. The constables staggered to their feet and made their way to the gate. I followed. 'Now', I said, 'bring me the camp leaders.' Three surly-looking captives were brought to me half-an-hour later. I told them in no uncertain terms that any further trouble of this sort would almost certainly result in some of their number getting killed. Rations for that section would be cut for two days and the guilty men would be sorted out and severely punished. On my way back to my camp I met Paddy McKinney. He hadn't even heard the alarm. On later reflection I thought that my impetuous action in entering the trouble area was probably unwise. It could have led to unfortunate consequences. However, in the event, it had turned out well enough.

To hammer home the lesson which the prisoners had been taught in the mornings encounter I decided to fire a few bursts from the machine gun over the top of the encampment, into the side of the hill 1,000 yards away. Going to the machine-gun emplacement I found that a belt of 50 rounds was already loaded in the gun. I fired this off in three long bursts into the hillside. The prisoners below ran for cover. I gave orders for the gun to be stripped, cleaned and reloaded. As I was leaving the emplacement, David Sharp poked his face round the edge of his door. 'What's going on?', he shouted. 'Just showing them that it might be unwise to repeat this mornings performance',' I replied. 'You shouldn't fire that without consulting me', he yelled. 'I shall report you to the D.C. when he gets back.' 'You do that', I said. 'When I want your advice on how to do my job, I'll ask for it!' I must give David his due. After thinking matters over for about an hour he sought me out and apologised for his remarks.

During the afternoon a fresh batch of detainees were expected. The open plain beyond the detainees encampment, between it and the volcanic outcrops had been cleared of obstructions and an airstrip had been constructed. At about 3 o'clock, I took Paddy McKinney in the Land Rover and we drove down to the landing strip. A group of guards, consisting of newly-recruited warders and part of my Uganda police detachment was already in attendance. Shortly afterwards, to the south, the roar of an aircraft was heard. A twin-engined D.C.10. then appeared and, after circling the airstrip, came in to land. The assembled guards made their way to the plane and a group of about 30 handcuffed and very airsick Kikuyu prisoners stumbled to the ground. After their handcuffs had been removed the prisoners were marched, at the double, over to the nearby volcanic outcrop. Here, each one was made to pick up a boulder and then run with it to a building site near the encampment, where a new hospital was being constructed. This, Paddy informed me, was the method of greeting all the new arrivals. Prison labour was being used in the construction of the hospital, and during the day, gangs of prisoners and their warders, could be seen running backwards and forwards between the hill and the construction site, carrying rocks. I thought it a bit hard on the warders and police constables who had the weight of their uniforms and rifles to cart around with them on both trips.

After an eventful day, I joined Paddy for a further expedition into the delights of his curry. This time I had followed his example and dressed, or rather undressed, for the occasion. From one of the nearby *dukas*, I had obtained a highly coloured *kikoi*, which I wrapped around my waist, held in position by the belt from which hung my revolver. One of my somewhat worn towels completed the ensemble. I must say that it was a most comfortable outfit for the occasion. At the conclusion of the evening, after consuming more curry and beer than was wise, I staggered somewhat unsteadily to the Land Rover and made my way to the camp. One great advantage of the *kikoi* I found, was that it was unnecessary to get undressed at the conclusion of a boozy evening.

The following morning I was awakened with my usual cup of tea. I must admit to having something of a hangover. I staggered from bed and got dressed, remembering to knock out my shoes. What I didn't do was to pay sufficient attention to my other clothing. I was fully dressed when I suddenly felt a terrific pain on the calf of my left leg. Glancing down I was in time to see one of the little yellow scorpions drop from my leg onto the floor. I quickly stamped on it, but the damage was done. The little bugger must have been caught up in my shorts. I could only thank my guardian angel that it had not caught me in a much more vulnerable part. The pain was intense and my leg was already beginning to swell around the wound. I quickly got out a fresh razor blade from my toilet gear and made a deep slash across the sting, about an inch in length. I'm not sure which was the more painful, the sting or the cut. I pressed the wound and allowed a fair amount of blood to escape. I don't know if this action was beneficial or not, but I had read that this was what to do in the event of a snake bite, so I hoped for the best. Then, wrapping a wet towel around the wound, I got into the Land Rover and, with some difficulty, drove to the wooden building where the prison doctor was housed. After cleaning up the wound he dressed it and gave me a couple of injections. My leg by this time had started to swell and was very painful. With some difficulty I drove round to Paddy's house. He was having his breakfast on my arrival. On hearing of my unfortunate accident he insisted that I move my gear up to his house where he could keep an eye on me. He had only one bedroom, but during the day I stretched out on his settee, and at night my camp bed was placed on the floor of the lounge. I spent the next couple of days with Paddy, by which time my leg had reduced to its normal size and, although still sore, I felt that I was fit to make the return journey to Lokitaung.

On our arrival at Lokitaung I was greeted by a very relieved Lofty. He was also very happy to see the return of Kesi since he was no great shakes at the art of catering. I related the events which had taken place during my trip to Lodwar. He was full of enthusiasm at the manner in which Whitehouse had been dealt with, but when I told him of the incident with the scorpion he was less so. 'Bloody man must have put a hex on you', he commented.

The beginning of March saw the commencement of the rains. These only lasted a short time in Turkana, but were especially violent in intensity. The river running through the gorge was a raging torrent for short periods and the way to the forts became completely impassable for several weeks. The cataract, roaring by a few yards from our house, was most impressive. At times the whole building shook with the impact of the torrent. Fortunately, the onset of the rain had brought an end to the raids and incursions by the Merille tribesmen. It also meant that it was practically impossible to make our usual safaris to check on the day-to-day running of the forts. The pay safari at the end of the month had to be made by a light aircraft. Neither Lofty not myself went on this as Murdoch Mackenzie decided that this was one which he would do. I regretted being unable to take a trip in this plane as I feel sure that a flight over Lake Rudolf would have been the trip of a lifetime.

At about this time we had two new arrivals. First was that of Inspector Ryan. As a result of a crash recruitment program, a number of new Inspectors had entered the Kenya force from the U.K. Ryan was not one of these but he had been replaced at his previous unit by one and thereby released to take up a posting to Turkana. Clearly it would not be too long before we should all be returning to Uganda. The other arrival was Superintendent Hutchins who arrived to replace Murdoch Mackenzie, who was due for U.K. leave. The recruitment programme had also included a large increase in the numbers of rank-and-file police into the Kenya force. These were now completing their initial training and being sent to their units. A number of the original police who had left Lokitaung at the outbreak of the Emergency now started to return. Gradually the Uganda contingent started to be brought in from the forts. Those who had been unfortunate enough to have been stationed at Namaraputh were particularly overjoyed at being able to return to the comparative comfort of the township, and set about relating the lurid details of their sojourn. It was finally decided that the entire Uganda contingent should be transferred to Lodwar, where there was still something of a shortage of guards for the rapidly enlarging population of detainees. It was with mixed feelings that Lofty and I packed and vacated the old building which had been our home for the past six months. At least it was been bricks and mortar. Now we were to be accommodated under canvas until our return to Uganda.

In the event we made ourselves quite comfortable at our riverine camp. Each of us had a large tent, 'officers for the use of.' Kesi had his tent nearby and, after my unfortunate experience we were all exceptionally careful in looking out for the scorpions and other creepy-crawlies of which there were multitudes. We had a reasonably easy existence during our stay here and I became quite expert at preparing curry under Paddy's watchful eye. We made frequent use of the pool, except Paddy who, I was surprised to find, was unable to swim. Being reasonably proficient in this, I took it upon myself to teach him and in a couple of weeks had him giving a good imitation of a hippopotamus. The Land Rover came in very handy and we were able to make trips to the west in the direction of north Karamoja, where the countryside was far more pleasant. Several of Jomo Kenyatta's other henchmen were being held in this area in varying degrees of discomfort. During this period Whitehouse left us severely alone, though his dog tried his luck with Barney once more and got badly savaged in the process.

One day Paddy informed us that a prisoner had escaped from one of the working parties. What he had hoped to gain was difficult to assess. The surrounding terrain was hardly friendly and he would have to make his way through some 200 miles of desert and scrub before making any contact with his friends. Paddy seemed not the least put out. 'I've passed the word to the local chiefs', he said. 'He'll be brought in within a couple of days, dead or alive.' Sure enough, the following day a very chastened looking Kikuyu was dragged back into Lodwar by a couple of Turkana tribesmen. He had been found less than six miles away. Paddy made quite a ceremony of returning him to the prison compound. The two captors were formally thanked in full view of the assembled detainees, and presented with a one hundredweight sack of sugar. 'This is for bringing him back alive', he said. 'Had you brought him back dead you would have been given two sacks.' We had no further escapes reported, at least, not during the remainder of our stay in Lodwar.

One of the constant threats to our existence at our camp was the number of snakes which shared our environment. Most of these were tree snakes and cobras which I was continually having to kill when they came into the camp area. There were also a large number of small black vipers which buried themselves in the sand with just their noses sticking out. These could be quite dangerous if stepped on so, somewhat unwillingly, while we were in the camp area, we both took to wearing calf-length leather mosquito boots, which were sufficiently thick to absorb any bites.

A letter arrived from police headquarters, Kampala. It contained two excellent pieces of news. The first was that our time was up. We were to return to Uganda on 24th April. Lofty was going back to the P.S.U. at Bombo. I was to return to Karamoja. The second piece of information was even better. It had been decided that all officers who had been seconded to Kenya would receive an upgraded allowance back-dated to their original date of departure. Instead of the Shs 12/- which we had been claiming, the night-allowance had been increased to Shs 35/-. Clearly this decision had been made for the benefit of the officers who had been sent to the more civilised areas of Kenya, where the cost of living in hotels must have been a great strain on their resources. However, they could hardly differentiate between them and us, so we had the benefit, even though it had cost us practically nothing to live in Turkana. I did a quick calculation. I had an additional sum getting on for £250 coming my way. This, in addition to the £200 which I had received for the crocodile skins, would make me a rich man! I should be able to pay off my car loan straight away! Any mileage allowance would be clear profit. What about Pearman? It seemed that he was still in Moroto. I certainly didn't fancy working with him again. I should have to apply for a transfer!

The great day dawned. Out of the dust storm which daily blighted our lives, appeared four lorries emblazoned with the Uganda Police badge. It was too late in the day for an immediate start, but a great celebration commenced among the Uganda contingent. Early the following morning we clambered aboard the lorries and took our departure. Paddy and the two D.Os were there to see us off. Whitehouse remained in his office, no doubt celebrating our departure in his own way. He and his dog both had plenty to remember us by!

It was about 4 p.m. by the time we arrived in Moroto. We were greeted by a flood of wives and children who swarmed from the police lines to greet the returning heroes. Overnight accommodation was found for the policemen, while Lofty and I made our way to my house. We had no sooner reached it when a beaming Tom Hinett arrived bringing Randy and pumping my hand in welcome. Randy was ecstatic in her welcome, both for myself and Kesi, but especially for Barney, who greeted her with stolid good humour. In the absence of any provisions in my larder Lofty and I were invited round to Tom's house for a meal. I was pleased to note that my car was in good order in my garage. Tom had even kept the battery charged during my absence. If Pearman was aware of my return he didn't indicate it by coming to see me. Possibly he was no more keen on renewing our acquaintanceship than I was. Peter Oades, who had taken my place was, however, more forthcoming. He turned up at Tom's house during the evening and gave us his opinion of working with Pearman. He was hoping that, with my return, he would be able to leave for Kampala once more. I, in turn, was hoping that I would now be able to leave immediately for my long-delayed local leave at Mombasa. In this, however, we were both to be disappointed. Early the following morning I took Lofty down to the police station, where the police lorries were fueled up and ready to leave. By 7 a.m. to the accompaniment of much tooting of horns and shouted farewells, the Bombo contingent were on their way. The Turkana episode was, once and for all, at an end.

I entered my office and looked around. All was much as it had been when I left. I wondered what sort of reception I was going to get when Pearman arrived at the police station. I could foresee a flaming row in the offing. Possibly I should have to give him a bloody good hiding. As I was perusing a pile of investigation files which sat on my desk, (now the responsibility of Peter Oades I was pleased to note,) the signals constable came in with a message. It was from the police post at Nabilatuk. Its content was grim. A major raid had been carried out by the Suk on a village about four miles from the police post. Several people had been speared and some 2,000 cattle had been stolen. A party of Karamajong together with Ekapalon Nanyiro and the government agent Lorika had set out in pursuit and had caught up with the rearguard of the raiding party. In the ensuing battle, both Lorika and Nanyiro had been speared to death, together with a number of the Karamajong party. The remainder of the outnumbered Karamajong had fled.

The killing of the two major personalities of Upe County could only result in the most serious of repercussions. It was not difficult to imagine what the reaction of the Karamajong was going to be to this. For some years, the relations between the two tribes had simmered gently, with the occasional minor raid by one side or the other, resulting in the odd few spear-bloodings. This situation had been more or less acceptable to both sides. Now, however, the case was altered. Killing the two most prominent individuals, plus a number of other rank-and-file tribesmen, and accompanied by the theft of a vast number of cattle was, without doubt, going to lead to the outbreak of civil war.

Taking the signal with me I went up to see Sandy Field. He was still at his house, it not yet being time to go to the office. After welcoming me back from the wilds and offering me a cup of coffee, he read the message. 'G-g-good God', he exclaimed. 'Lorika and Nanyiro killed. The bastards. This is serious. Has Pearman seen this yet?' I replied in the negative. 'We'd better go and have a word with him', he said. By this time it was turned 8 o'clock so Sandy and I went down to the police station where Pearman had just arrived. As I had expected, he tried to ignore my presence. I handed him the message. After reading it through he eventually grasped the enormity of the situation and started to panic. 'You had better get out to Nabilatuk and stop any follow-up party', he said. 'Yes, I'll do that', I replied, 'but there are a number of other things which must be done immediately.' 'What, for instance?', he enquired. 'First, a message to Karita. Get them out on patrol around Loporokocho. It's just possible that they may yet be able to intercept the raiders. Second, we shall want massive reinforcements to Karita, Amudat and Nabilatuk. Unless I am very much mistaken this is going to mean a major civil war between the two tribes. We don't have anywhere near enough personnel to handle this so we must ask headquarters to supply the additional men from the Police Service Unit at Bombo. Thirdly, we are going to have to ask Gareth to come out with me to examine the bodies. Clearly there are too many of them lying out in the bush to warrant bringing them all back to Moroto for autopsy.' Pearman's mouth dropped open. I had the impression that it was only the presence of Sandy Field which prevented him from telling me that it was he who would make whatever decisions were needed to handle the situation. As it was he was unable, on the spur of the moment, to think of a better line of action so he had to agree. At this time Peter Oades arrived and was put in the picture. 'Right', I said, 'I'm going home to start getting my safari gear together again. I'll leave you to get on with sending the signals.' I left the office wondering if Lofty Wells and his merry men would be able to get as far as Bombo before they had to come back to Karamoja.

Tom Hinett was very understanding when I explained to him that I was once again away into the bush. I was still hopeful of eventually getting my local leave, but it was clearly not going to be for a while yet. Once again he agreed to look after Randy for me. Kesi for once looked down his nose a bit when I told him that we were off into the bush again. After all, he had yet to properly celebrate his return from the last period of danger and discomfort. However, he regained his good spirits soon enough when I told him that there would be an extra Shs 5/- a month in it for him, assuming that we were out that long. It was clear that I was going to need the Land Rover for this expedition and somewhat grudgingly Pearman agreed to this. 'I would suggest that you signal headquarters and request that a further couple of Land Rovers be supplied. You will need one here to replace the one I'm taking, and a second one for whoever is sent up with the P.S.U.' was my parting shot.

Since I should not be returning to Moroto in the foreseeable future, Gareth made the trip to Nabilatuk in his own car. Once there we set off in the Land Rover, together with four constables and one of the tribesmen who had been present, to visit the scene of the battle. Flocks of vultures and marabou storks circling overhead indicated the location of the fight. Some of the bodies had been covered with tree branches fairly soon after the battle had ceased, when reinforcements had arrived. Others had been left unprotected. The bodies, we found, were scattered over a distance of half-a-mile, where some of the outnumbered Karamajong had tried, unsuccessfully, to escape. None were intact, however. The covering of branches had been insufficient to protect them to any great degree. Nanyiro and Lorika were identified by a few articles of torn clothing. Some of the other tribesmen were identified to us by the remains of the clay dressing on their hair. A total of 12 bodies were found, of whom three were Suk and the remainder Karamajong. While Gareth got down to the business of deciding what were the very obvious causes of death, I interrogated the tribesman who had been present. Nanyiro, he told me, had been armed with a double-barrelled shotgun. Lorika had been unarmed, the other tribesmen had carried their spears only. On sighting the rearguard, Nanyiro had called upon them to stop and had pointed the shotgun in their direction. Undeterred by this, about 30 of the Suk tribesmen had approached in a threatening manner, armed with bows and arrows, spears and shields. Seeing that an attack was imminent, Nanyiro had fired one shot over their heads. This had caused them to stop but, finding that none of them had been hurt they then rushed the follow-up party. Nanyiro had then fired his one remaining cartridge hitting several of the Suk, before being overwhelmed, when he and Lorika were speared to death. The Karamajong had then engaged the Suk in hand-to-hand fighting but, being heavily outnumbered, had finally retreated after the loss of a number of their party. Many more had been wounded in the battle and were at the dispensary at Nabilatuk.

Gareth completed what can only have been, a very cursory examination, and I photographed each body as it lay. We returned to Nabilatuk. A huge gathering of tribesmen was taking place. My first job clearly was to address these in an attempt to defuse the situation. This I did to the best of my ability. Feelings, as I had anticipated, were running very high and I felt it likely that too much pressure at this time might put my own life and that of my few policemen at risk. I contented myself with stressing that it was the work of the government, in the form of the police, of whom many more were on the way, to deal with the outrage that had taken place, not the tribesmen themselves, and that any warlike action by them would be severely dealt with. There was a lot of dissatisfied muttering at this, but I was glad to see the crowd begin to melt away. I was quite sure, however, that revenge attacks would follow as surely as night follows day. I could only hope that we should be reinforced pretty damn quick.

Some of the survivors of the battle had sustained nasty-looking spear wounds but had already been treated at the local dispensary. Gareth reckoned that with a bit of luck they would survive. He returned to Moroto and I spent the rest of the day recording statements from the other tribesmen who had been present at the battle. All confirmed the details given by the first witness. Nanyiro's shotgun was missing and had presumably been taken by the raiders.

The following morning I received a signal. Sixty men from the P.S.U. were on their way under the command of John Docherty, whom I had met at the Police Training School, and who had now reached the rank of Superintendent. I was glad in a way that Lofty Wells and his detachment were not on their way back. After Turkana, I felt they all needed a break. I spent the day patrolling as far as possible into and beyond the area where the battle had taken place. The bodies had by now disappeared, apart from a few fragments of bone, having been disposed of by the vultures and hyenas.

News reached me the following morning that, despite my threats to the assembled tribesmen of punishment should they carry out any revenge attack, such an attack had nonetheless taken place on a *manyatta* not far from Katabok. Six Suk, including two women and three children, had been killed and 40 head of cattle stolen. Things were warming up! I was glad when, at mid-day the first reinforcements arrived. Twenty men under the control of Head Constable Opondo turned up and established a tented camp near the police post. Opondo was a Jaluo tribesman, very thin in build and around six-feet-seven inches tall. I felt quite dwarfed by him. My instructions now were to head for Amudat where John Docherty had established his headquarters. I was more than pleased that I should be working with John in this situation. He had struck me as being a reliable individual, unlikely to panic in a crisis and someone with whom I could discuss a situation and, hopefully, reach a sound course of action.

It was dark by the time I reached Amudat. John had already set up camp and my own tent was soon erected. I joined him at the camp fire for a discussion and to work out a plan of campaign. Transport and mobility was clearly going to be the most important aspect of our operation. John had his own car plus a Land Rover. He suggested that I return to Moroto on the following day to collect my car, plus the police driver for my Land Rover. I should then be based at Karita and responsible for controlling the raiding from that area by making frequent mobile patrols. He would do the same from Amudat to cover the Katabok and Namalu areas. These would be reinforced by more prolonged foot patrols of heavily-armed police. Loporokocho would be re-opened by personnel from Karita and the area to the south of Kadam Mountain thereby covered as far as possible. One big advantage to all this was that I was to be granted an unlimited mileage allowance at full-rate and would be responsible for trips to Kitale to collect rations to supply the various units. Wow. I could foresee 'loads'a' money coming in my direction.

Early the following morning I set off for Moroto. I called at the police station and informed Pearman of the course of action which had been decided on. With great relish he then informed me that, since I would now be living in the bush for an unlimited period, and no longer under his command, that I should have to give up my house, which would be taken over officially by Peter Oades. The bastard. I suppose this was his petty way of trying to get back at me. I certainly didn't have time to spend in packing up my belongings, and I was not prepared to hand the job over to Pearman. I went off to see Tom Hinett, who willingly agreed to pack my property away and put it into store until I again needed it. I now collected my car and set off for Karita, followed by the Land Rover.

On my arrival I found that the police detachment of 20 constables and N.C.Os had already arrived and had set up their tents in the police compound. I ordered them to fall in and had a chat for ten minutes or so during which I outlined what would be their activities for the foreseeable future.

The police patrol which had been sent out to operate around Loporokocho had failed to intercept the returning raiders with the stolen cattle. Such a vast number of cattle must by now have been split up into smaller herds and scattered throughout the bush. It would be necessary to collect up the owners of the stolen beasts and take them out with the patrols in the hope that, sooner or later, some of the stolen animals would be identified and the thieves arrested. Meantime, I found that two Suk tribesmen had been arrested when they went to the local dispensary suffering from shotgun wounds. These I interrogated and was somewhat surprised when they readily admitted to having been part of the raiding party. They denied, however, having taken part in the subsequent killing of Lorika, Nanyiro and the others. They did however, let slip the names of two other tribesmen who had been present. Things were looking up.

The next couple of weeks passed quickly. Each day was spent patrolling the bush. As far as possible I used the Land Rover, but inevitably most of the patrols were on foot. On one memorable occasion my patrol unexpectedly encountered a large body of heavily-armed Suk tribesmen who were clearly embarking on a raid. Each of these carried a war shield and two spears. It was of course illegal to carry a shield. One spear was permitted but not two. I was now faced with a rather difficult decision. The war party numbered around 50 warriors. My party consisted of myself and five constables. If I took aggressive action and tried to forcibly seize the shields and spears I should almost certainly precipitate a fight in which I and my party would be wiped out. I was a bit loath to end up as a vulture's breakfast so, deciding that discretion was the better part of valour, I bent down and plucked a bunch of grass from the ground. Holding this above my head I approached the warrior who appeared to be in charge. Grass, I knew, to be a sign of peaceful intent. Fortunately, it was accepted as such and, grasping their shields and spears firmly the war party squatted on their haunches to hear what I had to say. 'Why are you carrying shields and two spears each?', I demanded. The elected spokesman replied, 'The Karamajong have raided our village, killed three people and driven off 20 cattle. We are following them to get our cattle back.' This was a fairly understandable reaction, but clearly it could not be allowed to continue. I then addressed the group in Swahili, of which most of them seemed to understand. 'This war was started by your people when Lorika and Nanyiro were killed. I will not tolerate any of you taking matters into your own hands to escalate the fighting. We have many policemen now throughout the area. Many more will come if needed. It is now our responsibility to investigate the killings and thefts, not yours. This we shall do whether you like it or not. If any of you are found in future carrying war shields you will be arrested and dealt with. Now, my men will take your names and you will return peacefully to the police post at Karita, where your statements regarding this latest raid on your village will be recorded and any other necessary action taken.' My bluff worked. The war party accompanied by my patrol made their way back to Karita. I breathed a sigh of relief, as I am sure did the men in my patrol. I couldn't help wondering if I should have been as successful had I been in a position to use *safi* (correct) Swahili. Few if any of the tribesmen would have understood me and the outcome might have been very different.

The interception of this war party certainly didn't bring a stop to the raiding and killing. If anything they were intensified over the following weeks. Large numbers of cattle changed hands at frequent intervals. The bodies lying in the bush became so prolific that it was no longer practicable for them to be examined by medical staff. As far as possible I viewed them myself and photographed them for future reference. Numbers of wounded tribesmen also came to my camp, in the hope of receiving treatment. My meagre first-aid kit was soon depleted and I met up with Gareth at Amudat and obtained fresh stocks. Bandages and penicillin powder were my main standby. Most of the wounded tribesmen were interrogated and arrested for taking part in the warfare. Eventually, only those who were really seriously injured presented themselves. One day two warriors were brought to me. One had received a spear through his upper arm. This was wrapped in a dirty piece of cloth. The other had a quite horrific injury. It appeared that a spear had been thrown at him. At the last moment he had seen it slicing towards his face and had thrown his head backwards in an effort to avoid the weapon. Instead, the spear had entered underneath the upper lip and, slicing upwards had removed the entire front of his face up to the forehead. His eyes were undamaged, but the flap containing his upper lip, one cheek and the complete nose had been opened up. As a first-aid measure his colleagues had pulled the flap back into position, securing it with half-a-dozen two-inch long thorns. Not a pretty sight. I decided to deal with this one first and got out my needle and cotton. After cleaning the wound up as far as possible, I dusted the area liberally with penicillin powder and stitched the face back into position. Throughout the procedure he made not a sound. I wanted to send him on to Moroto Hospital but he would have none of it. He wasn't going to take the risk of getting finished off in Karamajong territory. The second wounded warrior, having closely studied the treatment his friend had received at my hands decided that he wasn't going to submit to this. Both then departed for their homes. I was somewhat dubious about the outcome of this, but three weeks later the man with the face turned up at my camp. His wound had healed well. He would never be the prettiest ever, but at least he was alive. Unlike his friend with the spear wound in the arm. He had died within three days I was told.

Each day started with a sick parade. After my success with healing the various wounds presented to me, my reputation had improved by leaps and bounds. Now my policemen started turning up with various real and imaginary illnesses. Most of them complained of having malaria, the others had stomach upsets. At first I put them off duty for a couple of days, which seemed to do the trick. Eventually, however, with half my men lying around doing nothing, I decided that enough was enough. I had a good supply of mepacrin tablets, which were extremely bitter to the taste, also a large quantity of Epsom Salts. I took to crushing the mepacrin and mixing the powder with the Epsom Salts. A spoonful of this mixture dry, followed by a glass of water had miraculous results. The sick parade became practically non-existent overnight. The few who persevered were clearly genuinely sick and received appropriate treatment. Looking back, I suppose I was lucky that none of them perished. I might have been accused of manslaughter!

After the first couple of weeks at Karita, we were running short of rations. I was also almost out of the basic needs so I decided to make a trip into Kitale. John Docherty asked me to get him various bits and pieces, including plenty of fruit, which we both urgently needed. During his stay at Amudat he had been as active on his patrols as I had. I set off for the bright lights after lunch and by dusk was driving up to the hotel. The following morning I went to the local store and stocked up with sacks of *posho*, rice, salt and *matoke*. I left Kitale and returned to Amudat where I spent the night at John's camp.

Sporadic raiding still continued and it was decided that the possibility should be examined of establishing a police post between Nabilatuk and Loporokocho. One possible location to be considered was at a place called Lochuolongolomoi, where a permanent water supply existed, near a spur of Kadam Mountain. This was in the form of an extensive pool, fed by an underground spring which, no doubt, was fed from the mountain. After consulting with John, I undertook to make the journey from Loporokocho, a distance of some 30 miles across the bush. I hoped to be able to roughly map out the area during the journey and to this end obtained a small prismatic compass. The night prior to making this expedition I spent at Loporokocho, the half-dozen police who were permanently stationed there, plus my own police party, two guides and myself, crammed into the three aluminium rondavels which comprised the post. Early the following morning we wedged ourselves into the Land Rover and drove through the rough bush, determined to get as far as possible before starting our walk. In the event, we managed about five miles before coming to a deep ravine which took storm water from the mountain during the rains. After reconnoitering this for some distance, it became clear that this was as far as we were going to get. The rest of the journey would be on foot. Leaving the driver to make his way back to Karita we set off across the open countryside. Never had I seen so many animals. This was an area virtually untouched by humans. The only people who ever passed this way were the raiding parties going out on their murderous business or returning with the herds of stolen cattle. Great herds of kongoni and topi ranged in every direction. Buffalo, giraffe, zebra, grants gazelle, eland. A true garden of Eden. Several prides of lion stared at us as we passed but their lack of interest only indicated how well fed they were. I wondered where such vast numbers of animals could obtain their drinking water. There was no sign of any permanent water. Maybe they made the same trek that we were on, to Lochuolongolomoi, each time they wanted to slake their thirst. My police party each carried a water bottle containing about two pints of water. In the absence of any other supply, this was going to have to last us the full journey.

The morning began to warm up. At about 10 a.m. I called a halt for ten minutes and we sat under a convenient fig tree. As we set off again our two guides chattered to one another and we set off at right angles to our previous route. I thought that possibly we were going to be shown a water hole. The party followed eagerly. After a detour of about half-a-mile we came to a rocky outcrop on which grew a tree of a type I had not previously encountered. A sparse crop of fruit, the size of a small plum grew from the branches. Our guides swarmed up and started to pluck and eat the fruit. One or two of the policemen managed to clamber up and collected about a dozen of the fruit. By this time the entire crop had vanished. The guides had done quite well out of it. No one else had. I was given one of the ripe fruit. It was sweet, tasting of honey, a bit like a plum but with no stone. I thought it hardly worth the detour. Now, had there been a couple of pounds of fruit each it might have been worthwhile. We continued on our way, which now passed over an area of broken rock. Nearby, and stretching into the distance, were a range of volcanic outcrops. On enquiry, my guides told me that each of these had a name which identified them. None of them were marked on my map, and it struck me that any of them could be used as a lookout point. From the top of them a superb view of the surrounding countryside for many miles would be obtained. I made my way to the nearest outcrop. which was about 200 feet high. Leaving the guides and the police party below I made my way to the top. As I had thought, a wonderful vista opened up. The scattered herds could be seen in every direction. From a point like this, any raiders would be spotted from miles away. Looking towards Kadam I could just make out one of the trig points which had been erected on a summit by the early surveyors. I took a bearing on this, and then further bearings on three of the nearest volcanic outcrops. Making my way down, I enquired from the guides the names of the outcrops I had so recorded. We then headed towards the other outcrops and I climbed each in turn, taking bearings and noting down their names and approximate height. In this manner I was able to roughly map this area, fixing the positions of the outcrops by triangulation. At about 2 p.m. we stopped for a well-earned rest and a bite to eat. Apart from one or two sips of water, I had reserved my supply. I now treated myself to about half-a-pint. We had about a further ten miles to travel and four hours to do it before nightfall. Some of the constables were showing signs of distress and most of them had finished their water supply. The afternoon was oven-like. Not a breath of wind to relieve the heat. I was thankful that my recent stay in the deserts of Turkana had taught me the importance of conserving the water supply. With a bit of luck I should stay the course.

As dusk was falling we staggered up to the waterhole at Lochuolongolomoi. I was grateful to find that my driver had managed to make the round trip to Nabilatuk and had somehow driven across country with our tents and camping equipment. Even better, he had brought Kesi and Barney. I slaked my thirst with a cool bottle of beer and slumped into my chair at the side of the camp fire. I estimated that I had covered at least 35 miles during the day, 30 of these on foot.

During the night, our slumbers were frequently disturbed by the sounds of the herds of animals drinking nearby. From time to time, a thunderous roar would announce the arrival of the lions. Hyenas chuckled and gurgled over the remains of the kills. 'How splendid this is going to be for any police unit we station here.' I thought.

Chapter 19

Shortly after I returned to Karita, I received a letter from police headquarters. It was not entirely unexpected, but I thought that, in the circumstances, it was a bit unfair. Its content was to draw my attention to the fact that my two years probationary period was now up and, although I had passed the law examinations and the written Swahili, I still had not passed the oral Swahili. I was therefore now losing seniority to those who had passed these examinations and, unless I passed within the period of my initial tour of duty, my appointment would be terminated, in accordance with the current regulations.

I wrote a reply to this, pointing out the fact that my entire tour to date had been spent in Karamoja, mostly living in tented accommodation in the bush, where I had not the slightest chance of obtaining the tuition which I felt I needed to pass the one remaining examination. In the circumstances I felt I had no alternative but to apply for a transfer to Kampala or some other town where tuition might be available. Needless to say, I received an answer to this after a lengthy delay, to the effect that there was no one else available to fill the post which I was presently engaged in, but that consideration would be given to my request in due course. It reiterated the point that unless I passed the final examination, my appointment would be terminated. I carefully filed the correspondence in case, at some subsequent time, I needed to lodge an appeal with the Colonial Office.

The next Swahili examination was scheduled for August, less that two months away. I formally submitted my application to take this, as I had on the previous occasions. I also discussed the matter with John Docherty the next time I saw him. As a result, John started to give me tuition in the spoken language each time we met. John gave me an invaluable tip. 'Learn a bit of conversation and intersperse it with as many proverbs and phrases as you can. *Haraka, haraka, heina baraka*', he said. 'That doesn't mean Hark, hark, the dogs do bark. It means, Haste, haste, has no blessing, I'm sure you can easily insert that into your conversation. Here's another one for you: *Simba ngurumopo, michezi ni nani*. That means, 'Who stops to play about when the lion roars?' Describe the type of terrain in which you've been living. *Nchi iliokimonginyoka*. That means, Eroded land. I made a note of these words and phrases and many others, and learned them off by heart. Of course, I still used the same old Swahili in everyday use as I previously had. Otherwise no one would have known what I was talking about. However, gradually over the next few weeks, my conversation in *safi* Swahili improved. The examination was held in Soroti, and I took a day off to attend. I was reasonably happy with the conduct of the examination. I rather feel that a few words had been said to the examiner about the problems I had been experiencing. Anyway, he went to a great deal of trouble to put me at my ease. The conversation followed the course which John Docherty had predicted. Nothing was said directly to me at the conclusion of the examination, but I left with some degree of confidence. I was delighted to hear that this was not misplaced when, a few weeks later, I received a letter from headquarters informing me that I had now passed all of the examinations and was confirmed in my appointment and promoted to the rank of Assistant Superintendent! I had however lost three months seniority. I determined that, somehow, I would get this back!

While all this was going on, life in the bush continued much as it had previously. Each day saw heavily-armed police patrols setting off into the bush. Sometimes they took with them Karamajong owners of stolen cattle, and considerable success was achieved by these in identifying many beasts by means of brands and earmarks which had not been sufficiently disguised. I usually accompanied these patrols, either in the lorry with the main force, or travelling separately in the Land Rover. Generally, each patrol would be completed on foot. On one occasion I was driving across a dried-up river bed, about eight-feet deep. A drift had been cut across this to enable the vehicles to traverse the banks on each side. As I drove up the slope on the far side, my head came level with the surrounding ground. I saw a sudden movement and glancing round was confronted by a cobra, its head up and hood fully-expanded within a few inches of my face. Yells came from the policemen in the back as they ducked out of range. Then we were past the serpent. I couldn't have dodged the fangs if I had tried, had the snake decided to strike. Maybe it was as startled as I was at being suddenly confronted by a moving vehicle within a few inches of where it was basking in the sun.

A splendid piece of news filtered through. Pearman was

going on leave. He had been transferred from Moroto and who else but Lofty Wells had replaced him. Maybe I should be able to return to Moroto again at the end of the present emergency. I felt that I should have no problem working with Lofty again. However, Peter Oades was still there, so maybe I should have to go after all — considering I had already applied for a move!

The rainy season was with us again. Life under canvas for my detachment at Karita became very uncomfortable. The patrols also became difficult. Fortunately, the flood-water in the stream beds ran off very rapidly. Each day the rain would fall in a torrent for about an hour. The streams and rivers would rise, and drop just as rapidly. It was an interesting phenomena to watch as a dry stream bed gradually started with a trickle of water coming round the corner, gradually increasing in volume and carrying with it an assortment of debris left by previous floods. Within two hours the stream would, once again, be dry.

I had a note from Willie Hagstrom, inviting me to visit him. I found that he was working near Katabok, about 18 miles away. This could be reached either by going all the way round on the main road via Amudat, a distance of about 90 miles, or directly to it on a fairly rough track through the bush. I decided to take the direct route. After all, either of the two alternatives could become impassable should there be heavy rain. I did know, however, that there was only one dubious point on the bush track and that was within a mile of where Willie was camped. I set off at about 10 a.m. taking one constable with me and driving my own car as the Land Rover with its driver were off in the bush on patrol. We reached Willie's camp without incident. Fortunately, the stream a mile from his camp was quite dry and presented no problem, apart from the boulder-covered bed which bounced the car about somewhat. Willie greeted me with a beaming smile and invited me into his caravan trailer. I noticed that the linoleum covering the floor had been ripped to pieces. Willie explained the damage. He had found a baby warthog wandering in the bush some weeks earlier. An absolutely charming little creature, a tiny caricature of its ugly parent, from whom it had become separated. Anyway, Willie, being as soft a touch as myself, had rescued the little creature which had quickly become very tame. However, it had also rapidly developed little tusks and, the previous day had spent the entire morning, while Willie was outside working, in ripping up the linolium. Needless to say, the meal which Willie offered me was roast pork. It was delicious!

By 3 o'clock, the rain had started. I was a bit worried about negotiating the nearby stream and so took my leave and set off on the return journey. I seemed to have left it too late, however. There was already nearly 18-inches of water rushing down between the banks. I should have had no problem with the Land Rover of course, with its four-wheel drive and low-ratio option. It was a bit dicey with my car though. The main thing was to stop the water from running up into the exhaust system. I had prepared for just such an exigency as this by providing myself with a twelve-foot length of rubber pipe which I fitted over the exhaust and attached to the side of the car. Then, in low gear and revving the engine at a good speed, I drove into the water. Half-way across, one of the front wheels struck a boulder and the car came to an abrupt stop. 'How annoying!', I said, or words to that effect. I gave my instructions to the constable. 'Get out and run back to Bwana Hagstrom. Tell him I'm stuck and ask him to bring his lorry to pull me out.' The constable needed no second bidding. He was out and running. Meanwhile, somehow or other, I needed to keep the engine running. Once it stopped the water would flood back into the engine and do all sorts of damage. I sat in the driver's seat with my foot on the accelerator, watching the rising water. It was already well over my ankles. I hoped Willie wouldn't be too long or I might be washed away down stream. For some reason, I began to feel very strange. My head began to swim and I felt myself swaying in the seat. I took plenty of deep breaths in an attempt to retain consciousness. What the hell was happening? I heard the roar of an engine as Willie arrived behind me. Then darkness overtook me. I vaguely felt very wet and then I was lying on the stream bank. Willie told me later that I had only been unconscious for about ten minutes. He had arrived on the scene just as I had forced open the car door and fallen head first into the water. I suppose that at the last moment I had realised that it was the fumes from the car exhaust, blowing back into the vehicle that were causing the unpleasant symptoms I was experiencing. My first concern on recovering consciousness was for my car, but I was pleased to see that the water level was already falling and, with a bit of luck, no serious damage would have been done to it. Willie pulled it out of the water and left it on the bank to dry off. Then, helping me into the cab of his lorry we set off back to his camp. Back inside the caravan, I happened to catch sight of myself in a mirror. I was bright red. I should have made a very healthy-looking corpse.

I received a signal from headquarters. I was ordered to Kampala to compete in the East and West African Revolver Shooting competition. This was an annual event in which a team of four officers from each territory fired off at targets which were then sent in to London to be assessed. It was the first time I had been invited to take part in this and I considered it something of an honour to be chosen. Of course, I had fired off each year on the annual Revolver Course, but clearly my marks must have been considered fairly reasonable to be chosen for the team. I normally favoured a .38 Smith and Weston for everyday use. However, on my arrival in Kampala it was suggested that a .45 might be better since it made a bigger hole in the target and might hereby stand a better chance of cutting the line for a higher score. I spent a while on the day of the competition, practising with the heavier weapon. At first I didn't like it much. The recoil from the heavy charge caused the bullet to lift off target. However, once I got used to the weapon, I found that it had considerable advantage. I decided to stick with my .38 when out in the bush though. When the competition was fired, the other three competitors were Jack Bourne, Pip Bate and John Thompson, the O.C. of the Police Training School. Mine was not the best score. Neither was it the worst. By and large we had not done too badly. Well enough, in the event, to win the Cup. I eventually received a medal for being one of the winning team.

During my absence from Moroto a rather nasty incident had occurred. One of the many Suk prisoners remanded on a charge of murder had starved himself to death. Oddly, no one had noticed him getting thinner and thinner, until one morning he didn't come out of his cell and was found dead on the floor. This, of course, resulted in a major enquiry. Blame was eventually laid at the door of Dr Lubega, one of whose daily duties was to visit the prison and check on the health of all the prisoners. I couldn't help wondering though if he had not been made a scape-goat. As a result of the enquiry, it was recommended that a new prison be built to take the place of the old one, which really belonged in the dark ages. Now discussions were to be held to decide where the new building should be sited. I was invited to attend the meeting, since it was pointed out that I knew the area as well as anyone, and that the prison had been one of my responsibilities. During the discussion I put forward a strong argument that the new building should be sited to the east of Moroto Township, in the area nestling between two spurs of the mountain. This had the advantage of having a seasonal stream on each side of it, which would be useful, if dammed, to supply water for agricultural purposes. My suggestion was carried and Tom Hinett was forthwith set the task of constructing this major project.

The rains continued. It was now the middle of the rainy season. Fortunately, with the ground becoming more and more waterlogged, the raids had reduced in number and it was announced that a Judicial Enquiry would be held at Amudat, Karita and Nabilatuk, when witnesses from both sides would be called to give their evidence and a communal punishment inflicted to, hopefully, bring the matter to an end. Because of the difficulty in supplying the police unit at Loporokocho it was decided to close the post down until weather conditions improved. The Land Rover went out from Karita and collected all the equipment. The constables and N.C.O. followed on foot or on their bicycles. While they were on their way a particularly heavy downpour occurred. On reaching the river at Karita they were confronted by a raging torrent. On the far side they could see the lights of the police post through the driving rain. One of the constables, P.C. Obonyo decided that he wasn't going to hang about waiting for the water level to fall. He started to wade into the water. The river was about 25 yards wide at this point and the torrent was raging past like an express train. The corporal ordered him to get out of the water. 'I can swim this easily', said the P.C. These were the last words he was heard to speak. He was washed away down stream and out of sight. I was informed of the incident a few minutes later by a constable from Karita who had witnessed from our side what had happened. I immediately sent off search parties downstream to see if any trace could be found of P.C. Obonyo. By now, however, it was pitch dark. The following morning search parties were again sent out and P.C. Obonyo's body was found four miles downstream. He had already begun to bloat, but at least the vultures had not found him, as he was wedged under a pile of branches. The body was brought back to Karita and I sent it through to Moroto on the lorry. Gareth performed the autopsy which indicated that P.C. Obonyo's head had been bashed in on one of the rocks in the river bed before he had drowned. I took the opportunity of having a chat with the other police staff, in case any of them decided on playing silly buggers in the future.

Kesi reported to me at the end of the month. He had received a letter from his uncle to the effect that his father had died. Very inconsiderate of him I thought. He had decided to leave my employment forthwith and go back to Toro for a while. 'Bloody marvelous', I thought. 'I was really being left in the lurch. No possibility of getting another cook-houseboy while living in my present primitive conditions. Well, I had managed on my own in the past, I suppose I could do it again.' I paid Kesi the wages which were due, and sent him off to Amudat, from where he could get transport to Moroto and on to Kampala. I was sorry to see him go, especially since he had learned to make excellent bread, though I hadn't seen any of that since we had been living in the bush. I decided to make another trip to Kitale in the near future, since I might find a suitable servant there.

A few days after Kesi's departure I had a message from John Docherty. He had decided to visit me for a couple of days. I didn't want him to get the impression that I was unable to cope, foodwise, in the absence of a cook. I decided that the ubiquitous stew would do for the main meal. What about a sweet though. Then I had a rather brilliant idea. Treacle tart! I hadn't had one since my arrival in Africa. I got out the copy of *The Kenya Settlers' Cook Book* which I had purchased during one of my trips to Kitale. From this I got the recipe. Next I needed an oven. I decided to try out a suggestion which the book made. Hollow out a termite hill, and insert a paraffin *debi*, the front of which had been cut round to form a lid. Super idea! I found an empty paraffin *debi*, and a suitable termite hill nearby. Getting out my trenching tool I set to work. The termite mound would act as a natural chimney. I lit the fire and started making the pastry. Soon I had the treacle tart prepared. *The Kenya Settlers Cook Book* told me that I should need to bake the tart for 25 minutes in a hot oven. The fire was drawing well. A splendid roaring noise, with flames shooting out of the top.

I popped the tart into the paraffin *debi* and closed the lid. Three minutes later, I decided to have a quick look to make sure that everything was going O.K. The tart was already a dark brown in colour. Clearly it was already overdone. I whipped it out. It didn't look bad at all, but, cooked in three minutes? Could this be right. Well, the proof of the pudding is in the eating. It was a great success! John complimented me on my culinary skill. I must do this again. When I looked at the 'oven', however, I found that it had melted. The fire had got so hot that it had turned into a furnace.

The following week I made one of my occasional visits to Kitale to collect the rations. Here, after a visit to the local police station, the local fount of all knowledge, I was put in touch with a new cook who would be prepared to accompany me into the bush. He was a Kipsigis by tribe and had a totally unpronounceable name. So I christened him Oscar which was fairly close anyway. He didn't seem to mind particularly. On our return to camp I set him to work on a fairly simple meal. It was edible — just. But beggars can't be choosers.

The radio constable brought me a signal as I was having my breakfast. It was from Nabilatuk. 'P.C. Abinyi has tried to murder Head Constable Opondo by shooting at him with a .303 rifle. Please attend urgently.' I didn't stop to eat any more. Normally John Docherty would have dealt with this one, he being some 60 miles nearer to Nabilatuk. However, two days earlier he had gone to Kampala for a couple of days break with his wife Audrey. I was left in charge and would have to sort out, what looked like, a very unpleasant incident. I drove through to Nabilatuk, using my own car, and reached the police post by lunch time. To my surprise, a corporal reported to me. 'Where is Head Constable Opondo?', I enquired. 'He is in his hut, Sir.' was the reply. I went to the mud hut which Opondo was occupying. I called out to him but received no reply. Had I misunderstood the message? Maybe he had been hit by Abinyi's bullet. I entered the hut. Opondo lay on his bed shaking like a leaf. 'What's the matter Head Constable. Have you been hit?' I enquired. 'No Sir', was the reply. 'I dare not go outside in case Abinyi is waiting for me.'

I gradually extracted the story from Opondo. For several days P.C. Abinyi had been acting strangely. Opondo had thought that he was malingering and had given him a couple of punishment drills. This had evidently had the effect of tipping the balance and Abinyi had suddenly gone stark raving mad. At 5 a.m. he had left his hut, taking with him the 50 rounds of .303

ammunition with which he had been issued, plus a further 50 rounds taken from the P.C. in the next bed. Then, going to Opondo's hut he had fired ten rounds through the mud wall at about the position of Opondo's bed. After which he had run off into the bush, and had not been seen since. Opondo then showed me the holes in the mud wall. I was surprised that Opondo had not been hit. He must have come very close to becoming a vultures breakfast! One of the bullets had actually passed through one of the boots which had been left at the side of the bed.

I was now faced with an unpleasant situation. I had a stark-raving-mad constable somewhere outside, armed with a .303 rifle and 90 rounds of ammunition. He had already tried to murder the Head Constable. Who would be his next victim. At this juncture there was a disturbance outside. One of the local Karamajong tribesmen had arrived with news of the missing man. I questioned him. Abinyi had been seen in an area of thick bush about half-a-mile away. He still had the rifle with him and had levelled it at the tribesman who had rapidly withdrawn. 'Right', I said. 'Head Constable, you can come with me and we'll take half-a-dozen men and see if we can spot him.' Opondo sat down quickly on his bed. 'No Sir. I've been shot at once. I'm not going to give him another chance.' I didn't argue with him. Opondo clearly wasn't the most courageous individual and, after all, he had been the previous target. However, someone was going to have to sort Abinyi out and it looked as though I had just been nominated. I took off my Sam Browne belt and revolver holster and placed my revolver into my jacket pocket. Taking the Karamajong as a guide and half-a-dozen constables as backup, I set off. After a stealthy approach which lasted about ten minutes, the Karamajong pointed ahead to indicate the whereabouts of Abinyi. Then he rapidly left. I had a few words with the constables. 'If he shoots me you are to open up with your rifles and finish him off', I said. I advanced at a half-crouch towards the thicket where P.C. Abinyi was concealed. I kept my hand in my jacket pocket so that my revolver could not be seen, but I could, if necessary, fire it through the material. 'Abinyi', I called out, 'I'm coming in. Don't try anything silly.' No reply. I rounded a patch of bush. There stood Abinyi. A distance of less than ten yards separated us. His rifle was clasped in both hands and half raised towards me. I momentarily wondered if I could get off a shot from the hip before he could loose off at me with the rifle. I thought it unlikely. No point in hanging about. I took half-a-dozen paces towards him. No movement. His expression was dazed. Another couple of paces and I reached out and grabbed the rifle. He made no attempt to struggle or to retain it. I dropped it on the ground and took out my handcuffs. I cuffed him and wiped the sweat of fear from my brow. I picked up the rifle. It was unloaded. 'Where is the ammunition?', I demanded. 'Sir, I dropped it somewhere when I was running away from the camp.' he said. I couldn't help wondering if I should have survived the encounter if this had not happened. Indeed, there is no telling how many of the other constables and N.C.Os might have been picked off by Abinyi from the cover of the undergrowth. I recorded a few statements from Opondo and the others and then took Abinyi through to Moroto, where he was charged with attempted murder. In the event, he never stood trial. Gareth certified him insane and I never saw him again.

The Judicial Enquiry now commenced. Evidence was heard at the three main centres which had been involved in the tribal warfare. This, of course, was not the trial of the 200-or-so prisoners who had been charged with murder and cattle theft. They would be dealt with separately. This was purely an enquiry to establish the collective responsibility of the two tribes involved in the warfare. At the conclusion of the hearings an announcement was made by Rennie Beare, the Provincial Commissioner. Each adult tribesman was to be fined one head of cattle. These were not to be any old cattle, but the best in the herds. It could be either an ox or a bull or a young heifer. This last was a crafty move to try to reduce the size of the herds, which in turn would relieve the pressure on the overgrazed land. It was estimated that the fine would total some 5,000 head of cattle. It was going to be a major operation collecting this lot, let alone the problems of driving them through to the quarantine at Iriri and thence to the railhead at Soroti.

Now Wreford Smith came into his own. For over a month he toured the area. Oddly enough, none of the tribesmen objected to the fine. I think they were all rather relieved that the raiding was now at an end, for the time being anyway, also that the fine had not been considerably heavier. John and I spent a lot of the time attending at the collecting points and following the slow progress of the herds on their way to Iriri. Of course there were incidents. Some tribesmen tried to get away with handing in inferior beasts. Wreford quickly weeded these out, however. As each animal was selected it was branded on the rump and placed in the stockade. Wreford's own porters carried out the herding of the cattle, closely guarded by bands of police. Eventually, the last ox was driven through the crush into the stockade, helped by Wreford, armed with his branding iron. The police reinforcements were withdrawn from Karita and Nabilatuk. On the last evening John and I sat at his campfire and demolished a bottle of champagne. This was not just to celebrate the successful conclusion to the operation, it was also a personal celebration for each of us. We had both picked up commendations for our work in putting down the war. More importantly from my point of view we had each claimed 2,000 miles a month for seven months at the full rate of Shs 1/23 per mile! I was rich, beyond the dreams of avarice!

John Docherty now returned with his men to Kampala, and a much relieved Audrey. I made my way to Moroto to see what lay in store for me. Of course, I didn't even have a house. Peter Oades had been sufficiently inconsiderate to get married during my absence. I moved into the Rest House —but not for long. The signal from headquarters arrived two days later. Clearly, my continued presence in Moroto had become an embarrassment. I was posted to Jinja, where I should be accommodated in the hostel. Well, I only had myself to blame I suppose. I had, in a moment of pique, applied for a transfer!

The news of my imminent departure from Moroto spread rapidly throughout the community. Having been virtually absent from the town for well over a year. however, the reaction was somewhat muted. A number of new officers had arrived on the departments during my absence in Turkana and at Karita and of these I knew nothing. My departure was so precipitate that there was only time for a couple of parties and, to my regret, neither of these took place at the *dukas* where, invariably, a good spread and plenty of booze was available. I was a bit sad that after two-and-a-half-years in and around the district, I should be shunted off to a place like Jinja at such short notice. However, I only had myself to blame. I shouldn't have bitched about not being able to get proper facilities for learning Swahili. Now I was hoist with my own petard. I consoled myself with the thought that once I was settled in at the hostel I should be able to apply for some local leave at Mombasa, with a fair degree of certainty of getting it. There was also the likelihood of finding some crumpet in Jinja. There were a lot of nurses and stenographers working in the various government departments. Some of them might even be living at the hostel. That would be convenient. Possibly, I might even find myself a wife!

I was amazed at the amount of bits and pieces I had accumulated during my comparatively short career in Uganda. It filled several large wooden crates, kindly provided by Tom. One of these was completely filled with hunting trophies. I certainly wasn't going to have room for them at the hostel. Some would have to go into store once I reached Jinja. On the due date I got into my car, accompanied by Barney and Randy. Oscar sat in the back and a lorry followed along behind carrying my three crates.

It was growing dusk by the time I drew up outside the hostel at Jinja. A motherly woman appeared and showed me to my quarters. These consisted of a small lounge and an even smaller bedroom. An electric stove was provided, should I need to do any cooking though this, I found, was discouraged. A communal ablution block was provided, with separate male and female facilities. Likewise. a communal dining-room provided meals at set times. I suppose that it was O.K., but, having become used to living in my own home, be it ever so humble, this came as a bit of an anticlimax. Also, there were no females currently living at the hostel. Things looked black indeed. Oh well, roll on the next five months, when I should be able to go on leave to the U.K. Meantime, I had to make the best of it.

I found that pets at the hostel were discouraged, and it was suggested that get rid of Barney and Randy as soon as possible. This time I dug my heels in. No way was I going to give them up. I pointed out that I had no wish to be in the bloody place anyway. I should have been allocated a house where I could have continued my independent existence. In the event, no one made an issue of the subject. In fact the manageress at the hostel soon became very fond of both of my companions, particularly Barney, when I told her of his exploits. Oscar, it seemed, was going to do pretty well out of this move. His duties, it seemed, would be confined to laundering my uniforms, cleaning and tidying my couple of rooms, and looking after the two dogs.

The following day I made my appearance at the police station at Jinja. I wasn't very impressed. True it was a much larger and more modern building than that at Moroto, but I got the feeling that it was totally impersonal. I had to share an office with a young Inspector, still wet behind the ears. I was given a few crime files to investigate and then left to my own devices. No doubt I was being sized up to see how I settled in.

Jinja was a great disappointment. Where was the crumpet I had so confidently expected? It turned out that most of the stenographers were already married and the nurses, an unprepossessing bunch, were all being courted by randy coppers already. Maybe I had been so long in the bush that I had lost the touch. Anyway, the few females who turned out to be available were the scrapings at the bottom of the barrel. After about ten days spent exploring the various possibilities without success, I decided that the time had come to apply for my long-delayed local leave. I submitted my application and received the necessary approval. I was to leave for Mombasa in two weeks time — I thought!

The order to appear instantly at police headquarters came as something of a surprise. What had I done to warrant such a peremptory summons? I racked my brains on my way over to Kampala but could think of no dastardly deed, recently perpetrated, to warrant this. 'Maybe', I thought, 'they are going to relieve me of all the ill-gotten gains I had accumulated during my sojourn in the bush during the past 18 months.' I had already thought that my luck couldn't be this good. Well, I should soon find out. I pulled into the car park and made my way into the holy of holies. I thought I detected an air of suppressed excitement about the place. I knocked on the door of the Staff Officer and entered the office. 'You've made very good time, to get from Moroto', said Tomley-Evans who had replaced Stan Forte. 'Yes, indeed', I said, 'except that I've only come from Jinja!' Know why you're here?', he demanded. 'Yes of course. It's because I received a message demanding my immediate appearance!', I replied. 'Ah, then you don't know the reason', he said. 'I've got a feeling that you are about to tell me', I replied. 'Well', he said, 'The *Kabaka* was arrested this morning and is being deported to the U.K.' This was pure politics as far as I was concerned, and I was neither interested nor affected by the news.

I had never met the *Kabaka*, and for the life of me couldn't see why the arrest and deportation of a minor dignitary should have any bearing on my day-to-day activities, unless I was required to act as escort. That might not be a bad idea. A free trip to the U.K. I thought. 'Well, I think the Commissioner is waiting for you, so I'll let him know you've arrived.' So saying, the staff officer went off to report my presence. A couple of minutes passed and he returned and ushered me into Joe Deegan's office. I was greeted in a friendly enough manner, though I thought that he was a bit preoccupied. 'Ah, Beaden', he said, 'glad to see you back in civilisation at long last. I hope you've not lost all the social virtues during your life in the bush', I said that I thought I had retained a few of them, and waited to see what pearls of wisdom came forth. I had not long to wait. 'How does a posting to Government House strike you?' I think that the expression on my face told it all. 'Of course, you can refuse it if you wish, but it wouldn't do you career a lot of good.' 'Why me?', I enquired, thinking of the fate of Alan Hussell as a result of a similar posting. 'Well, you're spare at present. We need someone to go there as personal bodyguard to the Governor. I expect you've already been told of the *Kabaka's* deportation. He's at present on a plane, on his way to London. There have already been death threats made against the Governor so we've decided to provide him with a bodyguard and, after your success in the East and West Africa Cup, you seemed to be the obvious choice! You won't need any uniform. Just take plenty of civilian clothes with you.' Well, that was a laugh for a start. Civilian clothes! I had none! I was going to have to buy a complete new wardrobe. I said as much to the Commissioner. And what about my dogs! 'Well, you'll have to get out a bit sharpish and buy some. I'm sure you're not short of a few quid after living in the bush for so long! Your dogs will have to stay at the hostel. I'll have a word with the manageress.' I desperately cast about for some good reason for refusing the posting, but could come up with nothing on the spur of the moment. 'Is there any way of telling for how long the posting might last?', I enquired. 'None at all, I'm afraid', said the Commissioner. You're going on leave next May, I believe, but you should be out by then. Right, that's settled then', he added. 'Go along to see Sid Grimley in Special Branch. He will issue you with a revolver and armpit holster. Just one thing to bear in mind. Wherever the Governor goes, you go. Even if he tells you to bugger off, take no notice of him. Just go along. We are relying on you.' I could just imagine myself having a slanging match with Sir Andrew Cohen. Feeling somewhat numbed, I made my way along to Sid Grimley's office and collected a very neat .38 Smith and Weston revolver with a barrel no more than two inches long, and a leather strap and holster that fitted quite comfortably under my left arm.

I made my way to Drapers, the Kampala equivalent of Harrods, and spent what seemed to be a vast sum of money on shirts, underclothes, pyjamas, shoes, swimming trunks and so on. My next port of call was the little Asian tailor where my original uniforms had been made. Here I was measured for a variety of jackets and trousers, including a white evening jacket, making sure that plenty of room was left under the left arm pit to accommodate the weapon which was to be with me night and day as long as this assignment lasted. 'We shall have this ready for you within two weeks', I was told, to the accompaniment of much obsequious hand-rubbing. 'I am on my way to Jinja, and will be returning in four hours', I said. 'I shall expect to be able to collect at least one jacket and pair of trousers when I arrive back here. The remainder is to be delivered to Government House, Entebbe, by this time tomorrow.' These words seemed to ignite a magic firework under the tailor's bottom. He moved into top gear and started to rush round his shop like a scalded cat. I left his shop, confident that this was one order which was going to be completed in good time.

I made my way back to Jinja and was greeted by the manageress. 'Don't worry about your dogs.' she said. 'I'll make sure they're taken good care of.' Joe Deegan had evidently done a good job on her. After giving Oscar his instructions I collected up the few articles I felt I might find a use for at Government House, and made my way to the police station where I shoved my few investigation files over to the Inspector and took my departure.

By the time I arrived back in Kampala, all of the shops and offices were closed and dusk was falling. The tailors shop, however was still the scene of frantic activity. I made my way inside and was greeted by the beaming owner. 'We have one jacket and one pair of trousers ready as promised. The remainder will be sent to you at Entebbe tomorrow.' I tried on the two garments. Perfect. Evidently, I had stumbled on the formula for obtaining first-class work in the absolute minimum time. It was a system I should have to try again.

I drove to Entebbe wondering just what had hit me. There seemed to be few vehicles on the road. Groups of people stood around outside the huts which lined the roadside. They did not seem particularly hostile. From what oddments of information I had gleaned since arriving in Uganda, the *Kabaka* was not a particularly popular figurehead with his tribe. It would be interesting to see how matters developed now that he had been deported. I wondered if 'absence might make the heart grow fonder'. Someone must object to his deportation or threats would not have been made against the Governor's life, and it would not have been considered necessary for me to take up my present occupation of bodyguard.

I drove up the shrub-lined road leading to Government House. At the top was a barrier and two constables on duty. I was duly challenged at gun point and had to identify myself. I didn't know either of the constables and, clearly, they had never heard of me. 'Not really surprising', I thought. 'After living for years in the bush it would be difficult to find anyone who had heard of me.' Eventually I was admitted and drove up to the entrance to the beautiful Colonial-style house where the Governor lived. By this time, it was quite dark, but a series of floodlights lit up the whole area around the house. Before I could get out of my car, an African clad in a very ornate uniform appeared and asked me my business. Having satisfied himself he enquired if he could take my luggage, so I passed over the brown paper parcel containing my jacket and trousers. I thought that a look of scorn flickered over his features but he made no comment. I was invited into the reception area and left to wait. Shortly afterwards a young man dressed in the uniform of an R.A.F. Flight Lieutenant appeared and greeted me warmly. This, I found, was Mike Brown who had the unenviable job of A.D.C. to the Governor. 'Where's your car?', he enquired. I told him that it was parked at the front entrance. He blanched. 'Christ, let's have your key quick. We must get it shifted before H.E. sees it.' I thought that this was a pretty unfriendly attitude to take and told him so. 'Oh, no one parks at the entrance. There's a car park at the back.' I had a feeling that I was going to enjoy living at Government House. An African in chauffeur's uniform then appeared and, taking my key, removed my car to its proper position. I was now escorted to a bedroom which had been allocated to me in, of all places, the nursery wing. Again I was strongly reminded of the fate which befell Alan Hussell in these very premises, almost certainly in this same nursery wing, and under the auspices of the same Governor and his wife!

My parcel containing my jacket and trousers lay on my bed so I quickly changed and, with the unaccustomed bulk of the revolver under my left armpit, made my way back downstairs. During my absence Sir Andrew Cohen and his wife Lady Helen had made their appearance in the lounge. Clearly, this was going to be a stage-managed meeting, during which we should all have the opportunity of summing one another up. I had already met Sir Andrew briefly at the recent Police Review, on which I had had to put in an appearance in order to be presented with the medal I had won at the Revolver Shooting Competition. He was a rather peculiar-looking individual, I thought. Standing about six-feet-two-or-three-inches in height, he had a very pale, ugly schoolboyish face, a fat paunch and practically no shoulders. I took an instant dislike to him. It saved time. He commenced showering me with questions, clearly designed to make me feel as insignificant as possible, and to find out what quality of individual police headquarters had fobbed him off with. Sir Andrew was a very left-wing civil servant, appointed by a very left-wing government. We were never going to see eye-to-eye, so there was no reason, I thought, to discuss anything of a political nature with him. Not that he would have been interested in my views anyway. Many years later I found from Peter Wright's book, *Spycatcher* that Sir Andrew had been one of the Cambridge undergraduate group who, together with Philby, Blunt and Blake, were recruited by the Russians. This, however, was not known until many years afterwards and, when he found that he was being investigated, Sir Andrew conveniently died of a heart attack! Meanwhile, we had been thrown together by circumstances. I think that he took the same instant dislike to me. Lady Helen Cohen seemed quite a pleasant person, at least six-feet in height and having a vast pair of tits. She, I found later, had been married to a Cambridge Professor, by whom she had produced identical twin girls, now about seven years old. They were the most obnoxious brats it had ever been my misfortune to encounter. The Cohens had a further two children. Two small boys aged about four and three years. These two seemed reasonably normal, though I didn't have a lot to do with them. The menage was made up by the Governor's secretary, Marjorie Ives, a very high-powered thin creature, clearly at risk of being returned unopened, and the Nanny, whose name I can't remember, a very plain-looking little creature from South London. Evidently, the Cohens were not going to chance a recurrence of the Hussell saga.

The next few days passed rapidly and were, generally, quite interesting. True to my instruction I hung around, ready to move off at a moment's notice. Cohen would appear. 'Off to Kampala', he would bawl. My job was then to rush out to the limousine, open the door for him, see him inside then fly round to the other door and try to get in alongside before the vehicle took off at high speed. As the days went by, however, he would call for me and, on my appearance, would shout, 'Shan't be needing you today. You can go with Lady Cohen to open the Hospital Fete.' Off I would go and spend hours following Her Ladyship around, carrying the handbag. Needless to say, I didn't find this terribly amusing after my life in the bush, especially when I got back to Government House to find that the evil bugger had slipped off to Kampala no sooner had he got rid of me, taking his A.D.C. instead. One day I spotted Sir Andrew sliding furtively out of the side of the house into his car. Not a word had been said to me. He didn't even have the A.D.C. with him. I ran out to find the limousine heading off down the drive. I rushed to my car and belted off after it. I caught up after about a mile after which I followed at a more sedate pace. Suddenly, miles from anywhere, the limousine skidded to a halt. Sir Andrew emerged from the rear door and stormed back towards me, a look of fury on his face. 'If I want you to accompany me', he bawled, 'I shall tell you. I gave you no instructions to follow me. NOW GO AWAY.' By the time he had reached me I was out of my driving seat and making a desperate effort to control my temper. This man was a menace to himself and everyone else. We were five miles from Entebbe, 15 from Kampala. We could be within feet of an ambush, and here the bloody fool was, shouting at me to go away. I took a deep breath, stood my ground and let him rant on. Eventually he ran out of steam. 'Have you finished, Sir', I said. He clearly had. I was about to get the sack. I couldn't have cared less. 'I must tell you that I did not volunteer for this job.', I said. 'As far as I'm concerned I don't mind leaving this instant and returning to do things I enjoy more. I've been sent here to be your bodyguard because I am considered, rightly or wrongly, to be the best-qualified police officer available to do that job. However, if for some reason, best known to yourself, you feel that I am not up to the job, I shall happily go on my way. But, only after a direct order from Mr Deegan, whose instructions I am carrying out to the best of my ability. If you care to contact Mr Deegan when you reach Kampala and if, as a result, I receive instructions not to accompany you, then nothing will make me happier. Now, Sir, please return to your car and let us get under way. We are both somewhat vulnerable here.' So saying I got back into the driving seat of my car. Cohen returned to his and once again we were on our way. For the remainder of the journey I fretted and fumed. Obviously I should not have spoken to Her Majesty's representative in this manner. Could I be sacked out of hand? I was confirmed in my appointment, so I thought, probably not. Things could be made mighty unpleasant for me though. Maybe I should apologise! Not bloody likely! Let the bastard do his worst.

Cohen's visit to Kampala took him to the Town Hall. I parked my car as close as I could and sprinted across, in time to accompany him into the building. He glared at me but said nothing. At the conclusion of the meeting he snarled at me. 'You're to come back in my car.' I handed the keys of my car to the nearest corporal with instructions to get a police driver to bring it back to Entebbe. When I reached the limousine he was already seated and waiting for me. We exchanged not a word on the return journey. Clearly he must have contacted Joe Deegan by telephone while in Kampala and had been told that if he didn't like the situation, he would have to lump it.

After breakfast the following morning, I received a phone call from Tomley-Evans. 'What have you been up to now?' he demanded. 'The Commissioner wants to see you urgently. Not the nanny is it?' I set his mind at ease on that count. 'I'll have to find out what Sir Andrew's programme is first. If he's not going out I'll be right across.' Cohen was in his office dealing with some official papers when I knocked at the door. His A.D.C. answered my knock. 'It's Beaden Sir', he reported. 'Send him in', I heard. I entered and stood to attention. 'Good morning Sir', I said, 'do you plan on going out this morning.' He put on an evil grin. 'What's it to you?', he demanded. Well, I thought, in for a penny, in for a pound. 'Oh, I thought I made that clear yesterday, but if you don't plan on going out, I'm required at headquarters.' 'Good', he said. 'As far as you are concerned I shall be here all morning.' Well I suppose I didn't expect a direct reply to my question. Still it had been said in front of a witness so be it on his own head. I got into my car and headed for Kampala.

On my arrival at headquarters I made my way to the staff officers' office. He had a slight grin on his face. The Commissioner will see you straight away. Off we went and entered Joe Deegan's door. Tomley-Evans reported my arrival and departed. 'You've been having problems I hear', he said. 'You could say that', I admitted. 'But nothing you couldn't handle?', he pressed. 'Look', I said, 'I'll be more than happy to be taken off this job. I'm not cut out to be a wet nurse to a spoiled overgrown schoolboy. You told me to stay with him and that's what I've done. I'm not going to tolerate his stupid behaviour indefinitely though. Or his filthy temper.' 'Oh yes you are', said Joe. 'He's delighted with you.' 'Well, he's a funny way of showing it', I replied. I turned to leave the office. Deegan followed me to the door. He shook me warmly by the hand. 'Good luck', he said. I suddenly realised that Joe was a Freemason!

I would love to know what conversation had taken place between Deegan and Cohen about the situation at Government House. Now I never shall. Suffice it to say that the remainder of my stay at Government House was totally pleasant. Cohen went out of his way to be nice to me. I was invited to join in every function which took place. Something was scheduled for every day. Most evenings were taken up with official receptions or visiting the various departmental heads. People in high places started seeking me out and asking if I could put in a good word for them with Sir Andrew! At the receptions nothing was stinted. Whisky flowed like water. I recollect Mike Brown asking in a rather embarrassed tone on being pressed to his umpteenth whisky. 'Is this all right?', Sir Andrew overheard his and stated in a loud voice, 'Well it's the best I've got!'. Of course it was all duty-free so that whisky was cheaper than the local beer. Mike and I split the bodyguard duties between us. If Sir Andrew and Lady Cohen were going out together to a function I would usually accompany them in my official capacity. If, on the other hand, Sir Andrew was going out and Lady Cohen remaining behind, we would toss to see who accompanied whom. I well remember one evening when an official reception was being held for the representatives of the 'World Press', covering what had become known as 'The Buganda Crisis'. Sir Andrew loathed them all and legged it, accompanied by Mike. Being the only male member of the Government House staff present, I was made to sit at one end of the table, while Lady Cohen took the seat at the opposite end. How I loathed it all. Bloody reporters creeping to me for snippets of unpublished information. Eventually, Lady Cohen left for the drawing room, accompanied by the 'ladies'. 'Give us five minutes before you bring the men through' had been Lady Cohen's instructions. The party was getting a bit out of hand I thought. Dirty jokes were going the rounds. I rose to my feet. 'Shall we join the Ladies', I suggested. 'Fuck the Ladies', was the reply from a very drunk representative of a famous American publication, and the whisky bottles continued their rounds. Eventually, after what seemed an age, I managed to entice the drunken mob from the dinner table and into the drawing room where polite conversation was taking place. Lady Cohen glared at me. I shrugged my shoulders. I thought I'd done pretty well to shift them at all!

One of the advantages of living at Government House was that it had a swimming pool. Most days, when I knew that I should not be required for a couple of hours, I would indulge in a dip. Even during these periods of relaxation, however, I was never parted from my .38 revolver. After all, it would not look good at an enquiry into an assassination if I had to say that I had left my weapon behind at the crucial time because I was having a swim! It wasn't a large pool but it was about 7-feet deep in the deepest part. I was making my way there one afternoon when one of the terrible twins rushed towards me with the information that her sister had drowned. I dropped everything and sped to the pool. Sure enough, the other sibling was floating face down in the deepest part. I managed a racing dive and hauled the limp body to the side and out onto the bank. I had been working on the 'corpse' for several minutes before I found that, what I had thought were signs of returning life, were in fact helpless giggles of laughter. Bloody little beast. Both of them could swim better than I could. I was forced to abandon my afternoon's relaxation and spend the time cleaning the revolver — plus a report writing off the ammunition. Also, I never knew which one had had me over. They were identical.

Christmas was now upon us. The Buganda Crisis was not to be allowed to interfere with the multitude of celebrations taking place all over Entebbe. I accompanied the Cohens to a number of boozy parties, though I was unable to join in to the degree I would have liked. I had to keep my aim steady at all times. One afternoon immediately before Christmas a party was held at Government House and all the European children from Entebbe were invited, together with their mums. Tables were set up on the lawns and vast quantities of cakes and fizzy drinks were consumed. Lady Cohen wore a very low-cut frock and looked very fetching. As she leaned across the laden table with the cake plate her vast bosom came very close to having an unexpected airing. I got a very good shot of this with my trusty Kodak. One for the 'Family Album'.

Mike Brown roused me at about 2 a.m. one morning. 'Get dressed quickly', he said. 'There's a meeting in the office.' I needed no second bidding. It must be serious to get Mike out of bed at that time. I was dressed and in the office within three minutes. Sir Andrew sat behind his desk. Other members of the European staff and family began to arrive. When all except the children were present Sir Andrew made the awaited anouncement. 'I have been informed by one of the African staff that an attempt will be made tomorrow to poison us', he stated. Lady Cohen made a rather uncalled-for remark to the effect that similar attempts were being made every day by Mrs. Moore, the cook-housekeeper. I had always thought Mrs. Moore's efforts absolutely first class. Mrs. Moore said nothing, but if looks could have killed Lady Cohen would not have needed poison. A certain amount of chit-chat followed. I tried not to get involved until forced to do so. This didn't take very long. 'What do the police advise?', said Sir Andrew, looking very directly at me. Trapped! It was being demanded that I give an opinion on behalf of the Commissioner, Special Branch, C.I.D. and the entire Uganda Force. Everyone stared at me. 'I'd like to know who gave you this information, and when', I said. 'Can't tell you that', came the reply. 'Promised I'd not disclose his name.' I thanked my lucky stars. I was saved from a miserable admission of defeat. 'Well, if

I'm not to be told the source of your information, so that I can interrogate whoever it is, then I regret that I am unable to voice an opinion on its reliability', I answered. This was the end of the meeting. In the morning, I would be able to pass the whole thing over to Special Branch. They'd bloody soon find out who the informant was and interrogate him to extract anything useful. We all returned to our beds.

By now I had been at Government House for six weeks. During this time, nothing startling had happened. There had been no riots or killings. The local peasantry seemed totally unconcerned by the removal of 'King Freddy'. Even the politicians seemed unprepared to make a big issue of the matter. Finally a decision was made that my presence was no longer required at Government House. By now I had adjusted to the easy life I'd been leading, and to the lazy routine. Still — as well to get out now, before I got fat and soft. I packed my bags and went round saying my good-byes. Sir Andrew gave me a parting gift of two bottles of duty free whisky, shook me by the hand and I was on my way to see what else life had to offer. I called in to headquarters to hand back the revolver and ammunition. Tomley-Evans appeared from his office. 'Commissioner wants to see you', he said. I made my way to Deegan's office. 'I expect you're raring to go now after your holiday', he said. 'Which holiday was that?' I replied. 'Well, you can hardly class a few weeks at G.H. as work, can you?' he answered. I had to agree that it had not been particularly onerous. 'Good. I'm glad you've had a pleasant relaxing time, because I've got a special posting for you'. My ears pricked. This sounded interesting. Maybe, at last there would be some crumpet at the end of it. 'Are you going to let me know where it is or do I have to play guessing games?', I said. 'Oh, I'll put you out of your suspense', he replied. 'Mr Docherty has made a special request for you to go back to Moroto! You are to leave immediately!'

CHAPTER 20

Three days later, I drove past the familiar sentinel of Akisim Rock at the entrance to Karamoja. Packing my few belongings and arranging for the P.W.D. lorry had not taken long. Barney and Randy were, of course, delighted to see me on my return from Government House, and to hear of our return to less civilised parts. Personally, I had mixed feelings about my return to the wild! On the one hand, it would be like coming home to the familiar surroundings and faces. On the other hand, was I being type cast? Had a decision been made that I was too far gone, too bush-batty to be allowed back into civilised society? It would have been nice to have found a bit of reasonable crumpet while in the fleshpots of Entebbe or Kampala. My 'celibate' condition looked likely to continue until I went on leave in four months time.

I drove into the police post at Iriri to report my arrival in the district. Nothing had changed, except that a new corporal had taken over from my old friend, Corporal Okeng, whom I had managed to get on to a promotion course. The usual wild consternation on the sleepy faces on their perceiving the unexpected arrival of an officer. However, I did manage to forestall the full parade, followed by the general salute as I left. I made a quick check in the Occurrence Book. It was a bit more slovenly than usual. I signed it and made a mental note to pay a bit more attention here than it appeared to have been receiving. Then we were off again and an hour later I was driving through the familiar outskirts of Moroto Township.

I pulled up in front of the police station. Welcoming smiles from a couple of the N.C.Os who came to the office doors to greet me. Then John Docherty and Peter Oades emerged from their office. Both greeted me with enthusiasm. 'I've booked you into the Rest House for a couple of days', said John, 'You'll be moving into Peter's house as soon as he's handed over to you.' I wondered why Peter was being transferred, but decided not to enquire too closely.

I gave instructions to Oscar about the unloading of my crates and dropped him at the Rest house where the lorry driver was already waiting. Then I followed John to his house. He had done rather well for himself I decided, having been allocated one of the very large, swish bungalows which Tom had completed. Tom was in fact, his next door neighbour, similarly housed. Audrey Docherty was sitting on the verandah at the front of the bungalow, under the shade of a large ornamental sun-umbrella. She rose on seeing me and came to my car to greet me. I had met Audrey before, during the time that John and I had been living in the bush. Audrey had just happened along one day while John and I had been conferring at Amudat. She was one of the high- powered stenographers recruited by the Crown Agents and had met John in Kampala. She was about four-inches taller than John, who tended to be of stocky build, and as fair complexioned as he was dark. However, she was very pleasant.

Over a cup of tea we discussed local events. Raiding was still taking place, but on a much-reduced scale. The money collected from the sale of the communal fine cattle was going to be used to build an 'all weather road' to the south of Kadam. My mapping of the area would be invaluable in deciding the best line of country through which this should pass. Of course, this would be terrific as far as controlling the raiding was concerned, but I couldn't help thinking how vulnerable that 'Garden of Eden' was going to be, to the depredations of poachers from Teso and Bugishu Districts.

Finally, the subject of my return to Karamoja was raised. It appeared that Audrey Docherty, and Peter's wife Jean, didn't hit it off too well so Peter had asked for a transfer. I couldn't help but wonder if the old system of not allowing wives on uncivilised outposts such as Karamoja, hadn't been justified in some ways.

On leaving John and Audrey, I called on their next door neighbours. Tom and Vi were delighted to see me back in Moroto. The children were still at home on their Christmas holidays, but were due to return to school at Eldoret within the next day or two. Young Violet was starting to blossom into a very attractive young woman. I considered matters and then decided not! At 15-and-a-half she was a little on the young side. After all I was now an old man of turned 30!

The next few days passed rapidly. The official handing-taking-over, took but a few hours since we had no need to visit the outposts. I met Peter's wife just before they left for their next posting. She was quite pleasant. Peter obviously found her attractive. I believe she had come out on a Crown Agents' appointment to fill some clerical job and was clearly anxious to shake the dust of Karamoja from her feet, and get back to Kampala or some other large community where she would be able to enjoy the bright lights. Within a couple of days all was achieved. The Oades went off on transfer and I moved into what had been Noel Caunce's old house up at the base of the mountain where I had spent my first night in Moroto. Only one thing was absent. I quite missed having Kesi around. Oscar was passable, but hadn't a clue on making bread. Still it would only be for a few months!

I soon got back into the saddle and was off investigating raids and murders as though I had never been away. I rapidly met and made friends with the stations new arrivals. We now had our own game warden, Tony Henley, who, with his new wife, Priscilla, had arrived about six-months earlier. Tony was the archetypal Kenya 'white hunter', as seen on television. Indeed, this had been his occupation before joining the Uganda Game and Fisheries Department. About 24-years of age, blonde, five-feet-ten-inches and heavily-built, I could well imagine him servicing all the bored American millionairesses on safari, in the time-honoured manner. None the less I took considerable liking to him. We enjoyed the same things. It was just that he was getting more of it than I was. Priscilla was an attractive creature, just the sort which I would have expected him to team up with. She seemed a bit highly-strung though. However, I found that this was probably due to a tragedy that had occurred a couple of months prior to my return to Karamoja. Her sister had made a visit to the Henleys. I had the impression that she had been getting over a recent divorce. Anyway, the three of them had gone off in Tony's four-wheel-drive truck up to the Kidepo Valley, where they had established a tented encampment and gone out to see the multitude of game in the area. After dinner at the campfire they had turned in for the night. The following morning an alarm was raised by one of the boys when, on taking the early morning tea, the sister could not be found. Tony set off straight away with a tracker and the missing woman was found about half-a-mile from the camp, swinging from a tree. During the night she had taken a length of rope and wandered off into the bush. The tree she had chosen was not very tall, so when she had jumped from the branch to which she had tied the rope she had finished up not far off the ground. The hyenas had found her shortly afterwards, but it was uncertain whether her legs had been eaten while she was alive, or after her death. Fortunately, she had been found before the vultures arrived, so her body was intact from the thighs upwards. It struck me that in committing suicide in this gruesome manner she had been totally inconsiderate. She clearly needed a good talking to. Her remains had been taken back to Moroto and the investigation had been done by Peter. I didn't envy him that one!

Another new boy was John Wilson. He was living in my old house, the one which I had taken over from the Hinetts. John was in his early 20s and employed by the Geological Department. Notwithstanding his youth, he was a very bright paleontologist. He had discovered an extremely rich source of fossils at Napak, near the Karamoja/Teso border. We got on very well together and I rather regretted being unable to take advantage of his discovery. I should have loved to have joined him in his fossil hunting!

Tom had pressed on apace with the construction of the new prison during my absence. Gone were the old communal cells, where 60 or 70 prisoners huddled together for most of each day, and where remand prisoners and convicts could only be distinguished by the colour of their clothing. The new prison buildings were spacious and clean. No more than five to a cell, and plenty of room for exercise and recreation. Workshops had been set up and some of the prisoners were even being taught carpentry and other skills. Of course, on conviction, the prisoners had their heads shaved. Away went the fine clay-moulded coiffures. Some of the prisoners requested that they be allowed to retain the hair to turn it into a sort of wig. I raised no objection to this and the results were interesting. Quantities of coloured clay were saved from the old hair and these were re-used. A base to fit the head was very cleverly made from cords plaited together then, onto this, a base of hair was woven so that it appeared to become a heavy felt material. Then the various coloured clays were applied and the head-dress built up. At various stages little coils of wire were inserted, into which ostrich feather pompoms and various ornaments could be placed. The finished product, which represented hundreds of hours of work, was absolutely magnificent. I was delighted when, one day, I was presented with two of these, one of which had actually been made to fit me. I imagine that one of the warders had surreptitiously obtained some measurements from my cap. I found later that on leaving prison with their new style wigs they had become so much admired that a completely new fashion swept the district. Of course, it had the enormous advantage that head lice could be coped with. Previously, these little beasts had to be either tolerated under their clay fortresses or scratched at with bits of wire.

I arrived home for lunch one day feeling a bit jaded. I sat down in the lounge and poured a well-earned beer. Oscar appeared looking rather more glum than ever. '*Iko mtu moja, taka ku ona wewe*', (There is a person who wishes to see you.) he said. I went to the kitchen. '*Iko wapi?*' (He is where?), I demanded. Oscar pointed outside. At that moment, Kesi's head popped round the door. '*Jambo bwana. Habari ya siku nyingi?*' (Hello Sir. What is the news of many days?), he enquired, beaming broadly. '*Jambo Kesi*', I said, 'What are you doing up here? I thought you were living in Fort Portal.' 'Sir, I have come back to work for you. Am I not your son? Are you not my father?' 'Kesi', I said, 'you can see that I have a boy. I do not need anyone else.' His face fell. 'Sir, could I not be cook and Oscar could be houseboy?' Cunning little beast. He must have heard that I was missing his bread. How did he know that I had come back to Karamoja? Here was an example of jungle drums. Eventually I relented. Warning him that the job would only last about three months, I agreed to employ him at a reduced wage. He then introduced me to his 'wife'. I don't know if he had actually married her. I rather doubted it. She was young and pretty and nubile. Or maybe I HAD been in the bush too long! Far too good for him. 'No drunkenness', I warned, as a parting shot. I don't know what happened during the night, but I was somewhat surprised on the following day, when Oscar came to me with the sad news that his father had died and that he was going to have to return to Kenya! I paid him off and away he went. What an extraordinary coincident that Kesi had turned up so fortuitously!

John Docherty had gone off on pay safari taking Audrey with him. Wise man! Tom and Vi were off to Eldoret visiting their children. I had an unexpected visitor. Jack Redman, the Deputy Commissioner of Prisons, turned up unannounced. I had not previously met Redman but since I was responsible for the running of the prison I suppose he was technically my boss. I didn't let it go to his head though, treating him as casually as possible. 'Just happened to have a couple of days to spare so, since I was just over the border in Soroti, I thought I would pop up and see how the building is going', he announced. 'Sure', said I, 'Welcome any time. Should have sent a signal though. Lucky I wasn't away as well.' We went off in my car, leaving his driver to unload the suitcases at the Rest House. I gave him a conducted tour of the almost-completed prison complex and could see that he was greatly impressed, both by the location which had been chosen and by the architecture and quality of the building. Since he knew no one else in Moroto, I invited him round to my house for drinks and a meal that evening. During our conversation he told me of a big prison-building programme which had just been approved and which it was hoped to commence as soon as suitably-qualified officers had been recruited. As a matter of interest I enquired what qualifications the officers sought might need, and what rank and pay scale they would obtain on entry. Clearly they were thinking of a high-powered administrator with a great deal of practical building and teaching experience since it was hoped that most of the work would be done with available prison labour. The rank on entry would be Superintendent of Works, equivalent to Prison Superintendent, and the pay-scale set at a very high rate. 'I think', said I, 'that it's just possible that your visit here has been fortuitous. Tom Hinett, the P.W.D. officer who is responsible for building the prison here and a number of the houses, might just possibly be interested. I'm making no promises mind you, but he would certainly be your man. You will do no better. Most of the prison has been built using prison labour for whose training he has been responsible. Also, of course, he makes locally all the bricks which are used. He has made lime kilns and most of the mortar and all the whitewash are made by him.' I could see Redman becoming more and more keen on the idea which I had successfully planted. 'I'll tell you what', I added, 'tomorrow, I'll take you round and show you some of the houses Mr Hinett has built. We can also have another look at the prison if you wish, and then, if you wish, I'll have a word with Mr Hinett when he returns from Kenya, and find out if there's any chance of him being interested.' By this time, I could see that the Deputy Commissioner had well and truly swallowed the bait. Had Tom walked into the house at that moment, Redman would have been down on his knees beseeching him to take the job.

The following day, I devoted a further couple of hours to showing off Tom's good works. I knew then that the job was his for the taking. Redman left after lunch. He even gave me a sheaf of application forms for Tom to fill in, if I could get him sufficiently interested. 'Do your best for us Mr Beaden', were his parting words as he set off on his return journey. Needless to say, Tom was rather more than interested in my news. The job of Superintendent of Works would at least double his present salary. I had my work cut out in restraining him from setting off for Kampala instantly. 'Tom, take my advice. Leave it a few days. Don't seem too interested. Write a letter in about a week's time, asking for further details. Make sure that it's not a job on local terms. Enquire about promotion prospects. Find out how high up the salary scale you can go.' I am happy to report an eventual positive outcome to this. A couple of months later Tom received a well-deserved appointment and he and his family moved to Tororo on the Kenya border, very handy for visiting the kids. Later, after the building program there was finished, he moved to a number of other districts, and eventually transferred to the Kenya Prison Service where he finished up as an Assistant Commissioner. I like to feel that I repaid him in some part for the many kindnesses he and his family had shown me.

Tom's departure from Moroto left a gap in the P.W.D. staff. Shortly before his departure his replacement arrived. This was Arthur Kessel. A vast, mountain of a man. At least 20-stone in weight, exuding goodwill to all men and with a thirst to match his size. 'Kess', as he insisted on being called, was a Cornishman. He was in his mid-40s and unmarried. Although he had served several tours in Uganda, he was still a comparatively junior officer. Consequently, he was unable to take over Tom's house, which had been allocated on the basis of the size of Tom's family. Two days before Kess's arrival, Sandy Field came to me, cap in hand. 'Would I mind if Kess shared with me?' 'Yes', I replied, 'I bloody well would mind.' At this time of course I knew nothing about Kess. Also, I was just going on safari for a couple of days, and Randy was very close to producing pups which, I hoped, were Barney's. Barney, I know, had the same hope. I had allocated Randy the bedroom into which this Kessel fellow was trying to wheedle his way. The thought of a total stranger, moving into my house during my absence, installing his own furniture without my say-so, moving my stuff out of his way, ordering my staff about — it was all too much! In the event however, I had no option but to agree, which I did with very bad grace.

I went on safari feeling very annoyed with the world in general and Kessel in particular. In fact I left him a rather curt note telling him which bedroom was mine, which quarters I had allocated to him for his staff, and laying down certain ground rules. To this day, I bitterly regret not making him more welcome. Of course, he no more wanted to share with me, than I wanted to share with him. In the event I got on extremely well with him. He had a wonderful sense of humour and was very good company. He had been a great athlete in his day, and showed me photographs of a very different Kess, taken at a time when he had a reputation as an international swimmer.

The day after I returned from safari, Randy produced 12 pups. Clearly, Barney had had nothing to do with the process, and was totally disgusted at such infidelity. Must have been one of those rotten Alsatians from Jinja. Barney had been no luckier in civilised parts than I had. However, there was no way that I was going to dispose of Randy's pups around the *dukas*. John Wilson spoke up for one and Willie Hagstrom for another. The others, I got Sandy Taylor to destroy.

An outing had been suggested. There was a big dam at a place known as Lorengakipi. The lake formed behind the dam was some eight square-miles in extent and had been constructed some years earlier, It straddled the border between Teso and Karamoja Districts, was easily accessible from either sides of the border and was teeming with duck and geese. The suggestion was that a party from Soroti and Mbale and one or two other places would meet up with the Moroto contingent, for a good day's shooting. Actually I wasn't terribly interested. The shotgun was not my weapon. In fact I didn't possess one. I was so expert with the rifle that I doubted whether I would be able to revert to the shotgun. There had been a time during the War when, on an air gunner's course, I had been reasonably proficient. However, that was some time ago. However, I was eventually persuaded and Sandy Field loaned me a fairly elderly shotgun. We set off in the early morning. The Moroto contingent numbered eight officers, including Tony Henley, whose territory this was. Tony had a number of game guards based at Lorengakipi, basically to prevent the poaching and illegal trapping of the vast herds of animals attracted to the permanent water supply. At about 10 o'clock, we arrived at the dam and parked our cars. I had decided against bringing Barney, knowing his loathing for cold water. He would never have retrieved a duck had his life depended upon it. The Teso party had already arrived. No shots had yet been fired and it was decided that the parties would split, taking in both sides of the dam. Half-an-hour would elapse before firing would commence. I drove off down the very reasonable track which ran down the eastern shore. On arriving about half-a-mile from the dam wall I took up my position and waited for the firing to commence. Ducks and geese were there in their millions. Eventually, the first shots sounded. A great cloud of waterfowl arose from the dam and started to circle at great speed. I could see that some of the party were having great success. But not me. Every shot was a clean miss. I wouldn't have thought it possible to fail to hit anything in such a cloud of birds. Eventually, after about 20 shots, I managed to wing a small duck. How, I don't know. It was a goose I had been aiming at. Poor little sod. It landed in the water about ten yards off-shore and started feebly swimming in circles. Feeling very sorry, I put my gun on the ground, took off my shorts and shirt and waded in to retrieve it. Unfortunately, it didn't seem to appreciate my good intentions. I only wanted to kill it! As I neared it the little bird swam a few yards further out. I waded in further. Again it swam just out of reach. I was now up to my waist and the water was rapidly deepening. One more effort and then, if it didn't want to be killed it could bloody well stay alive! As I was about to reach out my hand to grab the duck, from the depths rose a vast pair of jaws which removed the duck from this life. My hand very nearly accompanied it. The bloody reptile actually had the cheek to wink at me as I froze in horror. Why had the croc taken the duck instead of me? I didn't know. Maybe it wasn't hungry. Maybe it had a warped sense of humour. Maybe it only liked human faeces. I now made my very best impersonation of Jesus Christ, and arrived on shore in three-seconds-flat. I looked round expecting to see the croc pursuing me out of the water. Not a sign of it! Sod duck shooting I thought. Fancy people sending their pet dogs into waters like this. I put the shotgun back into my car and took out my .22 rifle. With the next 20 shots I downed 15 good-sized geese. Not one of them went anywhere near the water. On my way back to our meeting point I passed the huts where the game guards lived. There, pegged out on the ground, were the belly-skins of seven crocs, all of them in excess of 12-feet in length. I stopped to enquire how they had killed them. This was just one day's catch, I was told. The dam was alive with them. The method used to trap them was to put out a bait on the shore where tracks indicated a croc's regular usage. To get to the bait the croc had to put his head through a wire noose to which was tied a float and a heavy rock. On taking the bait, the croc would find the wire noose tightening round its neck. It would then panic and rush back to the water dragging the boulder after it. The boulder sank to the bottom and the croc drowned. The float indicated its location and it was later retrieved. The remains of the crocodile would then become the bait for the next traps. A very lucrative occupation.

It was time to commence my plan of campaign for home leave. I was going to have six months of paid leave before my return to Uganda. During this time I felt that it was essential that I found myself a wife. Financially, I was now reasonably secure. Clearly the first thing to sort out was transport. Without a reasonable-looking car I would be at a distinct disadvantage. My correspondence with the various import companies produced a flood of brochures. Making a choice from this lot was not going to be easy. The Standard Vanguard Van, now fully-paid-for and producing a substantial income in its own right, had proved itself a good reliable vehicle. I eventually decided to go for the same make but in the saloon version. This was superb. All the latest gadgets, over-drive gear, leather upholstery, metallic blue paintwork. In fact, perfect 'wife bait'. I arranged to have it delivered to the airport to meet me on my arrival. Later, at the end of my leave, it would be shipped on board the liner on which I intended making my return trip, and I would take possession of it a few days after my arrival in Kampala.

A nasty raid had taken place in the north of the District. This was a bit of a blow. We appeared to have got the raids between the Suk and the Karamajong down to acceptable proportions. Now, a comparatively new problem had arisen. A raid by the Turkana on the Karamajong in Dodoth. True, it wasn't a very big raid, there only having been four people murdered and quite a small quantity of cattle removed. The fact was, that it had happened at dead of night. The four herdsmen were a nomadic party and had been speared to death while they slept by a raiding party which had climbed the 3,000-foot escarpment from the Turkana desert. A similar raid some years earlier had developed into a full-scale tribal war and this incident had every indication of following the same lines. Already, the war parties were being called out by the Karamajong. Once they made their way down the escarpment, there was no telling what scale the fighting might reach.

I set off for the scene of the raid in my car. There was no point in taking the Land Rover this time. In the first place it could have only carried around three or four fully-equipped policemen. In the second place, good vehicle though it was, there was no way that it could have negotiated the narrow, or non-existent track down the escarpment. A lorry hired from Madan Tandon followed along behind me, carrying a dozen armed constables and N.C.Os.

That night we made camp at Kaabong, about 20 miles from the scene of the raid. The local *mkungu* chief reported to me. His news was not good. A large band of warriors including the owners of the stolen cattle and relatives of the murdered men was gathering. 'Go and tell them that if one of them sets foot down the escarpment before I arrive, I shall personally execute him', I said. The *mkungu* scuttled off to do my bidding.

Early the following morning we set off for the scene. I left my car at Kaabong and we all crammed onto the lorry as best we could and managed to get to within about five miles, after which we set off on foot. A dozen porters whom I had hired carried our camp equipment as head-loads. An hour later and I was examining the few bones remaining from the victims. Relatives informed me which fragments represented each of the deceased. I wondered how they were so sure but decided not to overcomplicate the situation. The large band of warriors who had assembled were informed in no uncertain terms of their fate, should they try taking the law into their own hands. In fact I must say, that I found them surprisingly malleable. I took with me three of their number who would, I hoped, identify the missing cattle, should we come across them. Then, leaving the majority of our equipment under the guard of a constable at the top we were away down the 3,000-foot drop. I wasn't too sure of my legal authority on this expedition. I was now back in Kenya, *de jure* and *de facto*. I hoped that the rules of 'hot pursuit' might cover me.

The track down the escarpment was about five miles in distance. I couldn't help but marvel as we made our way. The great cataclysm, millions of years ago, when the Great Rift had been formed, had constructed a sort of 'Time Machine'. Each few yards we progressed down the escarpment wall, represented a million years or so in 'time' terms. Near the base of the track a number of Turkana *manyattas* were built. These, I thought, would be particularly vulnerable in the event of open warfare. I could make capital out of this given the opportunity. As we neared the desert floor, we were obviously observed by the residents. A party of Turkana gathered and set off towards us. I took the opportunity of ordering the rifles to be loaded before they arrived. I didn't want to come under a sudden attack, unprepared. The Turkana, when they arrived, numbered about 60 — all armed with spears. A number of others similarly armed, could be seen drifting across from the other *manyattas*. Not wanting to precipitate the instant opening of hostilities, I plucked a handful of dry grass from the ground as a sign of our peaceful intent. One of the warriors, clearly a local chief, plucked a similar handful and came towards me. I greeted him with one or two words of Turkana, which I had taken the opportunity of learning during my desert sojourn. This took him somewhat by surprise and he chattered away in the same language, losing me instantly. We then conversed for a while in Swahili with one of the Karamajong cattle owners helping out where necessary. I enquired if he had any knowledge of the raid. 'Yes', he replied. 'It was made as a reprisal for a recent Karamajong raid on the Turkana.' In fact, his own son was one of the raiders. He seemed quite sure of the legality of the action. Either that or he was sure that we would never get away with any prisoners. 'Is your son here?', I enquired. 'Yes I am here', said a voice from behind me. I turned and found a strapping warrior at my back. I addressed my questions to him. 'Yes, I went on the raid. I speared two of the Karamajong. My friends also speared them and the others.' I could hardly believe my ears. They were very sure of themselves. Three other warriors came forward and identified themselves as being the other culprits. 'Where are the stolen cattle?', I enquired. A nearby *manyatta* was indicated. I ordered that the cattle be produced and the owners identified them. Now the tricky bit. I spoke to the two corporals in English. Fortunately, most of the constables present also understood my instructions. I made my way round to the back of the four warriors who had admitted taking part in the raid, on the pretext of looking at the cattle. Then I drew my revolver and at the same time my policemen aimed their rifles at the group. They were completely outfoxed by this and dropped their weapons to the ground. My prisoners were quickly handcuffed. I didn't hang about after this, but contented myself with telling the chief that any further raids into Karamoja would bring death and destruction on him and his people. Then, with the Karamajong owners and my porters driving the cattle, we set off back to the top of the escarpment. I must say that I fully anticipated an ambush on our route and sent out scouts and rearguard but there was none. What had happened. This should have been a difficult investigation. Instead it had turned into one of the simplest! What should by every rule have turned into a bloodbath, had turned into a confrontation with pussy cats. Well, who was I to complain.

At the top of the escarpment we were greeted by a delighted band of Karamajong warriors, who wanted to deal with my prisoners by spearing them immediately. I warned them that any further raids would bring me down on them like a ton of bricks. Then we returned to our lorry and started off back to Moroto. It was late evening by the time I had housed the prisoners, after which I made my way to see John Docherty. He was amazed at my early return, and full of congratulation on the outcome. The outcome of this expedition was that the four Turkana were duly convicted and hanged. I got a commendation for good work and Sandy Field, who had not set foot outside his office, got an O.B.E. for avoiding a tribal war. Well, they do say that O.B.E. stands for Other Buggers Efforts!

Now at long last I was to leave Karamoja. This time I received the full treatment. A full fortnight of boozy parties led up to my departure. I had long lost count of the number of different O.Cs I had worked with or suffered under. Maybe I had learned something from each of them. Maybe they had each learned something from me. Kess was going to look after Barney and Randy for me during my leave. This at least ensured that I should have to make a return trip to Karamoja to collect them, albeit a brief one. On my drive down to Jinja, where I was to leave my car for storage, I mused that I never had managed to get that leave. Strangely, I didn't feel the least bit fed-up about that. After all the last three years had been one continuous paid holiday. One regret sprang to mind. Three months of this leave was to be spent attending a Senior Detective Course at Hendon Police College. How was I to find a wife in the remaining time. Love would find a way. Now what was the name of that nurse whose particulars I had taken down? Margaret something?

CHAPTER 21

My flight to London Airport was without incident and, on arrival, I found the 'passion wagon' which I had purchased as 'wife bait' awaiting me. This was a rather smart, blue Standard Vanguard saloon, smelling strongly of its new leather upholstery. Equipped with such an advantage, I felt that my quest for a suitable wife could hardly fail.

After three years of driving on the rough but virtually deserted roads of Uganda, I found the London traffic somewhat daunting, particularly in a car with which I was not familiar but, with a bit of luck, I picked my way through the dense traffic and was at last on the open road.

My parents seemed quite pleased to have me back home again, particularly when I unpacked the large ham and the quantities of exotic fruit which I had brought with me. My new car was duly admired and a half-hour tour of the countryside with them put the finishing touches to my homecoming.

I had mapped out a plan of action for the following day. Little did she know it, but Margaret, the little nurse I remembered from some four years earlier when I had dealt with an accident involving her brother, was the lucky girl on whom I had set my sights! With some trepidation I made my way to the address in Hastings at which I had met her. It was essential, I felt, to discover if she was still available. I wished that I could remember her name. I felt disinclined to enquire at the front door where my carefully-laid plans might be shattered by the appearance of a hostile parent or, worse, by an enraged husband! On reaching the house, I parked a short distance away and lurked. On reflection, I suppose that the chances of seeing Margaret were somewhat remote, but my plan of campaign had not extended beyond this first reconnaissance.

My efforts were wasted. No sign of her. After about an hour I accepted the fact that early success was unlikely to come as a result of lurking! I went to find my old friend and ex-colleague Wally Kimber. Wally would at least be able to remind me of Margaret's name. Might even know a bit more. After all, she had been a member of the first-aid team that he ran!

Success! Wally not only reminded me that her name was Sutton. He also informed me that she was now a Staff Nurse at the Royal East Sussex Hospital where she now resided in the nurses quarters. I might have lurked for a long time at Barley Lane with singular lack of progress! I telephoned the hospital without further delay. Margaret, I was informed, was on duty. Eventually I was put through to her. To my amazement she not only remembered me, she also recalled my old police number — 77. Better still, she accepted my invitation to a meeting the following day. My cunning plans were making good progress — I thought!

Margaret, on that first meeting after three years, was exactly as I had remembered her. Very pretty, intelligent, well-spoken and a charming companion. I was smitten.

Oh, headstrong youth! At the end of that first evening my mind was made up. Not for me a tentative and lengthy relationship culminating after several months, or years, in a proposal of marriage. No, I jumped in with both feet. Margaret was, without doubt, the one I was looking for and, in the saloon bar of the Robert de Mortain pub on the Ridge at Hastings I told her that I intended marrying her! Somewhat to my surprise she turned me down flat. Told me that she knew nothing about me and that, in any case, she was embarked on a career in nursing and had no intention of getting married for a considerable time, to me or anyone else. What had gone wrong with my 'cunning plan'? What about the 'wife bait' — the beautiful car which formed the basis of my 'cunning plan'? She didn't even seem to notice what an excellent 'catch' I would be! Neither did she seem to care. She wasn't even impressed about the life of luxury in the wonderful climate of Uganda that I promised her! She did, however, agree to meet me again the following evening so all was not yet lost.

In the meantime I gave the subject some serious thought. Could it be that I had taken too much for granted? Maybe I had expected too much from the first meeting! I made up my mind to be a bit cagey next time.

The following evening I again collected Margaret from outside the nurses home. I noticed that she came out with several friends, all of whom seemed to be inspecting me covertly before going their separate ways. This time I played it cool. We had dinner at a restaurant and I made no further reference to my proposal of marriage — until just before I returned her to the nurses home at eleven p.m. Once more I was turned down flat.

This was depressing. The way things were going I should be returning to Uganda with my single status unchanged. Over the next couple of weeks I repeated my proposal each and every day. Bugger playing it cool. I had tried that once without success. Margaret's refusal was as inevitable as it had been the first time I proposed.

It was now time for me to report to Hendon Police College. At least I should be able to get home each weekend. Maybe the enforced absence would help matters along. The course at Hendon was one for which the sergeants and inspectors from a variety of U.K. forces who were attending it might have been expected to give their eye teeth. Indeed, most of them confided that they had been hoping and praying for it for many years past. Having been finally selected they were ecstatic at the prospect. However, glancing through the syllabus, which was presented to me on the day of my arrival, I could see little in it which might prove to be of value to me in Uganda. The lectures by Professors Camps and Simpson on forensic medicine might indeed be worthwhile, but for the life of me I could see no value in subjects such as the Children and Young Persons Act, Peddlers and Hawkers, Diseases of Animals and Vagrancy. These and allied subjects seemed to form the bulk of what I was expected to learn during the next twelve weeks.

Fortunately, I was not expected to reside at the college. I had been allocated lodgings in a house about a mile distant where I was fed and watered by a pleasant enough young couple who were taking in college students for three months at a time to help out with the housekeeping. I think they were particularly pleased that they did not have to put up with me from after breakfast each Friday until Monday evening when I next appeared.

At the end of the first week at the college I made my way back to Hastings. During my enforced absence I had cracked the problem. I knew precisely where I had gone wrong with my proposals of marriage! I had forgotten to tell the poor girl that I loved her. Maybe if I got down on bended knee and told her this it would make a difference 'What silly creatures women are'. I thought, 'Surely she must know by now that I loved her. I'd hardly be asking her to marry me otherwise.' Still if that was what was missing from my 'cunning plan', so be it. I would tell her next time I saw her.

As luck would have it, my return to Hastings coincided with Margaret's late duties, so it wasn't until the Saturday that I was able to see her again. As usual, I collected her from the nurses home and off we went for a drive around the countryside. I shall gloss over the next hour or two. All I will say is, that it's damned near impossible to get down on one's bended knee in the back of a Standard Vanguard saloon. Still, I did my best and remembered to tell her that I loved her passionately and the thought of returning to Uganda without her was impossible to contemplate. As I recollect it, she told me that I'd better get used to the idea.

The next few weeks slipped by. The routine remained the same. Each weekend I would return to Hastings, spend the next couple of days proposing to Margaret and being turned down, and back to the college by 9 a.m. on Monday morning.

The course was following the line which I had anticipated. Few gems came to light which might have been of value to a practical Colonial policeman. Occasionally some snippet would turn up, such as the method which might be successfully used to reinstate the frame number on a bicycle where it had been filed off after being stolen and later recovered. The thing that I found most disturbing was the hidebound attitude of the British police.

Occasionally we would be lectured by very senior detectives who had spent their entire careers investigating crime. They would relate, with relish, 'Their murder.' In some cases it would be the only murder they had ever had to deal with. Others might have dealt with half-a-dozen during their 30-years service. Every episode related included references to the 'team' that had been working under them. This would often amount to some 20 or 30 detectives and uniformed personnel who would be used for the routine enquiries. As a member of an overseas police force, I was asked if I had ever taken part in investigating such a crime. I made the mistake of admitting that I had. 'How many?', I was asked. 'Oh, a fair number', I replied. Knowing grins all round. Here was a bullshitter they decided. 'Did you deal with them yourself or were you one of a team?' 'Well, as part of a team I suppose', said I. 'I usually had a corporal to help with the translation and maybe a couple of constables to trace and escort witnesses but that was usually about the lot.' Never have I seen such blank disbelief! 'Come on then. How many murders have you dealt with and over what period?' 'Well, to be perfectly honest, I've lost count but certainly during the past three years it must amount to well over 200. Some cases involved as many as 20 victims in a single incident.' After this I was treated as something of a pariah. No one wanted to associate with such a barefaced liar.

I began to long for each weekend to arrive so that I could get away from the confines of the police college and from the other students with their narrow-minded attitudes. I had not actually fallen out with any of them. I guess their outlook on the course was so totally at variance with my own. Anyway, I was also missing Margaret quite badly. I had really fallen deeply in love with her and the enforced absence was getting on my nerves.

I had now been on leave for nearly two months and had practically accepted the fact that I should be returning to Uganda without a wife after all. Consequently, it came as something of a shock to the system when, one evening, after my usual proposal, Margaret said, 'Yes'. I was so astounded that it took me some time to realise that my 'cunning plan' was going to work after all.

Not that Margaret's acceptance had come any too early. Frantic arrangements had to be made. First, however, I was taken to Margaret's home. This was not the first time I had met her parents and I thought that I got on well enough with both of them. I understood from Margaret, however, that they didn't get on with each other. 'None of my business', I thought. Any marital friction involving my prospective in-laws would be hardly likely to affect us when we were in Uganda. About half-an-hour after our arrival at her home, Margaret's father, Percy, returned home from work. To my astonishment, I found myself alone with him, Margaret and her mother having departed to another room. After a while, I gathered from the way in which the conversation was being steered, that Percy was expecting me to formally ask for his daughter's hand in marriage. This had never occurred to me. Margaret was, after all, 22-years-old, and a Staff Nurse. I quite imagined that her own acceptance would be fully adequate. However, if that was what was expected of me, I was quite prepared to go along with it, part way at least. 'You've no doubt been told that I've asked Margaret to marry me, and that she has accepted my proposal', I said. 'May I take it that you have no objection?' There. It was said. Possibly not in the way that he had expected. If he wanted more, hard luck! 'Any chance of taking her mother as well?', said Percy. I declined his offer.

It was Margaret's wish to be married at Christ Church, St Leonards, where she had been baptised and confirmed, and where her father was a leading light in the choir. This was in a totally different parish to either her home, or the Royal East Sussex Hospital where she resided for most of the time. However, it was in the same road and only about half-a-mile from where I was currently staying with my parents. We went along to see Canon Marion-Wilson who was the rector of Christ Church. After a lengthy conversation with him it was decided that Saturday 4th September would be a good day for the wedding. Arrangements were made for the banns to be read three times in the church, as was required. In fact, Margaret and I went along once to hear them being read.

Meanwhile, I wrote to the Crown Agents to inform them of my forthcoming marriage. I also told them that I wished to return to Uganda by sea and not by air as had been planned. This would have the advantage of being an additional holiday which, I felt, would go some way towards compensating me for the time I had spent on the course at Hendon, and also prolong the honeymoon in rather pleasant surroundings. It also had the distinct advantage of enabling us to take out to Uganda a very considerable quantity of household effects with which we should be able to set up home with the minimum of expense.

An extensive exchange of letters then followed, in which it was suggested by the Crown Agents that we travel to Uganda in separate cabins, Margaret sharing with two other women and me similarly sharing with two men. Needless to say, I dug my heels in pretty hard on this one. This was eventually sorted out during the course of an acrimonious meeting at the Crown Agents' premises at Milbank between a supercilious clerk and myself in which voices were raised and tempers frayed. Needless to say, I got my own way.

The course at Hendon finally came to an end. I had not, I felt, derived a great deal of benefit from it. Fortunately, there was no examination at the conclusion. Everyone passed and, in an interview before leaving the premises, I was told that a glowing report was to be submitted regarding my progress. I sincerely hoped it would not be too complimentary. I had no wish to join the ranks of the C.I.D.

Saturday 4th September arrived. The wedding was scheduled for 1 .a.m. Many of the guests had already arrived, having travelled from far and near. At 9 a.m. there was a ring at the front door bell. I answered it. The verger from Christ Church stood on the doorstep. He was somewhat out of breath. 'Mr Beaden', he gasped, 'I've been sent up to collect your banns certificate.' 'Why come to me?', I replied. 'You must already have it at the church. I know they were called there because I was present at one of the readings.' 'Ah!', he said, 'but you're living in the parish of St John.' 'Well', I said, 'how the hell was I expected to know that? The rector knows full well where I am living. He made no comment on it. I was never told that anything else was required. What happens now?' All this talk of hell seemed to have an adverse effect on the verger. He turned rather pale and backed away. 'I'm afraid you won't be able to get married', he gasped. Just as well he was out of range or he might have had something to be afraid about.

My next stop was Christ Church. The rector was awaiting my arrival with some trepidation. He was full of apologies but confirmed what I had been told. 'It never crossed my mind that you didn't realise that you were in a different parish', he said. 'Well, having never been married before, it didn't cross mine either', I replied. 'I thought it was your job to advise me of what was required. Anyway, I'm sure there must be some way round this problem. Can't you issue a Special Licence or something?' 'I'm sorry', was the reply. 'Only the bishop at Chichester can issue a Special Licence and he wouldn't be able to do it today.' I cursed under my breath. 'Well, when can he issue it?' I enquired. 'Not till Monday at the earliest', he answered. I now had the job of breaking the news to Margaret. It was not a pleasant situation. I fully expected floods of tears from her and total uproar from her family. In the event there was none. Everyone took the news calmly and we sat down to decide on the next step. Clearly the wedding would have to be re-scheduled for Monday. This would mean setting out very early in the morning for Chichester, where we should both have to swear affidavits before the bishop who would then issue the Special Licence. Then a speedy trip back to Hastings where Margaret would be left to get ready, while I returned to St Leonards to do the same. The wedding was now to be at mid-day in two days time. However, all the guests were expecting the wedding now. The reception to be held at a local hotel could not be cancelled or postponed. We decided that there was no alternative to going ahead with the reception for the benefit of the guests who had travelled distances to attend, followed by a smaller affair at the later date for those who could still make it! What a balls-up! To this day, however, I can't see that I was entirely to blame for it. If I ever get married again I shall know better. The trouble is, I don't know if Margaret would have me second time around!

The wedding guests were duly gathered up and informed of the changed circumstances. To their credit none of them made the expected comments about piss-ups in breweries. Just as well I guess since I wasn't in the mood for falling-about-laughing. On second thoughts, maybe they were just hiding their true feelings.

The reception at the hotel was, to tell the truth, a somewhat muted affair. The food was excellent. The speeches were non-existent and the telegrams and cards were retained for use at the later date. Owing to the shortage of accommodation and the sudden influx of guests who would be spending the next couple of days in Hastings instead of returning home, I slept — on what should have been my wedding night — with my brother! Great!

In the event, the delayed wedding went without a hitch. True, the schedule was a tight one and I may have broken the speed limit more than once while going to and from Chichester, but eventually I was waiting at the church. My brother Ralph was best man. The wedding march commenced and I glanced round to see Margaret walking down the aisle with her father. She was beautiful. My 'cunning plan' had worked and I would be returning to Uganda with a wife I could be proud of, who was an asset and who would be the centre of admiration among my colleagues.

The second wedding reception, though catering for a considerably-reduced number of guests, was nonetheless reasonably successful. There was, I felt, still a feeling throughout, that an almighty balls-up had occurred somewhere along the line. I remember making a somewhat halting speech to the guests who had made the effort to attend this second attempt. I was conscious throughout that there wasn't a lot to be said in my defence!

Eventually, to our relief, we were able to leave and commence our honeymoon. It had been decided that we would spend a couple of weeks touring the south of England and the west-country in the passion wagon, making a sort of circular trip which led us eventually to Oxford and then back to Hastings. This turned out to be quite successful, though I don't know that I would recommend it to anyone else. But then, Margaret was quite exceptional.

On our return we viewed the wedding photographs and the newspaper coverage. The former were very good. The latter, submitted by my mother-in-law, seemed to concentrate on the fact that Michael, the bride's brother, was in the army and serving in Korea and had, as a result, been unable to attend the wedding. I was, personally, never quite able to equate this with the minimal coverage of the wedding itself.

We now had about six weeks left before we were due to sail. The time sped by. We were both very happy and looking forward to embarking on our married life in Uganda. I hoped against hope that I should be posted to an up-country station. Another tour in Karamoja would suit very nicely. I had told Margaret all about this and she seemed keen on the idea, though possibly, not so enthusiastic about the snakes that I had mentioned.

The next few weeks were spent in purchasing those essentials which, while cheap and easily obtainable in England, were nonetheless expensive and difficult to find in Uganda. A number of wooden crates were obtained and our belongings carefully packed and, ten days or so before we were due to sail, despatched to the shipping agents. My car also had to be delivered back to the agents a week before we were due to sail so that it could be shipped on board and come out to East Africa on the same boat that we were travelling on.

I still had no idea of where we should be posted on our arrival in Uganda and it was not until a couple of days before our departure that the fateful letter arrived from police headquarters. No, we were not going up-country. We were posted to Katwe Police Station just outside Kampala. This was without doubt the worst place in the Protectorate. Universally known as a total hell-hole! 'What', I wondered, 'had I done to deserve this?' It was situated about a mile outside Kampala on the Entebbe road. The posting entailed living over the police station, dealing with the greatest concentration of crime in Uganda and with the minimum staff to cope with it. This was not going to be a picnic and, certainly, was not going to be the paradise that I had promised Margaret. I wondered how she would cope with the situation. I felt that it was quite on the cards that she would up sticks and leave after a very short time. In the circumstances I should certainly be unable to blame her if she did.

It was about this time that Margaret announced that she was pregnant. What should have been subject for rejoicing, was now overshadowed by the prospect of living over a police station where violent crime could be expected 24-hours a day. A more difficult start to married life was difficult to imagine. Anyway, at this stage there was nothing I could do about it. We would simply have to make the best of a bad job and hope that things might improve.

Thus it was on a miserable November afternoon that we set out on the train bound for London Docks. At least we were able to look forward to nearly three weeks of relaxation on board the *Transvaal Castle*, one of the Union Castle Line's modern liners. Passing through Customs and Immigration checks necessitated standing in a seemingly endless queue. It was extremely cold and, after about 20 minutes, Margaret passed out. No doubt her condition had a lot to do with this, but it had the instant benefit of getting us both on board without any further delay, for which we were duly thankful. We were ushered into our cabin, which was small but quite comfortable. The Goan steward had already delivered our suitcases so we decided to go straight to the nearest lounge and relax with a drink. An hour-or-so later all of the passengers had embarked and we had our first pleasant dinner on board. Shortly afterwards it was discovered that Margaret was not a good sailor. Strange really, bearing in mind her many fishermen forebears. To this day I don't know of anyone else who has been seasick while the ship is still tied up at the berth in the Pool of London. At 10 o'clock the ship was still awaiting the tide so we went to our cabin and turned in. The following morning, on our awakening, it was to find that we were well under way and steaming somewhere off Hastings.

Fortunately, the weather remained fine and the sea calm for the next couple of days. Margaret suffered badly however. I suppose much of it was due to morning sickness, but in the event she was unable to keep down any food for the first part of the voyage. I think that she was bitterly regretting her decision to marry me and go to Africa. Going through the Bay of Biscay was particularly trying. Generally speaking, I am a good sailor. On this occasion, however, even I experienced some discomfort. Margaret remained in the cabin most of the time. However, by the time the ship reached Gibraltar, the weather was much improved. We were able to go ashore for a few hours. This, I believe, was Margaret's first experience of foreign travel, so it was especially interesting for her. The voyage, after this, became very much more enjoyable.

Our journey to Mombasa took the best part of three weeks. The luxury of life on board ship, relaxing by the pool, drinking Pims and generally enjoying ourselves, was interspersed with the trips ashore at Port Said, Suez and Aden. Eventually, however, our holiday was over. We arrived at the bustling port of Mombasa. I did get a glimpse of the passion wagon as it was slung by a crane onto the quay. I could notice no apparent damage. I should next see it at the agents in Kampala. Shortly afterwards we disembarked and boarded the train for our final destination.

The journey to Kampala took a day-and-a-half and, not having experienced it myself, I found it as varied and interesting as did Margaret. On our arrival, we were met by a staff car and, with our hand-luggage, whisked off to the Imperial Hotel where we were to spend the next couple of days sorting ourselves out. The following morning, I set off for police headquarters where I was to be told about my new posting.

CHAPTER 22

The next week passed quickly. One of my first priorities was, of course, to get my transport. I could not expect to see my new car for a while, so it was over to Jinja to collect the trusty old vehicle from the P.W.D. store. At this stage I decided to take Margaret on a quick trip to Karamoja in order to collect my two dogs Barney and Randy from Arthur Kessel with whom I had left them. Leaving very early in the morning I managed to reach Moroto by about 5 o'clock. Kess, having just finished work, greeted me like a long lost brother. Randy came bounding out to greet me and to inspect her new mistress. Of Barney there was no sight. Kess then broke the sad news. Barney had died the previous night and was already buried in the garden. He had been very sick for some weeks and it appeared there was nothing the vet could do for him. The night he died he had staggered to his feet to drive off a hyena which had been lurking nearby. This had been his final act and he had keeled over and expired shortly afterwards. I went with Kess to inspect Barney's last resting place. A mound of heavy rocks lay over him. The hyenas would not be able to get at him there. I think Margaret was as upset as I was. I had told her so much about Barney that she felt she knew him. However, Randy was her usual healthy self and she exuberantly tried to make up for the loss. Early the following morning we left Moroto and by evening were back at the Imperial Hotel. A couple of days later the crates containing my various belongings were delivered to Katwe police station and we were able to move in.

The police station was situated about a mile outside the environs of Kampala and was reached by a good tarmacadam road which avoided the minor road which passed through Katwe Village, an area of Asian and African *dukas*, a multitude of bars and so called dance halls and a large collection of mud huts, topped by corrugated iron roofs. Here lived a very considerable percentage of the criminal fraternity of Kampala. How different this was going to be to my life of the three previous years, virtually living in the bush.

Outside the police station was a large roundabout where five roads converged. The first was the main road from Kampala. The second led to Makindye Hill where the Governor's Lodge was situated with its wonderful view over Lake Victoria. Here he and his family would go occasionally for a break from Government House at Entebbe. Also on Makindye Hill was a large population of senior Government and Commercial staff. The third junction led to Entebbe, about twenty miles distant. The next one was to Masaka and all stations west as far as the Congo border. The fifth junction was, of course, the road which emerged from Katwe Village.

In front of the police station was a hard-standing which could be used as a car park or a parade ground. The police station building formed an L shape and boasted a ground- and a first-floor. The ground floor was given over to the usual offices, cells and store rooms while the first floor was the domain of the unfortunate resident officer and his family. Thus there was no way that the O.C. Police could escape his responsibilities. Here I was literally on duty for 24-hours a day, 7-days a week. It seemed small wonder in the circumstances that the previous incumbent had suffered a nervous breakdown and had been invalided out. The layout of the officers' quarters necessitated emerging from one room and following an open passageway before finding the entrance to the next room. The accommodation consisted of a lounge, two bedrooms, a bathroom, a kitchen and a storeroom. The last two were immediately over the top of the cells where a collection of noisy drunks were locked away every weekend and frequently at other times. At the rear of the police station was a small compound in which were two garages and a gate which opened onto the police lines. The accommodation for the police constables and N.C.Os consisted of lines of concrete block dwellings with tiled roofs.

The Charge Office was immediately beneath our lounge and remarkably noisy it was. In addition to the police radio, invariably turned up to its full volume, vociferous complainants and violent prisoners did their best to ensure that the incumbent police officer had as little rest as possible. A European complainant would invariably insist on being dealt with by the officer in charge. No one of lower rank would do regardless of the time, day or night.

The staff at this unit consisted of myself, two African Sub-Inspectors, Sali and Byamugenzi, Station Sergeant Odubu, Sergeants Lule and Matovu, four Corporals and 23 constables, including one Balikirungi of whom more in due course. I had considered my work-load somewhat excessive on my previous tour of duty in Karamoja. Now I awoke to the realities of life. Every day thefts, robberies and burglaries were reported. Murders occurred several times a week or, at some periods, daily. The road to Entebbe with its excellent tarmac road was a race track and a killing ground, as was the Masaka road for at least the length of it which lay within the area covered by Katwe police station. It rapidly became apparent that it was beyond the powers of myself and the minute staff at my disposal to cope with this quantity of work. During my initial taking-over of the station I had noted that the standard of the station records left a lot to be desired. Now I found out the reason for this. Nobody could hope to deal with the crime and traffic workload, let alone keep an eye on the multitude of book entries at the same time. I found myself working 16-hours a day in an effort to keep abreast of the work. Even so, I was too readily available and would frequently be called out at night to deal with anything which might be considered beyond the scope of the staff on duty.

After a few weeks spent somewhat unsuccessfully in trying to burrow out from beneath the great pile of paperwork, I found time to visit my old friend and former O.C. Noel Caunce. He was happily ensconced at the police barracks at Nsambya where he was in his element. The administration involved in running this unit where several hundred police constables and N.C.Os were housed was right up his street. Lines' inspections, parades, disciplinary hearings and postings to other units meant that he was in his element. Like myself he had recently returned from leave and had also used this as an opportunity to get married. His wife Peggy was a pleasant if somewhat plain girl whose premature dental loss meant her using a top plate. She reminded me of nothing more that Popeye's Olive Oyl. She towered over him and was not averse to taking a mighty swipe at him if he upset her. She would indulge in this practice in public as well as in private. I fancy Noel was somewhat dubious at the swop he had made from Sophia, his African mistress, who could always be relied on to do his bidding and not obtrude into his social life. It was then that I discovered that Noel was the author of my present discomfort. He proudly informed me that, during a discussion at police headquarters regarding a possible replacement officer to take charge at Katwe, he had strongly recommended that I be posted there. I am sure that he had acted in what he thought was the best interests of both the force and myself. However, when I started to relate to him the problems I was encountering he promised to do what he could to alleviate the situation. In this he was as good as his word. Within a few weeks my staff was doubled and a considerable building programme was under way to house them.

The staff increase, while welcome in itself did not, however, have a great effect on my personal workload. I was still far too readily available to be called out to deal with a great variety of jobs. Well I should just have to make the best of it.

Katwe had been the scene of a number of particularly unpleasant robberies. A particularly vicious criminal named Okello was thought to be responsible for these. One evening a man, later found to be Okello, was detained by a posse of the villagers from one of whom he had stolen a bicycle. A simple theft for which he would have probably been fined by the Native Court. On the way to the police station, however, he had produced a knife with a lethal 9-inch blade and had plunged it into the chest of the nearest villager. In the ensuing confusion he had made his escape. Now the victim was carried semi-conscious to the police station where the ensuing uproar alerted me to the situation. My first action was to try to obtain a vehicle to take the victim to the hospital for urgent treatment. Nothing was forthcoming, however. Our own lorry was undergoing repairs and none of the other units around Kampala were prepared to take a chance on letting their own transport go in case they required it themselves. After ten minutes it became clear to me that the only way to save the unfortunate's life was to take him to hospital in my own car, my pride and joy which had now taken the place of the old faithful which had been pensioned off and could now be found in Kampala being used as a taxi. Fortunately, the victim was bleeding very little. I wrapped him in a blanket and laid him on the back seat. By the time I reached hospital he was unconscious and clearly in deep shock. I was convinced that the knife wound in the chest was causing massive internal bleeding. On my arrival I had the victim carried into the casualty department which was as usual filled to overflowing with other patients all awaiting treatment. 'Just put him down over there', an orderly instructed. 'We'll see to him when his turn comes.' Having gone to the trouble of personally conveying him to hospital I was not prepared to see him die before some effort was made to save him. I demanded to see the duty European doctor. If people coming to the police station were able to demand to see me, I didn't see why a doctor should be immune. Eventually the doctor arrived in a not-very-good mood. I took him over to the victim and a cursory examination followed. 'He has a stab wound to the chest', was the diagnosis. 'Yes', I said, 'I am perfectly well aware of his injuries. Now how about doing something about it.' With somewhat ill-grace the patient was taken off to the operating theatre. 'Well', I thought. 'I've done all I can. At least he's in good hands.'

The following morning I telephoned the hospital to be informed that the victim had died during the night. This was now yet another murder enquiry. I went to the hospital. The corpse lay in the mortuary awaiting a post-mortem examination. I examined the body, fully expecting to find a massive operation wound. Instead I found just the entry wound, secured by two neat stitches. I took this as a personal affront. Having gone to a great deal of trouble over this poor wretch, I was furious to find that some stupid inefficient so-called doctor had not made the slightest effort to repair the damage. During the course of the ensuing enquiry I took a statement from the doctor to whom I had handed the victim, in which I insisted on a full account of the action he had taken. I later had the pleasure of hearing him severely censured by the Coroner.

Several weeks later Detective Constable Balikirungi came to see me one evening. Balikirungi was a tall thin untidy individual who, unshaven and in his filthy clothes looked far more like a member of the criminal fraternity than a policeman. However, in the field of obtaining information he was without equal. 'Sir, I have seen Okello down in Katwe Village. He is in a house there drinking *waragi*.' I judged from Balikirungi's breath and slurred voice and unsteady gait, that he had also been imbibing heavily in the same local brew at the same location.

I hastily gathered as many staff together as I was able and within a few minutes was on my way, followed by our lorry containing no less that ten policemen. Leaving the vehicles parked some distance away we silently approached the hut where the wanted man was said to be. It soon became evident, however, that our approach had not gone unobserved. I had no sooner directed my staff to surround the building and was just about to enter, when the door flew open and Okello rushed out brandishing his wicked-looking knife with the clear intention of killing anyone who stood in his way. It just so happened that I was nearest and he came straight at me, his intention all too obvious. As he closed with me, I managed to grip his wrists. Okello was a tall. muscular man and agile as a monkey. He was also desperate. Try as I would, I could see the knife getting closer to my throat. My policemen now saw that I was engaged in a desperate struggle and came to my aid. They did not, however, try to get hold of my adversary but contented themselves with bashing him over the head with their batons. This didn't seem to have any noticeable effect other than enraging him further. What it did do was to cause him to bleed heavily all over me. Within seconds my hands were wet and sticky with blood. This gave him an unfair advantage because in addition to his natural agility he was now as slippery as an eel. I could no longer hold him firmly. I grimly held on knowing that any relaxation on my part would result in my attending hospital with a chest or throat wound from which I would be unlikely to survive. Fortunately. the pounding that Okello was taking on his skull rendered him unconscious in the nick of time. He was securely handcuffed and taken to the police station.

Okello, in custody, proved as violent and truculent as he had been before his arrest. I took the precaution of ensuring that he was heavily-secured and guarded when he was taken to Court. As expected, he was remanded in custody pending his High Court appearance and I breathed a sigh of relief when I saw him handcuffed and being taken off to Luzira Prison on the outskirts of Kampala to await trial for the numerous offences which he had committed over a very long period. My disgust can be imagined when, two days later, I received a telephone call from the prison informing me that he had escaped, killing a prison warder in the process. Some weeks later Okello was ambushed in the act of committing a robbery. During the ensuing struggle, he was shot dead by an European police officer. It was later found that he had had an active role in the Mau-mau in Kenya. I would have dearly loved to have been responsible for his demise, but it was not to be.

I was seated in my office one morning trying desperately to escape from beneath the mound of paper which was threatening to overwhelm me when an agitated European charged in, having not bothered with the formality of asking if I was available. I was about to forcibly eject him when he gasped out, 'For Christ's sake get up the road quick. There's been a traffic accident and the locals are about to kill a European.' Clearly there was no time to be lost so, quickly collecting my revolver from the safe while getting a couple more details regarding the location, I ran out to my car, grabbing a couple of police constables who happened to be standing outside at the time. Sub-Inspector Sali had come out of his office to see what was going on and I instructed him to gather as many policemen as he could and follow me to the scene of the accident as rapidly as possible.

The accident was on the Masaka road, a couple of miles from the police station. On my arrival, I found a crowd of about a couple of hundred natives armed with sticks and *pangas*, (the African machete) blocking the road while gathered round a large American car. I forced my way through the crowd and found a Belgian man and two women crouched in the passenger seats at the rear of the vehicle. At the front of the car was an African and another Belgian man. At the side of the vehicle was the body of a young African boy of about six years. I enquired of them who had been driving. The African told me that he had. The crowd, in an obviously ugly mood, shouted that the Mazungu had been in the driving seat. Further questioning made the matter plain. The vehicle, being registered in the Congo, had a left-hand drive. The Belgian, having been in the right hand front seat had been seen to get out from that side and had been assumed by the crowd to have been driving. Fortunately, at this time Sub-Inspector Sali arrived with half-a-dozen reinforcements. I got them to push the crowd back and quickly examined the scene. Skid marks indicated that the car had been travelling quite slowly. It was plain that, as the driver and passengers alleged, the boy had run out in front of them giving no opportunity for evasive action. I got them back into the car and instructed the driver to go to Katwe police station and await my return. I then collected several of the members of the crowd who had stated that they saw what happened, and got them onto the lorry.

The law required that I take possession of the body in order that a post-mortem be carried out. Here was the rub! As soon as the relatives realised what I was about, I was attacked. The whole thing was totally unexpected and I was quickly felled by a blow from a heavy stick wielded by an old crone who turned out to be the victim's grandmother. Staggering to my feet I grabbed her before she could inflict any further damage. Another individual then struck a further blow so I grabbed him also and shoved them onto the lorry with the assistance of my constables. We thrust the victim's body up after them and, reaching the comparative safety of my car, made a somewhat ignominious retreat before the rest of the crowd could decide on any further action.

At Katwe Police Station I settled down to the inevitable hours of work it would take to sort out the incident. The four Belgians were taken to my flat where Margaret provided tea and sympathy. My leg, where it had been struck by the old woman's stick, was badly bruised but the skin was not broken. Neither, fortunately, was the bone. No lasting damage seemed to have been done so instead of charging her with assault on police I released her after letting her cool her heels in the cell for a few hours. I dealt with her relative a little more harshly, however. After providing the required statements the driver and passengers were allowed to continue on their journey somewhat shaken but intact. At the subsequent inquest a finding of accidental death was recorded.

Mesulum Otwao, the senior of my two clerks, was a cheerful little Muganda of about 20-years of age. He lived a mile or two from the police station with a young girl who was not his wife but whom, he assured me, he intended marrying eventually. In addition to being a pleasant character he was also extremely naive. From time to time my evil sense of humour caused me to take advantage of this trait. Oddly, he never seemed to resent this but took it in good part.

While on home leave I had attended a number of auctions where I had acquired, very cheaply, a number of items which I thought would be useful in setting up our home. Among the bits and pieces I had brought was a Victorian Electro-Therapy Machine, beautifully made, in a mahogany case and complete with the original Leclanche Cell which was intended to provide an electric current of 1.5 volts. The machine converted this into around 32,000 volts, though of course no amperes. Hardly an item which could be thought to become an essential part of life in the African bush — but it was in a job lot and I am an inveterate hoarder. Playing about with it, I discovered that it worked very well on an ordinary torch battery. One morning I was in my office when Mesulum entered. His eyes lit on the mahogany box which I had placed on the window-sill. 'What is that, Sir.' he enquired. I couldn't resist it. 'Well', I said, 'it's a machine for measuring the amount of electricity in one's body and increasing it if that amount is too little.' 'Please Sir, may I try it'? he begged. 'Are you quite sure', I enquired. He was. 'Right,' said I. 'You must wet your hands to ensure a good contact.' He did so and gripped the brass handles. 'Now whatever you do don't let go of the handles.' I said. With that I flicked the switch. After about 30 seconds of mind-blowing screams, I enquired if he felt that the amount of electricity in his body had reached a sufficient level. He failed to reply directly to this question but I gathered from his increased bodily activity that he thought it probably had. I switched the machine off and Mesulum was left examining his hands, under the impression that they had just been surgically removed. 'I'll bet you feel a lot better for that', said I. 'Sir, I'm sure that Mr Galiwango would also benefit from it', he said. Mr Galiwango the junior clerk had by this time come into the office. He was, however, not quite as green as Mr Otwao. And, having been alerted by the screams, declined the treatment. Pity really. It did cross my mind that recalcitrant prisoners might also benefit from the machine but, regrettably, never gave it the necessary field trials.

A new batch of European officers had entered the force. No longer were they called Inspectors. The lowest rank now was Cadet Assistant Superintendent. Joe Deegan, the Commissioner, had published some sort of apology to the general public in which he regretted that the recent intake of officers had been somewhat sub-standard. This upset some of us, myself included, but we were then assured that this criticism was directed at certain officers who were no longer with us.

Monty Locke was the police officer with the overall command of Buganda Province with the rank of Superintendent. He occasionally visited Katwe police station not, as yet, to carry out a full inspection but, I suspected, to see if there was any sign yet of my following my predecessor to the funny farm. During one of his visits I enquired if it might not be possible to post one of the newly-appointed cadets to take over some of the burden. I pointed out that we had a spare bedroom, and meals and the other facilities could be provided at a lower rate than were being charged at the hotel where the latest intake were being housed. The outcome of this was the arrival of Ray Viggor. He was an ex-army Captain in his mid-20s with ginger hair and moustache. He was married but his wife was still in the U.K. and not permitted to join her husband for at least six months. His police experience was limited to the short course he had received prior to coming to Uganda. However he was a pleasant enough chap. His main reason for wanting to come to Uganda, it seemed, was the exorbitant price of coal in England. Still I've known worse reasons than that! Now, hopefully, I should be able to catch up on the mountain of administration work which had so far defeated me. First however it was essential that I should take Ray under my wing and break him in gradually.

A few mornings after Ray's arrival, he and I were in the office which I shared with him. Margaret had just brought us down a cup of tea and we were enjoying an unaccustomed moment of relaxation when a tall, thin figure in police uniform and with the badges of rank of Deputy Superintendent strode in. I had not previous met Laurie Smith and assumed that this was just a social visit from a passing fellow officer. No such thing. I found out very rapidly why Deputy Superintendent Smith had become universally known as 'Snakey Smith!' 'I was given to understand that you were under some pressure of work here', he snarled. 'What's all this then. Having a picnic.' He removed his cap and revealed a tonsured head of hair that would have done justice to a monk. Margaret got out of the chair on which she had been seated and left the office. Snakey then seated himself behind my desk and glared at Ray and myself. 'I am a very senior Deputy Superintendent. You are a junior Assistant Superintendent.' What that had to do with anything was quite beyond me. 'I've heard about you from Mr Pearman', he snarled, looking me up and down. So, that was it. Here was a friend of the one person in the force I could have cheerfully slaughtered, who had led me such a rotten life in Karamoja. If Pearman had been dying of thirst I wouldn't have pissed on him! Now I was being pursued by his great friend. Well he wouldn't have to look very far to find fault here! A couple of weeks later and I might have been able to find sufficient time to make some inroads into the chaos which passed for administration here. 'Right', said he, making himself comfortable in my seat. 'I'll start off with the

Station Diary and the Occurrence Book.' My heart sank. Obviously any excuses I might make would play right into his hands. I should have to accept what was coming with as much stoicism as I could muster. The books which he had called for were duly produced and examined with a sort of fiendish delight. 'Disgraceful', he bawled. 'I've never seen such badly-kept records.' Two hours later I was mightily relieved to be called out to deal with yet another murder. On my return a few hours later I found that my persecutor had left. A curt note reiterated his displeasure. 'I shall be back on Saturday afternoon when I shall expect to find that the matters to which I have drawn your attention have been rectified.' Saturday! It was Thursday already. I was totally underwhelmed by this. I was fully aware of the shortcomings of the records at the station. Now, just when I was about to get the opportunity to put things right, I had been jumped on from a great height.

The station diary I could do little about. To start trying to touch this up would be to invite disaster. All I could was to ensure that the cross-referencing was brought up to date. The Occurrence Book was a different matter. I started off with this. It was a large, hard-bound volume in A3 size. Columns extended across both pages. Of the current book about 100 of the 200 pages had been used. With a heavy heart I set to work. I shouldn't get much sleep tonight. Ray would have to take any call-outs and do the best he could with them. I could only see one way of putting this book right. That was to completely re-write it. By 3 a.m. I had done it. Next the Traffic Accident Register By 8 a.m., when a cup of tea was brought to me, I had completed the re-writing of this. Cells Register, Exhibits Register, Crime Register followed. By mid-afternoon I had cracked it. I called for the Sub-Inspectors and the Station Staff and produced the new books. 'This is the way these registers will be kept from now on', I said. 'You, Sub-Inspector Sali, will be responsible for examining them each morning, putting right anything which doesn't comply with this standard, and producing them to me in my office as soon as I am on duty each day.' So — I had done it! Fortunately, there had been no major incident during the time I had taken to put matters right. I was now ready to take up the reins again. Apart, that is, from catching up on some sleep! Fat chance!

Saturday afternoon arrived. Snakey Smith also arrived,

keenly anticipating the opportunity of having another go. Seating himself in my chair he called for the books. As he waded through them a look of disbelief came over his face. An hour later he stalked out having written in the Inspections Book. 'The shortcomings to which I drew attention on my previous inspection, no longer exist.' That was it. Not a word was spoken! During my sojourn at Katwe he never made another visit — for which I was duly grateful.

I received a visit from the local Mkungu chief. There were problems, he informed me, at Kibuye village which was situated quite near Nsambya police lines. A lot of illegal beer and *waragi* was being brewed and *bhangi* (Cannabis) was being grown. Kibuye village was quite extensive, covering almost a mile square. The main problem as far as the Mkungu Chief was concerned was the beer-brewing. Anyone could brew beer but it required a licence to do it on a commercial scale. The Mkungu was the one to issue the licences and he was thereby losing out financially. *Waragi* was a raw spirit distilled from maize or bananas or other ingredients. It was the cause of much of the violent crime committed in East Africa and brewing it was an offence under the *waragi* ordinance. Bhangi was also illegal throughout East Africa and its cultivation was an offence. The Mkungu's problem was that he didn't have enough of his local native police to mount a raid on the village. Could I help? Yes, I thought I could. This would be a great opportunity for searching the village for stolen property, bicycles, etc, as well as the *waragi* and bhangi. I decided to go to town on this and sought the assistance of Noel Caunce. He promised to provide 50 constables and N.C.Os, I could muster a further 20. The Mkungu was going to bring a further seventy. We arranged to meet up at 5 a.m. at Nsambya Barracks. No information was to be given to any of the troops taking part in the raid or it would certainly abort our efforts. Ray Viggor was to take charge of half of the police detachment while I would be responsible for overseeing the remainder.

The following morning we made our way to Nsambya. The local police unit with the Makungu was already in attendance and it took very little time to get the show on the road. By six a.m. we had flooded the entire village area and the raid commenced. Each house was entered with scant respect for its occupants. Naked damsels and their boy friends came scampering out as their doors were forced open. Where illegal brewing was found it was usually contained in 40-gallon steel drums which were unceremoniously tipped over where they stood. *Waragi*, usually contained in lemonade bottles was carefully collected as evidence, as was the large quantity of dried *bhangi*. The *bhangi* under cultivation was pulled up and likewise taken as evidence. I happened to be passing the open door of a mud hut when one of the 40-gallon drums of beer was tipped over by one of the Makungu's police. The contents hit the rear wall of the hut and rebounded with the strength of a waterfall straight out of the front door and soaked me. The irate householder came rushing out brandishing her licence. I commiserated and complimented her on the quality of her brew. By 9 o'clock the raid was over. A large quantity of stolen property had been discovered, 20 arrests made, around 500 gallons of beer destroyed, including some which was completely legal, and my uniform would never need starching again. The beer had dried and it resembled a suit of armour. Divorce proceedings had also been commenced by one of the N.C.O's from Nsambya who had found his wife of three weeks in bed with one of the villagers. He thought she was visiting her mother!

Bicycle thefts had reached epidemic proportions. Every day the theft one or two, sometimes more, would be reported. Of these very few were ever recovered. Those that were had inevitably had their identification numbers filed off. My endeavours to restore some of these using sulphuric acid in the manner described during my recent course at Hendon Police College had but limited success. Occasionally we would have a bicycle brought in, having been found abandoned. Usually it was a case of 'finders keepers, losers weepers.' Of these few, I imagine that the majority must have been stolen, probably from other areas. The chance of these ever being returned to their owners was slight. If they were unclaimed at the end of 3 months they were taken to the premises of the local auctioneer for disposal. I decided to obtain one of these to try an experiment. I had no difficulty in getting a really smart-looking bike — for nothing. The auctioneer was only too pleased to present it to me in the hope that I should continue to use his services. Back at the police station I obtained a small steel hinge and drilled and bolted it onto the chain wheel, having first cut the free side of the hinge into a tongue shape. Now, by flicking up the free side of the hinge it acted as a lever and removed the chain from the wheel immediately the pedal was turned. I then put my plan into action. A couple of policemen in plain clothes were sent to hang about near the local market. After half-an-hour or so another plainclothes constable cycled nonchalantly to the market, parked it near the lurking constables and wandered off to do his shopping. The first catch came within five minutes. The thief approached the bike, swung his leg over the saddle and commenced riding away. Off came the chain leaving his feet rotating aimlessly. Over came the two lurking constables and the arrest was made. Great. The trio escorted the thief back to the police station and off they went back to the market. Another three arrests were made before mid-day. Sufficient unto the day, etc. The following day the trio moved to another market. Within a short time the first arrest was made. The second thief made a run for it with the police in hot pursuit. A large group of the local population joined in the chase and having caught the thief proceeded to beat him up. Most of the villagers had lost bicycles in the past or members of their family or friends had. Here was an opportunity for revenge. Before the policemen could intervene, the thief had been summarily executed by the mob. The crowd melted away leaving the corpse lying in the road. By the time reinforcements had arrived with the lorry to collect the body, my bicycle had been nicked by another thief! No arrests were ever made in connection with the death of the thief, but the number of cycle thefts dropped dramatically after this. Later I obtained another bicycle and rigged it out in the same manner but never experienced quite such a good result.

The arrival of Ray Viggor at the Station eased matters to such a degree that I was able to take Margaret out occasionally at weekends. One of our favourite jaunts was to Entebbe, where we would take lunch at the Lake Victoria Hotel. This was superb. The hotel occupied a prime site set as it was on a slope overlooking the lake. Sunday lunch could be chosen from a traditional English roast or unlimited curry or a cold buffet, again of unlimited quantity. I'm afraid I made a bit of a pig of myself on these occasions. The cost was minimal. I wonder what it is like now. After lunch we would make our way to the lake shore and sunbathe on the sandy beach. Swimming was considered safe as there were no crocodiles in the area. I was a bit dubious about it though, bearing in mind the ever present risk of contracting bilharzia from the snail population. Alternatively we would go to the nearby botanical gardens or visit the zoo where orphaned animals were kept, hopefully to be returned to the wild in due course. I don't know if there was ever a single success recorded in this.

One of my occasional duties, now that I had a bit more time to spare, was to visit the local bars in Katwe village, to examine their licences. This proved quite an experience. Prostitutes of all shapes, sizes and colours plied their trade at most of the bars. The bars varied greatly. Some of them were merely mud huts with thatched roofs where *pombe*, the local-brewed beer was on sale and a pot could be purchased by a group of old men who would sit around sucking the content through thin pipes with a crude filter on the end to stop the solid debris from being swallowed. More generally, however, the beer was of the bottled variety direct from the Nile Brewery at Jinja or Bell Beer from Port Bell near Luzira Prison on the nearby shore of Lake Victoria. The nearby shops were also worth a visit. About half of these were Asian-owned and staffed, the remainder belonged to Africans. I saw a notice on the front door of an Asian tailor one day which has always stuck in my mind. It said, 'IF NOT IN FRONTSIDES WILL BE UP BACKSIDES'. I decided not to take my custom there.

Mr Otwao came into my office one morning in great good humour. His wife, or rather, the young girl he intended to make his wife when he got round to it, had produced a daughter. I congratulated him warmly and on the spur of the moment decided to exercise my evil sense of humour. 'How old is your 'wife'?', said I. 'She is just 15, Sir', he happily replied. 'Oh dear', I said. 'I'm afraid you have committed a very serious offence. Sexual intercourse with a girl under the age of 16 is a crime, as you are no doubt aware.' Poor Otwao's face was a picture. 'Forgive me, Sir. I did not think about it. If you let me off this time I will never do it again.' 'I'm afraid your sins have found you out', said I. 'I shall have to speak on this matter with Superintendent Anderson who is in charge of the C.I.D.' I then picked up my telephone and, keeping one finger firmly on the button, carried out an imaginary conversation with George Anderson. It went something like this. 'Mr Anderson? Oh good morning, Sir. Yes, I've got a bit of a problem with my clerk, Mr Otwao. I wonder if

I could ask you for some advice regarding the action you think I should take. Yes. Apparently he has been living with a young girl who became pregnant by him and has now produced an infant. Problem is that she is only just 15 so he must have made her pregnant when she was 14. Yes. I agree. Clear case. No doubt about it. Right, Statement under caution. Charge him and stick him in the cell.' By this time poor Mesulum had gone an odd grey colour and was near collapse. 'Well', I said. 'You heard that. Which cell do you fancy for the night?' 'Please Sir', he gasped. 'Let me off this time. I will never do it again. I will send her home to her father as soon as she has recovered from the birth. Or sooner if possible!' I couldn't keep the farce up any longer and collapsed with laughter. Realising that he was off the hook, Mesulum joined somewhat mutedly in everyone's enjoyment. Mr Galiwango who had been listening at the door joined in wholeheartedly, and I sent upstairs for a few beers to celebrate the birth.

Chapter 23

A spate of armed robberies were occurring throughout Buganda. The gang of robbers, up to a dozen in number and known as the *Bakondo*, would drive out to an isolated village or small town, usually in stolen vehicles, smash open the door of the house of a wealthy farmer or a shop-keeper and steal whatever was available. This gang were violent and armed with knives or handguns. The slightest resistance on the part of the householder or his family would result in death or serious injury being meted out immediately.

As usual it was D.C. Balikirungi who eventually got the information regarding the robbers hideout. It turned out to be within 200 yards of Katwe police station. I decided that this would have to be a full-scale operation if we were to clear out this nest of criminals. Knowing that the gang were armed and would not hesitate to kill if necessary, I decided that a raid at about 3 a.m. would be the best course of action. My police party consisted of Ray Viggor and myself, the two Sub-Inspectors, two sergeants and 20 constables. At 2.30 a.m. we formed up at the police station and, led by D.C. Balikirungi, for once almost sober, made our way on foot to the house where the gang were holed-up. Before setting out I stressed to the party the importance of absolute silence. The N.C.Os and constables went barefoot to avoid as far as possible any breaking twigs, etc., which might give us away. The house was very large by African standards. Probably around eight rooms I thought. It was in total darkness and I wondered at first if the gang were currently away on a raid. By 3 a.m. everyone was in position and all doors and windows were guarded. A constable armed with a heavy sledge hammer hid with me in the undergrowth immediately outside the front door through which I intended smashing a rapid entrance before any of the occupants woke up.

Just as I was about to give the signal for the raid to commence the front door opened and a man clad only in underpants came out stretching and yawning. He stood against the wall of the house and relieved himself and was just about to go back inside when something alarmed him. To this day I don't know what it was. His reaction was instantaneous however. Without a sound he bolted — in my direction. Rugby is not my favourite game. As far as I'm concerned it's a nasty, dirty dangerous pastime where one can sustain some unpleasant injuries. However, I made a perfect rugby tackle from a crouching position and grabbed the fleeing robber round the ankles bringing him heavily to the ground and knocking the breath out of his lungs. Unfortunately, I didn't notice a boulder the size of a football in the way. My tackle succeeded in bringing the robber down but the top of my thigh crashed straight onto the boulder. The pain of it took my breath away. Immediately a couple of the constables came to my aid and secured and gagged the prisoner. So far so good. The front door was open and no noise had been made to alert the occupants. I hobbled to my feet and gave the signal for the raid to commence. Fortunately, the house had electricity installed and the light switches were easily found. In the various rooms we found six of the gang and they were quickly overpowered before they could get to their weapons. A search of the house revealed a mass of stolen property and a considerable arsenal of handguns, rifles and shotguns, to say nothing of the knives and *pangas*. On reflection I guess we were very lucky that this operation turned out as well as it did. With the amount of firearms available to the gang we could have sustained any number of casualties and a siege situation could easily have been the outcome. By the following morning my right thigh was twice its normal size and turning attractive shades of purple and yellow. I went to the hospital where an X-ray confirmed that fortunately no bones were broken.

As a postscript to this, the same afternoon I went with Margaret into Kampala to pick up a new radiogram that I had ordered. Not being in a condition to carry this heavy article any distance, I parked immediately outside and went in. I was out within three of four minutes. However, within this time a traffic constable had given me a parking ticket. I later found that 'Snakey' Smith was responsible for this, having seen me park and hobble into the shop he had grabbed a nearby policeman and ordered him to report me. What a lovely man!

The telephone rang at about 5 a.m. It was my turn to respond so I staggered out to the passageway where the instrument was located. A European was in the charge office demanding to see me. I dressed and made my way downstairs. Mr French, I knew vaguely by sight. He was a director of one of the motor-vehicle importers and lived on Makindye Hill. As such he felt he could demand my services. I was not a happy man. However, I did my best not to be rude to him! I was informed that he had gone with his wife to a party, leaving at about 7 p.m. and, returning at about 4 a.m. had found his house had been entered by a rear window and ransacked. Nothing particularly unusual in this. I accompanied him to his house and examined the broken rear window. A beautiful set of fingerprints could be seen on one of the unbroken panes of glass. Cautioning him and his wife to touch nothing, I made a cursory examination of the house. The thief or thieves had apparently only been interested in cash and jewellery, apart from a few bottles of spirits which were also missing. There was clearly nothing I could do for the time being so, promising to get a member of the C.I.D. to attend later in the day to photograph the fingerprints, I returned to my bed. The stolen property turned out to be valued at several hundred pounds. The criminal responsible was never traced, the prints found being unrecorded.

Several months later an insurance assessor visited the police station and asked to see me. He seemed desperate to ingratiate himself with me. Eventually the reason became clear. Mr French's household insurance policy had expired at midnight on the night of the burglary. He was keen for me to give my opinion that the crime had taken place after this time. 'On the contrary', I said, 'It is almost certain that it took place before midnight. In my experience, thefts of this nature take place almost immediately after the owner leaves the premises. I would put the probable time of the crime at between 7 p.m. and 8 p.m.' The Assessor left my office in a rather bad mood. I must say that it left a nasty taste in my mouth to think that a well-known insurance company would scratch around in this manner in the hope of avoiding payment on a legitimate claim.

The birth of our daughter Alison added a new dimension to married life at Katwe. She weighed in at seven-pounds-eight-ounces at Nakasero Hospital on 29th June 1955. There was, I believe, a certain amount of calculation on fingers regarding the time between our wedding on 6th September 1954 and Alison's arrival, but she was legitimate. Just. One of the major problems was the constant noise. During the day it didn't matter too much. At night however the situation became serious. The heat, even at night, made it essential for the windows to be open. Alison proved to be a light sleeper and every night was broken trying to get her back to sleep. Apart from the inevitable shouting of complainants, prisoners and drunks, the police radio had no volume control on it. It blared out endlessly, not only from control speaking to Katwe, but also by every other station contacting one another. There was no means of isolating only the messages which concerned us. The volume was probably maintained at full blast to ensure that dozing policemen would not be able to ignore the messages. The time came when I felt that we could take no more of this. I obtained a large wooden box and liberally padded the inside. This I then upturned over the top of the radio. Peace at last. Each evening I would fit this silencer to the system. The volume was immediately reduced to an acceptable level. Great. First thing in the morning I would remove the cover and bedlam would once again return. Three days later, however, the radio ceased to function. The radio engineer attended immediately and carried out a repair. A week went past in blissful comparative silence. Then the radio again ceased to function. Again the engineer attended. This time he installed a new set. That evening I fitted my silencer. A week later the puzzled engineer carried out a further repair. This situation continued for several months. I got to know the engineer quite well. Eventually I invited him into my office where, over a cup of tea, I pointed out the problem as I saw it. With a look of relief at the solution to the puzzle he removed the set and replaced it with one which had a proper volume control. Thereafter we had little trouble from this source.

The respite afforded by the temporary inclusion of Ray Viggor on my staff at Katwe was at an end. Ray's wife had arrived in Kampala and he had received a new posting, this time to Mbale in the Western Province. I must say that I was somewhat envious of his move but I didn't begrudge it. He had worked hard since coming to help me out and the relief to the pressure I had been under had now diminished. The station was now working as an efficient unit. The books and records were being correctly kept and I could confidently leave their day-to-day supervision to Sub-Inspector Sali. I had succeeded in training Sub Inspector Byamugenzi in the basics of crime investigation and Sergeant Lule was able to cope with most of the traffic accidents, which were as prolific as ever. The problem of night calls was as bad as ever but I was able to delegate some of them to one or other of the Sub-Inspectors. Life at the police station continued to be somewhat fraught, but at least I had the satisfaction of knowing that I should not be caught out by any further snap inspections.

The weather had turned hot and humid. Sleep at night had become more and more difficult and Alison, in particular, was extremely fractious when her sleep was disturbed. Neither Margaret nor myself enjoyed much rest at night even with the window of the bedroom wide open. This latter, while allowing a welcome breeze to penetrate from time to time, had the disadvantage of also allowing every sound to disturb us. Since the window opened directly on to the front of the police station, the noise of cars and lorries coming and going, bringing in prisoners and complainants, violent drunks and noisy witnesses was causing considerable tension. One night a particularly noisy group in a police lorry arrived and pulled up immediately below our bedroom window. Fortunately, both the accompanying policemen and the others soon went into the charge office and the noise abated to some degree. Within a very short time, however, a most appalling stench filled the room. I got up and went to the window. In the open back of the lorry lay a bloated body, clearly the source of the smell. I rapidly closed the window and got dressed. The charge office was filled with a mass of humanity including the police driver. My first action was to get the lorry moved as far away from our bedroom as was possible. Meantime my enquiries revealed that the body had been found in an area of marshland about six miles out from the police station. It had been burned and beheaded. Fragments of unburned skin and bits of clothing indicated that the victim was an Asian, possibly a Sikh. Of the head there was no trace. I decided that there was little that could be done until morning so, leaving one of the Sub-Inspectors to make a start on the statements, I returned to bed. Margaret was up and attending to Alison. The window was once again open and the stench had dispersed. The night breeze had, however, carried into the room liberal quantities of black ash-like substances, clearly bits and pieces of the corpse and its clothing. Alison was covered in the stuff and Margaret was busy cleaning her up and getting fresh clothing and bedding.

In the morning, accompanied by some of the witnesses who had found the body I went to the scene of their discovery. The marsh was traversed by a narrow causeway, just wide enough to facilitate the passing of the police lorry. The body had been found about 50-yards into the swamp and might never have been discovered had it not been for the stench which had caused one of the witnesses to investigate. The marsh was covered in a thick growth of reeds about 6-feet in height. The ground, although waterlogged, was just about firm enough to take the weight of a man. At the edge of the causeway, between it and the reed area, a stream of fairly fast flowing water carried the outflow from the marsh under the road via a culvert. Fortunately, I was able to find an overgrown area nearby where the stream of water had ceased to flow. Here I crossed into the reeds and made my way to where the body had been discovered. There was no indication that the reeds had been burned here so clearly the body had been burned before being dumped. A patch of dried blood indicated, however, that the beheading of the corpse taken place here. Of the head, however, there was no sign. It seemed likely that the body had lain in the position in which it had been found for upwards of a week. Long enough for decomposition to become well-advanced. Clearly whoever had committed this crime was determined that the body should not be identified. Returning to Kampala I made my way to the police workshops where Willie Horn the senior Inspector of Vehicles was in his office. At my request, and while I waited, he had a large treble hook made out of mild steel. The hook ends were sharpened to needle points and the hook mounted onto a stout bamboo shaft. Armed with this tool I returned to the marsh. I reasoned that the most likely spot for disposing of the victim's head was the culvert under the causeway. However, we started with the stream carrying the outflow from the marsh and spent an hour dragging the hook backwards and forwards over a stretch of about 50 yards on each side of the culvert. This was singularly unsuccessful so the next step was to try the culvert itself. To do this it was necessary to send one of the constables into the water to poke the hook as far as possible under the road. After about five minutes we had the hoped-for success. Out came a bundle which on examination proved to be the victim's head wrapped in what had been a turban. The head was in an advanced state of decomposition but appeared to be that of a middle-aged bearded Asian man. Our find was taken to the mortuary where it was reunited with the remainder of the body. I now had the unpleasant task of taking fingerprints from those parts of the hands which had escaped destruction. I had devised a way of doing this by cutting the relevant strip of paper from the fingerprint form and wrapping this round and flat wooden batten about an inch-and-a-half wide. The ink-roller was then applied to each finger after which the strip of paper was rolled around the finger tip. This produced a passable fingerprint. A post-mortem examination of the body revealed that the cause of death was a single stab wound to the chest, which had penetrated the heart. Meanwhile, examination of the fingerprints succeeded in identifying the victim as one Ajit Singh whose family had not reported him missing but had, instead, put it about that he had gone on a visit to India. Ajit Singh had a criminal record for theft and violent crime. His wife still showed the signs of having suffered a vicious beating. Enquiries revealed that she had been a frequent victim of assaults by her husband. It took only a very mild interrogation for her to confess that during her most recent beating, she had grabbed a kitchen knife and plunged it into her husband's chest. Together with her relatives she had attempted to dispose of the body by burning it. This proving impossible a suitable place had been found and the remains dumped at night. Had it been taken a bit further into the swamp I doubt if the body would have ever been found and the remains would have been disposed of by the birds and small carnivores that inhabited the area. The outcome was that the woman was found guilty of murder, but having regard to the circumstances she received only a short prison sentence. The other members of her family, who were involved, were charged as accessories to murder and received considerably longer sentences.

A group of natives came to the police station one day and insisted on seeing me. I was informed by them that they lived about ten miles out near the lake shore between Katwe and Entebbe. One of them owned a number of cattle which were normally docile and well-behaved. On this morning, however, the herd bull had quite suddenly become a ferocious wild animal, charging a group of natives and succeeding in goring and killing one of them and seriously injuring two others. I was requested to attend and shoot the bull before it killed anyone else. I was a bit dubious about this never having come across a case of a domestic animal suddenly going mad and killing someone.

Clearly, however, something had to be done to prevent a recurrence. But how to get there? The location was way out in the bush with no roads leading to it. The tracks that were used were only wide enough for a bicycle and I didn't fancy a 20-mile walk. The problem was solved when one of the informants mentioned that he had come in on his motorcycle. A memorable ride followed. Perched on a pillion composed of an iron frame, I rode over extremely bumpy roads with my rifle strung across my back. Too late I wished I had taken the precaution of supplying a cushion to help me on my way. After about 7 miles we reached the lake shore and commenced our ride along the shoreline. Eventually, much to my relief, we arrived at the home of the cattle owner where the body of the victim lay. He had been virtually disembowelled and must have suffered a prolonged and most painful death. I felt sure that an inquest would be necessary but decided to deal with the cause of the problem before making arrangements for the removal of the body. I cautiously accompanied the owner of the cattle on foot through the bush. Great, this was just like being back in Karamoja. After about half-a-mile the offending beast was pointed out to me. It was standing on its own in an area of thick undergrowth. From what I could see of it, it didn't seem particularly ferocious. However, I certainly wasn't going to approach too close to ascertain its present temper. Best get the job over and done with. I could just make out the shape of the animal through the undergrowth about 100 yards away. I decided to make my way to a tree about midway between us, where I thought I should be able to get a clear shot. Stealthily, I crawled along pushing my rifle ahead of me. Without the slightest warning the bull suddenly charged me. The owner of the cattle who had been crawling along just behind me took to his heels. I had about three seconds to get to my feet take some sort of aim and fire. The bull had his head up and strings of foam and saliva dripped from his mouth. By the time I had got up he was virtually on me. There was no time to take careful aim. In fact there was no time to aim at all. It was a matter of pointing the rifle in the general direction of the animal and hoping for the best. Since he was by this time only about 5 yards away I could hardly miss. In my haste, my grip on the rifle was somewhat tenuous and as I pulled the trigger the weapon leapt backwards out of my hands. Fortunately the bullet struck the beast at the base of the throat and penetrated well into the chest, bringing him crashing to the ground at my feet. Within about 5 seconds half-a-dozen natives appeared as if from nowhere and set about the bull, their object being to cut its throat before it was dead — in the Moslem manner. If this was not done they would be unable to eat the meat. In a very short time the animal was skinned and butchered and taken back to the owners hut. '*Asante sana, effendi*', said the owner, and offered me about 20 pounds of prime beef. Thinking back to the behaviour of the animal just before its death and the strings of saliva trailing from its mouth, I declined the offer with thanks and, remounting my pillion seat, returned to the police station. To this day I puzzle over the bull's behaviour. I suppose it could have eaten some poisonous foliage in the bush which had caused the condition, if so, however, why were no other animals affected. I have discussed the symptoms on a number of occasions with veterinary officers but have never received a satisfactory explanation.

Mesulum Otwao came into my office as soon as I arrived one morning. He was clearly very upset and no amount of banter on my part could cheer him up. Eventually I found the reason. A small snake had entered his home the previous evening and had bitten his beloved daughter. He had taken the child to the local dispensary where it had received some fairly basic treatment but its condition was now clearly serious. Without any further delay I packed Otwa into my car and went with him to his home about 5-miles distant. Here I picked up his wife and the child and immediately took them to hospital. As usual I found a crowd awaiting treatment. Otwao reported to the orderly and in the time-honoured manner was told to sit down at the back and wait his turn. This really wasn't good enough. I demanded to see the European doctor in charge and he appeared after a few minutes. Surprise, surprise. It was the same individual I had fallen out with on the previous occasion I had taken a patient there. No doubt remembering the reprimand he had received on that occasion he could not do enough for me. The baby was rapidly taken off and injected with anti-venine. I returned to the police station leaving Otwao and his wife to stay at the hospital while the child was treated. Three days later Otwao re-appeared and was pleased to be able to report to me that the child was well on the way to recovery.

Buganda tribal tradition has it that an extraordinary individual named Kibuka lived several hundred years ago. Kibuka was able to prophesy the future and, while not endowed with wings, could nevertheless fly by levitation. Using this ability he used to get into tall trees and shower the enemy tribes, who were in the habit of attacking the Baganda, with spears, killing them by the thousand! Not unnaturally, when Kibuka died he was deified. As a God, Kibuka was credited with all sorts of powers, including that of making barren women fertile.

News arrived one day that the prophet Kibuka had been re-incarnated and was sitting in a tree on Matundwe Hill, a couple of miles from Katwe police station. Matundwe Hill rose about 300 feet above the surrounding countryside and could be easily approached from the south by a footpath. Otherwise it was surrounded by virtually impenetrable scrub. The top of the hill formed a plateau of reasonably clear ground, dominated by a single large tree, some 50-feet in height, in which Kibuka sat. It appeared that in addition to his powers of prophesy he had become something of a politician and was attended by a crowd of several hundred natives. The crowd was growing by the hour. It seemed that the object of his presence was twofold. The first was to encourage civil disobedience by refusing to pay taxes, etc. The second was to make a lot of money for himself by promising to make barren women fertile. I never discovered what his method was to be for the latter benefit! He was, however, collecting a great deal of cash and stock. I believe his fee was around 500-shillings a go. Nice work if you can get it! The crowd also brought with them numerous goats and cockerels to be used as sacrificial offerings. While seated in his tree and preaching to the crowd, Kibuka had a number of acolytes to collect the fees. The matter only came to the attention of the Protectorate Police when a detachment of the Kabaka's police, known as the Native Authority Police (or N.A.) raided the location one morning. hoping to arrest Kibuka for various offences. The police numbered about 30 and were under the control of a Head Constable. But not for long. Kibuka called on the crowd to resist and though he did not himself get out of his tree, he encouraged them to such a degree of violence that a riot resulted, in the course of which the Head Constable received a knife wound from which he immediately died. The police detachment retreated down the hill taking the body with them. Murder had now been committed and this was, of course, beyond the jurisdiction of the Kabaka's Police. The Officer-in-Charge of the N.A. police came immediately to see me. He held the rank of Superintendent but was not, of course, part of the Protectorate Police. Clearly the few police I had available at Katwe were going to be unable to deal with a situation of this seriousness. I reported the matter to Superintendent George Anderson who was in charge of Crime Investigation for Buganda Province. George decided that Katwe police station would be used as the main base for the operation and a meeting was called to decide of the plan of action. Information indicated that the crowd on Matundwe had now reached to over 1,000 and was still growing. It was decided that no action would be taken immediately, allowing time for a full reconnaissance to take place and to get the required plans drawn up. In the event, the operation started at 5 a.m. two days after the murder and the personnel to be used were 18 officers and inspectors and 300 other ranks. The route to be taken was from the east, through the dense scrub and onto the plateau. Hopefully, this would take the crowd by surprise, enabling the arrest of the prophet and his followers together with anyone who was thought to have taken part in the riot and the subsequent murder. Like all plans of this sort it had limited success. There was no way that 300 police could make their way silently through a belt of impenetrable bush and climb 300 feet onto the plateau. Barking dogs alerted the crowd long before the police arrived and they were met with a hail of missiles. However, by 6.30 a.m. and daylight, the police were more or less in control, much of the crowd was in full retreat and the prophet and his followers, together with about 50 of the rioters were in custody. A fleet of vehicles then brought the prisoners back to Katwe where they were herded together in the police station compound. Kibuka and his acolytes were placed in the cells in rather less than comfort since they were about 15 in each of the two cells meant for two prisoners. Still, if they can't take a joke they shouldn't have joined! The other riotous prisoners were immediately transferred to N.A. police custody. A large crowd gathered outside the police station and I wondered if we were about to be attacked. With this possibility in mind I armed a detachment of my police with rifles and Greener Guns and had them standing by. It soon became clear however, that the crowd had gathered hoping to see Kibuka come flying out of his cell. They dispersed, rather disappointed after a few hours. Up on Mutundwe Hill the N.A. police had set to work cutting down the offending tree to ensure that there was no repeat performance. The Prophet Kibuka was then interviewed in my office. He was still clad in his animal skins with the skin of an enormous python wrapped around him. I must say that his appearance with his long tangled hair and smelly body, reminded me strongly of Dedan Kimathi who had been one of the Mau-mau generals during the Kenya emergency. He was probably modelling himself on the Mau-mau leaders. George Anderson took charge of this investigation. A large number of exhibits had been brought in with the prisoners. In addition to a very large sum of money these included several sacrificial goats which were tethered in the compound and two cockerels which were in wicker baskets. For some extraordinary reason it was decided that this livestock should be retained at the police station pending Kibuka's court appearance. I was expected to look after them!

After their initial court appearance, Kibuka and his henchmen were remanded in custody to Luzira Prison to await trial on charges of murder. I managed to get the goats removed elsewhere, but I was stuck with the cockerels. After a couple of days these birds decided that they would settle down with us and they were released from their baskets and allowed the run of the compound. Any food which prisoners left would be hungrily devoured by them. Inevitably one of the cockerel went missing. Maybe it was one of the local dogs or more likely the wife of a hungry policeman. Anyway only one was left. This bird became the bane of my existence. Had it belonged to one of the policemen I would have given him the ultimatum of getting rid of it or being posted elsewhere. As it was, the responsibility was mine. Every night and all night it crowed. The security lights in the police station compound caused it to believe that it was continuous daylight. By the middle of the third night I was at the end of my tether. I arose from bed and slipped on a pair of shorts. Armed with my baton I crept downstairs. The two policemen in the charge office were sitting at their table playing cards. Apart from the occasional crow, the night was silent. The cockerel was sitting on top of my car in the open garage. To add insult to injury it crapped of the roof as I neared. I stealthily approached. It flew down to the offside of the car. I followed it.

It moved to the other side. I crept round after it. It went under the car to where I couldn't reach it. This went on for about five minutes. I was fed up by now. I slid silently over the bonnet. It hadn't expected this and was just within range. I swung it a vicious blow, catching it on the side of the head. It collapsed in mid-crow. 'Got you, you bastard', I said. I didn't wait for any more but went back to bed. 'I fixed him', I said to Margaret, pulling the covers over me. At that moment the crowing started up again. Not the same as before though. It was now more of a warble that a crow. Evidently my blow had damaged it but not enough to eliminate the problem. The following day I went to see George Anderson. I complained bitterly about having to put up with the cockerel. 'Why don't you just eat it?', said George. So we did!

During the ensuing investigation I was asked to carry out a search at Kibuka's house which was a few miles out on the Masaka Road. I took with me the key which, it was thought, fitted the lock securing the house. The building turned out the be a single-roomed mud-and-wattle hut having a galvanised iron door secured by a padlock. Sure enough the key fitted the padlock. I went in leaving outside the two constables who had accompanied me. My object was to search for any documentary evidence which might throw light on Kibuka's politics. In the event there was none. The furnishings were sparse in the extreme. A table and two chairs, a cupboard, cooking utensils, a rough wooden bed. That was about it. Under the bed was a 5-gallon paraffin *debi*. I tried to pull it out to examine it. It wouldn't budge. Eventually I had to shift the bed to see what the *debi* contained. To my amazement it appeared to be lumps of rough rock. I took a few bits out. They sparkled. Even to my inexpert eye, the *debi* was filled with practically solid gold ore. No wonder it was so heavy. I shifted the bed back to its previous position. Rightly or wrongly I decided not to even report my find. As far as I could reason it had no bearing on the case. I would have loved to know where he got this stuff from though. It must have been worth a very considerable fortune.

When the case came before the High Court, Kibuka was found guilty of manslaughter of the Head Constable. His henchmen were found guilty of being accessories. All received sentences of around 5-years in prison. Some months later Kibuka applied to have returned to him some 20,000-shillings in cash, which had been entered as an exhibit. To everyone's amazement he was successful in his application.

The cotton season was in full swing. Every day lorries belonging to the cotton ginneries could be seen tearing down the roads, loaded with vast bales of raw cotton, the owners of this produce usually sitting somewhat precariously on top of the swaying load. There was legislation covering the transport of this cotton and its owners. This stated that a maximum of 12 persons could accompany the produce between the point at which it was picked up by the lorry and its delivery to the ginnery where it would be weighed and the owners paid at rates set by the government. Viewing some of the lorries as they went by I often felt amazed that the number of passengers had been set as high as it was. It was not infrequent, however, that the lorries became overloaded. Sometimes, instead of just the owner of the cotton accompanying his produce to the ginnery, the entire family would treat the event as the opportunity for an outing and accompany him. When the drivers were caught with extra passengers they would be forced to unload any excess and then reported for the offence. One lunch time I was looking out of my lounge window when a cotton lorry arrived at the roundabout. It was a frightening sight. As it negotiated the roundabout the offside two wheels left the ground and I thought it was about to turn over. A multitude of passengers hung on precariously on top of the load of cotton. Then, off it went at high speed on the Masaka road. I raced down to my car and grabbed a couple of constables who happened to be nearby. It was nearly 5 miles before I was able to catch up with the vehicle and stop it. I ordered the entire load of passengers onto the grass verge where I lined them up and counted then. There were a 127, including the children. The lorry was driven by an Asian who turned out to be part-owner of a ginnery about 20 miles outside Kampala. The first thing he did was to offer me 500-shillings to let him go. That was his downfall. It led to his being charged not only with the overloading offence but also attempted bribery for which he was fined 10,000-shillings and imprisoned for 12 months with hard labour!

Chapter 24

Rumours were abroad that Frederick Mutesa, The Kabaka of Buganda, was to be allowed back into Uganda. After a prolonged period of rustication in the U.K. the British government, who had maintained all along that under no circumstances would he be allowed back, had done a U turn and were said to be on the verge of allowing him to return.

The Kabaka's Palace covered a site of around 50 acres and came within the jurisdiction of Katwe police station. From the moment that the rumours started the place became a hive of activity — and drunkenness. The Kabaka had, in the past, not been a particularly popular figure. However, this was clearly a case of absence-making-the-heart-grow-fonder. Hundreds of volunteers reported to the palace area and were set to work cleaning the place up and, in particular, cutting new reeds from the nearby swamps to replace the fence surrounding the palace grounds. The reeds which were to be used were around 12-feet in height and day after day the multitude could be seen toiling back from the swamp area, carrying vast bundles of the reeds on their heads. More volunteers were at work tearing down the old fence and preparing the reeds into the smaller bundles to be used in the new structure. Gradually, the new fence was built and, I must say, a very smart piece of work it looked. The reeds were of a uniform golden brown colour and the builders were clearly very skilled in their work. At the end of each day's labour, however, the entire work force made their way to the bars at Katwe village and proceeded to get roaring drunk. Fights and quite serious injuries were commonplace and the nights were made hideous as the victims, witnesses and assailants were brought in. Fortunately, unless the injuries were of a fatal or extremely serious nature, I was able to transfer the majority of these cases to the Native Authority. This was useful as it saved us a great deal of work and had also the advantage of swift retribution by the Native Courts and not only fines but compensation to the victims.

Eventually an official announcement was made that the Kabaka would indeed be returning on a particular date. He would, of course, be travelling by air and arriving at Entebbe airport. For two weeks prior to his arrival the road between

Entebbe and Kampala was the scene of great activity. Thousands of banana trees were cut down and used as a continuous line on each side of the 20-mile route. One might have thought from the number of plants being destroyed that a famine would be the eventual result. Not so. In this wonderful climate, bananas grew like weeds and it probably did a world of good to have them thinned out in this manner. The roundabout outside the police station was decorated not only with the banana plants but with great bundles of canna lilies and other blossoms as well.

My instructions for this event were to deploy as many of my staff as possible in the immediate vicinity of the police station, covering the approach road from Entebbe and the roundabout. I anticipated that for a comparatively short period, while the Kabaka and his entourage were passing, we were going to be somewhat busy.

The night before the Kabaka's arrival, Katwe was in uproar. Drunkenness reached new heights and the fights reached the proportion of open warfare. I had instructed that arrests were to be kept to an absolute minimum in order to have the cells cleared by the time the Kabaka arrived. As a result, most of the drunks were dealt with on arrival and they were released into the hands of various relatives to be taken before the Native Court at a later stage. At around 2 a.m., however, a particularly noisy individual was brought in. Since he refused to be quiet and since there was no one with him to accept custody, he was placed in one of the cells where he proceeded to make our life intolerable. Alison was awakened for the umpteenth time that night and added her complaints to those of the prisoner. After phoning down to the charge office several times to tell them to sort this individual out, but without any noticeable improvement I decided that the time had come to take more direct action. I got dressed in shirt, slacks and bedroom slippers and went to the charge office. There I demanded the keys to the cells and, accompanied by one of the constables, went to the cells. The prisoner was an extremely large Acholi who was bent on destroying the cell door. Time after time with a great scream he would charge at the door, apparently totally impervious to the damage he was inflicting on himself as well as to police property. I opened the door intending of course to remonstrate with the demented creature. However, no sooner was the door open when he came at me like a charging bull. Remonstration went out of the window! I hit him as hard as I could on the jaw. He spun round and to add emphasis to the message I wanted to give, I kicked his behind, propelling him into the corner of the cell where hitting his head on the wall, he subsided to the floor. Christ! What had I done to my right foot? The big toe, which I had smashed years before on the day I was de-mobbed from the R.A.F. had fractured again! After re-locking the door I hobbled back to bed. Silence reigned. I was unable to get to sleep. Visions kept coming back of the prisoner smacking his head on the cell wall and subsiding to the floor. What if he was dead? After half- an-hour I hobbled back downstairs. Again I called for the cell keys. The prisoner lay exactly as I had last seen him. He hadn't moved a muscle. I went over to him and turned him over. He snored loudly and was clearly fast asleep. I returned to bed and enjoyed the untroubled remainder of the night. At 8 o'clock I made my way back to the cell. The prisoner beamed at me.

'*Jambo Bwana*', he said. He clearly had not the slightest recollection of the previous night's activities!

After dealing with the morning's paperwork I made my way to the hospital where my foot was x-rayed. Sure enough, the big toe was broken in two places. A collodian splint was applied and I made my way back to the police station. My activities outside the police station at 2 p.m. that day were somewhat hampered by my carrying a walking stick and having to wear on my right foot, my bedroom slipper with the front cut out. I don't think the Kabaka noticed though. He certainly didn't stop to commiserate.

Proof that other police stations around Kampala were facing much the same problems as those at Katwe were enforced when a directive was issued by George Anderson regarding the recording of 'statements under caution'. A number of these police stations were under the control of Asian or African police inspectors and clearly at one of these something had gone badly wrong. Instead of getting the offending officers to police headquarters to give them a couple of days intensive instruction, the directive stated that in future ALL 'statements under caution' were to be recorded by an European officer of at least the rank of Assistant Superintendent! As can be imagined this created absolute chaos. Now, in addition to my taking all of the 'statements under caution' in cases relating to Katwe police station, I would suddenly find myself faced with an Asian or

African inspector, each accompanied by several prisoners from whom I was expected to take the necessary statements. In order to adequately record any statement it was necessary to read through the evidence in each case before interviewing the prisoner. Resultantly, each request for the recording of a statement took a minimum of 2 hours to complete, often much longer. Sometimes the unfortunate officers would have to tote their prisoners around 3 or 4 police stations before finding a European officer who was willing, or mug enough, to undertake this additional task. What had obviously not been realised was that as a result of taking the caution statement the recording officer was then subject to being summoned to appear in court to give evidence that he had in fact recorded the statement. This could result in a complete day being wasted, hanging about in the court building. Fortunately, after a few weeks the total impracticality of the directive was realised and things reverted to the previous system.

On a similar subject, I was made to realise how little of the legal system had been drummed into my own staff at Police Training School. D.C. Balikirungi, while being an excellent thief-taker was totally illiterate. During one case, a statement was recorded from him by Sub-Inspector Byamugenzi prior to his court appearance. During the hearing he was cross examined by Philip Wilkinson Q.C. one of Uganda's leading lawyers. 'You say you cautioned the accused. What did you actually say?' Balikirungi was floored by this. It was quite clear that he had not the faintest idea what it was all about. 'What is the caution?', Wilkinson persisted. After several minutes of embarrassed silence by Balikirungi I had to come to the rescue by withdrawing the case. This experience exposed a dangerous fault in the police system of investigation. Clearly, at the Police Training School the trainee policemen had not been adequately taught this basic tenet of investigation. Or else they had forgotten it. The next day I paraded all my staff to find out how many knew what the caution to prisoners was. Only about three of them actually knew. I had the caution typed-out and a copy issued to each policeman. 'I may call on you at any time to tell me what the caution is', I said. 'You had better know it or you will be on a charge.' This threat worked well and we had no further problems of this sort in court.

A noisy altercation in the charge office drew my attention

one morning. After around five minutes there was no sign of it abating so I went to see what the problem was. A group of 7 or 8 Africans all shouting their heads off in Luganda. I hadn't the faintest idea what was going on so I bawled at them to shut up and enquired from the police corporal on the front desk what it was all about. 'Sir, they are alleging that D.C. Balikirungi has raped one of their women.' This could have serious repercussions. 'When was this supposed to have happened?' I enquired. 'Last night', was the reply. The alleged victim was among the group of complainants so my first concern was to have her medically examined. She was a rather unattractive creature in her 40s and looked like one of the prostitutes who frequented the Katwe bars. Accompanied by one of the other women in the group and taking a police constable with me, I went up the hospital leaving Sub-Inspector Sali to make a start on the recording of the others' statements. At the hospital I had the woman examined by the doctor on duty. The report indicated that she had engaged in sexual intercourse recently but there was no sign that any force had been used. I returned to the police station where I recorded her statement. Yes, she new Balikirungi well. The previous evening she had met him in a Katwe bar and from there had gone to her house where they and others had continued drinking. He had spent the night with her and this morning had gone off without paying her! As far as she was concerned this amounted to rape. The whole episode was a waste of time. I didn't even bother to interview Balikirungi about it but had the whole group ejected from the police station where they hung about uttering threats of complaining to the Commissioner of Police, etc.

A group of women ululating outside the police station warned me that a problem was requiring my attention. I went to the front office. By the time I got there, a group of people were inside shouting for attention. One of them, seeing me there, came to tell me that a young boy was missing in the Kabaka's Lake where he had gone swimming. I immediately got into my car together with a couple of police constables. The lake was only about half-a-mile away and we were there within a few minutes. A large crowd stood on the shore of the lake. \Where had the victim last been seen?', I enquired. A number of different areas were pointed out to me. None of the crowd had ventured into the water. They just stood and watched. Well, the boy had already been under the water for nearly an hour so there was absolutely no chance of his still being alive. 'Can any of you swim?', I enquired of the crowd. No reply. If they could they weren't going to volunteer. Neither of my policemen could swim — or so they told me. As usual it was muggins turn. I stripped to my underpants and waded into the water. The next half-hour was spent ducking and diving in about 12-feet of water to the great enjoyment of the assembled crowd. Eventually I found the unfortunate child and, dragging him to the shore, tried artificial respiration. Total waste of time. I fear that I was neglectful in my duty on this occasion. I simply couldn't take the child away from his grieving parents for the autopsy which clearly should have been carried out. It occurred to me, however,, that there was a strange quirk in the African makeup. Where else would a crowd have just stood around while a child drowned, without making any effort to save it!

I had now been a full year at Katwe police station and the unit was now running reasonably well. It was time for me to make a decision. A tour of duty could be either 3-years followed by 6-months' leave or 18-months followed by 3-months leave. If I opted for the full tour of 3-years, I should probably have to spend 3 months of my hard-earned leave on a course of some sort, as had happened during my previous leave. I had little hesitation in opting for the shorter period. It was unlikely, I thought, that I should have to return for a further period of suffering at Katwe. In any case, Margaret was keen for our respective parents to see the new arrival. Let some other bugger take the strain of life at Katwe. I'd served my time in this hell hole. I could hardly be sent anywhere worse so whatever I got on my return had to be an improvement. I put in my application for leave and prepared to stick it out for the next six months.

I was heading up Makinde Hill one morning on a routine enquiry involving a member of the European community who lived up there. About a mile from the police station I came across a battered old estate car which had apparently broken down an was blocking the road. An ancient European was standing at the side of the vehicle peering at the engine from which poured clouds of steam. I parked my car and went to him. The old boy was about 90 and appeared to be in about as dilapidated a state as his car. It was clear to me that there was little I could do to revitalise the vehicle. It was going to have to be towed to a garage for a major repair. The best I could do was to take him back with me to Katwe from where I could obtain a breakdown vehicle to remove the clapped-out car. I suggested this course of action to him and he accepted the offer gratefully. He introduced himself as Harry Boazman. He lived, he said, about 2 miles further on up the hill. At that time the name meant nothing to me. On our arrival at the police station I took him to my flat from where I phoned for a breakdown vehicle to attend. Margaret provided the old boy with tea and sympathy and while we waited he proved interesting company. He informed us that he had been one of the first European settlers into Uganda, having walked up from the coast in the late 19th century. On the arrival of the breakdown vehicle I took him in my car back to his vehicle and, having seen it towed away, continued on and deposited him at his house —which was about as derelict as his car. On shaking hands with him before my departure I realised that he was a Freemason. 'You must come to a meeting as my guest', he said as I left.

Several weeks later I received an invitation from him to attend a Lodge meeting in Kampala. I had not been to a Masonic Meeting for some years and was extremely rusty in the ceremonial. This would be the first time I had been to a meeting in Uganda and I thought it would be an interesting experience. I turned up at the Masonic Hall at the due time. Shock, horror. There was Joe Deegan the Commissioner of Police waiting for me! 'I've been hearing about you from Harry Boazman', he commented. 'Understand you rescued him from the bush when his car broke down.' 'Well, hardly that,' said I 'He was only on the road leading to his house.' 'Well, he's very grateful to you', said the Commissioner. 'And to your wife, I understand. You know who he is of course?' 'No idea', I replied. 'He's the Provincial Grand Master for East Africa', said Deegan. 'You're to be on the top table.' I now spent the most terrifying few hours of my life. In the first place I had great difficulty in remembering the ceremony. At the dinner afterwards I was expected to make the speech in reply for the visitors. My Masonic career had been, to say the least, sparse. Since being initiated during the war, I don't suppose I had been to more than a dozen meetings. The last time I went to a meeting was well over 4-years earlier. This was totally unexpected but somehow I stumbled my way through it. I vowed that I would never go to another meeting without some sort of preparation beforehand. As I write this I have been a Freemason for well over 60 years but I still feel uncomfortable when I'm invited as a guest to a Lodge. It is probably due to this incident that I based my decision never to take any office in any Lodge.

It was at about this time that I made the acquaintance of Bob Astels. He arrived one day at the police station bringing with him a vervet monkey which appeared quite tame, even though its condition was clearly very poor and its right arm ended in a raw stump. Bob was an employee of the Public Works Department and was engaged in road-building and maintenance. He was incensed at the state the monkey was in, having found it tethered outside an African hut. I shared his view on cruelty to animals but, having seen far worse cases in Karamoja, was quite sure that it would be a waste of time trying to prosecute the offender. However, more to placate him than anything else, I went with him to where the monkey had been found and gave the owner a severe bollocking. Bob had decided to keep the unfortunate animal, but in the event it only survived a few days. After this incident Bob Astels was constantly calling in at the police station with various complaints about animal cruelty and other things, which I dealt with as best I could!

One day he invited Margaret and me to his house in Kampala for dinner. On our arrival he introduced us to his wife, an attractive dark-haired woman of about 30. We had a very pleasant meal and were then introduced to his menagerie. He had two dogs, several monkeys and a number of reptiles. He then opened the door of the spare bedroom and introduced me to the biggest python I've ever seen. It was coiled up in a corner and was about 18-feet in length and as thick as a man's waist. It was not caged. I doubt if it could have been housed in a cage. It just occupied the whole of the room, which stank of it. Bob had found it in the Mabira Forest, between Kampala and Jinja where it had been caught by a crowd of Africans who, unusually, had not killed it but were carrying it along. It took 8 of them, to carry it. I duly admired the creature but decided that, even though I am interested in snakes, I would not want to have one, thanks very much. Several weeks later Bob called at the police station and informed me that the python had escaped and eaten one of his dogs. His wife had left him and had commenced divorce proceedings.

One of Bob's major interests was photography and in particular cine photography. On finding that I had an interest in rifle-shooting he suggested that we make a trip to the Mabira Forest where he knew of an area thick with guinea fowl and buck of various sorts. He would come along with his cine camera to see if he could get any interesting shots. I thought this would be a good idea since I had not had any guinea fowl since leaving Karamoja. The two of us left early one morning and I took both of my guns with me. Not one of my more successful trips it turned out. The guinea fowl were certainly there but they were shy and kept well out of the way. I saw Bob talking to a local native. 'They've got a problem with a buffalo', he said. 'It's attacked and injured several of them. I've told then that you'll find it and shoot it for them.' 'Bastard', I thought, 'he's deliberately led me into this. I haven't even got a suitable rifle for buffalo-shooting.' All I had was my old .22 rifle and the .375 Lawn and Alder which might stop it if I could get a deliberate aim but would be useless in a charge. I should have refused out of hand and told the locals to report to a Game Ranger. However, somewhat foolishly I agreed to see if I could dispose of the animal. I was led to the area where it had last been seen and crept into the thick bush. Several times I found traces of fresh blood on the foliage and it was clear that I was tracking an injured beast, probably the most dangerous situation a hunter could find himself in. For half-an-hour I crept on. The buffalo was nearby and several times I heard him rushing through the undergrowth. I wondered where Bob Astels had got to. Then I spotted him. He was 30-feet up a nearby tree with his cine camera, clearly hoping for an interesting sequence as I was gored by the enraged beast. I decided to disappoint him and called it a day. He later told me that he had seen most of the tracking sequence and had observed the buffalo circling me ready to make its charge as soon I was near enough. Next time he came to the police station I politely told him to piss off. A very dangerous man and, I think, mentally unbalanced.

The telephone awakened me at around 5.30 a.m. 'Sir, we have a report of a body lying in the road near Nsangi Village.' This was a location about 5 miles out of Kampala on the Masaka Road. I got dressed and made my way to the charge office ready to interrogate the informant. 'Sir, he has left to go to work, but he has told us exactly where the body is lying.' I cursed. 'You should not have let the informant go. It's important that he remained to show the exact location and to make a statement regarding the discovery.' It was still an uphill task getting the constables to carry out the most obvious of tasks. 'Sir, I know exactly where the body is lying. The informant told me.' I hoped he was right and, collecting a couple of my detective staff, headed for the location, taking with me the constable who assured me that he knew where it was. An hour later we were still searching! We returned to the police station. By the time we got there a further 3 witnesses had arrived, all of whom were reporting the same body. We set off again, this time ensuring that we took one of the witnesses along. Sure enough the body was found — about a mile from where we had been searching previously. I examined the corpse. It was a stockily-built male age about 30-years. Rigor mortis had not set in and at a rough estimate, judging by its temperature, death had occurred about 4 hours earlier. The body was nude and the first thing I noticed was that the testicles and scrotum had been cut off and stuffed in the victim's mouth. I took a number of photographs of the body and its location while my staff made enquires of the bystanders and in the local houses in the hope of establishing the victim's identity.

No luck in that direction. There appeared to be no blood on the road so it seemed safe to assume that the body had been dumped where it was found after death had occurred. I had the body removed to the mortuary and returned to the police station to start the paperwork involved. Later that morning I went up to the hospital mortuary where an African pathologist was busy performing the day's quota of autopsies. I handed him the forms relating to the victim and stayed to view the post-mortem. I could see no obvious wounds on the body apart from the removal of the scrotum and testicles. This would no doubt have smarted a bit but was unlikely to be the cause of death. It occurred to me that a possible motive was a sexual one. The removal of the testicles and stuffing them in the victim's mouth could well have been a revenge attack by an aggrieved husband finding his wife in *flagrante*. I soon had to revise this thought though when quantities of smegma were found beneath the foreskin of the victim. There was no doubt at all that he had not had sexual intercourse for a considerable time. The absence of bleeding then led the pathologist and myself to suspect that a blow on the head might be the cause of death. However, a closer examination of the head soon revealed the truth. A piece of wood about four inches long had been hammered into the victims right ear. The end of it was just visible to careful scrutiny. There didn't appear to be a suitable tool among the pathologist's instruments to extract the offending article and, eventually, I had to get a pair of stout pliers from my car, which did the trick nicely. Examination of the cranium showed that the wooden stake had penetrated the brain for a full 4 inches and had caused instant death. Tribal markings on the body indicated that the victim was most likely a native from the other side of the border in Tanganyika. This was, regrettably, one of the many murders which I failed to solve. With the number which were reported to me and the tiny staff at my disposal this was an inevitable consequence. I include reference to it as a matter of interest and because of its unusual details. Subsequent enquiries produced some interesting theories. The most likely of these pointed to a witchcraft killing. Apparently, in Tanganyika it was not uncommon to kill a witch by driving a stake into his or her brain, and particularly with the type of wood from which the stake had been made. As to the removal of the testicles no theories were forthcoming.

Disposing of a witch in Buganda took a different form. Since the staple diet of the Baganda was bananas of one sort or another, these were used to speed the witch on his or her way. The cooking banana was called *matoke* and was a different member of the plantain family. The banana plant looked very similar to the sweet eating-banana but the fruit was much larger, each being around 10- to 12-inches in length. It was usual to peel these with a knife, as is done with a potato. The *matoke* is then cooked in a pot with water until soft and then mashed. The consistency is similar to that of boiled potato. The *matoke* was also a main ingredient for making the native beer. Should a thief be found in someone's *shamba* at night, he or she was immediately suspected of being a witch. The punishment for this was death! It was immediately carried out without the formality of a trial. The method was to tie the victim nude and in a crouching position. The *matoke* were then stuffed up the anus one after another until the victim literally burst. Not nice! Very effective though. Not many thieves went into their neighbour's *shambas* after dark. Certainly not a second time!

At last the 18 months was up. With a sigh of relief I handed over the police station to my successor. The best of luck to him. At least he'd got a better deal than I had when I went there. Margaret and Alison and I boarded the plane at Entebbe. Noel and Peggy Caunce came to see us off. Alison proudly informed them that we were going to Wingland. Our flight was uneventful. I had made arrangements for a car to be delivered at the airport on our arrival in England. This time, however, it was obtained on a sale or return system, one which Ford Motors did not maintain for very long. During our leave I had nothing but trouble with this vehicle. It rattled. It was difficult to start. It was impossible to switch off unless one left it in gear and made it stall. The doors would not lock, or if they did they wouldn't open. Smoke billowed from the exhaust. It spent more time being repaired than it did on the road. In answer to my complaints I was told by the chief mechanic, 'It's just because it's new!' 'Christ', said I, 'What's it like when it's old?' I was so relieved that I didn't have to buy this load of junk.

It was a matter of some relief that my hard-earned 3-months' leave was not, on this occasion, to be interrupted by having to attend a course. Needless to say, after what was to them a prolonged absence, most of our leave was spent staying with either Margaret's parents or mine. Alison proved popular with both sets of grandparents, so much so that Margaret decided to delay her return to Uganda for a further 6 weeks in order for her to meet up with her brother Michael who, being in the army, had been absent at the time of our wedding and was about to return on home leave a few weeks after our intended return to Uganda.

A few weeks before my leave came to an end, I received news of my new posting. Again I had been hoping for a return to Karamoja. However, this was not to be. Instead I was to go to Teso District which was in the Eastern Province and actually bordered onto Karamoja District. Not this time as a lowly second-in-command. This time I was in charge. I had also been promoted to Deputy Superintendent. This was an accelerated promotion being several years before it was due and I like to think that my efforts in turning Katwe into a reasonable working unit had something to do with it.

Chapter 25

It was an unseasonably cold blustery July day when I boarded the train for Heathrow. My car had been returned to the Ford dealers and I had no regrets whatsoever at seeing the last of it. The flight to Entebbe was uneventful and it came as a relief to be back in the predictable sunshine of East Africa after the typically wet English summer. After collecting my car from the P.W.D. store at Jinja and arranging for the transport of our belongings, I set off for Soroti, my new station.

On my arrival at the Awoja ferry, some 20 miles south of Soroti where, for many years, vehicles and foot-passengers had been transported to the northern bank of Lake Salisbury on a raft supported by 44-gallon oil drums. I found that work was in progress to construct a substantial bridge that would undoubtedly contribute to opening up the northern area of Uganda to trade and industry. Heavy machinery was being used to drive piles into the bed of the lake at its narrowest point. I was informed by Mike Payne, the European engineer in charge of the project, that the construction would be completed within the next year. This would certainly simplify travel to Mbale and Kampala.

By late afternoon I had arrived in Soroti where accommodation had been booked for me at the local rest-house. The following morning I made my way to the P.W.D. where Bert Muddle, the officer in charge, took me along to view my new accommodation. This proved to be the excellent and spacious bungalow set in about an acre of land where I had spent a night with Dick Hook and his family some years earlier when I was on my way to Moroto on my first posting. After checking the furniture inventory and accepting the keys, I decided to make a quick visit to the police station.

Soroti police station was an elderly, sprawling building of typical colonial construction, built in the form of a square. The various offices, cell block and storerooms enclosed a quadrangle. The general impression was that the place was in severe need of tidying-up and organising. However, I decided to keep an open mind on the subject until I had completed the taking-over procedure. It was at this stage that I found that the previous O.C. Police had been removed in something of a hurry for reasons which were never made clear to me, though rumours abounded. The day-to-day running of the unit had been left in the hands of the second-in-command, Don Robertson, a newly-promoted Assistant Superintendent. He, I found, was absent on pay safari, though expected back on the following day.

I was greeted by the chief clerk, Mr Andrades, a friendly dapper little Goan of about 25. He took it upon himself to show me around the police station and to introduce me to the various members of staff. I felt that here I had a unit which I could easily mould into something I could be proud of. A little later a P.W.D. lorry arrived bringing my belongings from the store. I went to my bungalow to supervise the unpacking.

The following morning I made my way to the police station at the front of which was a parking area sufficient to accommodate about half-a-dozen cars. Leaving my car in this area I went to my office. Shortly afterwards a constable arrived bringing the Station Diary. Checking the Diary, Occurrence Book and other daily records should initially be carried out by the second-in-command. I made a note to take this up with Don Robertson to ensure that this was done in future. However, on enquiring as to his whereabouts, I found that A.S.P. Robertson had not yet arrived. At about 9.45 a.m. a thin, bald-headed, ferrety-faced individual of about 25 years came barging into my office. I presumed that this was Robertson only because he was wearing police uniform with the Assistant Superintendent badges of rank on his epaulettes. '*Jambo Bwana*', he said, without the formality of introducing himself. 'Is that your car outside. I'm afraid I've just run into it.' 'What a great start', I thought. 'Here we have an European officer who arrives 45 minutes late. Takes off his hat so that he doesn't have to salute on his arrival. Doesn't introduce himself and then tells me that he's crashed into my car. I'm going to love this guy.' Clearly he had been in the habit of dealing with the previous incumbent of my office in this casual manner. If I was going to get anywhere in the running of this station I was going to have to put things right from the start. 'I take it that you are Robertson', I said. 'Yep, sure', was the reply. 'Right', said I. 'Now I suggest that you go outside again, get properly dressed and then report yourself in a proper manner.' Robertson's face was a picture. For a minute I could see that he was deciding whether to comply with my order or not. Then he turned on his heel and walked out. Five minutes later there was a knock on my office door. In answer to my invitation to enter, in came Robertson, this time properly dressed and wearing his cap. With a face like thunder he made a casual salute. I decided to take no further action at this time. 'Good morning, Sir. I'm Assistant Superintendent Robertson, your second in command reporting for duty.' 'That's a little better', said I. 'I believe you were saying that you have damaged my car. Possibly we should go and see how much this is going to cost you!' Accompanied by Robertson we went outside. My car was still where I had left it. Parked nearby was a battered Morris. A deep scratch ran down lengthways down the offside of my otherwise immaculate Vanguard. There were no other vehicles in the parking area. 'How did you come to do this?', I enquired. 'There appears to have been no reason for your parking anywhere near my car. Were you by any chance drunk?' Robertson ignored the implication. 'Sorry about this', he said 'It's just that I usually park just there.' 'Well', said I 'You'll just have to get used to parking somewhere else now. I shall be using this space from now on! I shall be taking this down to the local garage later on today. You will be sent the bill for the repair and re-spray.'

I returned to my office and resumed checking the various records. Without exception they left a great deal to be desired. It was going to take longer than I had expected to get this station running efficiently. I phoned Robertson's office and asked him to join me. 'I'm not too happy about the way in which the books have been kept. Later on I shall have a session with you to show you how I shall require them to be kept from now on. I think that for the time being we will get on with the handing-taking over. I take it that you have now completed the pay safari so we will start with the contents of the safe.' 'Well, actually', he said, 'I was going to tell you about that. I've not yet completed the pay safari. There are still three outposts to be paid. I'm afraid I've lost the safe key so I can't hand it over to you.' I couldn't believe what I was hearing. For a few seconds I was speechless. 'I see.', I said at length, 'When and how did you lose the key and what steps have you taken to rectify the matter?' 'Well', he said, 'I don't know how I lost it. I noticed it was missing soon after I did the main pay parade. I was hoping it would turn up so I haven't done anything about it.' This was getting worse and worse. Now I was faced with a situation in which the key of the safe, containing not only a considerable amount of money but also the confidential and secret police files, had been missing for several days and police headquarters had not even been notified. With an effort I kept my temper. I said, 'I think you had better return to your office and get on with some work. We will continue with your handing over of the station when we get the safe opened.' Robertson glared at me and left.

My telephoned report to police headquarters was not well received. However, I was promised that an engineer would attend within a couple of days with the spare key and with a replacement lock. In the meantime I sent for the Head Constable and arranged for a guard to be put on my office at all times when I was not present. It was possibly too late if someone had already found the key and rifled the safe, but at least I could make sure that it would be intact from now on.

I decided to walk across to the *boma* which was the name by which the offices of the District Commissioner was universally known. On my arrival I was met by the D.C's stenographer, an extremely plain girl of about 25 years of age, named Joan Woodall. On my enquiry I was informed that Owen Griffiths, the D.C., was in his office.She accompanied me there and introduced me to him. I was cordially greeted and found that Owen and I had something in common. We had both been at Government House with Sir Andrew Cohen. He had been posted there as A.D.C. to the Governor shortly after I had completed my stint as his bodyguard.

I decided not to tell the D.C. of the problems I had found at the Station. It was none of his concern anyway. 'I'm glad that we're having a change in the police command', he said. 'Things have been going from bad to worse over there. You may find you've got a job on your hands in sorting it out.' He did not go into any detail but from my short experience of the day so far I could understand what he was getting at. Owen took me along and introduced me to his staff. His A.D.C. was Arthur Watson, a pleasant young man in his late 20s. In addition, there were two District Officers. Edward Cunningham who had lost a leg during the war and Pat Walker. It transpired that Arthur was Owen's brother-in-law, being married to Mary, the sister of Rosemary Griffiths. Mary was still in her early 20s and had been married to a D.C. in Kenya. He had been murdered by the Mau-mau who had captured him and buried him alive. Owen suggested that I come along to the European Club that evening to meet other members of the community.

During our conversation, I found that in addition to being O.C. Police in Soroti, I was also O.C. Prison. I wondered if I should get an additional salary for this but in this I was disappointed. However, I decided that since I was unable to continue with taking over the police unit, I would visit the prison instead. After lunch I set off to find it. My information indicated that the prison was on the road leading to the railway station. I duly found it about half-a-mile outside the township. To my surprise I noticed a convict herding half-a-dozen cattle nearby. I drew up outside the prison door. An eye regarded me through a slit in the door — then disappeared. A couple of minutes passed. I was about to hammer on the door when it opened and a smartly-dressed African prison officer appeared. After a smart salute he informed me of his name and invited me inside. The prison was clean and tidy, but carried the unmistakable sour smell that pervades all African prisons. I carried out a quick inspection of the building. All seemed to be satisfactory. I was informed that Soroti Prison had a usual complement of around 80 prisoners and 20 staff. 'I will chose a prisoner to assist at your house, Sir', said the officer. 'Also, I will send along a work party with a warder to attend to your garden tomorrow.' I wondered if this was usual but decided to say nothing at present. I enquired about the prisoner I had seen with the cattle outside. 'Yes, Sir. They are the prison cattle. The milk is used to supplement the prisoners' diet', I was told. I privately thought it more likely that the milk was used by the prison staff, but said nothing. 'Sir, your pigs are becoming very many. Shall I have one of them slaughtered and brought to your house?' 'What pigs?', I demanded. It transpired that a previous O.C. prison had acquired a couple of pigs which he had placed down at the prison. A convict trustee walked round with them all day and brought them back each evening. There were now 40 of them! According to the African officer they were all mine. Clearly I should have to do something about these in the near future or I should have more pigs than prisoners.

That evening I presented myself at the European Club where I became a member. I was introduced to a number of European officers. Don Robertson was, I gathered, still licking his wounds and was, fortunately, not present or the evening might have been soured. However, in addition to Rosemary Griffiths and Mary Watson and the other two D.Os whom I had already met, I was introduced to Les Todd, the Agricultural Officer who, it turned out, was my next-door-neighbour, Paddy Foley, the Geological Officer, Keith Batten the doctor, Viv Colley the Principal of Teso College which was about 5 miles out of town, near the railway station and Tony Hatch-Barnwell the District Magistrate, who was, of course, already known to me, he having been the visiting magistrate when I was stationed in Moroto. After a very convivial evening I returned to my bungalow and my lonely bed.

A couple of days later the engineer sent by police headquarters arrived and the lock on the safe was changed. I inspected the contents as thoroughly as the circumstances permitted and as far as I could see they were intact. Robertson had finished the pay safari to all of the police posts in the southern area of Teso District. I made a rapid inspection of these posts before setting off with him in the police Land Rover to finish the delayed pay safari and to inspect the police outposts along the Karamoja border so that the taking-over procedure could be completed. Generally speaking, I was well-impressed with the standard found at the outposts. I did, however, notice that there were none of the aluminium 'uniport' buildings at any of them. The entire outpost system was constructed from mud-and-wattle with grass-thatched roofs. I decided that I would arrange, as soon as possible, for at least some of these buildings to be replaced with the more secure aluminium rondavels. I considered it most unsatisfactory for rifles and ammunition to be stored in such a way that they could be stolen with a minimum of effort by anyone so inclined. Complaints were made by the staff at all of the outpost units regarding the lack of assistance being given by the local village chiefs. I found this surprising since the whole object of establishing these outposts was to dissuade the Karamajong tribesmen from their periodic raids over the border. The outposts had initially been agreed only after numerous representations by the local inhabitants who had been subjected to raids, cattle thefts and murder at frequent intervals. Largely, the substance of the complaints was that food, in the form of meat, vegetables and eggs, was virtually unobtainable from the villagers. I knew that when it had been decided to site the outposts in these areas it had been made clear to the local chiefs that they could only be maintained there on condition that supplies were provided at reasonable rates. I sent messages to the chiefs concerned instructing them to attend. On questioning them, I found that the reason for the non-supply of the food was that the police staff seemed to expect to have these commodities provided free. I advised the N.C.Os at each police post accordingly and to ease the situation until the food was forthcoming, I shot a buck for each post I visited on my way. Fortunately, there was no shortage of game in the area.

Robertson had, for the most part, kept himself very much to himself during the safari. Now, with the handing-taking over completed, he appeared to be trying to ingratiate himself with me. 'Are you coming along to the club this evening?', he enquired. I indicated that I should be. 'How about coming along for a bite to eat at my place afterwards?', he suggested. I could see no way of refusing this without appearing churlish so I agreed to meet him at the club at about 6.30 p.m. On my arrival there he bought me a drink and we sat down with several of the other officers and their wives. 'When is your wife due to join you?', he enquired. I had already told him this, but assumed that he had forgotten. 'About five weeks', I said. There was some conversation about this from the other officers and their wives. This was what the bastard had been waiting for. 'There's a favour I wanted to ask you', he said. 'Well, ask away', I said. I felt that I could hardly turn him down in front of the assembled audience, at least not until I knew the nature of the favour he wanted. 'If it's something that I can do to help, I'll do my best.' 'I'm getting married in eight weeks time. My fiancee has no relatives out here and I would be very grateful if you would attend the wedding and give the bride away.' Christ. The cheek of it took my breath away. If Robertson had got off on the right foot with me to start off with it might have been considered reasonable. Here was a man I had only just met, had engaged in a series of acrimonious exchanges, had damaged my car and whose entire attitude could be best described as insubordinate, having the nerve now to ask me to play a leading part in his wedding. Not only this. Instead of approaching me privately, he had done it in such a public manner that I could not very well refuse outright. 'Well', I said, bowing to the inevitable, 'You'll have to discuss it with me later on to let me know what is required.' Now the assembled officers and wives joined in. Clearly this was a put-up job. I suppose Robertson had approached most of those present in the hope that one or other of them would agree to give the bride away. Now they had someone who hadn't refused out of hand. 'We'll give you a hand with the reception,' they said. It was then that I realised that I had not only taken on the job of giving the bride away, I was also saddled with having the wedding reception at my house. This would entail the provision of the wedding breakfast plus all the booze. Was there no end to the presumptuousness of the sod? What was Margaret going to have to say about this lot?

The police barracks at Soroti had, for many years, consisted of a crowd of mud huts. The only permanent buildings had been the orderly room and the cells in which recalcitrant or drunken policemen were occasionally confined. Now new barracks were being built and to the delight of all concerned were nearing completion. Already I was able to move a number of constables and N.C.Os into their new quarters. A further occasion for celebration was that Soroti was, for the first time, to have a fire brigade. The fire brigade in Uganda, of course formed part of the police force so would become my responsibility. It was intended that the ancient fire engine currently stationed at Mbale, 80 miles to the south, would be sent to Soroti as soon as it was replaced by the slightly more up-to-date fire engine currently at Jinja. Now that I had completed the taking over of the unit, I felt that I must spend as much time as possible at the new barracks supervising the planting of trees and grass. Decisions made at this stage could affect the entire appearance of the unit. I went out to the Agricultural Research Centre at Serere, about 20 miles out of Soroti to obtain advice on this. The grass decided on was pasipalum which was provided in the form of large bundles. It had to be broken down into individual rooted stems and each planted about 4-inches apart. Runners rapidly sprang out from the parent stem and quite soon formed a hard-wearing coarse surface suitable for parade grounds, etc. The trees I chose were Cassia Spectabalis and Delanix Regia. The first type grew into a most beautiful tree covered with brilliant yellow flowers while the second had a dense dark-green foliage covered with red blossoms. Both types had the advantage of forming a spreading canopy under which the wives and families of the police personnel could relax at their leisure during the day. I arranged to have alternate rows of these trees planted between the rows of dwellings throughout the barracks. They were also planted alternately round the edge of the parade ground.

A couple of weeks after arriving at Soroti I decided that, in view of Robertson's obvious difficulty in grasping the basic requirements of keeping station records I would have to take this job upon myself. I therefore designated him o/c crime. This, I thought, might keep him occupied and out of my hair. The investigation staff who would be working under him were reasonably efficient I had found, and he could probably do little damage in this job. It would also free me to concentrate on the administration side of the running of the station.

I had by now been introduced to the bride-to-be. Her name was Joan. She was a South African. She had come to Uganda as a stenographer in Kampala some years earlier and, I can only suppose, had spent this time looking unsuccessfully for a husband. She was certainly one of the least attractive women I had ever come across. She and Don Robertson, I felt, deserved one another! God help any infant they might produce. Joan visited her husband-to-be several times during the period leading up to the wedding. I had not yet had the courage to tell Margaret of the treat I had in store for her soon after she rejoined me. I felt it quite possible that she might decide to stay in England until after the happy event if I let her know too early.

One of the chief recreations of the members of the Soroti Club was golf. An excellent 9-hole golf course had been laid out on the plentiful open space around the European Quarter. The course started and finished at the club house and included one · tee which had been constructed at the top of a hillock about 60 feet above the surrounding area. From here, with a mighty swing one could drive the ball hundreds of yards towards the next hole or, in my case, into the garden of one or other of the European officers' houses. Not that I achieved this very often. I turned out to be the worst golfer ever. Still, I suppose it was good exercise. During the three years I spent in the station, I developed enormous shoulder muscles which enable me to hurl the golf club vast distances and over the tops of trees. Several times I wrapped the club round the neck of a sniggering caddie. None of them seemed to mind though. Well not too much!

During one of my occasional visits to the local *duka* to replenish my depleted stock of beer I was approached by a dapper little Indian whom I instantly recognised as Madan Mohanlal Tandon and whom I remembered well from my days in Moroto when he had been the owner of the local garage, from which the police and other government departments occasionally hired transport. I assumed that he was on a visit from Moroto and invited him to my bungalow for a chat. 'Thank you, Sir', he replied, 'but I am now living just here in Soroti. Please Sir, do me the honour of entering my house for refreshment.' In the circumstances I was only too pleased to accept his invitation and accompanied him a couple of hundred yards to his house. Madan informed me that he had engaged a manager to run the garage in Moroto and had now purchased the piece of land on which the house we now entered had been built. This turned out to be a pleasant, substantial building. I was shown to a comfortable easy-chair and a bottle of iced beer appeared as if by magic, together with a great array of toasties. A very attractive Indian lady entered the room and was introduced by Madan as his wife Sneh Lata. She spoke little English but was most welcoming. Madan had married her a couple of years earlier during a visit to India and had thereupon decided to move to Soroti which was a much more civilised place for a sophisticated woman. Instead of opening another garage Madan had built a cinema which now operated 7 days a week and was proving very popular. One of my duties as O.C. Police was, of course, to carry out an annual inspection on the cinema to ensure that all safety regulations were being complied with. It occurred to me that this might be one of the reasons for this effusive welcome. However, I cast aside the idea as being unworthy. Before I had finished my beer another one had taken its place. However, I wasn't going to be caught this time. I remembered too well the boozy parties in Moroto when more alcohol had been consumed than was wise. It would not look too well for the O.C. Police to be found drunk in charge of his motor car! 'Please, Sir, do me the honour of taking a meal with me tomorrow evening. I will invite many important people to meet you.' I accepted this invitation with alacrity having fond memories of previous curry parties at the garage in Moroto. The following evening I presented myself at Madan's house. The place was crowded with all of the local businessmen and their wives. In between sips of beer I was introduced to them all which process alone took quite a while. I felt snowed under with the number of invitations which were showered upon me. In the event I declined them all as politely as I could, requesting that they be renewed when Margaret had arrived. All seemed happy enough with this arrangement. After a splendid evening, I made my way to my car. Fortunately I have always been able to hold my liquor so I had no difficulty in making my way home.

Soroti was about to enter the 20th century. In the first place, a supply of piped water was being installed. Almost all of the houses in the European quarter were reliant on concrete water tanks which collected water from the roofs. This was fine during the rainy season, but not so good during the months of drought when water had to be severely rationed and was brought round in bowsers. The first house in the European quarter to receive the supply was, of course, that of the D.C. However rapid progress was being made and, with luck my bungalow would be on system soon after Margaret's arrival. Furthermore, with the completion of the Owen Falls Dam at Jinja, practically unlimited electricity was now available. Power lines and pylons were creating a spider web across Uganda and now, at last, houses in Soroti were being wired for electricity. The actual supply was unlikely to be finally connected for 6 months or so. Meantime, cooking throughout the town continued as it had for decades on wood-burning stoves, while lighting continued in the form of oil lamps. It occurred to me that Margaret had never had the doubtful pleasure of cooking on a wood stove. Even though it might only be required for a comparatively short time, it would probably pay me to buy a paraffin cooking stove for her to use when she arrived. To this end I examined what was available locally and finally settled on a rather smart two-burner job which had a good-sized oven facility and all of which was easily controlled. I think this set me back about £50 which, in those days, was a not inconsiderable sum of money.

Shortly before Margaret's return to Uganda, Soroti was struck one evening by a tremendous storm. The duration was not much more than an hour but on inspecting the new police barracks the following day I found that the roof had been ripped off the canteen building and a large tree had fallen onto the new fire station. It was fortunate indeed that the fire engine had not yet arrived, or it would have certainly been written off before it had been taken into use. Minor damage had been caused to some of the new police houses in the barracks but, fortunately, no one had been injured. Damage had also occurred in the township itself and repairs were in progress in many places.

Six weeks had now passed since my arrival in Soroti. I made my way to Entebbe Airport where the plane carrying Margaret and Alison was due to arrive at about 10 a.m. It touched down only about an hour late and by mid-day we were heading north, passing our old home at Katwe police station on the way. The journey was uneventful and by 6 p.m., as darkness fell, we turned into the drive leading to our new home. It was, of course, far too dark for Margaret to see our new domain and, in any case, after her long journey she needed rest more than anything else. After inspecting the house in the light of the oil lamps, we had a meal that the cook had prepared on the wood stove and by 9 p.m. were heading for bed. A commotion occurred in the drive and half-a-dozen cars pulled up outside. In came Paddy Foley and 8 or 9 other residents of the European quarter, all of them somewhat the worse for booze. I had no option but to invite them in to meet Margaret and to offer them the liquid refreshment they had clearly arrived for. Alison, now two years old, was awakened by the noise and had to be bought in and duly admired. Eventually, having satisfied their curiosity and their thirst, I finally managed to dispatch the last of the visitors at about midnight.

The following morning, having left Margaret to sort out the domestic arrangements, I made my way to the police station. On my return at lunch time I found her in the throes of interviewing prospective candidates for the job of *ayah* for Alison. Eventually, with my help, she decided on a stout, middle-aged Musoga woman named Josephina. The references produced by this woman were more than satisfactory for the post and she was engaged at the princely salary of Shs 100/- per month. One of the things in her favour was that she was extremely ugly and therefore unlikely to be bringing boy-friends back to her quarters. However, Alison took a great liking to her and we never had reason to regret employing her.

Two of Soroti's residents were going on leave. These were Pop Neilson and his wife. Pop Neilson was a Swede and was the local boss of Craelius Drilling Company who were permanently engaged in drilling boreholes for water in outlying areas. This was a task which was going on all over Uganda. Neilson was responsible for the Eastern and Northern Provinces and as such was the immediate boss of Willie Hagstrom, the Swedish driller with whom I had become friendly in Karamoja. During Pop's three-month absence in Sweden, Willie was to take over the responsibility for doing his job. To this end he had moved his mobile home into the grounds of Neilson's house. A party was now held in the European Club to wish Pop and his wife a good leave and to welcome Willie and his remarkably attractive Finnish wife to Soroti. Willie confided to me during the evening that his wife was already pregnant and I wondered how the couple were going to cope with a new-born infant in the confines of a comparatively small caravan.

The day of the wedding was rapidly approaching. On hearing that I had been conned into giving the bride away and that we were to be responsible for the wedding reception at our house, Margaret had accepted the matter with far greater equanimity that I had imagined possible. At least we should not be responsible for housing the bride the night before the wedding. One of the other residents had been conned into this. Knowing the capacity of the Soroti residents for putting away booze, I laid in a vast stock of beer, spirits and a small amount of soft drinks. A few of the wives did in fact help out in providing sandwiches and other edibles. The bride had actually managed to provide the wedding cake herself, for which I was duly grateful. Don Robertson had kept very much in the background, making no offer to contribute to the cost of his wedding reception, contenting himself instead with the arrangements for the actual wedding ceremony which was to be held at the Native Anglican Church on the outskirts of Soroti. I decided to keep well clear of any involvement with this. The wedding ceremony was to be conducted by Dr Lee who was the missionary in charge of the Kumi Leper Settlement, which lay about halfway between Soroti and Mbale. I had in fact met Dr Lee on one occasion during the 8 weeks I had been in Soroti, he having called in to the police station to make some final arrangement with Robertson. He struck me as being vague to the extent of being unworldly. I hoped he wouldn't make too much of a hash of the only European wedding at which he would now or in the future be likely to officiate.

The great day dawned. Fortunately, it was a Saturday so most of the invited guests would be available to attend. I made my way to the police station as I invariably did at weekends and went through the books. Apart from one murder at Katakwi village the previous night, which was already under investigation by my detective staff, the district was peaceful. I doubted that I should miss Robertson's contribution to the running of the unit during the next couple of weeks. I returned home to get dressed in my best ceremonial uniform ready for the 11 o'clock ceremony. The Best Man, Assistant Superintendent Geoff Grace, a very pleasant New Zealander, had arrived with his attractive wife the previous night from Moroto where he was stationed. One of the A.D.Cs arrived to take Margaret along to the church while I made my way to the house where the bride was waiting. With her veil pulled well down over her face she looked almost passable! I drove to the church where the tinny organ was belting forth. To the strains of *Here comes the bride* I escorted her on my arm to the altar. The floor of the thatched building had been liberally coated with fresh cow dung. This treatment was so recent that the coating was still wet. The farmyard stench added to the unusual nature of the ceremony. Eventually, to my relief, I was able to hand the bride over to her spouse. 'I do', they both announced. To which Dr Lee bellowed, 'WHAT MAN HATH PUT TOGETHER, LET NO GOD PUT ASUNDER!' Somehow it didn't sound quite right but a snigger running through the congregation confirmed to me that I had not heard amiss.

Good organisation on the part of Margaret ensured that the wedding reception was a great success. The effort had cost me a lot of money for which I should certainly see no return. However, at least we could not be accused of failing to make the effort to ensure success. Neither Robertson nor his wife had the courtesy to even thank us for our contribution.

CHAPTER 26

With Margaret's arrival at Soroti, I could no longer evade the many invitations I was receiving from the Asian community on the station. One of the first to issue his invitation after her arrival was Gordonbhai Patel who seemed determined to ingratiate himself with me. Gordonbhai was a local businessman who, it seemed, had his finger in many pies. He resided in a very select quarter of the Asian community in a large, newly-built, two- storey house. It appeared that he had interests in transport, building, cotton-ginneries and a host of other things. I was reliably informed that he was a multi-millionaire. I accepted his invitation to dinner and on the due date arrived at his house with Margaret at about 7 p.m. The house was quite magnificent but the decoration decidedly tacky. Expensive display cabinets housed cheap and tawdry baubles. The place was crowded though we, it seemed, were the only Europeans present. I hoped that others would have been invited but in this was disappointed. It soon became evident that Margaret and I were the guests of honour at the gathering. We were plied with drinks and conducted by our host from group to group to be introduced to the other guests. Eventually, we were informed that the food was to be served. Before taking her seat at the table, Margaret turned to Gordonbhai's wife and, with her usual delicacy of phrase, said 'If you will excuse me, I'd like to wash my hands.' Her hostess thereupon conducted her along a passage to a small bare room with a concrete floor. All that this contained was a small drain hole in one corner, a tap above it and an ornamental brass pot. This stymied Margaret for a while but being completely ignorant of the customs of her host she eventually concluded that she had to pee in the brass pot, and tip it down the drain hole! This, with some difficulty, she proceeded to do and a few minutes later re-joined the party. The party consisting of some 20 local businessmen, their wives and ourselves, then seated ourselves at the several tables which had been set up. A little later, while we were enjoying our excellent meal, to her horror, a servant appeared carrying the brass pot, now containing water and proceeded to top up the whisky glass of one of the guests. The pot was then left on the table for the other guests to help themselves. Fortunately, not being a spirits man, I had stuck to beer during the evening.

A message arrived one morning from Mbale. They had finally received their replacement fire-engine and would be dispatching their old one, together with a new crew, to Soroti that day. The journey was only 80 miles so, hopefully, we should be in possession of the vehicle by mid-day. I went to the new barracks to make sure that all was ready. The fire station had been re-built since the tree had landed on it a few weeks earlier, the crew's quarters nearby were all ready and I could see no reason why, by evening, I should not be O.C. Fire Brigade in addition to O.C. Police and O.C. Prison. By mid-day there was no sign of the vehicle and at 3 p.m. I was quite worried at its continued non-appearance. I telephoned Mbale police station to be told that the vehicle had set off at 9 a.m. but had broken down a couple of miles outside the town and had been towed back by a breakdown vehicle. A mechanic was now investigating. The following day I received a call from Mbale. The new crew, it appeared, had thought that the engine ran on diesel and had filled it up accordingly. Since it was a petrol engine it had declined to go after a very short time. The engine was now being stripped down but should be ready in a day or two. Two days later a further message arrived informing me that it was now on its way. This was followed a couple of hours later by a phone call to tell me that, because one of the fuel pipes had not been tightened properly, the engine had caught fire 20 miles out of Mbale. Fortunately, having all the equipment handy, the crew had succeeded in putting out the fire and the vehicle had once again been towed back to Mbale for repair. I began to wonder if I should ever become O.C. Fire Brigade after all. However, after a further week of nail-biting tension, the machine turned up outside the police station one morning quite unannounced. I had a quick look at the engine before having it escorted to its new home. It had apparently originally belonged to Noah, prior to the flood. What a magnificent old machine. The large, shiny brass bell had a leather strap attached so that it could be rung by the crew member sitting in the open cab next to the driver. How I wish I still had it. I could have entered it in the London to Brighton run each year.

About a month after Margaret's arrival, the electricity supply to our bungalow was finally connected. We were among the first of the inhabitants of Soroti to reap the benefits of the 20th century and Margaret was mightily relieved. The oil stove which

I had purchased for her shortly before her arrival had performed yeoman service but the electric stove she now had was far superior. Robertson and his new bride had now returned from their honeymoon but their bungalow had not yet been converted and Joan was clearly somewhat out of her depth in trying to cope with the old-fashioned wood-burning stove she was expected to cook on. In an attempt to reduce the ill-feeling that they clearly still felt towards me, Margaret offered them the use of the oil stove until such time as their electricity supply was connected. This was gratefully accepted and the stove was duly installed. It was not until months later, long after their bungalow had been connected, that I remembered the stove, when I wanted to give it to a needy new officer in Moroto. Robertson duly returned it and on examination I found that it was totally ruined by a thick layer of rust, having been left outside his garage for an entire rainy season. Not a word of explanation or apology was offered. This did not do a lot of good for the relations between the two of us.

The police station was now running as a reasonably efficient unit and I decided to inspect the various storerooms for which Robertson was responsible. The 'found property' store contained so little found property that, apart from needing a good sweeping out, it passed muster. The records store, in which were kept all of the old occurrence and diary books together with a host of other records, clearly needed firm handling. All records had an official 'life' after which, with few exceptions, they had to be destroyed. It appeared that nothing had been disposed of during the past 30 years. No wonder it was practically impossible to get through the door. I gave Robertson the necessary instructions regarding the checking of the documents and their subsequent disposal. The next to be examined was the exhibit store. This had to be seen to be believed. I thanked my stars that we had not as yet been subjected to an inspection by the Provincial Commander. Apart from it being practically impossible to get into the storeroom the place was indescribably filthy and smelly. Few of the exhibits still bore their labels. Identifying them was going to be a major exercise. I decided to make a start early on the following morning. Obviously this chaotic state of affairs had commenced long before Robertson's arrival so he couldn't be blamed for all of it. However, he had knowingly allowed the storeroom to continue in this state doing nothing to rectify it or even report it to me.

On the following day, Robertson and I started by clearing out the entire room. The source of the smell soon became apparent. A virtually complete skeleton, still with lumps of flesh adhering to it and wrapped in brown paper was unearthed from beneath a quantity of other exhibits. A label still attached to this indicated that it was the victim from a murder which Robertson had investigated nearly a year earlier. The accused in this case had already been prosecuted and executed. No explanation was forthcoming from Robertson as to why the skeleton had been placed in the exhibit store in the first instance, and second, why it had not been rapidly disposed of. The majority of the exhibits, when eventually identified, were found to refer to cases long since dealt with. Many of them consisted of property, the subject of theft or robbery, which should long ago have been returned to the rightful owners. No attempt had been made to do this. By the end of the day, all of the exhibits had been identified and re-labelled and three-quarters of them disposed of, either by destroying them or returning them to the rightful owner. The skeleton went into the incinerator. The exhibit room looked almost tidy!

Pop Neilson returned from his leave in Sweden. To the regret of everyone on the station he told us that his wife had died shortly after returning to her native land. Poor old Pop didn't look at all well himself but was coping as well as he could. It had been decided that Willie Hagstrom and his wife would continue to live in his house for the time being. One of the first things he had told everyone on his return from leave was that should he die in Uganda he wanted to be cremated and his ashes returned to Sweden to lie with those of his wife. It was as well that he made his wishes known because about three weeks later he had a massive heart attack and died. The sudden death was reported to me and I had the body conveyed to the hospital where our newly-arrived Dr Prem Kapoor carried out a post-mortem. The cause of death was rapidly confirmed and I went to see Owen Griffiths regarding the disposal of the body. 'Well, there's no way that he can be cremated', said Owen. 'We simply don't have the facilities.' 'Couldn't we get the Asian community to do it for us?', I enquired. 'No. Sorry, I can't approach them on a subject like this. Wrong religion you know. Cause racial tension! We'll have to

get him buried quickly though. Don't want him going bad on us.'
That was the end of the conversation. By the following afternoon
a grave had been dug in the local cemetery and the funeral
service arranged.

Pop Neilson had been a popular figure on the station and
there was no shortage of attendance at his funeral. There was a
general feeling of discontent that Pop's wishes had not been
respected. It seemed, however, that there was little that could be
done. Dr Lee from Kumi Leper Settlement attended to take the
burial service. I hoped that we should not, this time, have the
hiatus that had occurred at the recent wedding. Six pall-bearers
carried the coffin to the newly-dug grave.

Paddy Foley and I supported the leading end. Willie
Hagstrom was one of the other bearers. When we were about 20
yards from the grave I murmured to Paddy Foley, 'I think that
hole's too small.' 'Nonsense', he replied. At ten yards I said, 'I'm
bloody sure it's too small.' This time he made no reply. We arrived
at the graveside and deposited the coffin alongside. The hole was
the exact size of the coffin. 'Going to be a tight fit', I muttered.
The coffin was lifted by the straps and lowered down. Calamity.
After 6 inches it stuck. It was pulled up again. 'Try the other way
round', suggested the D.C. This was tried but with the same
result. 'Tip it a bit', said Owen. Down went the head of the coffin.
This time it got to 2 feet below the surface at an angle of 45
degrees — and stuck. All attempts at raising it failed. With the
coffin firmly wedged just below the surface Dr Lee performed
the funeral service. 'Ashes to ashes, dust to dust', he intoned, in
his best funereal voice. Shortly after this debacle a leading
member of the Asian community arrived at the graveside. He had
just heard of Pop Neilson's death. 'But Mr Neilson came to see
me when he returned from leave', he said. 'He requested that,
should he die, we arrange his cremation and all is ready.' After a
further half-an-hour, the grave diggers released the coffin and off
it went to the Hindu burning *ghat*. It struck me that Pop Neilson
had been as determined in death as he had been in life. Clearly
there was no way that he was going to be buried so far away
from his wife, and certainly, not standing on his head.

Christmas arrived. A series of boozy parties had been
arranged at the European Club. Among these was to be a fancy
dress function on Christmas Eve. After some considerable

thought Margaret and I decided that she should go as a headless lady while I went as the headsman, carrying a wooden axe. My costume presented no problem. I simply stripped to the waist and donned dark trousers and a black half-mask. Margaret's costume was more elaborate. With her help I made a dress of red velvet. A ruff made of muslin on a wire frame through which she could see, covered her head and I made a *papier-mâché* head with crushed-up newspaper and painted it in gory colours. The effect was quite startling. 'This', I thought, 'will take first prize. No problem.' The costumes were judged shortly after everyone arrived. We didn't even get a mention. One of the committee approached me afterwards. 'Good costume', he said, 'but we have a rule that the costumes have to be home-made, not bought in.' I decided that it was not even worth discussing the subject with him. We went home and got changed.

Trouble was reported from Lira. This was the next station to the north-west of Soroti and was the headquarters of Lango District. At the time I was unaware of the cause of the unrest. It later transpired, however, that 'Land Tenure' was at the root cause of the trouble. Most agricultural land throughout the Protectorate was deemed to be Crown Land, which meant that, unlike Kenya, no European could actually own land. By the same token no African could be given title to land because he might sell it to a European. In practice, agricultural land was administered by the local chief. As a result of this system, the occupiers of land could not use the same to obtain a bank loan should he wish to develop his holding. At this time the Protectorate Government had decided that this system should be altered so that title to their land could be offered to those wanting it. This decision was bound to cause dissent among the Africans and particularly the political parties now rearing their ugly heads. The outcome was that rumours became rife that the Protectorate Government intended by these means to steal land from the Africans and give it to Europeans. Crowds began gathering at various locations and were being whipped into action by the politicians. The immediate outcome was that a large crowd of rioters armed with stones, clubs and spears, mobbed the Administration offices in Lira and commenced stoning the Administration staff. My old friend Lofty Wells who was at that time O.C. Police in Lango took out a riot party and when, eventually, after reading the Riot Act, this party came under attack, he had no alternative but to shoot one of the attackers dead. The rest of the crowd dispersed but continued in an ugly mood. I received a radio message from Lofty, addressed to the Commissioner of Police, copied to me, detailing the action taken and asking for assistance. Officially I should have waited for instructions from Headquarters before doing anything. If I sat back and awaited this, I felt, a bloodbath might be the result. Time, I felt, was of the essence. I told the Head Constable to sort out as many men as were available and then phoned round to gather up adequate transport. It was unlikely that we should be required for more than 24 hours, but this would allow Headquarters to send reinforcements in the form of the Special Force which had been formed with this specific purpose in mind. A couple of hours later, having sent a signal to headquarters detailing my action and without waiting for an acknowledgement, I was on my way with Robertson in the Police Land Rover followed closely by two lorries containing 50 constables and N.C.Os. On the outskirts of an ominously quiet Lira I stopped my vehicle and got out. I then disembarked and paraded my detachment of policemen and explained that it was possible that we might at any time come under attack. I caused all our weapons to be loaded but not cocked. Should we run into trouble we could be in action within seconds. We then drove into the township. Small groups of natives were collected in various places on our route. They were clearly belligerent but offered no violence to our party.

We arrived at the Administration Offices where I was greeted with some relief by Lofty Wells. Not wanting to interfere with Lofty's control of the situation, I handed them over to him for his disposal. The situation continued to remain quiet. It became clear that the arrival of the additional force of police had had the desired effect. I decided, however, to stay at least until the Special Force unit arrived to ensure that there was no further trouble. That evening Robertson and I went to the European Club where a very relieved population made us welcome. One of the least attractive wives seemed somewhat disappointed that it now seemed unlikely that she would be ravaged by the local tribesmen. Looking at her I found it difficult to believe that even the most sex-starved tribesman would have wanted to indulge.

Robertson and I spent the night on camp beds in one of the Administration offices where, if there was trouble, we should be on hand to deal with it. Fortunately, the situation remained quiet. In the morning, however, I discovered my uniform soaked with paraffin. Robertson had turned out the pressure lamp hanging immediately above, but instead of leaving the valve open, had closed it again. The residual heat of the lamp had renewed the pressure inside and the entire contents had dripped all night onto my uniform. Robertson's uniform was, however, unaffected since in occupied a different position. I was, as can be imagined, absolutely furious about this. Had Robertson been my size I would have relieved him of his uniform. Unfortunately, he being a little weedy creature, his uniform was no good to me. The man was a walking disaster area. I donned my paraffin-soaked uniform and prayed that no one would strike a match near me, or I should be incinerated! Fortunately, during the morning, the detachment from Special Force arrived to relieve my unit and we all returned to Soroti.

It was at about this time that we lost Randy. She was only a little, half-shenzi half-Alsatian bitch, but she had a very placid nature and had become very dear to us. Alison loved her. I had left her in my car under a shady tree outside the European Club. All of the windows were partially open, though not sufficient for her to get through. When I came out 20 minutes later she was sitting on the back seat, alongside Robertson's dog which had somehow got through one of the windows. Both had broad smiles on their faces. From the state of the inside of the car it was obvious what had gone on. I certainly didn't want any pup with Robertson's creature as father, but it was too late to do much about it! This however was not the cause of her demise. About 6-weeks later, while heavily pregnant, she suddenly became very ill. I got the veterinary officer to examine her. He had no doubt what the problem was. Leptospirosis. Otherwise known as Weil's disease. This deadly disease was carried by rats and evidently she had picked up the bug somewhere in her travels. The only hope was penicillin. And the vet didn't have any. I rushed her straight round to the hospital and persuaded Prem to give her a shot. All to no avail. She died the same evening.

One of the local natives turned up one morning carrying a tiny Dik-dik. This was offered to me for one-shilling and I purchased it as a pet for Alison, rather than having it finish up in someone's cooking pot. It was a delightful creature and, naturally, was christened Bambi. I imagine that its mother had been killed. It was probably no more than three days old and had to be bottle-fed. Surprisingly, it survived and was very tame. I built a wire-netting run for it in the garden, more to keep it safe from the station dogs than to stop it from running away. It showed no sign of wanting to leave and in the evenings it would come into the house and would wander round on the polished concrete floor before settling down on the carpet. The little animal was a male and grew the sharpest pair of miniature horns I had come across. One day Sam, the dog belonging to Hatch-Barnwell the District Magistrate, came to visit us. Seeing Bambi walking around on the polished floor, Sam decided that lunch had arrived. Bambi, however, was totally unperturbed and proved more than a match for his giant attacker by impaling Sam with his horns. Sam squealed and tried to escape but was pursued by Bambi who was determined to leave no doubt as to who was boss. The two combatants rushed round the polished floor skidding all over it. Bambi got in another two stabbing wounds before Sam in desperation climbed up on to the cushions on the back of the settee and stayed there until Bambi had been removed.

Both Margaret and I were meticulous about taking our anti-malarial drugs. Alison was, of course, given the dose prescribed for her age. Somehow, however, she still went down with a mild attack of the disease. For a couple of days she ran a high temperature and was quite miserable. It was at this time that I was called out to the police post at Katakwi to deal with a disciplinary matter. Katakwi consisted of the police post, half-a-dozen Asian and African *dukas*, a cotton ginnery and a number of mud huts scattered over a wide area. As I was leaving on my return journey, I saw a number of sheep outside one of the huts. My attention was drawn to one particular tiny lamb in the flock. The markings were extraordinary. The front of the body was pure white. The rest of the animal was a gingery-brown colour. It was exactly as though it was wearing a white sweater and a pair of brown trousers. I went to the owner who was seated nearby and, after due negotiations, purchased the lamb for two-shillings. I triumphantly took the little creature home and presented it to our sick daughter. She was suddenly cured. The lamb proved to be a male and Twinkle was the name that she decided on. It settled down well with Bambi in the wire compound. Both animals had the run of the house and garden during the day.

Hatch-Barnwell invited Margaret and me to take dinner with him. I had no great love for the man but we had agreed on a sort of armed neutrality since my arrival in Soroti. He had attended one or two parties we had thrown at our house and on this occasion we had been invited to meet one of the judges who was on circuit. The meal commenced with thin slices of raw kipper served on toast. Years later, having forgotten this particular occasion, he confided to us that thinly-sliced raw kipper could be disguised as smoked salmon when served to the ignorant. I don't know how he expected to get away with this to the judge. It certainly didn't work as far as we were concerned. However, we ate it without comment to keep the peace. On this auspicious occasion it had been suggested that a game of liar dice might be on the menu. Margaret had never played this in her life and the rules had been laboriously explained to her. I was also equally inexperienced but didn't admit to it. The stakes were small, a shilling maximum as I recollect. By the end of the evening Margaret had collected a small fortune. She was so transparent that none of us could tell if she was lying or not. Hatch occupied one of the very old colonial-style bungalows in the European quarter which was filled with heavy antique furniture which he had had shipped out in an enormous crate which he afterwards used as a stable for his horse. This unfortunate creature lasted several years before expiring from East Coast Fever. It was a well-known fact that Hatch, his horse and his dog were the thinnest creatures in Teso District. Hatch's dwelling was incredibly untidy and grubby. His houseboy lacked even the most basic supervision. I imagine that Hatch himself was probably unable to judge the degree of filth that his quarters presented. Now Hatch was going on leave. About a week before leaving he called in during my absence and persuaded Margaret to look after his dog, Sam, during his three-month absence. Being of a more kindly disposition than myself, she agreed to his request. Personally, I had nothing against the animal and, having been put in its place by Bambi, there should be no problem in housing him. After all we, at present, had no dog of our own. Hatch was being relieved by one George Farmer, an extrovert Canadian. In true Hatch-Barnwell fashion he laboriously typed out a *précis* covering the character of each of the European government employees in

Soroti. Then he started to hand over the office of Magistrate to George. George would have none of it. The files were, in his opinion, in a disgraceful state. A major row erupted between them which culminated with a strong letter of complaint being sent by Hatch to the Chief Justice in Kampala. By the time a copy of this reached George, Hatch-Barnwell had departed together with his furniture in the now somewhat dilapidated crate/stable. George Farmer, for whom I had great sympathy, now showed me the *précis* which Hatch had composed on each of the station officers. Much of it could have been considered libellous. I suppose I got away fairly lightly. 'What can one say about a man who has a snake named after him?', was his comment on me. Somewhat lacking in tact, I thought, towards someone who was doing him the favour of looking after his dog. I was also shown Hatch's remarks about George Farmer which the Chief Justice had forwarded to him for comment. In it the allegation was made that he was ignorant, rude, and lacking in civilised behaviour. George's return letter to the Chief Justice contained a memorable comment. 'I wish I had Mr Hatch-Barnwell's turn of phrase to describe the state of his toilet', he wrote. I don't think anyone on the station regretted the departure of this individual.

A few months later George Farmer went on local leave. He returned a couple of weeks later having got himself married. His wife was a rather plain woman of about 30. Where they had met I don't know. She was a pathologist of all things, and infinitely better qualified to carry out post-mortems than any of the medical practitioners in the Protectorate. However, she never offered her expertise in this field as far as I know.

Some months later I was driving home from the police station at about 10 a.m. I came across George's wife walking along the road and offered her a lift. As she got into the car I saw that she was weeping bitterly. 'What on earth is the matter?', I enquired. 'I'm in terrible pain', she said. 'I just don't know what to do. I don't want to upset George.' I was astounded at this remark from a pathologist no less. I turned the car round. 'I'll tell you what you're going to do', I said. 'You're going immediately to hospital and I'm taking you there.' Two minutes later we were there and I went in to see Prem Kapoor, taking her with me. 'I left her in Prem's capable hands and went over to the Court building where George was presiding over a case. I quickly wrote a note asking him to adjourn, and passed it to him.' He looked a bit put-out at being disturbed but, having read the note, he complied with my request and accompanied me to his office. There I explained the situation to him and left him to sort his problem out. I was later informed that Mrs Farmer had suffered a ruptured ectopic, where a pregnancy forms outside in the fallopian tube instead of within the womb. Fortunately, the rapid surgery she received from Prem Kapoor saved her life, but had it not been for this she would very soon have died.

It was time to take a bit of local leave. I had not had any during the five years I had been in Uganda. We decided that a couple of weeks at Malindi, north of Mombasa on the Kenya coast would be the place to go. It was going to be necessary to take Sophia (the *ayah*) with us to keep an eye on Alison while we were on the beach. It was also going to be necessary to arrange for some extra carrying space, since the car was going to be full to overflowing. To this end I made a large plywood box which fitted onto the roof rack. To streamline this I made a light sloping fairing which would attach to the front of the roof-rack. Great idea. I only wish I had patented the it. These days someone else has and, for about 50 quid one can buy the modern plastic version.

The holiday at Malindi was a great success. The Hotel Sindbad was beautiful as was the weather, the short rains having just finished. Unfortunately, the Tana River, a little to the north of Malindi, was in spate and carrying all sorts of debris into the sea. With the flow of the tide this brought it down to Malindi so the sea, instead of being its beautiful blue, was discoloured to an unpleasant brown colour. Still, it didn't stop us from swimming and surfing, using the surf boards which could be obtained from the hotel. We both got quite good at this. It was a matter of wading out until we stood in 4- to 5-feet of water, waiting for a substantial wave and then kicking off and lying flat on the surf board. If it was done properly the wave would take us in and land us right back up on the beach. What I didn't then appreciate, however, was that sharks love the murky water since it sometimes contains food, carried down by the river. Also I didn't know that 90 per cent of shark attacks happen in less that 3 feet of water. I was, therefore, rather more than startled one day towards the end of our holiday when, standing waiting for a suitable wave, while chatting to one of the other hotel guests, a great triangular fin passed between the two of us. Needless to say we made rapid progress to the beach and were unmolested. Having now read about shark behaviour, I believe that this particular one must have been a Bull Shark, they being the major culprits in shallow-water attacks. Presumably this one was not hungry at the time. No other hotel guests were reported missing so, seemingly, we had had a lucky escape. Both Margaret and I were a little dubious about surfing from then on!

I took the opportunity, while at Malindi of going out on a game-fishing trip. This entailed getting up rather earlier than I had anticipated and making my way to the harbour where, with two other holidaymakers, I boarded a modern game-fishing boat run by a native crew of two. After a trip of about 10 miles offshore, baited lines were cast overboard and we commenced trolling slowly along. Mine was the first catch. A 20-pound kingfish. Wonderful eating I was told. One of the other holidaymakers was next with an even bigger one. Then it was my turn again. This time I actually saw the fish swimming after the bait, apparently smelling it. Then it took the hook and the line screamed out. I lost about 300 yards of line before I could stop the run. Meanwhile, the boat had turned and we followed our quarry. I managed to gain a few yards of line. Suddenly, a couple of hundred yards from the boat a vast sailfin rose out of the water and, standing on its tail, tried to shake the hook from its mouth. It took me nearly half-an-hour to bring the fish alongside, by which time I was nearly as tired as the fish must have been. Finally, we boated it. No further fish were caught on this trip. The sailfin weighed in at 85-pounds. Not big by local standards but certainly the biggest fish I had ever caught, or am likely to catch. While we were at Malindi one of the local fishermen caught a record 600-pound blue marlin — on a hand line, while in a canoe! The Governor of Kenya presented him with a gold watch. I wonder what he did with it!

A trip to Gedi was one of the highlights of this holiday. Gedi is the site of an ancient Arab settlement, dating back to about 1500 A.D. The site had been discovered some years earlier, completely overgrown by the jungle. It covered a large area and the various dwellings were built from coral blocks which are a favourite local building material to this day. Many of the buildings were identified during the excavations. Interestingly, the settlement contained a large number of phallic monuments, some of them up to 15-feet tall. I'd like to have met the people to whom they were dedicated!

Finally, it was time to return to Soroti. I wondered what mischief Robertson had been able to get up to in my absence. I didn't have long to wait. I had not been in my office for more than 10 minutes when a furious Owen Griffiths strode in. Shortly after my going on leave, it transpired, a specie escort of two policemen had left on the Karamoja-bound bus taking cash, in coin and notes, to the value of about £5,000 to the Treasury office in Moroto. It was alleged, by the two constables, that they had deposited the boxes containing the specie in the luggage compartment of the bus where, they said, they could see them at all times. However, on arrival at Moroto the entire consignment was missing. Of course the two constables were the chief suspects. Robertson, as o.i/c crime, had interviewed them and on receiving a blank denial of guilt had done nothing further. He had made no effort to trace the other passengers on the bus who would almost certainly have witnessed the removal of the boxes. He had not even sought assistance of the C.I.D. in Kampala. I was absolutely certain of the guilt of the escorting policemen but, by the time of my return of course, the trail had gone cold. I immediately notified police headquarters about the incident and a C.I.D. officer was sent up. By now, however, it was too late. Whoever had the cash had had plenty of time to dispose of it. Shortly afterwards the two constables resigned from the Force and became businessmen!

CHAPTER 27

Urmila and Lila Patel sat in the squalid bedroom they shared in the squalid house in Soroti Township where they and their parents lived. Urmila was just 15-years old, while her sister Lila was nearly 18 and of a marriageable age. Lila had, in fact, been courted by a local lad for the past year, without the consent or knowledge of her parents. Her mother suspected some sort of liaison between the two but dared not mention this to her often violent husband. He, on the other hand, had been blissfully unaware that his daughter was having a sexual relationship with anyone, and was far gone in his negotiations with a related family in India, from where the husband chosen by him would shortly arrive. Now however, a chance remark by his wife had alerted him to the fact that his plans were about to go awry.

Being violent by nature, Ramanbhai Patel had had no hesitation in beating the truth out of his daughters. Lila held out for a while, but when her father started to beat Urmila, she sobbed out the entire story of her affair. Ramanbhai was, of course, furious, not only at his plans being thwarted, but at the thought that he would now become the laughing stock of the neighbourhood where he had openly boasted of the match he was arranging. Both girls received an unmerciful thrashing which only stopped when their mother physically intervened.

Now, as they sat in their bedroom weeping and trying to decide what action they should take to avert the further beatings which were sure to come, the future looked bleak indeed. Talk as they might, the problem seemed insoluble. After endless hours of discussion, only one avenue of escape seemed open to them. Suicide! The decision was made. A suicide pact. They would both die together. That would teach their father a lesson!

The means of committing this deed were readily at hand. A large stock of anti-malarial tablets together with a cocktail of other drugs were kept in an unlocked cupboard downstairs. After tonight their troubles would be over!

Their plans were interrupted at this stage by their mother calling them to come downstairs for supper. Ramanbhai was not present at the meal. Urmila managed to eat a substantial meal but Lila refused everything. Afterwards the girls made their way back to their bedroom taking with them the drugs they would use.

I was called out the following morning to deal with this sad affair. On my arrival I was taken to the bedroom where the girls lay in their shared bed. Lila lay on her back, eyes closed and seemingly quite peaceful. Urmila lay unconscious in a pool of vomit. This had saved her life. The majority of the drugs she had taken had been vomited up together with her last meal. Clearly my priority was to get her to hospital immediately. This done I turned my attention to Lila's corpse. A cursory examination of the body revealed the unmistakable signs of the beating she had received. Dr Prem Kapoor had by this time arrived and pronounced life extinct. I had the body taken to the hospital mortuary. Later the same day I visited the hospital where Urmila had regained consciousness. Prem Kapoor had recorded the injuries which she had received during the beating her father had administered. This might well be of value to the defence counsel in providing a reason for the action of the two girls. It could also form the basis of any charge I might, in due course, bring against their father. Prem gave his opinion that Urmila would be fit for discharge on the following day and gave his permission for her to be interviewed. I arranged for the local solicitor, P.B. Patel to attend to represent Urmila's interests.

The law, as it stood at that time, was quite specific. As was the case with the English judicial system, the survivor of a suicide pact was guilty of murder! Regardless of any personal feelings I might have regarding the matter, there was no lesser charge which could be brought. This put me in a difficult position. I had no facilities for detaining an Asian female juvenile for even the shortest period of time. I decided to complete the investigation, if possible, before Urmila was discharged from hospital. My first step was to record her statement under caution. This proved totally straightforward. I pointed out the offence that, in law, she had committed and the charge which she now faced. Urmila readily admitted the suicide pact and her part in it. She seemed only disappointed that she had failed where her sister had succeeded. The punishment for murder was, of course, death. However, this would not apply in this case as, being a juvenile, Urmila would not face this penalty.

The rest of the day was a flurry of activity. I rapidly recorded the remainder of the statements. I attended at the mortuary where Prem Kapoor performed an autopsy. On my instructions he examined the vagina of the dead girl and confirmed that she was not a virgin. Much of the massive overdose of drugs which had been taken were still in her stomach, some still in an identifiable form.

By mid afternoon my prosecution file was complete. I had found that the High Court was on circuit at Mbale, only 60 miles away. By applying a great deal of pressure I even managed to arrange for the case to be heard on the following morning. All that now remained was for me to get hold of George Farmer, the magistrate, and to get a formal Preliminary Inquiry held. By 6 p.m. it was done and Urmila had been committed to the High Court for the trial.

Early the following morning I was on my way to Mbale, taking Urmila and the escort. A police lorry followed close behind bringing the witnesses. In the event none of them were required. Because of her age, Urmila was permitted to plead guilty to the charge of murder. The evidence was laid before the Judge and at 11 a.m. she was sentenced to be Detained During her Majesties Pleasure.

This case had a number of interesting facets as well as some repercussions. First, it was the only case involving a suicide pact which had ever been brought before any court in Uganda. Second, it created a record in the time between the discovery of the murder and the sentencing of the accused. Twenty six hours to be precise. Third, it led to the law, in Uganda, relating to suicide pacts being altered. Never again would it be necessary for a murder charge to be brought. Fourth, it also led to a similar amendment to English law. As a footnote, I charged Samanbhai Patel with Assault Occasioning Actual Bodily Harm. He received 3-months in prison where he was made aware of what physical punishment really meant. Urmila spent a year in custody before being released.

I was seated in my office one morning when the telephone rang. Margaret was the caller, in something of a state! 'Can you get home quickly', she said, 'there's a great big snake in the garden. I was out of my office and into my car like a bat out of hell. I broke all speed records on my way home and pulled in at the gateway of the house. Sam was barking furiously and, on getting out, I saw that he was at the side of a shrub growing on the lawn. Rearing up and facing him was the biggest cobra I had ever seen. Its hood was fully extended and the head was some 4- feet off the ground, which would have made it at least 10-feet in length. Sam was keeping just out of range of the venom which these snakes can spit with deadly accuracy and by continual barking was holding its attention and preventing it from making its escape. The houseboy and the convict who helped in the kitchen and garden were standing to the rear, also watching the serpent closely. I quickly made my way through the kitchen door and collected my .22 rifle. Then I made my way to where Sam was still holding the snake at bay. It swung its head round to observe me as I arrived but made no attempt to escape. My exertions in getting home so quickly had left me a bit breathless, and as I fired at the head the snake suddenly turned its head back to Sam. My shot, instead of striking the neck where I was aiming, passed through the hood, doing little apparent damage. Immediately the snake dropped to the ground and disappeared into the long grass at the base of the shrub. Cursing my lack of accuracy, I told the servants to keep a close eye on the area to ensure that the cobra didn't make a break for it. I then went to my car and opened the petrol cap. It was the work of only a couple of minutes to siphon off a gallon of fuel and I returned to the place where the snake had been last seen. 'It's got to be still there in the long grass.' I thought. All I've got to do is to sprinkle the petrol around the area and put a match to it. That will bring the bugger out.' This I proceeded to do. Lighting a piece of paper, I threw it onto the petrol soaked grass. Nothing happened. I repeated the procedure. Still nothing. 'Bugger,' I thought. 'The heat has dried off the petrol already.' I bent down and with my lighter attempted to set off the fuel. Suddenly there was a tremendous whoosh. I leapt back and found myself in flames. I rolled on the grass to extinguish the conflagration and fortunately managed to succeed in this. My moustache, eyelashes and eyebrows had vanished together with the hair from my legs and arms. The hair on my head was less affected though I lost some of it. My nose and cheeks were well and truly singed and I looked a mess. Of the snake, however, there was absolutely no sign. To this day I cannot imagine how it escaped. There were plenty of people standing around observing after my inaccurate shot. There was at least 20 yards of very short grass in each direction around the shrub, yet no one saw its departure. I changed out of my singed uniform and returned to work. We never saw the snake again so maybe my shot had caused more damage than at first thought.

Hatch returned from his leave and collected Sam. He was being transferred to Kampala and George Farmer was staying. Evidently George had won the battle of the magistrates, much to the relief of most of the Europeans on the station.

After a couple of months without a dog around the house, we decided that this deficiency had better be made good. 'Bryn' arrived at Soroti railway station after a longish train journey from Nakuru. He was about 10-weeks old and a magnificent thoroughbred German Shepherd dog. His Kennel Club name was Dunlop's Telemon. It was obvious from the size of his feet that he was going to be a big boy so the Welsh for 'Mountain' seemed appropriate. Bryn he became! He rapidly settled down with the cat, the sheep and with Bambi, the now fully grown Dik-dik.

About this time we had a new addition to our family. The chief warder appeared at the back door early one morning carrying a cardboard box containing a tiny piglet. One of the sows at the prison had produced yet another litter. This time there were 10 piglets. However, all was not well. She had proceeded to kill them one after another. This was the only survivor from the litter. 'What did I want done with it?' Well, there could only be one reply. Alison had seen the tiny creature and wanted it! She was, after some consideration, christened Penelope. At first she was given milk from a hurriedly-obtained feeding bottle. Within a couple of days, however, she had found Bryn's food bowl from which all the meat had been taken. The maize meal which remained was just the job for a hungry piglet. She clambered into the feeding bowl and started to scoff. By the time she was discovered she resembled a small black football. Bryn didn't seem to mind too much about losing part of his meal, particularly when he was given some additional meat to make up for it. The myth of pigs being dirty animals was rapidly disproved. Instead of relieving herself on the floor, which is what I had feared when she joined the menage, she would go to the door and scratch on the wire inner-screen. When let out she would run out onto the grass, sniff around to find a suitable spot, do what came naturally and then rejoin us in the house. When one of my colleagues, Jim MacMullen came on safari and stayed with us for a couple of days, I enquired if he was Irish or Scots ancestry. On being told the former I said. 'Good, you won't mind having a pig under the table then.' Always the soul of tact, me.

One Saturday afternoon Madan Tandon arrived at the house in a state of great distress. 'Sir', he gasped, without preamble, 'Could you come quickly. A woman has burned herself.' I was a bit surprised at this statement. Why come to me. If she had burned herself, surely she should have been taken to the hospital for treatment. Why delay this by coming to me first. It occurred to me that maybe someone had already been to the hospital and found no doctor available. Anyway, assuming she had been badly burned, there was no time to lose. First-aid must be a priority. Subsequent treatment could be decided on at a later time. However, Margaret, being a qualified nurse, was better able to treat the woman than myself. She grabbed her first-aid kit and we both got into my car. With Madan in the lead showing us the way, we headed for the town. A group of Asians standing outside one of the houses indicated that we had arrived. Entering the house, Margaret carrying her first-aid kit, we were shown to a door leading from a short corridor. I opened it to be greeted by a smell of cooking. I found myself in a wash room with bare walls and concrete floor. Lying on this floor was the body of a young woman. Her body had adopted the classic pugilist attitude of death by burning. The clothes were burned from her body. Fat from the corpse ran through the drain hole in the wall and was already partly-congealed. An empty 4-gallon paraffin *debi* lay on the floor. Clearly the unfortunate creature had poured the contents of the *debi* over herself and set fire to her clothing. God. What a painful way to go. Margaret who had followed me into the room was a bit shaken by the sight and I pushed her outside again. Well, there was no need to call a doctor in this case. I had the body removed to the hospital mortuary and notified Prem Kapoor that a post-mortem should be carried out as soon as possible. Meantime, I had the grieving husband and other witnesses taken to the police station and commenced taking statements. The woman, yet another Patel, had been married about 5 years but had not so far produced any children. To her husband it now appeared that his trip to India to obtain his bride was money down the drain. Fingers were being pointed at him and the young woman had insisted that her failure to become pregnant was not her fault. Inevitably, considerable friction had built up in the household, made no better by the nagging of the in-laws. Friction had led to wife-beating and. finally. she had snapped and decided that suicide was better than continual beating and criticism. Ironically, the post-mortem revealed that she was in fact about two months pregnant!

On going to the police station one Monday morning I found that Robertson was, yet again, late on duty. I decided that, in his absence I would check the Station Diary and the Occurrence Book myself instead of waiting for him to report anything of interest. An entry for the previous day attracted my attention. An African woman, the *ayah* of one of the P.W.D. officers, going about her lawful business, had been attacked and quite badly bitten by Robertson's dog. Clearly Robertson, on being informed of the incident, had come to the police station to sort things out. Alongside the Diary entry he had written, 'No Further Action'. No statement had been taken from the complainant and, had I not noticed the entry, nothing would have been done. I was really angry about this and decided to check on the facts further before letting it go. I sent a constable to find the woman and to first escort her to the hospital to obtain treatment and a medical report, before bringing her to me to be interviewed. About an hour later I heard a commotion coming from Robertson's office. On going to see what was happening, I found that the complainant, having been brought in on my instructions, was now being ejected by Robertson. After interviewing her and recording her statement, there was no doubt in my mind that the attack by Robertson's dog had been totally unprovoked. The medical report indicated that the victim had suffered multiple deep bites to both legs. I sent for Robertson and asked for an explanation of his action in endorsing the Diary Book, 'No Further Action'. He was clearly embarrassed but could give no explanation. 'If a police officer is involved in any dispute involving injury to a member of the public', I said, 'it is not for him to decide on what action must be taken. This must depend entirely on the decision of his senior officer when all the relevant facts are known. Now I have investigated this complaint and clearly, had any other European officer or any member of the public been responsible for the behaviour of this animal, he would without doubt be prosecuted for failing to keep a dangerous dog under control. I would be failing in my duty if I decided to take no further action in this matter. I therefore have no option but to mark this file up for prosecution.'

Robertson stormed out of my office and I could hear him

cursing me in a loud voice as he returned to his office. This was clearly a matter which would have to be sorted out, and without delay. By pulling out all the stops the case was heard in Court 3-days later. Robertson was fined Shs 100 and ordered to pay compensation of a similar sum to the injured woman. An order was made that he should keep the dog under control. That was the end of the matter — I thought. Not so. A whispering campaign sprang up among the European officers and their wives. Robertson and his wife were at the bottom of it. In no time the station was divided. About half decided that I was a complete shit in prosecuting. The other half decided that I had had no alternative to the action I had taken. Meantime, relations between the Robertsons and myself reached an all-time-low. A couple of weeks later, Monty Locke, the Provincial Commander visited on his customary tour of inspection. I had by this time had more than enough of Robertson, so took the opportunity of informing Monty of the many problems I had experienced with him. A week later Robertson was transferred to Kampala and a Cadet A.S.P., Andrew Thomas, arrived to take his place. Andrew was a blonde curly-headed young man in his early 20s. Unlike Robertson, he proved to be extremely intelligent and hard working. The station rapidly returned to normality.

Dr Prem Kapoor was being transferred to Karamoja. In common with most of the officers on the Station, Margaret and I were very sorry to see him depart. During his short stay he had proved himself a competent and hard-working officer. One of his last acts in Soroti was to invite Margaret and me to spend a few days in Moroto with his wife, Santosh, and himself. This we accepted without hesitation, Prem's place was being taken by a short, fat Muganda, Dr Mukasa who was something on an unknown quantity.

A few weeks later, one Saturday afternoon, I made an unannounced visit to the police station. On entering the charge office I was surprised to find the place apparently deserted. I was about to make an uncomplimentary comment in the station diary, when a face appeared momentarily above the counter. On going round to the other side I found both constables cowering under mosquito nets. It was then that I noticed a considerable number of bees buzzing around the place. 'What's going on?', I demanded. From beneath the mosquito netting a voice answered, 'Sir, we are being attacked by these bees.' 'How long has this been going on?',

I demanded. 'About an hour Sir', was the reply. It suddenly occurred to me that, if the constables were under attack in the charge office, what was happening to the prisoners in the cells on the other side of the compound? I made a quick check of the prisoner's register and found that four prisoners plus a female lunatic were being held. I ordered the two constables to get out from their hiding place and bring the prisoners over to the charge office in handcuffs. Protesting loudly they started to cross the compound but rapidly returned when they were attacked by dozens of angry bees. Taking from them the keys to the padlocks securing the cells and a couple of pairs of handcuffs I draped a mosquito net over my head and crossed over the compound. In the process I was being badly stung. The mosquito net afforded some small protection to my head but my arms and legs were totally exposed. Gritting my teeth I opened the cells in which the screaming prisoners were cowering. They made no objection when I handcuffed them together and shepherded them over to the charge office. The female lunatic was a different matter. The woman who was engaged on a temporary basis as a police matron to attend to female prisoners, had left the station, taking with her the keys to the cell. The lunatic was crouching in the corner of her cell apparently not receiving the slightest attention from the bees. I retraced my steps to the charge office to seek for something with which I could force the cell door. After a quick search I found a crowbar which had been brought in as an exhibit. I returned to the cells. The padlock proved considerably tougher than I had hoped. I hammered it with the crowbar for what seemed like ages. The main effect seemed to be to enrage the bees still further. My legs and arms were covered with bee stings. The mosquito net had now proved totally inadequate, the bees having got underneath it. I could feel my head beginning to swell with the multiple stings I was receiving. Eventually the padlock broke open and I pulled the woman out. She had covered herself with excrement so this was not a particularly pleasant job. I staggered across to the comparative safety of the charge office.

Leaving the constables in the charge office to their own devices I made my way to the hospital where Dr Mukasa removed 120 bee stings from various parts of my anatomy. My face resembled a pumpkin. I suppose I was lucky in many ways. Many people have not survived attacks by these African killer bees and with many less stings that I had received. Dr Mukasa prescribed aspirin!

As though I had not had enough, I made my way back to the police station where I located the swarming bees inside the rear wall of one of the garages from which they were still emerging to form a solid mass some four feet by three feet and three inches thick. I went to my car and siphoned off a gallon of petrol into a can. Then making my way to the swarm and receiving more stings in the process, I doused the entire swarm and set light to them. The air was filled with angry bees trying to get back to the main swarm, flying into the fire in their efforts. None survived. Also the garage was now well alight. However, by this time a few more police had put in an appearance and between us we managed to put out the fire before too much damage had been done.

It was time, I decided, to put into effect certain building alterations which I had had in mind since moving to Soroti. I knew full-well that no money could be forthcoming from police headquarters for what I had in mind. However, this had never stopped me in the past and I saw no reason why it should affect my present plans. After all, as O.C. Prison, I had access to almost unlimited labour. Several of the prisoners were qualified in building skills and the prison had its own clay site where good quality bricks were produced and fired. Similarly, a very reasonable plaster was manufactured by burning a local limestone. My first project was to replace one of the three garage spaces in the compound by building an additional store-room. For some time it had become apparent that the existing storage space was inadequate. I first had the fire-damaged timbers taken out and by scrounging from the P.W.D. obtained new timbers to replace them. Cement and sand were obtained from the same source. Three prisoners were then set to work. These were all trusties who had been convicted of murder, but who, by reason of their trades in the building line, had been retained at Soroti Prison instead of being sent to Luzira Prison, just outside Kampala. It was considered quite safe to use these men without supervision, the theory being that, a thief could never be trusted not to thieve again, whereas a murderer was unlikely to re-offend. The tame prisoner who helped in my kitchen and garden was a convicted murderer. I never had any reason to doubt his reliability.

The rear wall of the garage was then cut away to expose the old bees nest. This was completely filled with nest debris and dead bee larvae. Having told the prisoner who was best qualified for the job, precisely what I wanted done, I left them to it. Sure enough, a week later the job was done and I had an excellent additional store at no cost. Again I went to see Bert Muddle who was in charge at the P.W.D. and scrounged a quantity of timber from which very adequate storage racks were made, and the job was completed. I learned from this exercise that, providing I didn't want to relieve this department of any part of their labour force, materials presented absolutely no problem.

Encouraged by my success in this I decided that it was time for my next project. A new office was badly needed. My own office was somewhat cramped and was situated next to the single office occupied by my clerical staff of one Goan and two Africans. By knocking these two offices into one. I would create that much extra room for them. My own new office would take the form of an extension to the frontage of the police station and could be reached only by passing through the clerks' office. This would have the additional advantage of stopping unwanted visitors from barging straight in when I was up to my eyes in work.

Once again I explained to my tame prisoners what I required and they set to work digging out the foundations. This was a little more complicated than the previous work but after little more than a month we were ready to break through the wall of my old office to make a door through to the new one. Finishing off and decorating took another couple of weeks and I was then ready to move in. My new domain was magnificent. It measured around 16-feet by 22-feet. My safe, instead of being free-standing, I had had built in. A large part of one wall was utilised to house a large-scale map of the district, which I personally drew, enlarging it from a map of standard size. On this I could mark the location of all our outposts and access tracks and marker pins indicated all crimes and incidents reported, including border raids by the Karamajong.

This, had it been financed through normal channels, would have been classed as major work. As it was it had cost the police force nothing. Owen Griffiths muttered about my failure to apply for planning permission but did nothing further. All the work had been carried out without reference to police headquarters or even to Monty Locke the Provincial Commander. As it happened, he made his twice-yearly visit a few weeks after the completion of the work. I wondered if I had gone too far in this latest episode but, in the event he was most impressed with the new office which, it appeared, was far more palatial that his own in Mbale.

Andrew Thomas had gone on safari to Katakwi to investigate the alleged burglary of one of the Asian shops. This was a fairly simple task which should not have taken him very long so I was surprised when, at about lunch time, I received a radio message from him regarding a totally different matter. It appeared that, during his investigation into the burglary, he had been approached by the local chief who reported that a woman had fallen into a pit latrine and had drowned. The body was still in the pit. He had viewed the scene but, clearly, was not too enthusiastic about dealing with it was a matter involving police. 'Is an exhumation order required before the body is removed?', he enquired. I decided to string him along on this one. I replied, 'What you have to ask yourself is, "Is the body properly inturd".'

The long rains were with us again. Every day violent storms would hit the area and the ground was soon waterlogged. Fortunately, the timing of the downpour could be more or less predicted each day, also its duration of about an hour. Margaret and I, together with about a dozen other officers and wives from various departments, were in the European Club at about 3 o'clock one Saturday afternoon when the day's storm struck. It became so dark that the lights had to be switched on. Lightning flashed and thunder rolled. The rain was so heavy that it was impossible to see outside for more than about 20 yards. Suddenly there was an immense flash and a instantaneous boom of thunder. The lights went out and we were left in almost total darkness. Stoically we continued to sup our drinks while we waited for the rain to ease off. This it did after about 10 minutes. We could then make out what had happened. The electricity sub-station about 100 yards from the club had been hit by lightning and was blazing away merrily. The telephone had also ceased to work so, as O.C. Fire Brigade, it was up to me to ensure that the blaze was dealt with. Margaret and I sped down through the flooded township to the police lines. The rain was at last easing off as I pulled up outside the front of the fire station. Fortunately the quarters occupied by the members of the brigade were close by and I managed to get three of them out. Of the driver, however, there was no sign. 'He has gone to do his shopping', I was told. 'Great.' None of the other members of the crew knew how to drive the engine. 'Right', said I, 'get the doors open and get aboard. I will drive.' As the doors were opened I realised that my car was right across the entrance. I jumped into the drivers seat and tried to start the engine. Nothing doing. Driving over the flooded roads had thrown water onto the plugs and the engine was dead. The fire engine crew got off the engine and pushed my car out of the way. Then they got back. Margaret sat in the open front of the fire engine alongside me in the driving seat. I turned the key and the engine came to life. I had absolutely no idea of the gear lay-out and my first attempts succeeded only in ramming the rear wall of the fire station in reverse gear. Eventually, I got into first gear and with Margaret pulling enthusiastically on the rope to ring the bell, we set off for the one mile trip to the burning electricity sub-station. Could I find any of the other gears? Could I hell! After a few abortive attempts in which the gearbox ground out its objections, I gave up and we roared through the township, bell ringing, at 5 miles an hour in first gear, all the way to the fire. I was gratified to find, on our arrival, that the sub-station was still blazing merrily. To my horror, however, I saw the fire crew busying themselves unrolling the hose pipe. I was just in time to prevent them from spraying the blaze with water and dying by electrocution. Where these people had received their training I do not know. I had to explain to them that the special foam equipment they were carrying on the engine was to be used for electrical fires. In any case, the first job was to turn off the power supply to the sub-station. I noticed a large switch at one side of the transformer, secured in the down position by a large padlock. Clearly, our main task at this stage was to turn off this switch. Fortunately, there were no direct flames in the immediate vicinity of the switch and a few well-aimed blows with an axe smashed the padlock. Having now turned off the mains supply, extinguishing the fire was child's play. Cedric Gunson, who was in charge of the Uganda Electricity Board for Teso District now arrived. Since he lived nearby and his was one of houses whose supply was affected by the blaze, he rapidly made emergency repairs to the system. However we were still without electricity for 24 hours.

CHAPTER 28

One of my many jobs as O.C. Police was the conducting of driving tests. Fortunately, I was not called upon to perform this duty too often and it was not too long before the job was taken over by an Inspector of Vehicles. However, at this particular time, I had to, occasionally, carry out a test. I was interrupted one morning by Dr Lee from Kumi Leper Settlement who arrived unexpectedly and was shown into my office. I had met him only twice before, once being when he officiated at the somewhat chaotic wedding of Don Robertson and his bride, the second at Pop Neilson's funeral. He began without preamble. 'I have brought one of my patients to you for a driving test', he said. 'I have been instructing him in driving our lorry and I consider that he is now ready to take the test.' I started to explain to Dr Lee that I was only prepared to take driving tests after a written application was submitted, followed by a proper appointment. Raising his voice an octave or two, he cut in on my objections. 'I am aware of the procedure', he announced, 'however, I must insist that you take this man for his test. I am urgently in need of him to drive our lorry as I shall be away on holiday for several weeks and without him we shall have no transport.' I must say that his attitude did not endear him to me. However, I felt that the police motto of *Salus Populi* must now come into play so I agreed to interview the applicant. Dr Lee duly brought him in. He was a Muteso of about 30-years-of-age. He was clearly a burnt -out leprosy case. The drugs he had been given had halted the disease. Not, however, before he had lost one of his feet and both hands which were missing just below the wrist joints. I was absolutely amazed that an apparently intelligent person such as Dr Lee could ever have envisaged that I would authorise a cripple with this degree of incapacity to be in charge of a 4-ton lorry on a public road. 'Dr Lee', I said, 'while I have the greatest sympathy for this unfortunate individual, there is no way that I would be a party to letting him loose on an unsuspecting public.' 'I am telling you', said the doctor, 'he is perfectly capable of driving our vehicle.' 'And I am telling you, Dr Lee', said I, 'that he is not. He might be able to steer the lorry and possibly change gear and maybe apply the brake. In an emergency, however, there is no way that he could be in total control. I am not prepared to risk the lives of the men, women and children who might be mowed down by your lorry as the result of my agreeing to give him a licence.' Dr Lee continued to argue the point and eventually I told him to get out of my office. He left with ill-grace and immediately wrote to police headquarters complaining of my lack of co-operation. Fortunately, I was backed to the hilt in this matter and I heard nothing further of it.

A letter arrived from police headquarters. This informed me that the Aga Khan, Prince Karim, was due to visit Soroti about two weeks hence. He had succeeded his grandfather the old Aga Khan, who had recently died, and was touring Uganda by air, with the object of visiting as many as possible of the Muslim community. My instructions were to liaise with the D.C. and the Muslims and to mount a guard of honour on the arrival of the Aga Khan at Soroti Airfield. I was further instructed that the Guard Commander was to be me! I made my way to Owen Griffiths' office. He had also just received notification of the visit and was running around like a headless chicken. Because of the security aspect, it had been decided that it would be unwise for the Aga Khan to be accommodated at any of the houses in the Asian quarter. The Government Rest House was totally inadequate. The alternative was for him to be housed in either the D.C's house or that of the A.D.C. Arthur Watson. In the event, Arthur Watson drew the short straw! The security arrangement were down to me.

The great day arrived and 11 a.m. found me at Soroti airfield dressed in my best bib and tucker and wielding my sword in charge of a guard of honour of about 40 policemen, many of whom had been hurriedly withdrawn from outpost duties. The entire European population were present in one group while the entire Muslim population of Teso district formed a rather larger gathering. The plane arrived, reasonably on time, and taxied to a halt nearby. The Aga Khan, together with an entourage of about 20, including several attractive young women, who didn't seem to be attached to anyone in particular, disembarked and formed up nearby. Owen Griffiths greeted the Aga Khan and accompanied him on his inspection of the Guard of Honour. All went well. Introductions were then made to the government officers and their wives after which senior members of the Muslim community made their own introductions. All this took about 20 minutes, after which the party broke up and the Aga Khan was taken to Arthur Watson's newly-decorated house for lunch.

It was planned that the Aga Khan would only remain in Soroti for one night so the Muslim community had laid on a grand meal and entertainment at a building adjoining the local mosque. The majority of the European officers had been invited to this, as had all of the important Muslims from throughout Teso District. The hall was packed to overflowing. Prince Karim had been seated at the end of the long main table. I noticed him eyeing the assembled guests. I had quite thought that one or other of the young ladies in his entourage would be seated next to him, or alternatively possibly the D.C's wife, Rosemary. To my astonishment, however, as well as Margaret's, he turned to an official standing by his chair who made his way to Margaret and without hesitation she was plucked from the crowd and offered this seat of honour. Poor Rosemary looked very sour about this. I decided to keep a very close eye on the proceedings from then on. Karim's father, Sadrudin, had a reputation as a playboy which was, presumably, why he had not been chosen to succeed the old Aga Khan. However, in the event, Karim acted as a perfect gentleman. (I think.) Why had he chosen Margaret to sit next to him? Well, clearly, he was a good judge of beauty and brains. Margaret was undoubtedly the best-looking and the most intelligent woman in the gathering!

Karim spent the night at the house of Arthur and Mary Watson. I was unable to discover which, if any, of his entourage spent the night with him. What I did discover was that Arthur's houseboy had filled every available container with the waste water from Karim's bath as it had come out of the drainpipe. He made a small fortune selling it to the local Muslim community. It seems highly likely that, once he found out the saleable value of this commodity he supplemented it with water of doubtful provenance! I wondered how he had not been discovered by my police guard during this somewhat dubious activity. Possibly the policemen were also involved. Best not to enquire too closely.

A couple of weeks later I received a personal letter signed by Karim thanking me for my efforts, both on the guard of honour and in regard to the security cover. A cheque for Shs 1000/- was enclosed, with a request that it be used for police recreational purposes.

I decided that it was time that Margaret learned to drive. I was not overly keen for her to learn on the Vanguard that was my pride and joy. However, there was no obvious alternative. Fortunately, the roads around the European quarter were usually virtually clear of traffic and made an excellent training area. Margaret made rapid progress. The end of the month came and with it the pay safari. The road to our outpost at Serere was 20-miles in length, practically straight and quiet. It seemed an ideal route for her first longish drive. She completed the drive without incident and at about 30 miles an hour. We arrived at the police post, which consisted of a dozen aluminium Uniport huts. The police personnel, warned of my imminent arrival, were already on parade awaiting inspection before receiving their pay. Margaret turned the car into the entrance to the outpost and made for an enormous tree, under whose shade she intended parking. 'O.K', I said, 'stop here.' Nothing. 'Stop here', I repeated. Nothing. 'STOP NOW', I bawled, trying to make a grab for the hand-brake. Too late! The front bumper hit the trunk of the tree full on at about 10-miles an hour! Worse still, it was in full view of the assembled ranks. 'Well', I said. 'It could have been worse. You might had ploughed into the parade!' I climbed out to inspect the damage. I should need a new front bumper. By and large, I suppose we had got off fairly lightly. Now, at least Margaret could appreciate the difference between the clutch and the brake! I completed the pay parade and drove back to Soroti.

A month later and Margaret had attained a fair degree of expertise. She could reverse into a parking space and round a corner and knew now how to stop in an emergency. I decided that it was time for her to take a driving test. Fortunately, this was one job that I had now managed to cast off. Stan Leedham, the Inspector of Vehicles, was now making a monthly visit and, over a period of two days, was undertaking all driving tests and vehicle examinations. 'Stan', I said. 'It's time Margaret took her test. I don't want to pay out for it though, unless she passes. I suggest that you take her out on your usual test run as a practice. She need not know that you are testing her. If you think she's O.K. I'll get her a test application and you can fill it in after she has completed it.' So it happened. At the end of the day Margaret got her full licence and she didn't even know that she had taken her test.

H.E. The Governor, Sir Andrew Cohen, and his wife, Helen, were coming to Teso District on tour. Once again I had to provide the Guard of Honour to greet him. Once again I had the short straw and was the Guard Commander. Apart from this and the normal security measures, the police were not particularly involved. After my sojourn as Sir Andrew's body guard I knew him and his wife well enough to have no particular feelings, one way or another, about his visit. He was not, in my opinion, a particularly bright individual and providing one stood up to him and gave as good as one got he would invariably back down. This time he was to be in the district for three days, staying with the D.C. and visiting various localities during this time. One of the visits which had been arranged was to Kumi Leprosy Centre, about 30 miles out of Soroti, an establishment which was financed by a religious order and where a new Medical Centre had been built. Dr Lee, who was a Doctor of Divinity rather than medicine, was in charge of the Centre and had sent out invitations to all of the Government Officers and their wives to attend the ceremony at which Sir Andrew had been asked to formally open the new building.

Margaret and I arrived at the Centre a short while before the Governor was due. About 30 other Europeans were present and, on Cohen's arrival, we all trooped along after the Governor's party on the arranged inspection of the facilities. At the conclusion of this we were invited into the new Community Centre where Dr Lee and Cohen and his wife were seated on a raised dais. Dr Lee commenced the ceremony with a speech which he hoped would result in Cohen making some additional government financial help to the Leper Centre. His speech lasted about half-an-hour instead of the anticipated 5 minutes and I could see Cohen's face getting more and more annoyed at his being delayed. Eventually Dr Lee had said all that he wanted to say, and Cohen stood up. His speech lasted about two minutes. The gist of it was that, since this was a religious community, God would no doubt provide. Dr Lee was advised to pray hard! At the conclusion of this, from Dr Lee's position, rather unsatisfactory reply, Sir Andrew was asked to unveil a plaque celebrating his opening of the Centre. He gave a light pull on the cord which was supposed to operate a little curtain. Nothing happened. He gave a firmer tug. Still nothing. At the fifth attempt Cohen put his foot against the wall and put his full weight on the cord. The entire curtain then pulled out of the wall but, fortunately, did not bring the plaque down with it. A very red-faced and annoyed Sir Andrew then stalked out of the building and into his car. Kumi never did receive Government assistance.

Soroti had by now received a telephone link with the outside world. In many ways this made life easier. No longer did we have to rely on messages sent by the laborious morse code. At about 11 a.m. one morning I was beavering away in my office when I had a telephone call from my old friend Johnny Walker. I immediately assumed that he was going to ask me if we could accommodate him and Nan for a night or two. My immediate response was to complain to him of his recent failure to be in contact. Not so. His next words struck a feeling of great foreboding. 'Sorry to hear about your father', he said. 'What — about — my father', I managed to reply. There was a lengthy pause while Johnny collected his thoughts. 'Do you mean you've not heard?', he eventually said. He then told me. I packed up work for the day and told Andrew Thomas that I was going home and didn't want to be disturbed. On my arrival I told Margaret what I had been informed. My frequent attempts to telephone my mother were without success. No reply. I next tried to contact my brother but got no reply from him either. I decided not to make any immediate plans, but to wait until I received a letter from my mother. This arrived the following morning. It was dated some eight days previously. 'My old darling has died', she wrote. Apparently he had developed severe abdominal pains and had been rushed into hospital. 'I didn't write to let you know as I didn't want to worry you.'

I was now faced with a quandary. My father had died 10 days earlier. Although my mother had made no mention of his funeral, I knew that it was his wish to be cremated. If I now made arrangements to fly to the U.K. it would certainly be a further three or four days at the absolute minimum before I could get to Hastings. By this time the funeral would undoubtedly be over and I should have had no opportunity to bid my father goodbye. It seemed that any such journey would be wasted effort. My brother and sister were no doubt doing whatever was necessary to ease my mother's burden. Further efforts at telephoning my mother and brother were no more successful than before. I therefore dispatched a telegram to my mother telling her of my decision and offering whatever financial help she might need in the meantime. I have often wondered since why my mother or at least my brother had not taken immediate steps to inform me of the situation. Both knew that I was easily available by phone or telegram. Instead, I had been placed in a queue of friends and acquaintances to be informed eventually by letter. Even Johnny Walker had received the news before me! I felt somewhat bitter at having been denied the opportunity of seeing my father one last time.

A letter from police headquarters informed me that the police band, which was based in Kampala, was due to make a tour of the Eastern Province, starting at Jinja, then to Mbale, Soroti, Lira and finally Gulu. The European officer in charge of the Band no longer had the title of Bandmaster. This, when I had first joined the Uganda Police was Teddy Bear. On his retirement a couple of years previously the title had been changed to Director of Music. This was Ted Moon. I was asked to arrange accommodation for him at Soroti Rest House. However, no such accommodation was available so, in due course, Ted came to stay with us. The remainder of the band members were housed at the police barracks.

Margaret and I both got on well with Ted. He was an excellent musician, having received his training at Kneller Hall. Working with the rawest and least-talented material he had produced a brilliant band which was not only used on ceremonial occasions but performed excellent band concerts and had a very good dance-band section as well. Their arrival unfortunately coincided with the rainy season. This did not greatly affect the success of their Soroti visit since the band concert that was performed was timed to avoid the daily downpour. The dance section gave a very popular performance at the European Club.

Too soon the visit ended. Ted led the way towards Lira, the next port of call, in his car, while the remainder of the 20-odd strong contingent followed on in the bus which had been hired for the purpose. About four hours later, an African arrived at the police station bringing the news that the bus had run off the road about 40 miles out of Soroti and was now partially submerged in a swamp.

Clearly there was no time to be lost. I made my way to the local garage and hired a large breakdown truck which was fortunately available. Then I set off for the scene of the accident followed by the breakdown truck and two police lorries. A desolate scene met my eyes. The heavy rain had caused the swamp level to rise above a causeway which formed the main road. The road had, thereby, become practically obscured for about a mile though, for the most part, it was only under about six inches of water. Ted, in the lead with his car, had negotiated most of this successfully but the driver of the bus had not been so fortunate. The front nearside wheel had left the road leaving the vehicle stranded. Insufficient grip could be obtained from the rear wheels since the offside one was clear of the ground. Fortunately, the situation was not as serious as it first appeared. By carefully reversing the breakdown truck near to the rear of the bus we were able to attach a cable to it and draw it out of the swamp reasonably easily. Ted and the band members were greatly relieved to have been rescued and we all returned to Soroti. Regrettably the remainder of the band tour had to be abandoned and they returned to Kampala the following day.

One thing which was lacking from the facilities at the European club at Soroti was a swimming pool. Several times this had been raised at Annual General Meetings of the club. The inevitable conclusion was that such a project would be totally outside the financial reach of the club and the matter was thus shelved. However, a major contractor had now moved into the district and was engaged in a road-building programme. The roads involved were initially somewhat limited in scope involving, as they did, a stretch of some five miles of tarmac out to the railway station and a similar stretch between the township and the Awoja bridge which crossed over Lake Salisbury. However, Taffy Davis, the engineer in charge of the works was a frequent visitor to the club, where I had proposed him as a temporary member. Taffy was a small, dark-haired Welshman with whom the majority of the European officers had little contact. For some reason, however, he took a great fancy to Margaret and myself and, seemingly, couldn't do enough for us.

I don't think I consciously intended raising the subject of a swimming pool with Taffy Davis. I happened to mention it one day in the course of conversation over a beer. Taffy obviously considered this for a couple of minutes then said. 'I could use one of my machines to dig out a hole for you for the swimming pool if you like. If you could then provide a gang of prisoners to finish off the excavation, I could concrete the base, shutter off the walls and finish the job off for you.'

I was somewhat taken aback by this. 'Well, Taff', I said, 'it's a very kind offer. I'll have to get the O.K. from the club committee first, but I'm sure they will be pleased to accept your offer.' And so it happened. Three months later, the Soroti Club had its swimming pool. In the intervening time, however, we were all pleased when Mackay Imla, the rather unpopular manager of the local Standard Bank of South Africa, fell into the hole when emerging somewhat drunk from the bar. Unfortunately there was no water in it at the time!

The opening of the Soroti Club Swimming Pool was marked by a grand party. Various swimming competitions were organised together with such things as 'lovely legs', (male as well as female. I donated one of my many pigs which was roasted whole, and another which was jointed and distributed to the fortunate club members.

About this time we suffered some losses from our menagerie. Bambi, the Dik-dik, had grown into a particularly fine specimen. The tiny set of horns on his head were practically a record for his species. Having the run of the house and garden, I was never surprised to see him several hundred yards away from time to time. One day he did not return. We could never be sure whether he finished up in someone's cook pot or whether he found himself a mate. There were, to be sure, a few Dik-dik in the vicinity, though I never saw any others nearer that a couple of miles away. Hopefully he found them and lived happily ever after!

Our next loss was Penelope the pig. She had grown into a magnificent sow and, I suppose, I should have sent her back to her relatives at the prison. She was certainly becoming too large to continue as a household pet. She continued, however, to regard herself as one of the family and spent most of her time indoors with Bryn. Fortunately, at about this time, Tom Hinett and his family paid us a visit. Tom was going from strength to strength in his career. Having completed the prison-building programme in Uganda, he had transferred to the Kenya Prison Service, with a promotion and was engaged in a similar building programme in that country. When I suggested that Penelope might form the nucleus of a pig-breeding programme at one of the new prisons he jumped at the chance. A couple of weeks later a truck arrived and Penelope was on her way to start a new dynasty of prison pigs.

With the departure of Bambi and Penelope, Twinkle, the now fully-grown sheep, was left to wander around on his own. He took to wandering off from the garden and eating flowers and vegetables wherever he could find them. Our European neighbours didn't mind too much but their African staff took a dim view of having their little plots of vegetable raided. In the end we were left with no alternative but to sentence Twinkle to prison. Here he found his niche. He became the leader of the small herd of cows who formed part of the prison farm. The cows, with Twinkle in the lead, and with the prison trustee in charge went off each morning, into the grass which grew on the edge of the Township. Here they would graze until it began to grow dusk when all would return to the prison for the night. All went well for about six months, when the cow that Twinkle had displaced caught him with a well-aimed kick and broke his back leg. The vet, who attended, gave his opinion that nothing could be done for him so poor Twinkle appeared on the menu at the prison. I was presented with one of the legs, which was delicious. I wondered afterwards whether it was worth the hassle that I suffered from Margaret and Alison who, apparently, objected to me eating him.

The annual competition for the East and West African Cup was now due. This was the revolver-shooting competition entered into by all of the African police forces which came under the influence of the Colonial Office. By now I had been accepted as a permanent member of the team. I left in my car on the afternoon prior to the competition. On this occasion I was not accompanied by Margaret, who had taken a part-time nursing job at Soroti Hospital where she was employed as a theatre nurse. By the time I neared Mbale it was dark. On the outskirts of the town was a crossing where the railway passed across the main road. This was unmanned, unlit and without a barrier. On my arrival, I found that the accident waiting to happen had finally done so a couple of minutes earlier. A lorry, driven by an Asian, had arrived at the crossing. In the cab, in addition to the driver, was his wife who was carrying a three-month old baby on her lap, and an African turnboy. As the vehicle started over the crossing a train had struck its offside. It was 200 yards before the train was brought to a standstill. The train had come to a halt completely blocking the road and the engine had been derailed, so was unable to reverse away from the lorry.

I made my way along the track to the mangled remains of the vehicle. The cab was crushed but, surprisingly, the three adults were still alive. And shouting! I crossed the railway line in front of the vehicle and, finding a couple of cars on the road on the other side, I instructed the drivers to return to Mbale and inform the police, fire brigade and hospital of the occurrence. It was, however, an hour before assistance arrived. In the meantime, armed with a hacksaw which I happened to be carrying in the back of my car, I set about the lorry cab. The windscreen was, of course, totally shattered so I concentrated my efforts on cutting through the windscreen frame and the area round the door hinges. Fortuitously, an African doctor arrived during this time and was able to inject the driver and his wife with large doses of morphine. By the time other help had arrived I had succeeded in extricating the woman and child from the wreckage. She survived but the child was quite dead, having been crushed in the initial impact. Her husband and the turnboy also perished. Barriers were erected on the rail crossing shortly after this tragedy.

A few months later I was notified by prison headquarters that an African prison officer was being sent to Soroti to take over the running of the prison. I had mixed feelings about this. It was certainly high time that responsibility for the day-to-day running of the prison should be taken over by the Prison Service. I was, after all, spending a considerable time each week, sorting out the various administrative problems which arose. I received no additional remuneration for this. The plus side of the job was that I had as much prison labour as I required for my various building projects and my own garden. Also, the regular supply of fresh pork for myself and the other European officers would cease.

The handing-over of the prison took place in due course. The newly-appointed Prison Officer was a pleasant and apparently intelligent individual of the Basoga tribe who struck me as being an excellent choice to undertake the day-to-day running of the prison. At the conclusion of the hand-over he thanked me profusely for my guidance and asked if he could call on me should he run into any difficulties. This I was pleased to agree to. Regarding the prison pigs, I was assured that I should be provided with meat at any time I requested it. I was also invited to continue being supplied with prison labour at any time I wished. This struck me as being an excellent arrangement. A short while later I received a letter from the Commissioner of Prisons conveying the usual glowing thanks which I had long before learned to disregard.

The train from Soroti to Kampala ran about three times a week. Soroti station was about five miles outside the township and was the loading point for the Karamajong cattle which were one of the main sources of meat in the capital. The railway employed a number of very junior staff who job was to wander along a particular stretch of line a couple of times each week to inspect the line and ensure that nothing had come loose.

I was called out one afternoon to the track about 10 miles out of Soroti. One of the railway employees had been run over by a train. On my arrival, I found the train driver awaiting my arrival with some impatience. The body of the dead man was distributed over about 400 yards of track and much of it had already been consumed by the vultures and marabou storks who, circling high above, had been awaiting just such an opportunity. However, the remaining bits were gathered up and taken off to Soroti for post mortem. Apart from the train driver there was one major witness to the affair. This was a friend of the deceased who had been with him at the time. This individual was still very drunk. He informed me that the two of them had been drinking native beer at a local bar and had left at about mid-day much the worse for wear. Walking home along the rail track shortly before the train was due, the deceased had said, 'I am a very powerful and important man! If I step onto the track and signal this train to stop, it will have to do so.' So saying he did just that but, unfortunately, the train driver failed to recognise his importance.

I now had about two months left before my home leave became due. Two items of information now came to my notice. The first was that Margaret was pregnant. The second that, once again, half of my hard-earned six months leave was to be spent in attending a course. This time it was the Senior Command Course, and was to be taken at Bramshill Police College, near Hartley Wintney in Hampshire.

Our departure from Soroti was preceded by the usual round of parties both at the European Club and at a number of Asian houses where we had made many friends during the past three happy years. Eventually we had packed our belongings into crates and were off again to Kampala on the first step of our journey.

I decided that, on this occasion, I would not bother about getting a new car for home leave, but would wait until I returned for my next tour. To this end I wrote to my brother and asked him to sort out a reasonably cheap but reliable vehicle. Big mistake! On our arrival in England, we were presented with a small, ancient Ford Popular. What a load of crap. On my first drive in it I found that hot oil leaked from the pressure gauge, straight onto my trousers! The shock absorbers were completely shot so that the car bounced about all over the road. This also affected the steering rather badly. Sharp application of the brakes would sometimes cause the vehicle to spin in a complete circle. The clutch was also so badly worn that in order to get up a hill, a flying start had to be made at the bottom. I eventually disposed of it for scrap to a car breaker!

The course at Bramshill commenced a few weeks after our arrival in England. About 26 senior police officers were taking part and we were housed in the original Bramshill House. At that time a large building programme of classrooms and dormitories was under way, which would eventually cater for several hundred students. It was an interesting course and the students were divided into syndicates and set various problems such as organising Royal Visits, Major Emergencies, Civil Disorders and so on. There were several other colonial police officers on the course and we had to spend one of our weekends at Bisley where an army officers' course was under way. Here I had the task of lecturing the junior officers on dealing with riots in the colonial territories.

At the conclusion of the course, a dinner and dance was held for officers and their wives. Margaret, of course, attended — heavily pregnant — and managed to fall down the flight of stone steps at the entrance of the House. Fortunately, she was uninjured but she gave everyone an anxious few minutes.

On the final day of the course we had to attend assessment interviews with our tutors. No examinations were held and the assessment was entirely on our course work. It seemed that I had passed the course with flying colours and my future was assured. I had the inevitable final question. 'What type of police work did I enjoy least.' 'Training and parade work', I unwisely replied!

CHAPTER 29

I now had just over two months leave left before returning to Uganda. I had arranged for our return to be made by sea again. I felt entitled to the additional break gained thereby, having been robbed of half of my leave while attending the course. Unfortunately, I had not taken into account Margaret's pregnant condition. Our new arrival was due to make its appearance about half-way through the voyage. I deemed it wiser, therefore, for Margaret to have the baby in the U.K. and to follow me out by air at a later date. I wrote to the Crown Agents and made the necessary alterations to our travel arrangements.

Meantime, I received notification from police headquarters regarding my new posting. Prior to going on leave, it had been hinted that a posting to Gulu in the Acholi district was on the cards. This would have suited me superbly since the area took in the Queen Elizabeth National Park with the Nile and Murchison Falls and was alive with game of all sorts. The new posting came, therefore, as something of a disappointment. It was to Masaka, about 80 miles from Kampala. Reasonably civilised but where, unfortunately, political unrest was rife. This was quite an important posting but I was no longer to be in charge, my rank of Deputy Superintendent meant that I should be second-in-command to the Superintendent. After three years as top dog, this was going to come as something of an anticlimax. Still, it was infinitely preferable to a posting to Kampala itself.

During the three months which I had spent on the course at Bramshill, I had been giving some thought to the acquisition of a property in Hastings which we could use during the times we were on leave from Uganda and let while we were absent. There was also the problem of my mother. She and my father had been able to live in their flat at Winchester House rent-free during his lifetime, but with his death this arrangement ended as the odd jobs which my father had done in return for his accommodation, could not be expected of my mother.

My mother had already disposed of most of the best antiques which she and my father had acquired at various auction sales during his lifetime. She was now living with a friend of hers at Clive Vale in Hastings. The decision I made was to purchase a large property which could be converted into flats, one of which she could occupy in return for keeping an eye on the remainder. To this end I had been viewing potential properties during my weekends away from Bramshill. There were plenty of suitable buildings on the market at this time and, shortly after returning from Bramshill, I chose one at 6, Essenden Road, St Leonards. This I now purchased for £1,750. The house was a late-Victorian semi-detached property having three floors plus cellerage. Margaret and I moved into the ground floor which consisted of a large lounge, two bedrooms, a bathroom/toilet and a kitchen/dining room. We now visited a number of auction rooms and, for a minute sum, purchased sufficient furniture to make a very comfortable dwelling.

My talent for building and altering buildings now came to the fore. I spent some time re-wiring the house and converting it into three self-contained flats and then moved my mother into the first-floor flat. She was very happy with this arrangement since, in addition to it being rent-free, I let her have the top flat also which she let and which brought her a small income. Having achieved this major objective I now advertised for a tenant to rent our flat once we had returned to Uganda. In this I was fortunate in receiving an application from the R.A.F. who were looking for accommodation for some of their staff who were working at the radar site at Wartling. The necessary legal agreement was drawn up and, over the next few years, I had very reasonable tenants.

My heavy luggage having by now been delivered to the Union Castle Line agents for delivery to the docks, I now said my good-byes to Margaret and my mother. Margaret had moved to her mother's house which was only about half-a-mile from the maternity home where she planned to give birth to my son! So it was, in mid-September, that I boarded the *S.S. Transvaal Castle* on my journey to Mombasa. The journey proved uneventful until we entered the Red Sea when, on 7th October 1959, I was handed a telegram informing me of the birth, on the previous day, of a daughter, Jacqueline Ann. I was a bit disappointed at not having got a son, but made the best of it over a dram or two and sent a telegram of congratulation to Margaret hoping for better luck next time! The main thing was that Margaret and the new infant were both well and that I should be seeing them in a couple of months time. On my arrival in Kampala, I took possession of a new Peugeot 403 saloon which I had ordered prior to going on leave and, after a quick courtesy call at police headquarters set off for my new station.

Although I had driven through Masaka a number of times previously I had never paused long enough to take any note of the place. On the outskirts was a smart new hotel, The Tropic Inn. The main road through the town, heading towards Mbarara, the next large area of any note and onward to the Congo border, was littered with various Asian shops then, on the right-hand side, one came to the road leading to the Administrative Offices, Court and the old European quarter. On the left-hand side was a road leading to Bwala Hill, a new development of European bungalows where mainly junior officers of all the various government departments were housed.

The bungalows in the old European quarter were superb. Most of them were around 30 or 40 years old, and all were surrounded on each side by a deep cool verandah, protected from annoying insects by its mosquito netting. Each one stood in about half-an-acre of garden in which fruit and ornamental trees grew in profusion. Unfortunately, all of the old bungalows were occupied and jealously guarded by the departments whose officers were fortunate enough to be occupying them. I was, therefore, allocated one of the new development on Bwala Hill. This was adequate but nothing special. It did have the advantage of being 300- or 400-feet above the township and was pleasantly cool and enjoyed a superb view over the surrounding countryside.

After spending the first day of my arrival unpacking our now numerous possessions, I eventually reported to the police station. This proved to be an old building something on the lines of that at Soroti but very scruffy and badly in need of reorganizing and decorating. The Superintendent in charge was George Harrison, aged about 50, ex-Indian Police and nearing retirement. He had a large untidy moustache, a permanently-sour expression on his face and an extremely bad temper. He habitually carried a swagger-cane under his arm and was as unpopular with the other Europeans on the station as he was with the officers and other ranks of the police unit. He proved to be one of the laziest man I've ever come across. The only thing he ever did with any enthusiasm was to delegate responsibility to the other officers. I rapidly came to appreciate the reasoning behind my posting. I was to take over the policing of the District in every respect, apart from getting the promotion to go with it! The other officers on the unit were Len Holt A.S.P., David Vickers Cadet, and Mike Barber, Cadet. There were also a number of Asian and African Inspectors and Sub-Inspectors. In addition there was a Special Branch officer, Geoff Mitchell, A.S.P.

George Harrison greeted me with some relief and accompanied me to the office which had been allocated to me. 'You'll be in charge of the day-to-day running of the unit', he said.' 'Any serious crime that's reported I shall expect you to deal with. You can bring me the books each morning after you have gone through them. Crime files and occurrences you will check daily, marking up lines of enquiry or action to be taken. You will also be responsible for parades, records, weekly lectures, lines inspections, pay parades both here and on the sub-stations also prosecuting any serious cases that come to Court. I will deal with any disciplinary cases that arise, providing I'm not otherwise engaged!'

'That', I thought, 'is a fairly comprehensive list. I wonder what I shall do in my spare time.' I didn't have to wonder for very long what George Harrison did with his spare time. 'Right', he said. 'I'm going out to see the Gombolola Chief at Mukungwi. I'll probably be in tomorrow sometime.' Ten minutes later he was to be seen together with his orderly driving past the police station, his shotgun in the back of his car and with his wife alongside, together with her canvases and painting equipment. This, it turned out, was his regular routine, several times a week. Off into the wide blue yonder, shooting guinea fowl while his dutiful wife sat at her easel painting with watercolours.

I rapidly settled into the new routine. I even found time to carry out a bit of reorganisation in the various offices and storerooms. Getting onto good terms with the local Public Works Department proved a little more difficult than it had in Soroti, since Harrison and his wife were highly unpopular and no one wanted to do anything which might be for his benefit. However, eventually I managed to get a degree of co-operation which came in handy in my various projects. I didn't do too much of this, however, as I could seen no reason for carrying out any major refurbishment for which Harrison would get the credit.

By the time Margaret and my daughters arrived a couple of months later, I was reasonably well organised. Jacqueline Ann, our new addition was proving to be a most objectionable child.

She rarely seemed to sleep and had the most powerful lungs of any child I've come across. She wasn't very pretty either. At an early stage she was nick-named Khrushchev, after the Premier of the U.S.S.R. whom she closely resembled. Thank God she has improved over the years!

New neighbours were moving in next door but one. On my return home at lunch time I saw an attractive woman and a bearded man busily unloading their belongings from a lorry. They both looked somewhat harassed so I wandered along to enquire if they would like a cup of tea or a meal. 'No thank you. We're fully organised!', I was told somewhat curtly. I retreated! Thus it was that I made the acquaintance of Harry and Lota Stokes who were, regardless of the unpromising start, shortly to be numbered among our closest friends. Harry was a Telecommunications Engineer while Lota was taking over the Masaka Exchange. Both of them were passionately interested in wildlife and rearing young orphaned animals.

Life in Masaka went on fairly uneventfully for some months. Once I had sorted out the running of the police station to my satisfaction, I was able to relax to some degree and take Margaret and the children out to see what the district had to offer. I had, by this time, taken up one of my early hobbies — keeping tropical fish. Here, I had an ideal opportunity to catch and study fish of types I had never previously encountered. Collecting them was so easy. Tiny fish of dozens of different types and colours could be netted from any of the local swamps or the ditches running alongside the roads. In addition to one very large tank, I had several smaller ones in which I could isolate anything I was not sure about before adding it to the main collection. Suitable aquatic plants presented a problem at one time. Those I collected either grew too large too rapidly or else died off for no apparent reason. However, one day we went to Lake Nabugabo, about 20 miles out of Masaka. It was said that there were no crocodiles in this lake though, since it was not too far from Lake Victoria, I decided to be a bit circumspect. What I did find, once we had sat down to our picnic tea, was that the place was alive with snakes. A couple of hundred yards from where we were sitting was an old European house which had fallen into disrepair. Upon my going inside to investigate it I disturbed a couple of cobras and several other species which I didn't have time to identify. I wondered what circumstance had caused the previous occupants to leave. On returning to the picnic party I spent a little while scanning the branches of the large tree growing above our head. In a very short time I noticed movements and was able to identify a very large green tree mamba. Not wanting him to join our party I got half-a-dozen stones and with a lucky strike dislodged him and he fell into the lake. After our picnic I wandered along the lake shore where, in a shallow area, I saw exactly what I had been looking for. A large patch of valasinaria, a narrow-stemmed water plant a bit like coarse grass. This grew about ten yards from the bank which, at this point, was overgrown with coarse undergrowth and thorn bush. In order to reach the valasinaria I had to wade along in the water for about 50 yards. Fortunately the water was only about two feet deep for most of the way. I waded in, taking with me the net which I had made, mounted on a broomstick, in case I saw any likely looking fish. Having reached the area I was aiming for, I collected my prize and was about to retrace my steps when I was alerted by a commotion in the undergrowth. Then I saw a large shape break out and splash into the water. 'There are crocs after all', I thought, 'now I've got one coming for me!' I quite thought that my last moment had come. I could see the wake of the creature as it rapidly approached under the water. Mud from the disturbed lake bottom rose to the surface as the animal neared. I readied myself with the net. My only hope was that I should be able to catch it a hefty spear blow with the broomstick, maybe in its eye if I was lucky. If not I should be dead meat very quickly. As I was about to make my strike, the creature broke the surface. I breathed a gasp of relief. My 'attacker' was an enormous monitor lizard, probably far more frightened of me that I had been of it. On seeing me it dived and I lost sight of it. Now, I made my way to dry land by the quickest route. Forcing my way through the thorn bushes and undergrowth I was very conscious of the prevalence of the snakes. However, these were not to be the problem. I had only gone a few yards when I became conscious of excruciating pain all over my legs. I was being attacked by hundreds of red soldier ants. There was nothing I could do about this as I forced my way through. By the time I reached the open space I was covered with the angry little beasts. Most of them had taken a firm grip with their jaws and I had to get Margaret's assistance to prise them loose. I think that it was likely that the precipitate entry of the monitor lizard into the water was due to the attentions of these creatures rather that its being disturbed by my proximity.

A couple of months after Margaret's arrival I heard a rumour that one of the bungalows in the old European quarter was about to become vacant. I immediately went along to the *boma* where I saw the D.C. Bennett Jacobs, known as Jake, with whom I got on reasonably well. By dint of considerable persuasion, I managed to secure this dwelling and went off in triumph to inform Margaret. We moved shortly afterwards. Our new abode was superb. Although it was quite old the accommodation was palatial. In addition to the cool verandah which surrounded the building, there was a large lounge, a similar-sized dining room, three bedrooms, large kitchen and various storerooms. The garden, however, was the greatest triumph. This, having been lovingly cultivated for many years, grew fruit, flowers and vegetables in profusion. A great avocado pear tree stood near the gateway, laden with fruit, Half-a-dozen citrus trees grew near the hedge which bordered the golf course. These included oranges, tangerines, limes and lemons all of them simultaneously in flower, immature and mature fruit at the same time. One of the lemon trees was quite extraordinary. I don't know what variety it was (if it had one) but some of the lemons weighed three and three quarter pounds each. Thin-skinned too and full of juice. Also in our garden were tree tomatoes, mangoes and guavas. A large bed of strawberries was laid out in the vegetable garden and these produced fruit at all times of the year. A veritable garden of Eden.

A letter was received from police headquarters. The Commissioner was going to visit on an inspection. Had it been the Deputy Commissioner of one of the Assistant Commissioners, Harrison would have been able to make his escape. As it was he would have to, at least, put in an appearance. This did not please him over much. 'Well', he said, 'I shall expect you to take the parade. I shall accompany the Commissioner on his inspection. You had better get practising.' With my known dislike of parade work, this didn't meet with my approval but I didn't have much option. With somewhat ill-grace, I abandoned the various files I was wading through. The next couple of days I spent down at the barracks working out the routine for the parade. I hated every moment of it!

Two days to go before the Commissioners arrival. At 5.20 a.m. I was awakened by the bed moving around the floor. I switched on the light and woke Margaret. 'What's going on?', she enquired. 'Did you not notice anything?', I said. She had not. I thought I must have imagined it but then noticed that the bed head was several inches from the wall. About 20 minutes passed and I had just dropped off to sleep again when the telephone rang. This was a direct line to the police station. The charge office constable was on the other end. 'Sir, there has been an earthquake. A building at the bus station has collapsed and trapped people inside.' 'Right', I said, 'Get the fire brigade out, telephone Mr Holt and Mr Barber and get them to the scene. Get any constables and N.C.Os who are on duty down there. I am leaving immediately and will see them there.' I rapidly dressed and collected a torch. As an afterthought I put on my steel helmet and I was away.

On my arrival at the bus station all initially appeared normal. The compound where the buses were parked had, over the years, become a sort of dossing ground for tribesmen from Ruanda who, on their way to Kampala and other areas to seek work, would spend the night prior to their onward journey the following day. The compound was surrounded by a brick wall about 15 feet in height against which, in various places, several brick built shelters with corrugated iron roofs had been erected. Then I saw that part of the wall had collapsed onto one of the shelters. The collapse had brought down the walls of the shelter and the whole lot had fallen inwards. Muffled screams and shouts came from under the debris. Far from assisting, however, the natives in the other shelters had turned over and gone back to sleep. None of the assistance I had requested from the police station had arrived so I made my way to the collapsed shelter. My shouts soon produced a response from one area where at least one person was trapped. Shining my torch around, I saw that there was quite an extensive mound of heavy debris over the victim. On top of this was a long piece of corrugated iron which still leaned against the top part of the collapsed wall, at a height of about ten feet. My first object, therefore, was to get rid of the corrugated iron so that I could make a start on clearing the brick rubble. 'I really should have put some gloves on', I thought.

I took a firm grip on the corrugated iron and gave it a pull. Nothing happened. I tried again. Something gave and the next instant I was crushed under a piece of masonry which weighed some two hundredweight. What I had not noticed was that the corrugated iron was still attached to the wall. This caught me squarely on top of the head knocking me to the ground and then bouncing off down my back, finishing on my legs. The incident was over in less than a second and, apart from the initial blow to my head, I knew nothing of it. I must say that, had I been killed, a less painful method could not have been devised.

How much time passed in my unconscious state I am not sure. Probably not more than five minutes. I was eventually roused by the screaming which was still going on immediately beneath me. I struggled back to some degree of consciousness to find that I was lying face down with my legs pinned by the weight of the block of masonry which had struck me. Apart from the cries of those trapped below, the silence of the night was unbroken. No, I'm mistaken. Someone was groaning nearby. It took me a couple more minutes to realise that it was me! My torch was lying nearby, still functioning, and I could just reach it. I grasped it and shone it onto my legs. At first I thought that they must be both broken. They were certainly painful enough. I realised at this stage what must have happened and thanked my lucky stars for the last minute thought which had made me wear my steel helmet. Had it not been for this my brains would certainly now be scattered on top of the debris. I gingerly felt those bits of my body that I could reach. In the light of the torch, I could see that my right hand was bleeding heavily having been lacerated by the corrugated iron as it fell. Next I tried to turn over. I was held fast by the block of masonry. However, by reaching back and pulling at the block, I managed to release my right leg. Now I was able to move a bit more and by pulling out other smaller pieces of brick and rubble I eventually managed to release my left leg as well. I staggered to my feet and immediately fell over again. The world was gyrating madly and I sat, head in hands for a short while until I regained full conciousness.

I had, I estimated, now been at the scene of the incident for almost half-an-hour. Dawn was not far away. Still no assistance had arrived and still the occupants of the other huts slept on. I started shouting for assistance. Nothing happened. I got to my feet and started to shift the debris from immediately above the man who was making all the noise. After a few minutes I had cleared enough to see his face. He didn't look very well! I spoke to him in Swahili in an attempt to let him know that he would soon be released. I learned that two other men had been in the shelter with him at the time the earthquake occurred. No other voices could be heard so I thought that this was probably the only survivor. As I continued with the clearance, at long last the fire brigade arrived followed shortly by Len Holt. 'I thought they must be having me on', he said. 'I didn't feel any earthquake.' I thankfully handed over the remainder of the rescue to Len. 'I'm going to hospital to get sorted out', I said. 'Get this other poor sod out and to hospital and see if the others are still alive or not.' With this I got into my car and drove, somewhat erratically to the hospital. On my arrival I found that the only member of staff on duty was a junior orderly. I instructed him to phone the Medical Officer, Dr Cherry and sat down to wait. Dr Cherry arrived about ten minutes later, rubbing his eyes. In common with all the others he had not known of the earthquake until he had been telephoned. At this juncture the injured man from the shelter was brought in, together with his companions who were both dead, one having had his skull crushed and the other having suffocated. The injured individual had received a crushed pelvis and multiple fractures and lacerations. He wouldn't be going anywhere for a while. When I was cleaned up I found that I had got off pretty lightly with concussion, a lacerated hand and multiple-bruising to both legs and back. Harrison was most put out during the morning when I limped into his office to tell him that I would be off duty for a few days and that he would have to take the parade after all. True to character he immediately delegated this job to Len Holt. It was later found that the quake had measured six on the Richter scale, and in fact one other person had been killed as a result, though this was not discovered until some days later.

We and our friends Lota and Harry Stokes were invited to an Asian wedding. We were delighted to accept this invitation as it was well-known that such weddings were lavish affairs where splendid Indian food was plentiful and the booze flowed like water. On our arrival at about 7 o'clock we found that the wedding had already been in progress for many hours but the banquet was just about to begin. The bride and groom, decked out in their finery, sat on a raised platform while the multitude of guests sat at a number of long tables. Margaret sat on my right while Lota sat on my left. Alcohol, we found to our dismay, was not permitted by this particular caste, but there were plenty of soft drinks. If only we had known, we could have smuggled in a bottle of gin — but it was not to be. Of food, there was a surfeit — but we were not permitted to touch it until after the speeches. These seemed to go on for hours. Mostly in Gujerati or some such language which we could not understand. To pass the shining hour I, *soto voce,* told Lota a joke I had heard. 'There was this young subaltern in the Indian Army. Always getting himself into scrapes. At a mess dinner he found himself seated next to the Colonel's daughter. 'What lovely hands you have', he said. 'Tell me, how do you keep them so white?' 'Why, I wear buckskin gloves', she replied. 'How extraordinary', he said. 'I always wear buckskin breeches and my balls are as brown as berries.' Lota's sudden hoot of laughter came at a particularly crucial point in one of the speeches and the entire assembly glared at us. Our host did not invite us again. Pity really. The food was very good!

The local prison officer was Les Henry. He had been in the prison service for many years and was a very pleasant character. He and his wife lived on Bwala Hill and we got to know them very well. A fact that was not generally known but which he confided to me was that he was the official executioner. About once a month he would go off to Luzira Prison just outside Kampala where he would weigh and measure half-a-dozen or so condemned felons and, at the due time would adjust the ropes around their necks and drop them through the trap doors up to three at a time. On his return to Masaka, his wife would refuse to sleep with him for several days. I wonder why! Some people are just too squeamish!

Expatriate officers had, for some years now, been aware that their job could no longer be regarded as being 'for life'. Harold Macmillan, during his term of office as British Prime Minister, had made his famous 'Wind of Change' speech and the writing was now on the wall. African officers were being promoted to ranks which, a few years earlier would have been regarded as totally out of their reach. Now the terms of 'Compensation for loss of office' were announced. When they were implemented, expatriate officers could expect to receive a substantial 'pay off'. This would vary according to age and length of service of the individual, as well as the rank he had reached. It was proposed that such compensation would be made over a period of four years by five equal installments. The optimum age for compensation was 40 years. I was, at this time, 38 years old so would come out of it near the top. The prospect certainly gave everyone a great deal to think about.

We were, from time to time, invited to the homes of various Asian businessmen. both Lota and Harry and ourselves were keen on these outings. The Indian food was invariably of a very high quality and usually there was plenty of alcoholic beverages as well. At one of these dinners we were introduced to an Asian sweetmeat called *fulfaladah* (I think). This was like a very thick, spiced jelly. So thick in fact that it defied our best efforts to cut, let alone eat it. Not wanting to offend our hosts we surreptitiously hid the sweet in our handkerchiefs until the end of the evening. On the way home, going down the steep hill, we released it out of the window. We were surprised to be overtaken by it, travelling at the speed of sound and showing not the slightest sign of disintegrating. I wish I had the recipe. I feel sure that there must be some industrial application for the stuff!

We were occasionally visited by natives wanting to sell us various items of produce. Usually they were sent on their way since we were virtually independent as far as fruit and vegetables were concerned. and the rather crude wooden carvings, that were sometimes offered left much to be desired. However, on one occasion we were asked if we might be interested in a large glass carboy full of honey. I was tempted by this since I was, at the time, thinking of trying my hand at making mead. With this amount of honey I could manufacture an almost limitless supply. I bought the whole lot for Shs. 5/- and placed it on a high shelf in the food store. Our next visitor was a gentleman who had caught a young pangolin. Alison fell in love with it and called it Sammy. Sammy wandered all over the place like a small tank. He was incredibly tame, not even nervous of Bryn our large Alsatian. If ever he felt threatened he would roll into a ball like a very large wood louse, his scales giving him complete protection. Feeding Sammy was a bit of a problem. His diet of ant larvae was very difficult to duplicate. I telephoned the game department at Entebbe and received the suggestion that a diet of minced beef mixed with a small quantity of formic acid might suffice. In the meantime, until I had time to make a suitable cage for Sammy he was put into the food store from which everything on the lower shelves had been removed. Sammy was reputed to be largely nocturnal though I must say that I found him to be active most of the time. He consumed a fair amount of the suggested diet but I was not happy that he was going to survive for very long on this.

On the third day after his arrival, I was roused by a tremendous crash from the direction of the food store. I opened the door with some trepidation. Somehow Sammy had clambered onto the top shelf. Shards of broken glass littered the floor. About ten gallons of very runny honey was rapidly spreading in every direction. Sammy was paddling in it and helping to spread it liberally around. I grabbed him and stuffed him into a box. Much as we loved him he had to go. Leaving Margaret and the houseboy to clear up the debris, I got into my car and headed for an area of ant hills about ten miles out of town. I never attempted to keep a scaly anteater after this.

CHAPTER 30

One of my least favourite tasks was arranging a weekly lecture for other ranks in the police barracks. These lectures were usually attended by about twenty constables and N.C.Os. I took my turn as rarely as possible but drew up a roster giving a suggested subject for the other officers and inspectors to lecture upon. My turn came round and I racked my brains to find something which might be a little less boring than the norm. I decided on personal descriptions as my subject. Each of the audience was issued with a piece of paper and then given the task of describing an officer or inspector who was not present. The result was hilarious. George Harrison was universally disliked. 'He is a very UNGRY man.' 'He always shouts.' 'He carries a stick, having a moustache.' 'He hates everyone.' 'He does no work but shoots many birds.' I never mentioned this to Harrison but we and the Stokes had many a laugh about it.

Word arrived from the direction of Mbarara that a bulldozer which had been clearing an area for tea planting had come across a lioness and two cubs. The lioness had allegedly attacked and had been shot. The two cubs were unlikely to survive. I immediately phoned Harry and Lota. Without a moment's hesitation they were away to rescue the cubs. The next I heard was that they were busily engaged in feeding them every two hours day and night. They were in poor condition but with tender loving care they survived. They were christened Porgy and Bess. The Game Department at Entebbe agreed to allow them to be reared providing one was handed over in due course for the department to dispose of. Not a bad bargain really. The Stokes did all the hard work, after which the Game Department took one of the cubs and sold it for a considerable sum. Both cubs became very tame. Porgy, the male, was eventually sold to an American Zoo while Bess finished up in Bristol Zoo where in later years Harry would visit her and go into her cage where she made a great fuss of him. Unfortunately, Bess had become humanised and wanted nothing to do with any of the male lions who were introduced to her. She died childless at a great age.

During the time I had been in Masaka, I had been conscious of political activity simmering just beneath the surface of the apparently peaceful countryside. If Jeff Mitchell, the Special

Branch officer, had any inkling of trouble brewing, he was keeping it to himself. I knew, as did every other police officer, of the cause of resentment in some areas. This was the problem of the so-called 'Lost Counties'. During the early years of the British Administration, the Banyoro tribe under Kaberega, the *Omukama*, had engaged in warfare with the Baganda with whom the British had formed an alliance. The British forces under Captain Lugard then defeated the Banyoro. Kaberega was pursued and captured and finally deported to the Seychelles Islands in the Indian Ocean. The Bunyoro tribe were punished by the transfer of the counties of Bugangadzi and Buyaga and much of the land in Mubende to the Baganda. This is, of course, over-simplifying the entire debate but it serves well enough to illustrate the cause of dissent. Now the Protectorate government decided to hold a referendum to decide whether the 'Lost Counties' should be returned to their previous administrative areas. Polling booths were set up in villages throughout the district and the police had to provide mobile and static units to prevent trouble from breaking out. This was the signal for a large body of political activists to start their campaign. Polling was to take place over a period of three days. I did not have sufficient police at my disposal to man all of the booths all of the time. On a number of occasions the crowds waiting to cast their votes would be attacked or threatened and driven off as soon as the police presence had been temporarily withdrawn. In addition to this, riotous crowds started to attack various Gombolola headquarters. Fortunately, no one was killed during these incidents but a couple of the headquarters were burned to the ground and in almost every case safes and strong rooms were attacked and opened by force or threats and cash stolen. Much of the poll tax which had been collected was stolen during these raids and records destroyed so that it was impossible to know who had paid up and who had not. This was a most unsatisfactory state of affairs as, by the time an incident had been reported, the instigators were well away. Special Branch personnel and my own detectives investigated as far as was possible but with small success. The incidents finally ceased when the referendum results became known and the county boundaries were re-aligned.

We had now been in Masaka for about 18 months. My

mother wrote to us regularly giving news of herself and my flats. Apart from a problem with the roof which necessitated an outlay of a couple of hundred pounds all was going well. Her latest letter was an enquiry of whether she could come out to Uganda and stay with us for a while. Her suggestion was that she would be able to look after the two girls which would enable Margaret to take up her nursing career again. I must say that I was a bit apprehensive about this. Margaret and I had a very happy relationship and I didn't want to put this at risk. Live-in mothers-in-law had rarely worked out, in my experience, but I knew that she was depressed following my father's death and I was loath to refuse her request. After a considerable discussion, Margaret and I suggested a stay of about six months. Within a couple of weeks, mother was with us.

Visitors from the Belgian Congo were few and far between. Now suddenly we were overwhelmed with them. These, however, were not the normal visitors but refugees. Without any warning or preparation for handover, the Belgian government had decided to abrogate all responsibility for their colonies. This was an absolutely despicable act which put at risk every European, Asian and African member of the population. With the withdrawal of the central government, all of the local administrations instantly collapsed. Law and order became non-existent. European officials made a run for it, taking with them whatever valuables they could carry. Commerce and industry collapsed. Every shop closed. Rape, pillage and murder were the order of the day. Armed gangs roamed the streets. Convents were raided and the nuns, who had spent years of their lives caring for the poor and sick, were raped and murdered. Houses blazed and those belonging to Europeans or Asians were quickly commandeered by their erstwhile cooks and houseboys. The border between the Congo and Uganda became the scene of chaos. Belgian citizens in their large American cars queued up at the crossing trying to bribe their way across. The gangs were waiting for them. Some were permitted to cross with just the clothes they stood in. Some were fortunate enough to retain their transport but nothing else. A few who had plenty of ready cash with them managed to get across the border virtually unscathed. Some others who tried to crash their way through on the side roads, were shot out of hand.

In this situation the European population of Masaka were

mobilized to give what help they could to the flood of refugees now pouring into the District on their way to Kampala. I set up a road block on the outskirts of the town and directed each group of terrified humanity to a holding point where they were given food, clothing or accommodation as required. Sometimes I would see a vehicle approach only to quickly turn round and try to escape, the unfortunate occupants evidently fearing that yet another gang of robbers lay in their path. Initially a language problem arose since I could speak no French and the refugees could speak no English. I quickly found the way round this. We could all speak Swahili so the entire process was carried on in this language.

Only one slightly amusing incident occurred during this tragic period. A coach containing about 20 bedraggled men and women drew up at my road block. I commenced giving the driver directions for the nearest aid point. An enormously fat woman wearing a filthy dress dismounted from the interior of the coach. 'Say buddy', she said, 'We may look like refugees but we're American tourists. Now get out of our way.'

The refugee problem continued for several days and nights during which time the road block was manned continuously. At the end of this period, however, the influx ceased. It was too late for those unfortunates who had not managed the crossing in time!

Mother was, unsurprisingly, somewhat alarmed by these goings on. With the tales of attacks on Europeans featuring prominently in press and on the radio she, not unnaturally, formed the idea that our lives were in serious jeopardy. My attention was drawn to the situation when Kalori, our houseboy, brought to me a large kitchen knife which he had found under mother's pillow when making her bed. I had to take her aside and assure her that the situation was under control. The idea of her stabbing the houseboy or any of the other servants who might be bringing her her morning cup of tea did not meet with my approval.

With the arrival of my mother, it was clearly time to think about a spot of local leave so that she could have memories of East Africa to relate to her cronies when she returned to England. Lota and Harry Stokes were going to the Western Province for a break and they kindly took her along to show her that part. Margaret and I decided that we would plan for a couple of weeks at Malindi on the Kenya coast. This was an area we had loved on our previous visit. I had no problem in obtaining leave and duly booked with the Sindbad Hotel for a date a couple of months ahead.

Shortly after this I discovered that moves were afoot to remove George Harrison from Masaka. Bennett Jacobs, the District Commissioner, and heads of other departments were fed up with his laziness and it had become well known that it was in fact me who was running the police in the District. My first inkling of the situation was when I was called to police headquarters and closely questioned regarding what I was in fact responsible for as regards running the unit, and what Harrison considered to be his function. I tried to make it appear that he did more than was, in fact, the truth. I had no wish to cause him damage. He left me pretty much alone to get on with the running of the unit and this served my purpose quite well. It did not, however, suit the Commissioner of Police. He could see no reason why a senior police officer should be paid a large yearly salary to spend his time outside of his office shooting guinea fowl while his wife did her painting. It seemed that others had produced a pretty full picture of the true state of affairs.

The next move came out of the blue. I had finished work and was relaxing at home with a pint of beer when a constable appeared with a message. 'PROMOTION... D.S.P. J.A. BEADEN IS PROMOTED TO THE RANK OF SUPERINTENDENT OF POLICE WITH IMMEDIATE EFFECT.' I decided to say nothing of this to anyone except Margaret for the time being. The message had been addressed to me, not to Harrison, so I felt justified in not passing it to him either.

The following morning I set off to Kampala bright and early. I arrived at the Quartermasters Store as it opened and purchased my new badges of rank. By 10 a.m. I was back at Masaka and at my desk. As usual Harrison had not yet arrived and I carried out my usual checks of the Diary Book and Occurrence Book before going to his office. I had practically finished making my report when he caught sight of the crown on my shoulder. I feared for a moment that he was about to have a seizure. 'Why was I not informed of this?', he demanded. I pointed out that the message had arrived well after office hours and it was on his insistence that all late messages should be dealt with by me without disturbing him. Also, I pointed out that the message had been addressed to me, personally. Harrison stomped out of the office and left me to carry on.

I was now hopeful that, having now reached the rank of Superintendent, I should be given command of the District. Unfortunately, other moves were in the offing. The officer who was second-in-command at the Police Training School in Kampala had suddenly been taken ill and had gone to the U.K. for treatment. It was decided that Harrison would be the ideal candidate for this post while I should be given command in Masaka. Harrison, however, decided otherwise. He resigned after writing a strong letter of complaint to the Colonial Secretary. It got him nowhere!

Now there were two vacant posts to fill. Fate was plotting against me! It was decided that, with my known dislike of training and parade work, I was the ideal candidate to transfer to the Police Training School. Masaka was running so well that a less experienced officer could take over here! I had to view the situation philosophically. I had, after all, come out of it with a totally unexpected promotion which put me ahead, in seniority, of all of my old enemies!

In the event it was I who was the first to leave on transfer. The parties, which the Asian community wanted to throw, had to be severely curtailed due to the urgency of sorting matters out before the departure of both senior police officers. We were very sad to be leaving Masaka and particularly upset to lose our beautiful house and garden. I completed our packing and the handing over to my relief. We did have a farewell party at the European Club. Harrison and his wife did not attend! We had a choice of housing in Kampala. We decided upon a superb bungalow at a development known as Silver Springs, about three miles out of the city centre on the Port Bell road. This had been built a couple of years earlier and had four bedrooms, a very large lounge and similar dining room, splendid kitchen and four servants quarters. A newly-built hotel, the Silver Springs with restaurant and open-air swimming pool, was situated a couple of hundred yards distant. We rapidly made ourselves comfortable in our new surroundings.

One of the first items on the agenda in our new location was to sort out schooling for Alison. During the latter part of our stay in Masaka, she had attended an infant school, run by the wife of one of the European officers. It was essential that she was now found a new source of education. To this end enquiries were made and I was informed that the Director of Education, a Mr Bartlett, lived in a house a few doors away from us. Great. We could go to the top. To this end Margaret and I set off one evening to the address we had been given. We were greeted by the lady of the house who invited us in and introduced us to her husband. She then produced refreshment, both liquid and solid. We were entertained for half-an-hour or so and then broached the subject of our visit. Mr Bartlett seemed a bit startled by our demand for information regarding schooling for our daughter. He and his wife conversed for a short while Margaret and I looked at one another in amazement, to think that the Director of Education should have such an abysmal lack of knowledge of the educational opportunities available in his local area. After a prolonged discussion between them, they admitted defeat. 'Sorry, I really don't know what the answer is', Mr Bartlett announced. 'I should think that Mr Bartram, the Director of Education, would know. He only lives next door you know.' A little later, we made our confused escape.

Once I had satisfied myself that nothing of an urgent nature needed to be done in our new abode, I drove to the Police Training School and reported to my new boss. Oliver Lucas was about 50 years of age and, with the Africanisation policy now in force, was fairly laid back about his future prospects. He had reached the rank of Senior Superintendent and knew that further promotion was most unlikely. He was more than pleased to have a reliable younger officer to whom he could hand over most of the administration of the school. For my part, I had little experience of lecturing and hated the idea of parades. Oliver, on the other hand, quite enjoyed parade work and didn't mind giving the odd lecture. With his blessing I rapidly re-scheduled the working practices, taking most of the administration myself and ensuring that the other officers covered virtually all of the lectures and most of the parade work. I found, to my relief, that a Force Drill Instructor had been appointed with the rank of Assistant Superintendent. This was an ex-army officer named Spreage. He was responsible for the day-to-day supervision of the N.C.O. drill-instructors and was assisted in this task by Sub-Inspector Oloya, one of the finest African officers it has been my pleasure to meet. Oliver was more than satisfied with this new regime and left me very much to my own devices.

At the time of my arrival, practising for the Annual Police Review was in progress. I was delighted to find that I had been left out of the list of Company Commanders. With a bit of luck I should be able to dodge this task permanently once I became established in my new job.

The Police Training School varied in its complement in accordance with the number of new recruits which the Force was authorised to enlist. Under normal circumstances a new intake would be taken on about every two months. An intake would normally consist of about 100 recruits who would be divided into three classes. Each class would be under the direct control of a sergeant or corporal who would be responsible for teaching them drill, among other things, and ensuring that his particular charges got to their classes on time. At any particular time there could be up to 400 recruits at various stages of their training, plus around 100 staff of various ranks. The recruits were, of course, housed in dormitories and fed in the canteen. A small amount was deducted from the pay of each recruit to purchase their food. A sergeant cook was responsible for preparing the food, assisted by a couple of corporals and several constables. Classroom instructors were either N.C.Os, Inspectors or officers, each of whom had their own particular subjects to lecture on.

A couple of weeks after my arrival, having now taken up the reins in my new job, I broached the subject of my forthcoming local leave to Lucas. I don't think that he was particularly overjoyed at the prospect of doing without my assistance so soon after my arrival, but with the leave already approved and the hotel booked, there was little that could be done.

Our 600-mile journey to the coast was fairly uneventful apart from the occasion when, travelling through the Tsavo National Park, on hitting a boulder in the road, the exhaust pipe parted company with the engine. Rounding a sharp bend in the road at about 50 miles an hour while sounding like a machine gun, we were suddenly confronted by one of the enormous red bull elephants the area is famed for. I skidded to a halt about 20 yards from it and grabbed my cine camera. The elephant, ears flapping wildly, was clearly having difficulty in deciding whether to charge us or run in the opposite direction. Fortunately, it took the latter option and we went on our way. I managed to get a film of the last five seconds of the encounter but at least it gave mother something to relate to her cronies for years afterwards.

On this occasion, the weather was perfect for a holiday at the coast and the sea no longer carried the earthy stain of flood water washing down from the Tana River, which had been a feature of our previous holiday. The danger of sharks close inshore was thereby diminished and Margaret and I enjoyed our surfing to the full. We took mother to the lost city of Geddi where she was duly impressed. We also took her to Casurina Point, a most beautiful spot where the casurina trees whispered in the breeze while we lay on the pure white sand. A memorable trip was made in a glass-bottomed boat over the reef where millions of brilliantly-coloured tiny fish swarmed around the living coral. Some of the party with us went in swimming among the teeming shoals, until mother was sea sick all over them.

During one of our walks around Malindi Township towards the end of our leave, I was approached by one of the local tribesman carrying a small cardboard box. This, I found, contained a tiny Dwarf Mongoose. She was, I estimated, about a month old and the size of a large mouse. She was as tame as a kitten and we instantly fell in love with her. I bought her for Shs 1/-. I made a quick visit to the local carpenter who, on my instructions, knocked up a lightweight plywood box to house our new addition until we got her home.

I have never known an animal to be quite so fearless or so inquisitive. Within a couple of days of our return, she had taken over the entire household. At first she terrorised my Alsatian dog and my two cats. She would lie in wait and, at an opportune moment, would pop out of her hiding place, bite hard at the nearest foot, ear or nose and then, retreating to her hiding place, sit down chirruping while dog and cats flew in all directions. She very soon became accustomed to the other animals though and ceased tormenting them. Instead she would curl up and sleep with whichever of them took her fancy.

Within a week they were all great friends. Tickey, as she was christened, became a great favourite with the children whom she would allow to carry her about and play with her without any attempt at biting. One of her great delights was to play with a table tennis ball, which she seemed to think was a particularly stubborn egg. She would spend hours positioning it between her front paws and then hurling it through her back legs against the wall. She would be really furious when, after countless attempts, she failed to break it.

Mongooses, I found, are not the things to have around should you have a lot of breakables. As I have said, they are inquisitive and one of Tickey's favourite games was to get round the back of the books on the bookshelf and throw them onto the floor one after another. Vases of flowers also had a fatal attraction for her.

I had, by now, become established at the P.T.S. Because I was responsible for producing the Training Schedule, I was easily able to ensure that I kept clear of lecturing. I did a little parade work, but this was usual when carrying out the final inspection of each squad prior to their passing out. This entailed the choice of one individual to receive a prize at his passing out for smartest recruit. Not an easy choice as, by the end of nine months, the turn out was immaculate. I found time to have long chats with Oliver Lucas regarding our forthcoming retirements. Oliver pointed out that he was now 50 years old. He would normally have retired at 55 but the terms of compensation with the optimum age of 40 meant that the longer he stayed on the smaller would be the amount of compensation for loss of office he would receive. Oliver decided that it was time he went. So it was that on 25th July 1961 he left the Training School on leave pending retirement. The same day, I was appointed Commandant of the Police Training School with the rank of Acting Senior Superintendent of Police.

I now received a directive from police headquarters. With my new appointment, it had been decided that, for security reasons, we should be housed at the Police College Officers' Quarters at Naguru a couple of miles out of Kampala on the Jinja road. Our new house was not as grand as the one at Silver Springs, but the garden was magnificent. The previous occupant had been Ron Castle and his wife. Both keen gardeners. The area was not particularly large but it had been planted with a mass of flowering trees and shrubs. The front hedge was a blaze of scarlet hibiscus and a pergola of purple bougainvillaea stretched across the bottom of the manicured lawn. It was little wonder that the place had featured in an article in the British magazine, *Homes and Gardens*, a little while before.

Tickey soon established herself at her new home. For the

first few days she was kept indoors but soon escaped and set up her new range in the grounds of the Officers' Quarters. When she first went missing we thought we had seen the last of her. Not so. As it was getting dusk there was a scratching at the door and in she walked. Now we constantly received telephone calls from worried wives who had found her in the kitchen looking for eggs or generally making herself a nuisance. She was totally without fear as many a cat who stalked her found to their cost. The pounce of the cat would be countered by a lightning evasive move by Tickey and a swift counter-attack which usually took the form of needle sharp teeth through the cat's nose. The cat would depart through the nearest hedge with Tickey in hot pursuit. Dogs, regardless of size, fared no better. The only thing that made her nervous was the sight of a hawk overhead. This would send her scuttling for cover from which she would peer chittering with rage. One day, however, she did not return and all enquiries failed. I'm pretty sure that a hawk had finally accounted for her. Without her the house seemed empty.

About a month after her disappearance, I received a telephone call from one of our friends. Three very young banded mongooses had been found. Would we like them? The following day two of them arrived, the third having died in the meantime. The two survivors were a male and a female. We called them Widdle and Puke after two pups in one of Gerald Durrel's books. On arrival they weighed one ounce each. Both were still blind and very weak. Shortly after their arrival they developed a number of septic spots which made their hair fall out. For the first couple of weeks they needed to be fed every two hours with warm milk to which vitamin drops had been added. We were glad when they could go the whole night without waking us up. They both gained weight rapidly and soon had their eyes open. They were both very active and soon had the run of the house. Like Tickey they were quite fearless and would curl up to sleep with the cats and dog. Both seemed to think that the Alsatian dog was their mother and would search in vain for a nipple. Unfortunately it was a male dog and a bite on its tummy would send it in bellowing retreat. From the beginning Widdle, the male, gained weight faster than his sister and became a bit of a bully. They had a large cage in which they would spend the night and both were very possessive about what they considered to be their particular part of the cage. The slightest trespass by one or the other resulted in screams of rage and fights would break out at frequent intervals. Neither, however, seemed to suffer the slightest injury.

Both of them were greedy at meal times, especially Widdle. This, unfortunately, led to his downfall. One of the favourite item on the menu were the green grasshoppers (*nsenene*) which flew around the lights at certain seasons. These they would devour with horrible crunching noises and smacking of lips. Widdle, unfortunately, tried to swallow one alive and it stuck in his throat. He was choked to death before we found him. He was sadly missed by all except Puke who apparently could not have cared less.

Without competition Puke, now re-christened Pooky, grew fatter and sleeker. She eventually found her way outside but, like Tickey, always returned. She made friends with the *shamba* boy whom she would follow around until he did some digging when she would pounce on any insects he uncovered. She also made friends with the college porters whom she followed round waiting for the inevitable tit-bits. On a number of occasions we had to rescue P.W.D. workers who were marooned up ladders by this dreadful wild animal which sat underneath chittering at them.

It was at this time that I received a letter from police headquarters. I was invited to set one of the examination papers in the forthcoming half-yearly Police Law Exam. I must say that the thought of not only setting the questions but ploughing through literally hundreds of answer papers did not fill me with any great enthusiasm. I was about to draft a reply declining the offer on the pretext of having too great a work load when Paddy Field, one of my junior officers, came in. I told him of the letter. 'Lucky bugger', he said. 'Think of all that money.' 'What money', I enquired. 'Well you get paid a pound for every paper you mark.' he said. I decided that the greatest number of entries would undoubtedly be for the Penal Code and set to work the same day to produce a suitable question paper. Four hundred members of the Force sat the exam and I continued to make this one of my perquisites until my retirement.

On 10th November the first squad of policewomen completed their training and passed out with their male colleagues. These had commenced shortly before my arrival at the P.T.S. under the guidance of Miss Jennifer Robinson, Jeff to her friends. Jeff was a serving police Inspector from the U.K. who had been seconded to Uganda for one tour of duty to get the policewomen training programme off the ground. Basically they underwent the same training schedule as the men, attended most of the same lectures and were taught foot drill and firearms drill by the same instructors. Jeff was, however, responsible for ensuring that such offences as rape and such like facets of police work which would be best dealt with by women police were properly understood. In this she was proving her worth and other women recruits were already under instruction.

I was at this time faced with something of an ultimatum. I could either leave Uganda almost straight away or I could agree to stay for a further three years. The advantage of staying on was that the first payment of compensation would be doubled to around £4,000 pounds. No great problems of security were apparent in the soon-to-be-independent Uganda, so it was decided that we would stay on. However, bearing in mind that we had by this time now completed two years of the tour, it would be best if we went on home leave immediately for four months and then returned for a further three years. This time we didn't have to pack up our household belongings since we should be returning to the same quarters. Mother left us about a week before we ourselves were due to fly.

One problem now arose. While we had no difficulty in finding a temporary home for Bryn and our two cats, at such short notice we could find no one to look after Pooky and Kasu the parrot my mother had acquired. No alternative could be found so two boxes were made and our pets accompanied us. Thus it was that in November 1961 we once again boarded our aircraft for the U.K. Since the P.T.S. could not be left without a senior officer in charge, Bill Humphreys was appointed to take my place on a temporary basis.

Going through Customs at London Airport was a great experience. It wouldn't be allowed today, but at that time there was absolutely no objection to bringing a parrot and a mongoose into the country. The Customs officers were far too interested in playing with Pooky to bother about our luggage.

Chapter 31

Our leave in the U.K. was fairly uneventful. Our unexpected arrival made it impossible to give adequate notice to the tenants of our flat so, once again, we spent most of the time with relatives, mostly with Margaret's parents. Pookie succeeded, during the next few months, in making the life of Margaret's parents quite hideous. Having been used to the freedom of the house at Naguru, she refused to be confined to her cage in her new environment. She was not interested in going out in the garden as it was mid-winter. Instead she busied herself pulling the wallpaper from the walls. Any bits of paper within her reach on which the adhesive was slightly defective were rapidly found, long finger nails were poked underneath and a very satisfactory strip torn off.

One the few occasions that she was not scouting around, looking for the next bit of mischief, she would lie in front of the fire toasting herself. Nothing gave her more pleasure than to lie on someone's lap and be scratched. Then she would purr in a loud voice exactly as a cat does. Examining people's ears also gave her a great deal of pleasure and providing one was prepared to tolerate it, she would examine these appendages at great length, nibbling the lobes and poking with her fingernails in an attempt to find out what was inside. These activities would be accompanied by loud squeaks which, at such close quarters would be absolutely deafening. Needless to say, one could not put up with this torture for very long.

She could never resist investigating any interesting-looking orifice and one day crept inside my father-in-law's trouser leg. I shall never forget the look on his face as he hopped around trying to dislodge her while at the same time retaining his dignity. Pookie finally appeared looking a little the worse for wear out of his shirt front.

Being a very sociable creature she loved visitors and would immediately be up on the lap of anyone who sat down. Should they prove at all nervous, however, their life would be made a hell by crafty bites when they were not looking or by wiping her bottom on their shoes. Mongooses have a scent gland at the base of the tail which they can use very effectively should the occasion arise.

Eventually our leave came to an end and, packing Pookie back into her travelling box, we made our way to the airport. Within a few hours we were back in our house at the Police College at Naguru. The following day, I took up the reins at the Police Training School for the last time. Things had changed little in my absence. Within a couple of days, however, a letter came through from headquarters. I had been promoted to the rank of Senior Superintendent. Time to make my presence felt. My immediate boss was the Director of Training, George Johnson, a very experienced Assistant Commissioner, whose job it was to oversee training at both the College and the Police Training School. He was nearing his own retirement and wanted nothing more than a quiet life. I made my way to headquarters to tell him of various changes I had in mind in the way the P.T.S. was run. George Johnson was, I decided, a man after my own heart. He was delighted to have someone running the School whom he could leave alone in the knowledge that the job would get done.

One of the first tasks I decided upon was the total re-drafting of the training schedule. Up to now, each instructor had his own sheaf of notes on which he based his instruction. Naturally, any two instructors might vary slightly in detail. The recruits, in turn, were left to take what notes they could during a lecture and to use these notes for revision. Much got left out and there was no way in which information lost during a lecture could be accurately gleaned at a later date. I set to work and, somehow or other, in addition to the normal administration of the School, I produced a complete and up-to-date training manual comprising some 300 pages in a hard binder, a copy of which was issued to each recruit on his commencing training. My office staff were hard put to it to keep up with the production effort.

I was now given a further responsibility. In addition to the recruitment and training of hundreds of candidates for the Protectorate Police, it was now decided that three months' training should be given to every member of the Kabaka's police, both those already serving and any new recruits. It was intimated that, not only the Kabaka's police but local police from each and every district of Uganda would, in due course, receive three months of basic training at the P.T.S. This, not only placed a great strain on the dormitory accommodation at the School, it also placed an even greater strain on the instructors. I now had to draft a completely separate training schedule to cover the subjects considered necessary to be included in this new training load. A revised training manual also had to be drafted and prepared and for some weeks I was hard put to it to cope with this additional work load. Because of the limitation in dormitory space, I had no alternative but to reduce the number of recruits to be trained for the Protectorate Police. The Kabaka's police were a fairly motley collection. They were paid considerably less than my own recruits and did not have the same educational standards on which I was now insisting for my own recruits. Neither had they gone through the rigorous selection process which I had devised. However, eventually my new training programme was in operation. With luck, I might turn out a reasonable product at the end of the day!

A project which I had been considering for some time was a swimming pool. I felt that, during the nine months they spent on their initial training, recruits should be taught swimming and life-saving. Very few had any idea of swimming and none at all of life-saving. There was no suitable facility within Kampala and certainly no money would be forthcoming from police headquarters for such a purpose. Such details had never deterred me in the past. I had managed to get a pool going in Soroti with very little financial help so why not here. A friend of mine, Bob Browning, held a senior post in the Public Works Department Headquarters and I made my way to his office. As I had hoped, he was most helpful and, within a couple of weeks had produced detailed drawings of a pool which was to be 75 feet long, 21 feet wide and with a depth varying from four- to eight-feet. Discussions on the site resulted in a decision to build the pool on sloping land immediately outside my office. The filtration plant would have to be sited a further 20 yards further out. My fellow officers decided that I had gone completely mad to even contemplate such a scheme.

Now the subject of finance came up. The figures which Bob produced put the whole project completely out of the question as far as financial help from headquarters was concerned. The only finance I was able to contribute was a float left in the recruit's canteen account. While this was a fairly considerable sum, it was insufficient to even make a start on the construction work. I had been intending to dissipate some of it in the purchase of a couple of television sets and other recreational facilities. Television had only recently come to Uganda and I decided that since none of the staff or recruits had experienced it previously, it would do them no harm to wait a bit longer before exposing them to its doubtful benefits. With around 400 recruits under training at any one time, I decided that an increase of around 30 cents a day on the amount extracted from each recruit for his food, would result in a very considerable sum being produced in quick order. Bob, for his part, decided to bring pressure to bear on one of the companies who were negotiating for a road-building contract worth around a million pounds. For myself, I was able to offer a very considerable amount of labour for those parts of the construction where hand digging would be essential. I always had a large number of recruits who, having been selected, were waiting to commence their training. I was expected to feed them during this period and so could insist on them doing some manual labour to earn their food. Here was something that would keep them busy. Soon the site had been marked out and a large mechanical digger moved in. Within a very short time the pool was excavated and the soil removed. Now concrete was poured into the base and steel reinforcement put in place. Shuttering went up, more steel reinforcement and more concrete poured. A complicated filtration plant was manufactured with a back-flow system which would dispose of any debris collected by the plant. Chemical tanks were designed to ensure the purification of the water before its return to the pool. A brick building housed the filtration plant. Finally, the entire pool was covered with blue mosaic tiles and a six-foot surround of concrete slabs put in place. Within eight weeks of commencement, the pool was ready to be filled.

While all this had been going on, life at the school was hectic. The Annual Police Review was scheduled for July. This time I was unable to dodge it. It was to be the last time the Review was to be commanded by an European officer. As Commandant of the Police Training School it was down to me to fill this role. A.S.P. Spreag, the Force Drill Instructor had by now departed, his place being taken by the recently-promoted Inspector Oloya. The training programme for the Kabaka's police had, perforce, imposed a strict limitation on the number of my own recruits available to take part in the parade. However, by drawing on staff housed at the nearby Nsambya police barracks I was able to assemble sufficient men to form four Companies, each of around 40 men who made up the basis of the Review. Fortunately, I was able to leave Oloya to deal with the day-to-day practise for the parade. A major problem arose, however, when he came to me one day and confessed that he had no idea how to give a sword salute when marching past in slow-time. Neither had I. However, the devil was driving. I assembled the four Company Commanders on the parade ground, together with Oloya and a drummer from the band and for two solid hours we experimented. At the end of this time I was satisfied that I had devised a very adequate drill movement. I don't know how close this was to the real thing. I've never bothered to find out. All I know is that, on the day, it worked to perfection. The remainder of the Review comprised the police band, under Ted Moon, the dog section, under Vic Parker, two Special Force units, the fire brigade under Don Flint, a radio car section and a motor cycle section.

Friday 20th June 1962 was the big day. His Excellency the Governor, Sir Walter Coutts, was the inspecting personage. To say that I was nervous would be something of an understatement. I was bloody terrified. To make things worse, I was having to wear boots and puttees. I wore these inventions of the devil as rarely as possible and, as a result, would take ages getting the puttees wound on so that the tape holding them up finished up on the outside of the calf. I remember making at least six abortive attempts to get them right. Each time the puttee ended up a couple of inches out. Finally, I had to admit defeat and just did them up a bit tighter to make them come into the right position. Silly bugger!

The parade formed up and the Company Commanders commenced walking up and down to help relax while some 3,000 visitors were arriving. Finally, the motorcade bringing the hereditary rulers of Uganda's Kingdoms arrived and we were under way. The Governor's car arrived and I called the Parade to attention. The Governor mounted the dais and I gave the order 'Royal Salute, Present Arms'. The band played the National Anthem and I advanced to report, 'Parade Ready for Inspection'. Everything went to perfection. I accompanied the Governor on his inspection and then returned to my place. Medals were presented to various recipients and we then marched past in quick- and slow-time. Finally, I gave the command, 'Parade will Advance in Review Order'. Another Royal Salute and the parade came to its end. Though I say it myself, the standard to drill displayed by my men would not have disgraced a Guards Regiment. Indeed, I have since seen many such parades on television which the performance of my policemen would have bettered. Now we were able to march off. At last, I was able to hand over the parade to Inspector Oloya. My left leg was killing me. Now we were to adjourn to the Officers' Mess where the traditional piss-up was about to start. I took the opportunity of slackening off my puttees but the pain did not noticeably subside.

On the following morning, after a sleepless night, I found that my left leg had swollen like a pumpkin. The pain was excruciating and I could not put my foot to the ground. Margaret drove me to the newly-opened Mulago Hospital. Within an hour I was in the operating theatre and my leg was opened up to remove a large thrombosis from the vein. A little longer and I should have lost my leg. So much for the Police Review. I was relieved that I should never again have to undergo the trauma involved.

My sojourn in the hospital was not without incident. The small ward only contained two beds. I occupied one while a Catholic priest, Father Faupel, was in the other. He was suffering from Epididimitis which, I found, was something affecting his testicles. When he returned from the operating theatre I noticed him surreptitiously investigating his nether regions. I think he was quite relieved to find that he still had some. I presumed that, in his particular line of business, he didn't really need them anyway but I didn't make my thoughts known to him. We got on quite well in the circumstances and he gave me a copy of a book he had just had published about the Uganda Martyrs. I had the distinction of being the first person to use the new operating theatre. Being of an open plan, the ward was anything but soundproof. A clock on the nearby wall had the characteristic of jumping forward every minute with a loud click. Not noticeable during the day, but a night just enough to preclude any possibility of sleep. I found the next problem the following day when I limped out to take a bath. No hot water. Then I discovered that there was. It came from the cold tap. Naturally, I mentioned this slight problem. The following day, an Asian plumber appeared. Taking up various floorboards, he rectified the problem by switching the supply pipes round. It did occur to me at the time that he could have achieved the same result by switching over the blue and red buttons on the top of the taps. Too simple I guess. However, all was not well with the toilet cistern. When the toilet was flushed, a cascade of hot water descended! I was discharged from hospital after about a week and resumed my various tasks at the Training School.

Speaking of my various tasks, I had found, on being appointed Commandant of the P.T.S, that I had been bequeathed a daunting portfolio of jobs which, clearly, no one else wanted or had time for. I was Chairman of the Police Boxing Committee — though it was years since I had done any boxing. I was President of the Police Band, with administrative responsibility for around 80 personnel — though I couldn't play a note. I was Divisional Commissioner of the Police Division of St John's Ambulance Association — though my First Aid was, to say the least, rusty. I was Chairman of the Police Athletics Committee, a subject in which I had some small knowledge, though, at the approaching age of 40 I was a bit past my prime. I was Chairman of the Police Recreation and Welfare Association Central Council and I was Chairman of the Police Training School Recreation Committee. At the same time, I was Editor of *Habari* the quarterly police magazine. I didn't mind the latter job, though I hated having to rack my brains for a suitable subject for the editorial in each issue.

I had, since the outbreak of war in 1939, donated blood about once every six months. What had struck me since my arrival in Uganda was the unwillingness of Africans in general to make any such donation. This had been the subject of my lectures on a number of occasions in the past and all to no avail. On one occasion, while in Soroti, I found that the wife of one of my N.C.Os was dying because she urgently required a transfusion. I called the African staff together and put it to them that she could be saved if they were prepared to give blood. I thought that this was an ideal opportunity to press home the point. Not one volunteered, not even the woman's husband. I fell out with them badly over this and let them see my displeasure. I myself volunteered to give blood but unfortunately mine was not compatible. The woman died quite unnecessarily.

Now, it occurred to me that I had a wonderful opportunity to supply the blood transfusion service with enormous amounts of blood. Forthwith, I made it a condition of being considered for recruitment that the applicant must donate a pint of blood. Initially this had the effect of reducing the number of applicants dramatically. However, after the first few intakes had been bled with no noticeably detrimental effects, recruitment returned to its previous level. From now on bleeding sessions were held at the Drill Shed once a month. To reinforce the point, I personally gave a pint on each occasion. Far more than I should have, but I suffered no ill effects and my presence at each session helped to encourage the back sliders.

With the swimming pool nearing completion, the problem of finding a suitable instructor to teach the recruits swimming and life saving arose. Here I was lucky. About a year earlier a number of retired U.K. Inspectors of Police had been appointed, on three-year contracts, to fill various posts, mainly as Inspectors of Vehicles. One of these, a Scot named Clunie Inglis, seemed the most likely candidate. Having completed 30 years service in the Glasgow police, he was now in his early 50s. He was a qualified swimming instructor and a Grade 1 Life-Saving Examiner. This meant that he could not only teach swimming and life-saving but could also examine the recruits and staff in these subjects and examine and appoint suitable staff as life-saving instructors in due course. Clunie jumped at the chance of taking up the post of instructor at the P.T.S. He not only dealt with the swimming and life-saving aspects, I also appointed him Assistant Editor of the *Habari* and gave him responsibility for a few of the lectures, to fill in any spare time.

The completion of the construction of the swimming pool did not mean that I was able to sit back and take things easy. A large number of timber poles were obtained from the Forestry Department and an eight-foot fence, changing rooms and a shower were constructed. The area between the concrete slabs and the boundary fence was grassed over and the whole site tidied up. I made up a diving-board and a slide and the whole area was looking very smart. The inevitable teething troubles now arose. On the first filling, the water was cloudy. That couldn't be helped, it was the way it came out of the pipes. We set the pump going and started to pass the water through the filter. A large quantity of charcoal filter medium was deposited into the pool, most of it floating on the top. Back to the drawing board. Various other filter media were tried but, by the time we were ready to try again, the pool had turned green in the sunlight. At last, after much trial and many errors, we were at last ready for a grand opening.

Thus it was that in September 1962 the pool was officially opened by Michael Macoun the Inspector General of Police. Most of the African police staff attended, together with a large proportion of the officers and their wives stationed in Kampala. It was generally agreed that the pool was a resounding success and I was duly grabbed and thrown in! I was rapidly joined by most of the other officers attending the opening ceremony. Thereafter, every Saturday afternoon and Sunday the pool was reserved for officers, their wives and families. During the week only the recruits and staff were permitted to use it.

With self-government and Independence to follow now looming large on the horizon, it was announced that a competition was to be held to choose a new Uganda National Anthem. Budding musicians were invited to submit their compositions for this great work and a large number of entries were received. Ted Moon, our Director of Music went to work and produced an excellent and stirring entry which, I felt sure, should win easily. No way! The winner, not unnaturally, I suppose, was an African, whose dreary and lacklustre offering of music and words was judged to be the winner. Bloody pathetic! This, anyway, was about the last effort Ted would make to improve Uganda's image. Shortly afterwards, and just before his retirement, he handed over to Assistant Superintendent Oduka, who became our new Director of Music.

It had occurred to me during my various inspections of the buildings at the Police Training School, that the police crest which had been in place over the entrance to the main dormitory block was looking decidedly the worse for wear. It was painted on a wooden panel and had been in position since 1939 when the block was built. I felt that if anything was to be done about replacing it, it should be done fairly soon as, once Independence was achieved the crown surmounting the crest would be eliminated, which would be a pity. No doubt it would happen in due course but if I found some way of replacing the crest it would at least be there for a few years longer, hopefully.

After giving the matter some thought, I went to the rifle range near my office armed with a spade and, after digging around for about ten minutes, had extracted a large quantity of lead bullets. At home each evening over the next week or two I made up a series of sections of the police crest using wood and laminations of hardboard. When I was satisfied with the results, I made a series of moulds in plaster of paris and, when these were thoroughly dried, I melted the lead bullets and cast the new sections. The result was surprisingly good. After mounting the sections on to a metal plate and painting and framing the whole, I removed the old crest and mounted the new. Word of the new crest rapidly got around and visits were made to view it by the various senior officers from headquarters. No one commented about my inclusion of the Crown on the new crest.

The Uganda Amateur Boxing Championships were due. This year I had been asked if they could be held in the drill shed at the P.T.S. As Chairman of the Police Boxing Tournament Committee I could hardly object, even had I wanted too. My friend, Les Peach, one of the European officers stationed at nearby Nsambya Barracks, and himself Heavyweight Champion of Uganda, having knocked out one Idi Amin a corporal in the army, was the official referee. One of my staff, Corporal George Oywello was the Light Heavyweight Champion of Uganda and easily won his bout. In December the same year he was part of the Uganda Boxing Team that attended the Commonwealth Games at Perth in Australia. Here he achieved the impossible when, while boxing at heavyweight, a weight above his own, he won the Gold Medal. Tragically he was killed in February 1965 while riding a motor cycle on the Kampala–Entebbe road at night.

Fortunately, apart from attending in my official capacity, the Championships did not involve me in an inordinate amount of work. However, I was able to make my nomination for the person to present the prizes to the winners at the end of the evenings entertainment. I chose Margaret, though she didn't know about it until she was assisted into the ring at the end of the evening. My choice proved very popular!

On 9th October 1962, Uganda ceased to be a Protectorate. After sixty-six somewhat tempestuous years of benign British rule, Uganda had, it was to be hoped, reached a sufficiently viable economical and political state to be able to govern itself. Independence had arrived. Certainly politics were now playing a central role in everyday life. Political parties sprouted like mushrooms and violence played an increasing part in political life. One had to start treading a tightrope when discussing politics with any African. Personally, I was totally aware that tribalism played a major role in the various political groupings. What was even more clear to me was that every so-called politician was out not for his party nor for his country, but for himself, first and foremost. Elections had been held but, on various spurious grounds, had been boycotted. Benedicto Kiwanuka, one of the foremost politicians and President of the Democratic Party had, perforce, been chosen as the Prime Minister for the period between Self-government and Independence. With the arrival of Independence, however, he was eliminated from this position and Milton Obote, an Acholi, a one-time lorry turnboy and now President of the Uganda National Congress, had struggled to the top of the midden and became Uganda's first elected Prime Minister.

Numerous committee meetings were held prior to the great day to iron out any possible snags. I attended most of these and joint parades were planned to include both police and army units. To mark this historic event, the Duke and Duchess of Kent had been invited to represent Her Majesty at the celebrations. In the event the Independence celebrations passed off without incident and were, in the main, good-humoured and free of the violence which had been anticipated in some quarters. On one of my visits to police headquarters Mike Macoun called me into his office and informed me that he had nominated me for the award of the Colonial Police Medal for Meritorious Service. I was delighted at this news which I considered a great honour.

It was my practice to go back to Naguru each day for lunch. The back entrance to the P.T.S. led onto a road which arrived directly to the shunting yard of the Uganda Railway. The road passed over three different rail tracks before it passed through an industrial area and thence onto the Jinja road. One had to exercise extreme caution when passing over these tracks. When trains were being shunted onto new lines, it was the practice to have an African railway employee standing behind the engine to stop any traffic from crossing the line when the train was about to move. That this was fraught with danger I knew from experience. On one occasion I had been signalled across the line by the individual standing at the rear of the train and was passing over the track within a couple of yards of the engine when the driver, having misinterpreted the signal, decided to reverse. Only a very rapid bit of reversing on my part prevented my car from being flattened, and me with it. I got away with it, though I ran over the front wheel of a cycle following closely behind me.

On this particular occasion, I arrived at the rail crossing to find that a dangerous situation had occurred just before my arrival. A fully laden petrol tanker, whilst crossing behind a stationary engine, had been struck amidships and had tipped over. Three thousand gallons of petrol were now flooding out onto the track and the road and down the nearby drains. Abandoning my car I ran to the scene. The tanker driver was uninjured and had managed to clamber out of his cab. He stood nearby in a state of shock. The engine, with eight carriages and trucks still attached was, fortunately, still on its rails. Here was a situation in which I needed to do 100 different things with equal urgency. What should I do first. I decided to get the train shifted. With petrol now beginning to run underneath it, it could very rapidly be turned into an inferno. I instructed the driver to move. He complied with a speed seldom seen among rail employees. Fortunately, he took the train with him. Since it was now lunch time, the place was a milling throng of cars, bicycles and pedestrians. Most of them happily puffing on their cigarettes. I spotted a couple of my N.C.Os from the Training School nearby and directed them to stop all traffic attempting to cross the rail tracks. At this moment Les Peach. the O/C of the Nsambya Barracks. arrived, also on his way to lunch. I instructed him to return to the P.T.S. and gather up as many of my men as he could and to get them down to me at the double, then to order a general turnout of the others, to get to the scene to assist. I also told him, once he had done this, to telephone the Fire Brigade and get as much assistance as they could muster. I then turned my attention to the job in hand. Pools of petrol now covered a wide area. Drains were carrying it away under the nearby factories. A single spark or a back-firing car could ignite the lot and result in a massive fire and loss of life. For the next ten minutes I was rushing from place to place berating motorists, many of them Europeans, who were disregarding the orders given by my two N.C.Os. Eventually one or two of them, now appreciating the danger of the situation, got out of their vehicles and helped me to stop the passers-by from smoking. Shortly after this, the first of my recruits and instructors arrived and I was able to start putting out a cordon and to gradually push the crowds back to a safer area,

After a further 20 minutes, by which time the situation was reasonably under control, the Fire Brigade, under the control of the Chief Fire officer, Don Flint, arrived and commenced spraying the area with foam. Don Flint possessed a friend on the local newspaper who was his personal publicity agent. Don was later quoted as saying, 'This was the most dangerous incident I have ever attended.' No mention was made of myself, or of the others involved, prior to the arrival of the brigade.

CHAPTER 32

One of the first acts by our revered Prime Minister, was to order the erection of a structure known as Independence Arch. This was built outside the Parliament Building and stood about 70-feet in height. Suspended at the top of the arch was a vast bronze disc which bore the likeness of Obote's somewhat simian features. 'This', I thought, 'is the shape of things to come.'

Obote now decided to get married. Not that he needed to since he already had two wives. One for breeding and one to work in the house and *shamba*. No. This one was to be the social wife. What was needed was an attractive and photogenic African woman who could appear with him on important social occasions. The lavish wedding duly took place and hundreds of guests were entertained. Obote and wife departed on a three-week honeymoon. It was later disclosed that the entire cost of some £40,000–£50,000 had been born by the Uganda government. This raised criticism by the British Freedom from Hunger Campaign. Obote replied, 'I have not stolen the money. What about weddings of royalty in Britain? In young countries there is a tendency to overlook the important position held by a person and only accord respect to him as an individual.'

There were strong rumours abroad that Obote was impotent as a result of venereal disease. These were partially discounted a year later when Mrs Obote produced a child. It was later discovered that the father was a friend and fellow tribesman of Obote, A Kampala dentist named Martin Aliker.

Now came the news from Michael Macoun. 'Obote has decreed that there are to be no Colonial police medals, now or in the future. Nothing personal, but Colonial is a disgusting and evil word.' I tried to be philosophical about this by thinking, 'Oh well, what I've never had, I shan't miss'. I didn't succeed! In September 1963, Bob Browning, who had been largely instrumental in my getting the swimming pool constructed, visited me at the P.T.S. and happened to see the police crest I had made. I could see that it had made a considerable impression on him. I was a bit dubious when he asked if he could borrow it for a day to show someone. After all, I had included the Royal Crown in the crest, which could land me in trouble. However, I let him take it away. The following day he returned it. 'Do you think you could do something similar featuring the Uganda Coat of Arms?,' he enquired. 'Well, I expect I could,' I replied, 'but it would take a long time, and I'm pretty busy at present.' 'Let me put it this way', said Bob, 'Obote has seen this and wants a Coat of Arms made for inside Parliament Building. I have been trying for some considerable time to find a suitable source of manufacture within Uganda without any success whatever. Now you are being invited to make it.' My options were somewhat limited by this. If I refused to make the Coat of Arms, having already shown by making the Police Crest, that I was capable of doing so, things could be made difficult for me. Particularly bearing in mind the Crown which I had illegally included on the Police Crest which, with African Nationalism as it was at the time, could be made much of. I did a bit of rough calculation. I didn't want to be dragged into a lot of additional work with no financial reward at the end of it. I decided to make a very high estimate. That should get me off the hook. 'It will cost £500', I said. "O.K.,' said Bob, 'That's fine, go ahead and get it made as soon as possible.' I cursed. I should have said £1,000. In those days Uganda's economy was booming and could clearly well afford a substantial expenditure on nationalistic baubles if it wished. If the Uganda government could afford to pay for Obote's wedding they could presumably afford to pay well for my talents. Also, one could buy a very reasonable house in the U.K. for £1,000.

The next few weeks were very busy. Each day after work I busied myself making the patterns for the individual parts of the Coat of Arms. I did not want to use lead this time as I had noticed a tendency for it to bubble if the mould was the least bit damp. Instead, I found a car-accessory shop in Kampala and purchased a quantity of fibre glass filler and resin of the type used in vehicle repairs. I also sent off to a company in the U.K. for a large quantity of a type of powdered rubber which could be melted down to make moulds. By the time I had finished preparing the patterns for the Coat of Arms, the materials were to hand. I now encased each of the patterns in a wooden surround and poured the hot rubber over them to produce the moulds. I then filled these with a mixture of the fibre glass filler and resin. An hour later the fibre glass had set and I had the finished items. It was then just a matter of cleaning them up and painting them. I used polyurethane yacht varnish for this and, though I say it myself, the results were pretty good. The parts were then mounted onto a wooden frame which was successfully concealed behind them.

Bob Browning was ecstatic when he saw the completed article. He immediately took it to the Parliament Building where it was viewed by Obote and the full Cabinet. The following day he was back. 'They want another 20 for the Court Buildings throughout Uganda', he said. How the hell was I going to find time to make another 20? It was true that the administration of the Police Training School was not now proving particularly arduous, particularly since I was attending less parades, but I had all sorts of other ideas I wanted to work on. In addition, I was being expected to train up a senior African officer to take my place when I retired. I had already had three African Superintendents who, after a couple of months each as my 2 i/c, had either been shifted to a district or had proved incapable of learning the job. One consideration on the plus side was that, having prepared all the moulds, the actual construction of the Coats of Arms would take far less time than had the prototype. Supplies of the fibre glass filler and resin were going to be a problem though. I had already bought up all that the shop in Kampala had, and had been informed that no more could be expected for several months. I made a calculation of the amount I should require and telephoned the manufacturers in the U.K. No problem. A supply would be dispatched immediately by air. A similar request to the makers of the moulding rubber, produced a similar reaction. I was in business.

During the next few months, I worked ceaselessly each evening on producing the Coats of Arms. My time was limited if I was to get the work completed by the time I retired and we left Uganda. Eventually, I produced the first five and took them along to the office of Cuthbert Obwangor, the Minister of Justice. I also took along the bill for these. I fear that my conscience had got the better of me and I reduced the price to £200 each. Bloody fool that I was! Somewhat to my surprise, I left his office with a cheque in full payment. I was, however, requested to place the first one in the High Court in Kampala, behind the chair of the Chief Justice. The remainder were to be taken by me personally to various Court buildings throughout Uganda where I was to personally fit them. I was to travel by a light aircraft which was provided. I was quite enjoying this. The trip to the High Court in Kampala produced an additional bonus. I found that the original

Royal Coat of Arms, which had been behind the chair of the Chief Justice, had already been removed. I enquired where it had gone and was told the it was in a dungeon below the Court Building. Having fitted the new Coat of Arms I liberated the old one from its incarceration and nicked it. I still have it proudly displayed in my house. It is a beautiful item, hand-carved from a solid block of timber.

In November 1963, Clunie Inglis was promoted to Acting Superintendent and 2 i/c. This was during one of the periods in which the trainee for my post had proved particularly incompetent and I was glad to be rid of him. My only regret was that Clunie's promotion was obviously going to be of short duration since he would quickly be replaced by yet another 'trainee'. How short, I hadn't an inkling at the time.

On 11th December 1963, Kenya, our neighbouring East African State, gained its Independence. To celebrate the event, a number of rather ill-advised ex-patriate residents of Uganda, both government and commercial, decided to hold a party at the residence of one of them, at a location just outside Kampala known as Tank Hill. This was, incidentally, on my old stamping ground near Katwe. The party was publicised as 'The Casting off of the White Man's burden.' All done in a very light-hearted manner, the invitees being asked to attend in 'Sanders of the River or Native Costume.' We did not receive an invitation, probably because we were not 'Club' frequenters. Clunie Inglis, however, received one. He did not inform me of the forthcoming event or I should have advised him of its likely outcome. However, because of a previous engagement, he was unable to attend. All might have been well. Unfortunately, instead of telephoning his hosts, he called round at their house a couple of hours before the party was due to start. He was invited in for a quick glass to beer and then went on his way. The party duly took place and numerous guests turned up dressed for the occasion. At midnight, as the Union Flag was being lowered in Nairobi, the British National Anthem was sung. Two days later the story of the 'Tank Hill Party' was splashed all over the newspapers. It immediately blew up out of all proportion into an international incident. Demands were made for the perpetrators to be publicly flogged, imprisoned and then deported. Clunie was named as one of those who had attended. His denials went unheeded. The British government were involved and statements made in parliament. With the increasing sensitivity of the African population to such events, I could see what was coming. I called Clunie to my office and asked for his side of the story. He told me of his lack of involvement but, with the present political mood, I saw the inevitable outcome. 'Go home and start packing', I advised. 'If nothing happens, so well and good. Best to be on the safe side though.' It was good advice in the circumstances. On 23rd December 1963, Clunie was deported. He was a good friend and an efficient officer. I was sad to see his departure in these circumstances. The least I could do was to complete his packing and ensure that it was properly dispatched to him. Others similarly deported included Don Robertson and his wife!

While my spare time occupation involving the manufacture of the Coats of Arms had been an ongoing 'Cottage Industry', I was still very fully engaged at the P.T.S. One of the projects I was involved in was a fairly simple one. I decided to produce a new cover for the police magazine *Habari*. For the first time, a different photograph, hopefully featuring some aspect of the Force, would appear on each issue. There should be no great problem about this. The printers raised no difficulties when I mentioned my intentions to them and I managed to find an artist who was able to design the new cover.

Taking with me the Drum Major of the Police Band, a bugler, the seven trumpeters and a couple of drummers, all in full ceremonial uniform, I made my way to Parliament Building which also housed Police Headquarters. I ran off a couple of spools of colour film of them with various backgrounds. After getting the films printed I decided that one of the shots of the Drum Major would make a superb subject for the first and possibly last issue of *Habari*, featuring a colour photograph. When the new issue of the magazine was printed it proved very popular. I had arranged a larger than usual print-run but this was rapidly sold out.

Having the printing plates readily available, I decided that a Force Christmas Card, using the same photograph on the front, might be equally popular. After discussing it with the printers I ordered a run of 4,000 cards and a similar number of suitably inscribed inserts, to be held together by a ribbon bow in the Force colours to be provided by the Quartermaster. The printing posed no problem but a problem did arise when it came to the bows which held the two parts of the card together. This could not be done by machine and was too labour intensive to be financially viable. 'O.K.', I said, 'just supply the cards and inserts. I will get the assembly done.' I was determined not to be thwarted on this. I gathered together half-a-dozen of the more intelligent recruits awaiting their training. It took me over an hour to show them what I required. Initially progress was slow. A number of the cards were spoiled, but eventually the job was done and for about 30 cents I was able to offer a card, unique to the Uganda Police, which would have cost at least a shilling elsewhere. Needless to say, demand was high. I could have sold three times as many. What I found a little annoying about this was that the Uganda Calendar published by the same Company, included my photograph of the Drum Major on one of its pages, credited to the name of one of their African staff. Bloody cheek.

It was about this time that a troop of Chinese acrobats were touring East Africa. They were very good indeed. They were also, it transpired, members of the Chinese Army and were expert paratroops. Once they had completed their performances in Uganda, they went on to the other East African territories. They proved very popular. They completed their series of performances with a visit to Zanzibar where, on 12th January 1964 they organised a *coup d'état* and deposed the Sultan. I don't think it was ever proved that they had taken the major role in the uprising. In truth, the new government went to considerable lengths to deny any involvement by an outside influence. Methinks they did protest too much! A couple of years later, however, when we visited Zanzibar on our way back to the U.K, we noticed, on looking through the visitor's book when visiting the museum on the island, that the first visitors to this building when it re-opened after the *coup*, were all Chinese.

Eight days after the Zanzibar *coup*, it was the turn of Tanganyika. Here the army mutinied, ostensibly for more pay and better promotion prospects. The government had, however, in the preceding week, taken the precaution of requesting assistance from the U.K. Government. An aircraft carrier, *H.M.S. Centaur* arrived off Mombasa and 600 commandos were air-lifted to Tanganyika. The mutineers fled into the bush as soon as the British army personnel arrived but were rounded up by helicopter.

On the following day 21st January 1964 it was Uganda's turn. The Army, based at Jinja, mutinied and seized Felix Onama the Minister of Internal Affairs who was visiting the barracks at the time. Fortunately, the police remained loyal and a large contingent immediately manned roadblocks on the Owen Falls Dam, cutting the road to Kampala and confining the mutineers to the East of the Nile. The ringleaders of the mutineers now demanded very substantial pay rises for all ranks.

My immediate action on receiving the news to the mutiny was to increase the security of the Training School Armoury. Looking back on it, I suppose that my efforts were on a fairly trivial scale, but I felt I had to take some action. I sent a truck out to the Forestry Department plantation and collected a number of stout eucalyptus poles each about ten feet in length. These I had concreted into the ground around the armoury after which a large quantity of barbed wire was attached to them making a fairly secure outer perimeter. Properly manned, this might have held up any intruders for a few minutes!

The new Government of Uganda having, however, been forewarned by the events in Zanzibar and Tanganyika and had taken the precaution of requesting military assistance from the U.K. Now we had a situation where an independent government who, on being granted their independence, had nothing but bitter words to say about their European oppressors, with no gratitude for the multitude of benefits which had accrued over the years, were now clamouring for help from those self-same oppressors to put down an internal uprising. If it had not been so serious, it would have been laughable.

In true British fashion the U.K. Government dispatched 450 troops of the Scots Guards and the Staffordshire Regiment, who arrived at Entebbe Airport in 15 aircraft on 23rd January 1964. They were met on the runway by Mr Adoko Nekyon, the Minister of Tourism. The British troops, who were prepared for any eventuality, disembarked in battle order and immediately threw Mr Nekyon to the ground and stood with their rifles trained on him. They let him to his feet only when the British High Commissioner, Sir David Hunt, intervened. They then proceeded to 'capture' and secure the control tower and the main airport buildings which was a fairly standard procedure in such situations. This did not take very long since none of the buildings were guarded in any way! After this the commanding officers were briefed by the police on the true nature of the problems. They then embarked in the armoured vehicles which had been aboard the aircraft and were away in the direction of Jinja.

On reaching the army barracks at Jinja, it took the British Army unit all of ten minutes to put down the mutiny and to imprison those mutineers who had not already fled. However, they were with us for a couple of weeks, during which time they were made very welcome by the Uganda Government. They made full use of the swimming pool at the P.T.S. and various functions and dances were held. A section of the Band of the Royal Anglian Regiment arrived and made several performances.

One might have thought that the Government of Uganda, having had its bacon saved by British troops, might have reconsidered its position in regard to the unfortunate expatriate officers it had so hastily deported. Not a bit of it. As soon as the situation had been brought under control by the British troops, they could not wait to be rid of these 'foreign forces'. Without even a word of thanks!

Meanwhile, on 25th January, an army mutiny took place in Kenya at Lanet Barracks in the Rift Valley. The Centaur was still moored at Mombasa at this time and a detachment of 200 men of the Royal Horse Artillery were rapidly dispatched by helicopter to deal with the mutineers. This took a little longer to bring under control than had the previous mutinies. However after some 17 hours including the hours of darkness when little could be achieved, the 500 mutineers were arrested. After these incidents, East Africa returned to its normal peaceful state.

With the departure of Clunie Inglis, I was left without a 2 i/c. Not that I was particularly worried about this. The P.T.S. was running like clockwork by now and I could have managed quite well. At the end of December, however, Assistant Commissioner George Johnson the Director of Training departed on leave, pending retirement. I was now promoted to fill this rank and position on a temporary basis until another officer was appointed. I now found myself as Acting Assistant Commissioner of Police at headquarters part of the time and Commandant of the Police Training School for the remainder. This had some benefits. In my capacity as Commandant of the P.T.S. I could write to the Director of Training at headquarters, making some suggestion or other, and then go to headquarters as Director of

Training and reply to myself, approving my suggestion! However, after a six month stint in this rank, it was decided that Assistant Commissioner Gerald Murphy should fill the vacant post until a suitable African officer could be found. I was sorry to relinquish this post. I had found it a lot of fun! During one of my visits to headquarters, Mike Macoun mentioned to me that he had recommended me for the award of the M.B.E. I was pleased about this but, bearing in mind the fate of the previous recommendation, I decided not to hold my breath. Just as well really, since Obote decided that the British Empire was not an institution to which he could recommend any awards.

Meanwhile, in early January 1964, a newly-promoted Superintendent Kasuja arrived as my new 2 i/c. I was not overly impressed but decided to do the best I could with him. A letter arrived from headquarters informing me of a forthcoming visit by Haile Selassie, the Emperor of Ethiopia. He was scheduled to arrive at Entebbe by air on 17th June and was to be met by the *Kabaka*, President Frederick Mutesa. He would then inspect two Guards of Honour, one of which was to be provided by the Army, the second to be from the Police Training School. Clearly there was going to be some degree of competition as regards smartness and efficiency between the two. It was impressed upon me that all arrangements for the Guard of Honour which was to be provided by the Police Training School, should be carried out by an African officer. Mine was to be merely a watching brief. I sent for Superintendent Kasuja and informed him of the good news. The contingent from the P.T.S. was to be commanded by him and all the administrative arrangements also fell to him. It should be interesting to see how he managed with what was, in effect, a simple logistics exercise. His face blanched as I told him the news. 'Sir, what should I do?', he asked. I thought I had better give him a hand, in the initial stages anyway. 'You had better make a note then', I said. 'First, inform the Head Constable, who will choose the Guard of Honour. Second, inform Inspector Oloya. who will train them. Third, inform Mr Oduka The Director of Music who will need to practise with whatever part of the Band that he will need. Fourth, practise yourself with the Guard and the Band to ensure that you know what to do on the day. Fifth, arrange transport for yourself, the Band and the Guard of Honour. Sixth, make sure that you are there in plenty of time before the plane arrives. Do all that and you should have no problem!' Kasuja wrote it all down and left.

I inspected the Guard of Honour at it's practise from time to time. All seemed to be going well. Oloya was doing a great job of licking them into shape. I was particularly impressed by a phrase which he had obviously picked up on a Drill Course I had sent him on in the U.K. 'YOU HORRIBLE LITTLE BERLACKKK MAN', he would bawl. I could hardly intervene and accuse him of racism, since his remarks were totally accurate.

The Emperor was due to land at Entebbe at 11 a.m. on 17th June. It was, therefore, essential that the Guard of Honour, the Band and the officers be ready on parade at least 15 minutes before this. This meant that they should arrive at the airport by 10.15 a.m. at the latest. This, in turn, would require them to leave for the 22-mile trip to Entebbe by at least 9.15 a.m.

I arrived at the P.T.S. at 9.a.m. to find the Guard of Honour and the band ready to leave. Of Kasuja there was no sign. Neither had the transport yet arrived! 'He's cutting it a bit fine', I thought. Just to be on the safe side, I telephoned the Transport Officer at the Inspectorate of Vehicles. To my horror I found that he knew nothing about any transport requirements. To add to this there were no transport vehicles to be had since they were all otherwise engaged. I went into overdrive. By 9.30 I had scrounged an open truck from the police barracks and an enormous, closed, mortuary van which was the only vehicle the Inspector of Vehicles could lay his hands on. I packed the protesting police band into the mortuary van and sent them on their way, feeling rather sorry for them since it hadn't been cleaned and stank of rotting corpses. By 10.00 a.m. Kasuja had still not put in an appearance and a telephone call to his house failed to get a reply. 'Surely', I thought, 'he hasn't gone direct to Entebbe?'

I was now left with the problem of getting the Guard of Honour on its way. Already, according to my estimates, the time limit was upon us. I had the one open truck into which, at a pinch, I could pack maybe 15 men. There was but one alternative. The remaining 15 would have to be packed into the private cars belonging to various members of staff. At 10.25 a.m. the convoy was on its way. We had 35 minutes left to drive the 22 miles and get the Guard formed up. 'Maybe the plane will be delayed', I hoped. No such luck. As I drove into the airport, I could see the plane circling towards its approach run. I screeched to a halt beside the mortuary wagon. Thank God. The Band were already formed up and ready to go. The Guard of Honour extricated themselves from their cramped positions and formed up. No sign of Kasuja. 'Oloya, you will have to take the Guard', I said. He beamed. 'Thank you Sir,' he replied. The Guard of Honour ran the 200 yards to their positions and formed up alongside the army Guard. Considering the way they had been transported, they didn't have a bad turnout. Within 20 seconds of their arrival, the Emperor was mounting the dais. Oloya reported to him and the inspection was under way. I wiped the perspiration from my brow. Kasuja was going to have a lot of explaining to do. In fact he didn't have any explanation at all. He confessed that having forgotten to arrange the transport he panicked at the last minute when he finally remembered his error and, instead of reporting the matter to me he had done a runner, leaving me to sort it out. Two days later he was transferred to Mbale and replaced by an Asian Superintendent, Dev Kapoor. He was the younger brother of Dr Prem Kapoor who had been in Soroti with us. Dev was a pleasant and efficient officer but, like we Europeans, had no future in Uganda as he had not been born in the country, nor had he taken out Uganda citizenship. Quite clearly he had been posted to the P.T.S. as a stop-gap pending the choice of, yet another African officer for me to train to take my place.

I had, by this time, completed a total of 15 of the required 20 additional Coats of Arms. Surprisingly, I had been paid on the spot for each consignment. I could afford to relax a little on this front. I decided to make a few smaller and less complicated Coats of Arms which I could distribute to some of the police officers as they retired. Having now had plenty of practice in this field, it didn't take me too long to produce these. Instead of assembling the component parts so that the mounting could not be seen, I simply mounted them on a backing board and framed them. The effect, though less dramatic than the large- scale Coats of Arms was, nevertheless, quite pleasing. I gave one of these to Mike Macoun who was about to retire and kept one myself. The others I distributed to one or two particular friends in the police force.

On 4th September 1964, the Annual Police Review was held. This year the Inspecting Officer was to be the President, Frederick Mutesa. I was no longer required to command the parade, for which I was duly thankful. It was, however, my responsibility, in the absence of a suitable senior African officer, to organise the whole event. This was a reasonably straightforward procedure. Having carried out the same job for the past several years, putting the parade together presented little difficulty. What did exercise a few minds, however, was the question of who was going to command the parade. Our new Inspector General, Erinayo Oryema, decided that there were no Superintendents, Senior Superintendents or even Assistant Commissioners among the African officers who could be entrusted with this job. For a horrible moment, I thought he was going to nominate me to do it. Instead he chose a Senior Assistant Commissioner of Police, Inyalyo, to do the job. Poor Inyalyo did not have a lot of experience in parade work but I had him on the parade ground almost continuously for a couple of weeks prior to the parade and he made a reasonable showing on the day. A couple of months later he was promoted to the rank of Deputy Inspector General so, I suppose, his efforts had not gone unnoticed.

Time was now growing short. In less than six months we should be returning to the U.K. An African Superintendent, Drani, was posted to the P.T.S. to take over as 2 i/c. Dev Kapoor was transferred elsewhere. Drani was pleasant enough but was not, in my opinion, overburdened with brains. I had severe doubts about his ability to take over from me in due course. Well — not really my problem by then. I pressed on with the final five Coats of Arms. A month before we were due to leave Uganda they were finished and delivered and I was able to relax. A little later I was called to the office of Cuthbert Obwangor, the Minister of Justice. 'We would like you to make a further 200 Coats of Arms', he said. This took my breath away a little. He was talking about £40,000. 'I'm sorry', I said. 'I am retiring to the U.K. in about a month. If you like, I could make them there and get them transported out to Uganda in batches of say 20 at a time.' He looked disappointed at this, 'No, they must be made in Uganda. Many visiting dignitaries have seen and admired them. We must be able to continue to say that they are made by a Uganda resident.' That was that. The matter was not raised again.

Three weeks before my retirement a newly-promoted Senior Superintendent Majalya was posted to the P.T.S. to take over from me. Majalya was quite a useful officer who had served under me as a Sub-Inspector many years earlier. Given proper training, I thought that he could make an efficient Commandant. However, with only three weeks available, I had my doubts. Anyway, I did my best and as far as I know, he did reasonably well.

In March 1965, we boarded the train for Mombasa. We were sad to be leaving Uganda but had accepted the inevitable. We had enjoyed our years in the country and I think that there were some regrets among my African police. The band turned out to Kampala Railway Station and we pulled away to the strains of 'Will ye no come back again'.

Our route to the U.K. took us to Zanzibar and Dar es Salaam and then south to Port Elizabeth, Lorenzo Marques, Biera and Durban where I was approached on board the liner by the South African authorities who offered me an appointment as Superintendent of Police in Special Branch. After due consideration, I declined the offer. We disembarked and took a coach across the 'Garden Route'. Re-embarking at Cape Town we travelled back to the U.K. via Tenerife and Madeira.

Many years have now passed since we left East Africa. Over this span of time, I have, from time to time, had news of the characters I have mentioned in this account. Sadly, most of this concerns their deaths though some are still very much alive. Peter Godber, who received mention early on, when I was a member of the Hastings Borough Police, was appointed as Sub-Inspector in Hong Kong. He rose to the rank of Superintendent in that force but regrettably became involved in a corruption scandal in the '60s. He was, I feel, made something of a scapegoat since, I believe, very many other officers were similarly involved. He was sentenced to three years imprisonment in a Hong Kong jail. Not, possibly, a pleasant experience but since the amount he was alleged to have received in bribes amounted to £500,000, a lot of money at the time. Maybe he wasn't too unhappy. On his release he returned briefly to the U.K. before fleeing to Spain where, as far as I am aware he still lives in luxury. Joe Deegan died some years ago as did Mike Macoun. John Docherty died within a few years of his retirement as did Noel Caunce and his wife Peggy. Tom Hinett, on his retirement, lived at Tavistock in Devon. We visited him several times when we were on holiday. His wife Vi, died many years ago. Tom lived until quite recently at a nursing home in Plymouth. Arthur Kessel got married eventually and his new wife stopped his intake of gin. They retired to Australia where, sadly, he died not long afterwards. Sandy Field, on retirement, got a job as chief game warden in the Ngorogoro Crater in Tanzania. He bought a light aircraft and one day set off for his home. He never reached there and his plane has never been found. 'Snaky' Smith died a few years after he left Uganda, (shame), while Pearman died in 2004, (hurray). Clunie Ingles lived, at one time, quite close to us in Sussex and we would see him occasionally. He died a few years back. Bob Astels, because of his interest in cine photography, got an appointment to Uganda Television. When Idi Amin came to power he became a right-hand man to this homicidal maniac and was promoted to Major. As a result, he was responsible for putting the finger on anyone opposed to the regime. He was, directly or indirectly responsible for many hundreds of deaths throughout the Amin years. When Uganda was freed from Amin's yoke Astels was arrested, but instead of the execution he so richly deserved he was eventually released and fled to the U.K. I have heard nothing of him since. I think he must have changed his name or he would have, eventually received his just deserts. It transpired that he was the individual responsible for the deportations following the Tank Hill fiasco. Dev Kapoor retired to Canada when he was among the Asians deported by Amin. His brother, Dr Prem Kapoor, retired to England and had a practice in Hornchurch. He died in May 2009. Madan Tandon was deported by Amin and arrived in England, penniless. Through sheer hard work on the part of himself and his family he is now a multi-millionaire with a chain of filling stations. Sir Andrew Cohen died, unlamented, many years ago. *Kabaka* and President Frederick Mutesa fled to England in exile from Uganda with the arrival of Amin. He died penurious and in mysterious circumstances some years ago. His son worked as a postman in the U.K., but a few years ago was invited to return to Uganda as *Kabaka*. Idi Amin fled to the United Arab Republic where he died a few years ago. Haile Selassie didn't even manage to flee from Ethiopia. He was deposed by the Communist regime which seized power and was murdered. Lesley Whitehouse retired and continued to live in Kenya. Since he was classed as a local employee his pension was a tiny amount. He continually badgered Jomo Kenyata for an increase. Bearing in mind his treatment of Jomo during the time he was D.C. in Turkana I find it unsurprising that he was unsuccessful. He died in penury many years ago. Arthur Watson became Governor of (I think) the Windward Islands.

I have thought that one day I would like to return for a short holiday. Who knows? I have heard that the country, post-Idi Amin, is on its knees. Obote, it turns out, murdered as many — if not more — people as Idi Amin. The economy, without the Asian community to run it, is ruined. Where are all the roads the British built. Where are the hospitals and schools? What has happened to the Police Training School. I have heard on good authority that the swimming pool is still there, leaking, without a pump, half-full of green stagnant water and teaming with mosquito larvae. I do know that at least one of my Coats of Arms survived. I saw it in pride of place on a wall behind Idi Amin in a television film featuring him. Most of the police officers whom I helped to train have been murdered. Oryema, the Inspector General and later Minister of Internal Affairs in Idi Amin's government was killed shortly after attending one of Amin's rallies when he and the Archbishop of Uganda were denounced by Amin and shot. Poor Oloya was murdered during Idi Amin's reign of terror. I heard that he was promoted to Superintendent and posted to Entebbe police station. He made the mistake of helping some Asians, whom he knew to be my friends, to board an aircraft when they were deported. The army went to the police station afterwards and beat him to death with their rifle butts. Even the Karamajong, whose primitive but proud lifestyle I admired even as I pursued them through the bush, have virtually given up using their spears and shields during their cattle raids. Now they are all armed with Kalashnikovs Maybe it would be a mistake to go back after all.

FINIS
Bexhill-on-Sea, Sussex, October 2009

Appendix

Snippets from Recruit Applications

These are genuine extracts from letters of application to join the Uganda Police. You may feel that I have been cruel to have collected these bits of unconscious humour. After all, which of us, writing a letter in a foreign language, might not have done any better than these. I include them, nevertheless, for their humorous quality rather than to belittle the efforts of the writers, and have captioned each one accordingly.

Not if I see you first.
I am hoping to see you at your convenience.

Is this a record?
I have got five feet and eleven inches.

I can hardly wait.
I would be delectable if you turn up as soon as possible.

Poor fellow.
I am five feet and eight inches very tall and emasculation in appearance.

Like two short planks?
My height is five feet and seven inches and really if you can see me you can be amazed because I am very thick indeed.

Just a'wearying for you.
Should you like to know my character and conduct I refer you to my present headmaster, who will be homesick to write on my behind.

They saw it off in logs in Mobile.
I have been doing crapintree for the past two years.

Able to take his pick.
During my schooling I was good at spots and I still do it.

How else?

I should like to ask you kindly by having a pen in my hand and writing to you on paper that I wish to join the Police Training School.

Fencing for a position.

I beg to put in a post in your Police Training School.

Snap

I wish to serve the Police Force as a hole

I can hardly wait.

I would be delectable if you turn up as soon as possible.

Q.E.D.

When I was sending my application for training I showed my height (5ft 6ins) and now I have been 5ft 5ins. Therefore according to the first height you called me you should have allowed on this height I have because I am going to be over that height you wish in two weeks. Would you please enrol me on the list because I am going to be taller in a few days.

Any previous experience?

I wish to join up as a burglar.

It's a hard life.

My immediate family has kicked the barrel and left me poor and lonely.

Doesn't know when he's well off.

I could stay at home next year but I have a hard life at home.

We could do with a lot like this!

Nature of employment:- Teaching and carpentree.
Reason for leaving;_ Pregnating a school girl and sudden death.
Character given by employer:- I didn't demand for a recommendation.

What's new?

I have long time wanted to join the Police to be trained as a spy.

It's later than you think.

I think you will kindly consider my application and give me a chance to save you.

Sorry about that.

What happen my applicshon I send because you told me 'post early before Christmas'. Why no reply?

Well-qualified.

I love the police too much and I want to be a policewoman. It will be easy for me because I am strong and can walk quickly and know first aid.

Quite a sense of humour.

This year I am in Junior Secondary 1. I shall be very hilarious if my application is considered carefully.

No point in throwing this one out.

I am a Muganda girl aged 20 years. I am 5 feet 2 inches tall and have a sufficient chest.

My memory must be at fault.

You will be glad to take me in your place because I have taken you to be my father!! I beg you respond me quik.

Honesty, the best policy?

Since I can't get any other work, I am applying to join your Police Force.

Well qualified

Sir, I applicason for job in the Uganda policemotor cikles. I can drive foot cikle a alota years is not quik like pigi pigi I kno becos I mekanica.

You said it!

I will be very greatfool to receive your humble reply.

Don't mention it.
Hoping to be excused for the trouble I may cause you in thinking up a reply.

Lock up the policewomen.
I am male by nature and 19 years old.

How sad.
I am writing you about my miserable. When yong I hanged out with my parents. God called and both dead. Then hanged out with uncle. God called again. You can be my f ather.

Happiness
I am very merry to hold my pen and write to you, that if you give me vacancy at your Police Training School I will be delightful.

What more could he offer?
If at all let me com to join here and even the rules are hard, It is said in short story that many are called few are chosen even it is that I form you sir let me have a go or try. My blood, mine, heart and my joyer full are easy eager to join Uganda Police.

Never doubted it.
I belong to a highly respectable tribe.

Holy Post.
Please send me an early Communion.

Someone likes me!
From what I have gathered about you and when I consider myself fully, you are able to suit me best.

Breath out.
My chest is fit to go.

Don't wait too long.
I am wetting for your reply.

That's the long and short of it.
I am happy to send this short letter. How are you I am well. I want a place in your deportment. I am six feet and ten inches.

We'll see what we can spare.
I respectfully ask for the grant of a policewoman.

Try working.
I have no money to go with my education.

Beyond my control.
I beg to be trained as a man.

A common complaint.
Owing to shortage of fees I couldn't get any father.

Sweet surrender.
You may take me.

This I must see.
I have six feet and am hopping to see you.

Basic qualification.
I am male by nature.

Duty stallion.
I was doing stud at Buddu School.

What now?
I was long ago 5-feet 7-inches. Send me your calling card.

Guilty plea.
I have just done the junior school.

Fly — all is discovered.
I have a good knowledge of what you will do with my application.

Whew!
I can type 35 words per month.

Try again when I have retired.
I have really the greatest desire if you could just call me to
be trained as the Officer Commanding in your Police
Training School

Gosh thanks!
As far as character is concerned, I prefer you to my
headmaster